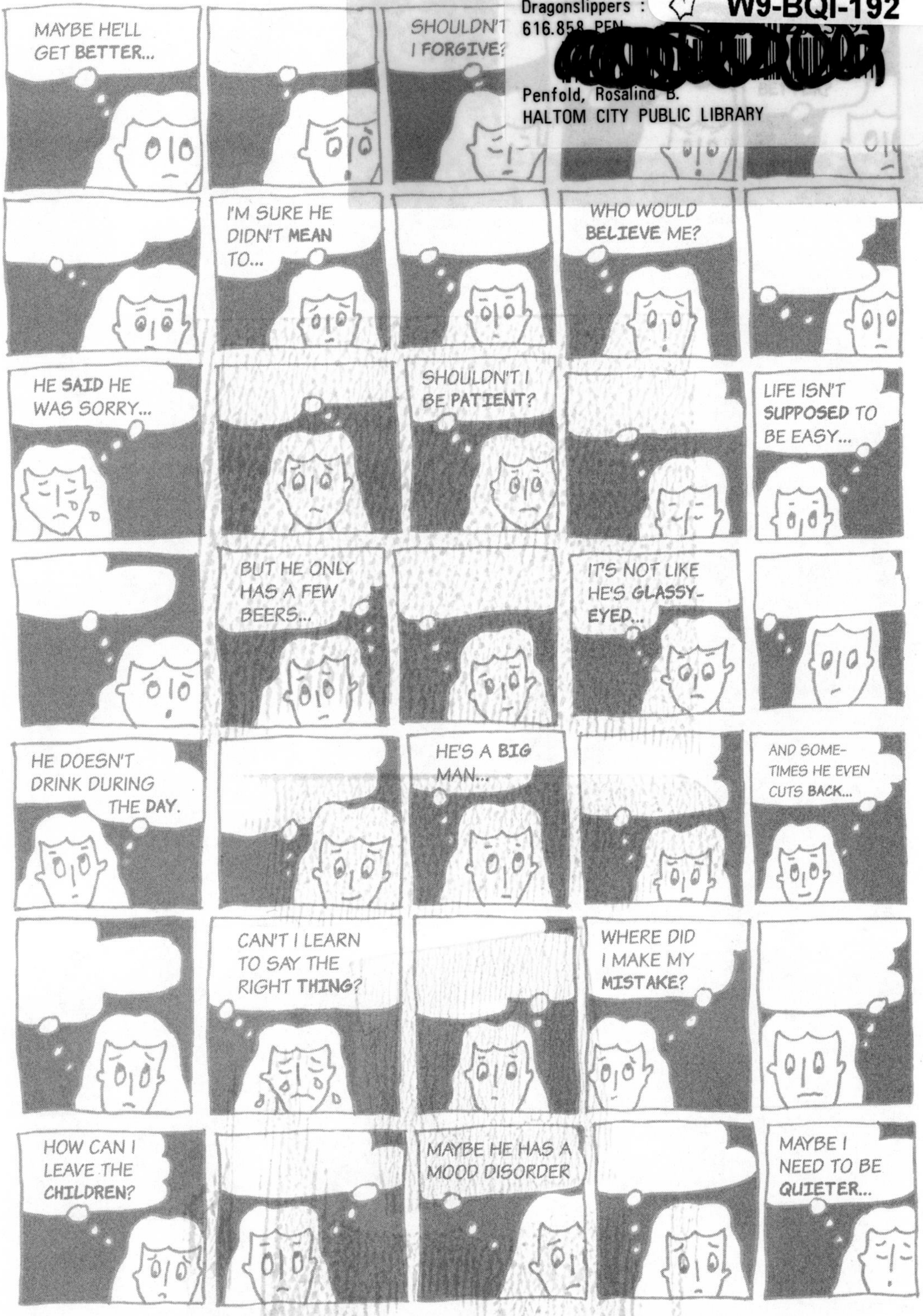
MAYBE HE'LL GET BETTER...
SHOULDN'T I FORGIVE?
I'M SURE HE DIDN'T MEAN TO...
WHO WOULD BELIEVE ME?
HE SAID HE WAS SORRY...
SHOULDN'T I BE PATIENT?
LIFE ISN'T SUPPOSED TO BE EASY...
BUT HE ONLY HAS A FEW BEERS...
IT'S NOT LIKE HE'S GLASSY-EYED...
HE DOESN'T DRINK DURING THE DAY.
HE'S A BIG MAN...
AND SOME-TIMES HE EVEN CUTS BACK...
CAN'T I LEARN TO SAY THE RIGHT THING?
WHERE DID I MAKE MY MISTAKE?
HOW CAN I LEAVE THE CHILDREN?
MAYBE HE HAS A MOOD DISORDER
MAYBE I NEED TO BE QUIETER...

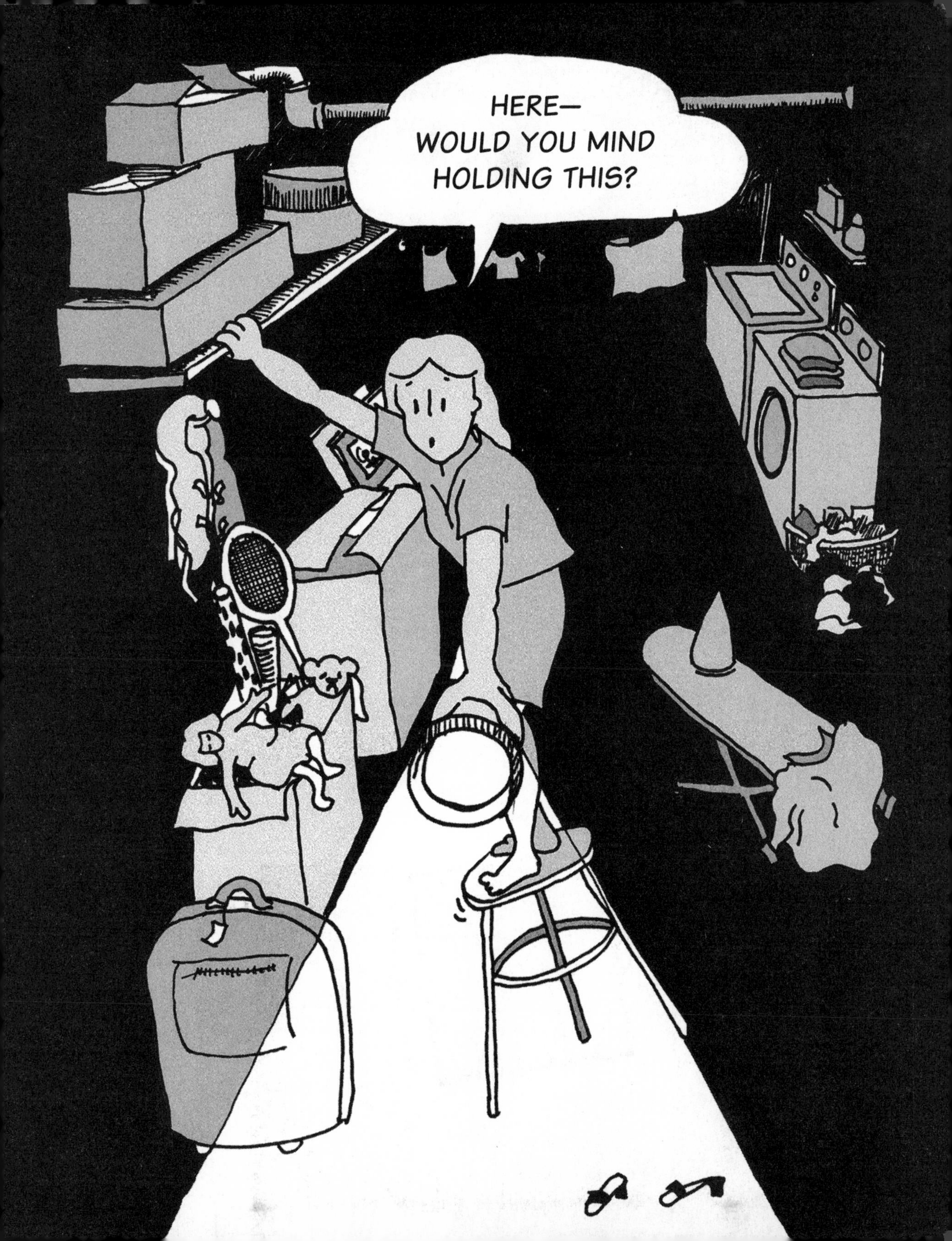
HERE—
WOULD YOU MIND
HOLDING THIS?

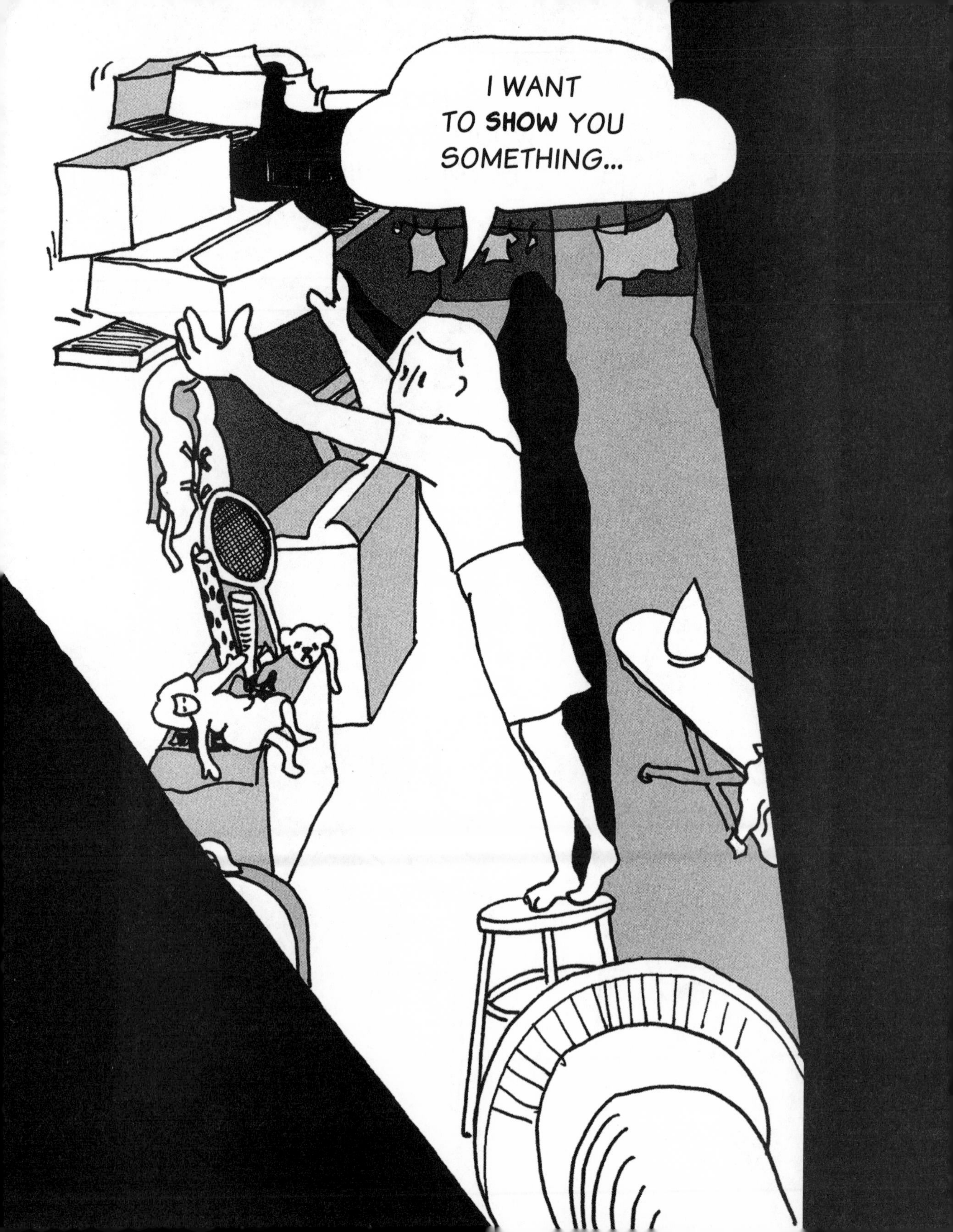
I WANT TO **SHOW** YOU SOMETHING...

Dragonslippers

This Is What an Abusive Relationship Looks Like

by Rosalind B. Penfold

BLACK CAT
New York
a paperback original imprint of Grove/Atlantic, Inc.

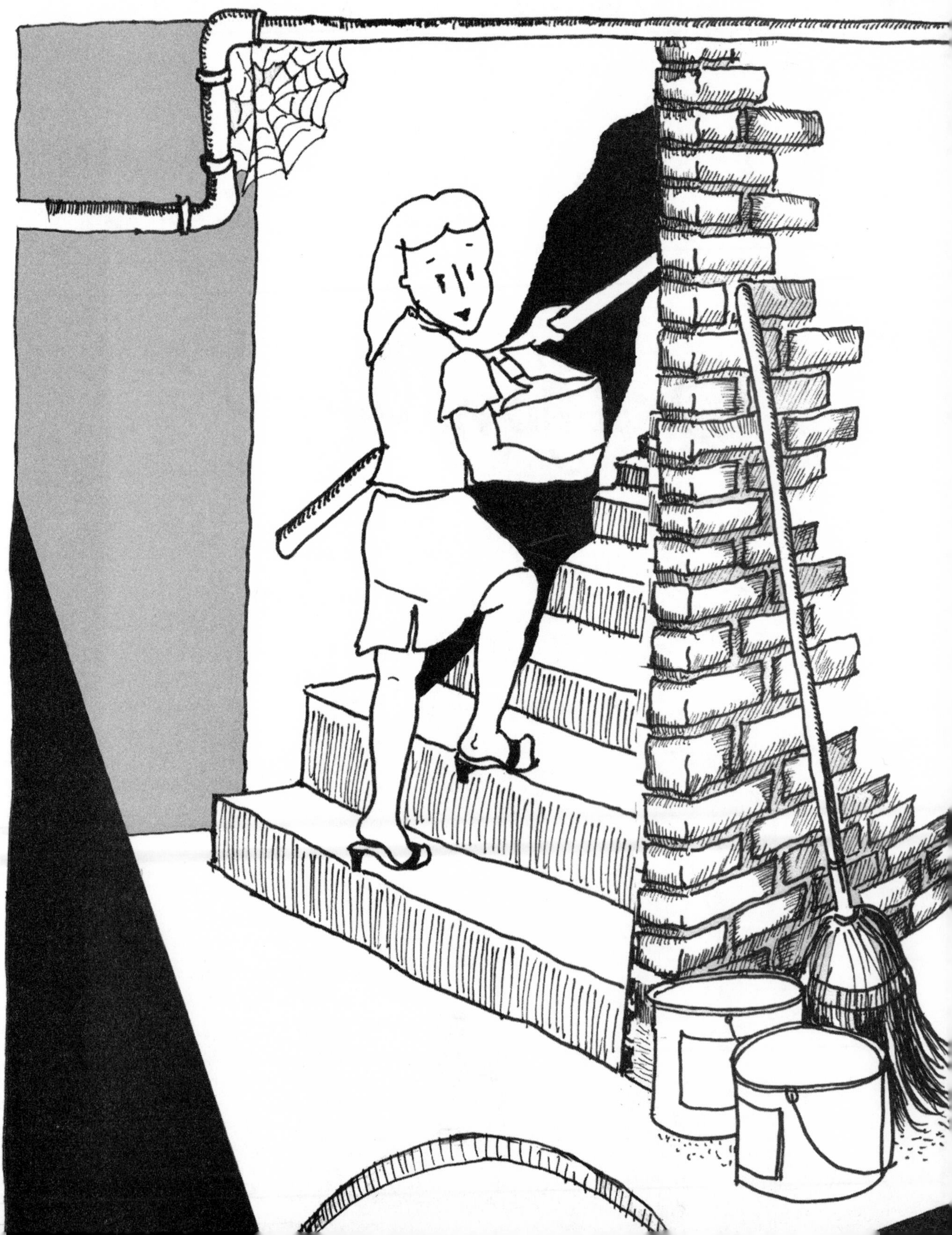

This Is What an Abusive Relationship Looks Like

WHEN I MET BRIAN, I fell deeply in love. I thought we were going to have a fairy tale romance. �֍ And we did ... briefly ... **UNTIL THINGS BEGAN TO CHANGE.** I ignored the early humiliations and subtle mind games, and refused to believe what was happening, until I was lost in **A QUICKSAND OF VERBAL, EMOTIONAL, SEXUAL,** and, ultimately, **PHYSICAL ABUSE.** My denial and shame kept me with Brian for 10 years. I clung to his promises, rather than what I saw and experienced. I spent all of my time trying to figure out what I was doing wrong and how I could make things better. I **COULDN'T ALWAYS REMEMBER** the abuse. There was **NO PREDICTABLE PATTERN,** and it seemed like my brain erased each instance— because it didn't fit in with my hopes. I didn't want to let go of the relationship— **I JUST WANTED BRIAN'S BEHAVIOR TO CHANGE.** I thought of myself as strong, but in this relationship I became so deeply confused that **I BEGAN TO LOSE ALL SENSE OF MYSELF.** ✖ People in abusive relationships often mistake *intensity* for *intimacy*. It *feels intimate* because it is **SO PERSONAL,** but intimacy requires trust—and there is no trust in an abusive relationship. The pattern feels like this: **KISS! SLAP! KISS! SLAP! KISS! SLAP!**

For every slap we receive a kiss, and for every kiss we receive a slap. Which do we want to believe? The kiss, of course. It is **WHAT KEEPS US THERE.** ❀ During the 10 years I stayed, I kept wishing there were cameras on the ceiling. I kept a diary, but **WHEN WORDS FAILED ME, I DREW PICTURES.** I remember thinking, "Maybe my brain just isn't processing this yet ... Maybe if I look at the pictures later, then things will make sense." But things never did, and I simply hid the pictures in a box in the basement. ❀ **WHY DID BRIAN BEHAVE THE WAY HE DID?** I almost died trying to figure that out. Why did I stay? It's the far better question. I believed one should turn the other cheek ... I believed that he loved me ... **I BELIEVED HE WOULD CHANGE** ... I believed I could protect his children ... I believed my love would make him better ... I used **SO MANY EXCUSES** to rationalize why I stayed, I refused to truly see. ❀ And then one day I found **MY PICTURES**. My brain could rationalize and deny, but my art went straight to the truth. I finally saw that the **MOST SHOCKING TRUTH OF ALL WAS NOT HIS BEHAVIOR, BUT MY OWN**—because I had stayed and allowed this damage to myself. **I KNEW I HAD TO GET OUT TO PROTECT MYSELF.** ❀ **ACCEPTING RESPONSIBILITY EMPOWERED ME.** It was not easy to let go, and I had many false starts. ❀ I never intended these drawings for publication. Sharing one's personal diary is not easy—and, at first, I felt shame. Then I decided that **SHAME WAS THE ENEMY**. I began to hope that my drawings could help others—even one other— to see what terrible, long-lasting **DAMAGE SUCH AN ENVIRONMENT CREATES** for a family. ❀ Looking critically at the drawings reveals some startling

"I sometimes think that shame, mere awkward, senseless shame, does as much towards preventing good acts and straightforward happiness as any of our vices can do." —C.S. Lewis

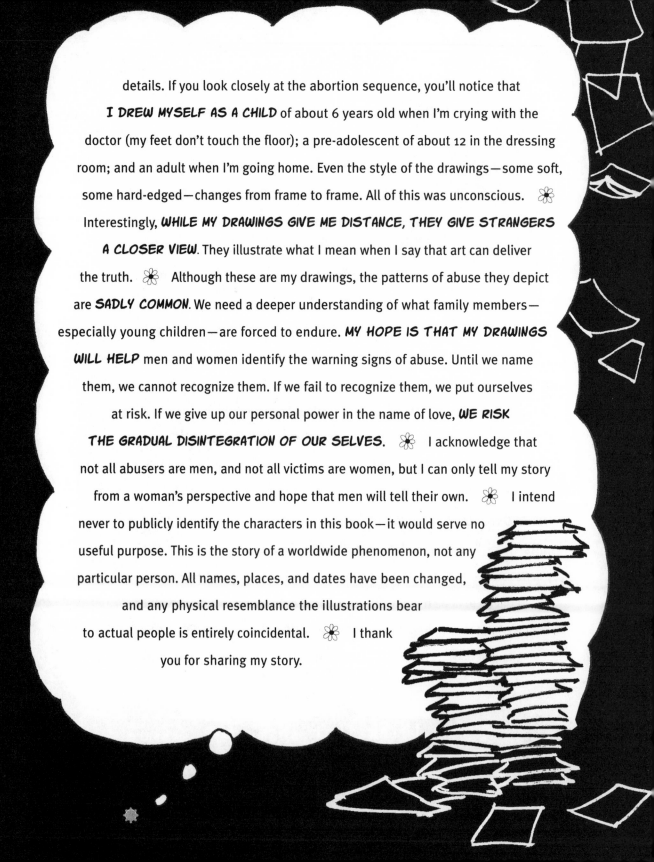

details. If you look closely at the abortion sequence, you'll notice that **I DREW MYSELF AS A CHILD** of about 6 years old when I'm crying with the doctor (my feet don't touch the floor); a pre-adolescent of about 12 in the dressing room; and an adult when I'm going home. Even the style of the drawings—some soft, some hard-edged—changes from frame to frame. All of this was unconscious. Interestingly, **WHILE MY DRAWINGS GIVE ME DISTANCE, THEY GIVE STRANGERS A CLOSER VIEW**. They illustrate what I mean when I say that art can deliver the truth. Although these are my drawings, the patterns of abuse they depict are **SADLY COMMON**. We need a deeper understanding of what family members—especially young children—are forced to endure. **MY HOPE IS THAT MY DRAWINGS WILL HELP** men and women identify the warning signs of abuse. Until we name them, we cannot recognize them. If we fail to recognize them, we put ourselves at risk. If we give up our personal power in the name of love, **WE RISK THE GRADUAL DISINTEGRATION OF OUR SELVES**. I acknowledge that not all abusers are men, and not all victims are women, but I can only tell my story from a woman's perspective and hope that men will tell their own. I intend never to publicly identify the characters in this book—it would serve no useful purpose. This is the story of a worldwide phenomenon, not any particular person. All names, places, and dates have been changed, and any physical resemblance the illustrations bear to actual people is entirely coincidental. I thank you for sharing my story.

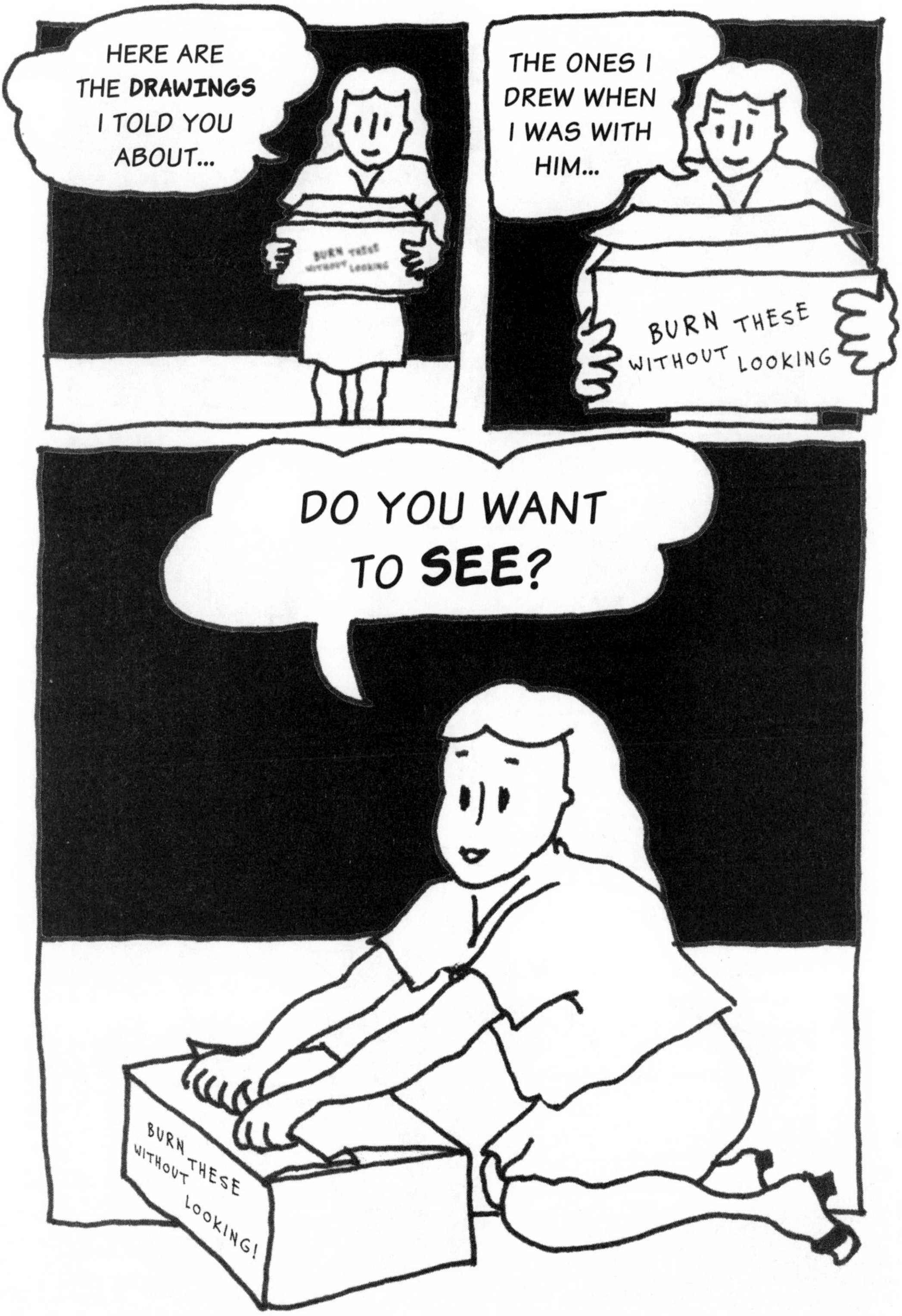
HERE ARE THE DRAWINGS I TOLD YOU ABOUT...
BURN THESE WITHOUT LOOKING
THE ONES I DREW WHEN I WAS WITH HIM...
BURN THESE WITHOUT LOOKING
DO YOU WANT TO SEE?
BURN THESE WITHOUT LOOKING!

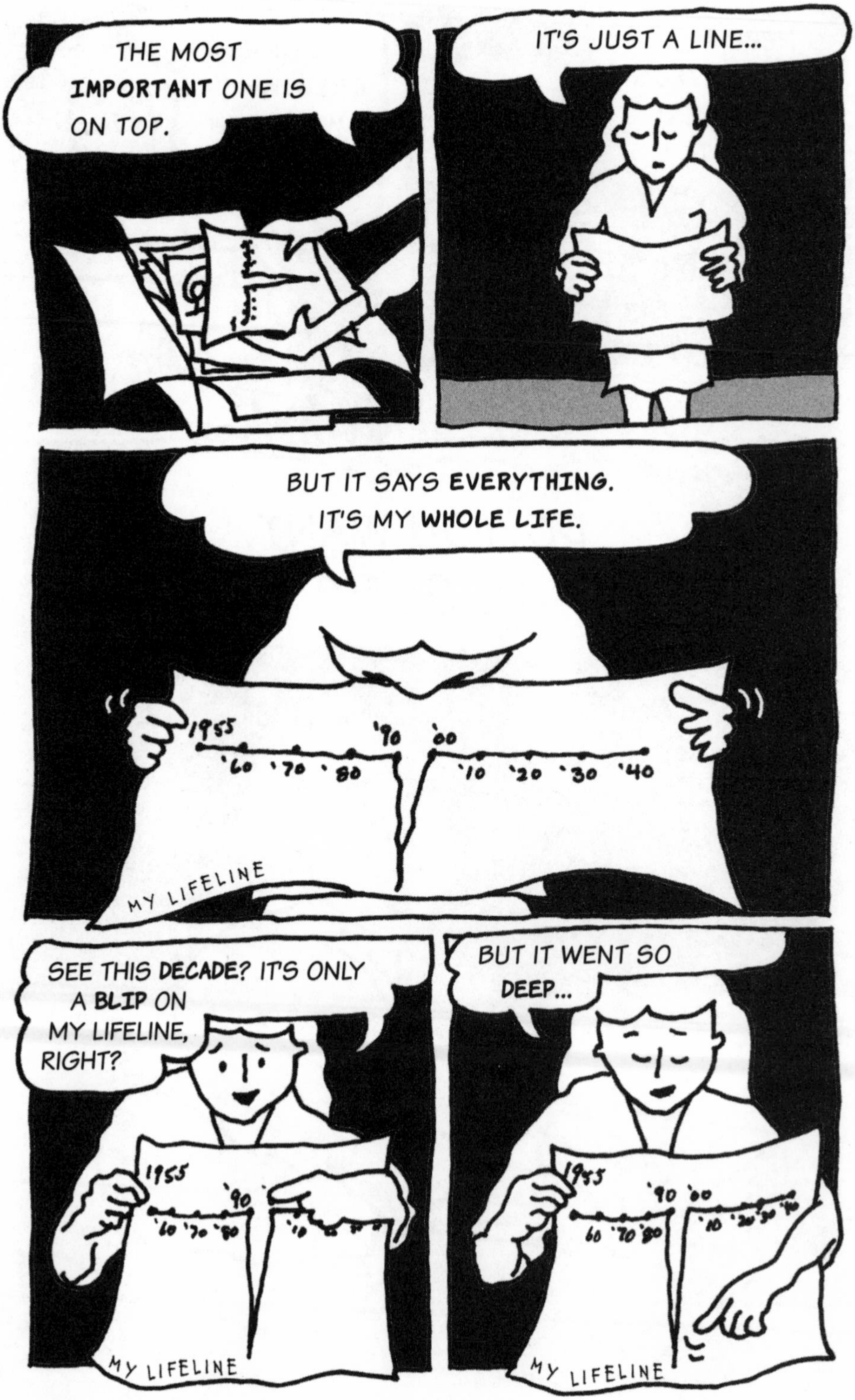
THE MOST IMPORTANT ONE IS ON TOP.
IT'S JUST A LINE...
BUT IT SAYS EVERYTHING. IT'S MY WHOLE LIFE.
1955
'60 '70 '80
'90 '00
'10 '20 '30 '40
MY LIFELINE
SEE THIS DECADE? IT'S ONLY A BLIP ON MY LIFELINE, RIGHT?
MY LIFELINE
BUT IT WENT SO DEEP...
MY LIFELINE

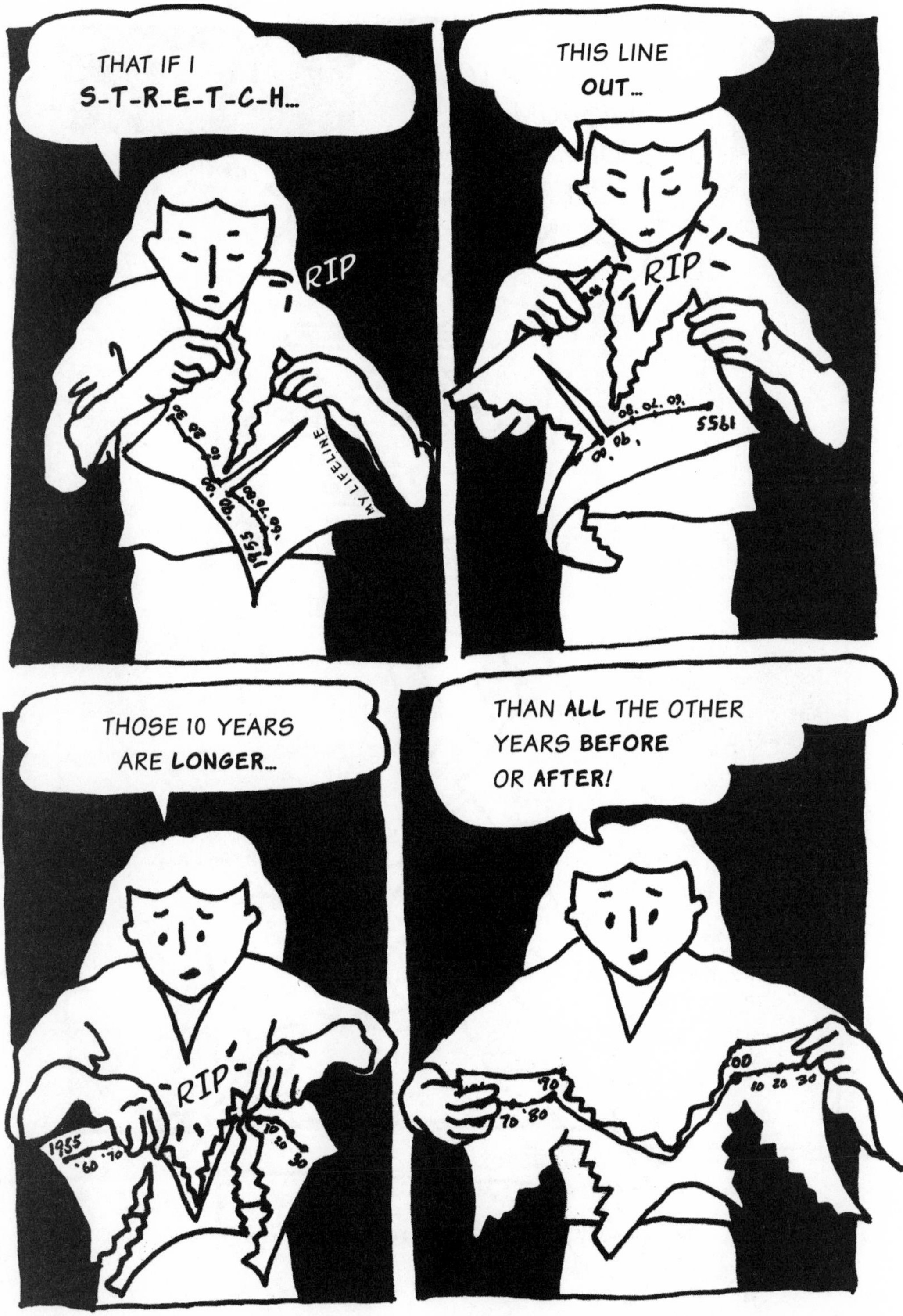
THAT IF I **S-T-R-E-T-C-H...**
RIP
MY LIFELINE
THIS LINE **OUT...**
RIP
THOSE 10 YEARS ARE **LONGER...**
RIP
1955
THAN **ALL** THE OTHER YEARS **BEFORE** OR **AFTER!**

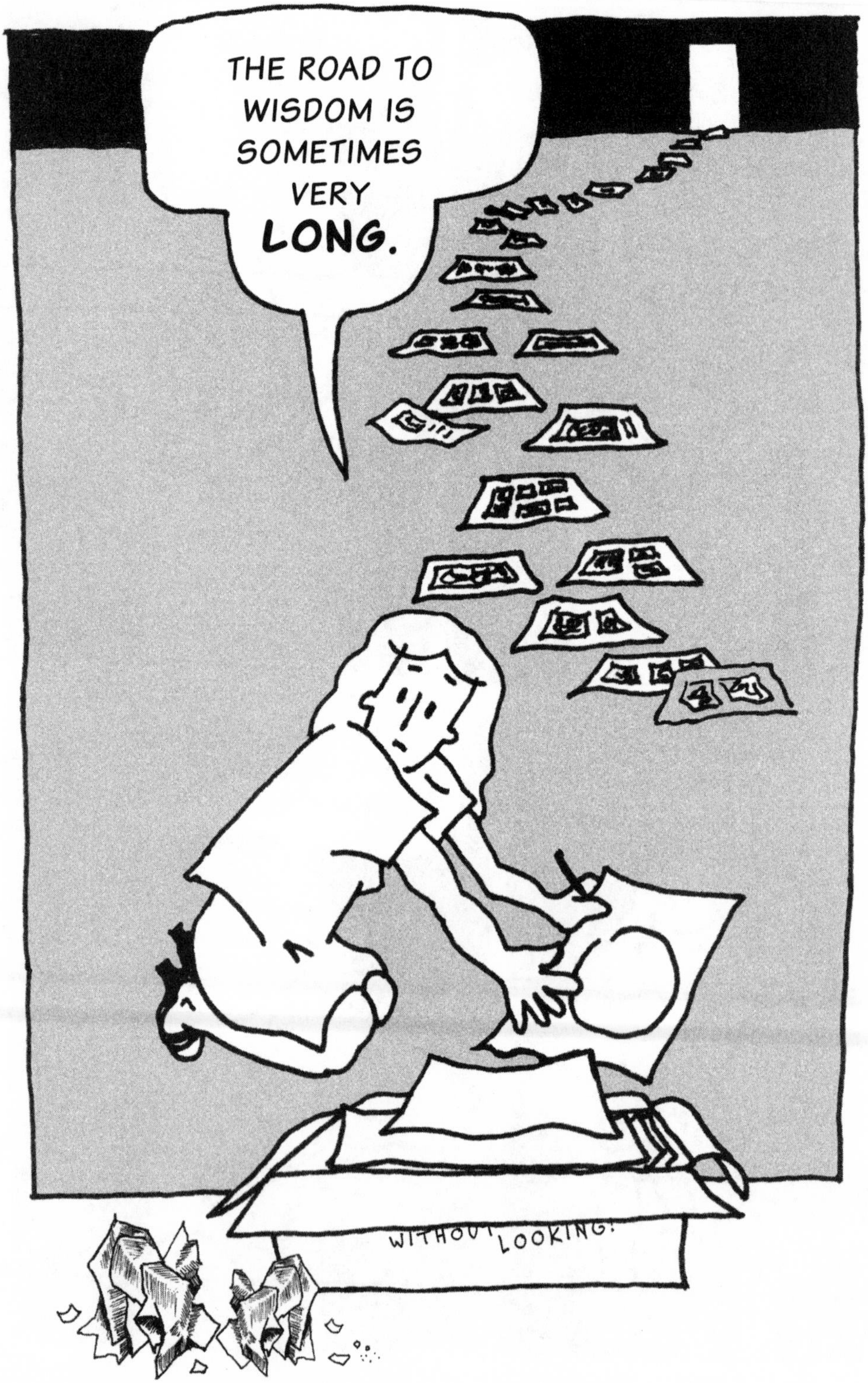
THE ROAD TO WISDOM IS SOMETIMES VERY **LONG.**
WITHOUT LOOKING!

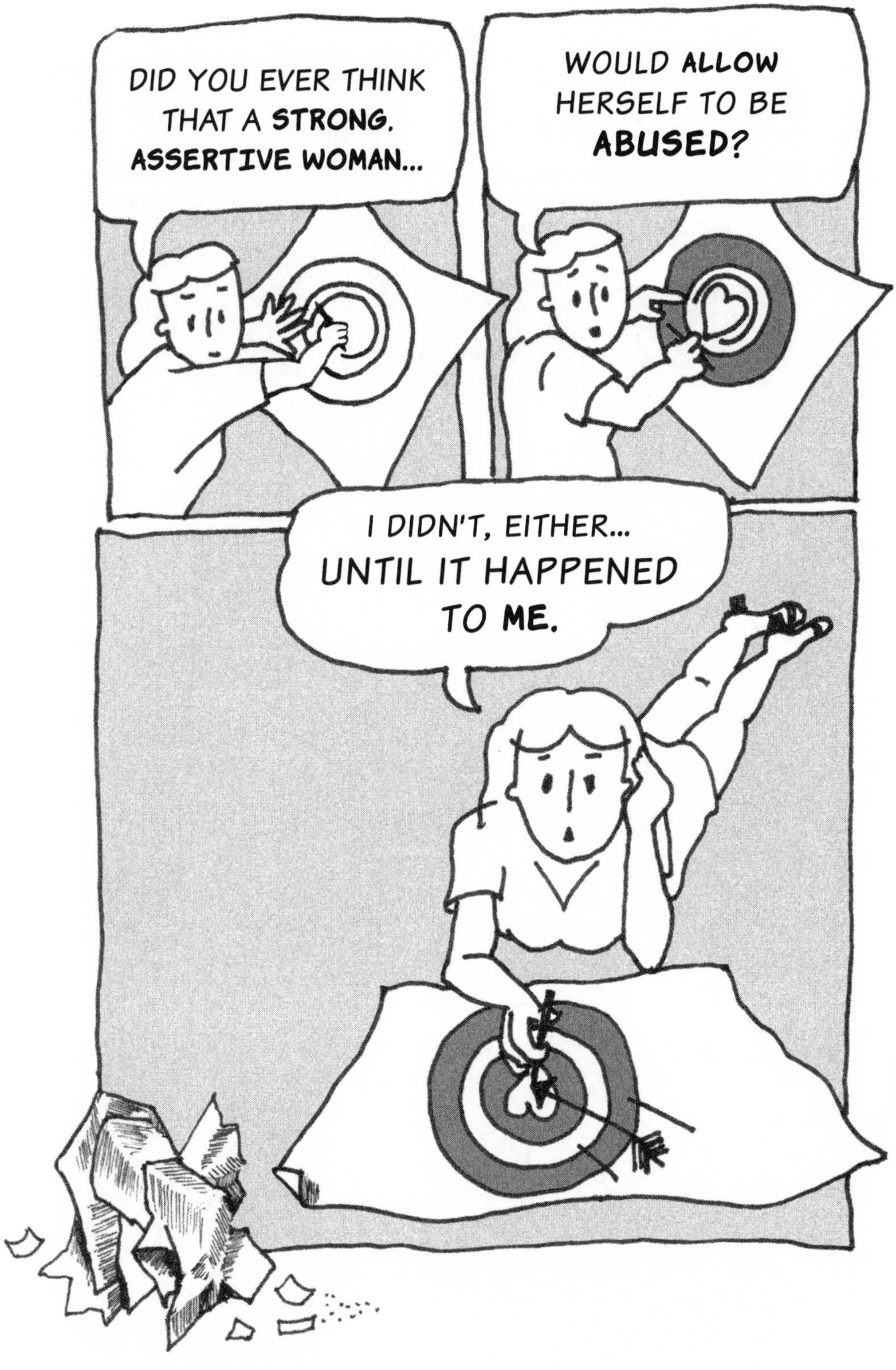
DID YOU EVER THINK THAT A STRONG, ASSERTIVE WOMAN...
WOULD ALLOW HERSELF TO BE ABUSED?
I DIDN'T, EITHER... UNTIL IT HAPPENED TO ME.

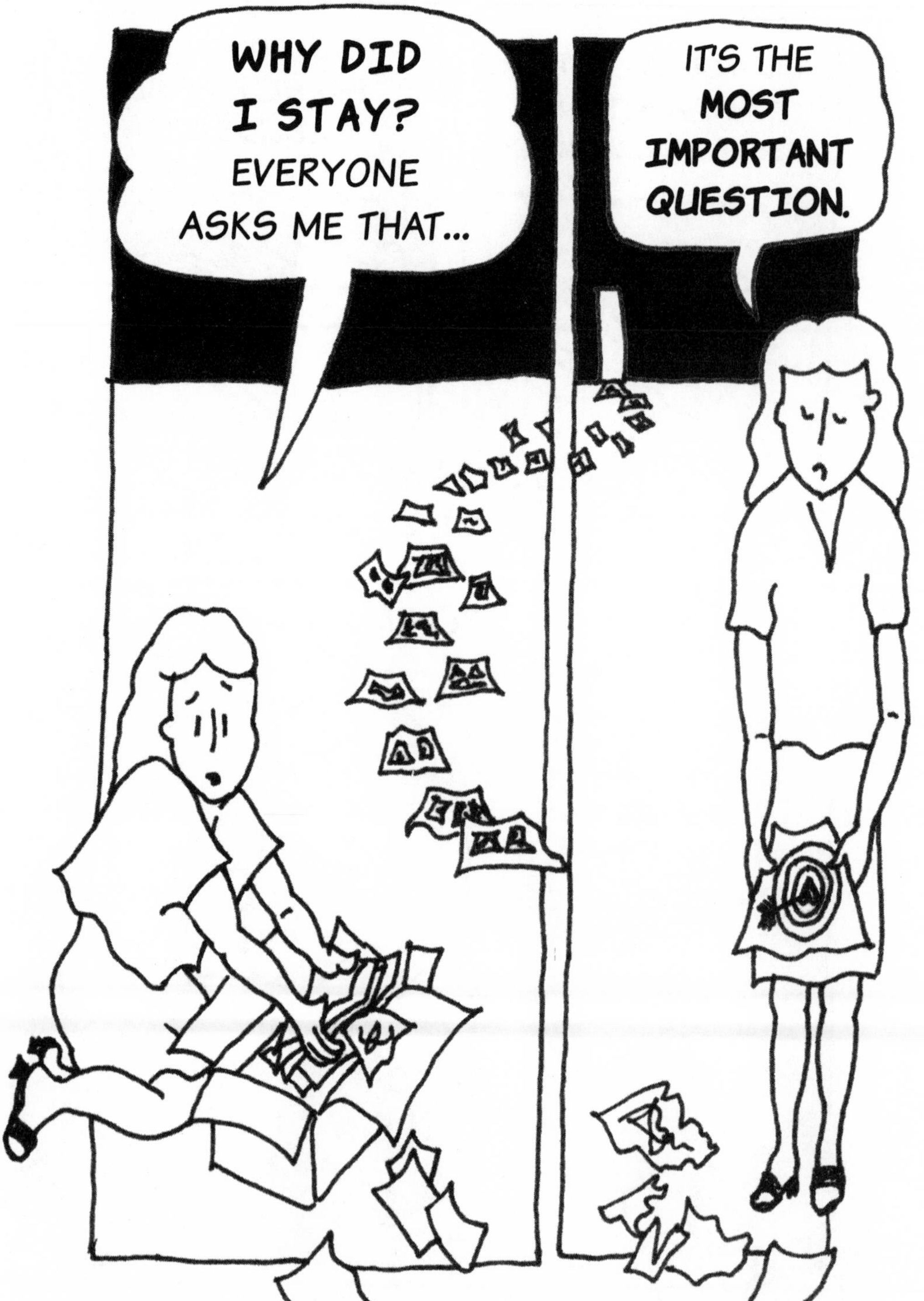
WHY DID I STAY? EVERYONE ASKS ME THAT...
IT'S THE MOST IMPORTANT QUESTION.

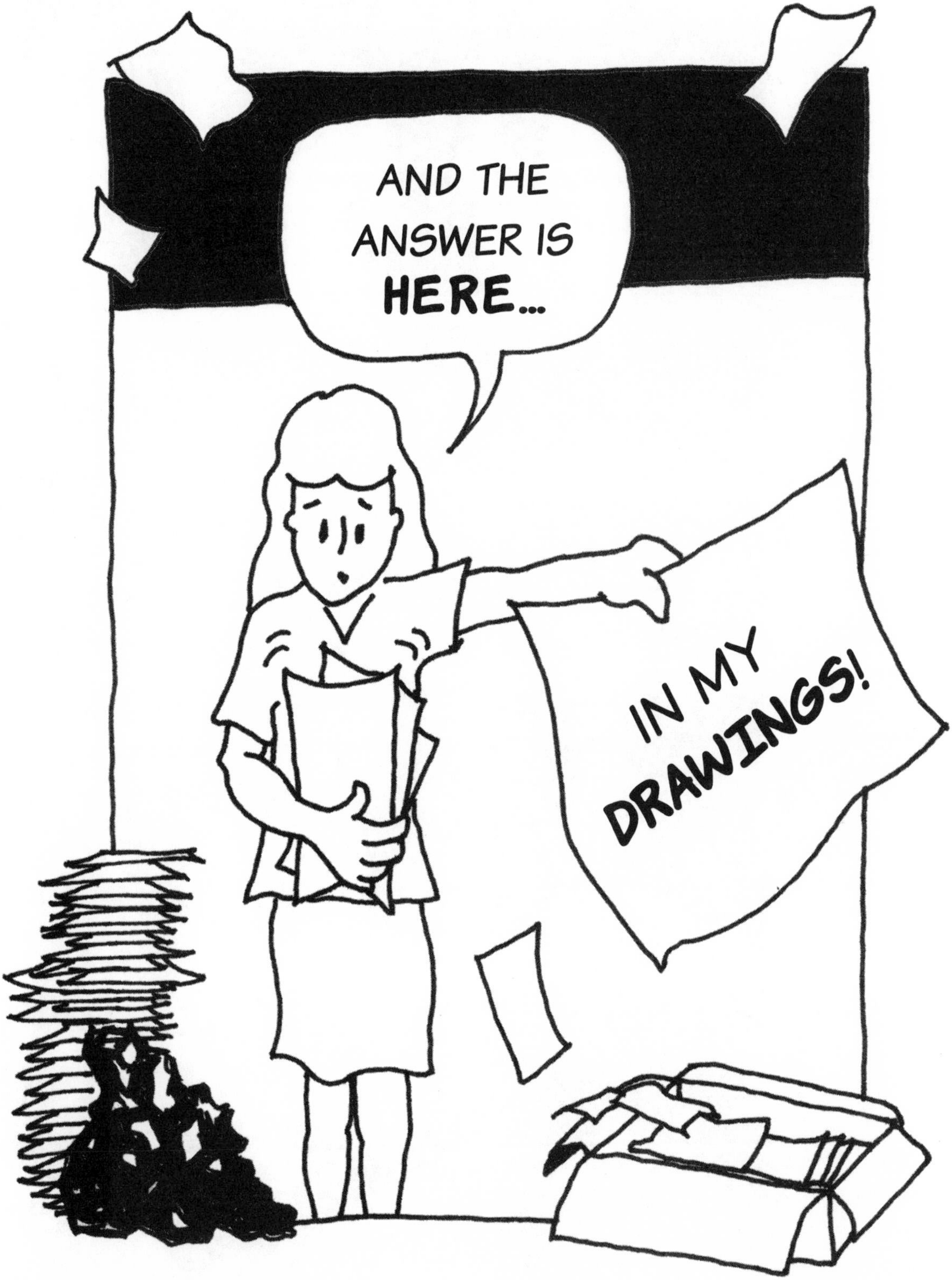
AND THE ANSWER IS **HERE...**
IN MY **DRAWINGS!**

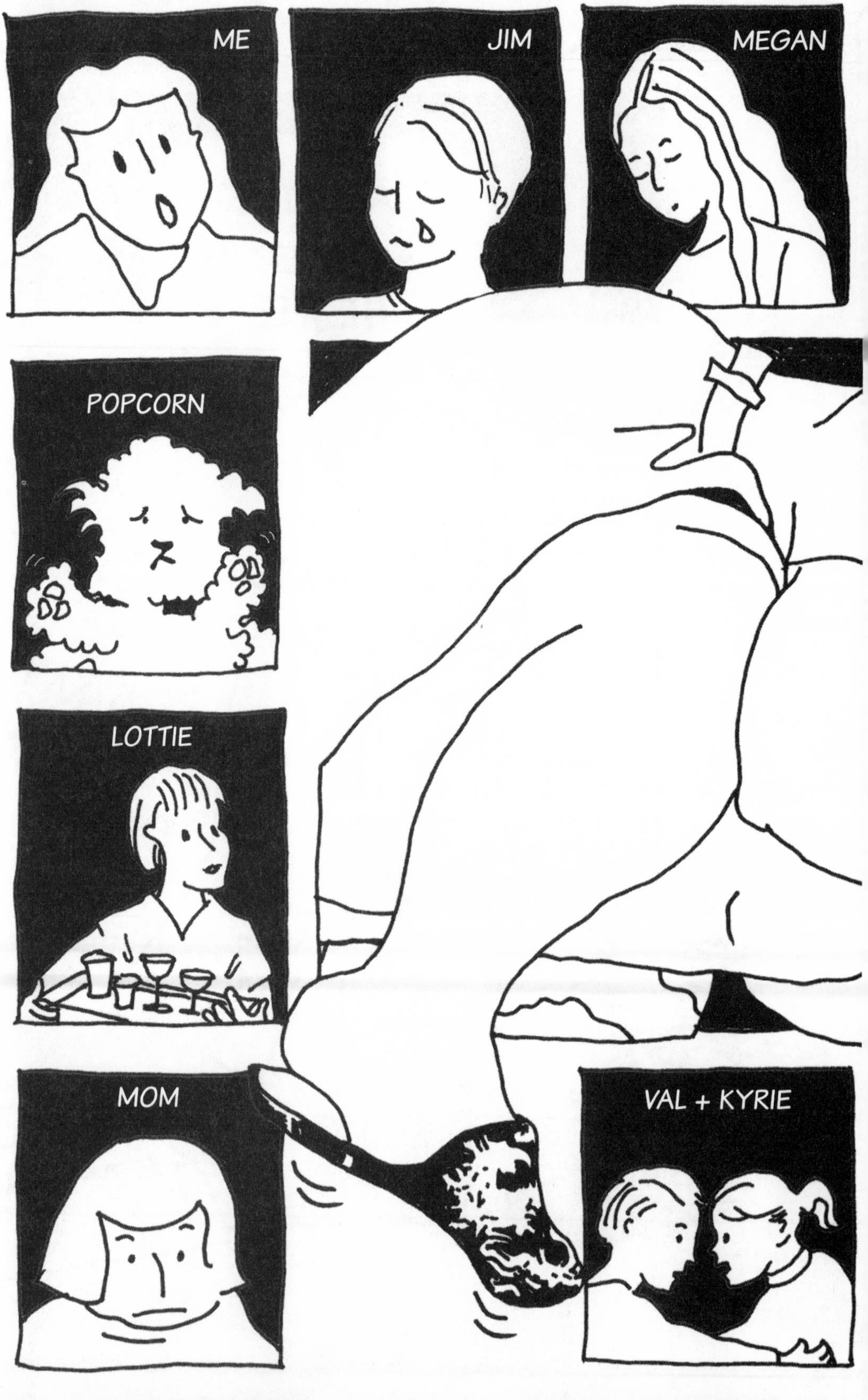

ME
JIM
MEGAN
POPCORN
LOTTIE
MOM
VAL + KYRIE

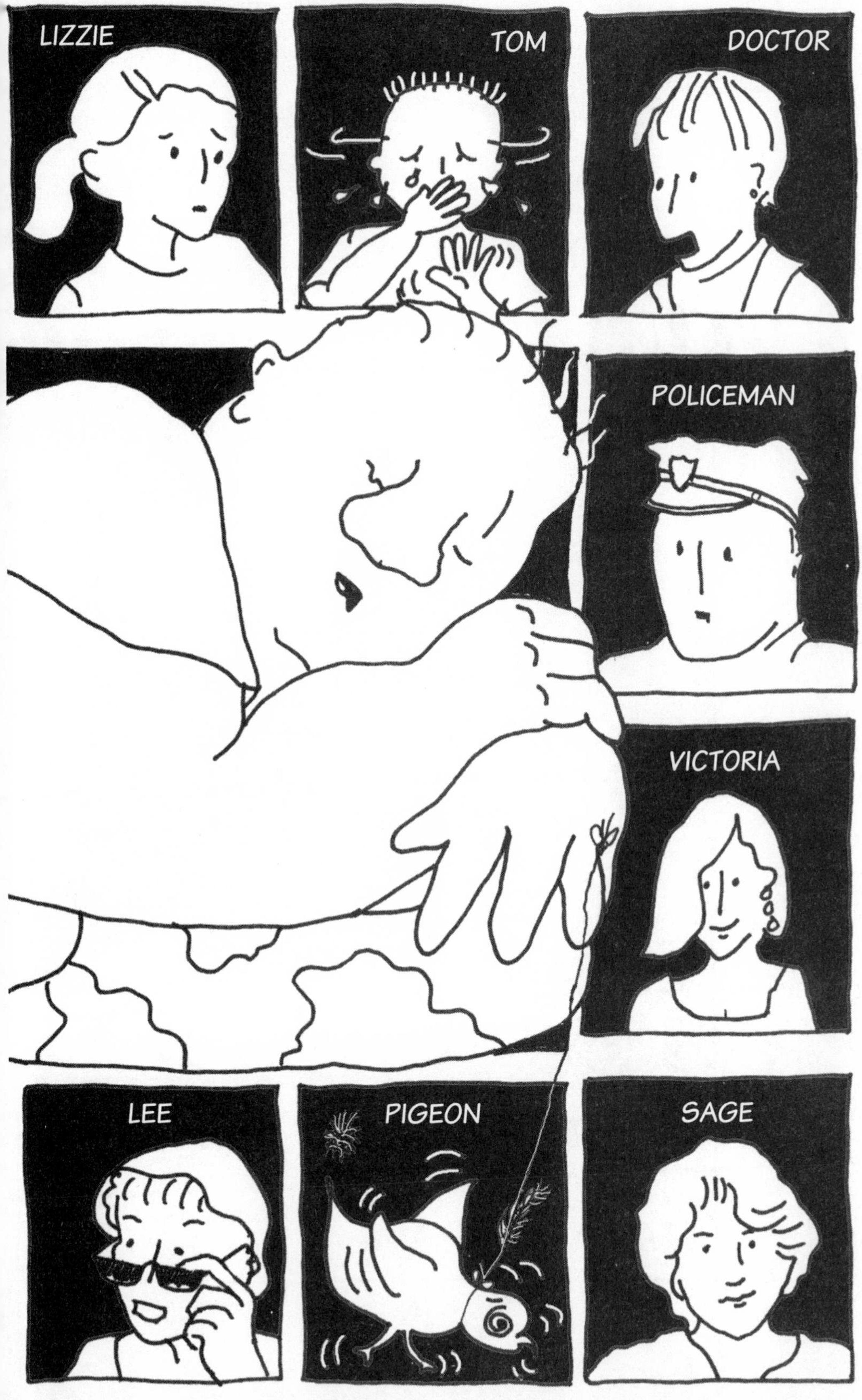
LIZZIE
TOM
DOCTOR
POLICEMAN
VICTORIA
LEE
PIGEON
SAGE

Getting In: The Honeymoon

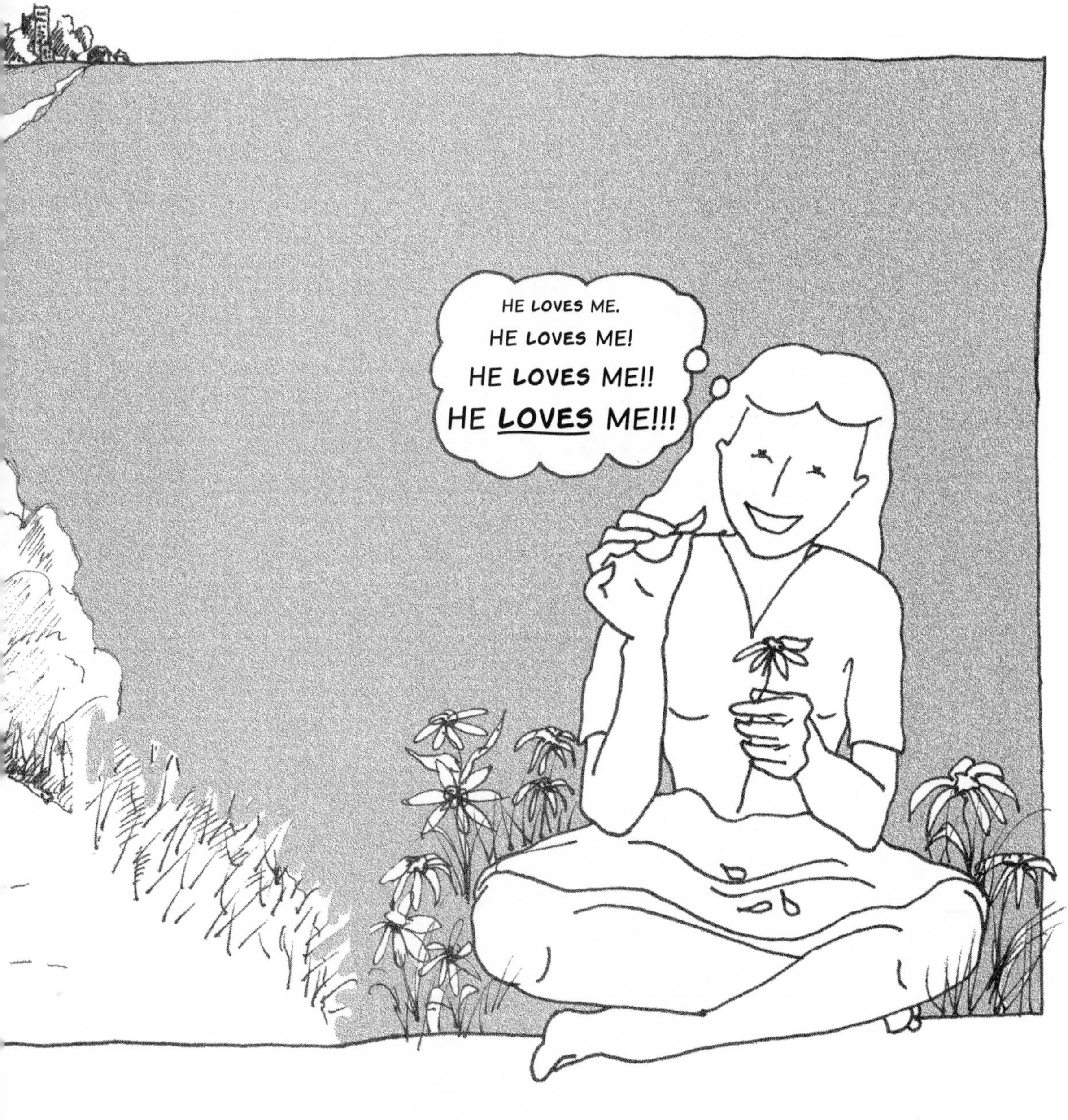
HE LOVES ME.
HE LOVES ME!
HE LOVES ME!!
HE LOVES ME!!!

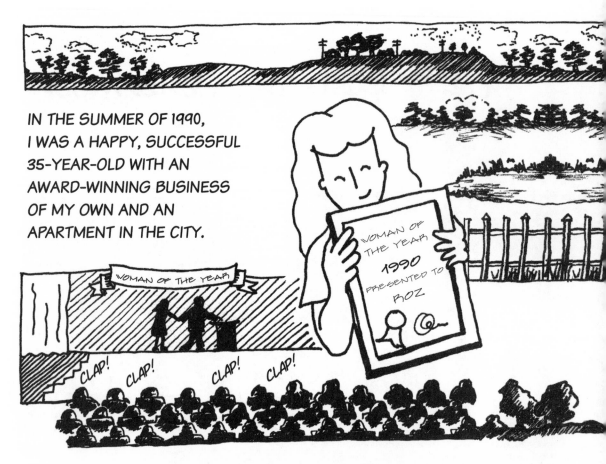

IN THE SUMMER OF 1990, I WAS A HAPPY, SUCCESSFUL 35-YEAR-OLD WITH AN AWARD-WINNING BUSINESS OF MY OWN AND AN APARTMENT IN THE CITY.
WOMAN OF THE YEAR
WOMAN OF THE YEAR 1990 PRESENTED TO ROZ
CLAP!
CLAP!
CLAP!
CLAP!
ONE DAY, MY PARENTS CALLED WITH AN INVITATION.
HOW WOULD YOU LIKE TO COME WITH US TO A PARTY IN THE COUNTRY TOMORROW? IT WOULD DO YOU GOOD.
YOU **WORK TOO HARD.** IT'S TIME YOU HAD **FUN!**
THANKS, MOM! THANKS, DAD!

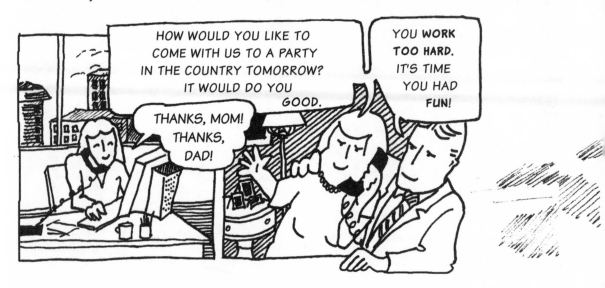

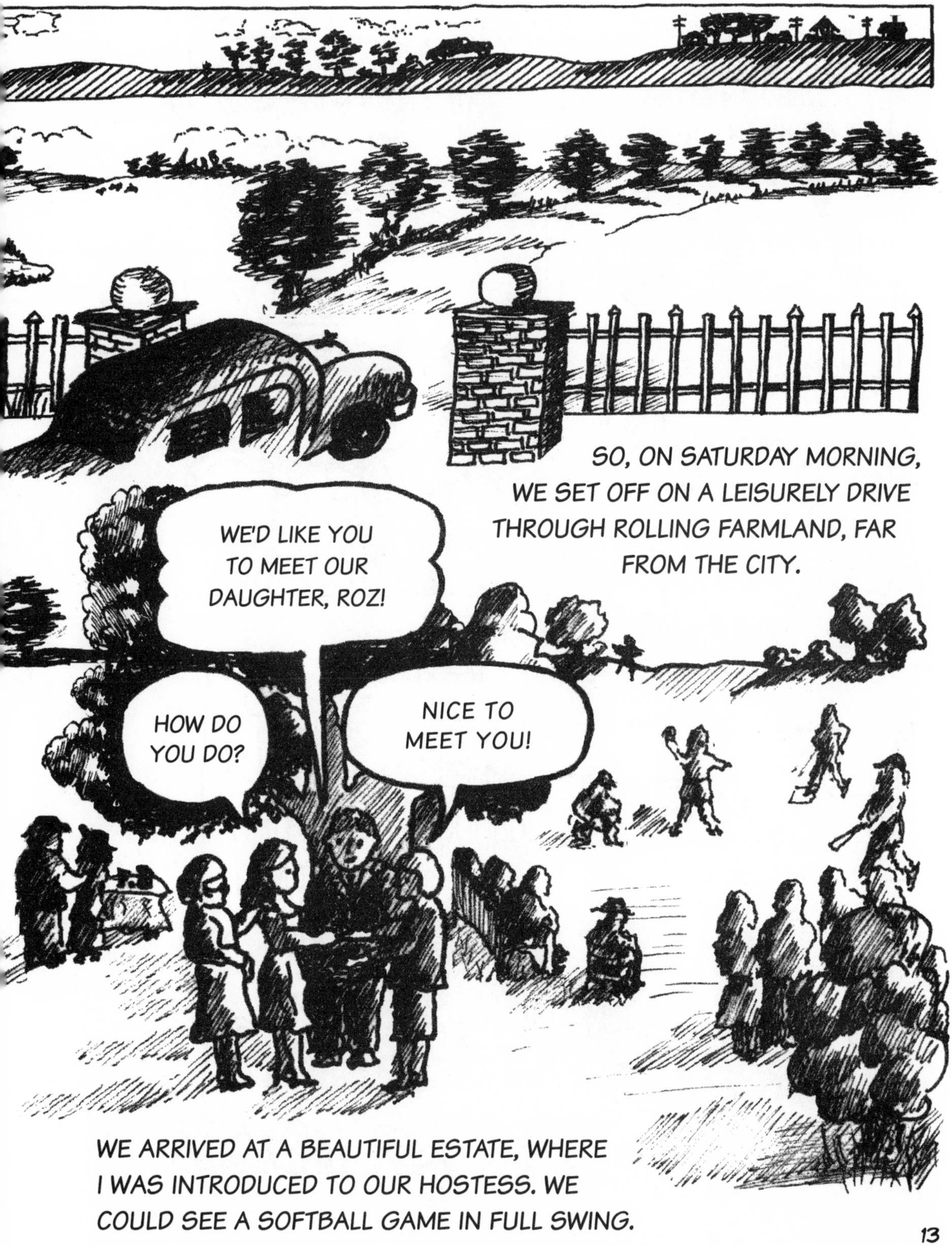
SO, ON SATURDAY MORNING, WE SET OFF ON A LEISURELY DRIVE THROUGH ROLLING FARMLAND, FAR FROM THE CITY.
WE'D LIKE YOU TO MEET OUR DAUGHTER, ROZ!
HOW DO YOU DO?
NICE TO MEET YOU!
WE ARRIVED AT A BEAUTIFUL ESTATE, WHERE I WAS INTRODUCED TO OUR HOSTESS. WE COULD SEE A SOFTBALL GAME IN FULL SWING.

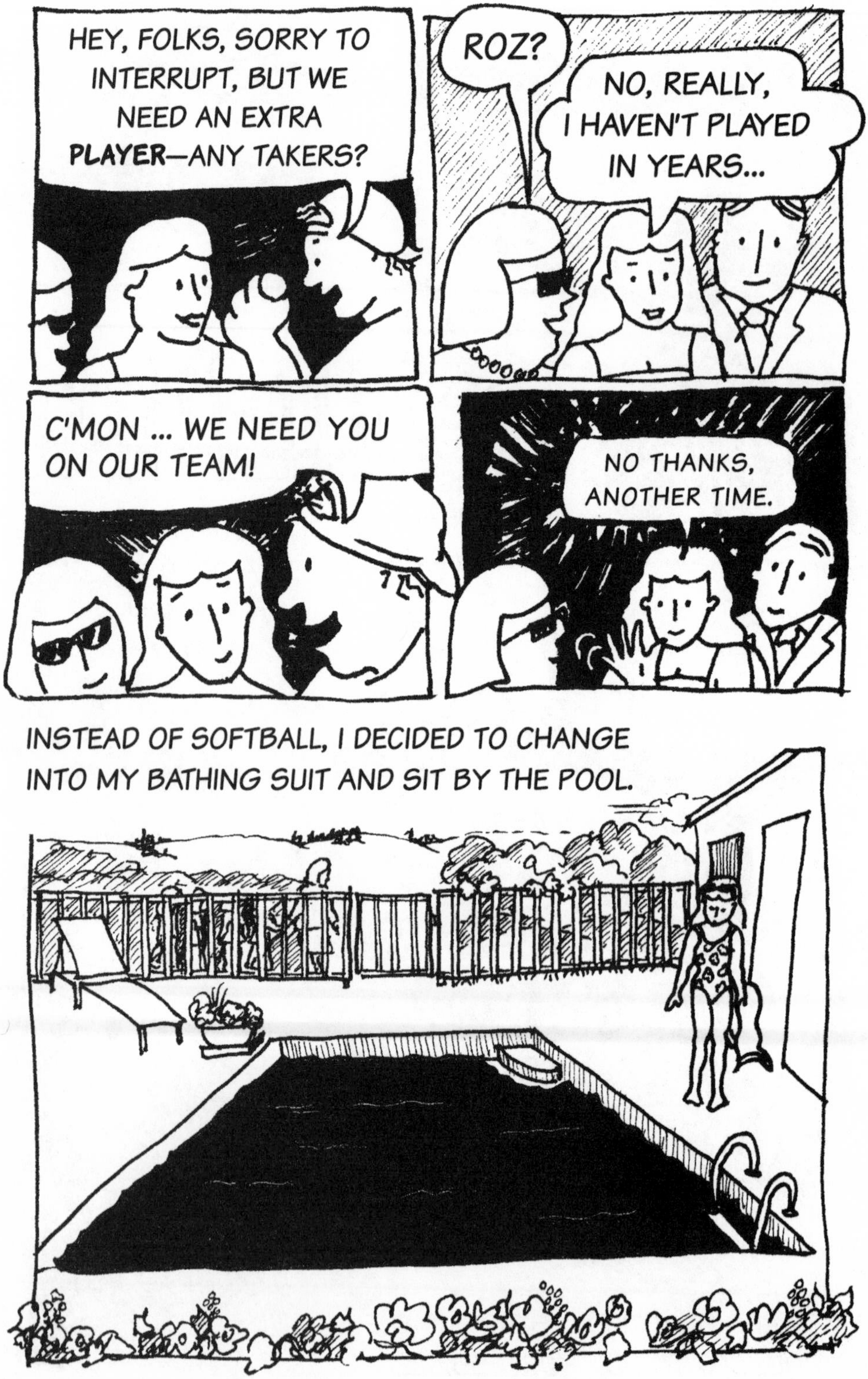
HEY, FOLKS, SORRY TO INTERRUPT, BUT WE NEED AN EXTRA **PLAYER**—ANY TAKERS?
ROZ?
NO, REALLY, I HAVEN'T PLAYED IN YEARS...
C'MON ... WE NEED YOU ON OUR TEAM!
NO THANKS, ANOTHER TIME.
INSTEAD OF SOFTBALL, I DECIDED TO CHANGE INTO MY BATHING SUIT AND SIT BY THE POOL.

SOON AFTER, IN THROUGH THE POOL GATE CAME OUR HOSTESS WITH 4 LITTLE CHILDREN. THEY LOOKED SAD. WHO WERE THEY?

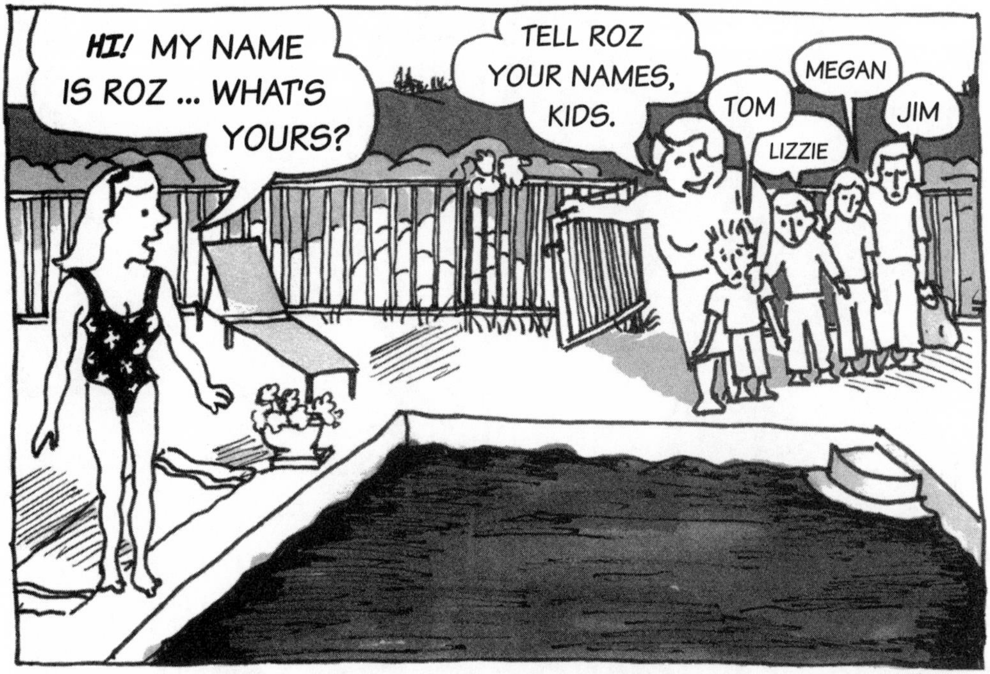

HI! MY NAME IS ROZ ... WHAT'S YOURS?
TELL ROZ YOUR NAMES, KIDS.
TOM
LIZZIE
MEGAN
JIM

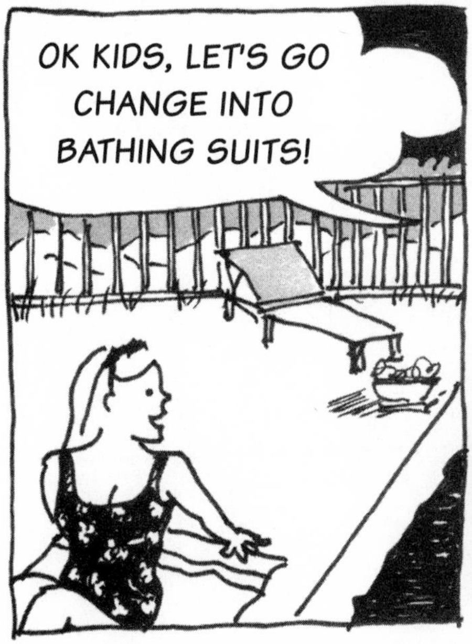

OK KIDS, LET'S GO CHANGE INTO BATHING SUITS!

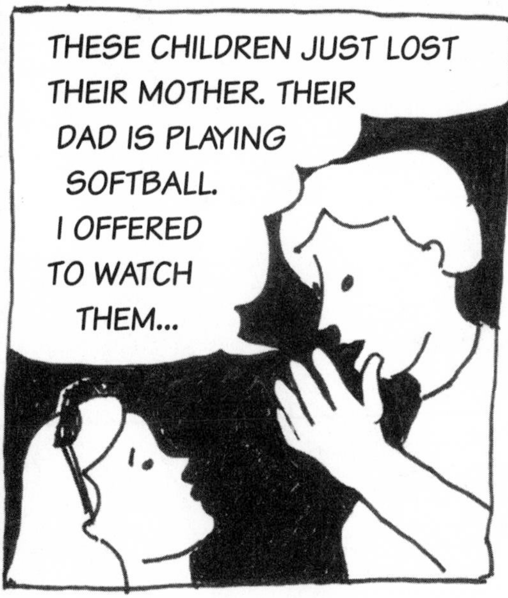

THESE CHILDREN JUST LOST THEIR MOTHER. THEIR DAD IS PLAYING SOFTBALL. I OFFERED TO WATCH THEM...

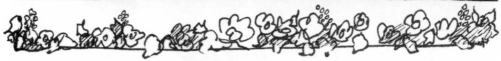

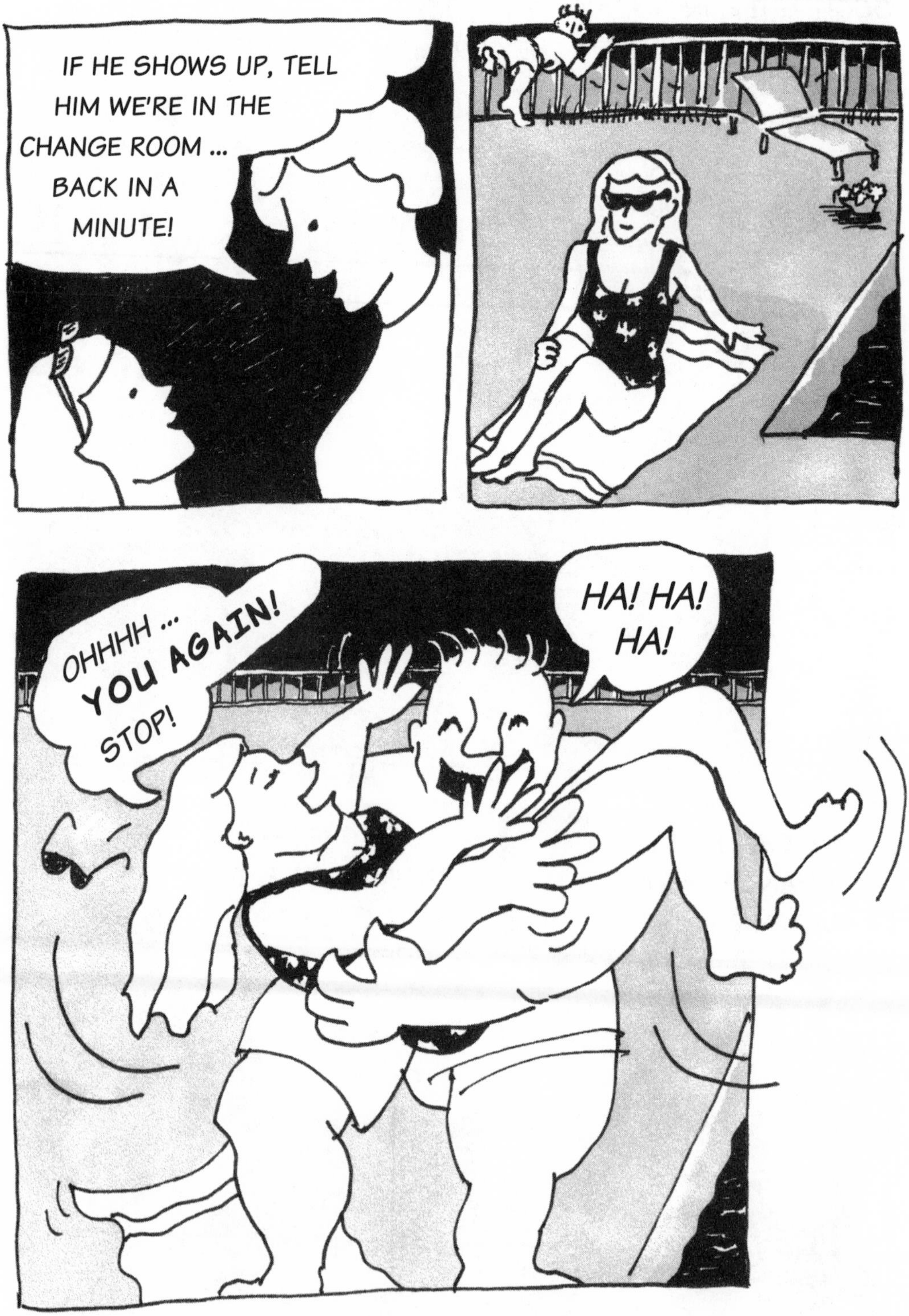
IF HE SHOWS UP, TELL HIM WE'RE IN THE CHANGE ROOM ... BACK IN A MINUTE!
OHHHH ... YOU AGAIN! STOP!
HA! HA! HA!

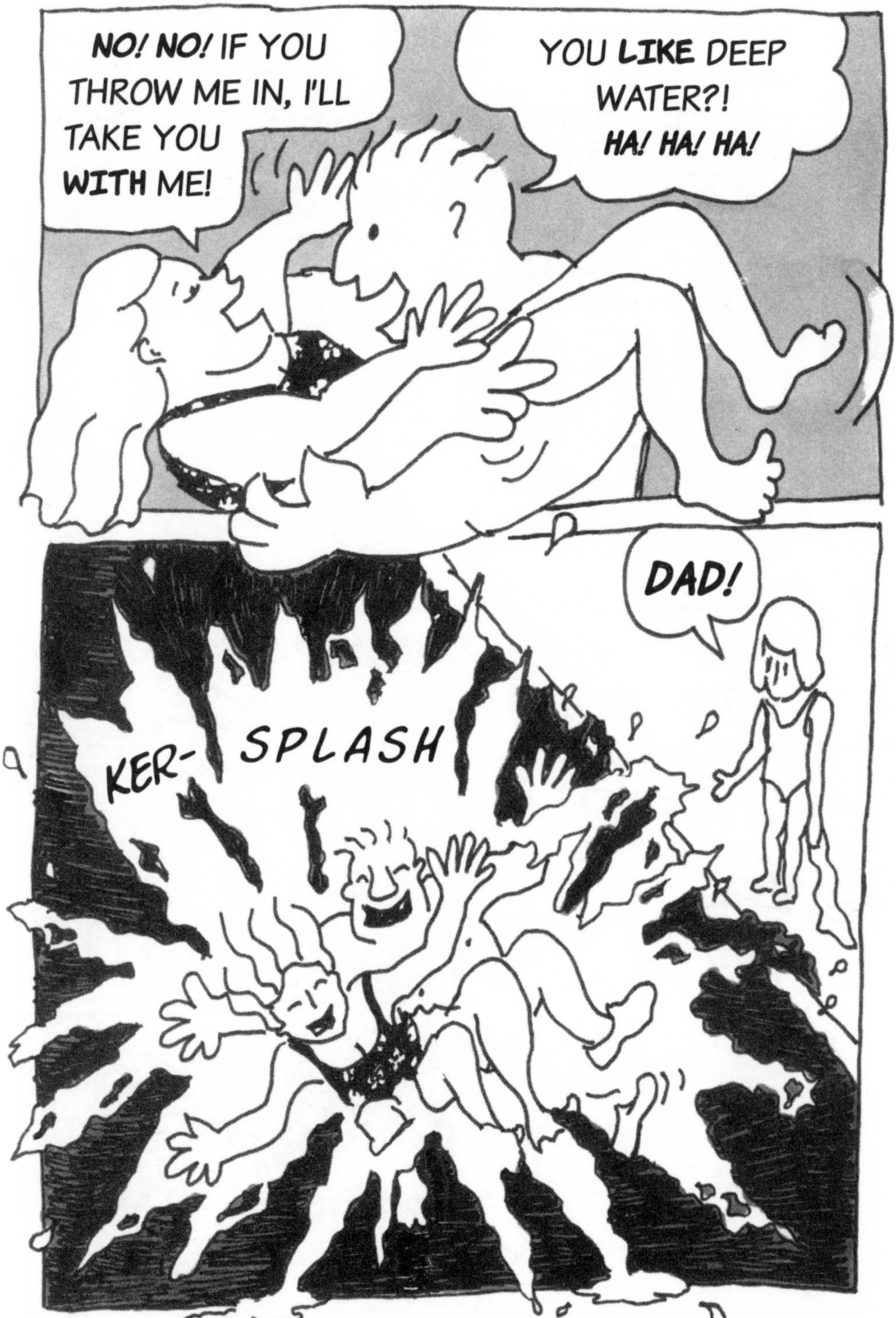
NO! NO! IF YOU THROW ME IN, I'LL TAKE YOU WITH ME!
YOU LIKE DEEP WATER?! HA! HA! HA!
DAD!
KER- SPLASH

DRIVING HOME, I FELT AS THOUGH SOMETHING FATEFUL HAD JUST HAPPENED.

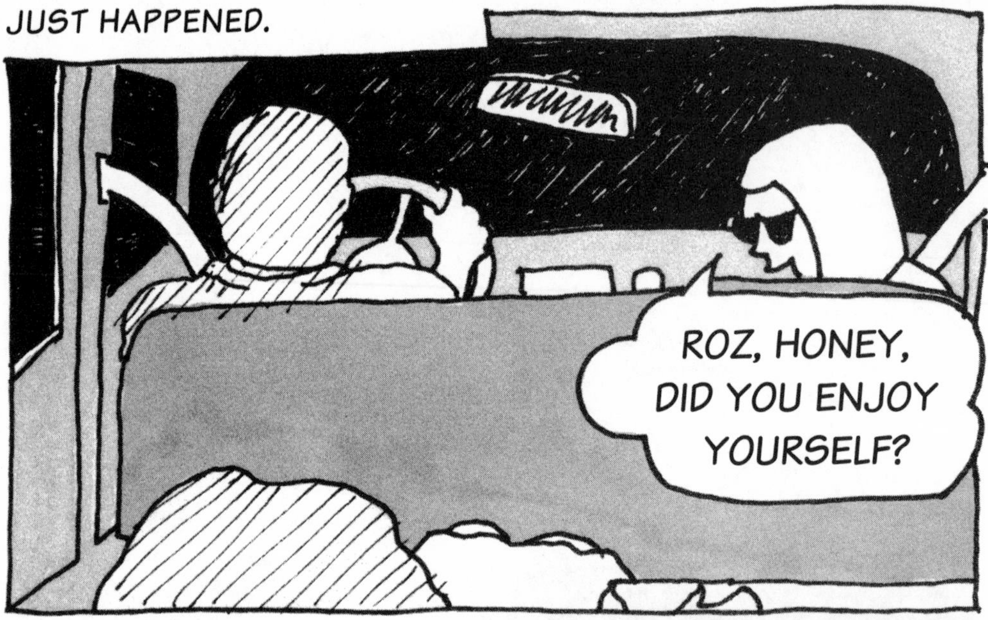
ROZ, HONEY, DID YOU ENJOY YOURSELF?

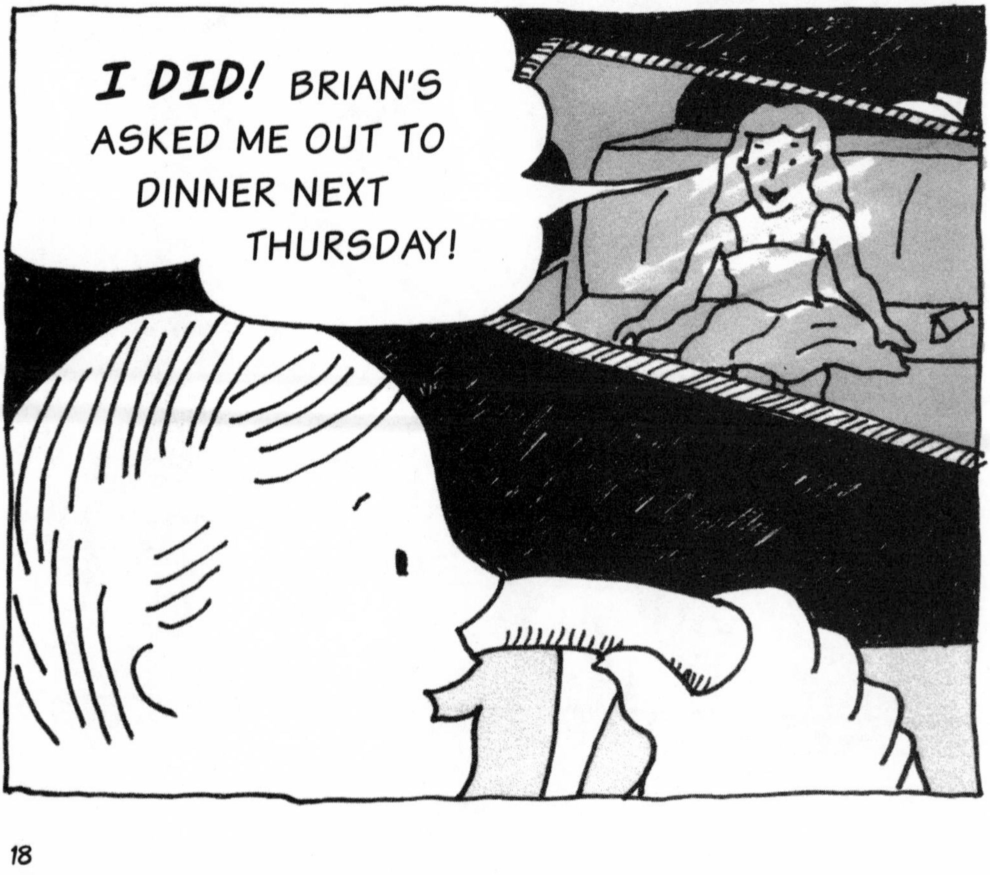
I DID! BRIAN'S ASKED ME OUT TO DINNER NEXT THURSDAY!

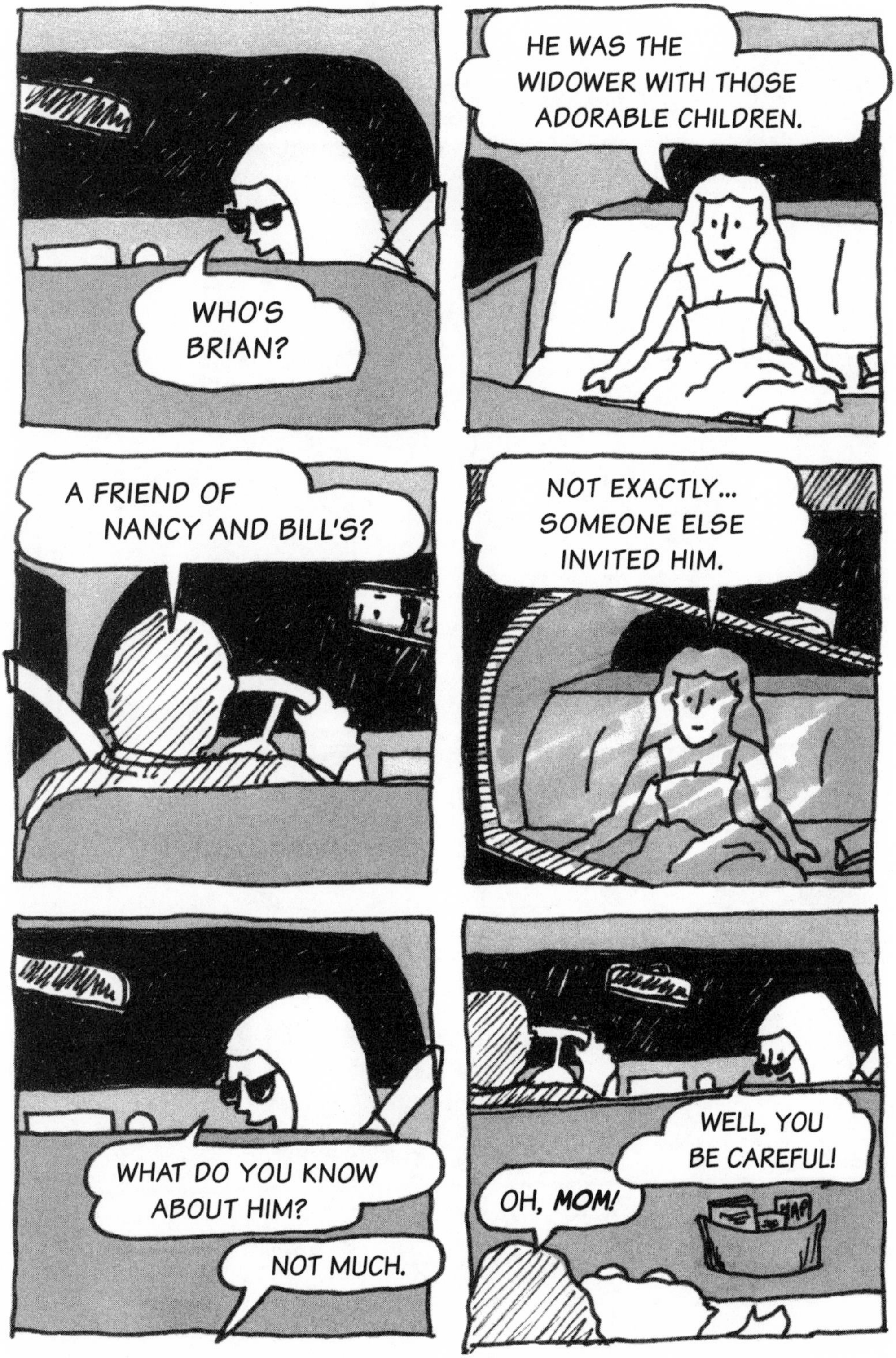
WHO'S BRIAN?
HE WAS THE WIDOWER WITH THOSE ADORABLE CHILDREN.
A FRIEND OF NANCY AND BILL'S?
NOT EXACTLY... SOMEONE ELSE INVITED HIM.
WHAT DO YOU KNOW ABOUT HIM?
NOT MUCH.
WELL, YOU BE CAREFUL!
OH, **MOM!**
MAP

THE FOLLOWING THURSDAY, BRIAN PICKED ME UP FOR OUR FIRST DATE. ON THE FRONT SEAT WAS A RED ROSE!

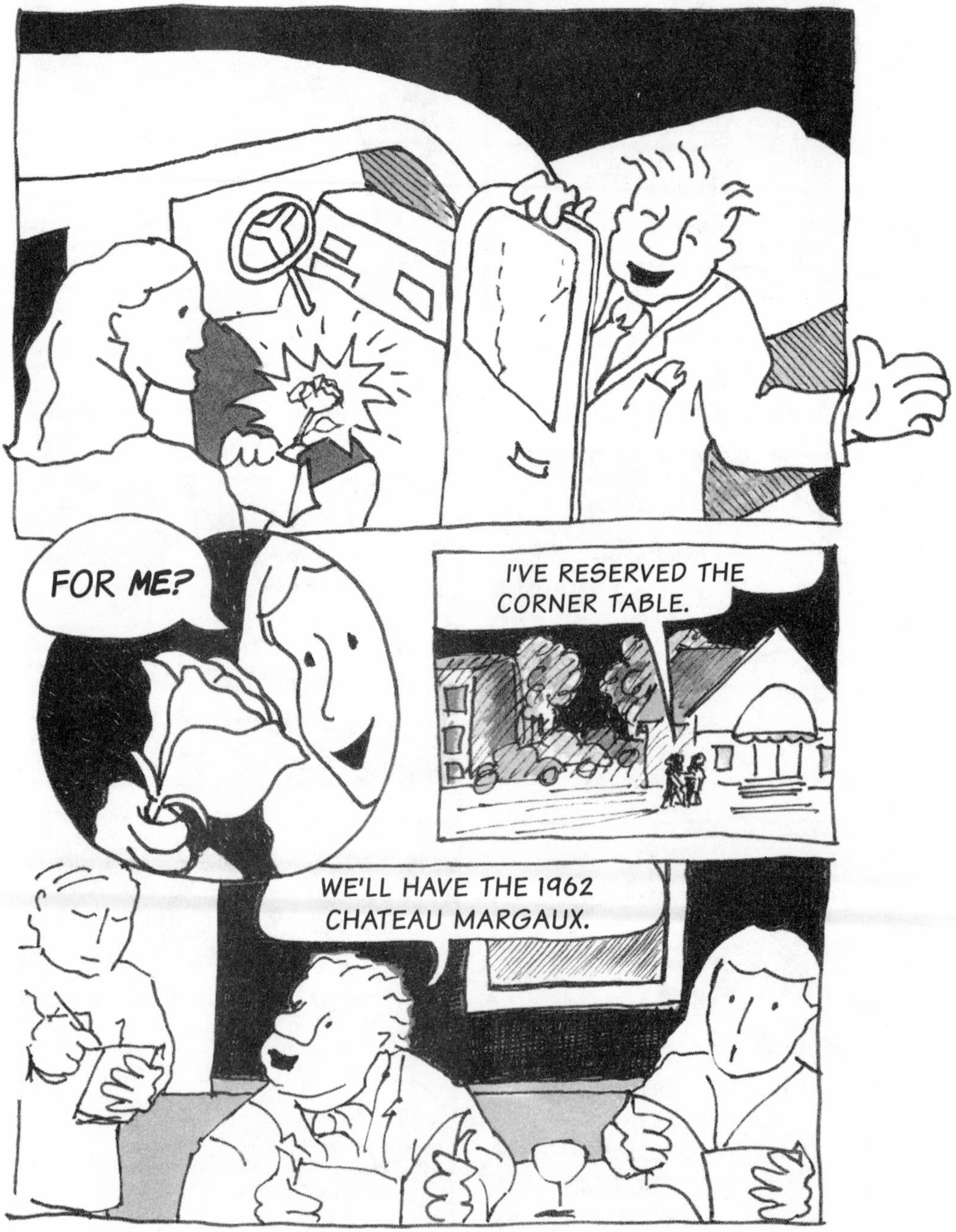

FOR ME?
I'VE RESERVED THE CORNER TABLE.
WE'LL HAVE THE 1962 CHATEAU MARGAUX.

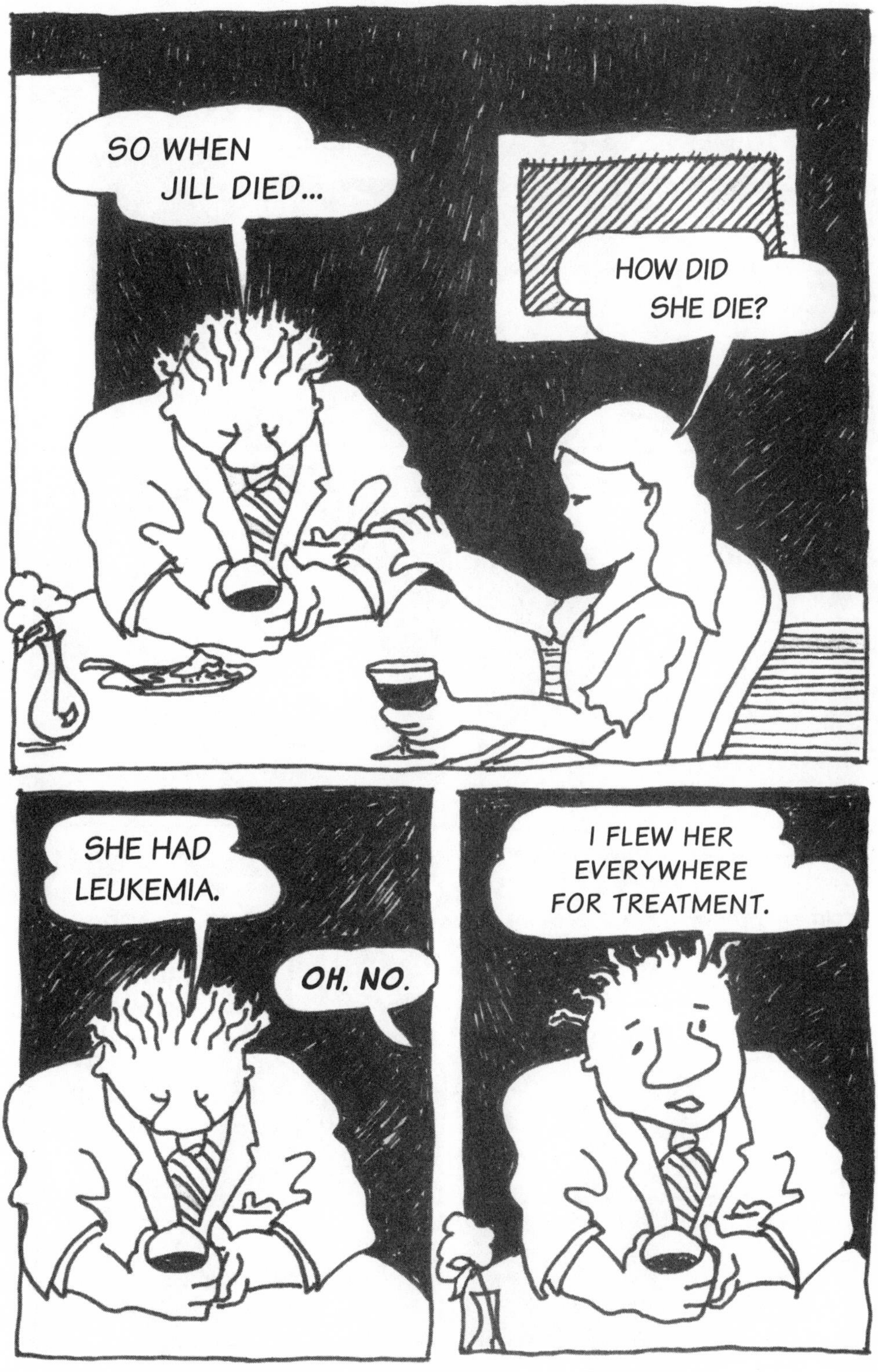
SO WHEN JILL DIED...
HOW DID SHE DIE?
SHE HAD LEUKEMIA.
OH, NO.
I FLEW HER EVERYWHERE FOR TREATMENT.

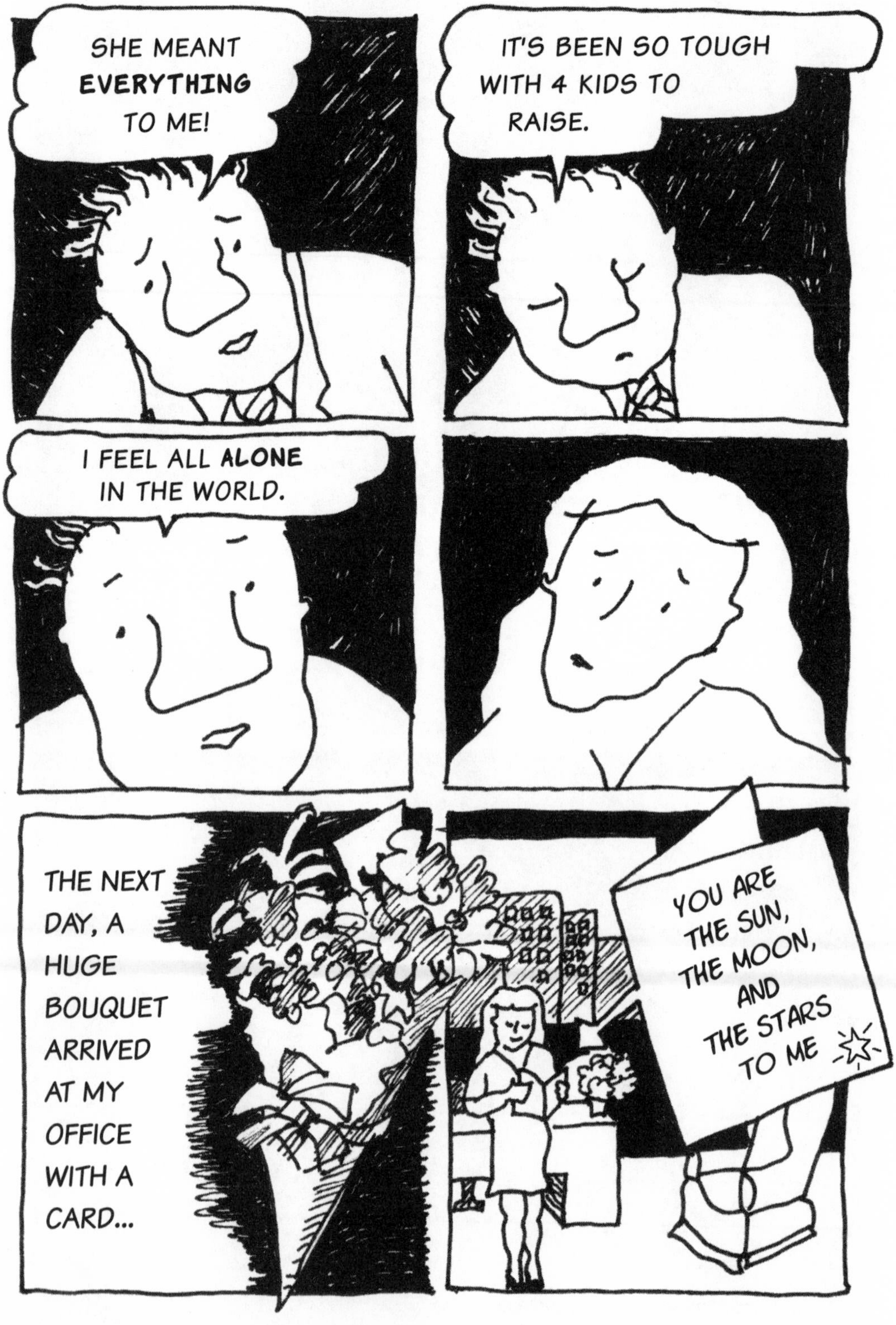
SHE MEANT EVERYTHING TO ME!
IT'S BEEN SO TOUGH WITH 4 KIDS TO RAISE.
I FEEL ALL ALONE IN THE WORLD.
THE NEXT DAY, A HUGE BOUQUET ARRIVED AT MY OFFICE WITH A CARD...
YOU ARE THE SUN, THE MOON, AND THE STARS TO ME

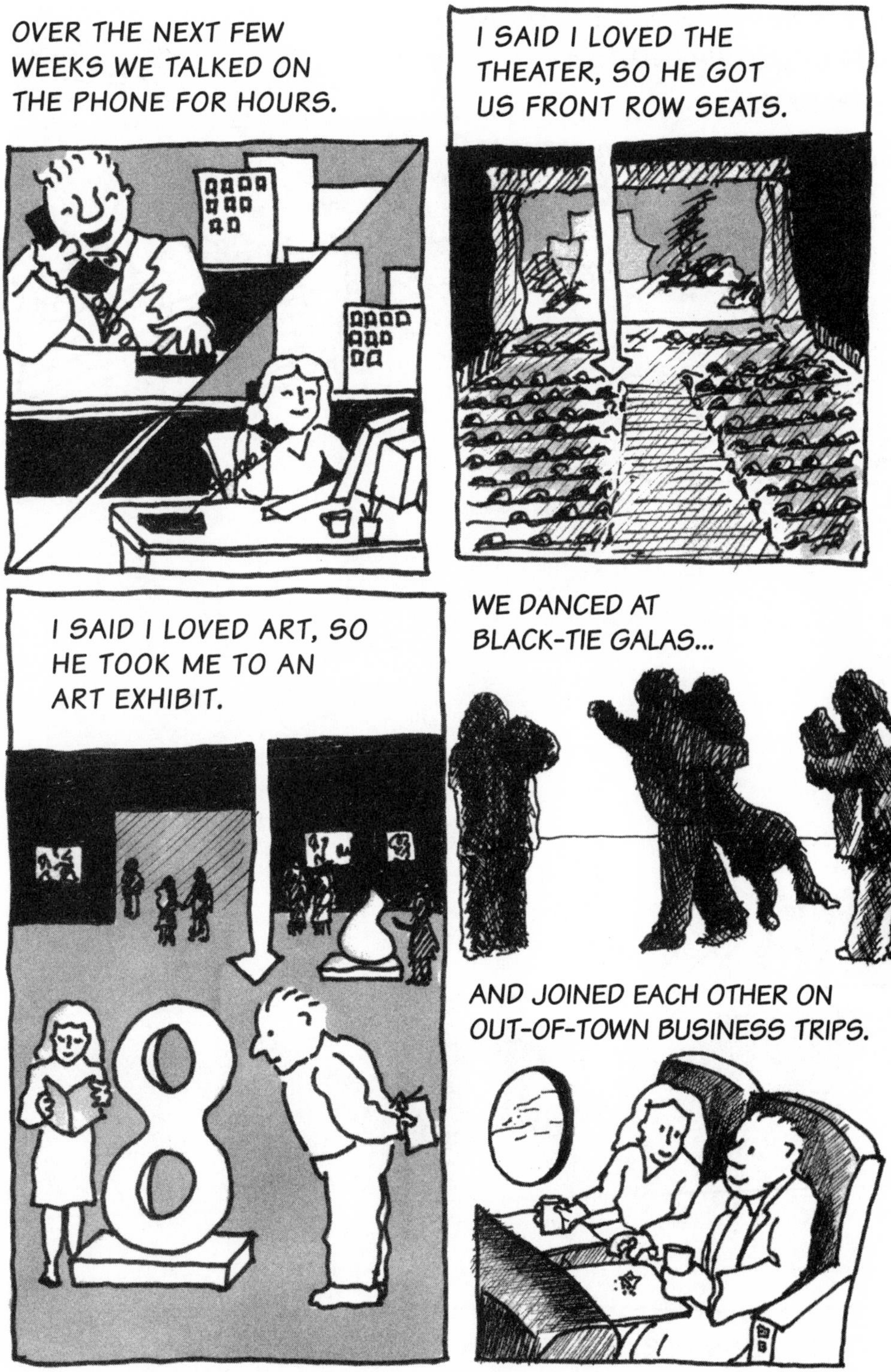
OVER THE NEXT FEW WEEKS WE TALKED ON THE PHONE FOR HOURS.
I SAID I LOVED THE THEATER, SO HE GOT US FRONT ROW SEATS.
I SAID I LOVED ART, SO HE TOOK ME TO AN ART EXHIBIT.
WE DANCED AT BLACK-TIE GALAS...
AND JOINED EACH OTHER ON OUT-OF-TOWN BUSINESS TRIPS.

FOR 5 YEARS I HAD WORKED 24/7 TO BUILD MY COMPANY, BUT NOW I BEGAN DELEGATING MORE SO I COULD SPEND TIME WITH BRIAN.

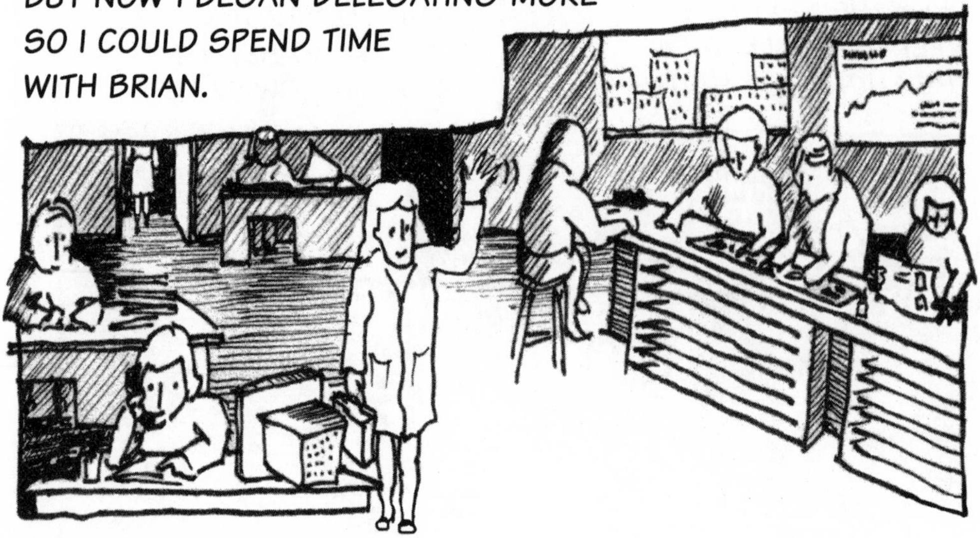

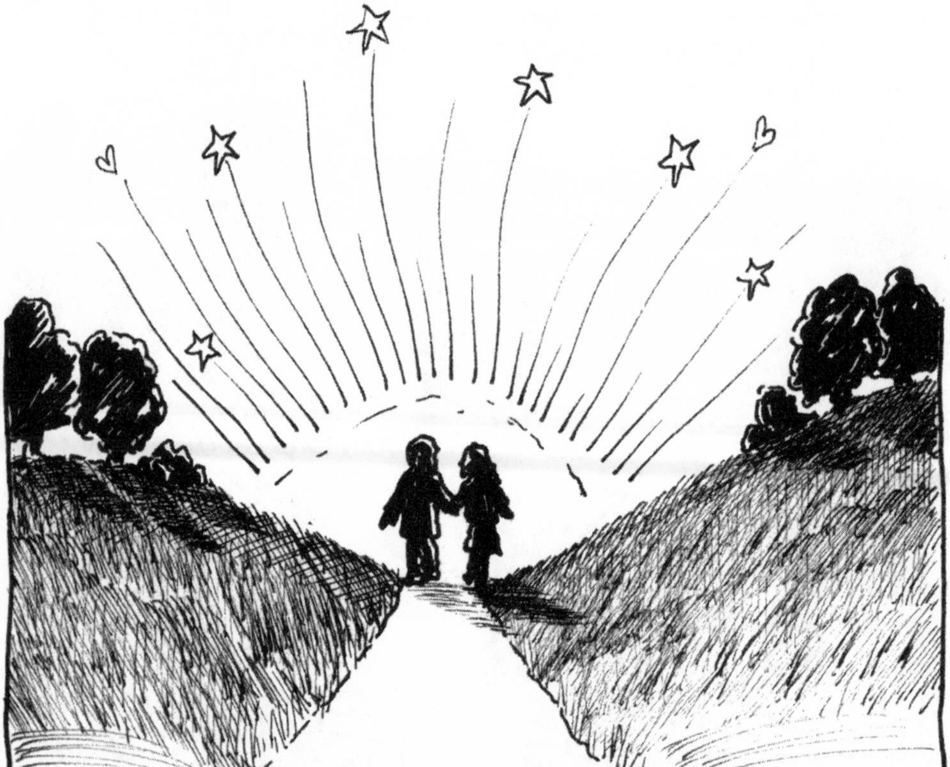

THE SUMMER PASSED IN A HAZE OF ROMANTIC LOVE.

MY FRIENDS WERE VAL + KYRIE, AND WE OFTEN JUST HUNG OUT AT VAL'S PLACE. THEY HADN'T MET BRIAN BECAUSE HE SAID HE WASN'T READY TO SHARE ME YET!

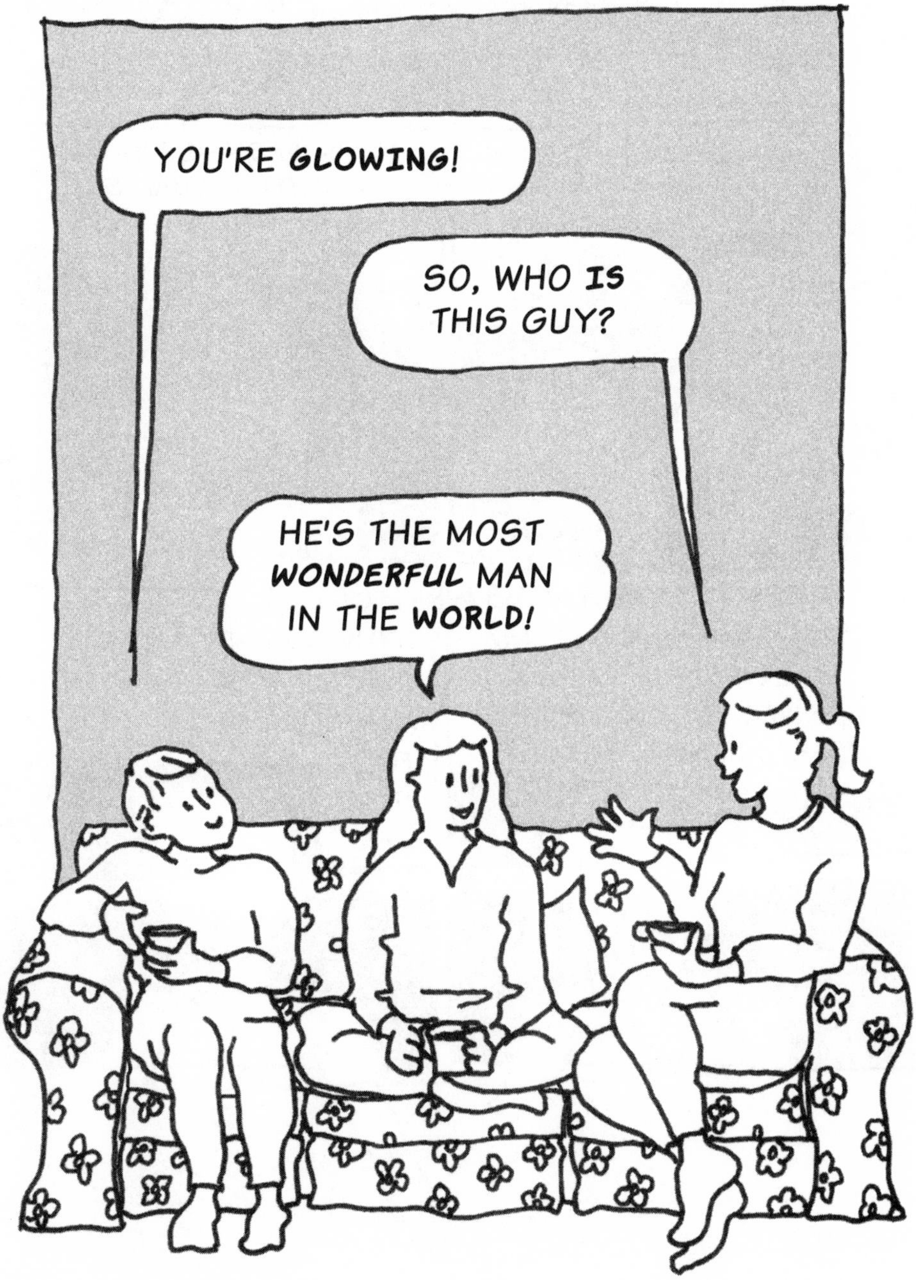
YOU'RE **GLOWING**!
SO, WHO **IS** THIS GUY?
HE'S THE MOST **WONDERFUL** MAN IN THE **WORLD**!

I GRADUALLY STARTED STAYING WITH BRIAN ON WEEKENDS, GETTING TO KNOW HIS CHILDREN.

JIM WAS 11—GENTLE AND ARTISTIC. HE SPENT MOST OF HIS TIME LOST IN HIS MUSIC.

MEGAN WAS 9—SENSITIVE AND INTELLECTUAL. SHE ALWAYS HAD HER NOSE STUCK IN A BOOK!

THE TWINS WERE ONLY 5.

LIZZIE WAS OBEDIENT AND RESERVED. SHE WAS AN OBSERVER, BUT SHE KEPT HER OBSERVATIONS TO HERSELF.

TOM WAS FUN-LOVING AND AFFECTIONATE, BUT HE SEEMED VULNERABLE. HE CLUNG TO LIZZIE FOR DEAR LIFE.

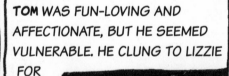

SUDDENLY, MY LIFE WAS DIFFERENT.

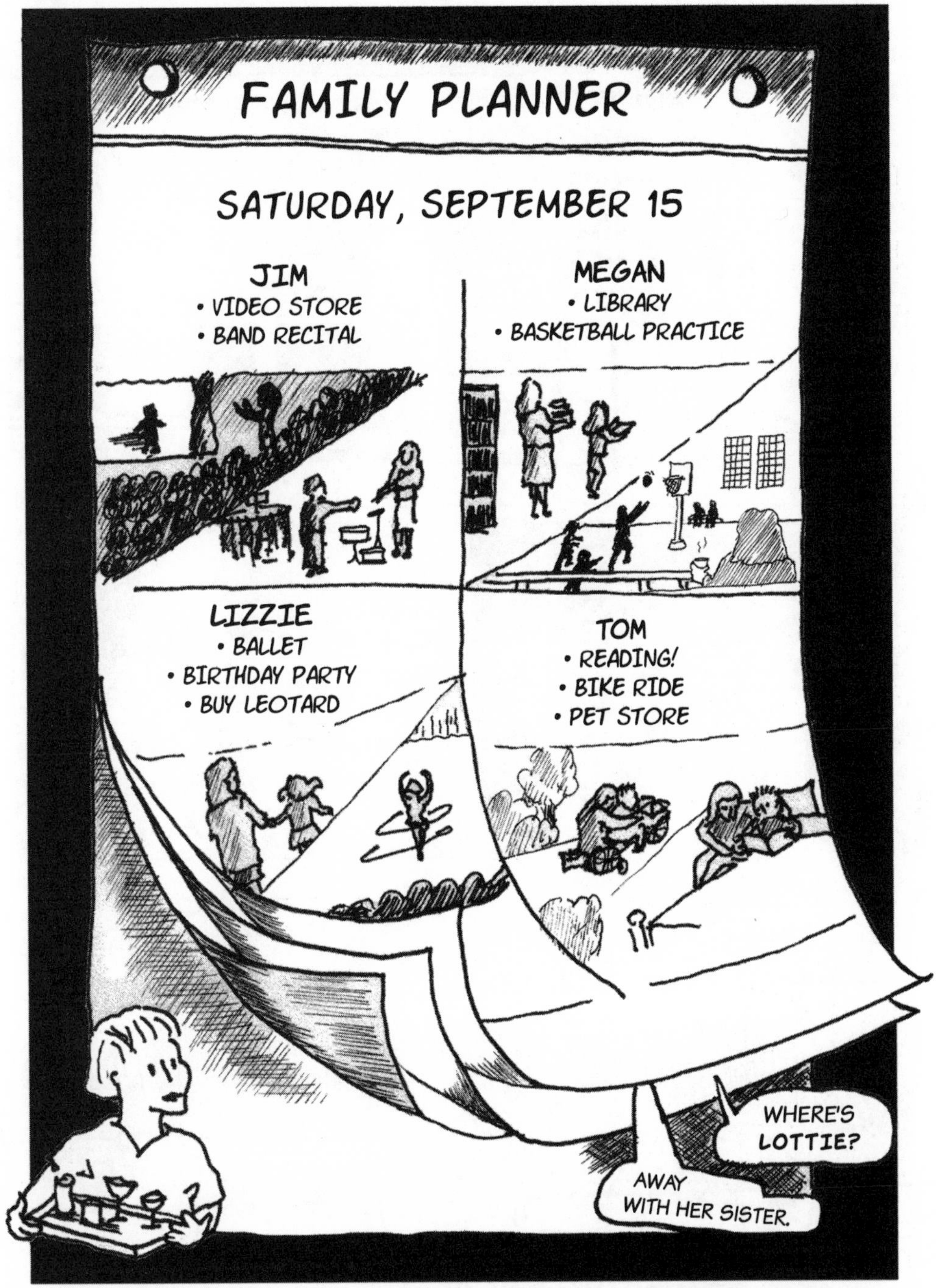
FAMILY PLANNER
SATURDAY, SEPTEMBER 15
JIM
• VIDEO STORE
• BAND RECITAL
MEGAN
• LIBRARY
• BASKETBALL PRACTICE
LIZZIE
• BALLET
• BIRTHDAY PARTY
• BUY LEOTARD
TOM
• READING!
• BIKE RIDE
• PET STORE
WHERE'S LOTTIE?
AWAY WITH HER SISTER.

BRIAN EMPLOYED A YOUNG SWISS NANNY NAMED **LOTTIE**. BUT I RARELY SAW HER. BRIAN GAVE HER EVERY WEEKEND OFF.

WHENEVER I ARRIVED, BRIAN WAS SO EXCITED TO SEE ME THAT HE LEAPT OVER THE RAILING.

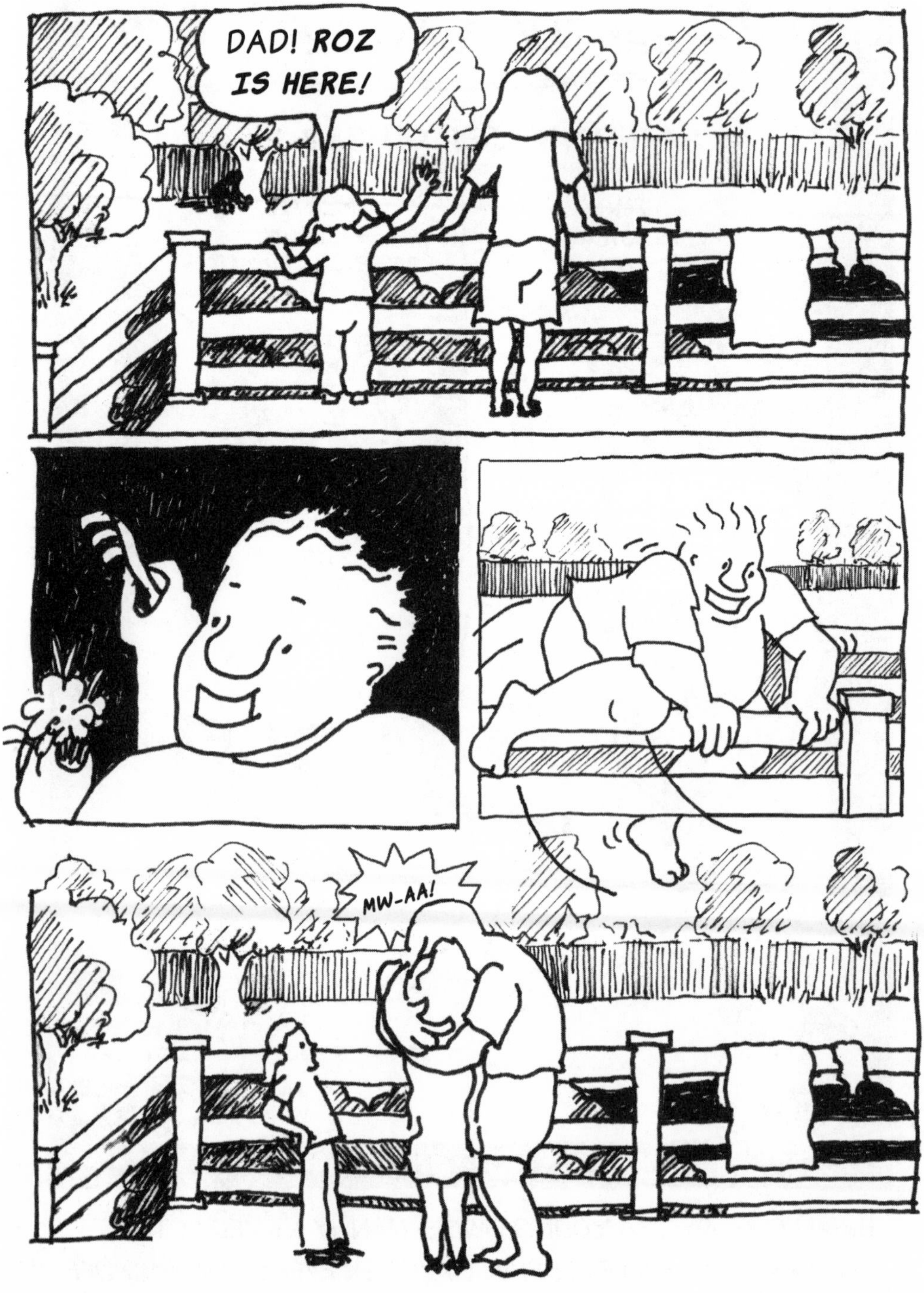
DAD! **ROZ IS HERE!**
MW-AA!

AND WHENEVER HE CAME HOME WITH *GOOD* NEWS, HE LEAPT UP ON THE COUNTER AND DID A DANCE—LARGER THAN LIFE...

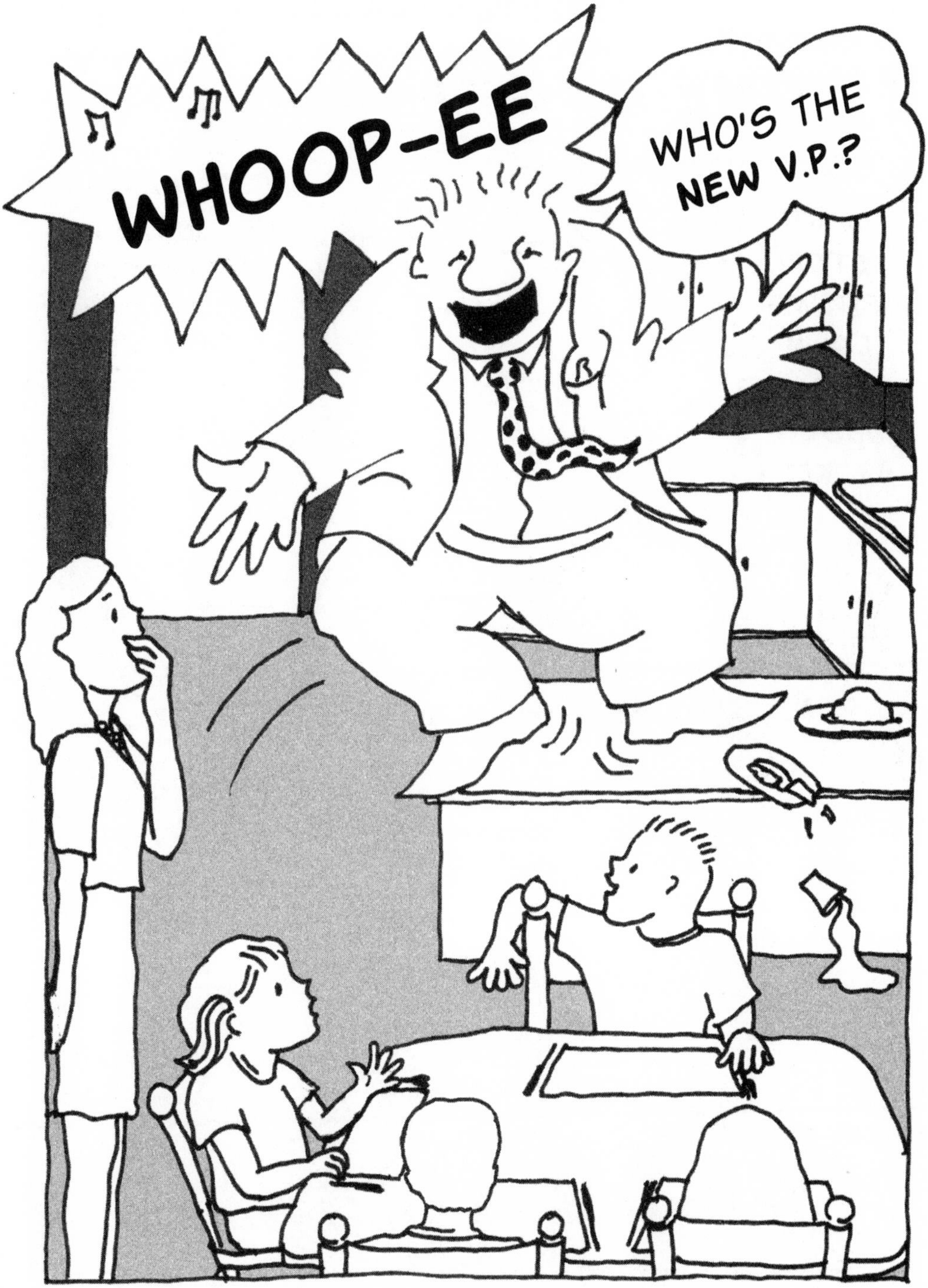
WHOOP-EE
WHO'S THE NEW V.P.?

THEN HE WOULD JUBILANTLY SWING ME AROUND UNTIL I WAS TOO DIZZY TO STAND!

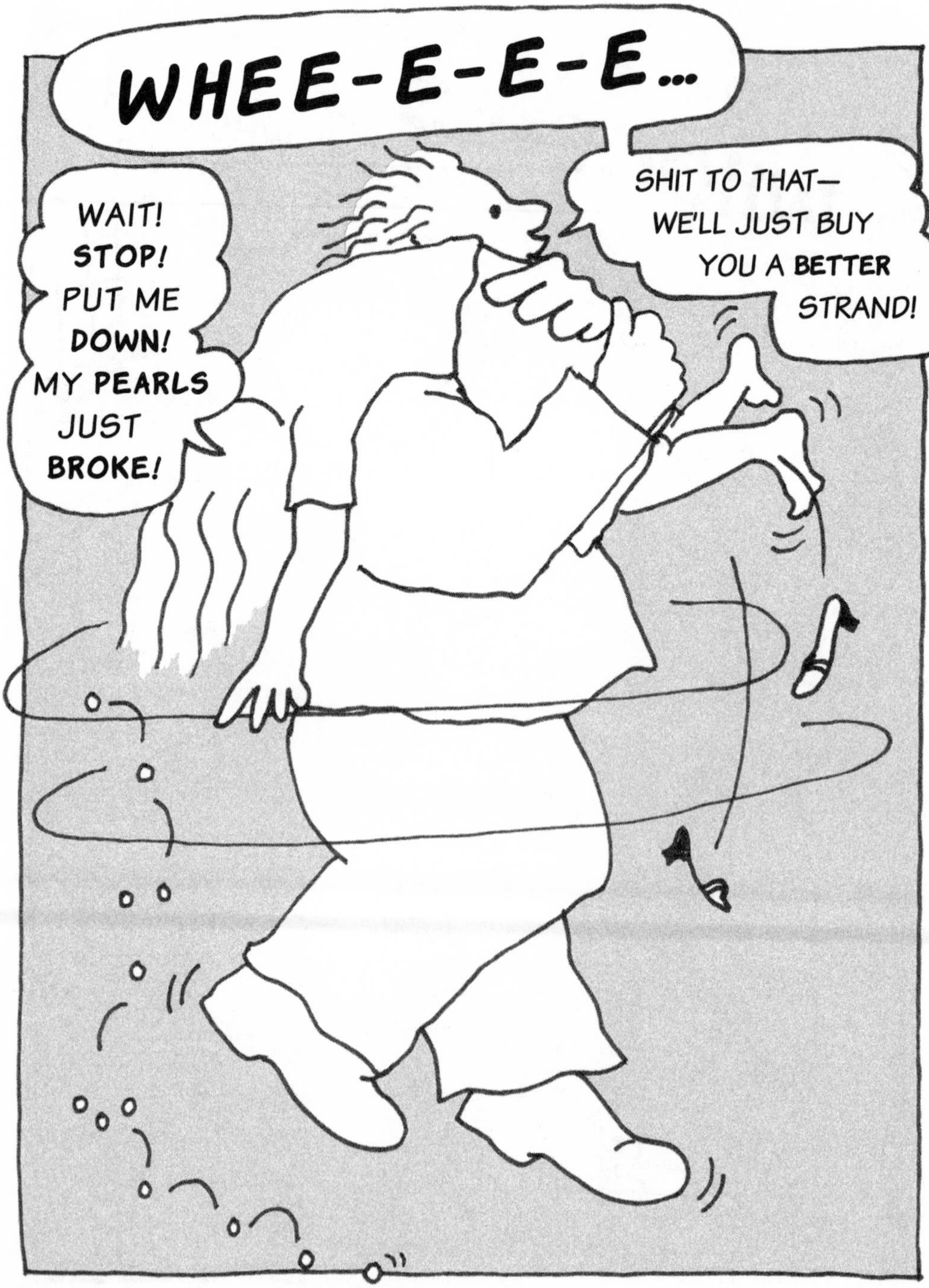
WHEE-E-E-E...
WAIT! **STOP!** PUT ME **DOWN!** MY **PEARLS** JUST **BROKE!**
SHIT TO THAT— WE'LL JUST BUY YOU A **BETTER** STRAND!

THERE WAS SOMETHING SO EXCITING ABOUT BRIAN'S IMPULSIVENESS AND DISREGARD FOR CONVENTION ... HIS EXUBERANCE AND ENERGY MADE ME FEEL SO ALIVE. HIS RECKLESS ABANDON WAS MESMERIZING.

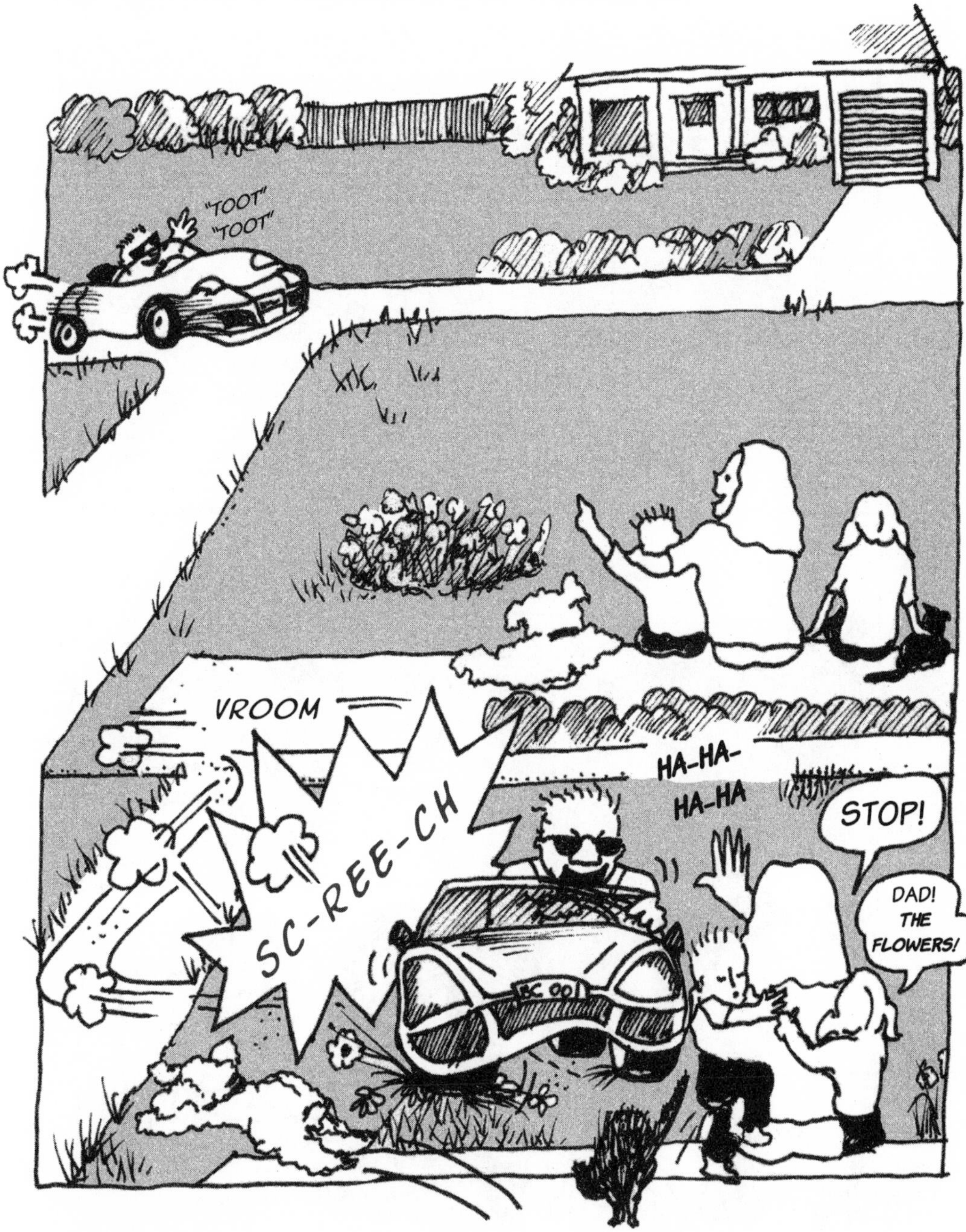
"TOOT"
"TOOT"
VROOM
SC-REE-CH
HA-HA-
HA-HA
STOP!
DAD! THE FLOWERS!

ONE WEEKEND WE TOOK HIS CHILDREN TO A WATERFRONT PARK TO SEE THE GEESE. IT WAS A BEAUTIFUL DAY.

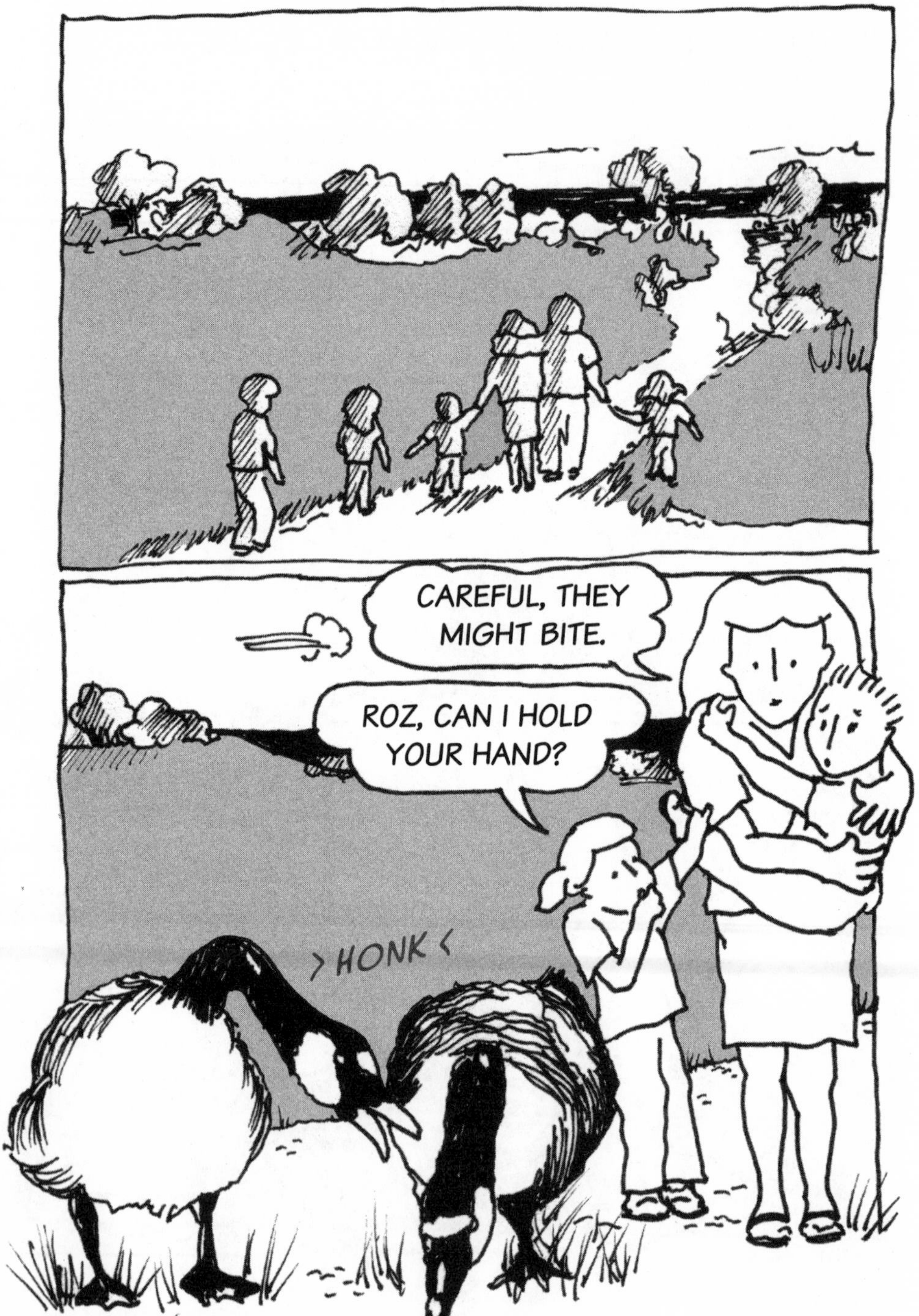
CAREFUL, THEY MIGHT BITE.
ROZ, CAN I HOLD YOUR HAND?
HONK

WE SKIPPED PEBBLES INTO THE WATER...

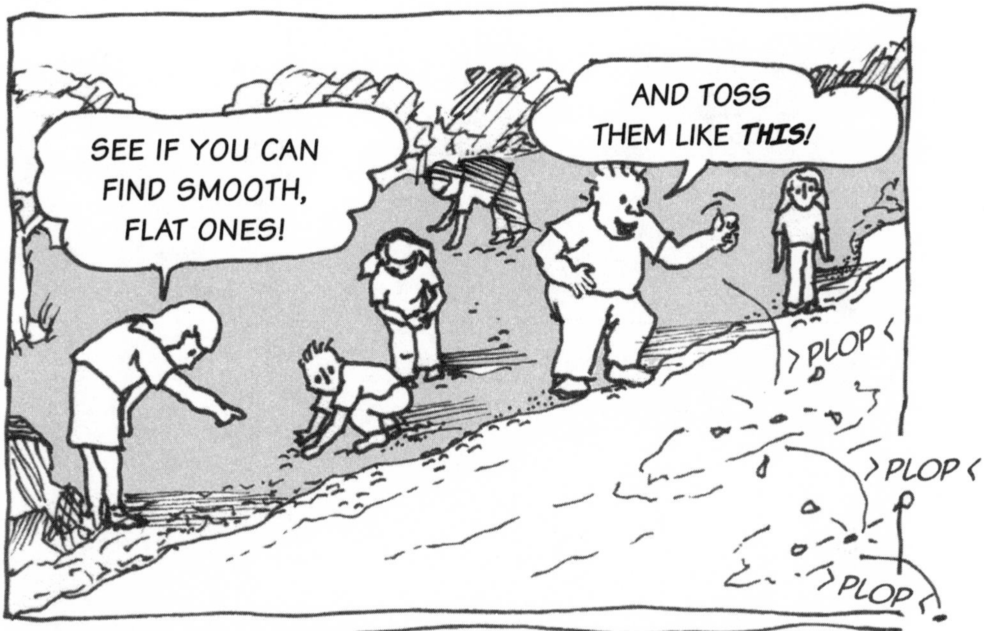
SEE IF YOU CAN FIND SMOOTH, FLAT ONES!
AND TOSS THEM LIKE THIS!
>PLOP<
>PLOP<
>PLOP<

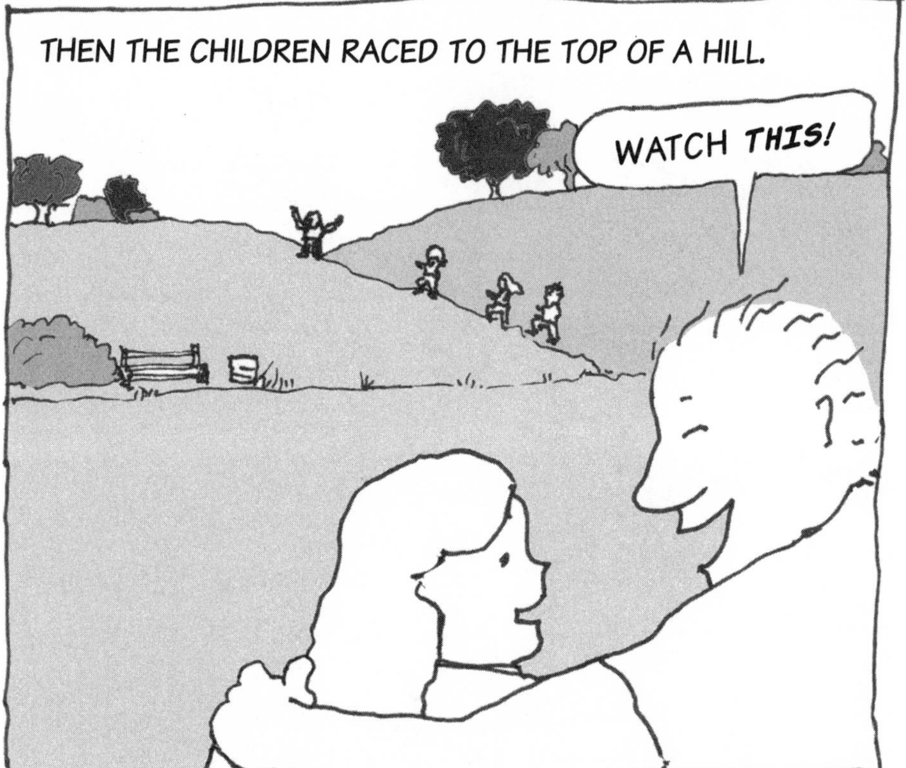
THEN THE CHILDREN RACED TO THE TOP OF A HILL.
WATCH THIS!

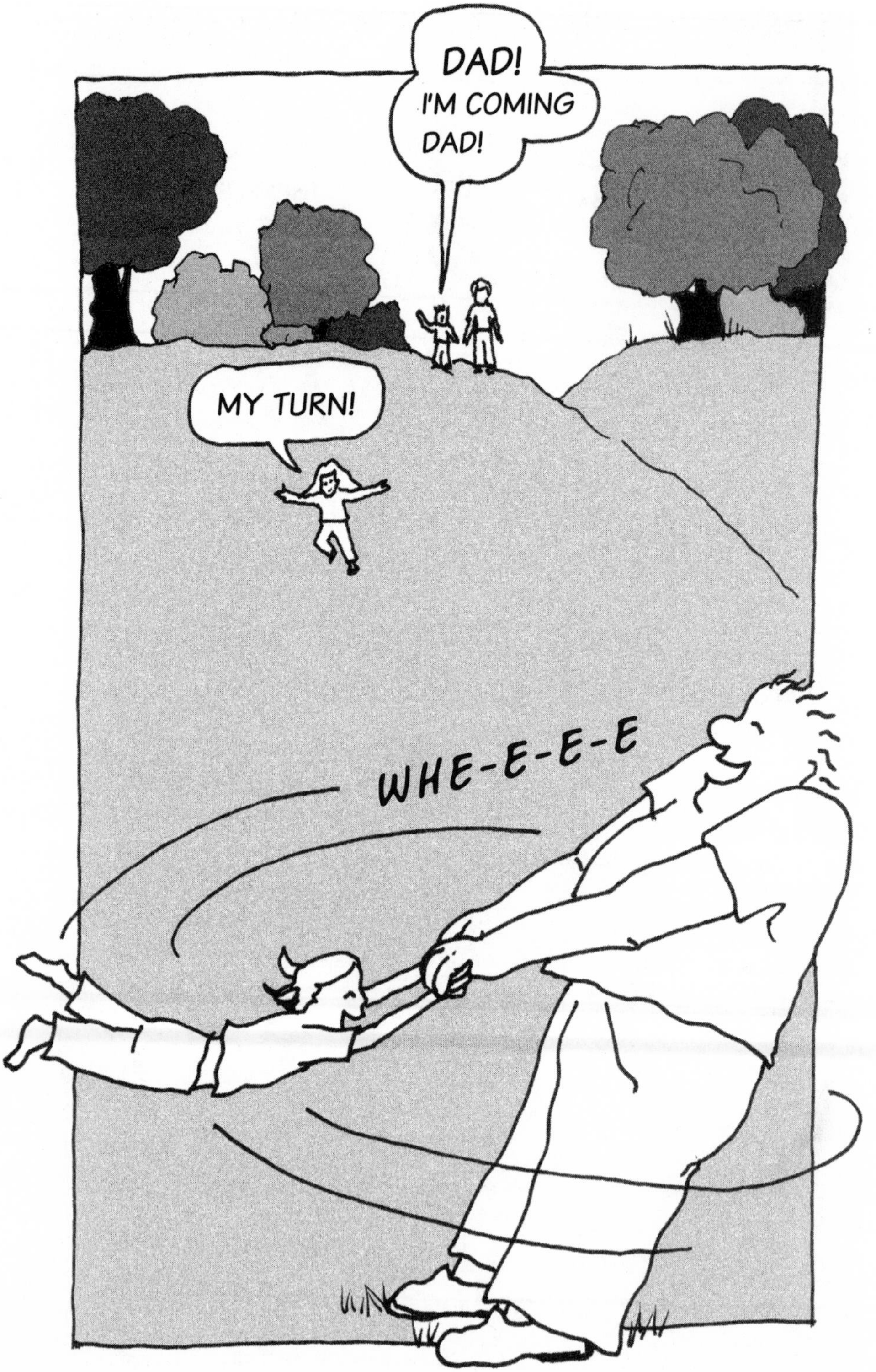

DAD! I'M COMING DAD!
MY TURN!
WHE-E-E-E

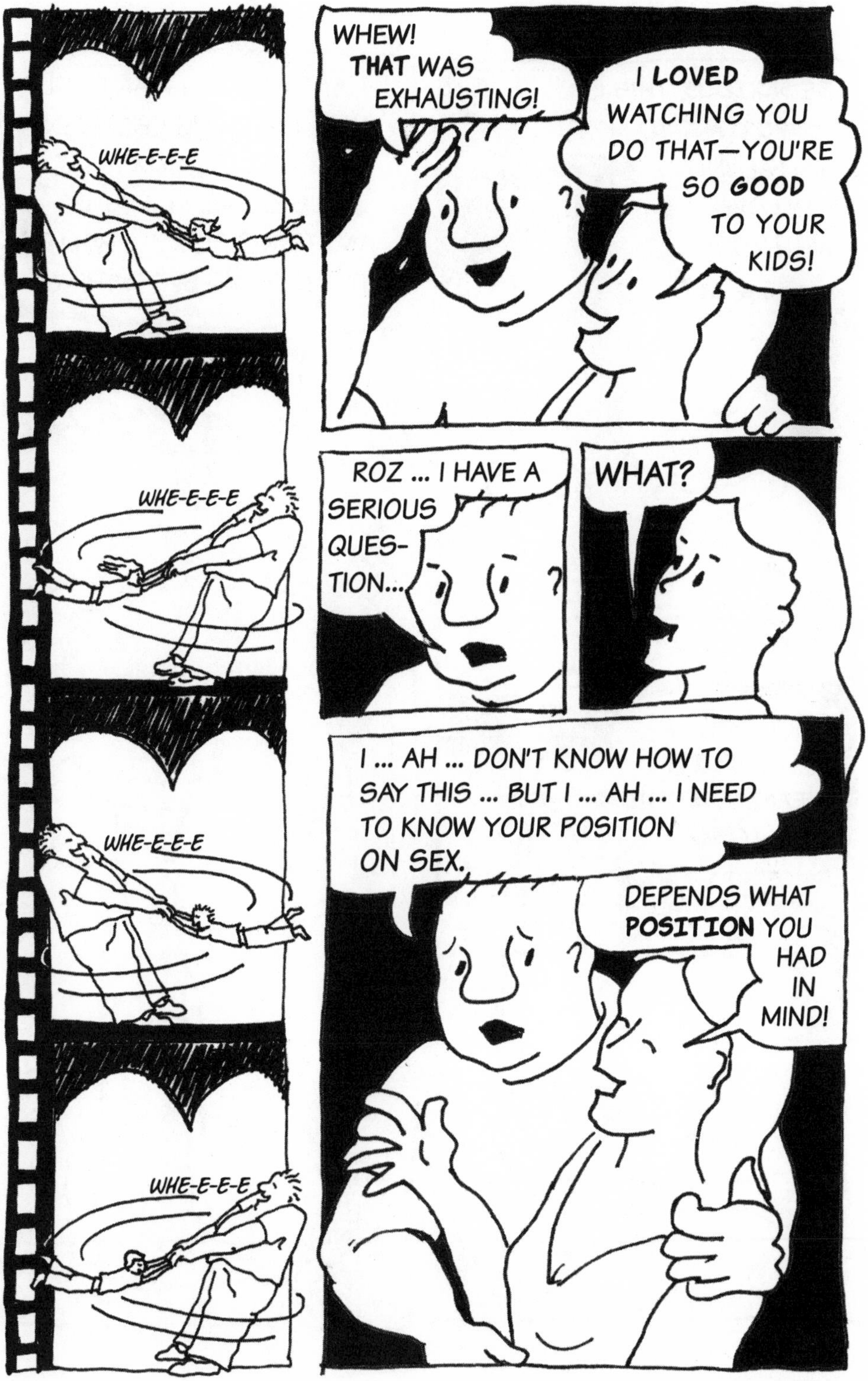
WHE-E-E-E
WHE-E-E-E
WHE-E-E-E
WHE-E-E-E
WHEW! THAT WAS EXHAUSTING!
I LOVED WATCHING YOU DO THAT—YOU'RE SO GOOD TO YOUR KIDS!
ROZ ... I HAVE A SERIOUS QUES- TION...
WHAT?
I ... AH ... DON'T KNOW HOW TO SAY THIS ... BUT I ... AH ... I NEED TO KNOW YOUR POSITION ON SEX.
DEPENDS WHAT POSITION YOU HAD IN MIND!

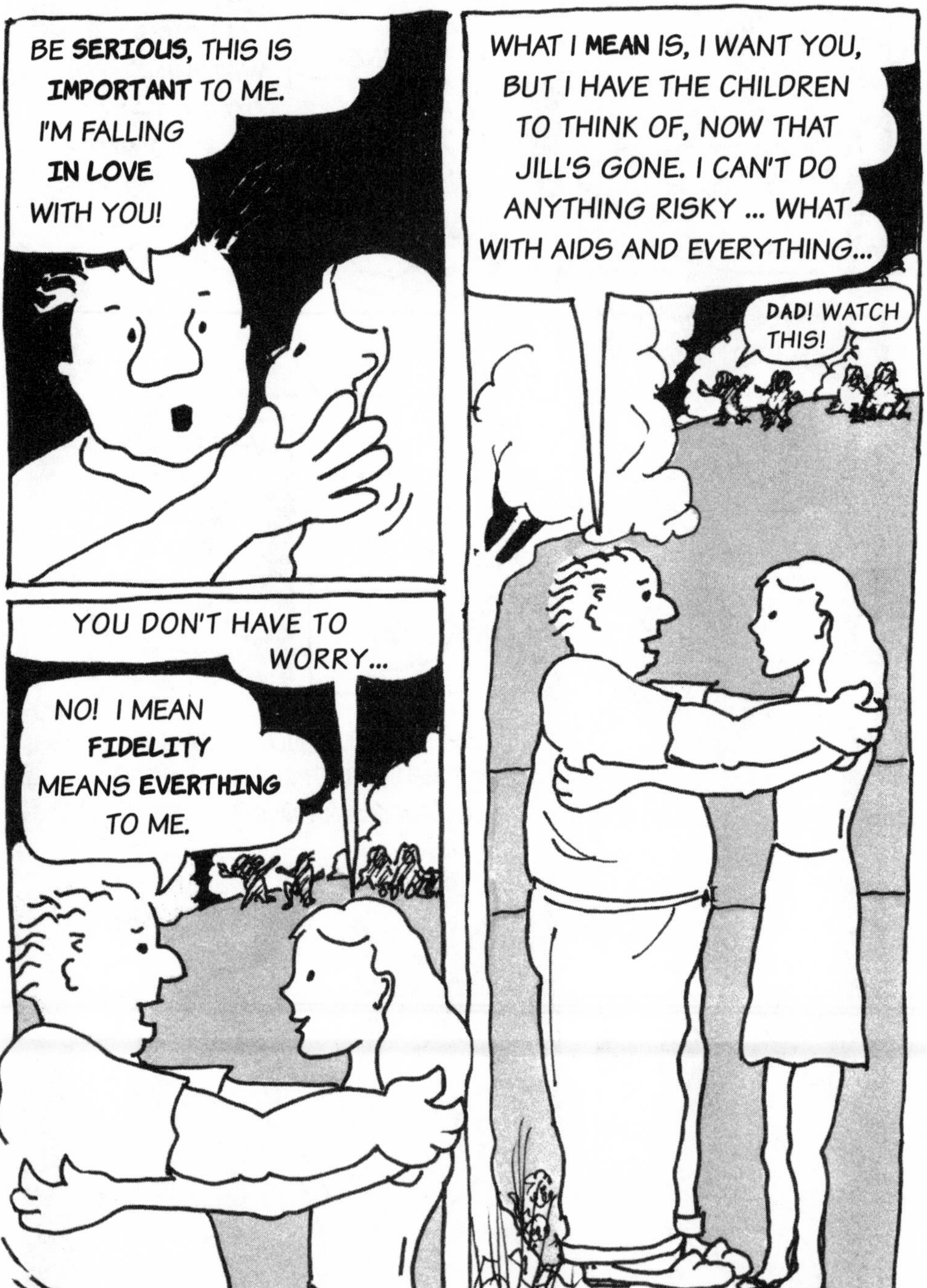
BE **SERIOUS**, THIS IS **IMPORTANT** TO ME. I'M FALLING **IN LOVE** WITH YOU!
WHAT I **MEAN** IS, I WANT YOU, BUT I HAVE THE CHILDREN TO THINK OF, NOW THAT JILL'S GONE. I CAN'T DO ANYTHING RISKY ... WHAT WITH AIDS AND EVERYTHING...
DAD! WATCH THIS!
YOU DON'T HAVE TO WORRY...
NO! I MEAN **FIDELITY** MEANS **EVERTHING** TO ME.

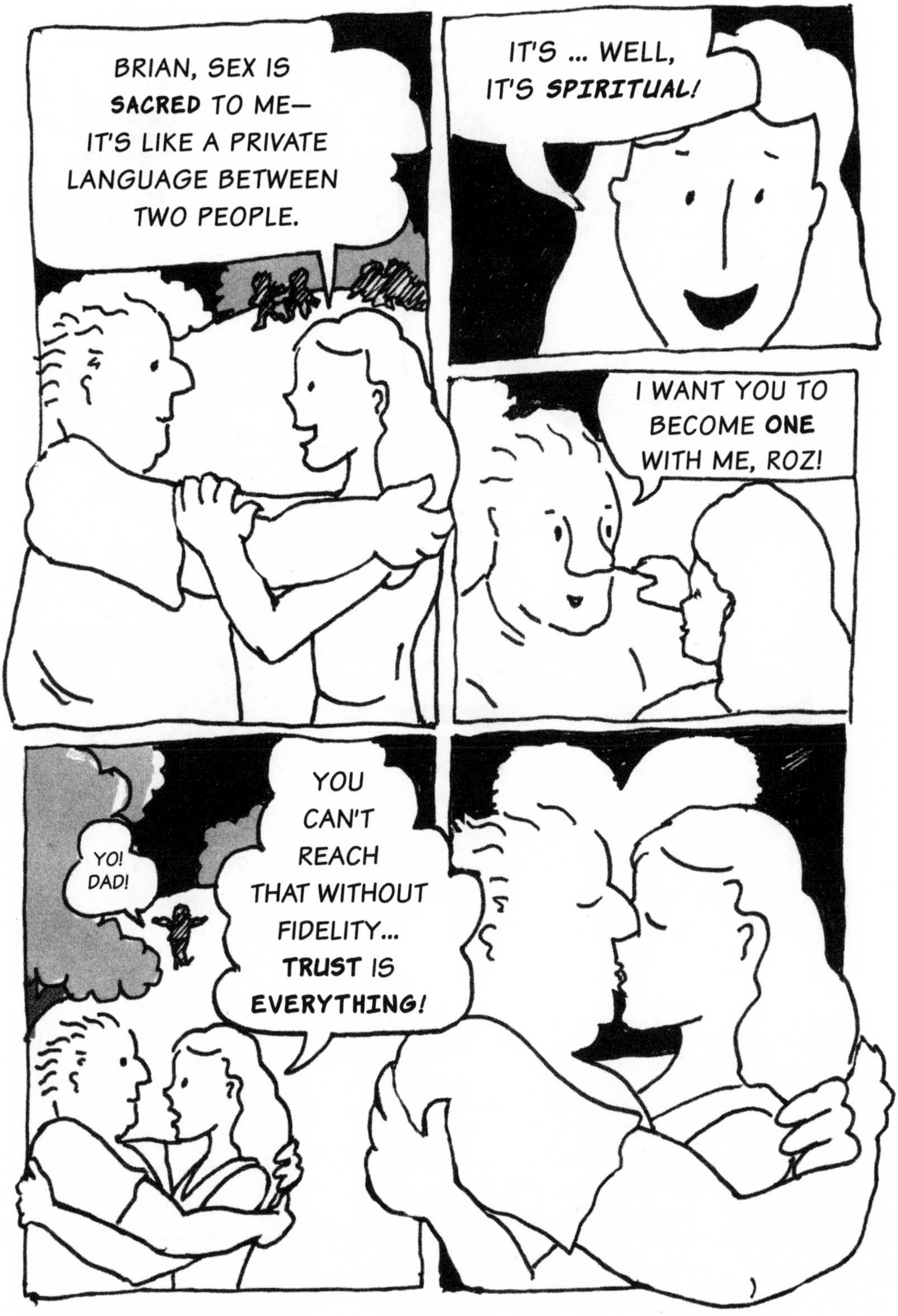
BRIAN, SEX IS **SACRED** TO ME— IT'S LIKE A PRIVATE LANGUAGE BETWEEN TWO PEOPLE.
IT'S ... WELL, IT'S ***SPIRITUAL!***
I WANT YOU TO BECOME **ONE** WITH ME, ROZ!
YO! DAD!
YOU CAN'T REACH THAT WITHOUT FIDELITY... **TRUST** IS ***EVERYTHING!***

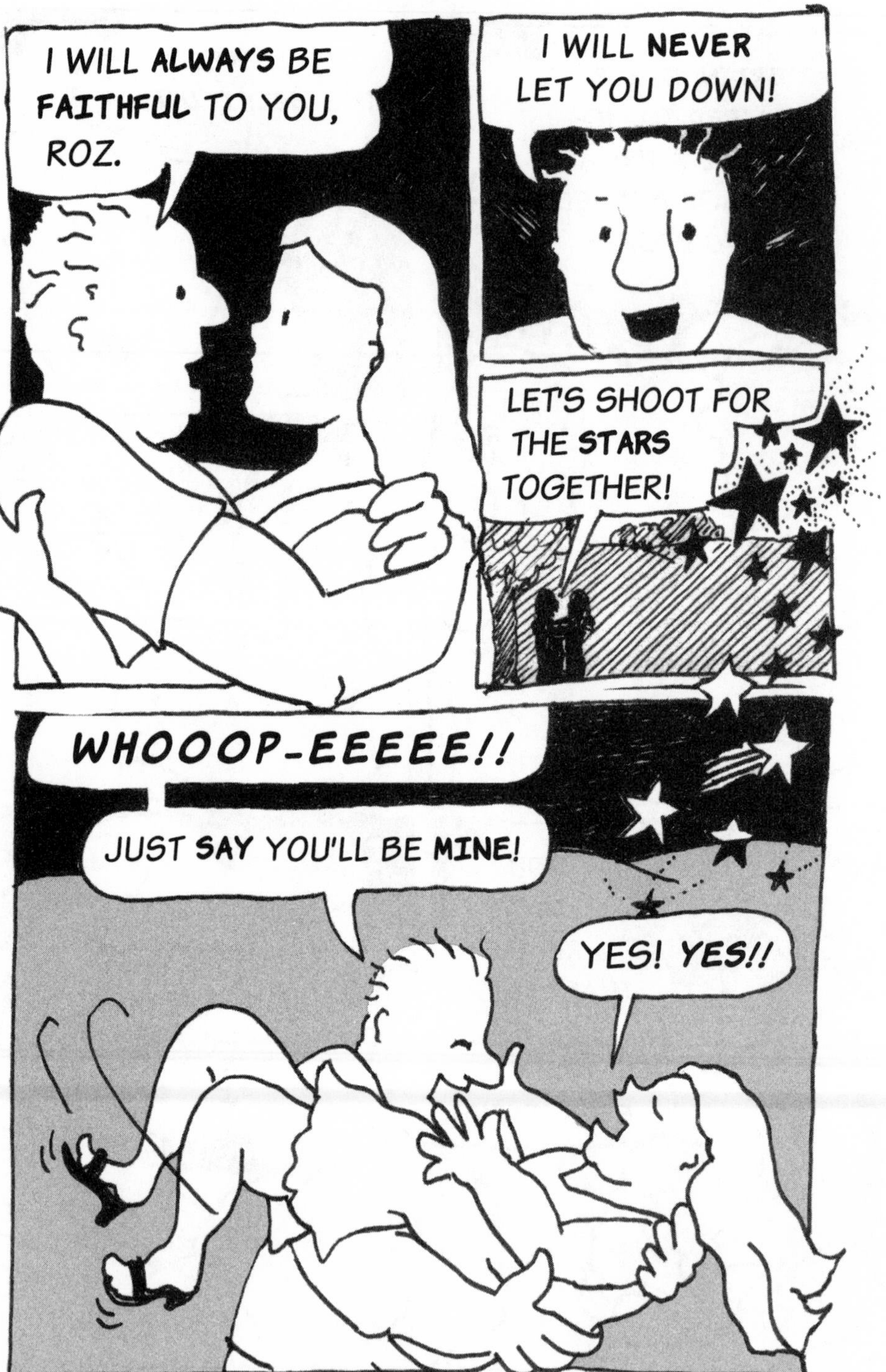
I WILL ALWAYS BE FAITHFUL TO YOU, ROZ.
I WILL NEVER LET YOU DOWN!
LET'S SHOOT FOR THE STARS TOGETHER!
WHOOOP-EEEEE!!
JUST SAY YOU'LL BE MINE!
YES! YES!!

BRIAN CALLED EVERY DAY. I FELT COMPLETELY ADORED.

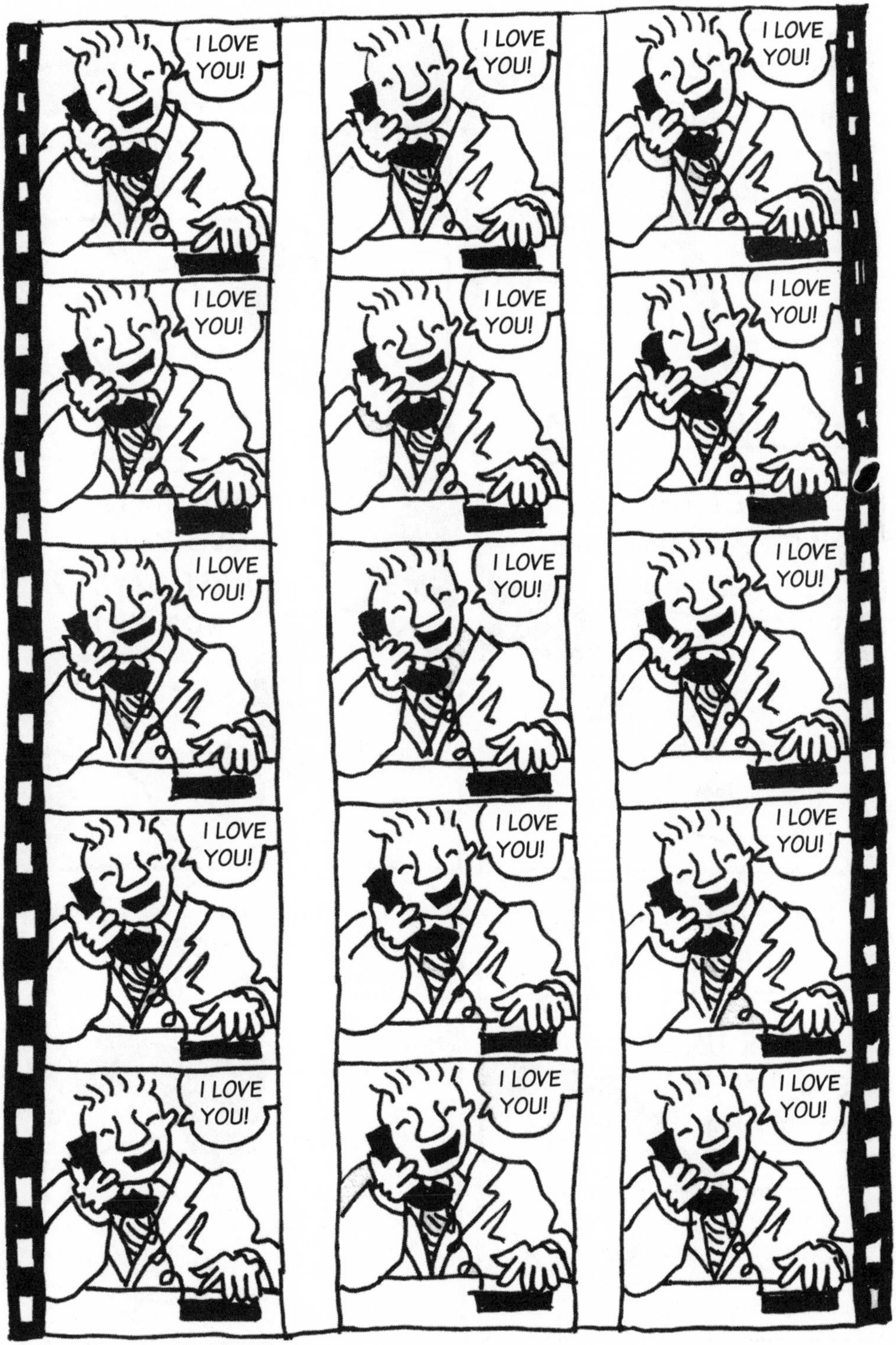

I LOVE YOU!
I LOVE YOU!
I LOVE YOU!
I LOVE YOU!
I LOVE YOU!
I LOVE YOU!
I LOVE YOU!
I LOVE YOU!
I LOVE YOU!
I LOVE YOU!
I LOVE YOU!
I LOVE YOU!
I LOVE YOU!
I LOVE YOU!
I LOVE YOU!

TWO MONTHS LATER...

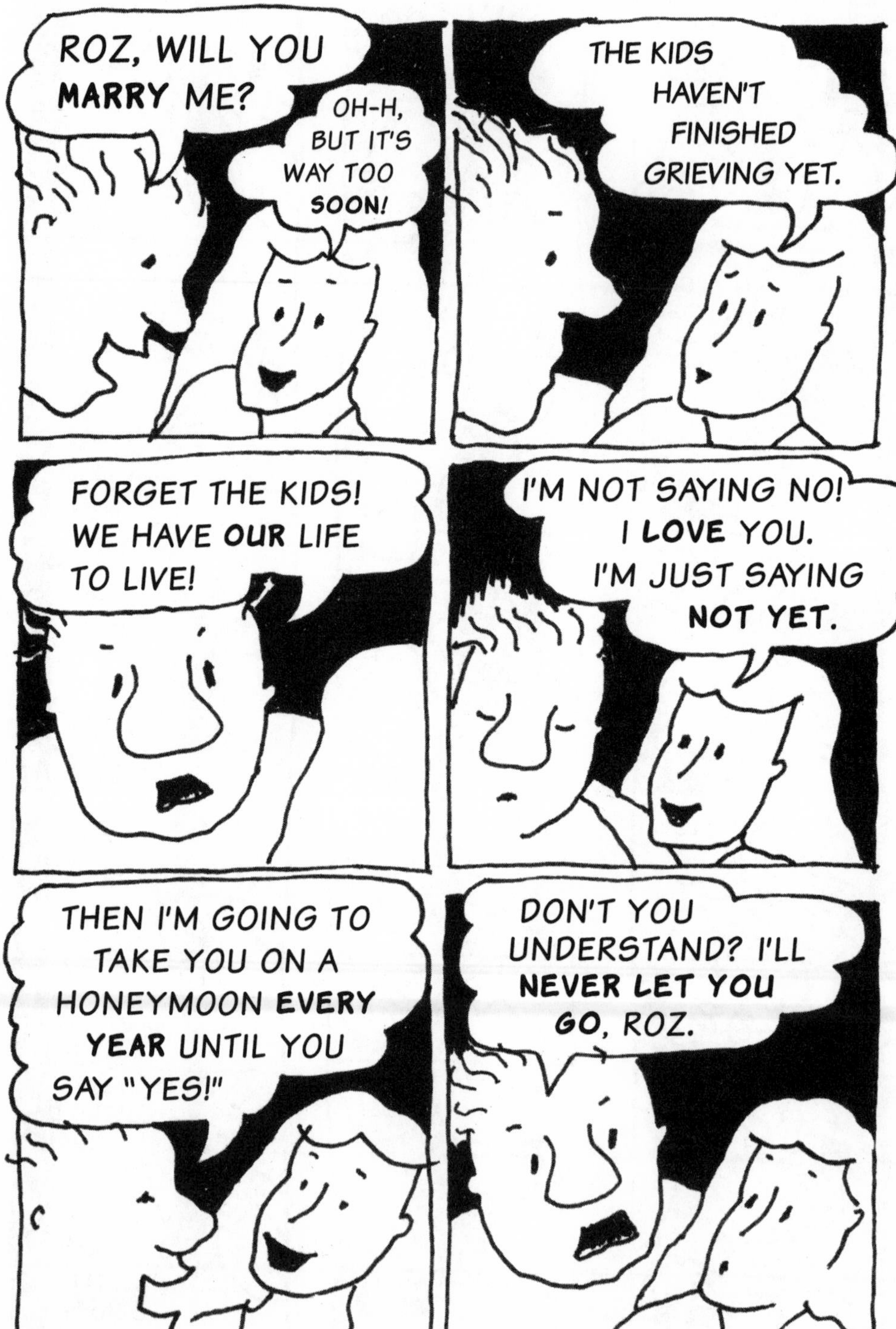
ROZ, WILL YOU **MARRY** ME?
OH-H, BUT IT'S WAY TOO **SOON!**
THE KIDS HAVEN'T FINISHED GRIEVING YET.
FORGET THE KIDS! WE HAVE **OUR** LIFE TO LIVE!
I'M NOT SAYING NO! I **LOVE** YOU. I'M JUST SAYING **NOT YET.**
THEN I'M GOING TO TAKE YOU ON A HONEYMOON **EVERY YEAR** UNTIL YOU SAY "YES!"
DON'T YOU UNDERSTAND? I'LL **NEVER LET YOU GO**, ROZ.

HE TOOK ME AWAY FOR A ROMANTIC WEEKEND —JUST THE TWO OF US...

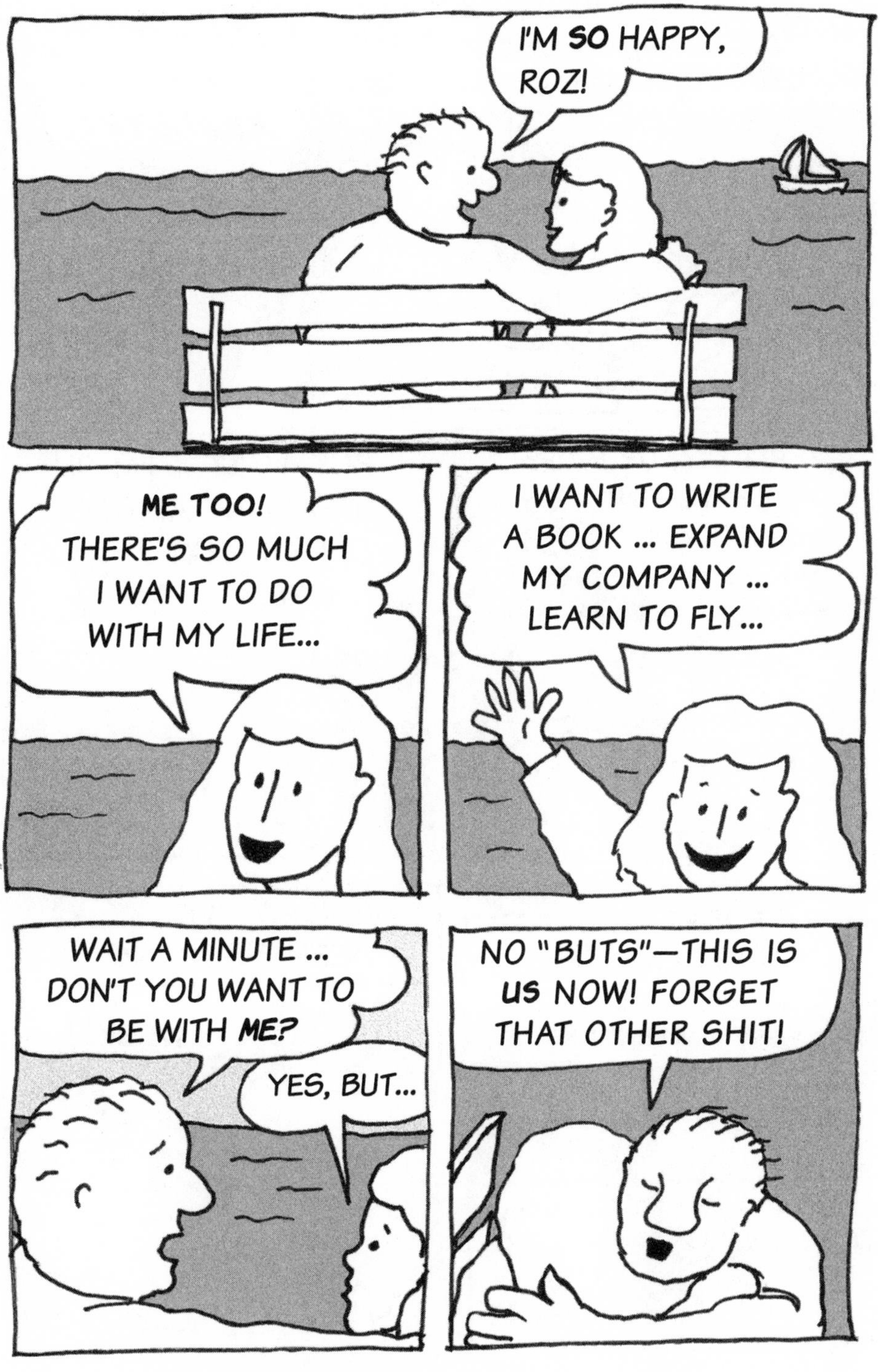
I'M **SO** HAPPY, ROZ!
ME TOO! THERE'S SO MUCH I WANT TO DO WITH MY LIFE...
I WANT TO WRITE A BOOK ... EXPAND MY COMPANY ... LEARN TO FLY...
WAIT A MINUTE ... DON'T YOU WANT TO BE WITH **ME?**
YES, BUT...
NO "BUTS"—THIS IS **US** NOW! FORGET THAT OTHER SHIT!

NOT LONG AFTER THAT, BRIAN SURPRISED ME...

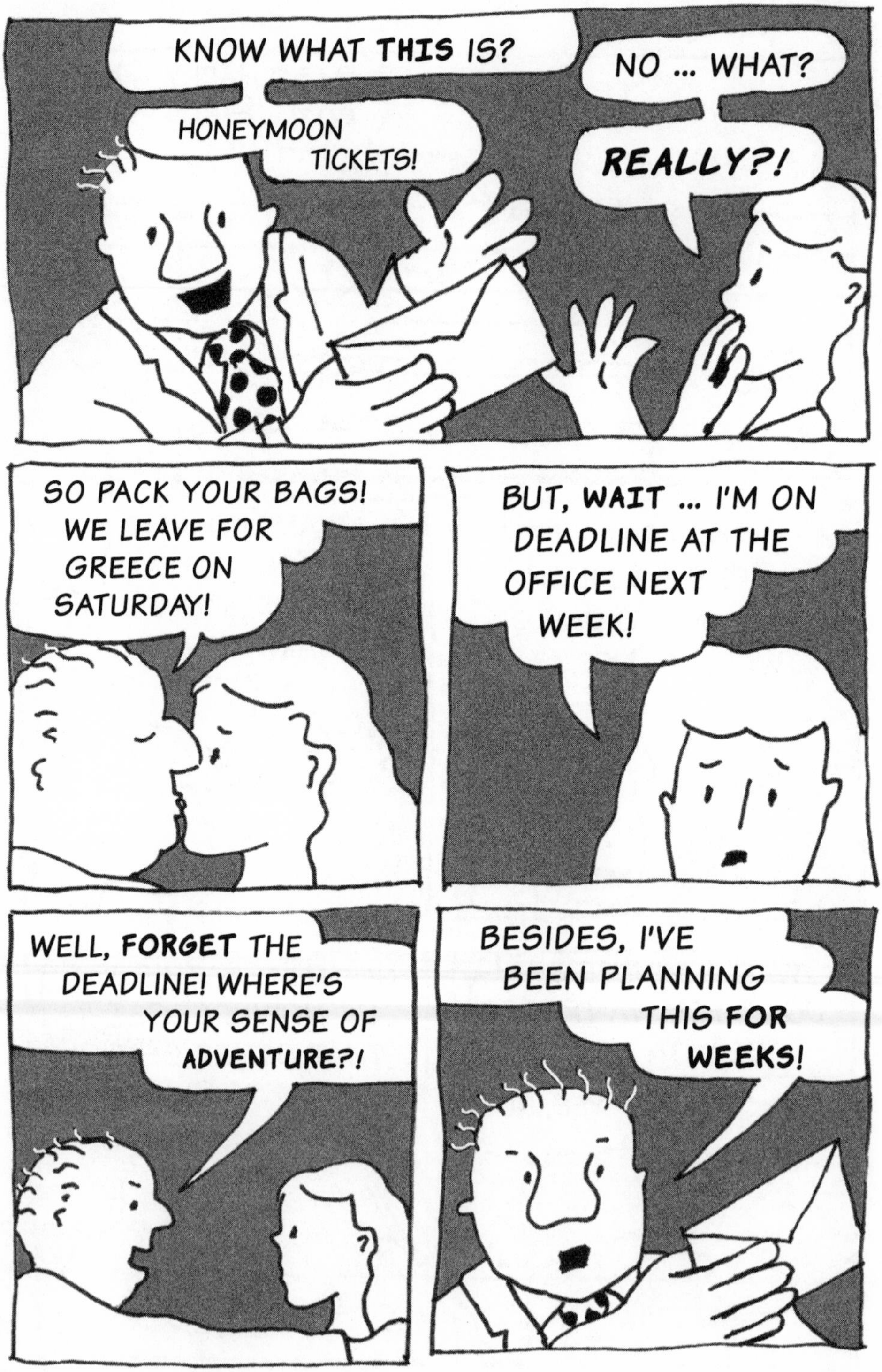
KNOW WHAT **THIS** IS?
NO ... WHAT?
HONEYMOON TICKETS!
REALLY?!
SO PACK YOUR BAGS! WE LEAVE FOR GREECE ON SATURDAY!
BUT, **WAIT** ... I'M ON DEADLINE AT THE OFFICE NEXT WEEK!
WELL, **FORGET** THE DEADLINE! WHERE'S YOUR SENSE OF **ADVENTURE?!**
BESIDES, I'VE BEEN PLANNING THIS **FOR WEEKS**!

SO I FRANTICALLY ORGANIZED ALL WEEK ... AND THEN FRIDAY AFTERNOON, BRIAN CALLED.

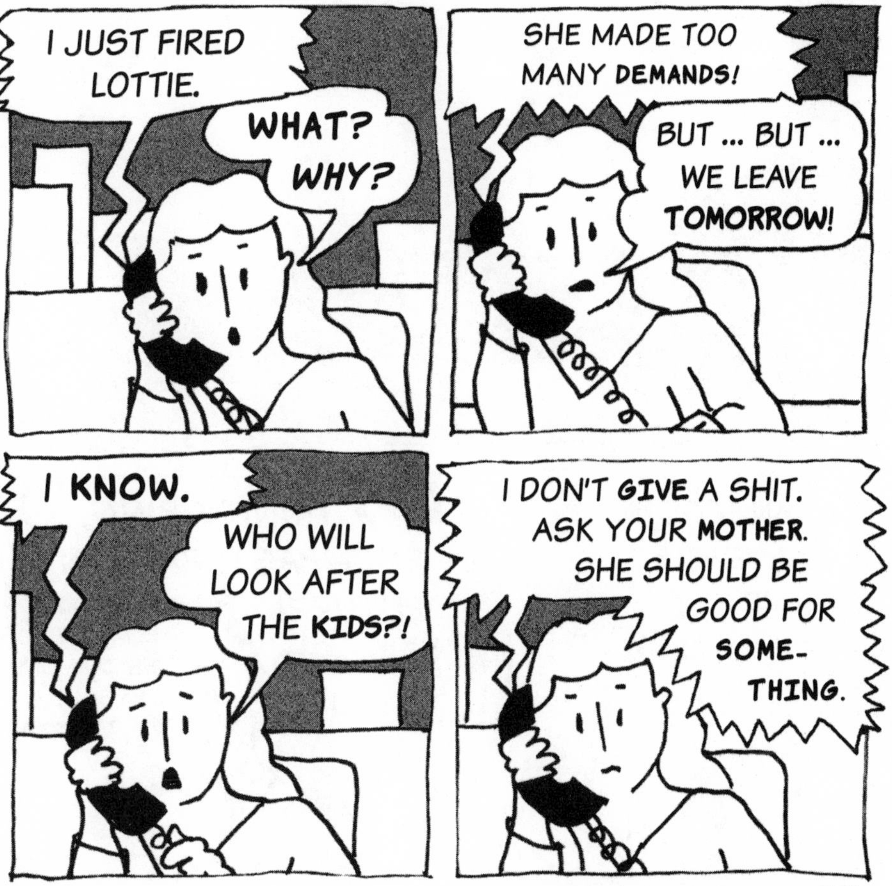
I JUST FIRED LOTTIE.
WHAT? WHY?
SHE MADE TOO MANY DEMANDS!
BUT ... BUT ... WE LEAVE TOMORROW!
I KNOW.
WHO WILL LOOK AFTER THE KIDS?!
I DON'T GIVE A SHIT. ASK YOUR MOTHER. SHE SHOULD BE GOOD FOR SOME-THING.

MY MOTHER STEPPED IN, BUT SHE WAS SUSPICIOUS.

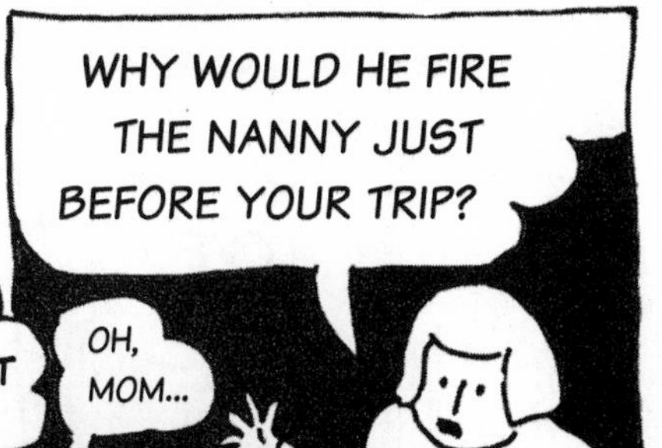
WHY WOULD HE FIRE THE NANNY JUST BEFORE YOUR TRIP?
OH, MOM...

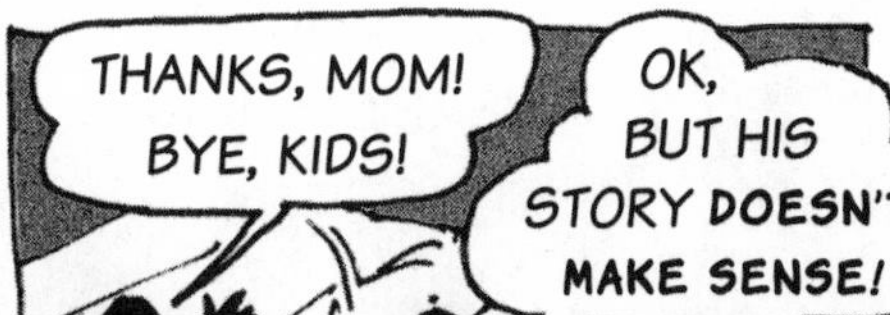
THANKS, MOM! BYE, KIDS!
OK, BUT HIS STORY DOESN'T MAKE SENSE!

AND THEN OFF WE WENT...

THE RESORT WAS LAVISH.

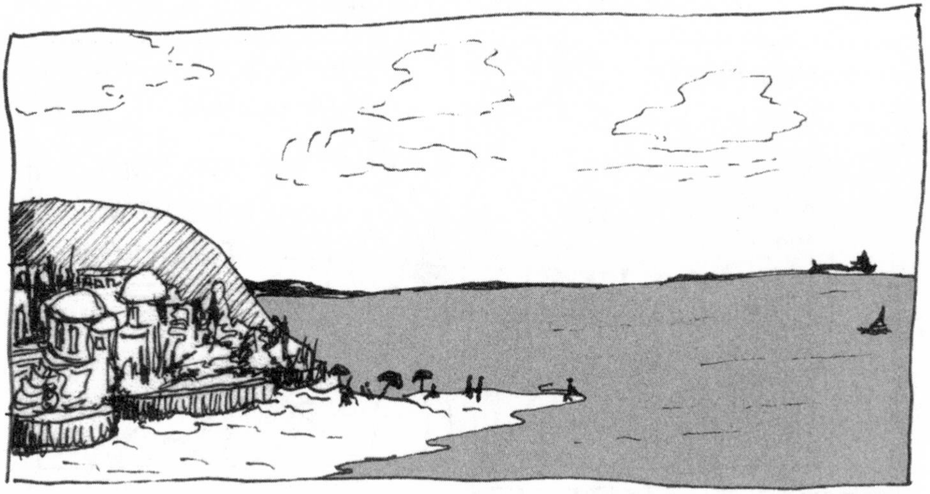

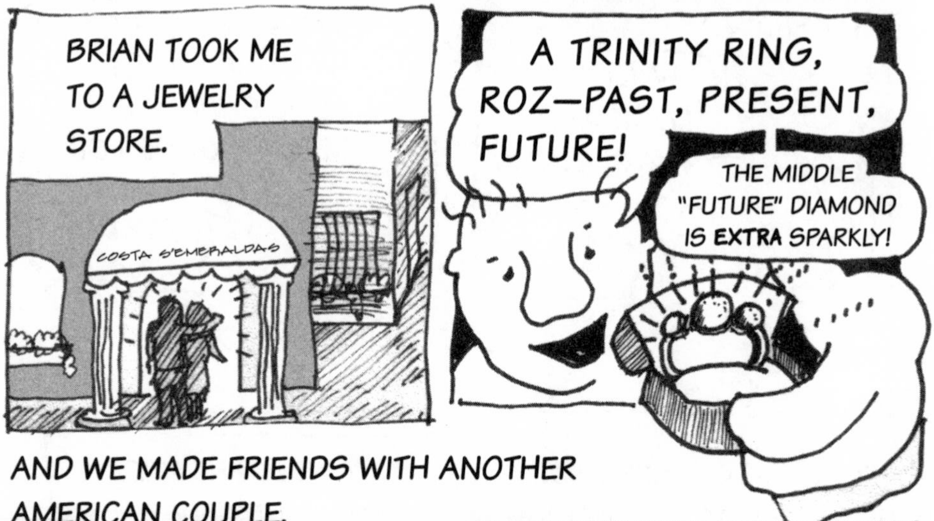
BRIAN TOOK ME TO A JEWELRY STORE.
COSTA S'EMERALDAS
A TRINITY RING, ROZ—PAST, PRESENT, FUTURE!
THE MIDDLE "FUTURE" DIAMOND IS **EXTRA** SPARKLY!

AND WE MADE FRIENDS WITH ANOTHER AMERICAN COUPLE.

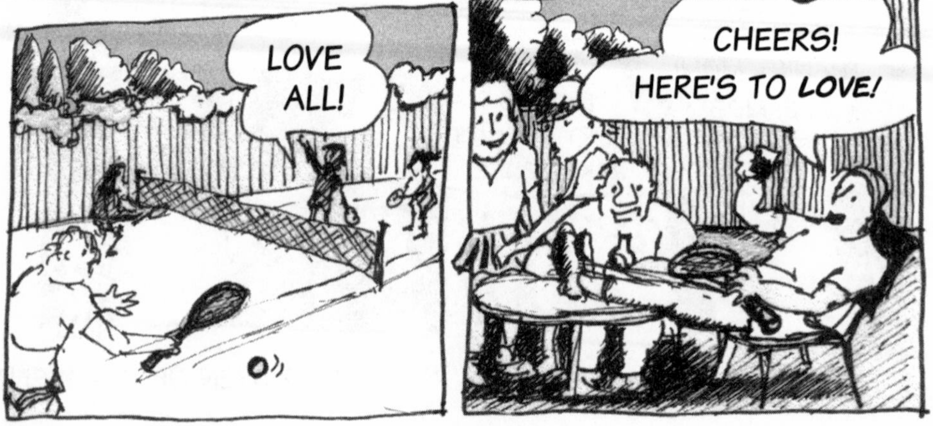
LOVE ALL!
CHEERS! HERE'S TO ***LOVE!***

STEVE OWNED A MARKETING COMPANY JUST LIKE MINE, AND I BONDED INSTANTLY WITH HIS WIFE, LEE.

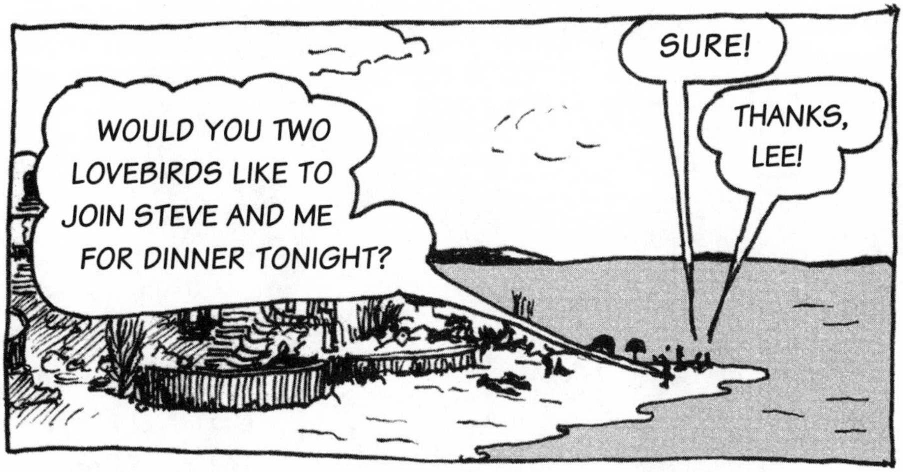
WOULD YOU TWO LOVEBIRDS LIKE TO JOIN STEVE AND ME FOR DINNER TONIGHT?
SURE!
THANKS, LEE!

DURING DRINKS, STEVE AND I HAD A LOT TO TALK ABOUT.

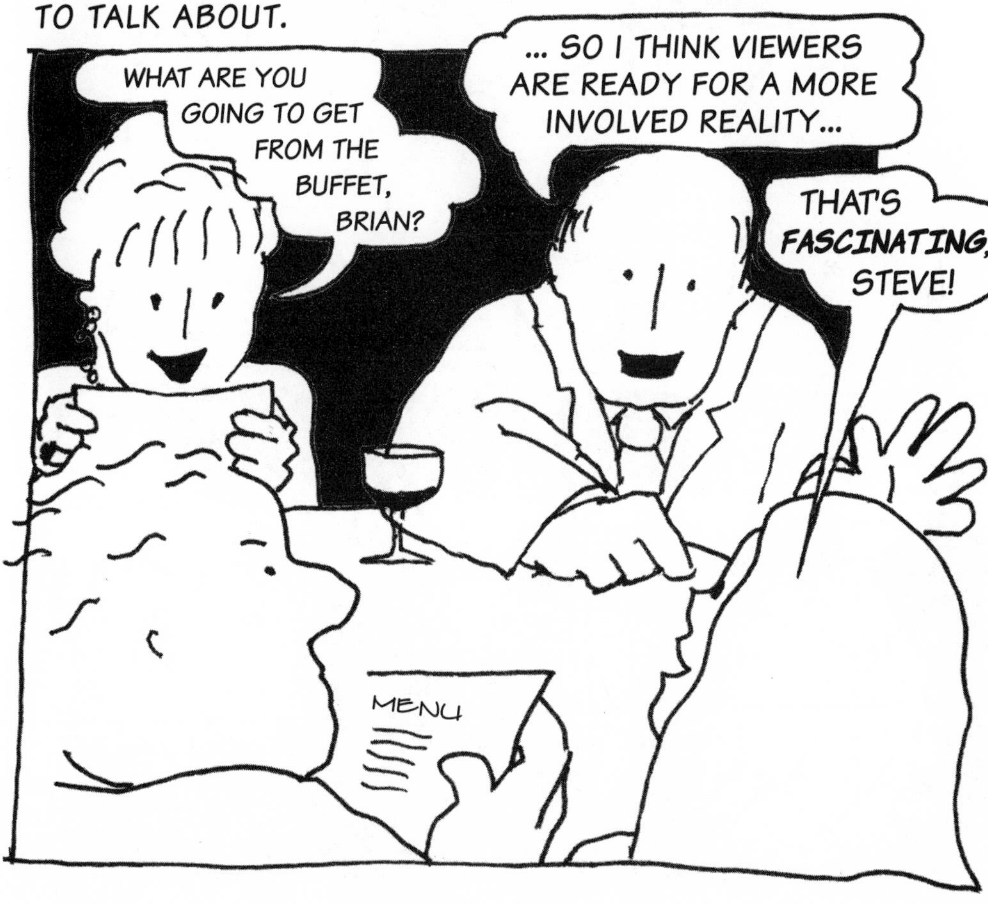
WHAT ARE YOU GOING TO GET FROM THE BUFFET, BRIAN?
... SO I THINK VIEWERS ARE READY FOR A MORE INVOLVED REALITY...
THAT'S **FASCINATING**, STEVE!
MENU

BRIAN AND LEE GOT UP TO GET DINNER, BUT STEVE AND I WERE TOO ENGROSSED IN CONVERSATION.

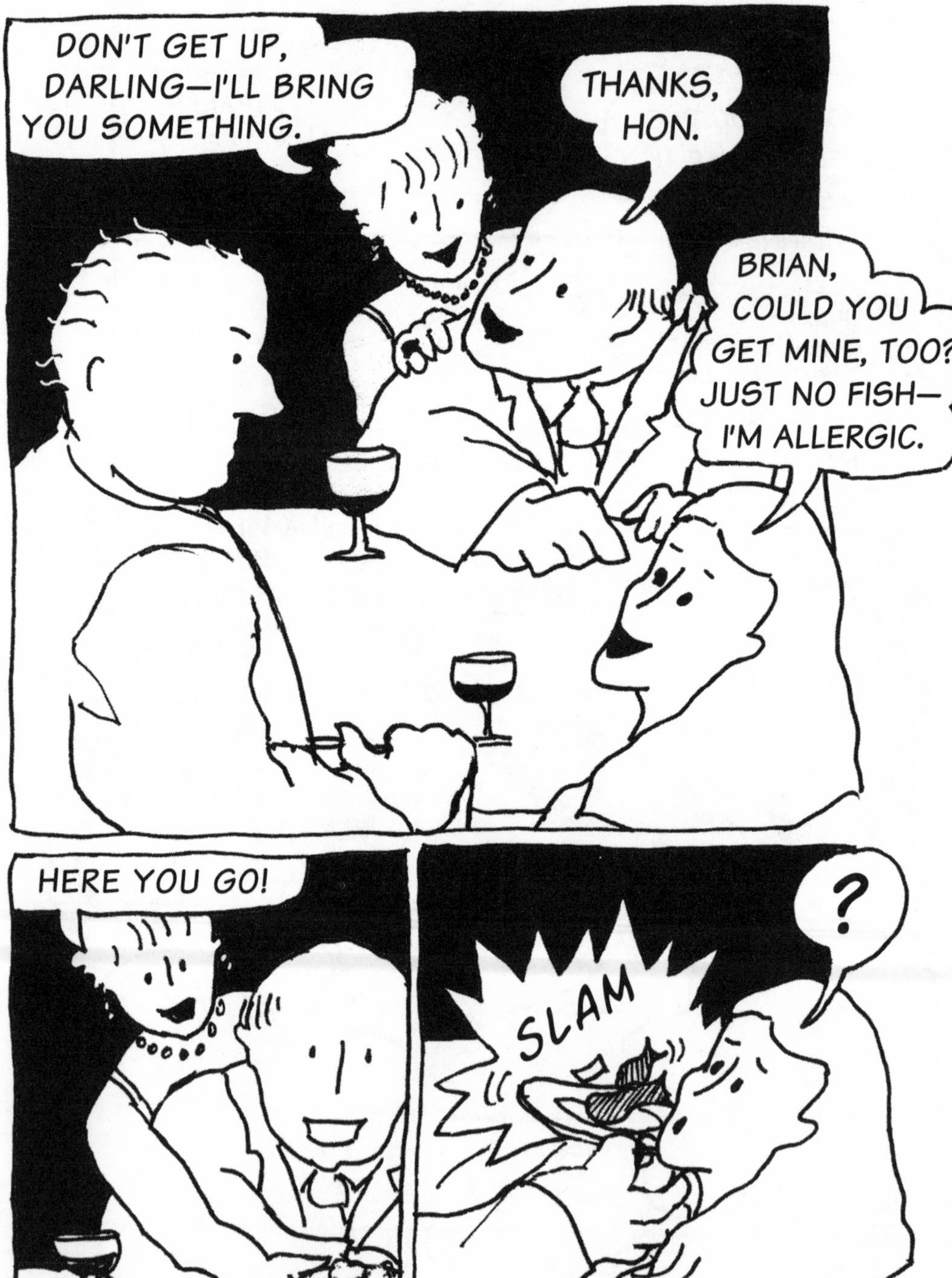

DON'T GET UP, DARLING—I'LL BRING YOU SOMETHING.
THANKS, HON.
BRIAN, COULD YOU GET MINE, TOO? JUST NO FISH— I'M ALLERGIC.
HERE YOU GO!
?
SLAM

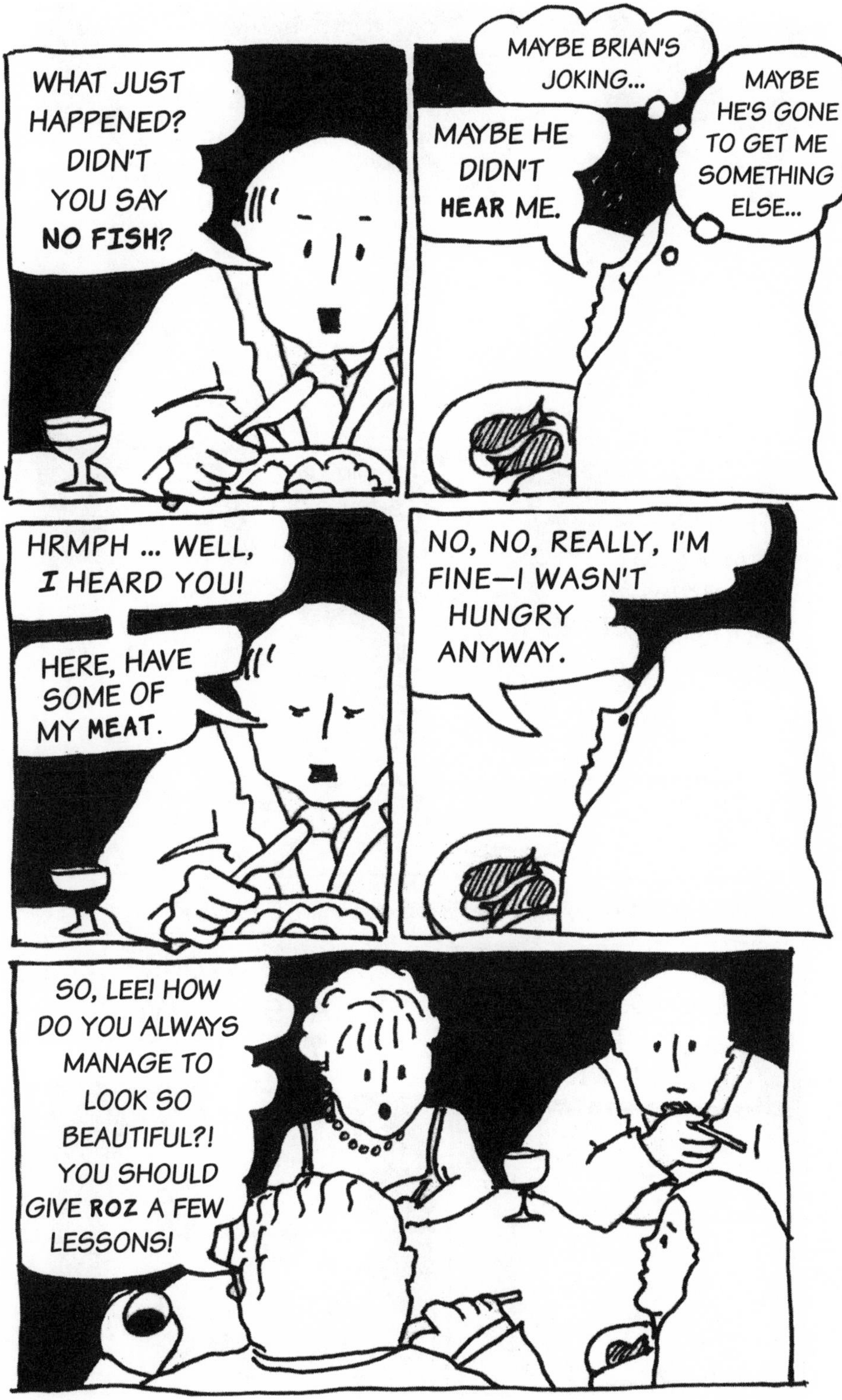
WHAT JUST HAPPENED? DIDN'T YOU SAY **NO FISH**?
MAYBE BRIAN'S JOKING...
MAYBE HE DIDN'T **HEAR** ME.
MAYBE HE'S GONE TO GET ME SOMETHING ELSE...
HRMPH ... WELL, **I** HEARD YOU!
HERE, HAVE SOME OF MY **MEAT**.
NO, NO, REALLY, I'M FINE—I WASN'T HUNGRY ANYWAY.
SO, LEE! HOW DO YOU ALWAYS MANAGE TO LOOK SO BEAUTIFUL?! YOU SHOULD GIVE **ROZ** A FEW LESSONS!

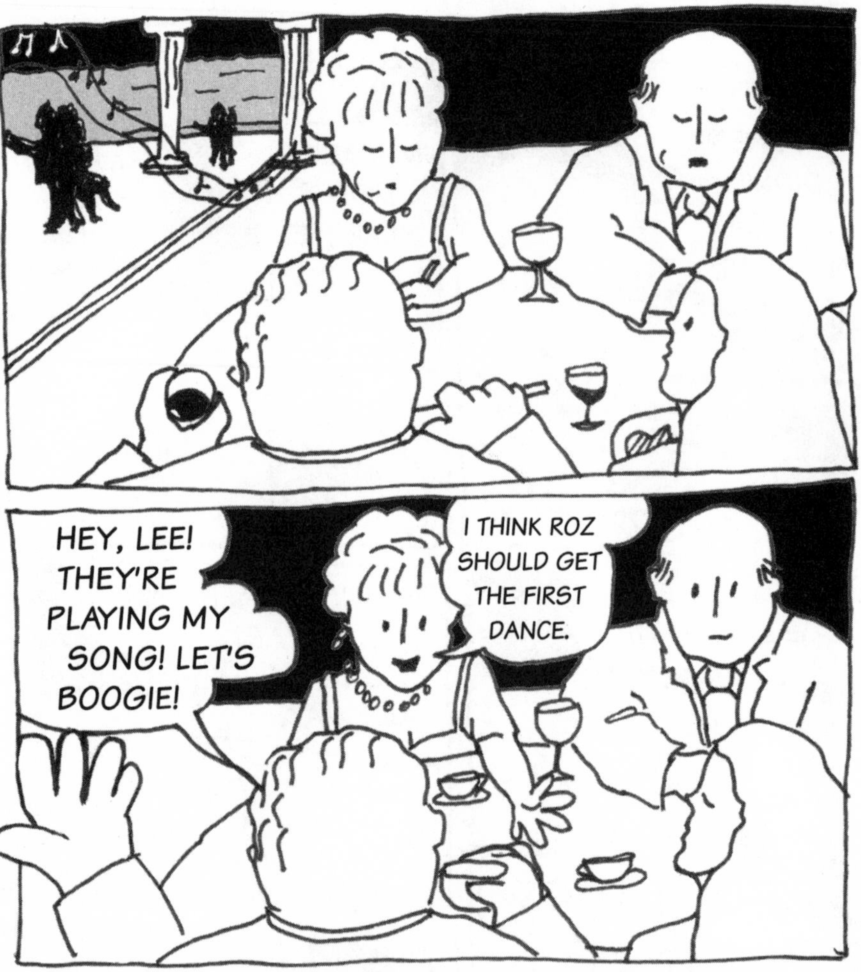
HEY, LEE! THEY'RE PLAYING MY SONG! LET'S BOOGIE!
I THINK ROZ SHOULD GET THE FIRST DANCE.

SO I FOLLOWED BRIAN ONTO THE DANCE FLOOR.

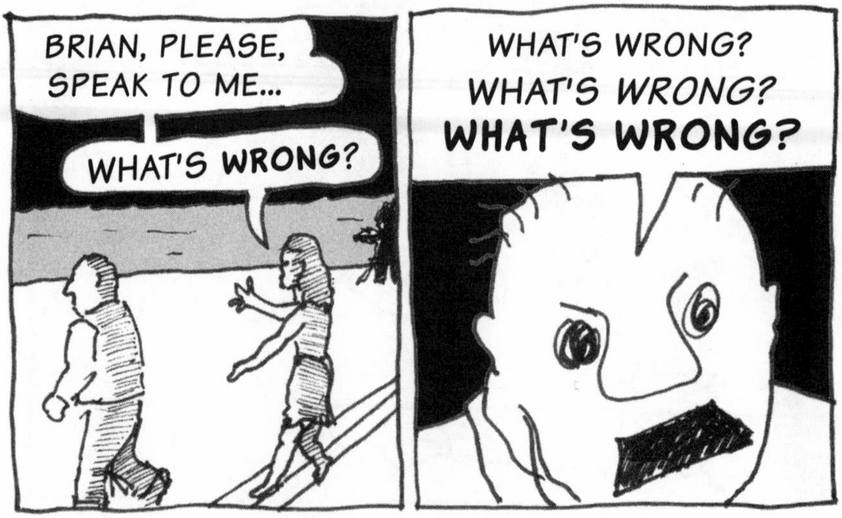
BRIAN, PLEASE, SPEAK TO ME...
WHAT'S WRONG?
WHAT'S WRONG?
WHAT'S WRONG?
WHAT'S WRONG?

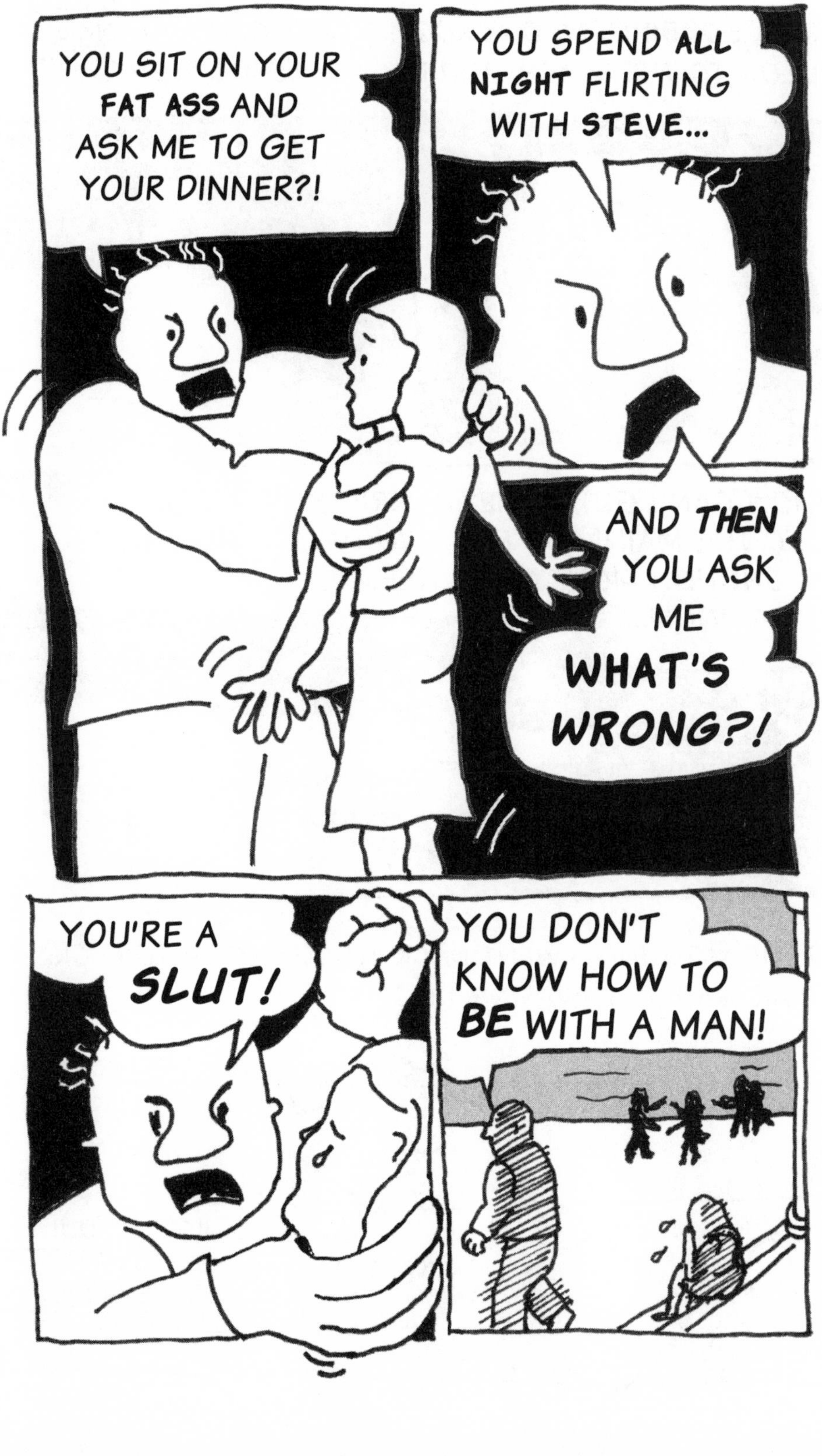
YOU SIT ON YOUR FAT ASS AND ASK ME TO GET YOUR DINNER?!
YOU SPEND ALL NIGHT FLIRTING WITH STEVE...
AND THEN YOU ASK ME WHAT'S WRONG?!
YOU'RE A SLUT!
YOU DON'T KNOW HOW TO BE WITH A MAN!

I RAN, SOBBING, TO OUR ROOM. I DRAGGED A BLANKET AND PILLOW TO THE BEACH, AND LAY AWAKE ALL NIGHT.

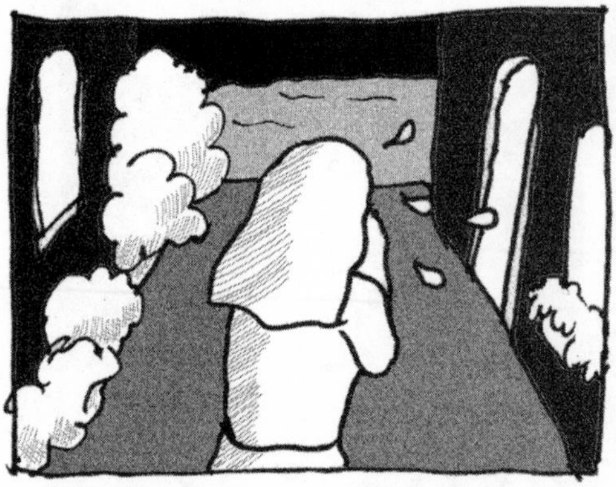

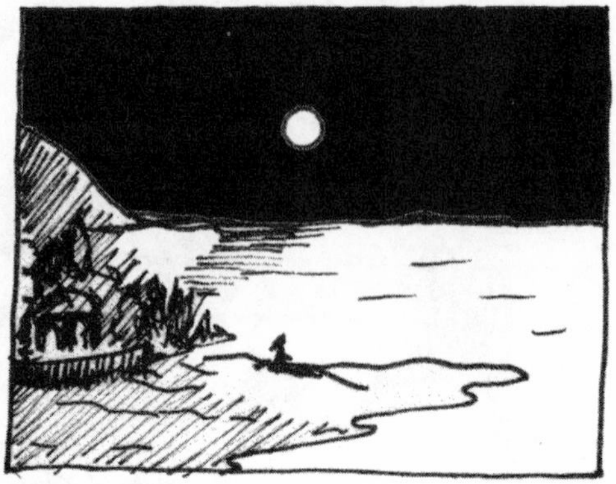

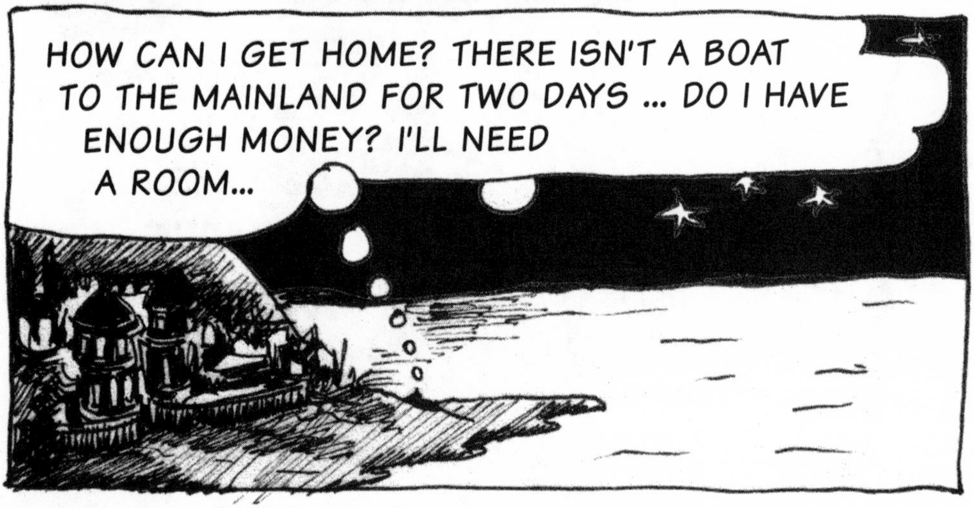
HOW CAN I GET HOME? THERE ISN'T A BOAT TO THE MAINLAND FOR TWO DAYS ... DO I HAVE ENOUGH MONEY? I'LL NEED A ROOM...

IN THE MORNING, I WENT BACK TO OUR ROOM TO PACK. BRIAN WAS JUST WAKING UP...

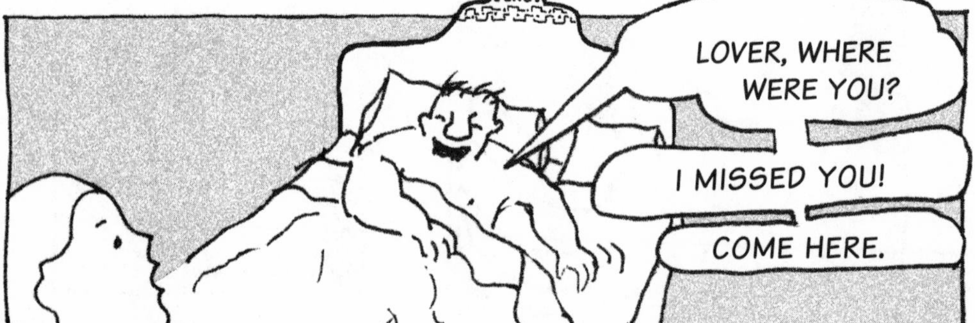
LOVER, WHERE WERE YOU?
I MISSED YOU!
COME HERE.

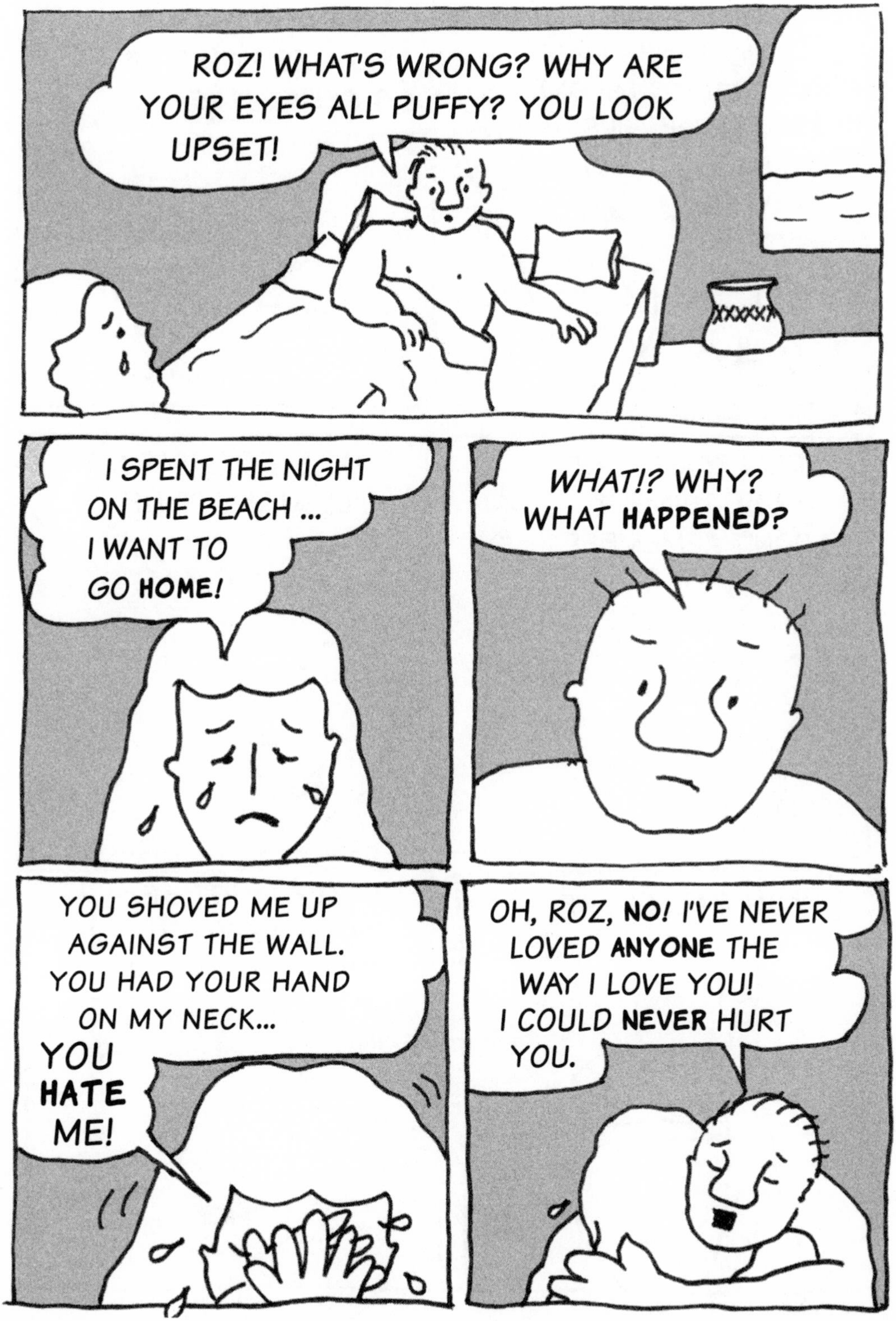
ROZ! WHAT'S WRONG? WHY ARE YOUR EYES ALL PUFFY? YOU LOOK UPSET!
I SPENT THE NIGHT ON THE BEACH ... I WANT TO GO **HOME!**
WHAT!? WHY? WHAT **HAPPENED?**
YOU SHOVED ME UP AGAINST THE WALL. YOU HAD YOUR HAND ON MY NECK...
YOU **HATE** ME!
OH, ROZ, **NO!** I'VE NEVER LOVED **ANYONE** THE WAY I LOVE YOU! I COULD **NEVER** HURT YOU.

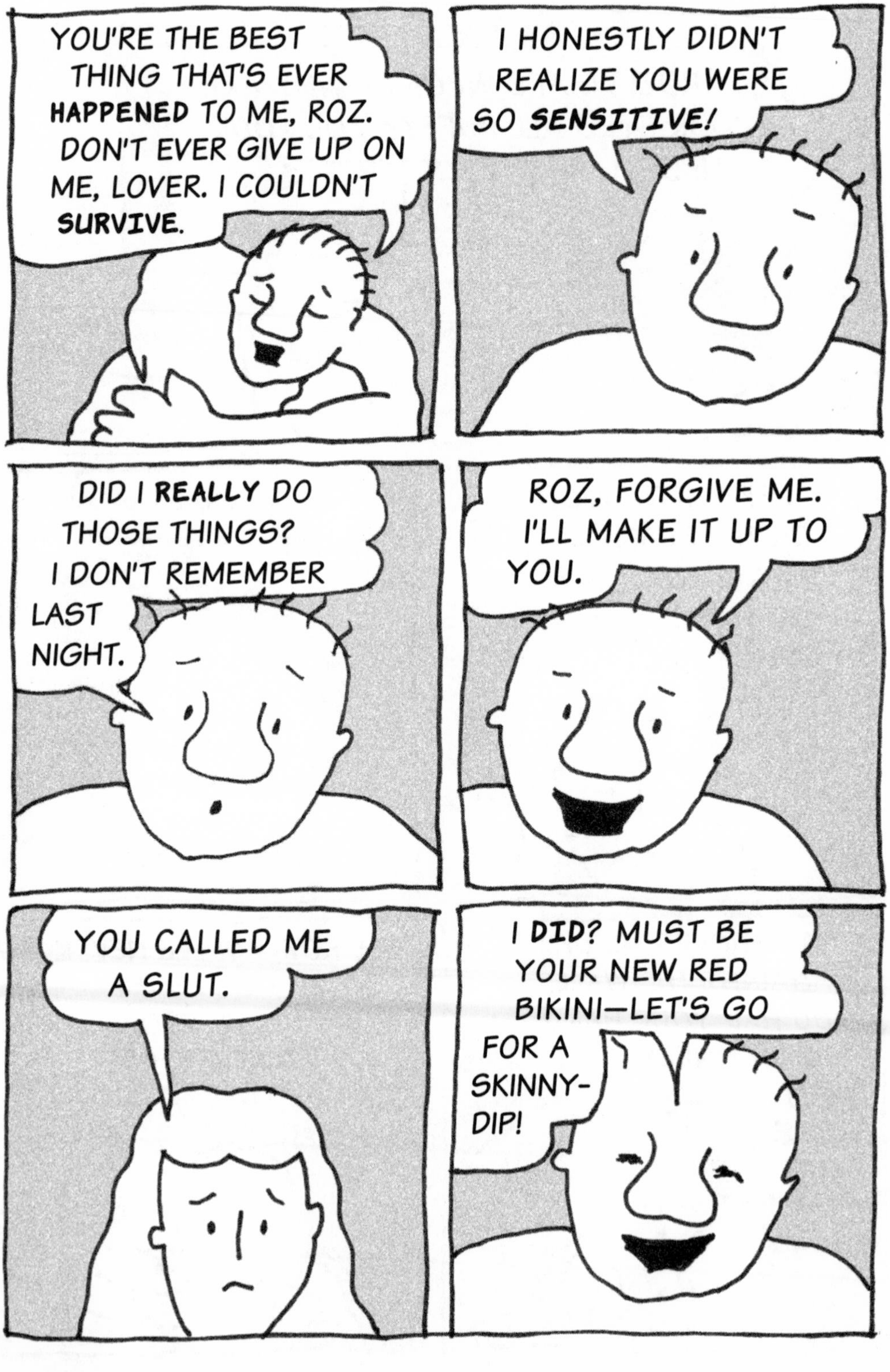
YOU'RE THE BEST THING THAT'S EVER HAPPENED TO ME, ROZ. DON'T EVER GIVE UP ON ME, LOVER. I COULDN'T SURVIVE.
I HONESTLY DIDN'T REALIZE YOU WERE SO SENSITIVE!
DID I REALLY DO THOSE THINGS? I DON'T REMEMBER LAST NIGHT.
ROZ, FORGIVE ME. I'LL MAKE IT UP TO YOU.
YOU CALLED ME A SLUT.
I DID? MUST BE YOUR NEW RED BIKINI—LET'S GO FOR A SKINNY-DIP!

AS WE SAT ON THE BEACH, BRIAN WAS SO SWEET THAT I WONDERED IF I HAD OVERREACTED. MAYBE I **HAD** FLIRTED WITH STEVE ... MAYBE I ***SHOULDN'T HAVE*** ASKED BRIAN TO GET MY DINNER ... MAYBE IT WAS ***ALL MY FAULT***.

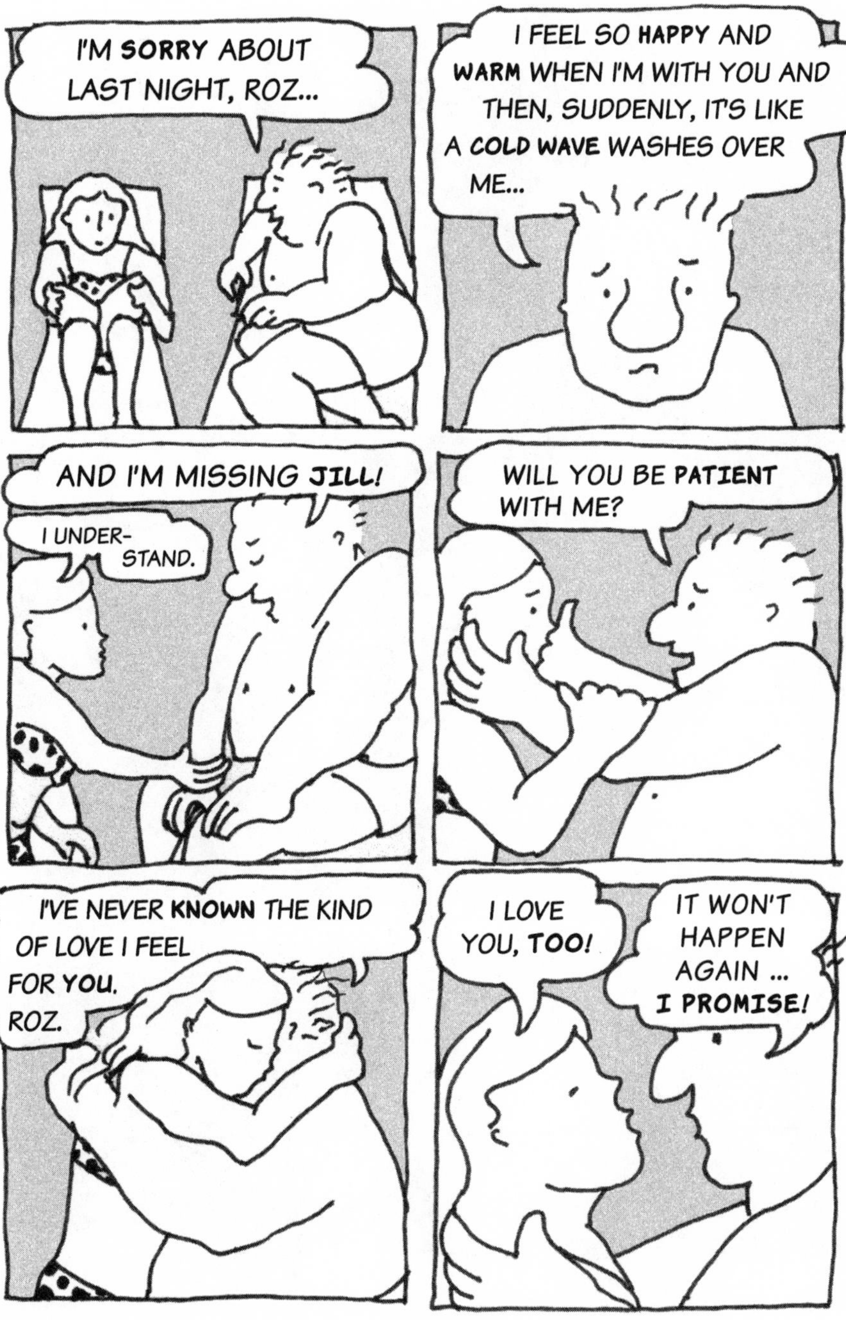

I'M SORRY ABOUT LAST NIGHT, ROZ...
I FEEL SO HAPPY AND WARM WHEN I'M WITH YOU AND THEN, SUDDENLY, IT'S LIKE A COLD WAVE WASHES OVER ME...
AND I'M MISSING JILL!
I UNDER-STAND.
WILL YOU BE PATIENT WITH ME?
I'VE NEVER KNOWN THE KIND OF LOVE I FEEL FOR YOU. ROZ.
I LOVE YOU, TOO!
IT WON'T HAPPEN AGAIN ... I PROMISE!

THE REST OF THE TRIP WAS **WONDERFUL.** SO I BEGAN TO WONDER IF THAT AWFUL NIGHT EVER **HAPPENED.**

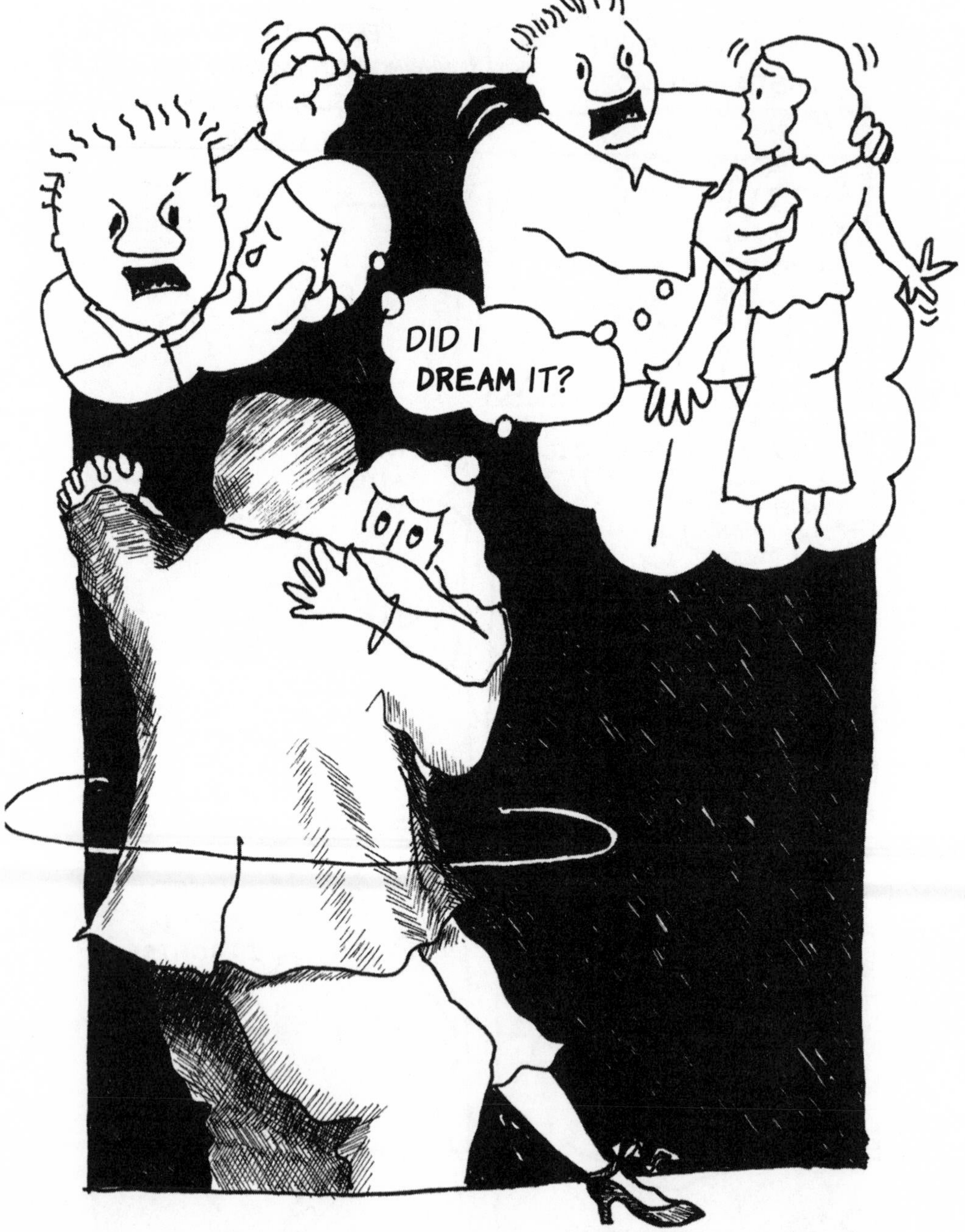
DID I **DREAM** IT?

BUT LEE INVITED ME FOR A LONG WALK THE NEXT DAY, AND I FOUND OUT THAT SHE AND STEVE HAD WITNESSED EVERYTHING.

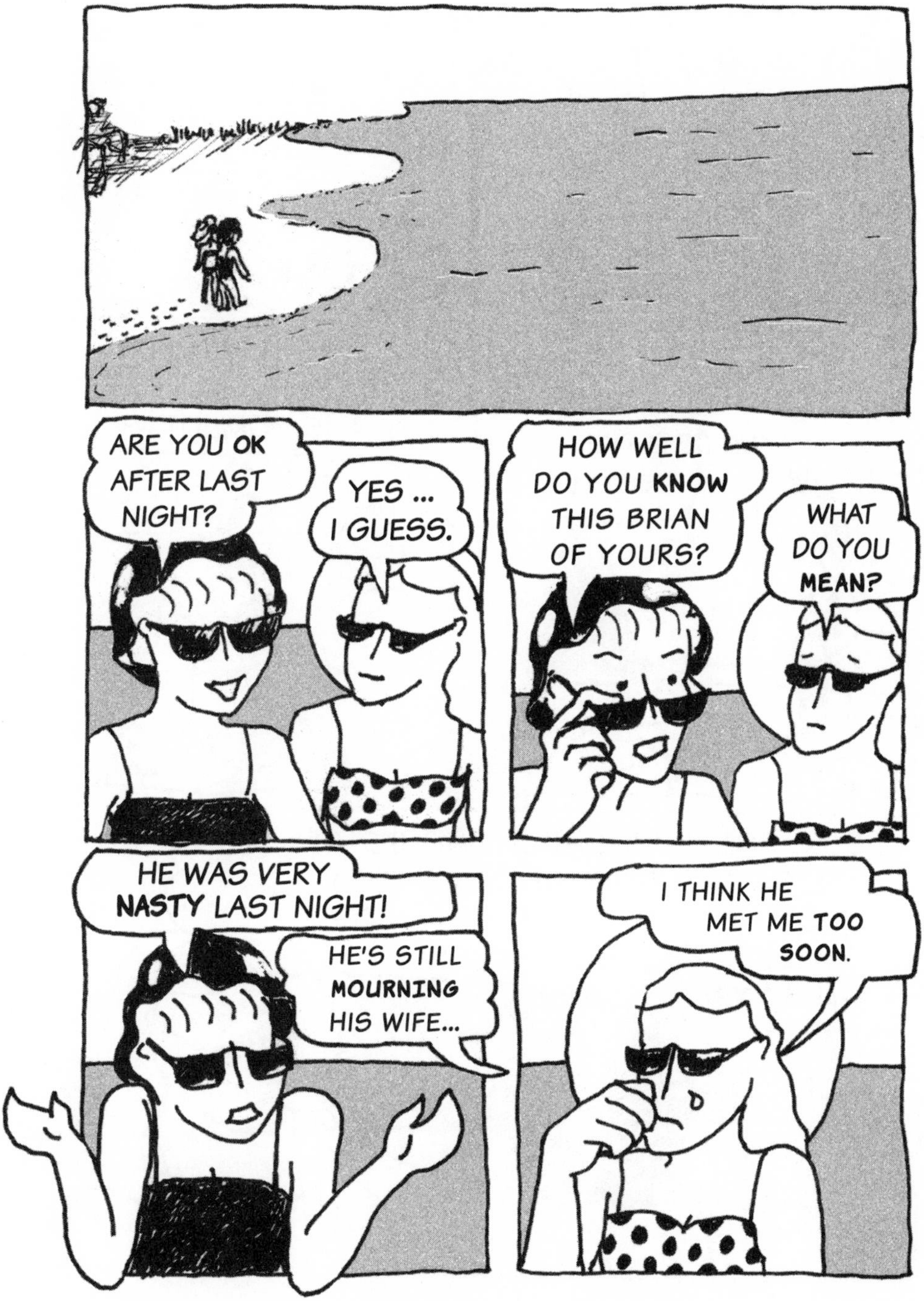
ARE YOU OK AFTER LAST NIGHT?
YES ... I GUESS.
HOW WELL DO YOU KNOW THIS BRIAN OF YOURS?
WHAT DO YOU MEAN?
HE WAS VERY NASTY LAST NIGHT!
HE'S STILL MOURNING HIS WIFE...
I THINK HE MET ME TOO SOON.

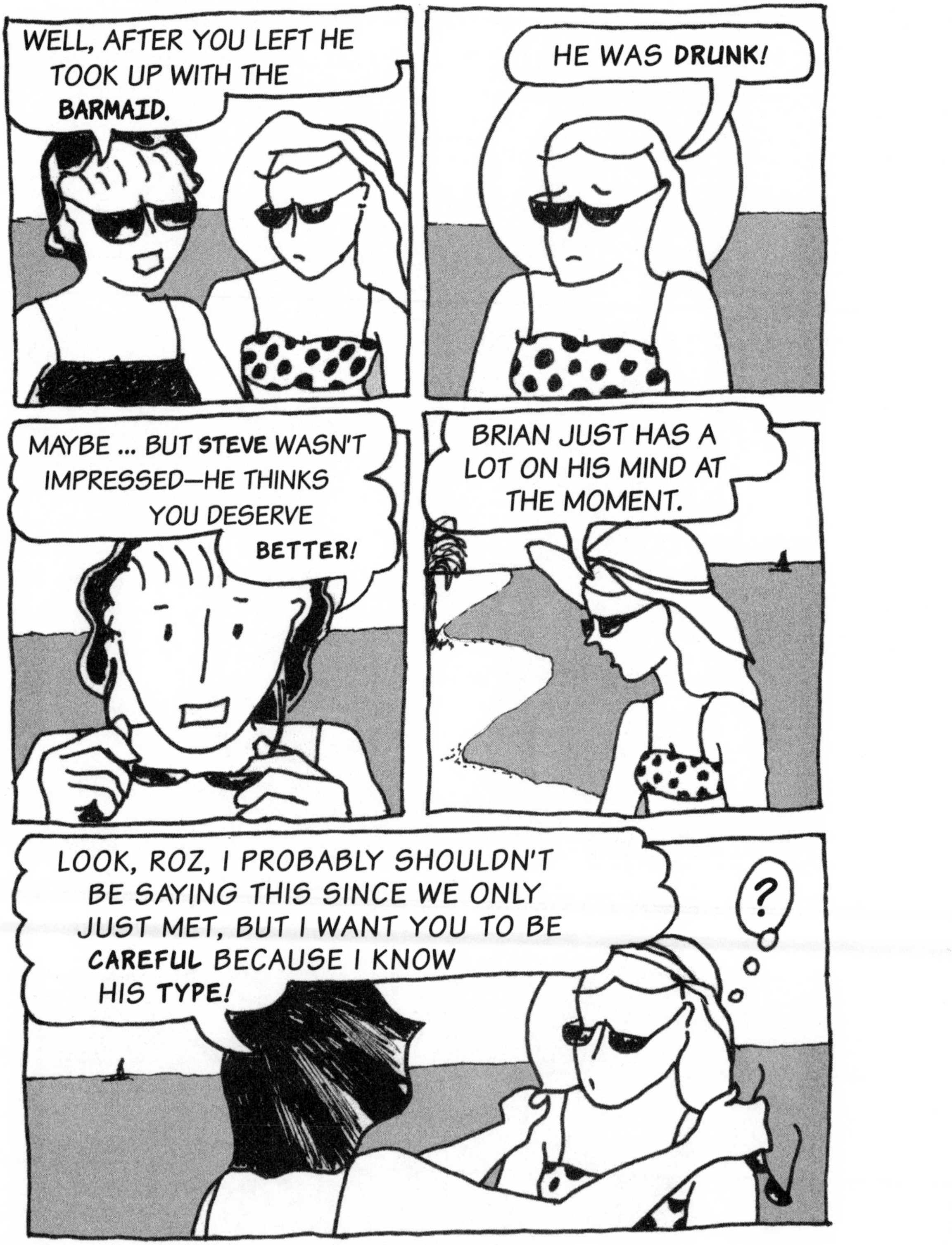
WELL, AFTER YOU LEFT HE TOOK UP WITH THE **BARMAID.**
HE WAS **DRUNK!**
MAYBE ... BUT **STEVE** WASN'T IMPRESSED—HE THINKS YOU DESERVE **BETTER!**
BRIAN JUST HAS A LOT ON HIS MIND AT THE MOMENT.
LOOK, ROZ, I PROBABLY SHOULDN'T BE SAYING THIS SINCE WE ONLY JUST MET, BUT I WANT YOU TO BE **CAREFUL** BECAUSE I KNOW HIS **TYPE!**
?

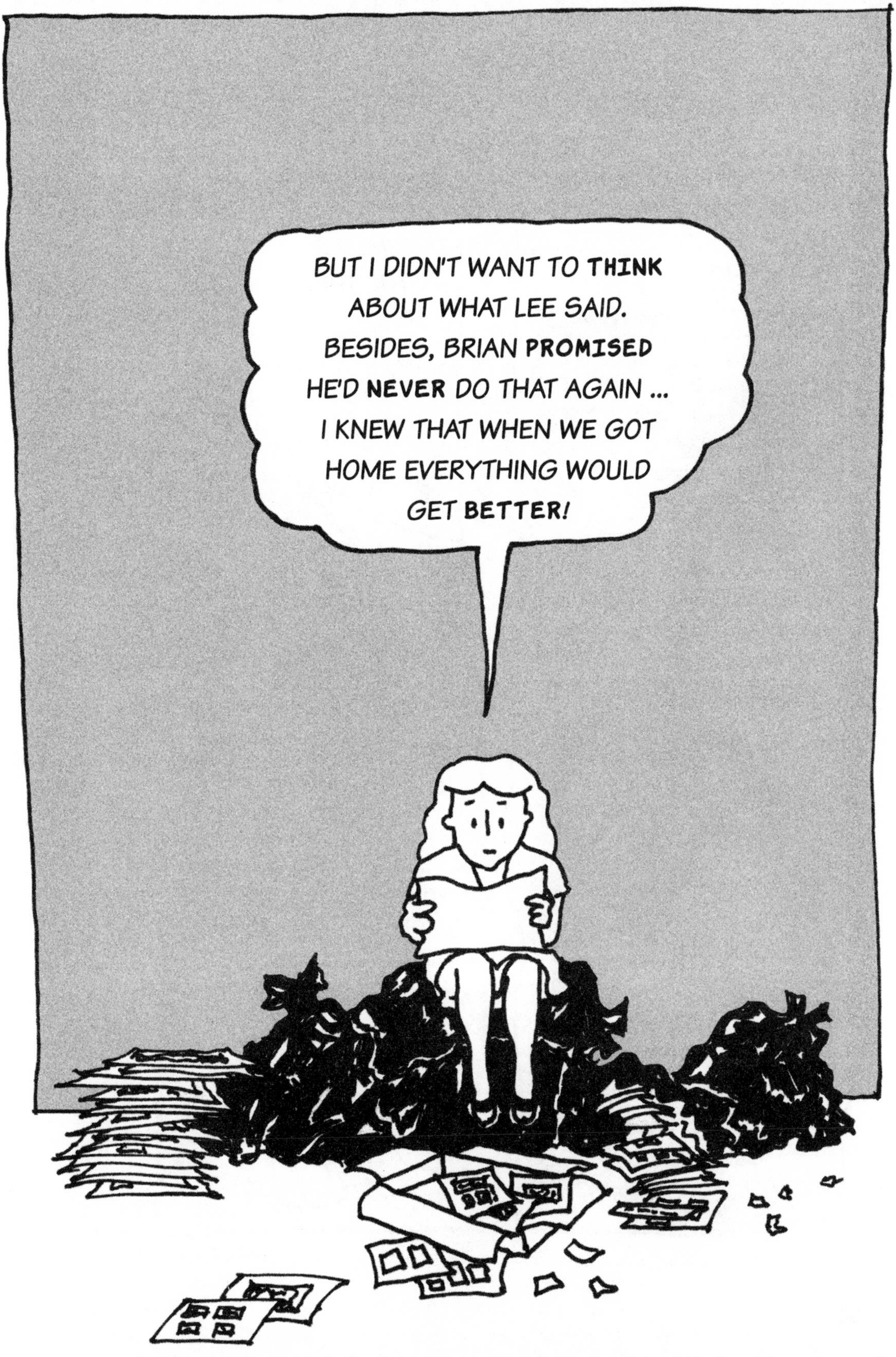
BUT I DIDN'T WANT TO THINK ABOUT WHAT LEE SAID. BESIDES, BRIAN PROMISED HE'D NEVER DO THAT AGAIN ... I KNEW THAT WHEN WE GOT HOME EVERYTHING WOULD GET BETTER!

AND IT **WAS!** OUR FIRST CHRISTMAS WAS WONDERFUL!

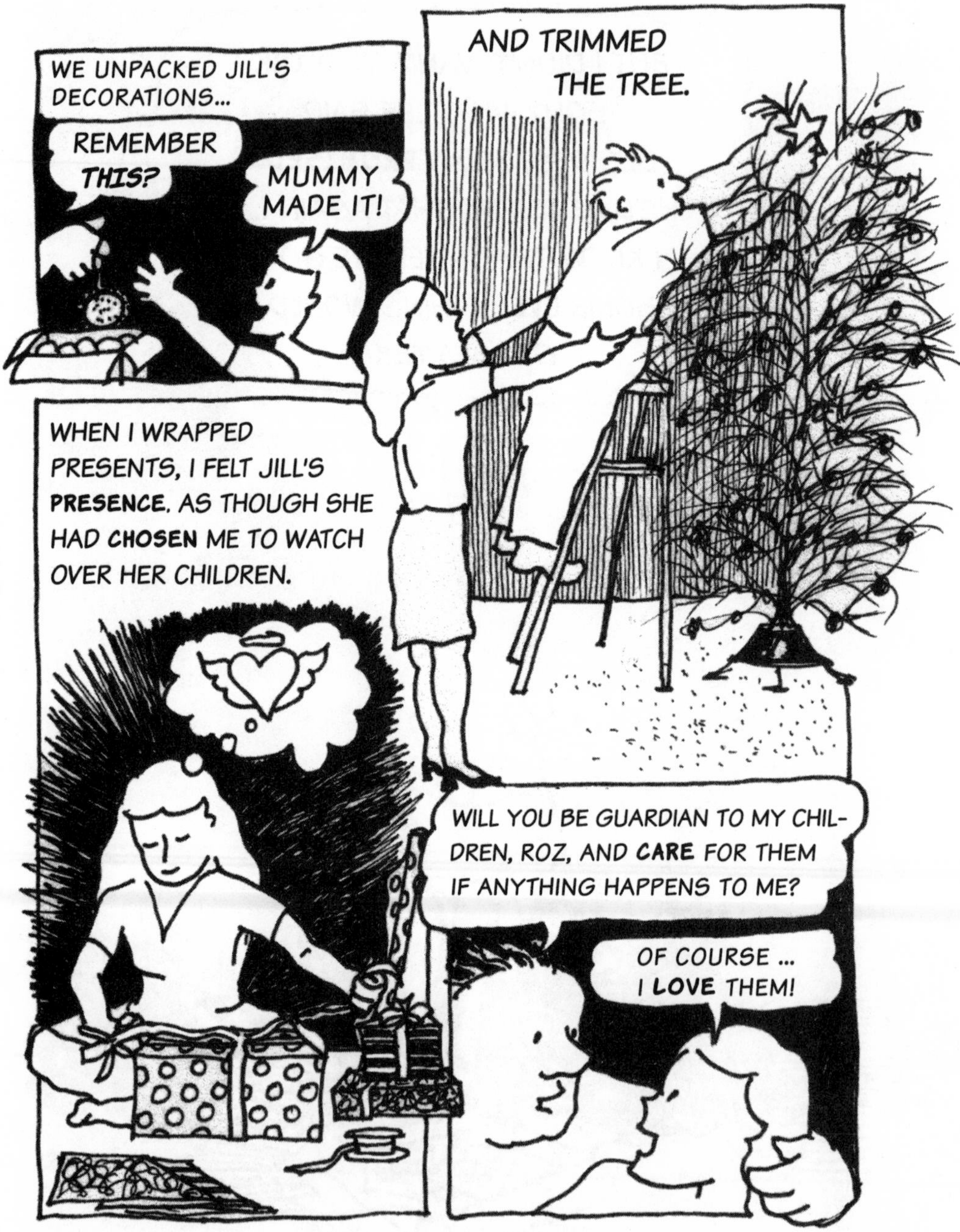
WE UNPACKED JILL'S DECORATIONS...
REMEMBER THIS?
MUMMY MADE IT!
AND TRIMMED THE TREE.
WHEN I WRAPPED PRESENTS, I FELT JILL'S PRESENCE. AS THOUGH SHE HAD CHOSEN ME TO WATCH OVER HER CHILDREN.
WILL YOU BE GUARDIAN TO MY CHILDREN, ROZ, AND CARE FOR THEM IF ANYTHING HAPPENS TO ME?
OF COURSE ... I LOVE THEM!

LATER THAT NIGHT...

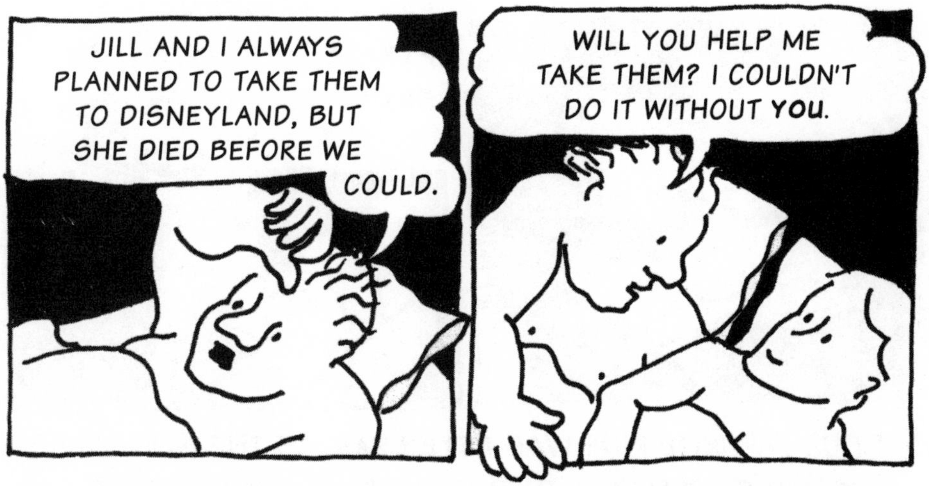
JILL AND I ALWAYS PLANNED TO TAKE THEM TO DISNEYLAND, BUT SHE DIED BEFORE WE COULD.
WILL YOU HELP ME TAKE THEM? I COULDN'T DO IT WITHOUT **YOU**.

SO, IN MARCH, WE FLEW TO CALIFORNIA AND RENTED A VAN.

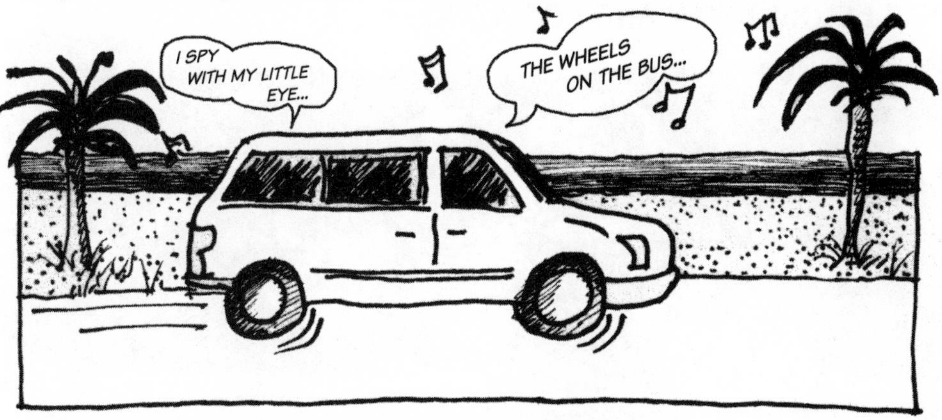
I SPY WITH MY LITTLE EYE...
THE WHEELS ON THE BUS...

OUR HOTEL OVERLOOKED AN ENCHANTED LAGOON, WHERE WE WATCHED FIREWORKS AT NIGHT. WE WENT TO A FAIRY TALE CASTLE...

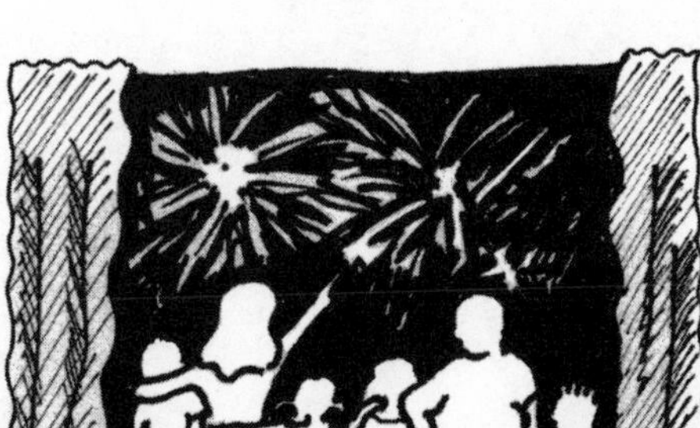

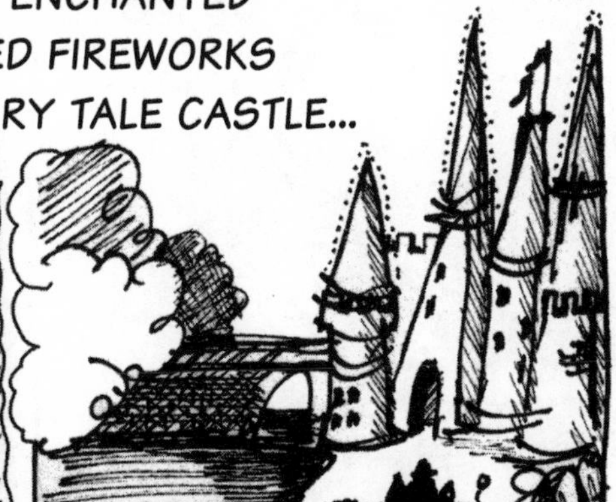

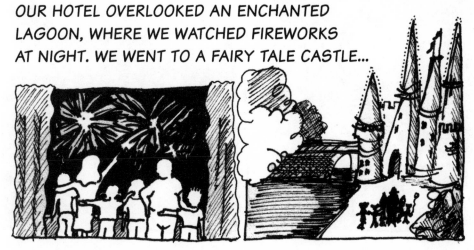

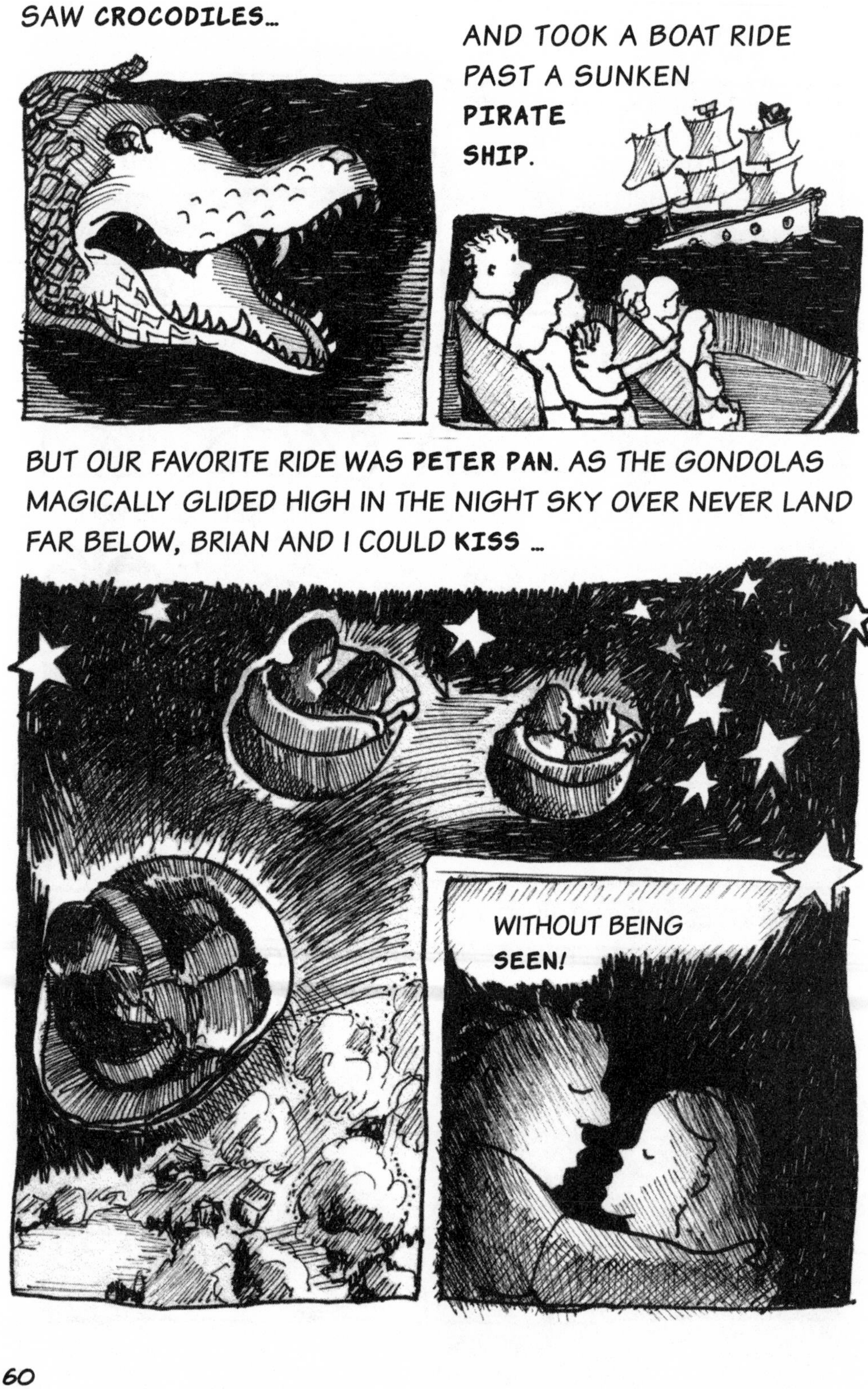
SAW CROCODILES...
AND TOOK A BOAT RIDE PAST A SUNKEN PIRATE SHIP.
BUT OUR FAVORITE RIDE WAS PETER PAN. AS THE GONDOLAS MAGICALLY GLIDED HIGH IN THE NIGHT SKY OVER NEVER LAND FAR BELOW, BRIAN AND I COULD KISS ...
WITHOUT BEING SEEN!

WE TOOK THE RIDE SO MANY TIMES, THE CHILDREN BEGGED US TO STOP!

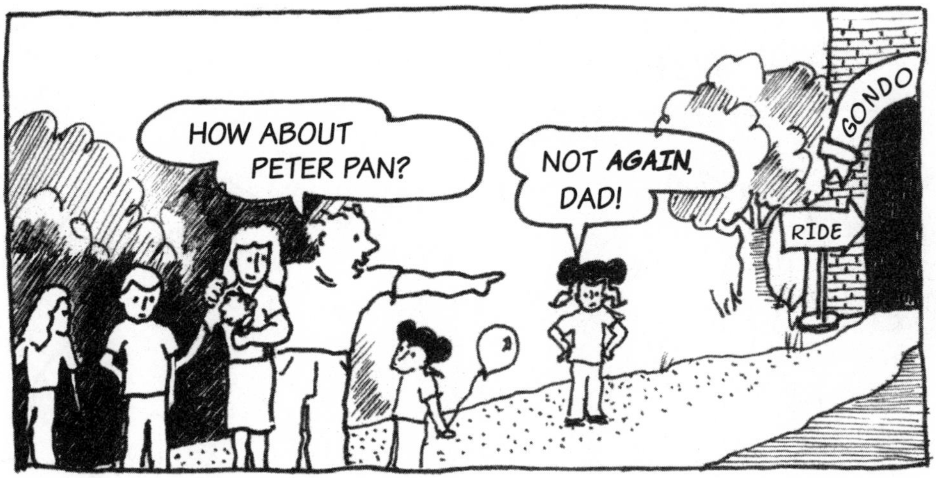

HOW ABOUT PETER PAN?
NOT **AGAIN**, DAD!
GONDO
RIDE

WE CAME HOME HAPPY AND IN LOVE, **TOGETHER** AS A **FAMILY**.

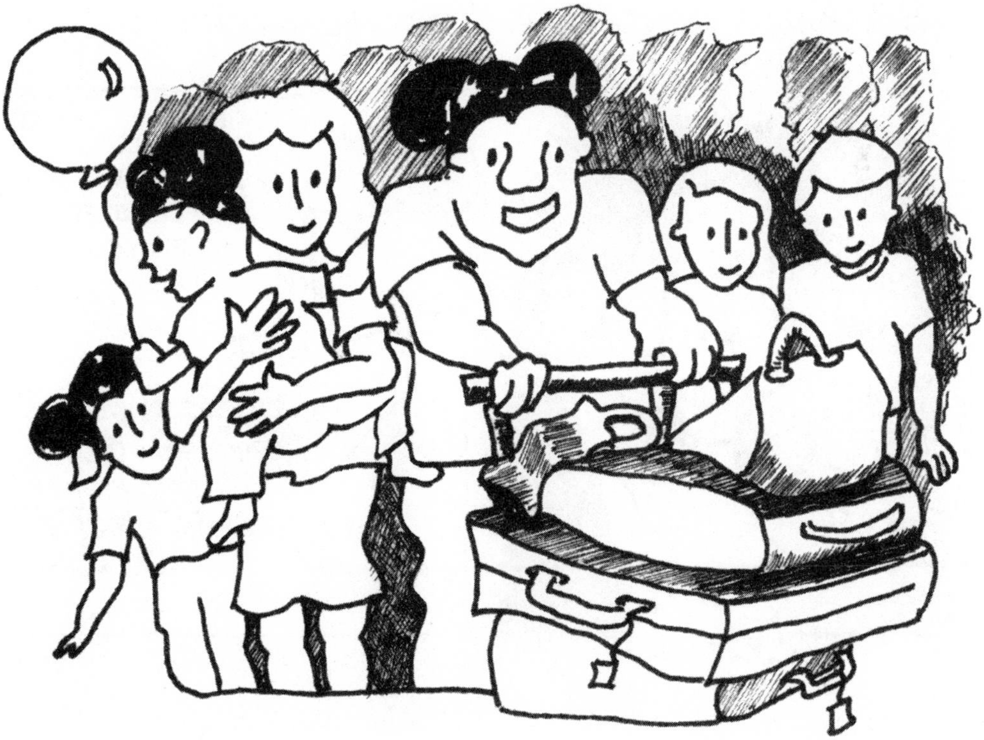

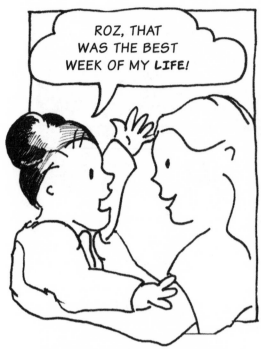

ROZ, THAT WAS THE BEST WEEK OF MY **LIFE**!
LIZZIE LEFT ME A SECRET NOTE.
DEAR ROZ I LOVE YOU VERY MUCH XXX OOO
JIM GAVE ME A SPONTANEOUS HUG FOR THE FIRST TIME...
AND MEGAN CONFIDED.
GOOD NIGHT, SWEETIE...
ROZ? I ALWAYS FEEL **SAFE** WHEN YOU'RE HERE.

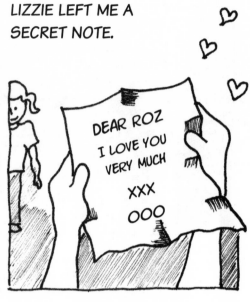

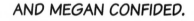

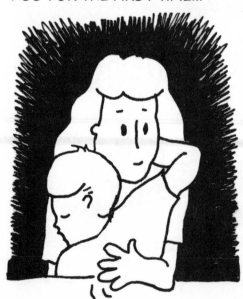

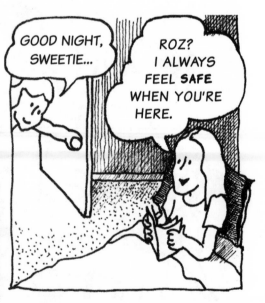

SPRING CAME, AND I SPENT MOST WEEKENDS PITCHING IN WITH HOUSEHOLD CHORES.

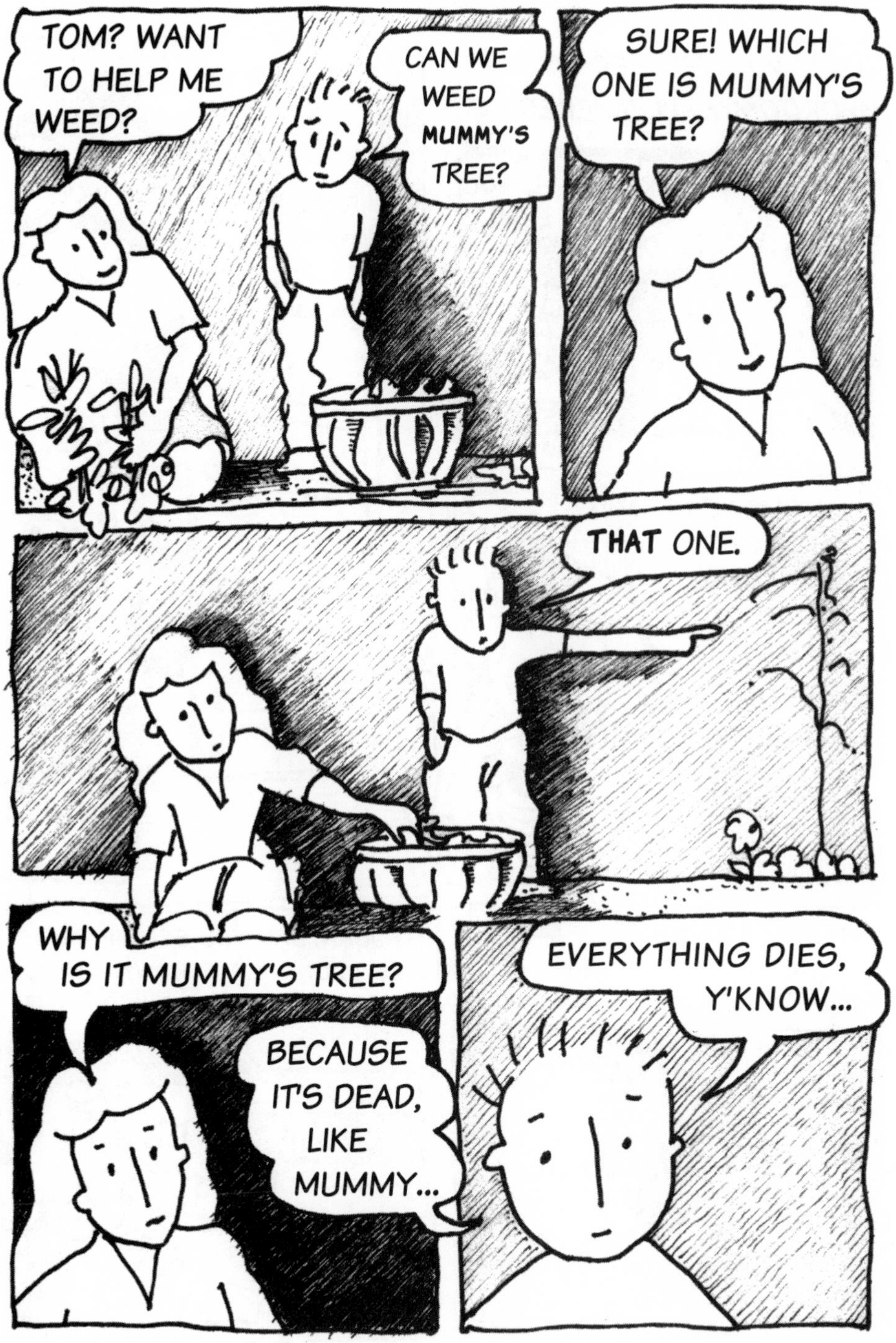
TOM? WANT TO HELP ME WEED?
CAN WE WEED MUMMY'S TREE?
SURE! WHICH ONE IS MUMMY'S TREE?
THAT ONE.
WHY IS IT MUMMY'S TREE?
BECAUSE IT'S DEAD, LIKE MUMMY...
EVERYTHING DIES, Y'KNOW...

WITH THE NANNY GONE, I WAS LEAVING WORK EARLY SO I COULD BE HOME WITH BRIAN'S CHILDREN AFTER SCHOOL.

LIZZIE WANTED HER BEDROOM WALLPAPERED.

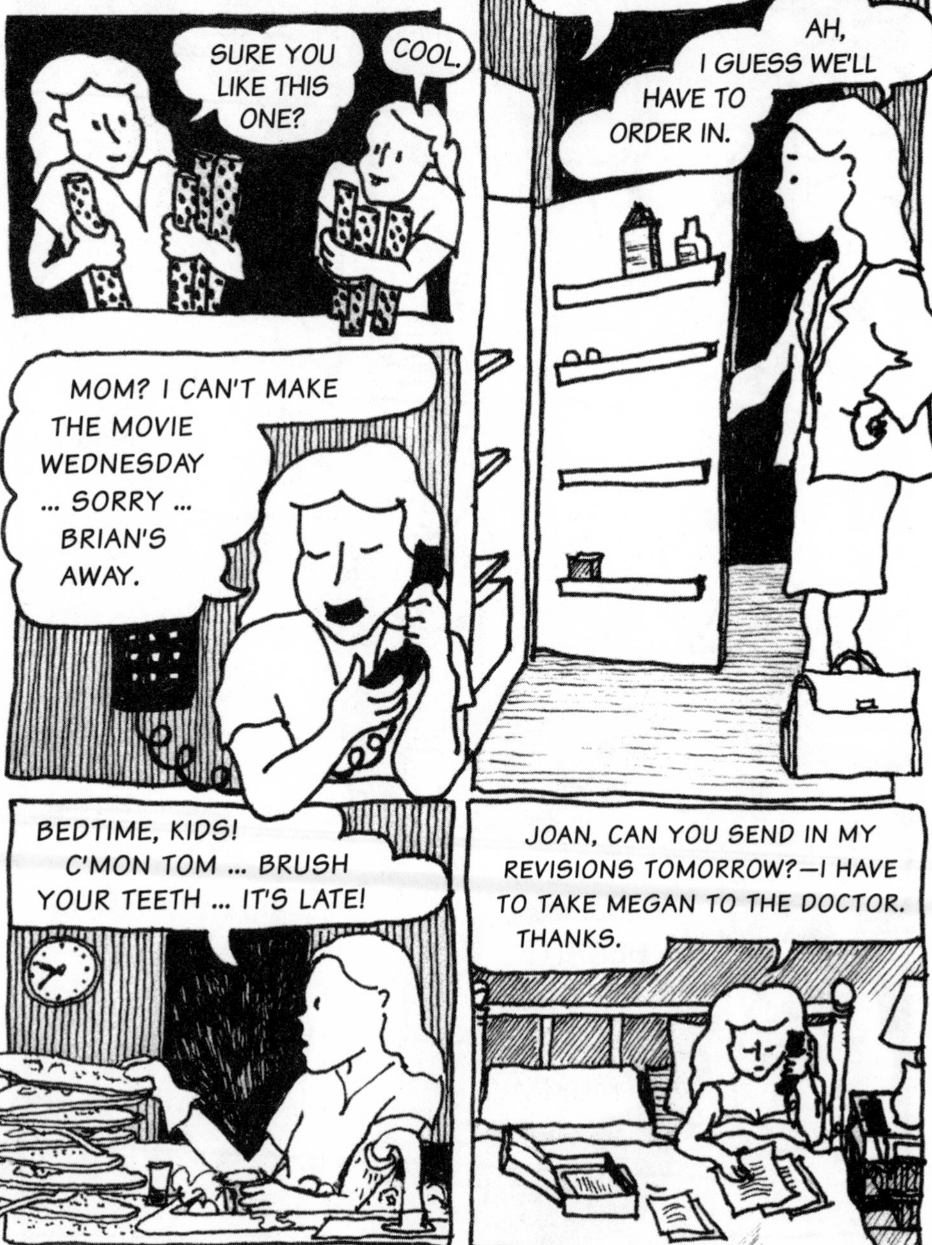

SURE YOU LIKE THIS ONE?
COOL.
ROZ, WHAT'S FOR SUPPER?
AH, I GUESS WE'LL HAVE TO ORDER IN.
MOM? I CAN'T MAKE THE MOVIE WEDNESDAY ... SORRY ... BRIAN'S AWAY.
BEDTIME, KIDS! C'MON TOM ... BRUSH YOUR TEETH ... IT'S LATE!
JOAN, CAN YOU SEND IN MY REVISIONS TOMORROW?—I HAVE TO TAKE MEGAN TO THE DOCTOR. THANKS.

BRIAN WANTED ME TO SELL MY COMPANY, BUT I FELT CONFUSED. WOULD I BE GAINING EVERYTHING OR LOSING EVERYTHING?

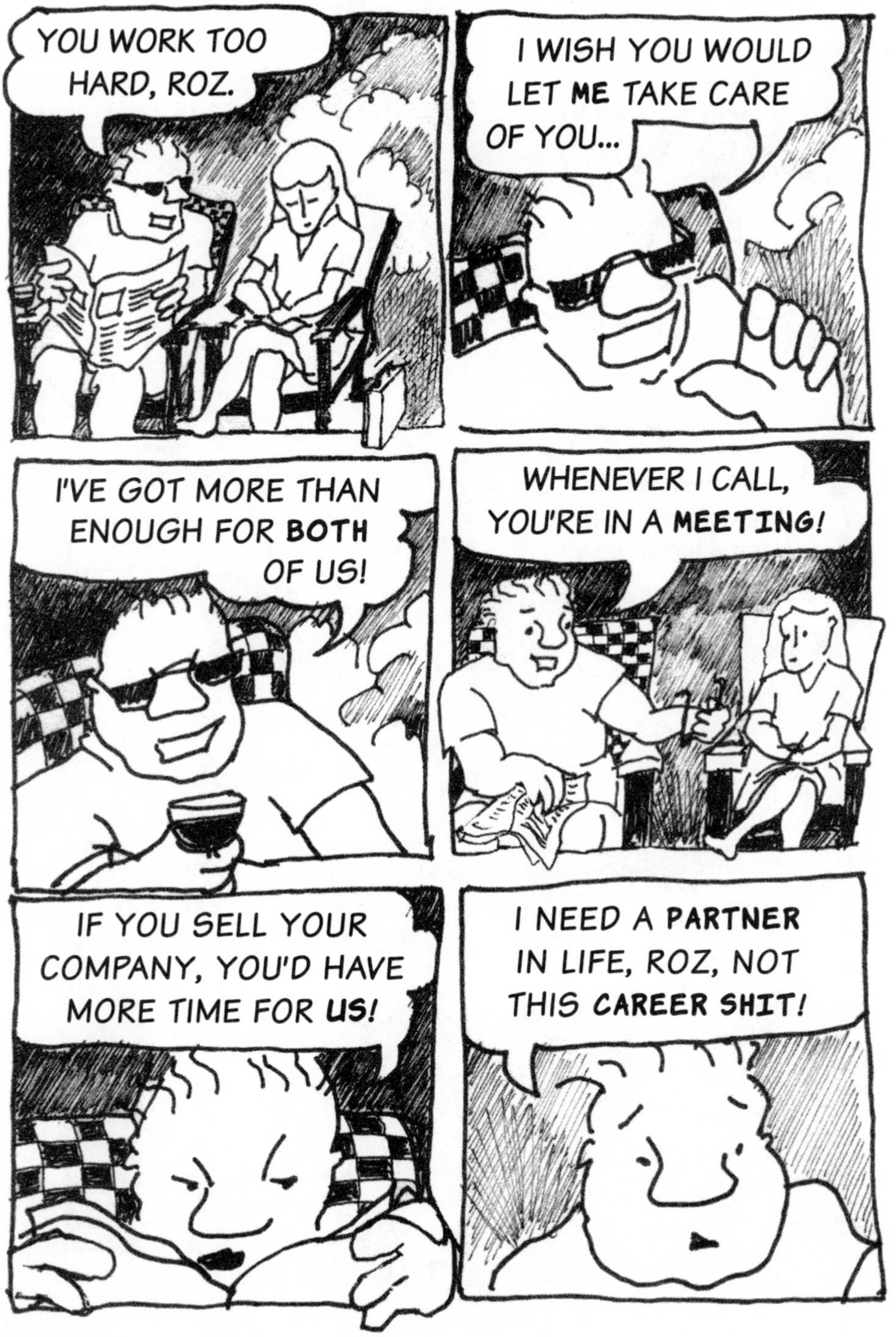

YOU WORK TOO HARD, ROZ.
I WISH YOU WOULD LET ME TAKE CARE OF YOU...
I'VE GOT MORE THAN ENOUGH FOR BOTH OF US!
WHENEVER I CALL, YOU'RE IN A MEETING!
IF YOU SELL YOUR COMPANY, YOU'D HAVE MORE TIME FOR US!
I NEED A PARTNER IN LIFE, ROZ, NOT THIS CAREER SHIT!

WHEN I TOLD VAL + KYRIE ABOUT BRIAN, I TRIED TO TELL THEM ONLY *GOOD* THINGS. I WAS TOO ASHAMED TO TELL THEM WHAT HAD HAPPENED IN GREECE.

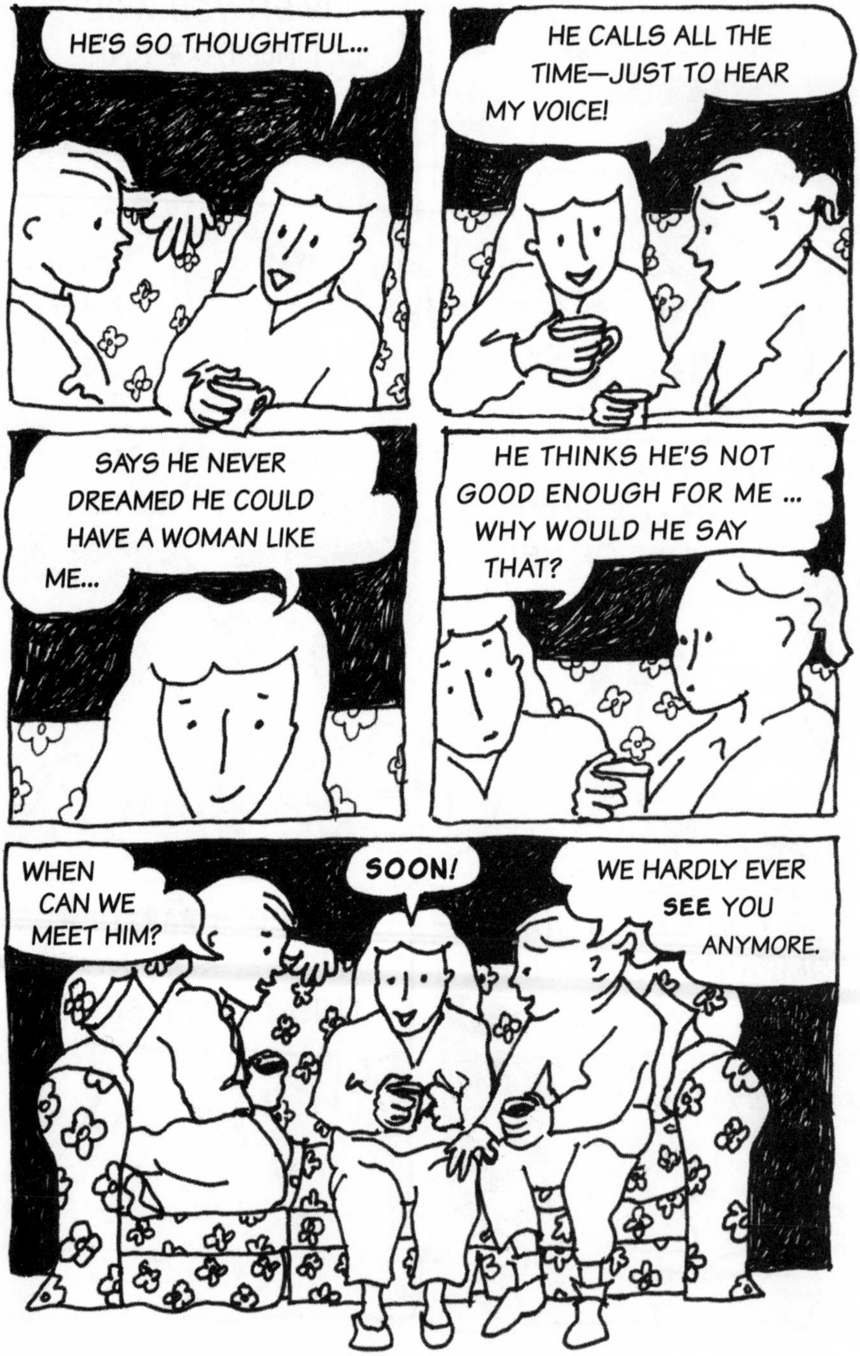

HE'S SO THOUGHTFUL...
HE CALLS ALL THE TIME—JUST TO HEAR MY VOICE!
SAYS HE NEVER DREAMED HE COULD HAVE A WOMAN LIKE ME...
HE THINKS HE'S NOT GOOD ENOUGH FOR ME ... WHY WOULD HE SAY THAT?
WHEN CAN WE MEET HIM?
SOON!
WE HARDLY EVER SEE YOU ANYMORE.

Getting Lost: Jekyll & Hyde

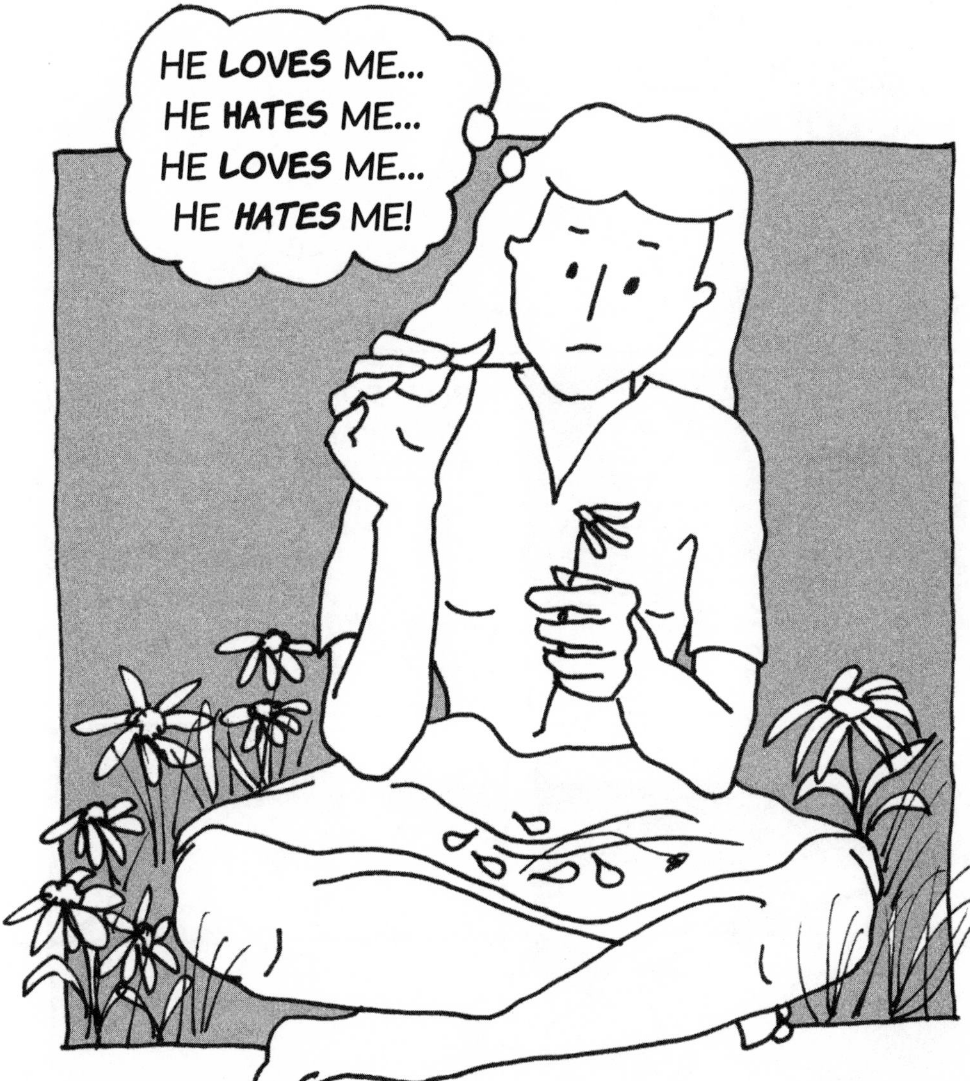
HE **LOVES** ME...
HE **HATES** ME...
HE **LOVES** ME...
HE ***HATES*** ME!

THE FOLLOWING WINTER I HAD AN IMPORTANT BUSINESS MEETING SCHEDULED EARLY ONE MORNING...

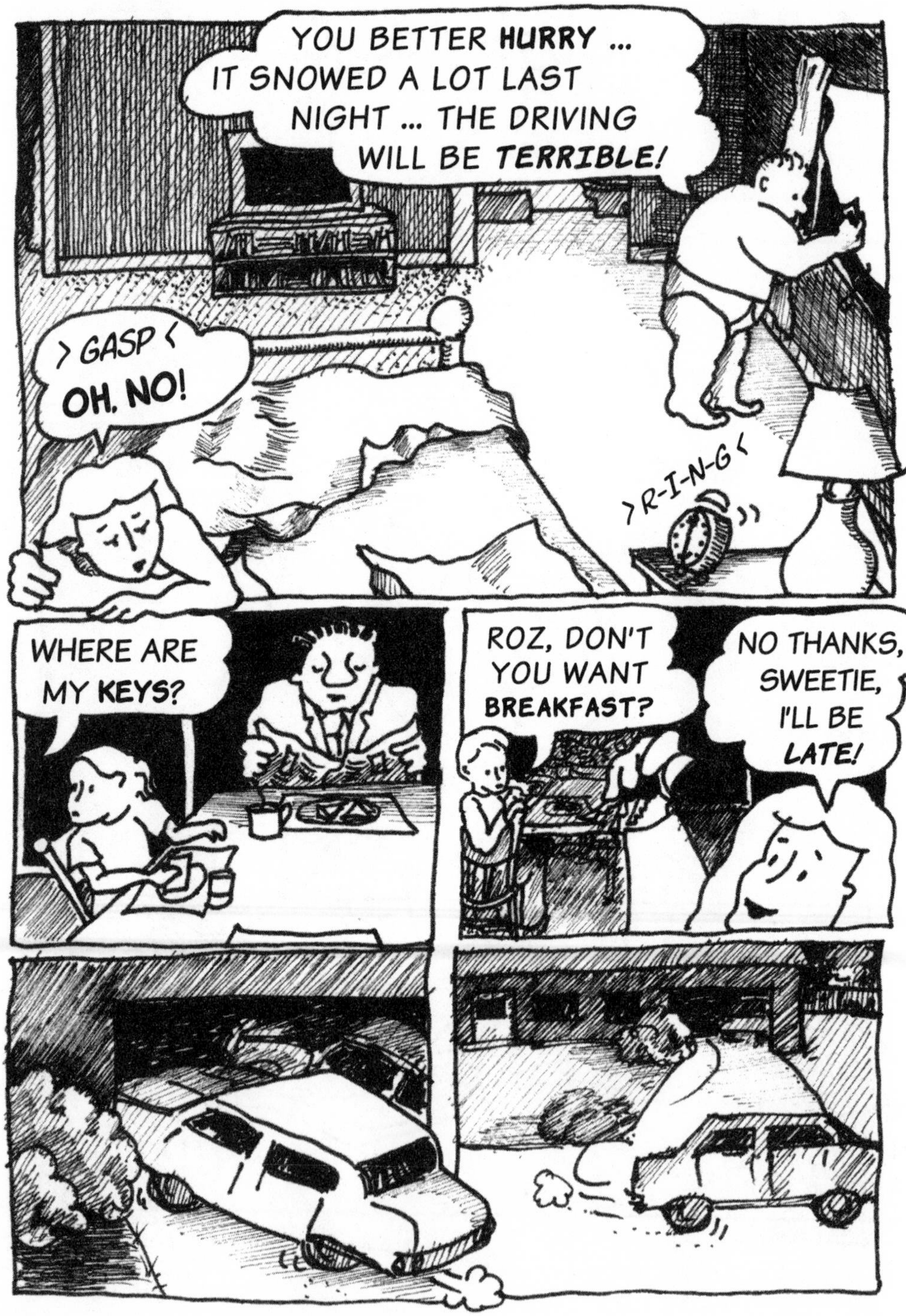
YOU BETTER **HURRY** ... IT SNOWED A LOT LAST NIGHT ... THE DRIVING WILL BE ***TERRIBLE!***
>GASP< **OH, NO!**
>R-I-N-G<
WHERE ARE MY **KEYS?**
ROZ, DON'T YOU WANT **BREAKFAST?**
NO THANKS, SWEETIE, I'LL BE ***LATE!***

BUT WHEN I GOT IN THE CAR, SOMETHING WASN'T RIGHT...

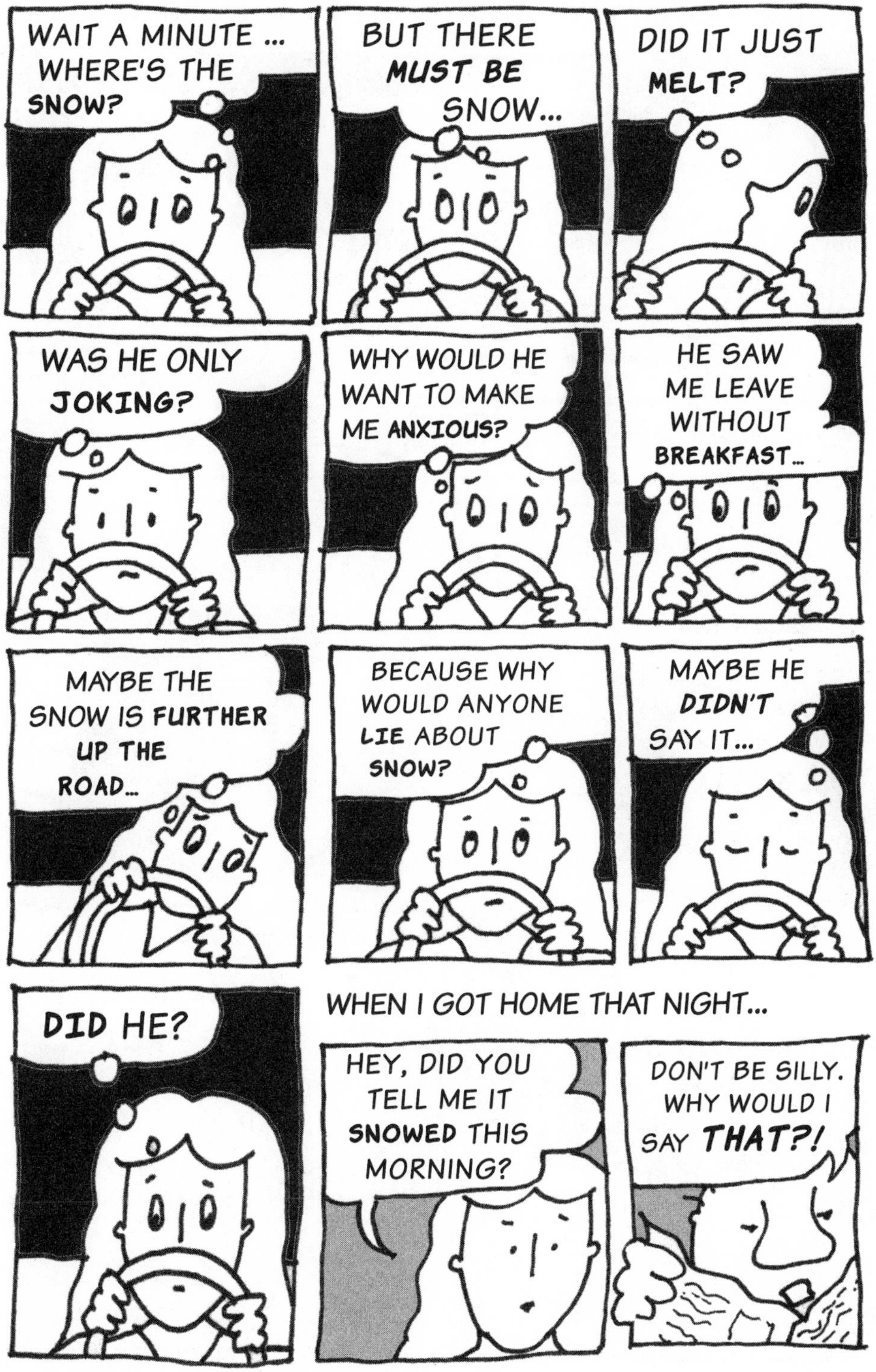
WAIT A MINUTE ... WHERE'S THE SNOW?
BUT THERE MUST BE SNOW...
DID IT JUST MELT?
WAS HE ONLY JOKING?
WHY WOULD HE WANT TO MAKE ME ANXIOUS?
HE SAW ME LEAVE WITHOUT BREAKFAST...
MAYBE THE SNOW IS FURTHER UP THE ROAD...
BECAUSE WHY WOULD ANYONE LIE ABOUT SNOW?
MAYBE HE DIDN'T SAY IT...
DID HE?
WHEN I GOT HOME THAT NIGHT...
HEY, DID YOU TELL ME IT SNOWED THIS MORNING?
DON'T BE SILLY. WHY WOULD I SAY THAT?!

AS THE WEATHER GOT WARMER, I BEGAN TO MEET THE NEIGHBORS, BUT BRIAN DIDN'T WANT ME TO. HE WANTED ME ALL TO HIMSELF.

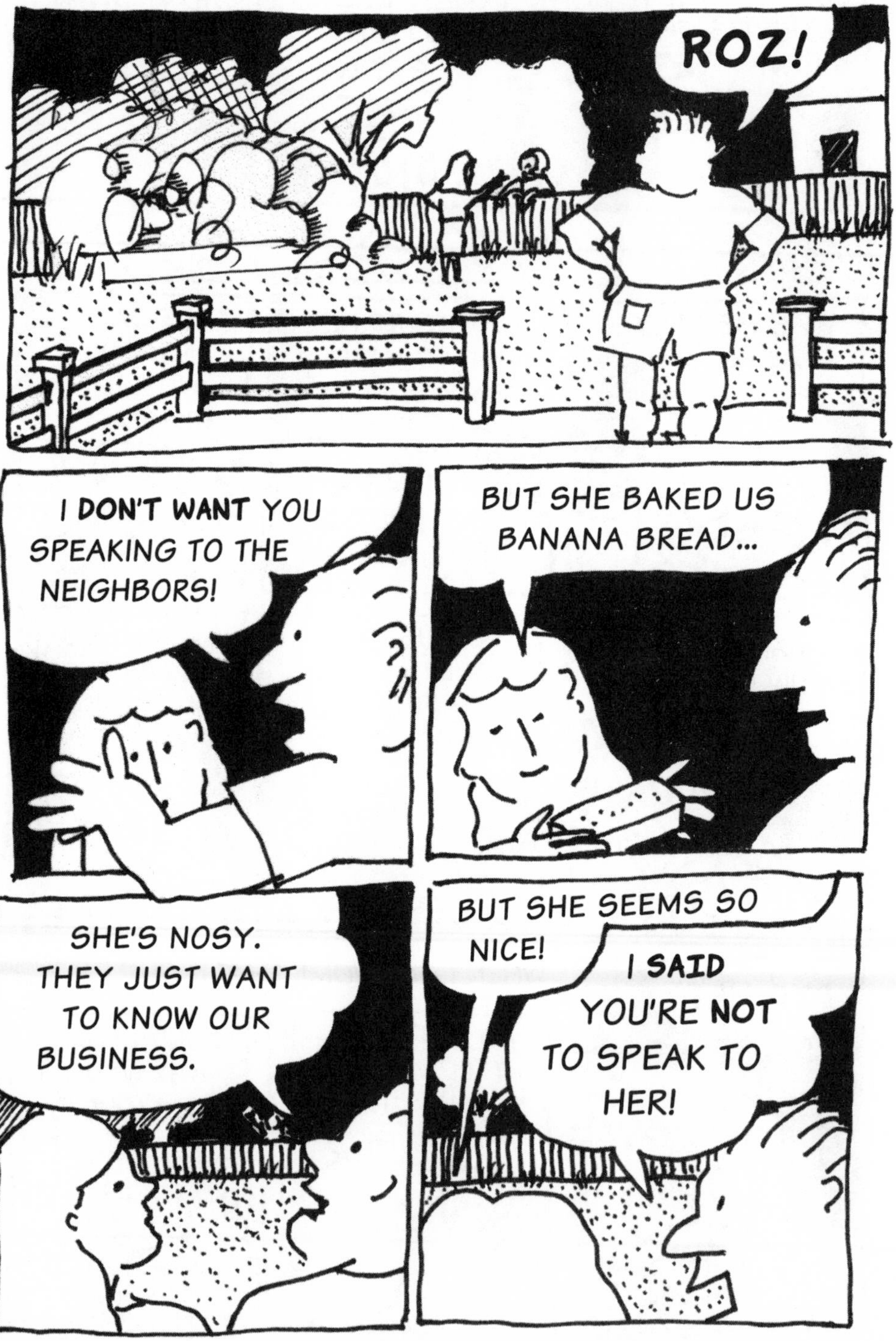
ROZ!
I DON'T WANT YOU SPEAKING TO THE NEIGHBORS!
BUT SHE BAKED US BANANA BREAD...
SHE'S NOSY. THEY JUST WANT TO KNOW OUR BUSINESS.
BUT SHE SEEMS SO NICE!
I SAID YOU'RE NOT TO SPEAK TO HER!

WHEN BRIAN TALKED ROMANTICALLY OF "BECOMING ONE," IT MADE ME FEEL UNEASY. I WANTED TO BE TOGETHER, SIDE BY SIDE ... BUT I DIDN'T WANT TO LOSE MYSELF IN HIM.

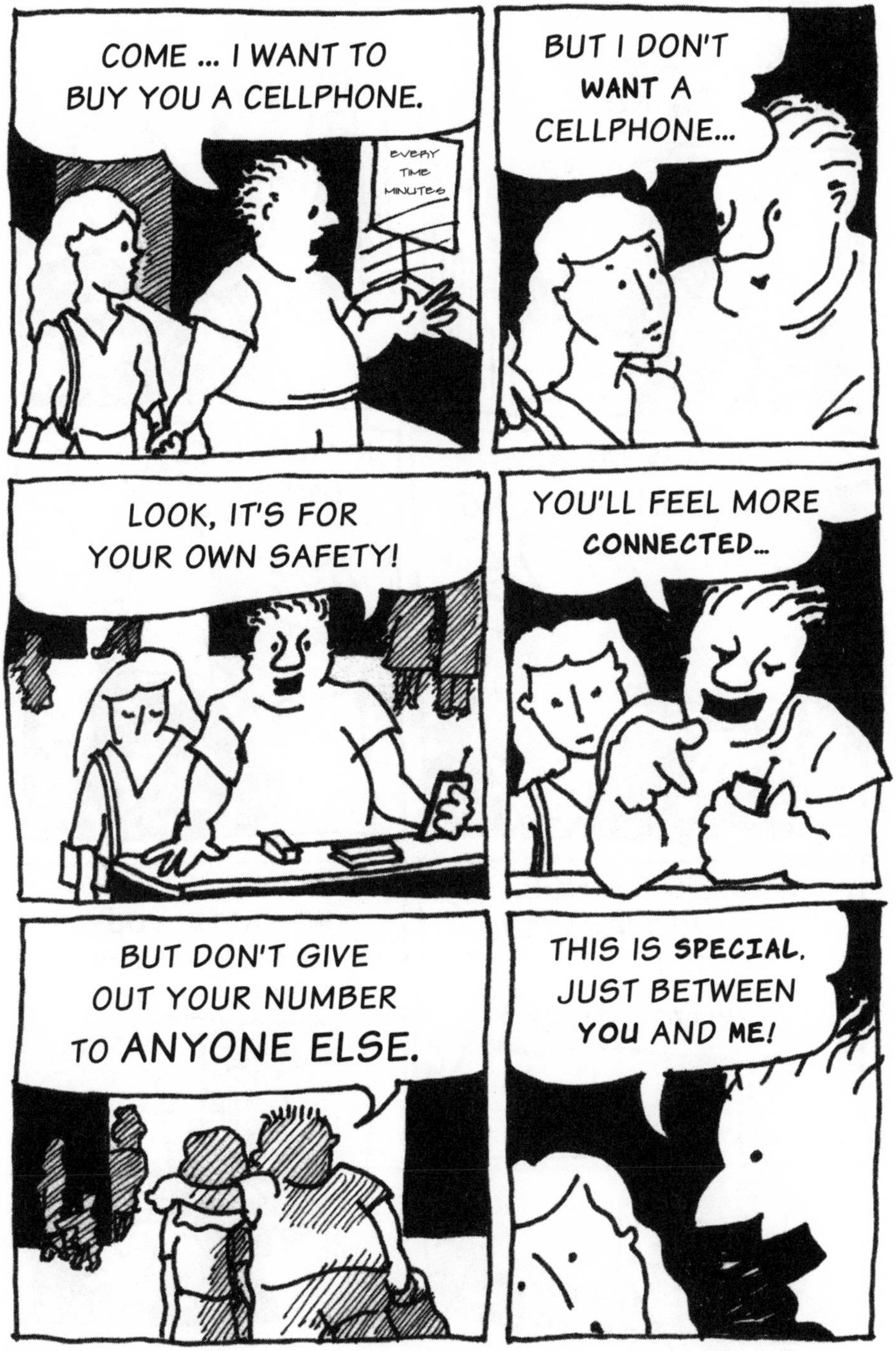
COME ... I WANT TO BUY YOU A CELLPHONE.
EVERY TIME MINUTES
BUT I DON'T WANT A CELLPHONE...
LOOK, IT'S FOR YOUR OWN SAFETY!
YOU'LL FEEL MORE CONNECTED...
BUT DON'T GIVE OUT YOUR NUMBER TO ANYONE ELSE.
THIS IS SPECIAL. JUST BETWEEN YOU AND ME!

FOR THE FIRST TIME IN MY LIFE, I STARTED TO FEEL INSECURE ABOUT HOW I LOOKED...

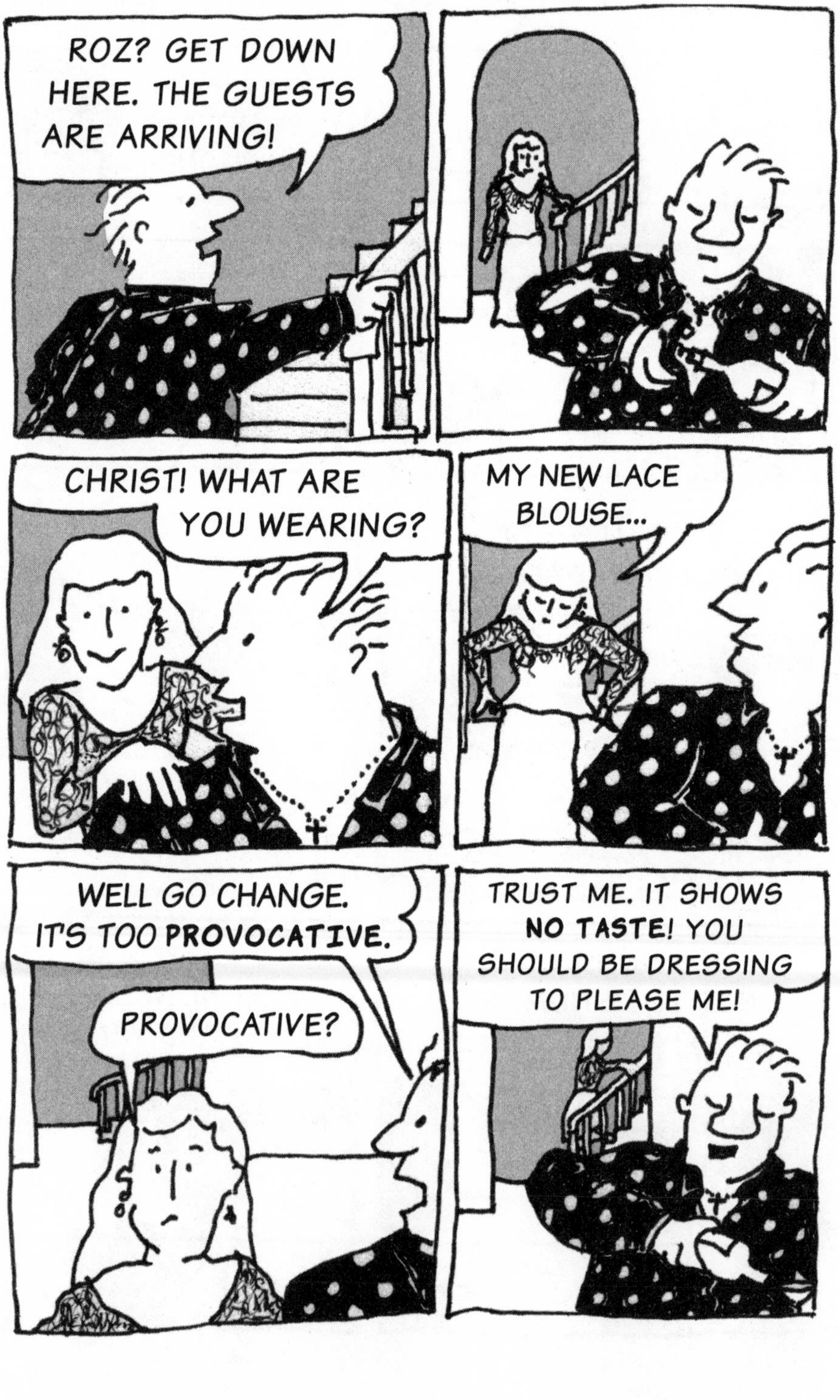

ROZ? GET DOWN HERE. THE GUESTS ARE ARRIVING!
CHRIST! WHAT ARE YOU WEARING?
MY NEW LACE BLOUSE...
WELL GO CHANGE. IT'S TOO **PROVOCATIVE.**
PROVOCATIVE?
TRUST ME. IT SHOWS **NO TASTE!** YOU SHOULD BE DRESSING TO PLEASE ME!

AND I BEGAN TO DOUBT MY RELATIONSHIP WITH MY MOTHER.

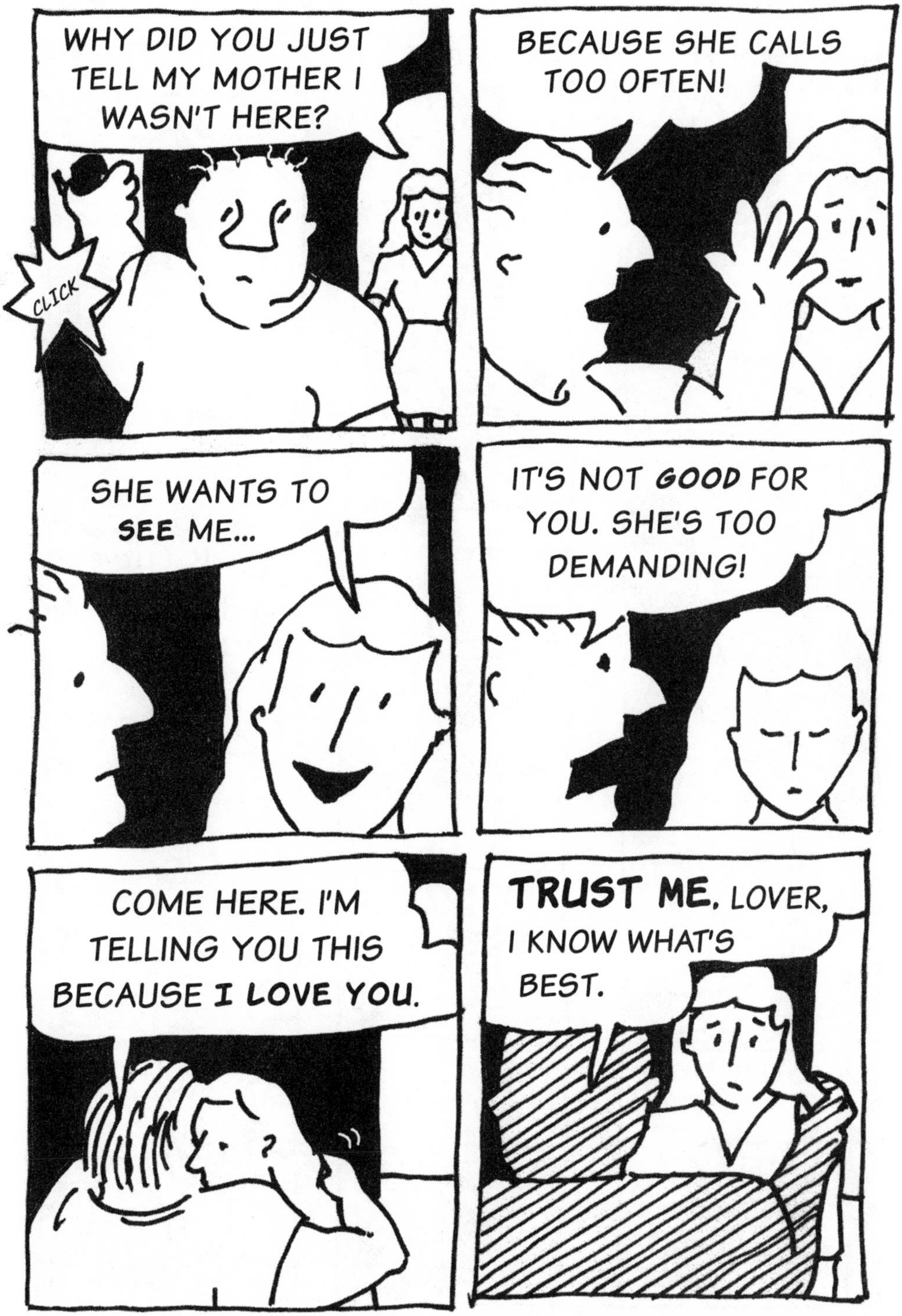
WHY DID YOU JUST TELL MY MOTHER I WASN'T HERE?
CLICK
BECAUSE SHE CALLS TOO OFTEN!
SHE WANTS TO SEE ME...
IT'S NOT GOOD FOR YOU. SHE'S TOO DEMANDING!
COME HERE. I'M TELLING YOU THIS BECAUSE I LOVE YOU.
TRUST ME, LOVER, I KNOW WHAT'S BEST.

IN FACT, I STARTED TO FEEL INSECURE ABOUT ***EVERYTHING.***
BRIAN SEEMED TO PULL ME CLOSE AND THEN PUSH ME AWAY.

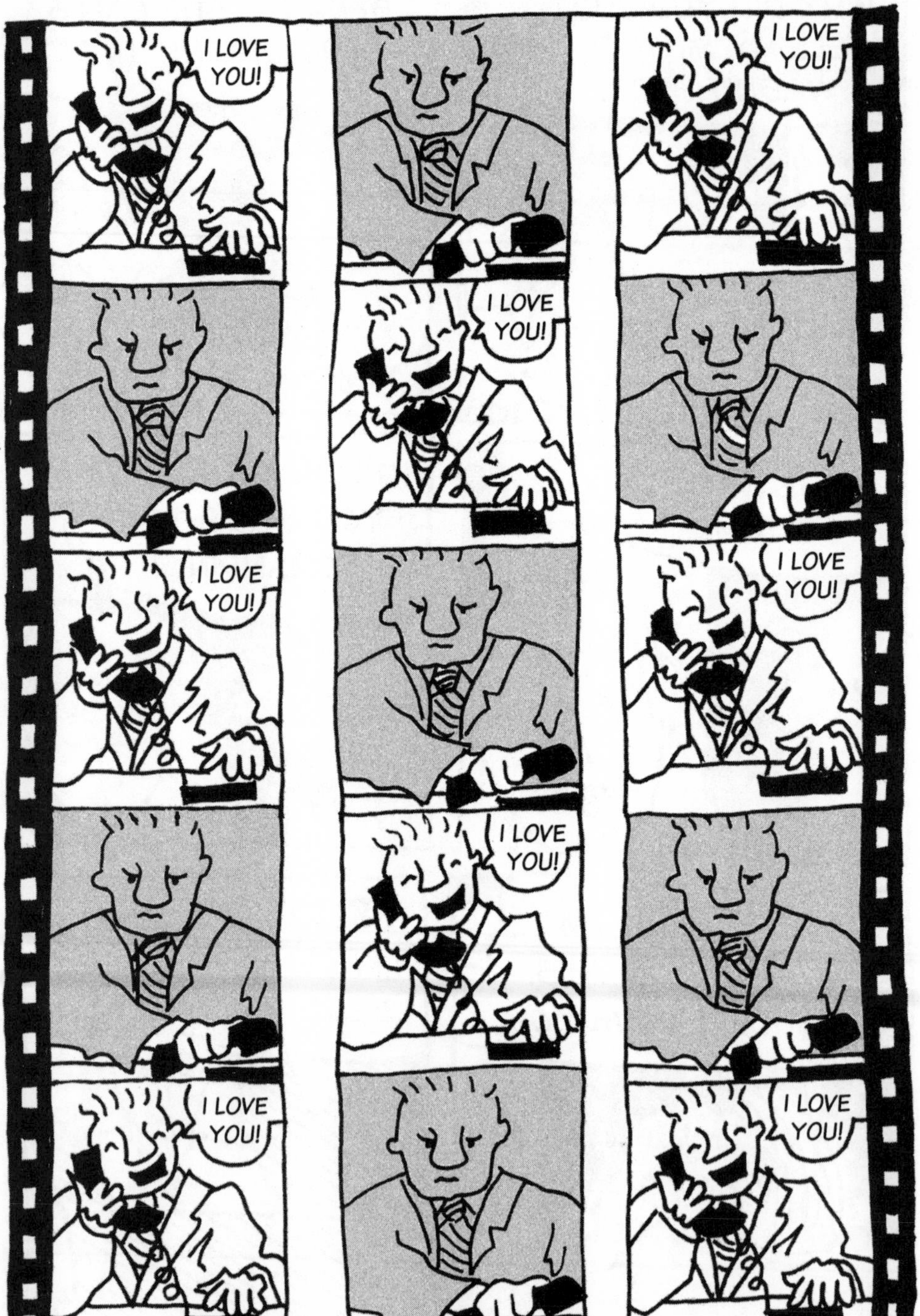
I LOVE YOU!
I LOVE YOU!
I LOVE YOU!
I LOVE YOU!
I LOVE YOU!
I LOVE YOU!
I LOVE YOU!
I LOVE YOU!

SOMETIMES HE ACCOSTED STRANGERS...

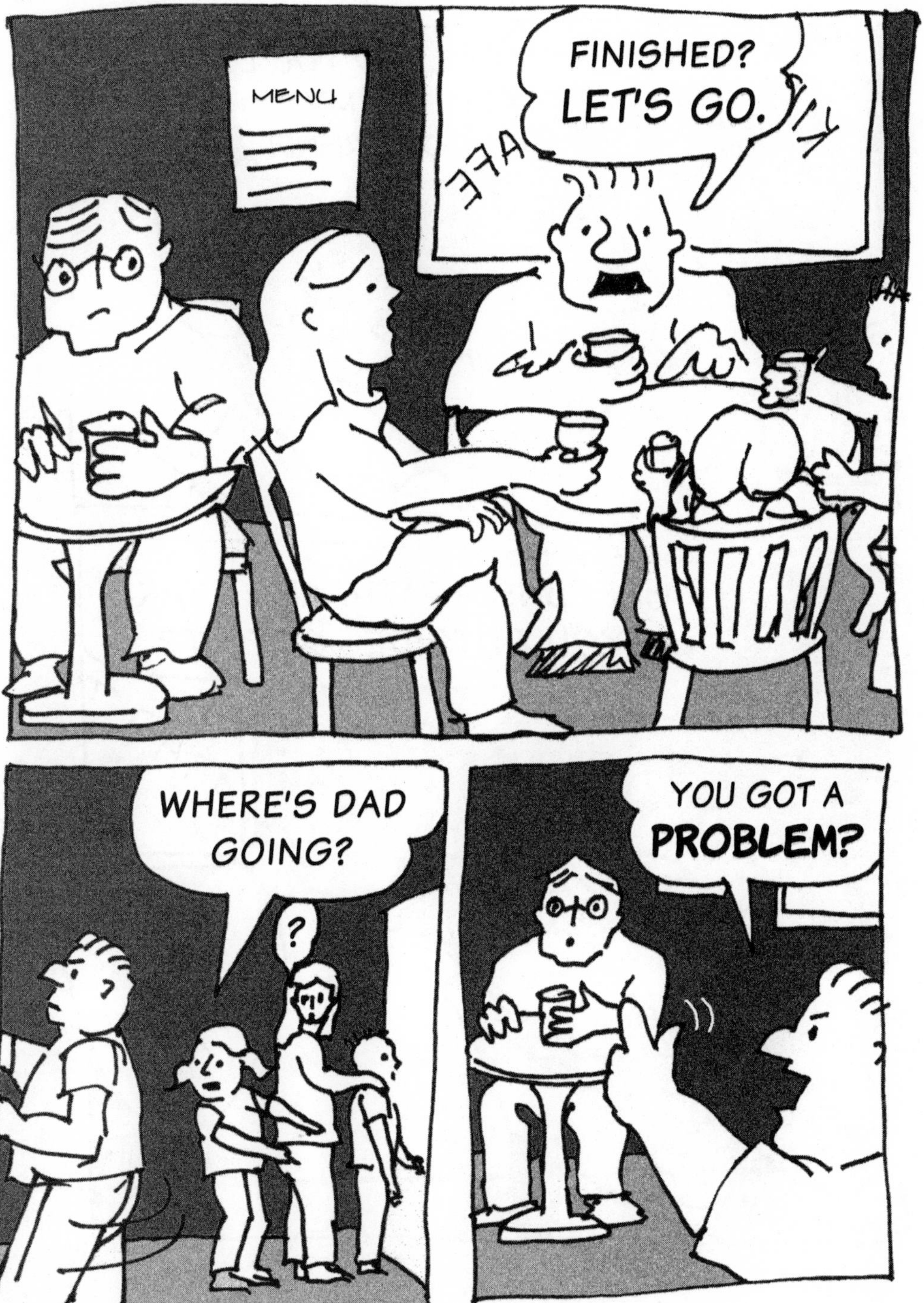
MENU
FINISHED? LET'S GO.
WHERE'S DAD GOING?
?
YOU GOT A PROBLEM?

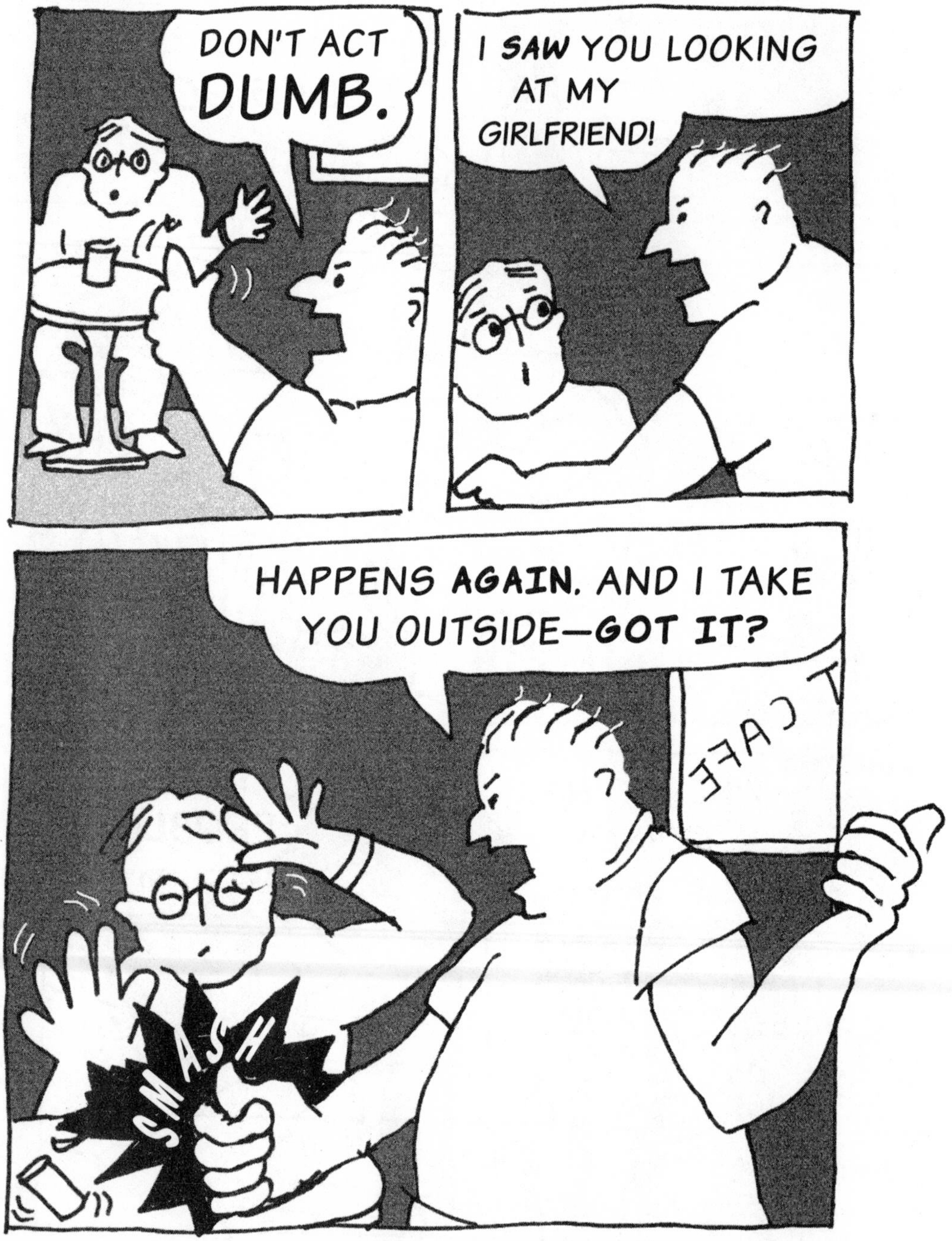
DON'T ACT DUMB.
I SAW YOU LOOKING AT MY GIRLFRIEND!
HAPPENS AGAIN, AND I TAKE YOU OUTSIDE—GOT IT?
CAFE
SMASH

AS TIME PASSED, BRIAN'S MOODS SEEMED MORE AND MORE UNPREDICTABLE. I FELT LIKE I WAS DEALING WITH JEKYLL & HYDE. I NEVER KNEW WHICH ONE WOULD COME HOME TO US.

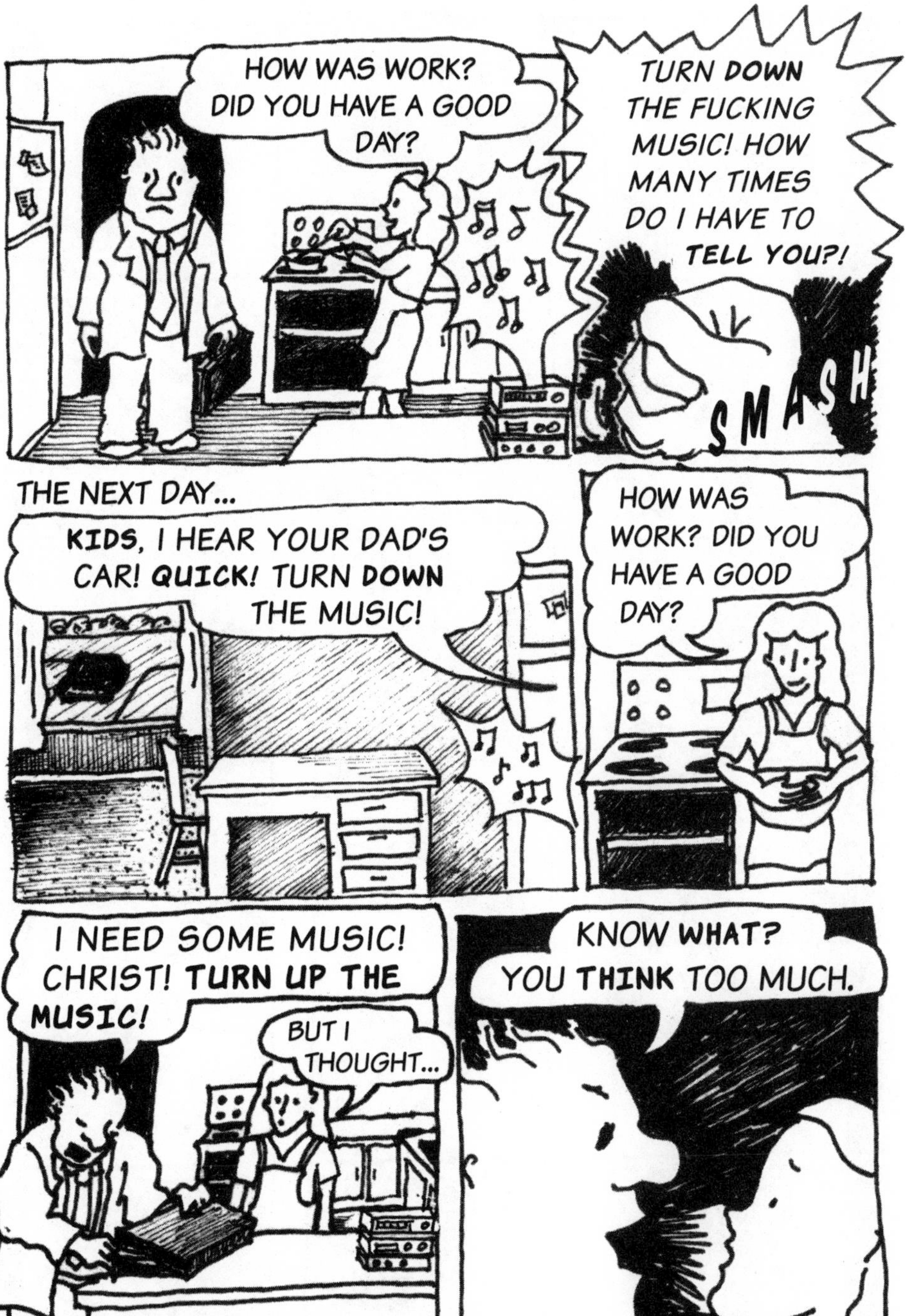
HOW WAS WORK? DID YOU HAVE A GOOD DAY?
TURN **DOWN** THE FUCKING MUSIC! HOW MANY TIMES DO I HAVE TO **TELL YOU?!**
SMASH
THE NEXT DAY...
KIDS, I HEAR YOUR DAD'S CAR! **QUICK!** TURN **DOWN** THE MUSIC!
HOW WAS WORK? DID YOU HAVE A GOOD DAY?
I NEED SOME MUSIC! CHRIST! **TURN UP THE MUSIC!**
BUT I THOUGHT...
KNOW **WHAT?** YOU **THINK** TOO MUCH.

I KEPT LOOKING FOR A **PATTERN** SO I COULD PREDICT ... OR AVOID ... OR MAKE THINGS BETTER. IT FELT LIKE WE WERE ALWAYS WALKING ON EGGSHELLS.

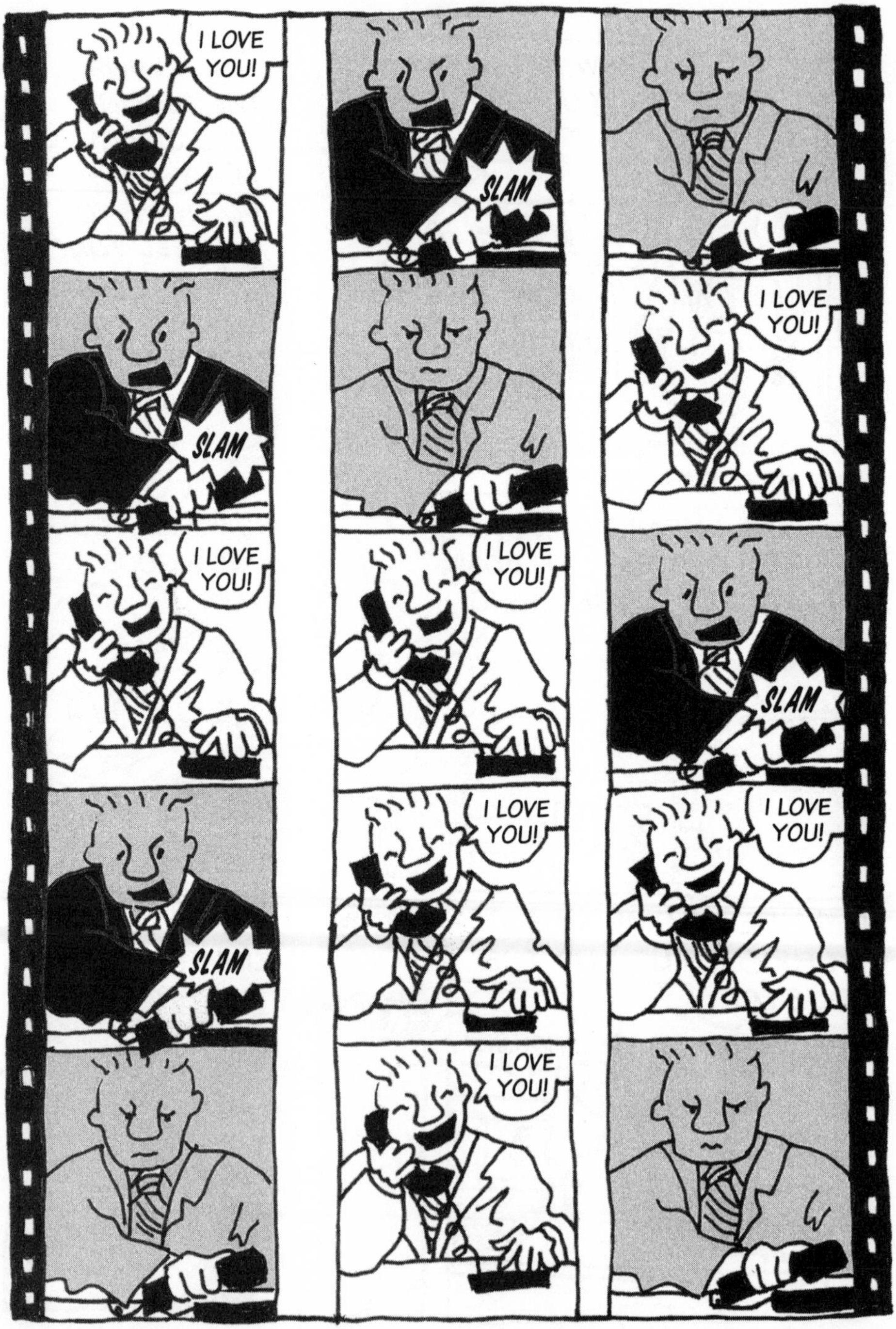

I LOVE YOU!
SLAM
SLAM
I LOVE YOU!
I LOVE YOU!
I LOVE YOU!
SLAM
SLAM
I LOVE YOU!
I LOVE YOU!
I LOVE YOU!

I BEGAN TO NOTICE HOW MUCH HE DRANK...

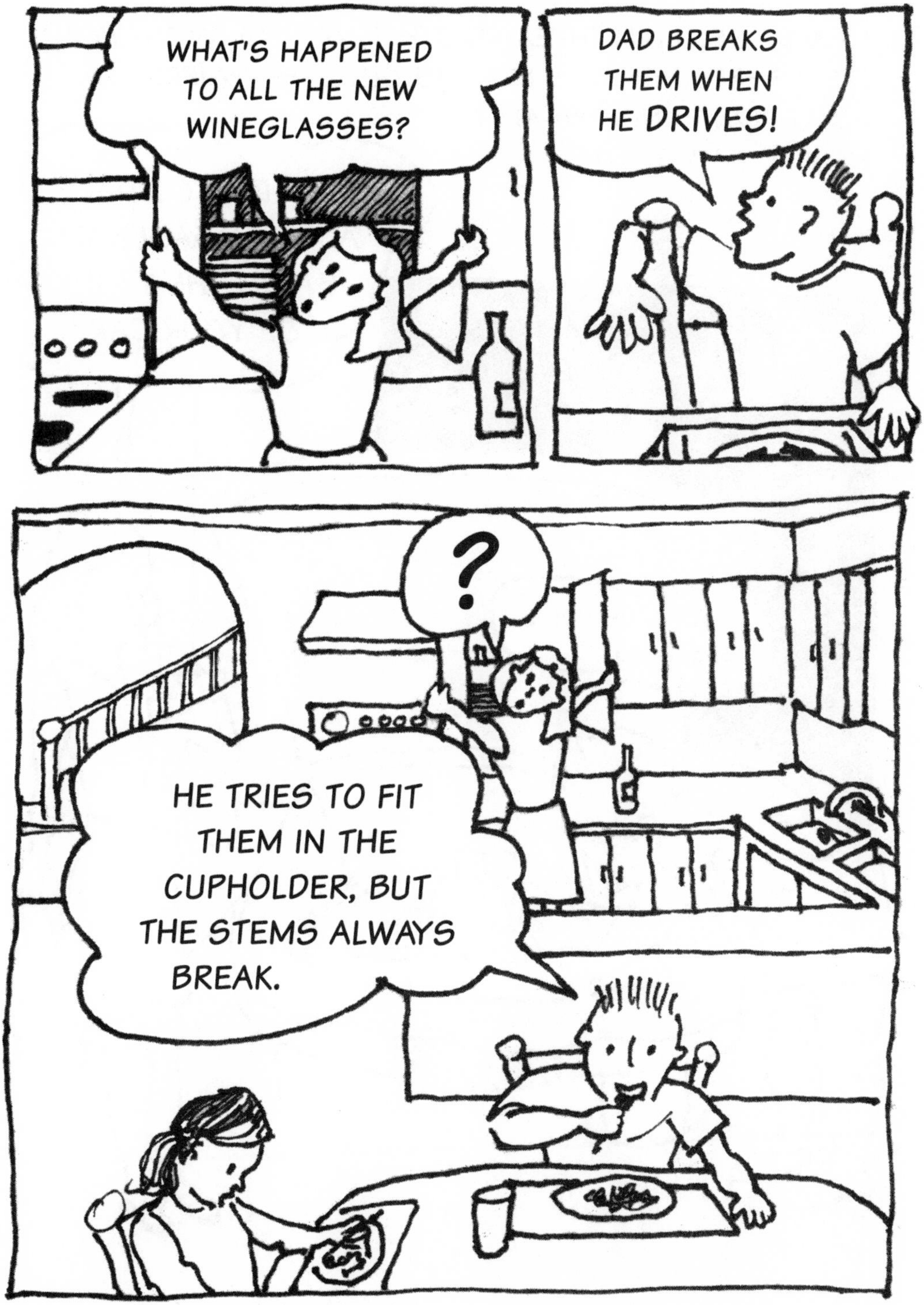
WHAT'S HAPPENED TO ALL THE NEW WINEGLASSES?
DAD BREAKS THEM WHEN HE DRIVES!
?
HE TRIES TO FIT THEM IN THE CUPHOLDER, BUT THE STEMS ALWAYS BREAK.

I'D ALSO SEEN HIM THREATEN OTHER DRIVERS ON THE ROAD. HIS AGGRESSION WAS LEAKING OUT EVERYWHERE, AND I DIDN'T KNOW WHAT HE WAS CAPABLE OF.

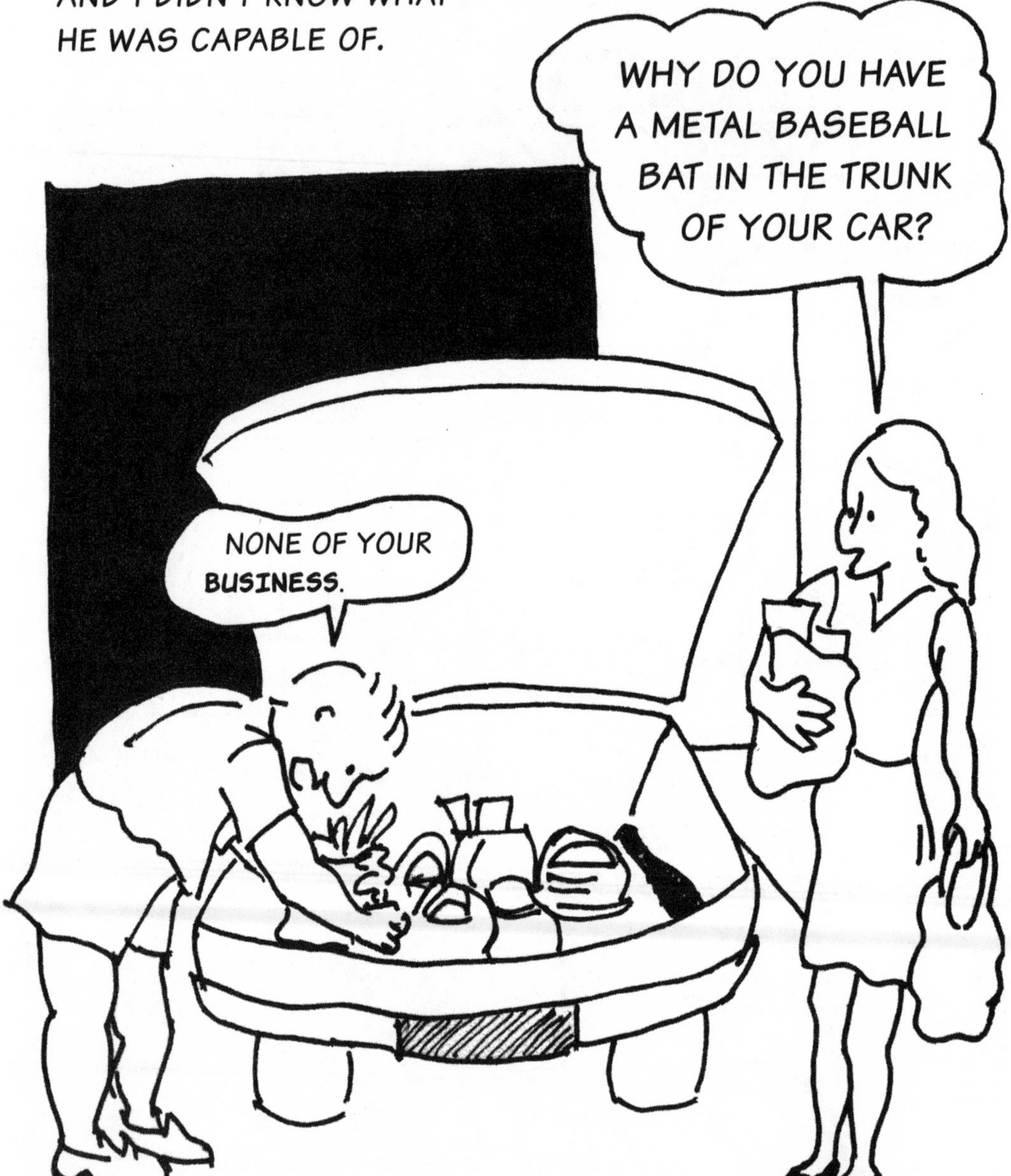
WHY DO YOU HAVE A METAL BASEBALL BAT IN THE TRUNK OF YOUR CAR?
NONE OF YOUR **BUSINESS**.

I WATCHED AS THE CHILDREN CAME TO FEAR AND HATE THEIR FATHER, EVEN THOUGH I KNEW THEY LOVED HIM.

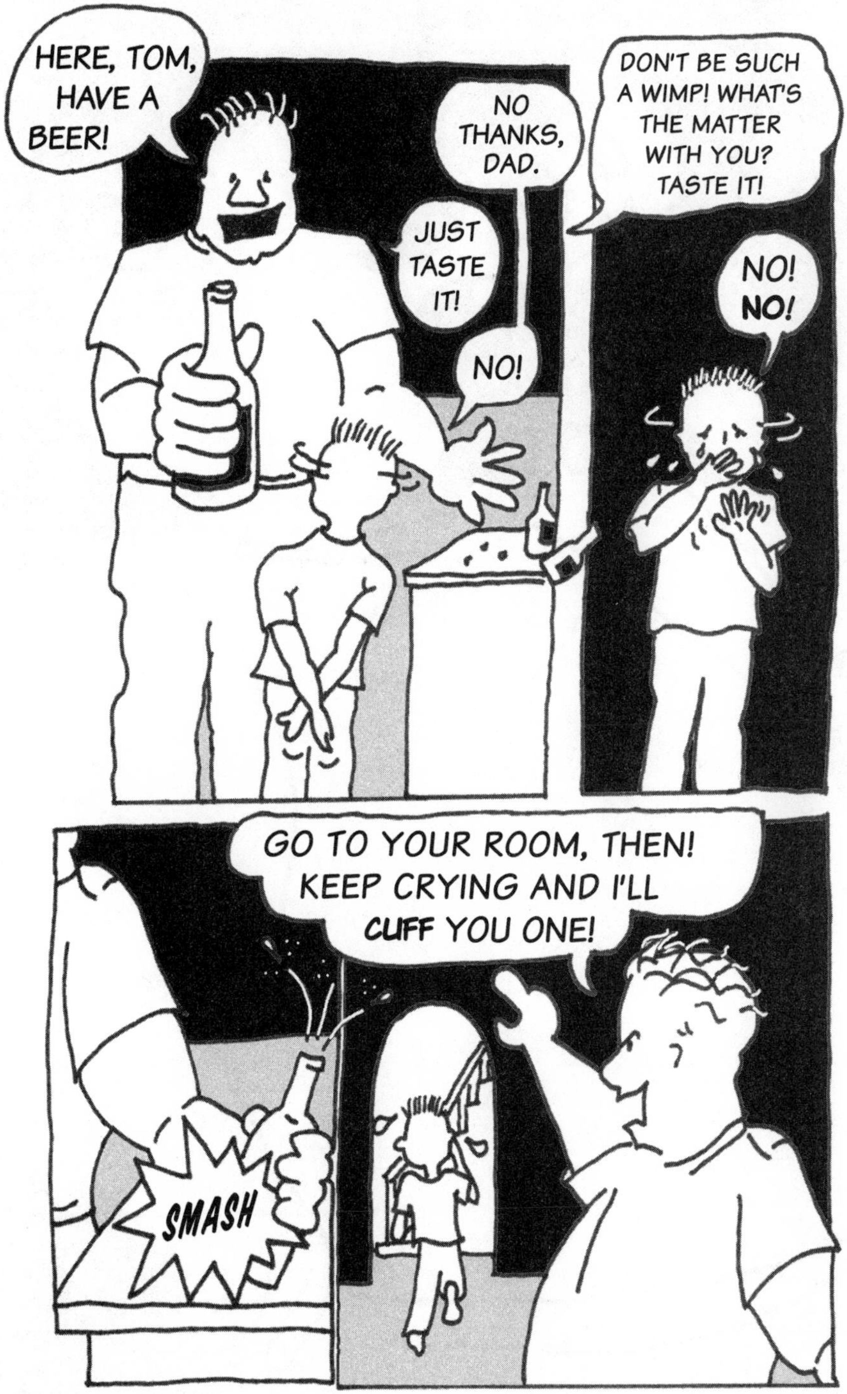
HERE, TOM, HAVE A BEER!
NO THANKS, DAD.
DON'T BE SUCH A WIMP! WHAT'S THE MATTER WITH YOU? TASTE IT!
JUST TASTE IT!
NO!
NO! NO!
GO TO YOUR ROOM, THEN! KEEP CRYING AND I'LL CUFF YOU ONE!
SMASH

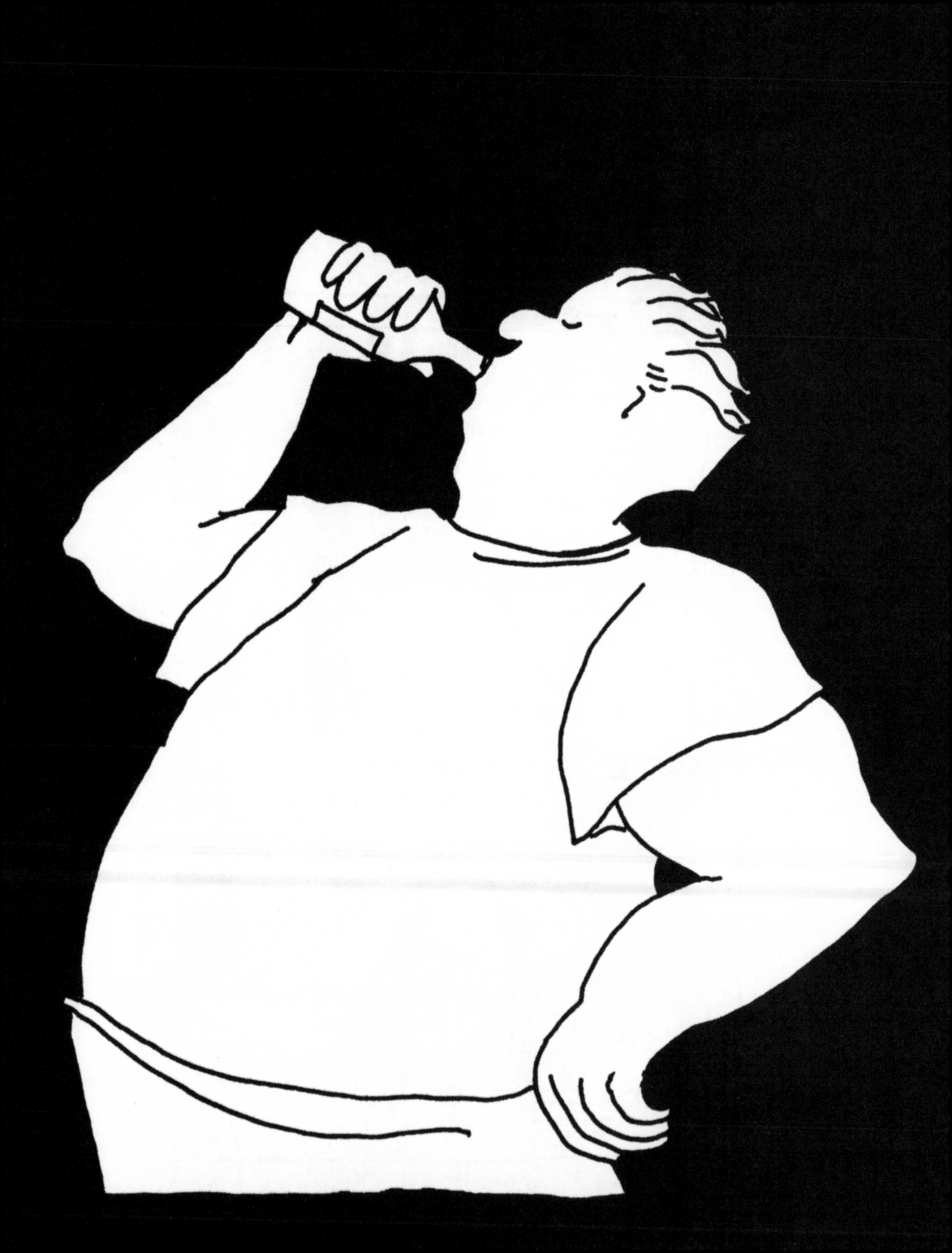

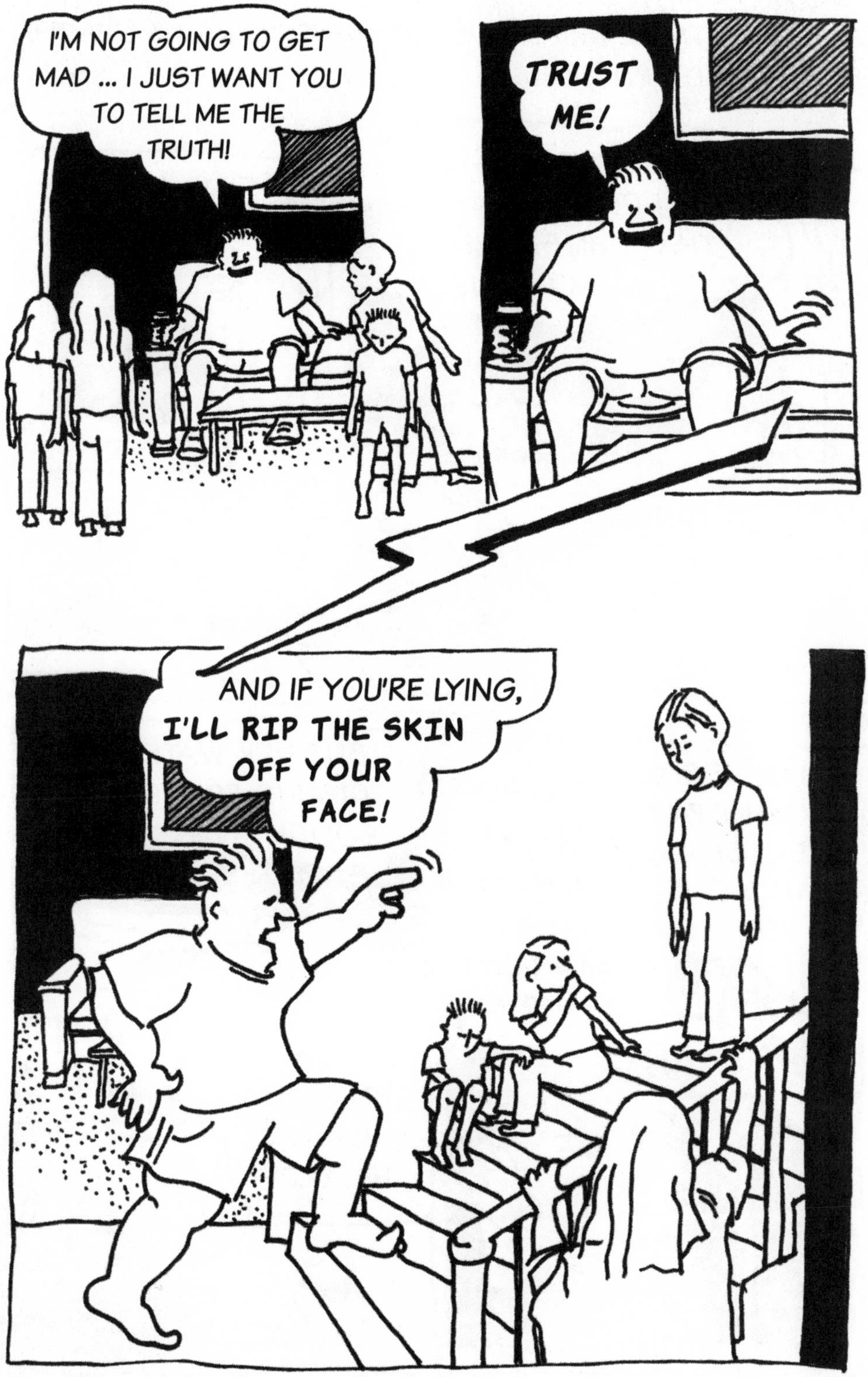
I'M NOT GOING TO GET MAD ... I JUST WANT YOU TO TELL ME THE TRUTH!
TRUST ME!
AND IF YOU'RE LYING, I'LL RIP THE SKIN OFF YOUR FACE!

ONE CHRISTMAS, BRIAN BOUGHT HIS CHILDREN A GENTLE, FLUFFY WHITE POODLE.

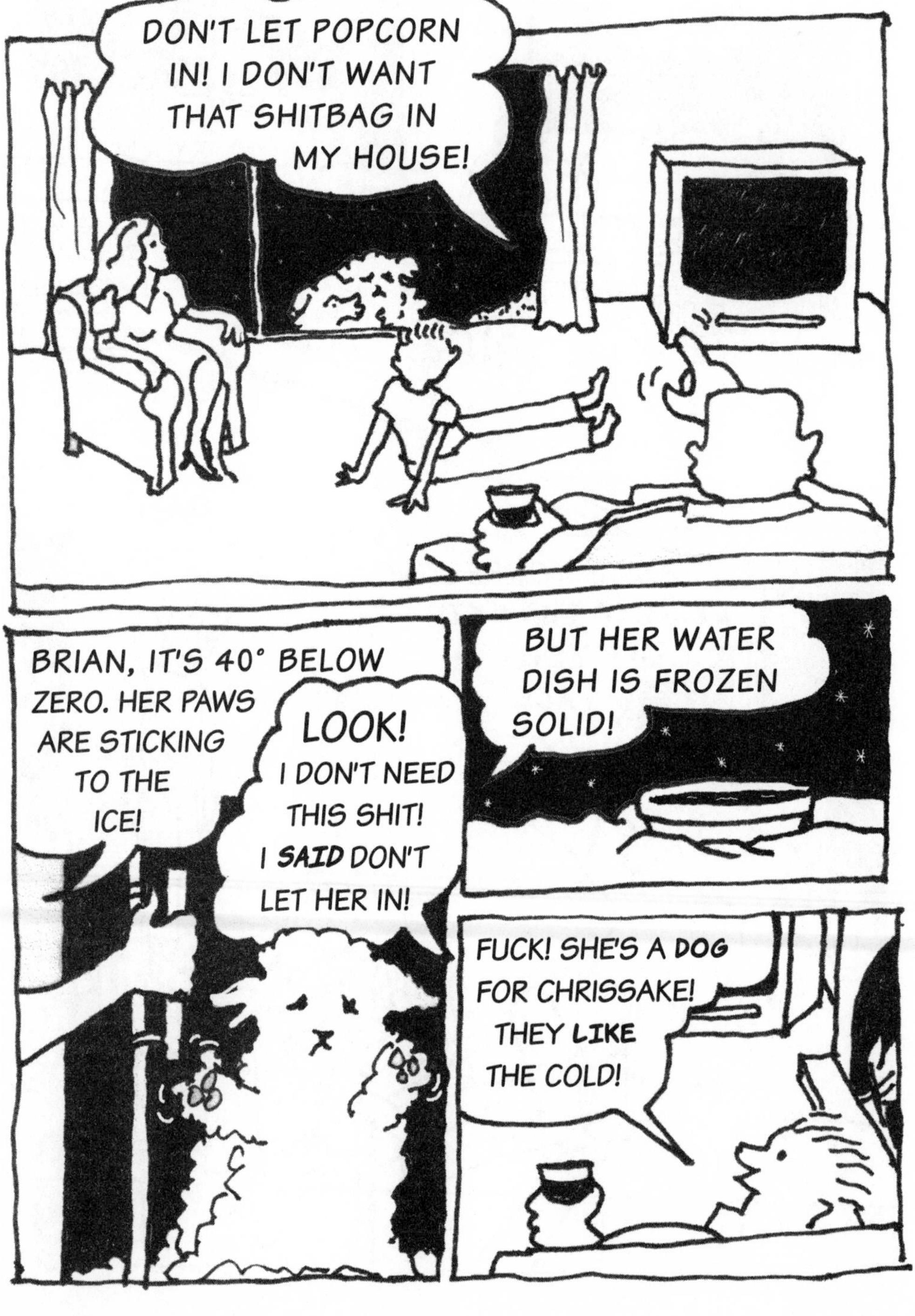

DON'T LET POPCORN IN! I DON'T WANT THAT SHITBAG IN MY HOUSE!
BRIAN, IT'S 40° BELOW ZERO. HER PAWS ARE STICKING TO THE ICE!
LOOK! I DON'T NEED THIS SHIT! I **SAID** DON'T LET HER IN!
BUT HER WATER DISH IS FROZEN SOLID!
FUCK! SHE'S A **DOG** FOR CHRISSAKE! THEY **LIKE** THE COLD!

THEN, IN AUGUST...

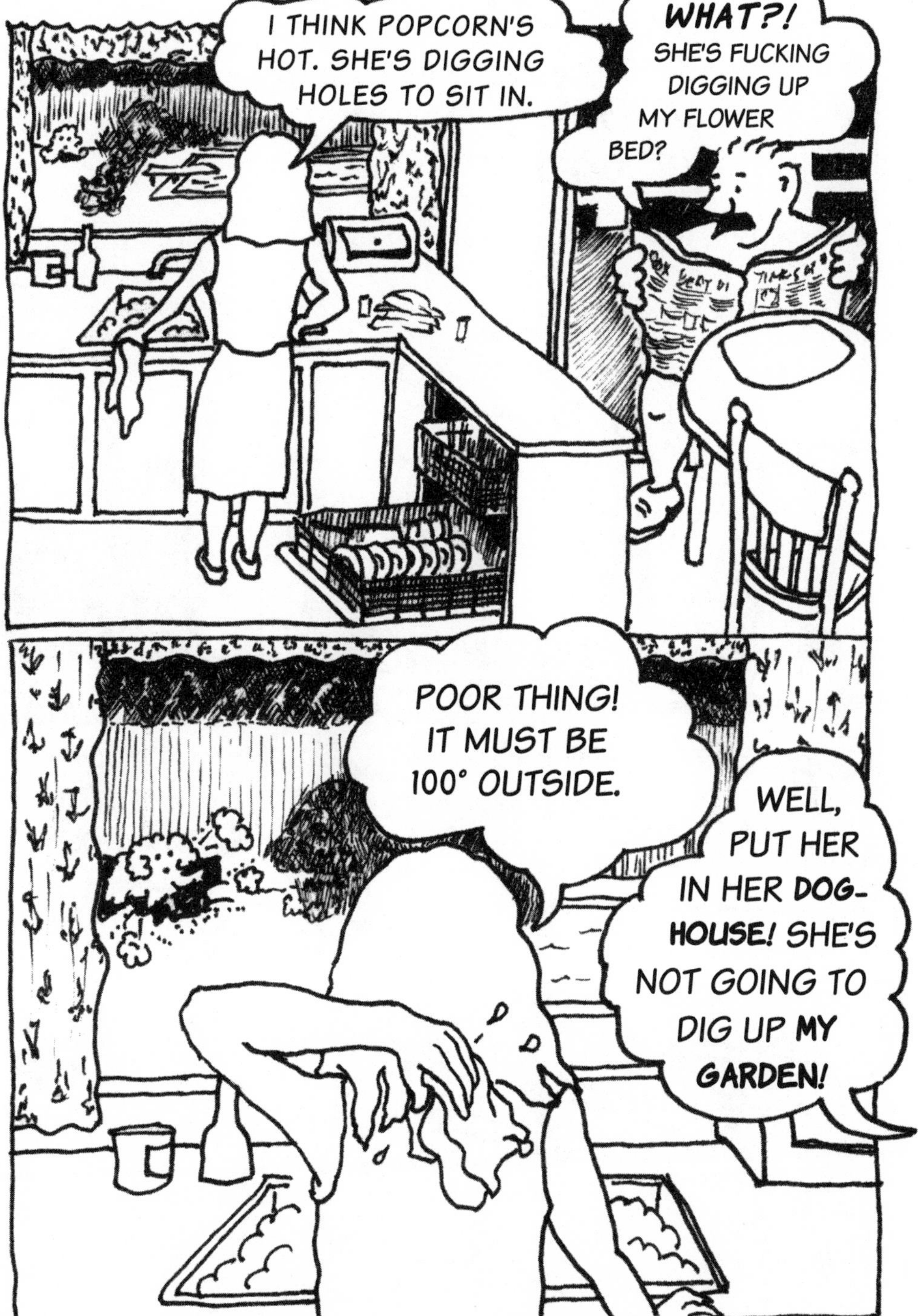
I THINK POPCORN'S HOT. SHE'S DIGGING HOLES TO SIT IN.
WHAT?! SHE'S FUCKING DIGGING UP MY FLOWER BED?
POOR THING! IT MUST BE 100° OUTSIDE.
WELL, PUT HER IN HER DOG-HOUSE! SHE'S NOT GOING TO DIG UP MY GARDEN!

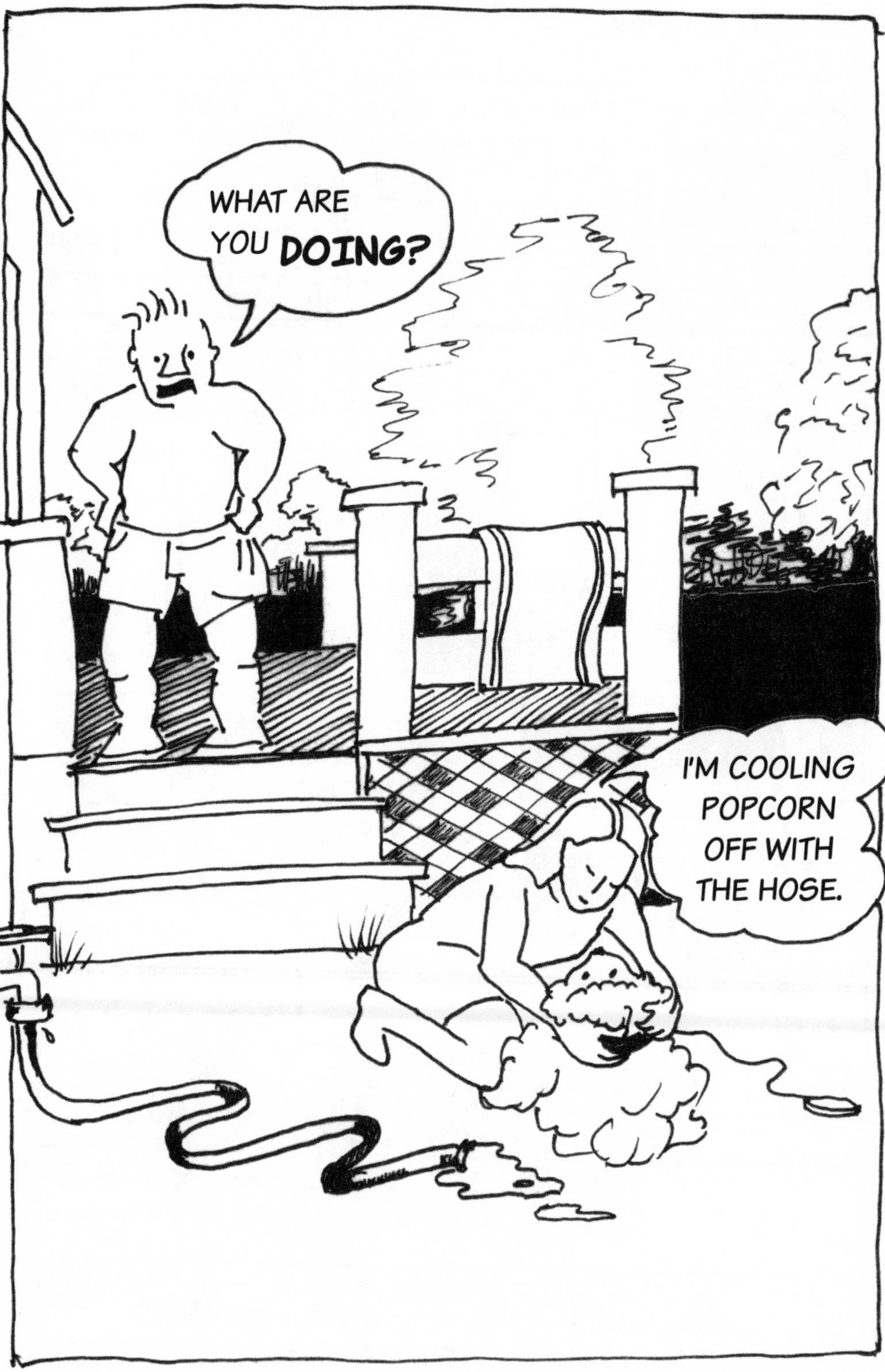
WHAT ARE YOU DOING?
I'M COOLING POPCORN OFF WITH THE HOSE.

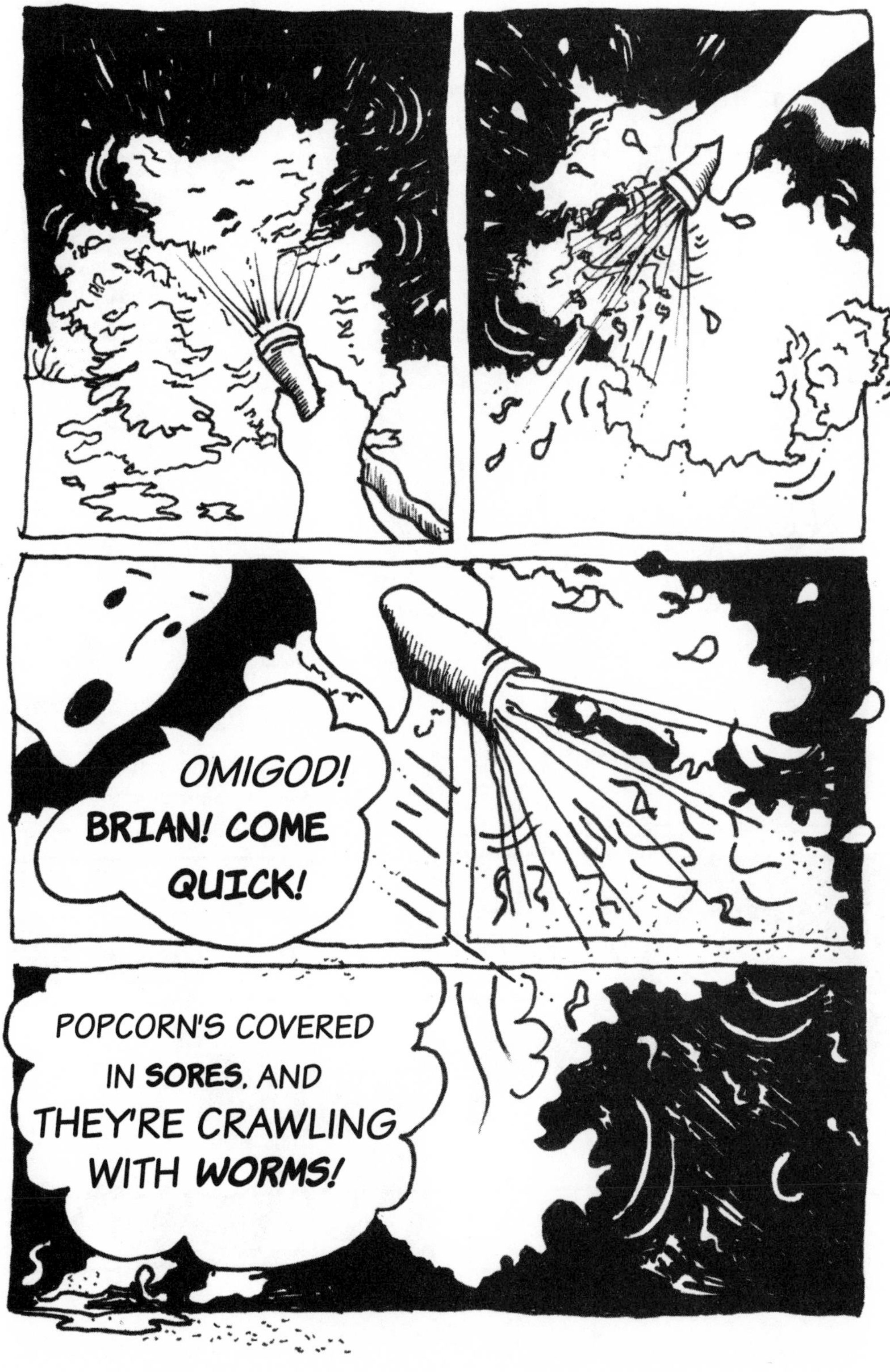
OMIGOD! BRIAN! COME QUICK!
POPCORN'S COVERED IN SORES, AND THEY'RE CRAWLING WITH WORMS!

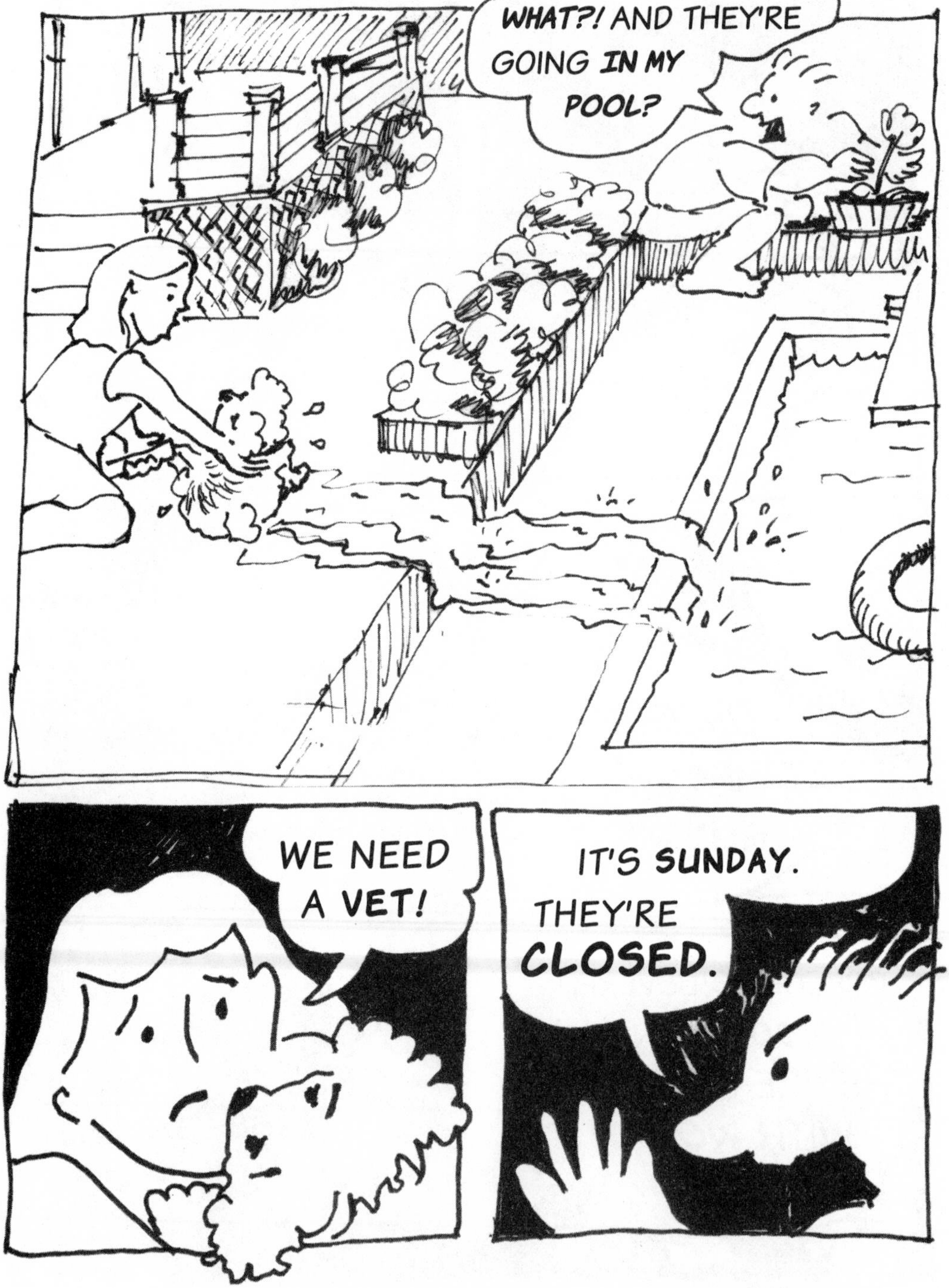
WHAT?! AND THEY'RE GOING IN MY POOL?
WE NEED A VET!
IT'S SUNDAY. THEY'RE CLOSED.

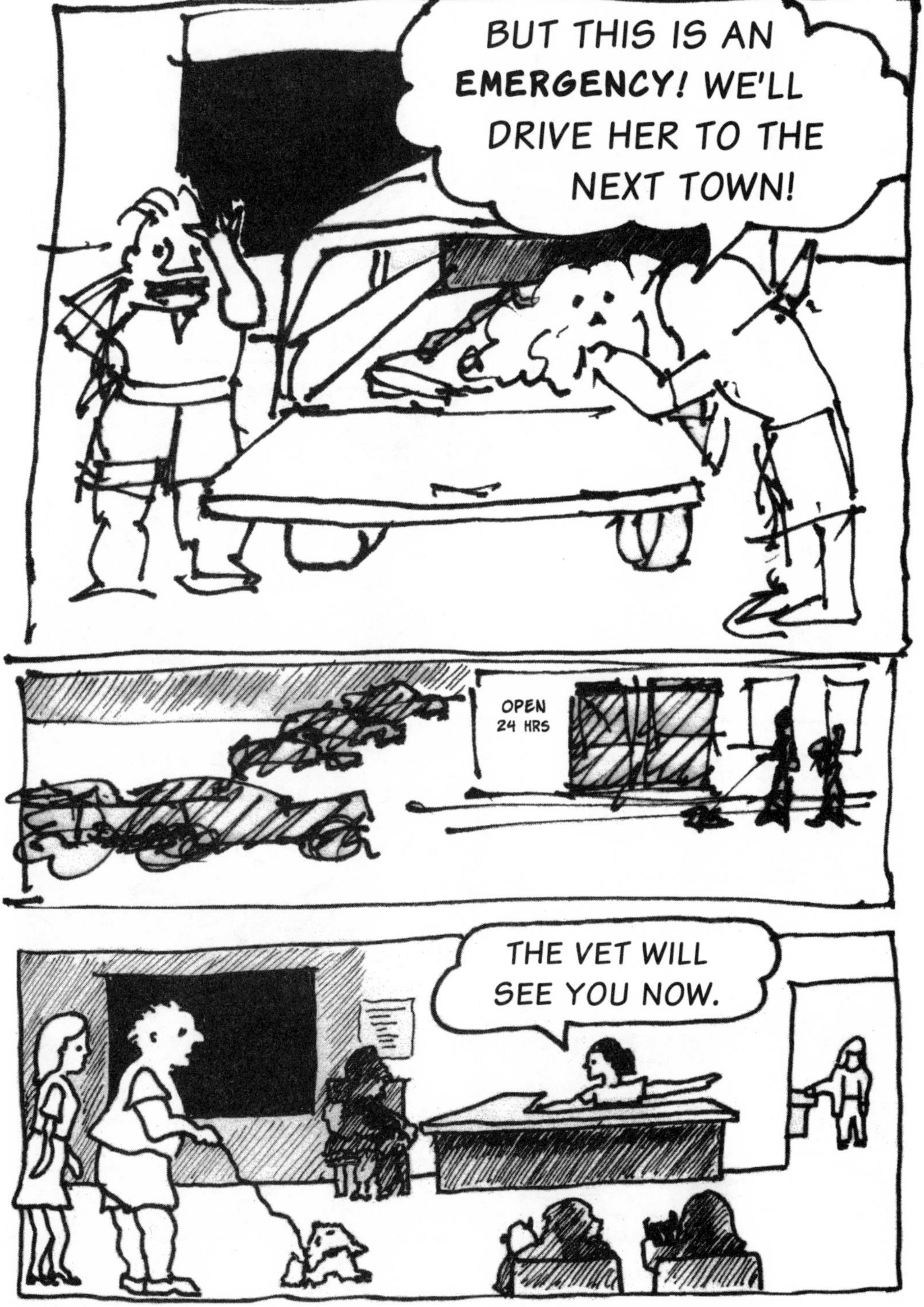
BUT THIS IS AN EMERGENCY! WE'LL DRIVE HER TO THE NEXT TOWN!
OPEN 24 HRS
THE VET WILL SEE YOU NOW.

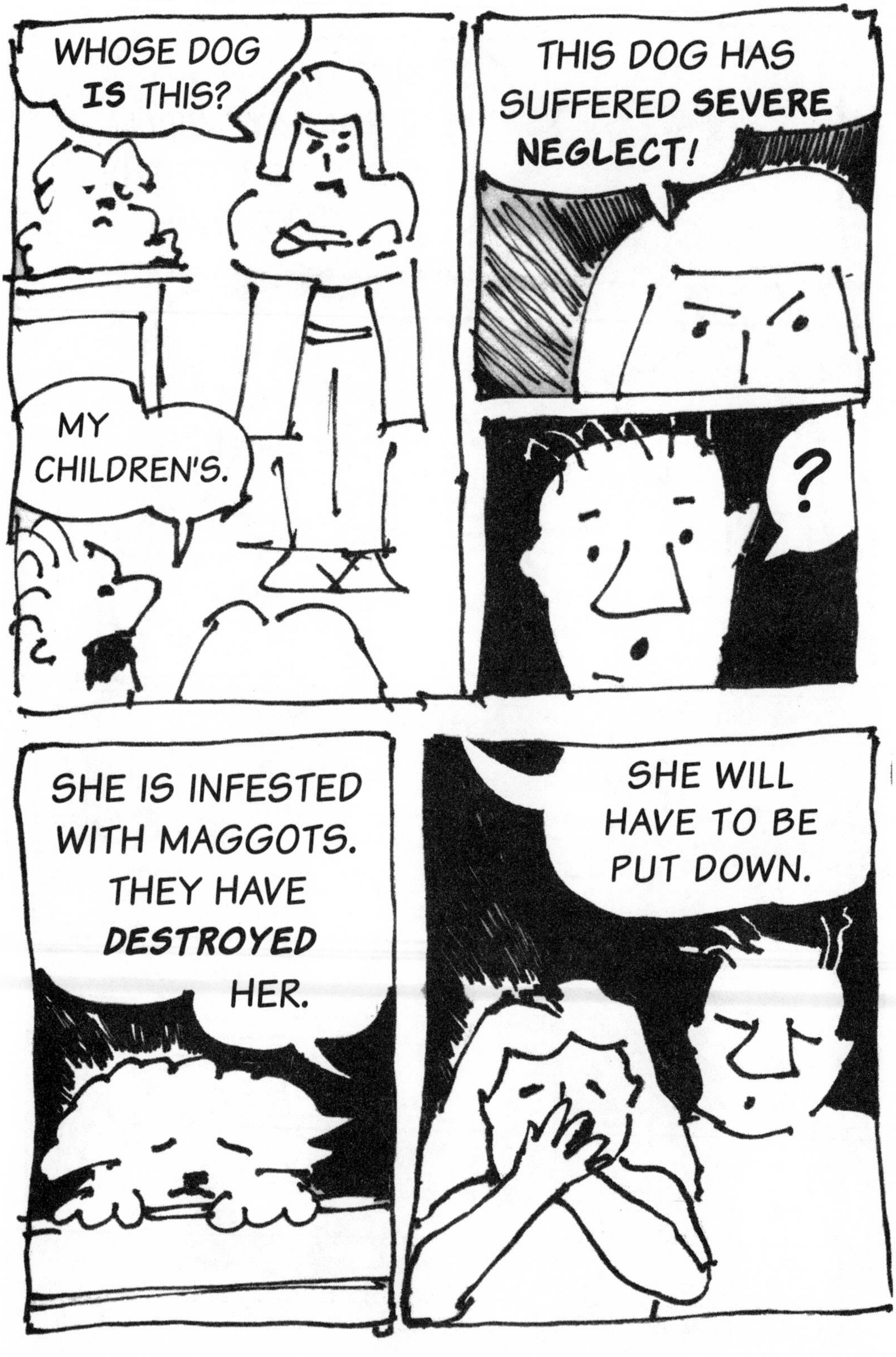
WHOSE DOG IS THIS?
MY CHILDREN'S.
THIS DOG HAS SUFFERED SEVERE NEGLECT!
?
SHE IS INFESTED WITH MAGGOTS. THEY HAVE DESTROYED HER.
SHE WILL HAVE TO BE PUT DOWN.

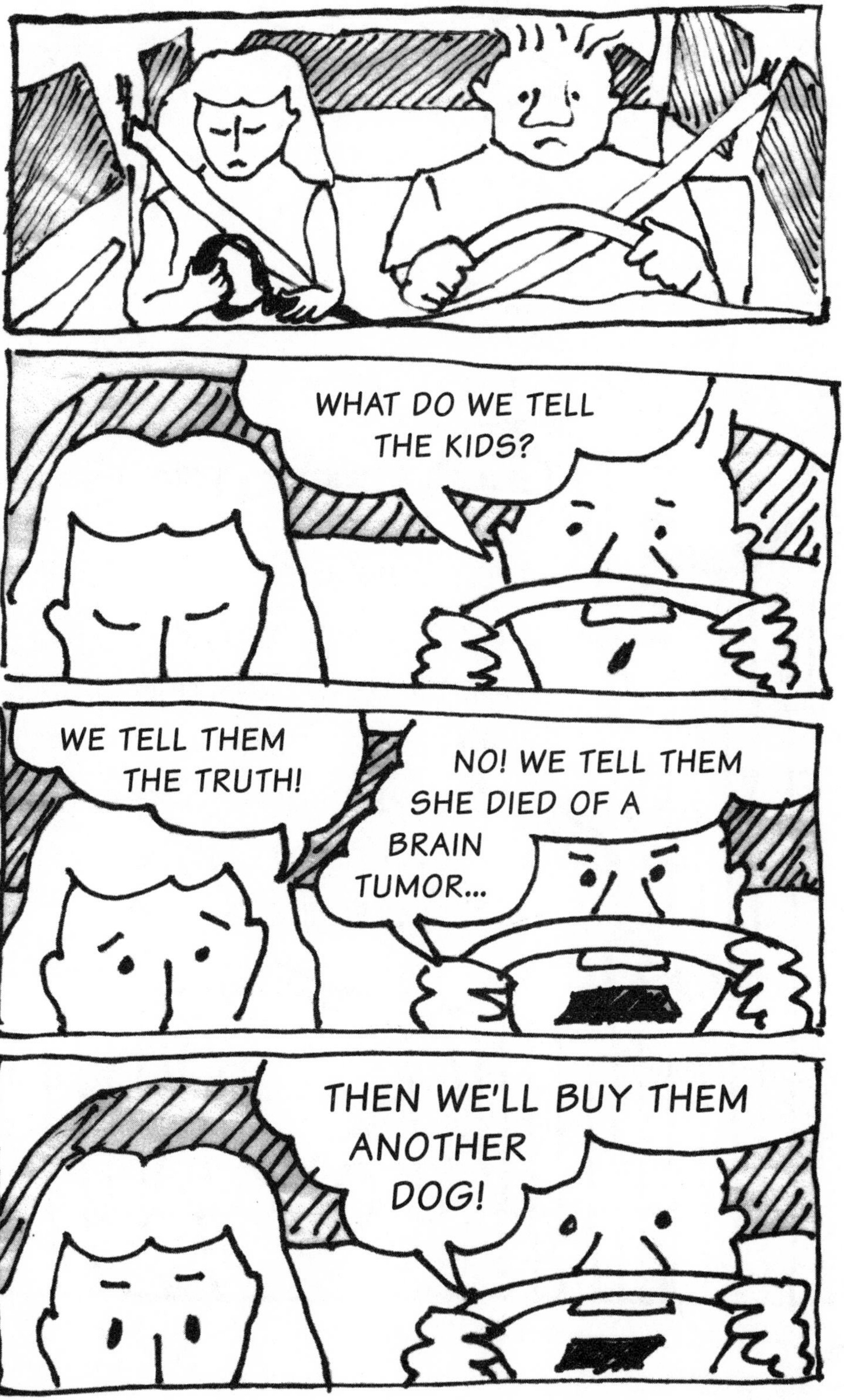
WHAT DO WE TELL THE KIDS?
WE TELL THEM THE TRUTH!
NO! WE TELL THEM SHE DIED OF A BRAIN TUMOR...
THEN WE'LL BUY THEM ANOTHER DOG!

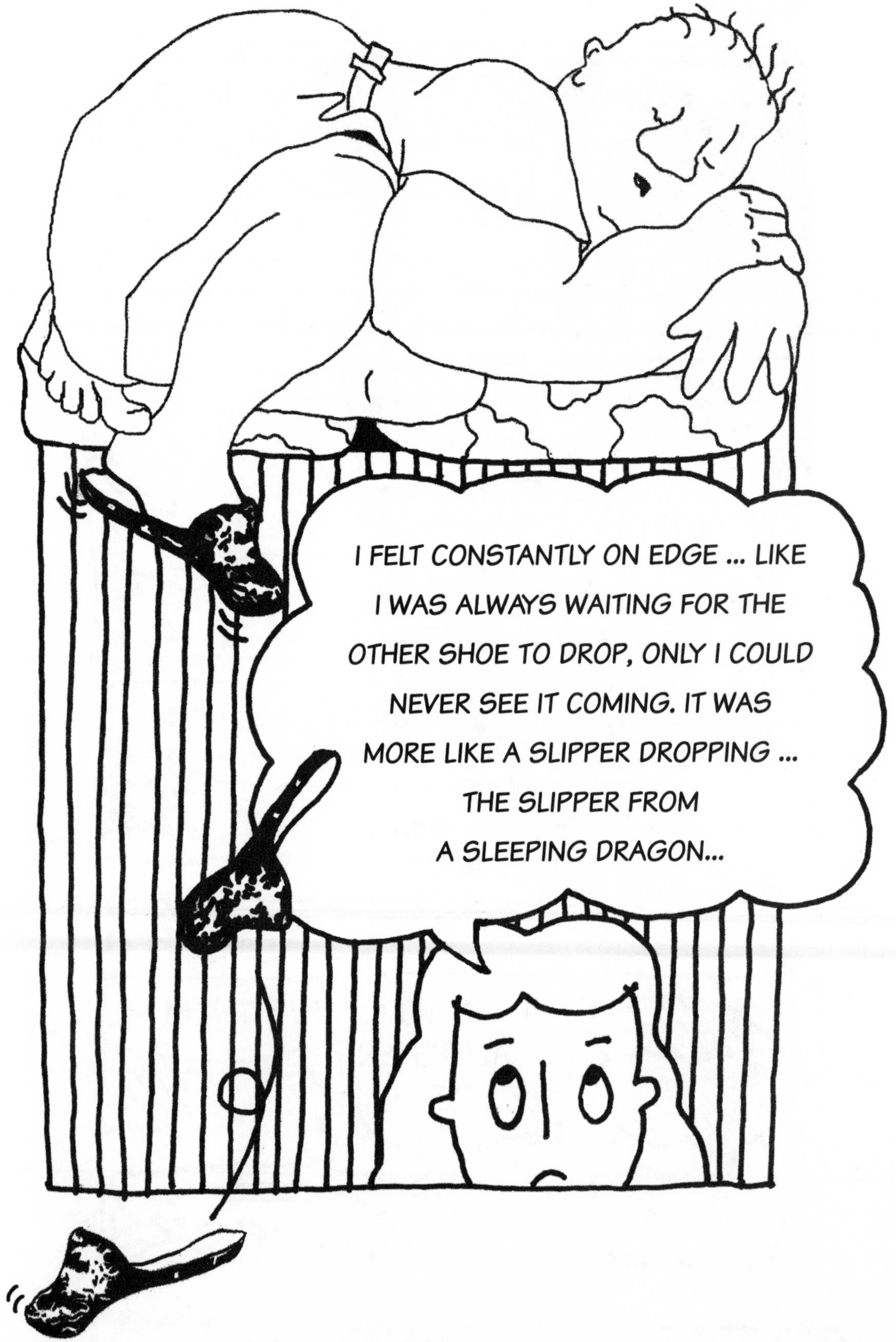
I FELT CONSTANTLY ON EDGE ... LIKE I WAS ALWAYS WAITING FOR THE OTHER SHOE TO DROP, ONLY I COULD NEVER SEE IT COMING. IT WAS MORE LIKE A SLIPPER DROPPING ... THE SLIPPER FROM A SLEEPING DRAGON...

I TRIED TO PLEASE BRIAN BUT, AS TIME PASSED, HE SEEMED TO WANT ME TO CHANGE SO MUCH ABOUT MYSELF THAT I WASN'T SURE I COULD REMEMBER WHO I WAS.

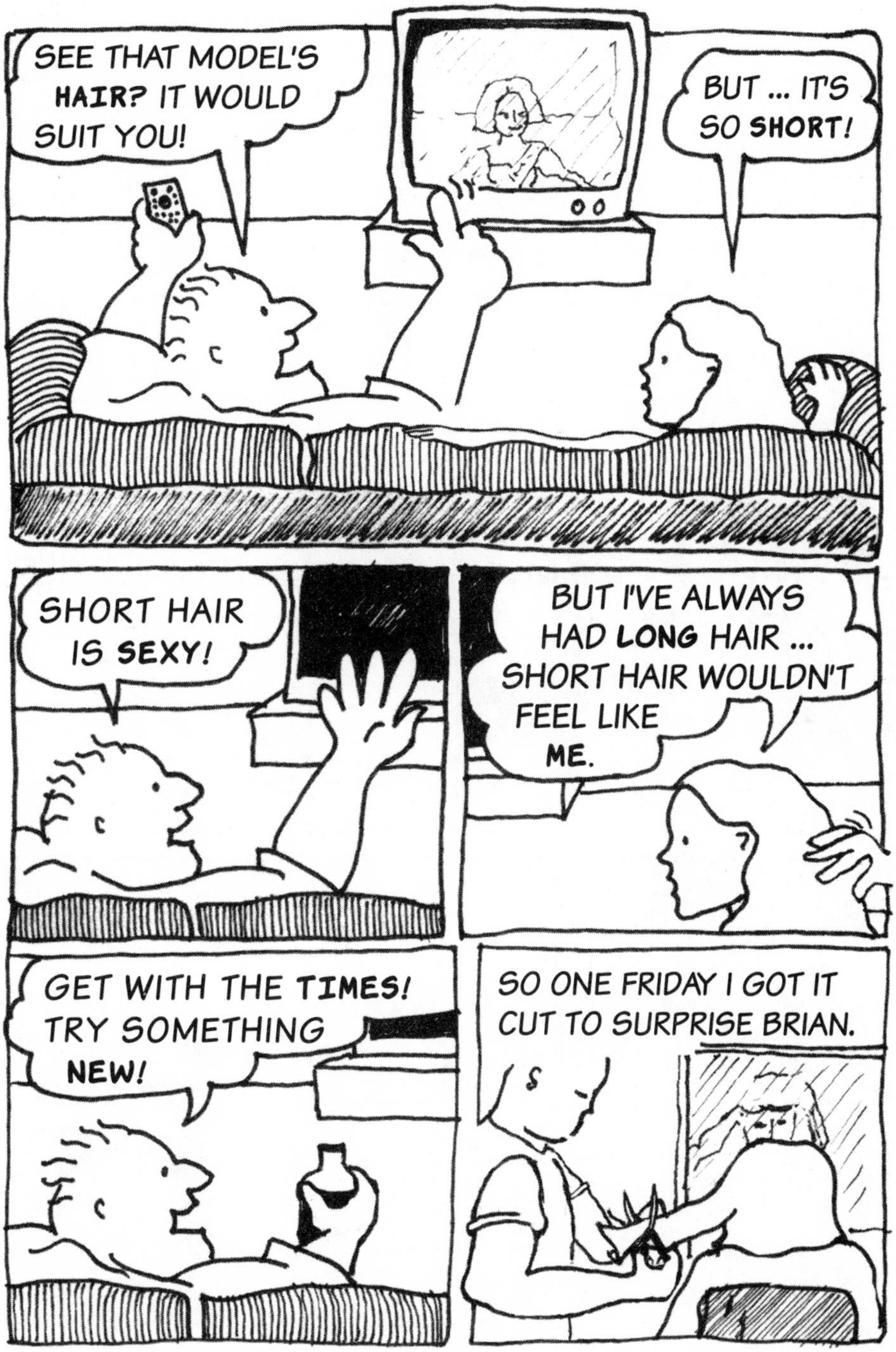
SEE THAT MODEL'S HAIR? IT WOULD SUIT YOU!
BUT ... IT'S SO SHORT!
SHORT HAIR IS SEXY!
BUT I'VE ALWAYS HAD LONG HAIR ... SHORT HAIR WOULDN'T FEEL LIKE ME.
GET WITH THE TIMES! TRY SOMETHING NEW!
SO ONE FRIDAY I GOT IT CUT TO SURPRISE BRIAN.

BUT WHEN I ARRIVED HOME FROM THE HAIRDRESSER, HIS INSULTS BEGAN ... AND THEY CONTINUED ALL WEEKEND.

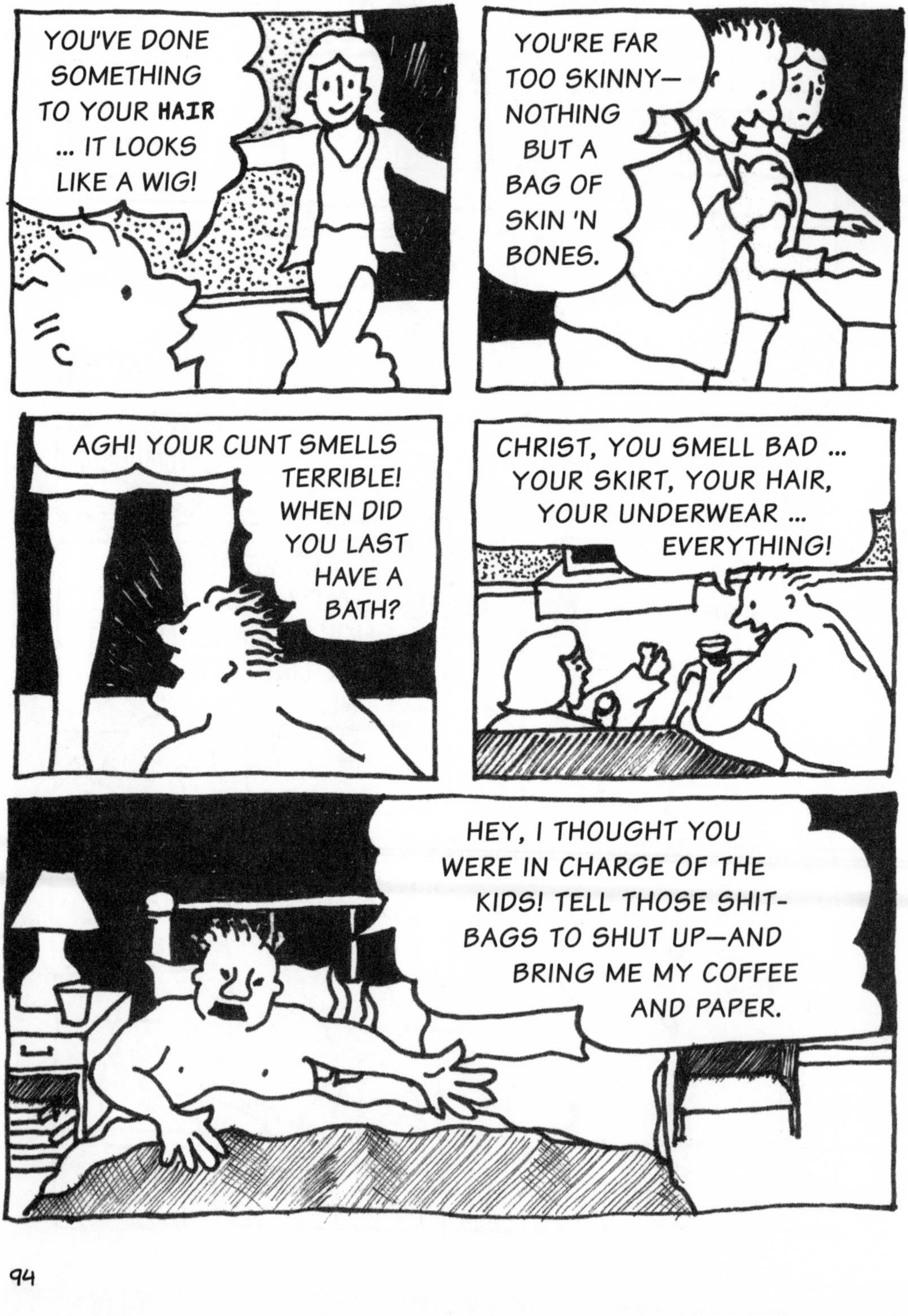
YOU'VE DONE SOMETHING TO YOUR **HAIR** ... IT LOOKS LIKE A WIG!
YOU'RE FAR TOO SKINNY—NOTHING BUT A BAG OF SKIN 'N BONES.
AGH! YOUR CUNT SMELLS TERRIBLE! WHEN DID YOU LAST HAVE A BATH?
CHRIST, YOU SMELL BAD ... YOUR SKIRT, YOUR HAIR, YOUR UNDERWEAR ... EVERYTHING!
HEY, I THOUGHT YOU WERE IN CHARGE OF THE KIDS! TELL THOSE SHIT-BAGS TO SHUT UP—AND BRING ME MY COFFEE AND PAPER.

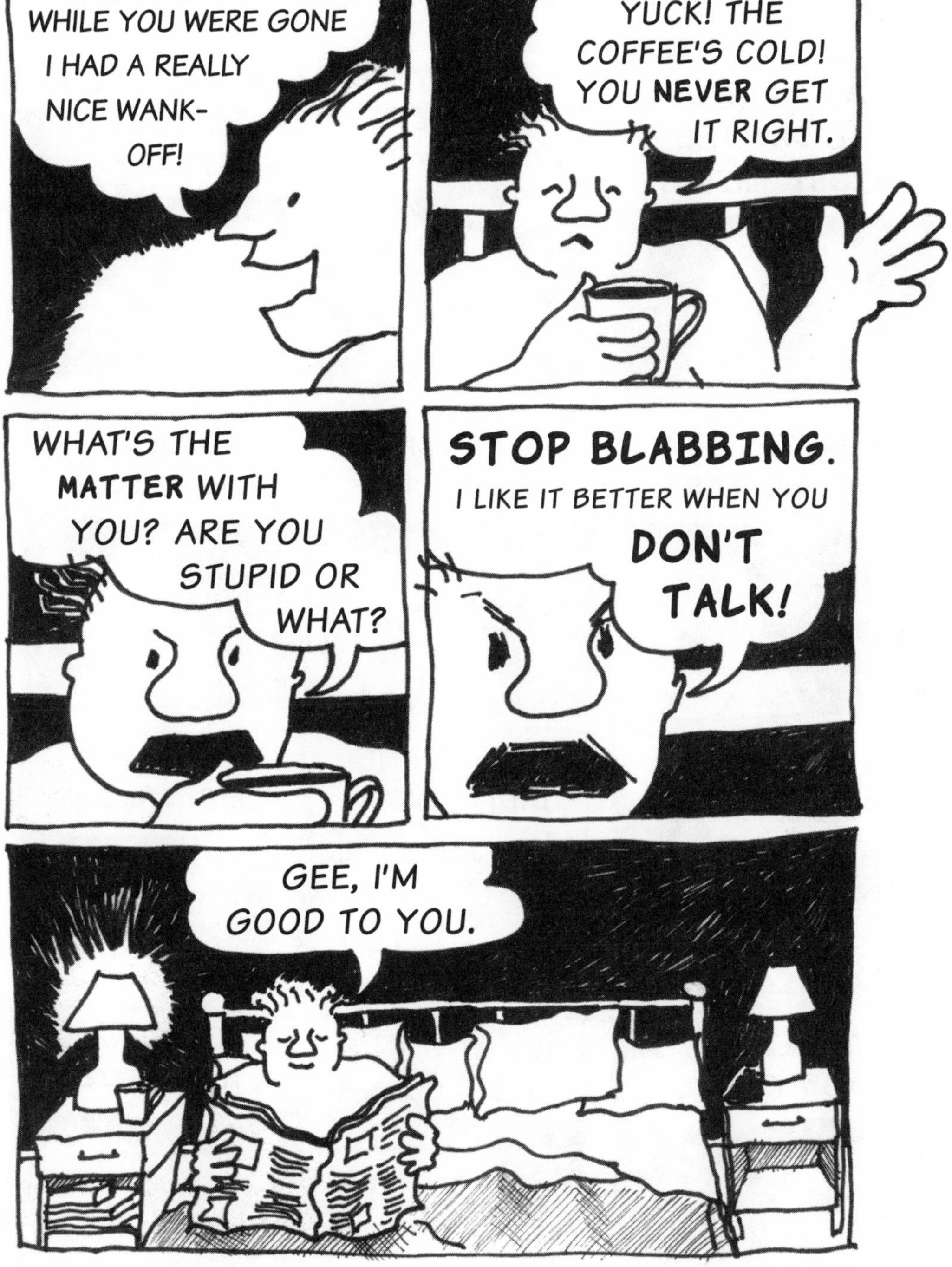
WHILE YOU WERE GONE I HAD A REALLY NICE WANK-OFF!
YUCK! THE COFFEE'S COLD! YOU NEVER GET IT RIGHT.
WHAT'S THE MATTER WITH YOU? ARE YOU STUPID OR WHAT?
STOP BLABBING. I LIKE IT BETTER WHEN YOU DON'T TALK!
GEE, I'M GOOD TO YOU.

THE MORE UNDERSTANDING I TRIED TO BE, THE MORE I HAD TO EXCUSE HIS BEHAVIOR AND THE MORE CONFUSED I BECAME...

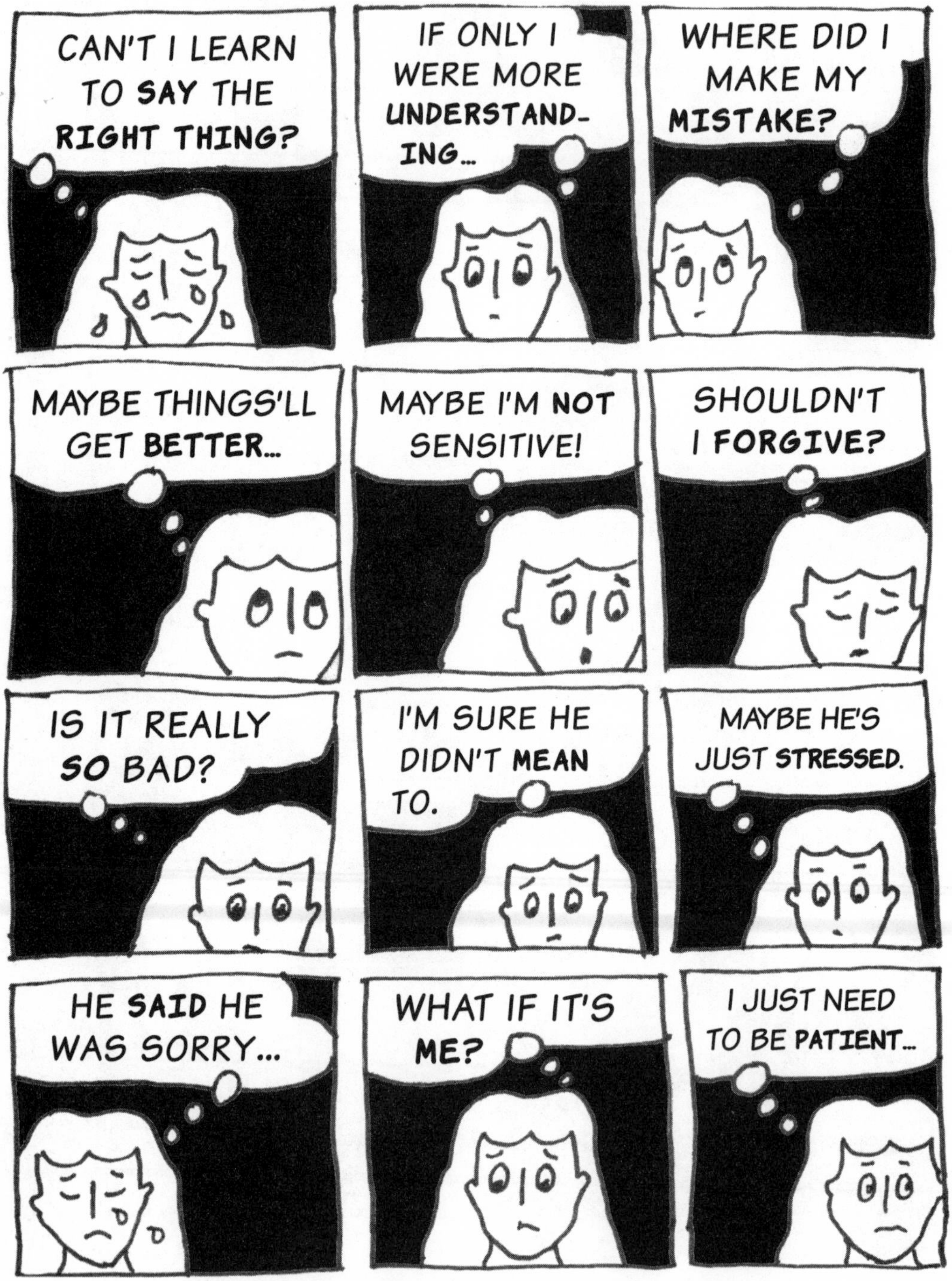
CAN'T I LEARN TO SAY THE RIGHT THING?
IF ONLY I WERE MORE UNDERSTAND-ING...
WHERE DID I MAKE MY MISTAKE?
MAYBE THINGS'LL GET BETTER...
MAYBE I'M NOT SENSITIVE!
SHOULDN'T I FORGIVE?
IS IT REALLY SO BAD?
I'M SURE HE DIDN'T MEAN TO.
MAYBE HE'S JUST STRESSED.
HE SAID HE WAS SORRY...
WHAT IF IT'S ME?
I JUST NEED TO BE PATIENT...

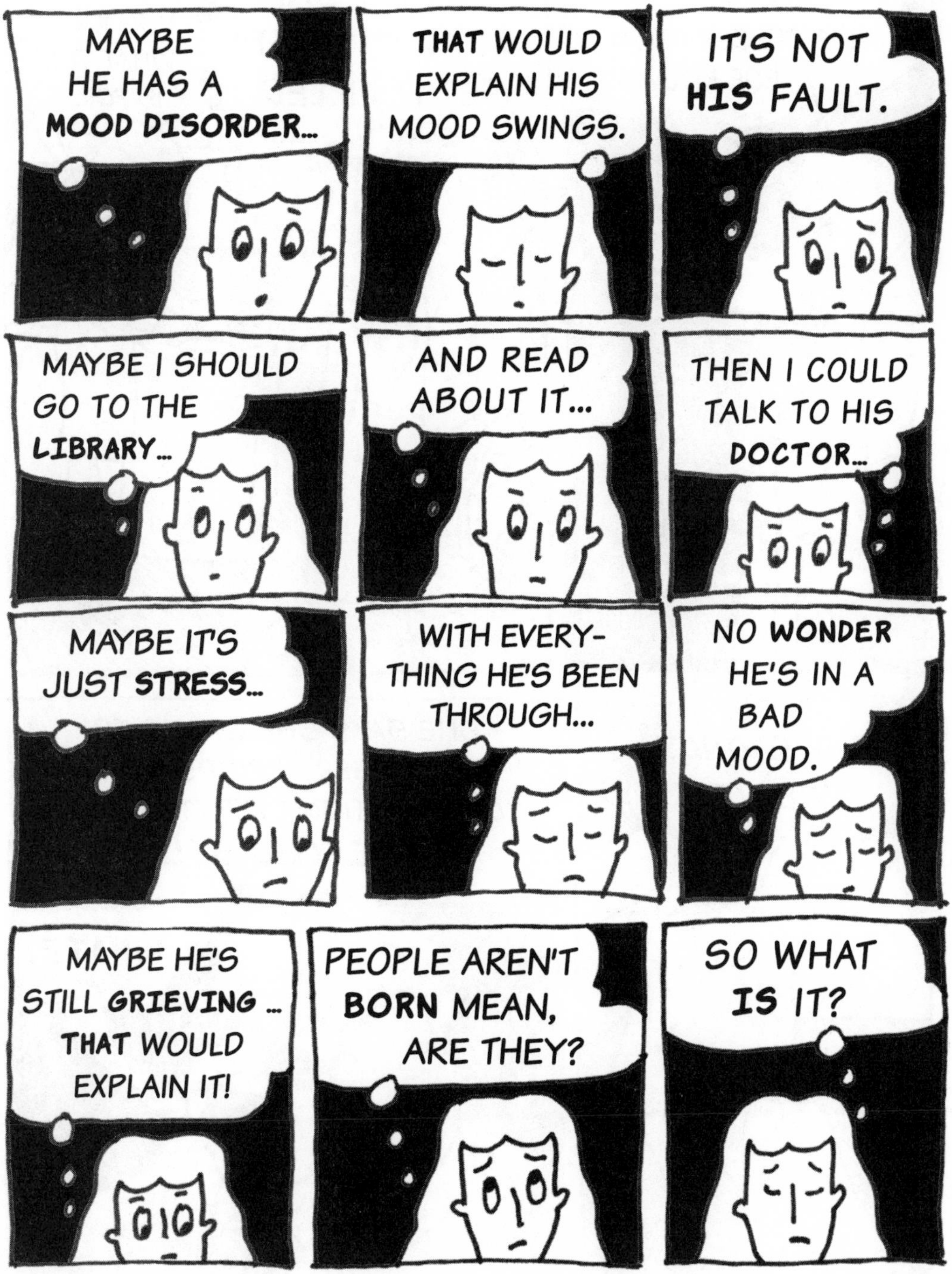

MAYBE HE HAS A **MOOD DISORDER**...
THAT WOULD EXPLAIN HIS MOOD SWINGS.
IT'S NOT **HIS** FAULT.
MAYBE I SHOULD GO TO THE **LIBRARY**...
AND READ ABOUT IT...
THEN I COULD TALK TO HIS **DOCTOR**...
MAYBE IT'S JUST **STRESS**...
WITH EVERY-THING HE'S BEEN THROUGH...
NO **WONDER** HE'S IN A BAD MOOD.
MAYBE HE'S STILL **GRIEVING** ... **THAT** WOULD EXPLAIN IT!
PEOPLE AREN'T **BORN** MEAN, ARE THEY?
SO WHAT **IS** IT?

BY MONDAY MORNING HE WAS STILL IN HIS MOOD...

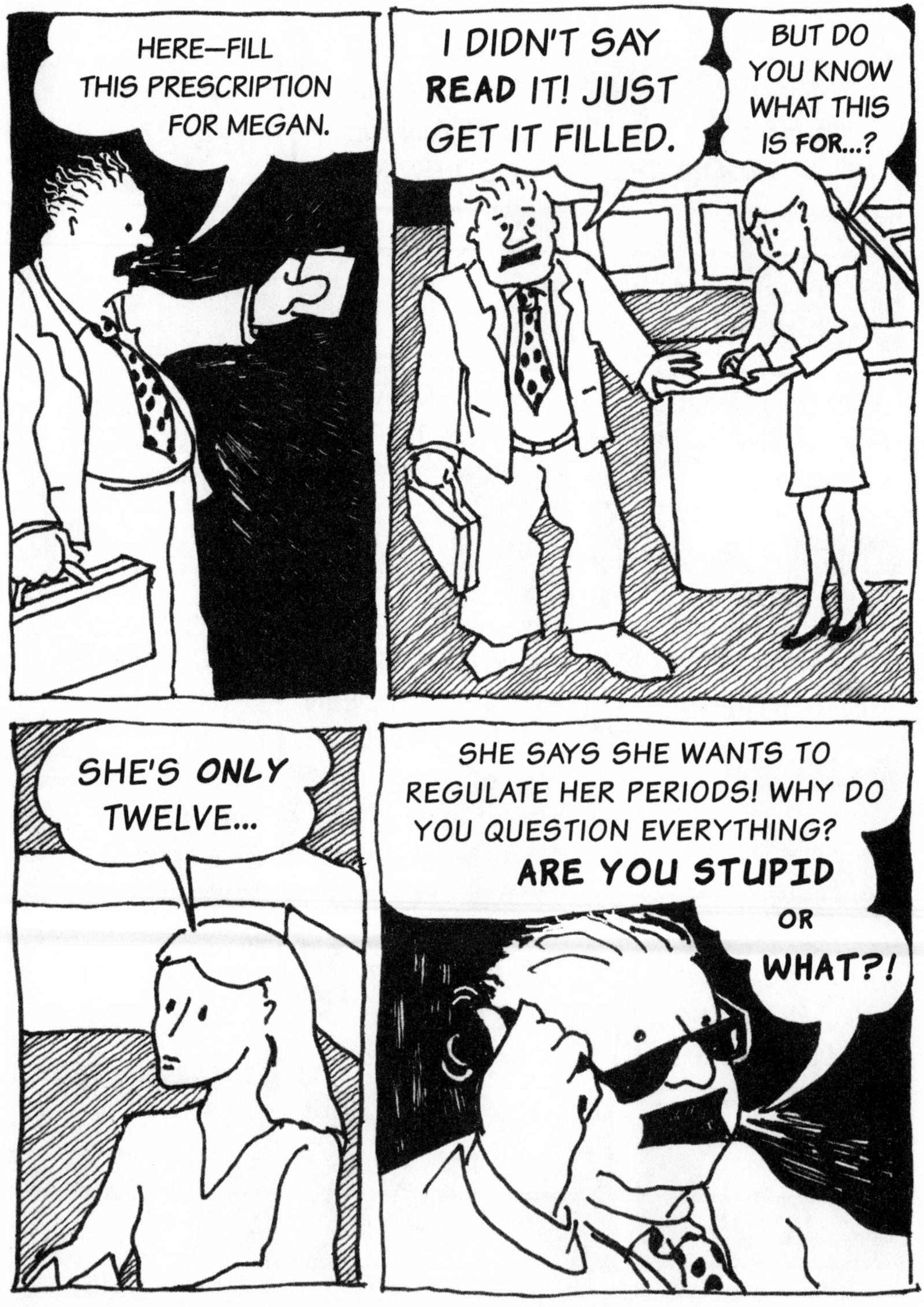
HERE—FILL THIS PRESCRIPTION FOR MEGAN.
I DIDN'T SAY READ IT! JUST GET IT FILLED.
BUT DO YOU KNOW WHAT THIS IS FOR...?
SHE'S ONLY TWELVE...
SHE SAYS SHE WANTS TO REGULATE HER PERIODS! WHY DO YOU QUESTION EVERYTHING? ARE YOU STUPID OR WHAT?!

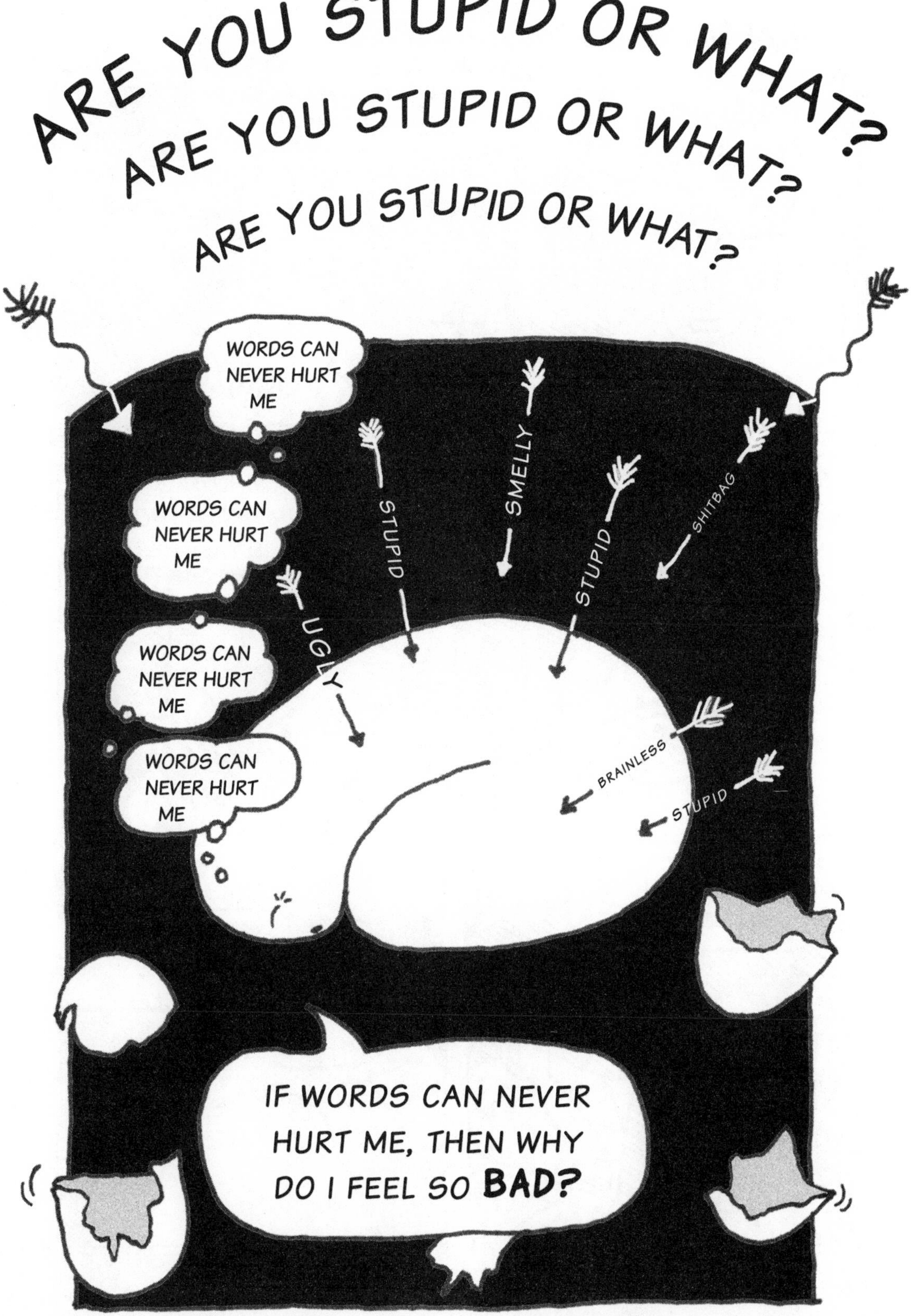
ARE YOU STUPID OR WHAT?
ARE YOU STUPID OR WHAT?
ARE YOU STUPID OR WHAT?
WORDS CAN NEVER HURT ME
WORDS CAN NEVER HURT ME
WORDS CAN NEVER HURT ME
WORDS CAN NEVER HURT ME
STUPID
SMELLY
STUPID
SHITBAG
UGLY
BRAINLESS
STUPID
IF WORDS CAN NEVER HURT ME, THEN WHY DO I FEEL SO **BAD?**

THEN, AT DINNER...

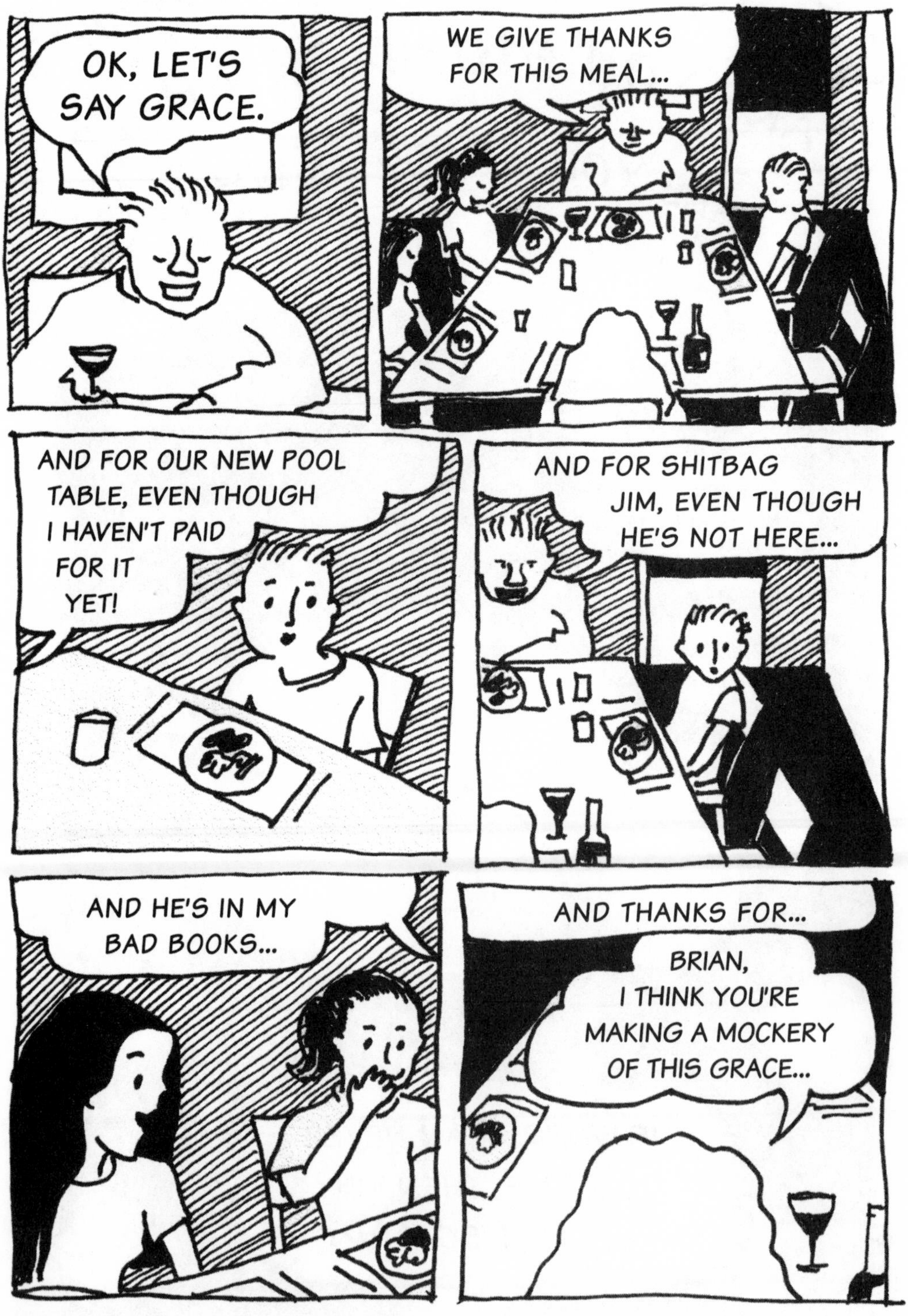
OK, LET'S SAY GRACE.
WE GIVE THANKS FOR THIS MEAL...
AND FOR OUR NEW POOL TABLE, EVEN THOUGH I HAVEN'T PAID FOR IT YET!
AND FOR SHITBAG JIM, EVEN THOUGH HE'S NOT HERE...
AND HE'S IN MY BAD BOOKS...
AND THANKS FOR...
BRIAN, I THINK YOU'RE MAKING A MOCKERY OF THIS GRACE...

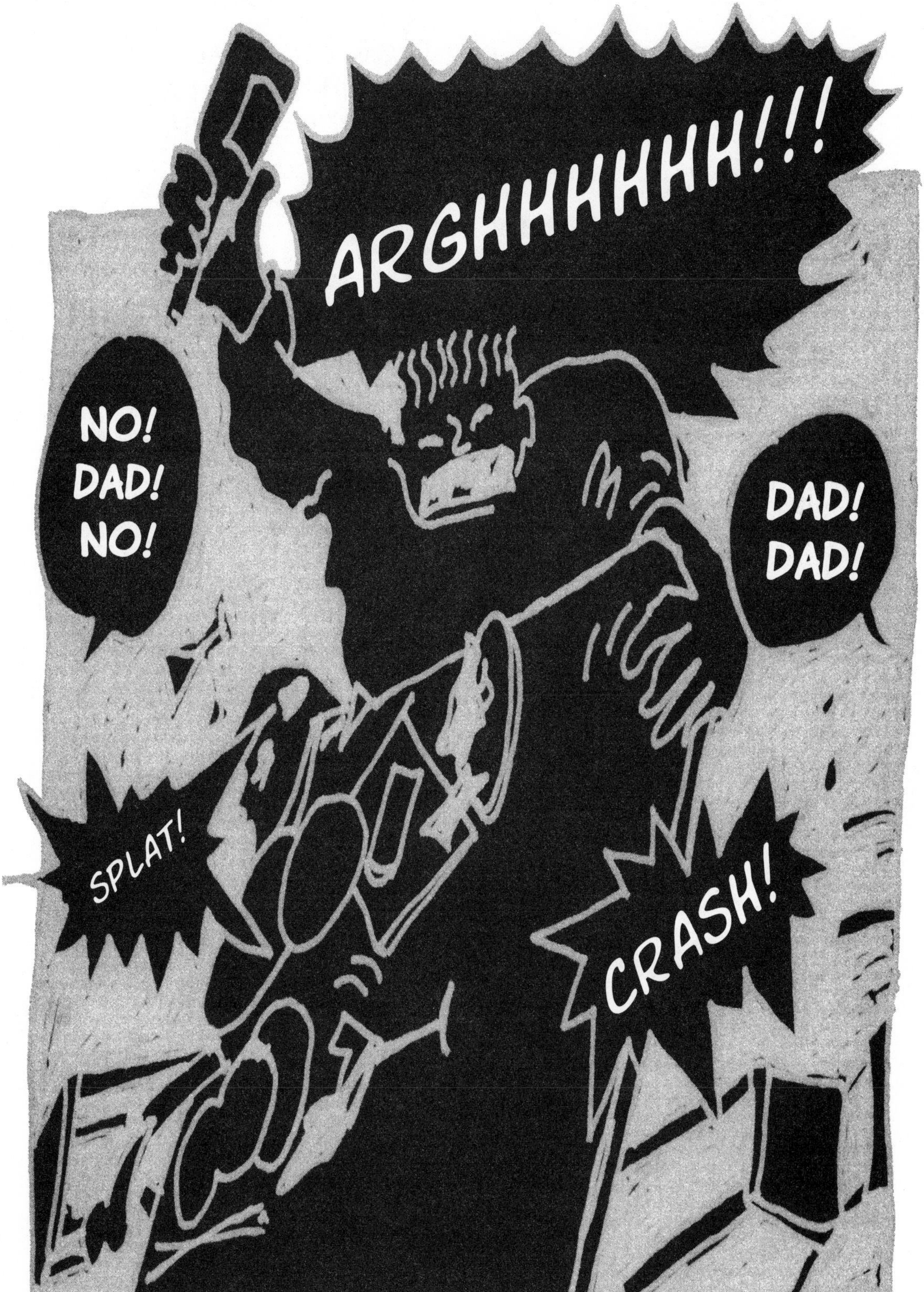
ARGHHHHHH!!!
NO! DAD! NO!
DAD! DAD!
SPLAT!
CRASH!

I WAS HORRIFIED. HOW HAD MY FEW WORDS CAUSED ALL THIS? I COULD SEE THE CHILDREN'S SCREAMING MOUTHS, BUT ALL I HEARD WAS AN EERIE WHITE NOISE, LIKE WE WERE IN THE EYE OF A STORM.

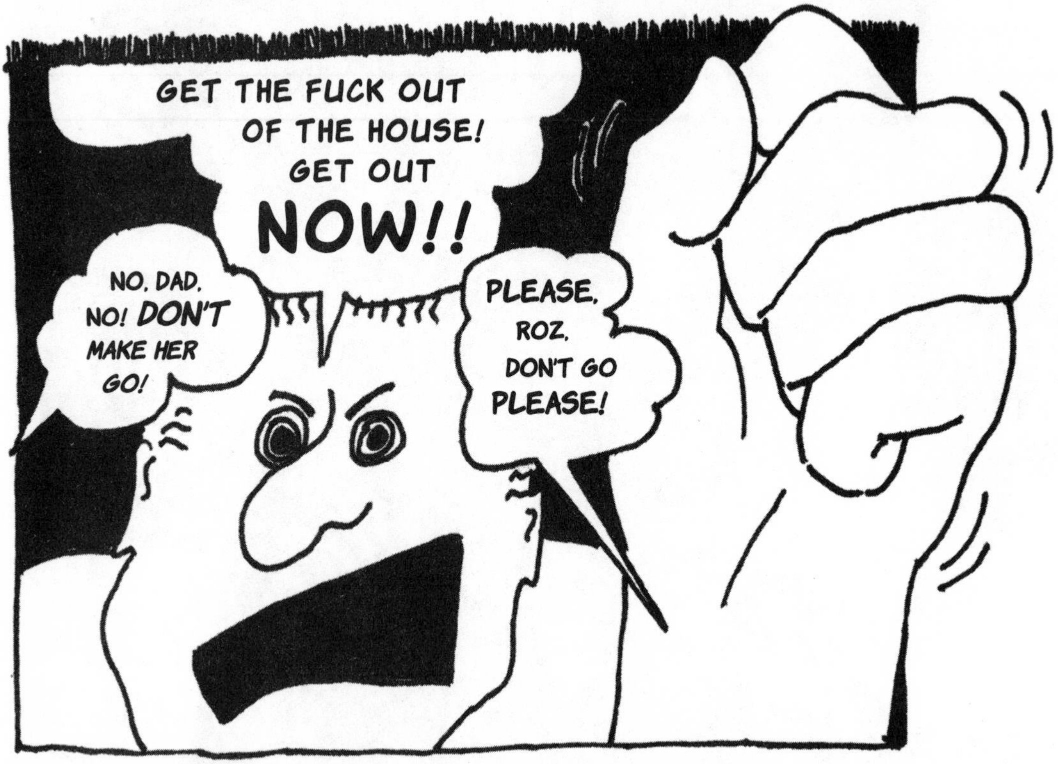
GET THE FUCK OUT OF THE HOUSE! GET OUT NOW!!
NO, DAD, NO! DON'T MAKE HER GO!
PLEASE, ROZ, DON'T GO PLEASE!

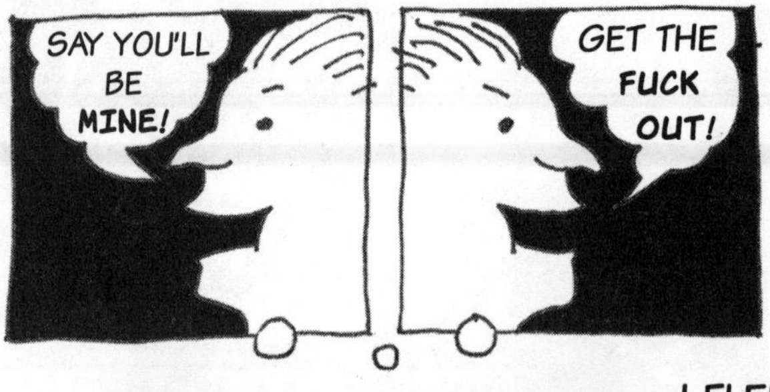
SAY YOU'LL BE MINE!
GET THE FUCK OUT!

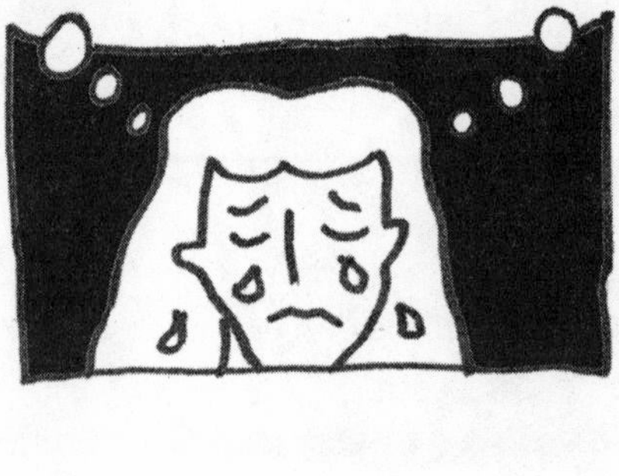

I FLED TO MY PARENTS' HOUSE AND CRIED FOR WEEKS, TRYING TO FIGURE OUT WHAT I DID WRONG...

ONE SUNDAY, MOM TOOK ME TO CHURCH.

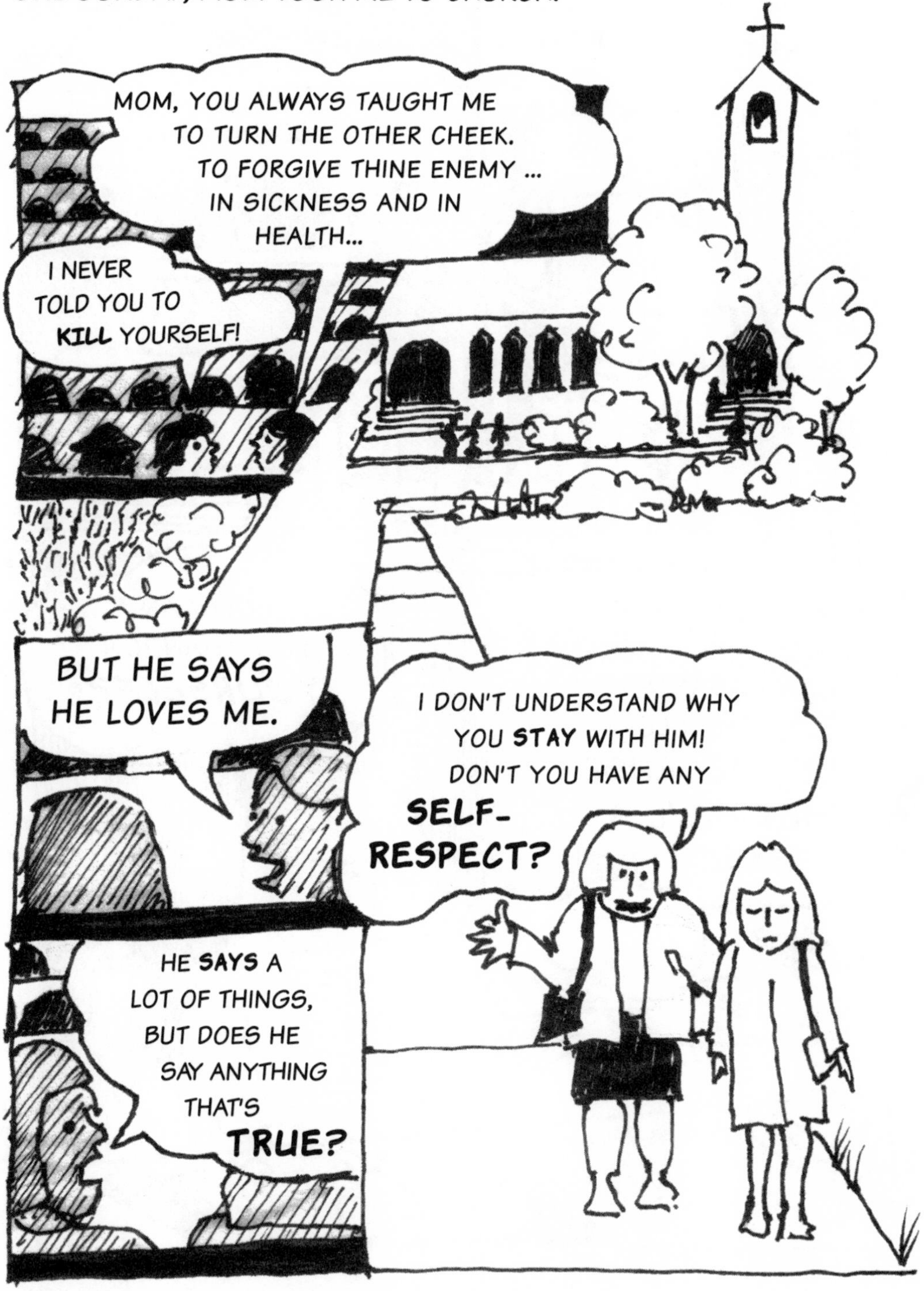
MOM, YOU ALWAYS TAUGHT ME TO TURN THE OTHER CHEEK. TO FORGIVE THINE ENEMY ... IN SICKNESS AND IN HEALTH...
I NEVER TOLD YOU TO KILL YOURSELF!
BUT HE SAYS HE LOVES ME.
I DON'T UNDERSTAND WHY YOU STAY WITH HIM! DON'T YOU HAVE ANY SELF-RESPECT?
HE SAYS A LOT OF THINGS, BUT DOES HE SAY ANYTHING THAT'S TRUE?

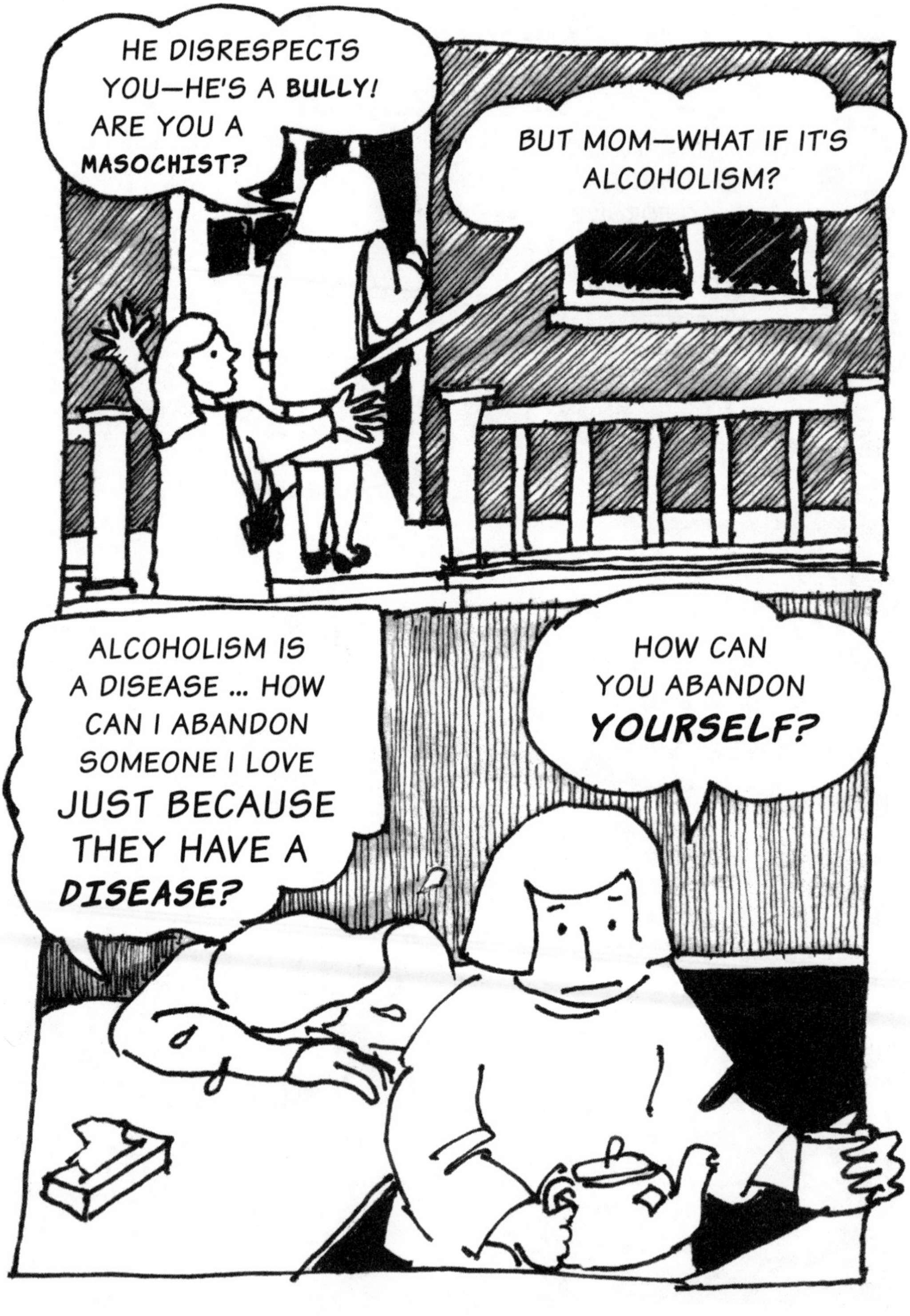
HE DISRESPECTS YOU—HE'S A BULLY! ARE YOU A MASOCHIST?
BUT MOM—WHAT IF IT'S ALCOHOLISM?
ALCOHOLISM IS A DISEASE ... HOW CAN I ABANDON SOMEONE I LOVE JUST BECAUSE THEY HAVE A DISEASE?
HOW CAN YOU ABANDON YOURSELF?

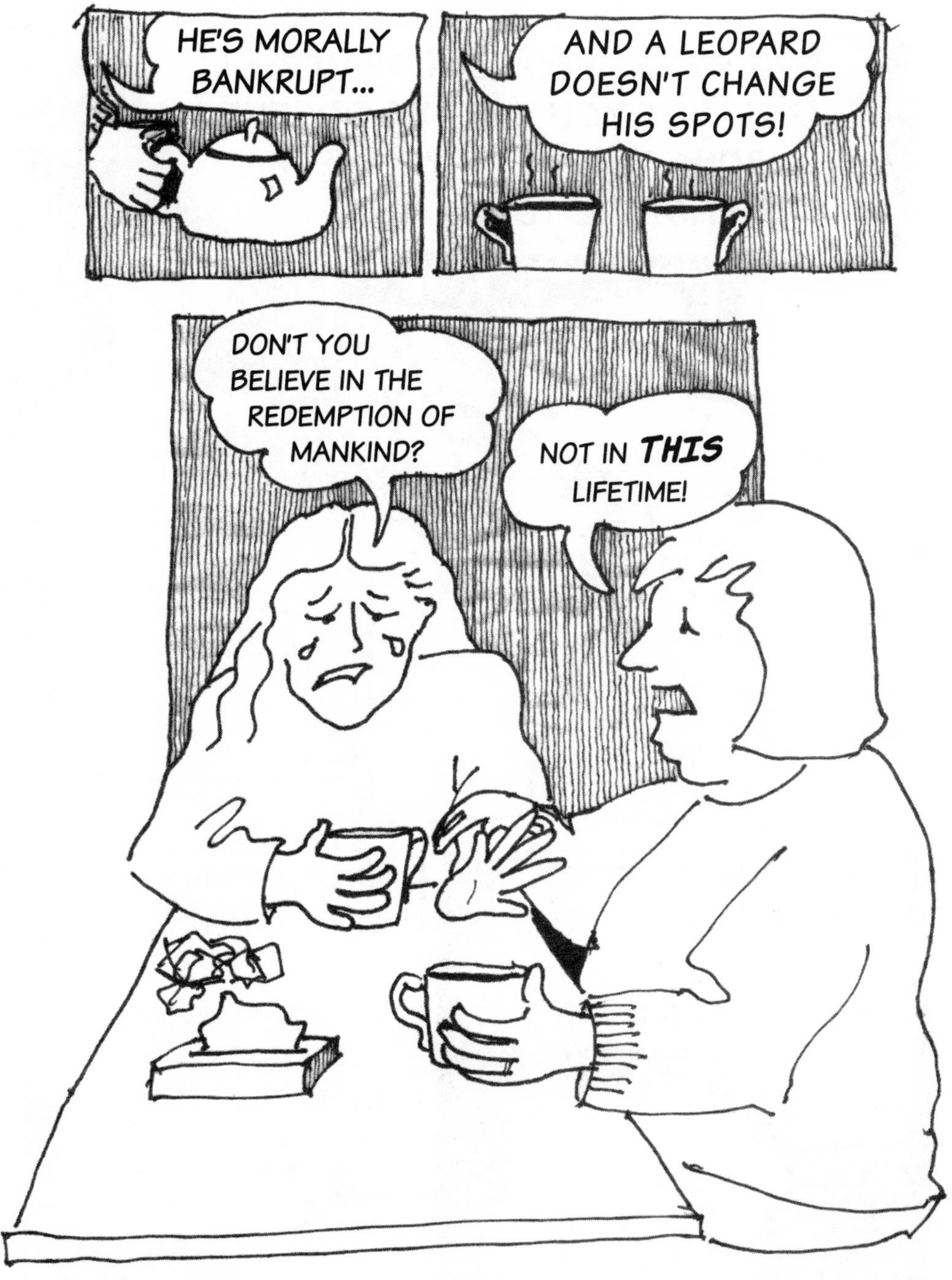
HE'S MORALLY BANKRUPT...
AND A LEOPARD DOESN'T CHANGE HIS SPOTS!
DON'T YOU BELIEVE IN THE REDEMPTION OF MANKIND?
NOT IN **THIS** LIFETIME!

3 WEEKS LATER, BRIAN FINALLY CALLED AND I WAS WEAK FROM MISSING HIM...

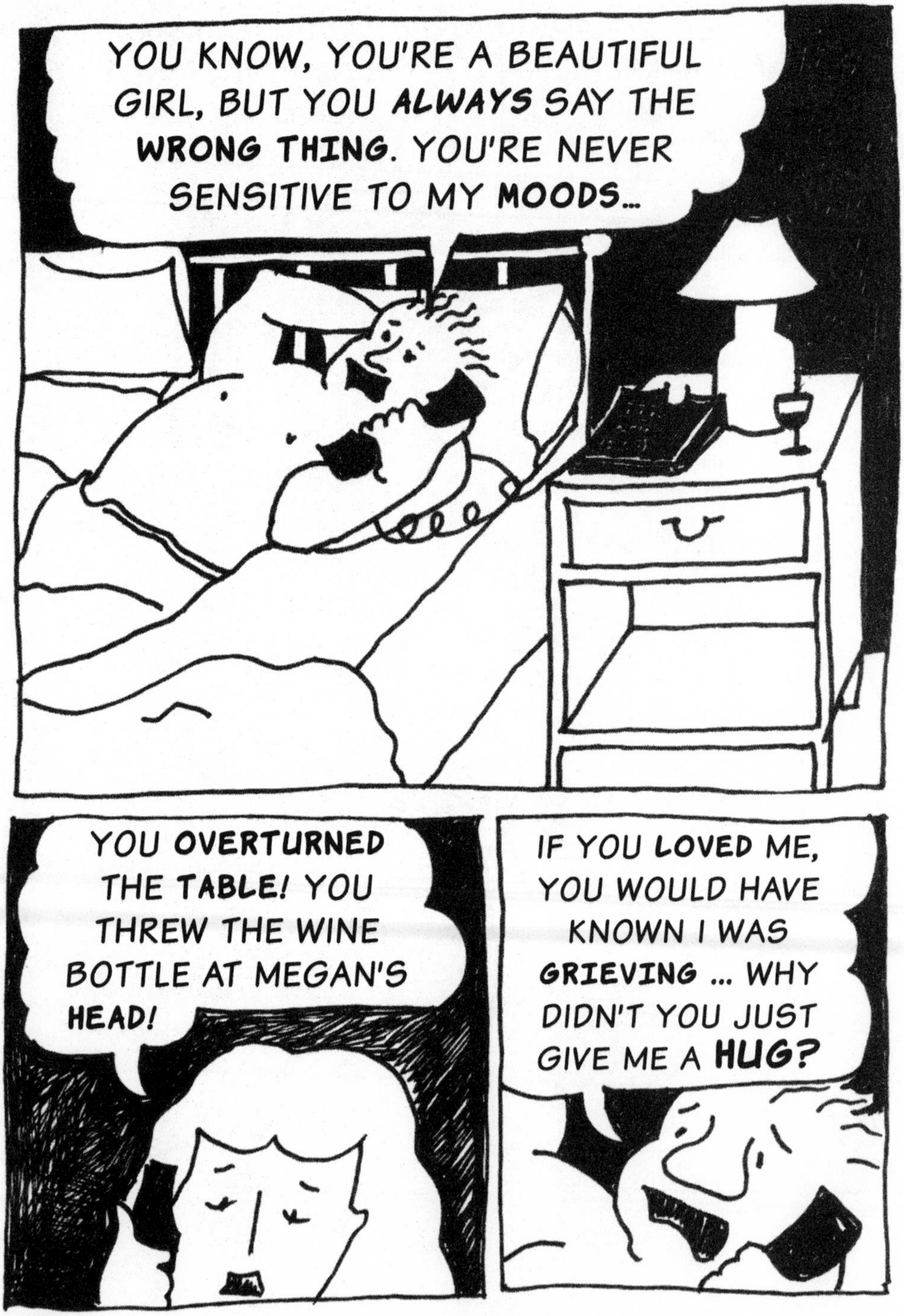
YOU KNOW, YOU'RE A BEAUTIFUL GIRL, BUT YOU ALWAYS SAY THE WRONG THING. YOU'RE NEVER SENSITIVE TO MY MOODS...
YOU OVERTURNED THE TABLE! YOU THREW THE WINE BOTTLE AT MEGAN'S HEAD!
IF YOU LOVED ME, YOU WOULD HAVE KNOWN I WAS GRIEVING ... WHY DIDN'T YOU JUST GIVE ME A HUG?

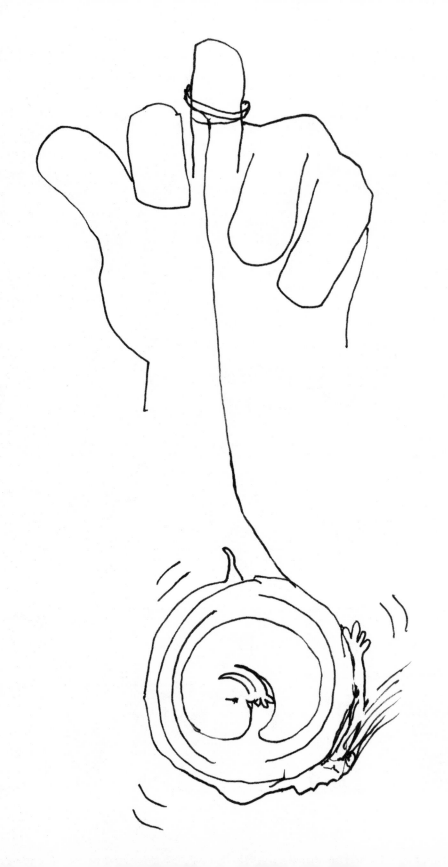

I FELT WEEPY AND WOBBLY, AS THOUGH WE HAD JUST SUFFERED AN EARTHQUAKE AND WERE EXPERIENCING AFTERSHOCKS...

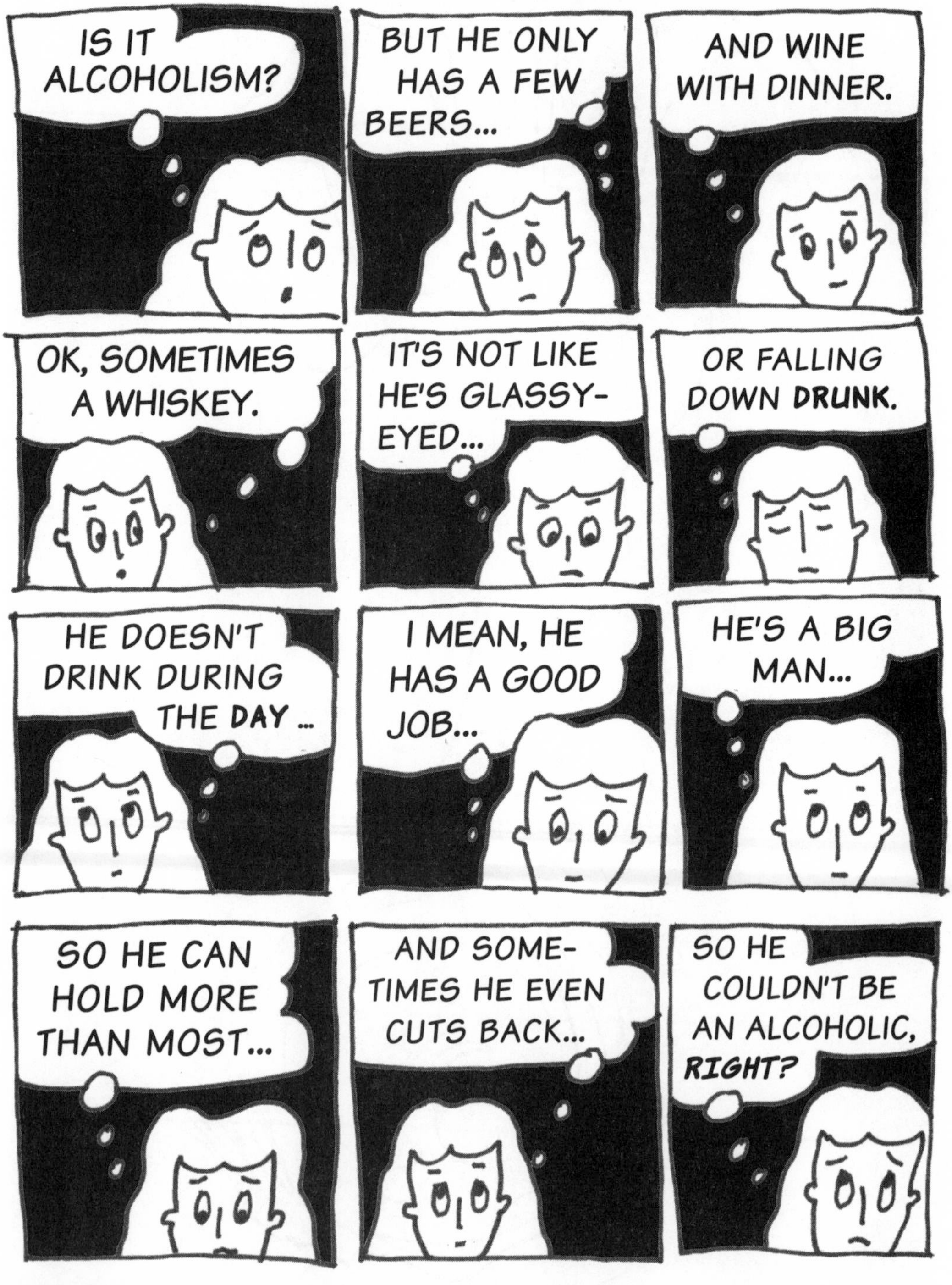
IS IT ALCOHOLISM?
BUT HE ONLY HAS A FEW BEERS...
AND WINE WITH DINNER.
OK, SOMETIMES A WHISKEY.
IT'S NOT LIKE HE'S GLASSY-EYED...
OR FALLING DOWN DRUNK.
HE DOESN'T DRINK DURING THE DAY ...
I MEAN, HE HAS A GOOD JOB...
HE'S A BIG MAN...
SO HE CAN HOLD MORE THAN MOST...
AND SOME-TIMES HE EVEN CUTS BACK...
SO HE COULDN'T BE AN ALCOHOLIC, RIGHT?

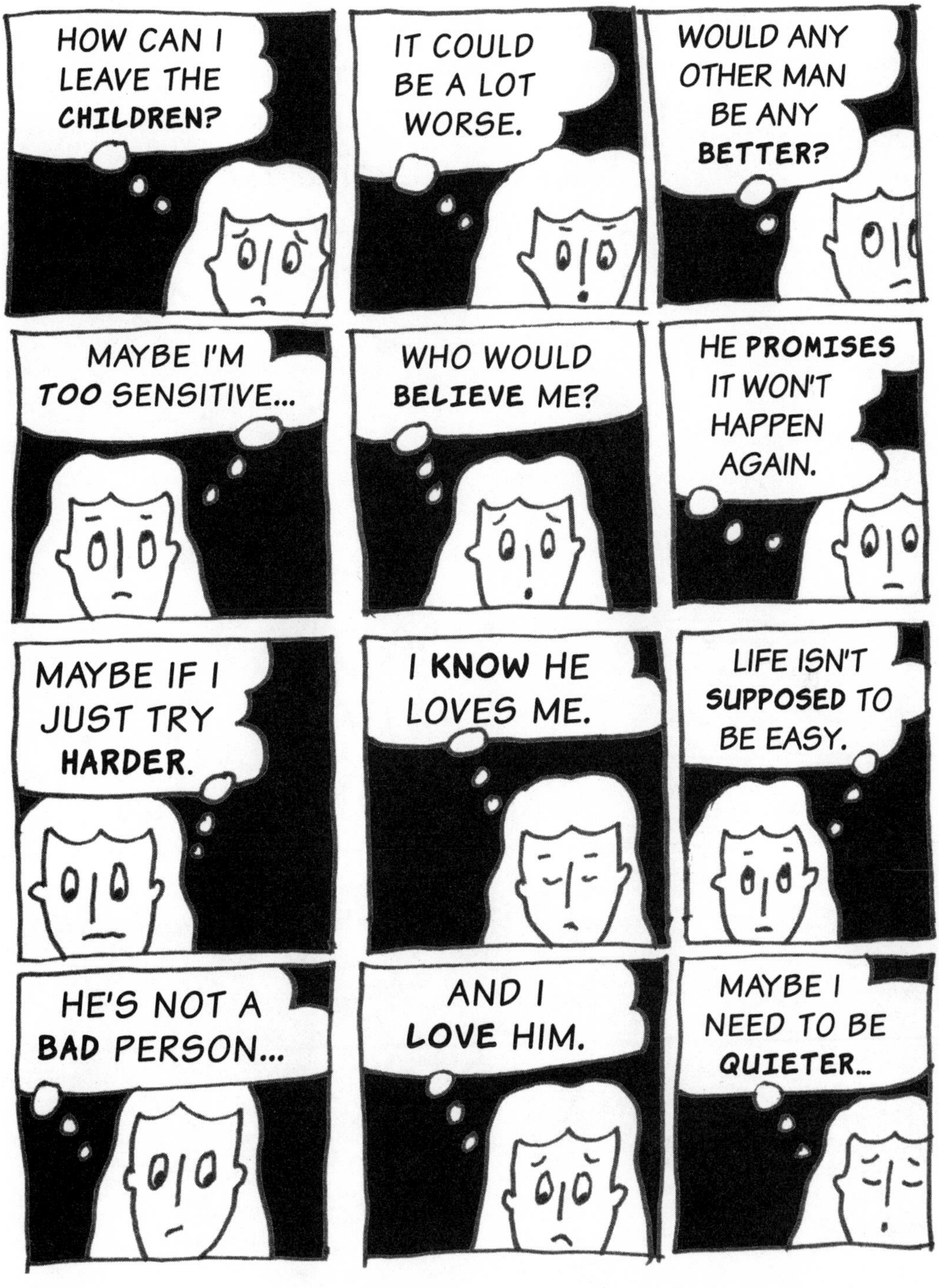
HOW CAN I LEAVE THE CHILDREN?
IT COULD BE A LOT WORSE.
WOULD ANY OTHER MAN BE ANY BETTER?
MAYBE I'M TOO SENSITIVE...
WHO WOULD BELIEVE ME?
HE PROMISES IT WON'T HAPPEN AGAIN.
MAYBE IF I JUST TRY HARDER.
I KNOW HE LOVES ME.
LIFE ISN'T SUPPOSED TO BE EASY.
HE'S NOT A BAD PERSON...
AND I LOVE HIM.
MAYBE I NEED TO BE QUIETER...

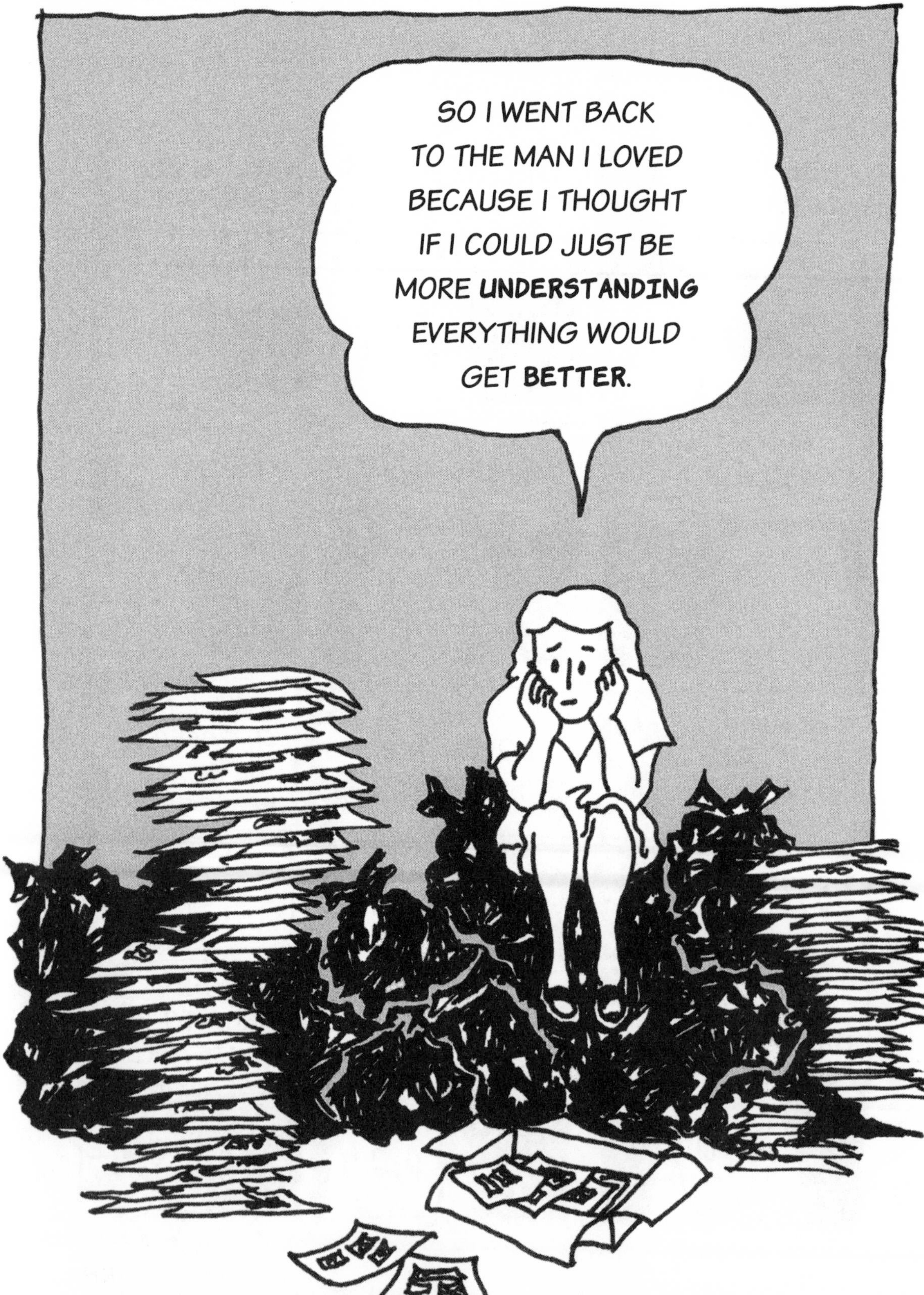
SO I WENT BACK TO THE MAN I LOVED BECAUSE I THOUGHT IF I COULD JUST BE MORE **UNDERSTANDING** EVERYTHING WOULD GET **BETTER**.

Getting Hurt: Holding On

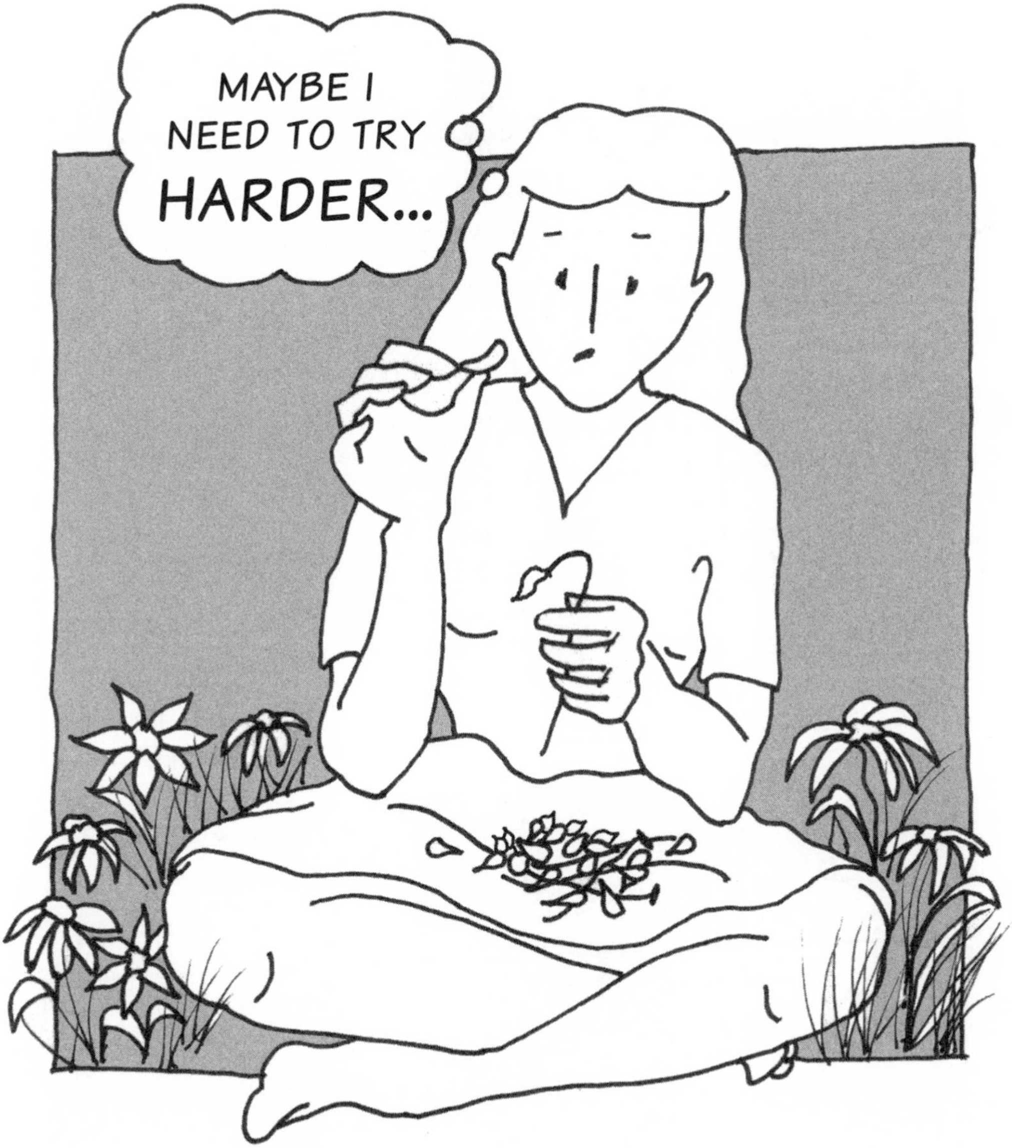
MAYBE I NEED TO TRY HARDER...

WE HAD A FEW GOOD MONTHS, WHICH GAVE ME HOPE AGAIN. THINGS SEEMED TO BE GOING SMOOTHLY, UNTIL ONE NIGHT...

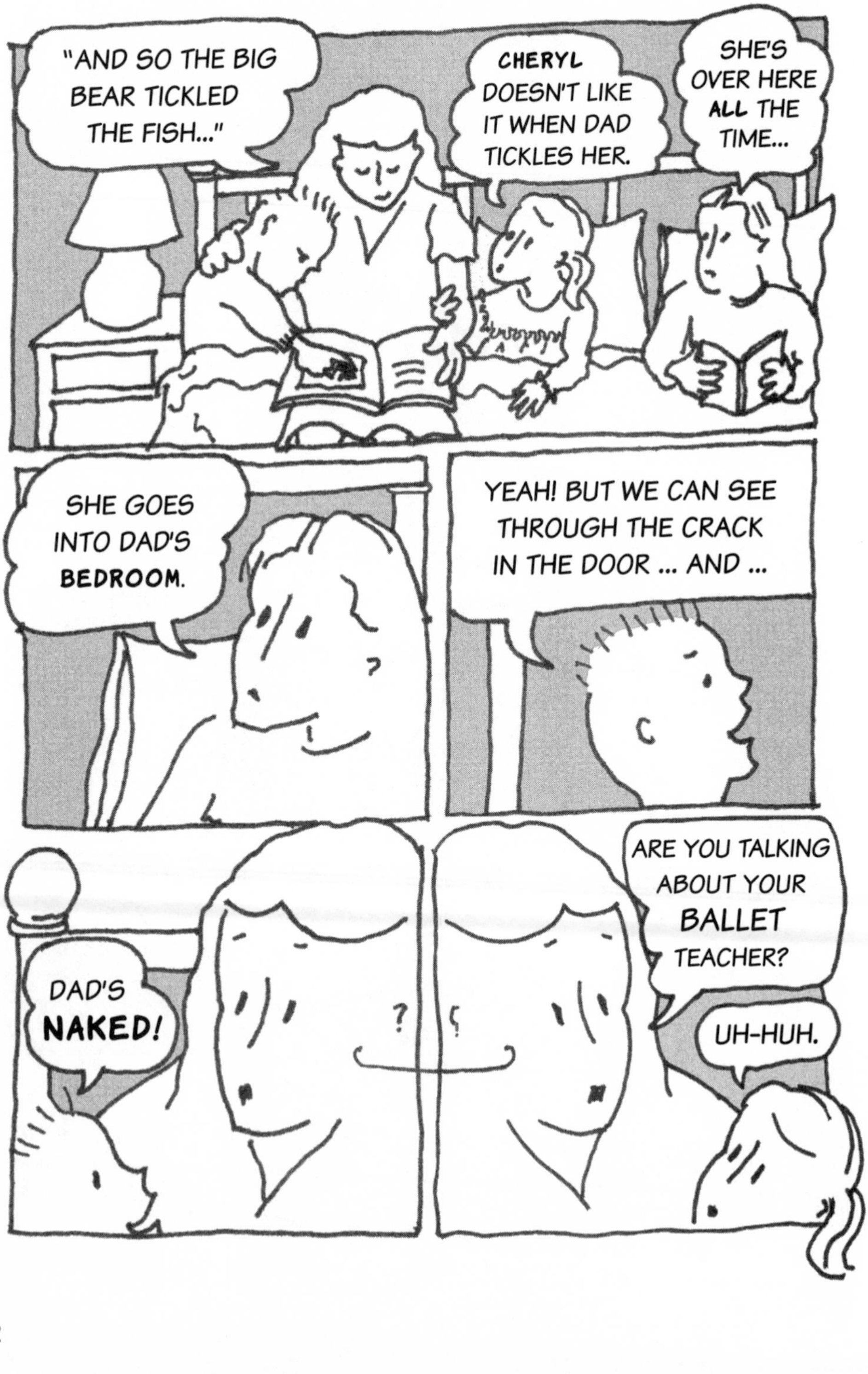
"AND SO THE BIG BEAR TICKLED THE FISH..."
CHERYL DOESN'T LIKE IT WHEN DAD TICKLES HER.
SHE'S OVER HERE ALL THE TIME...
SHE GOES INTO DAD'S BEDROOM.
YEAH! BUT WE CAN SEE THROUGH THE CRACK IN THE DOOR ... AND ...
DAD'S NAKED!
ARE YOU TALKING ABOUT YOUR BALLET TEACHER?
UH-HUH.

WHEN I CONFRONTED BRIAN, *HE LAUGHED!* HE SAID THE CHILDREN WERE JUST MAKING UP STORIES TO HURT ME, BECAUSE THEY WERE JEALOUS OF HIS LOVE FOR ME.

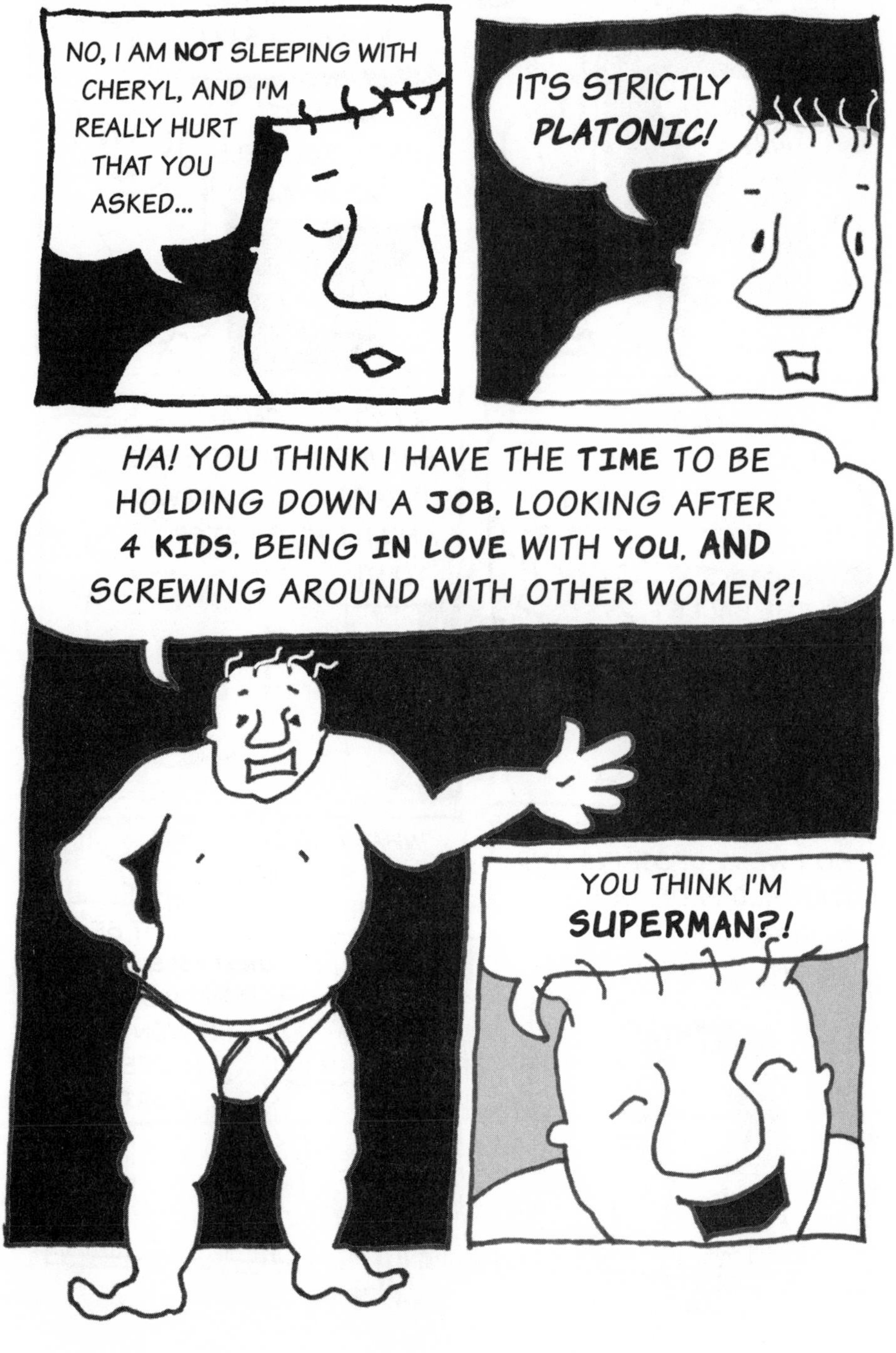
NO, I AM **NOT** SLEEPING WITH CHERYL, AND I'M REALLY HURT THAT YOU ASKED...
IT'S STRICTLY **PLATONIC!**
HA! YOU THINK I HAVE THE **TIME** TO BE HOLDING DOWN A **JOB**, LOOKING AFTER **4 KIDS**, BEING **IN LOVE** WITH **YOU**, **AND** SCREWING AROUND WITH OTHER WOMEN?!
YOU THINK I'M **SUPERMAN?!**

BUT SEVERAL NIGHTS LATER, BRIAN AND I WERE ENJOYING A ROMANTIC DINNER AT HOME. HE WENT TO GET WINE...

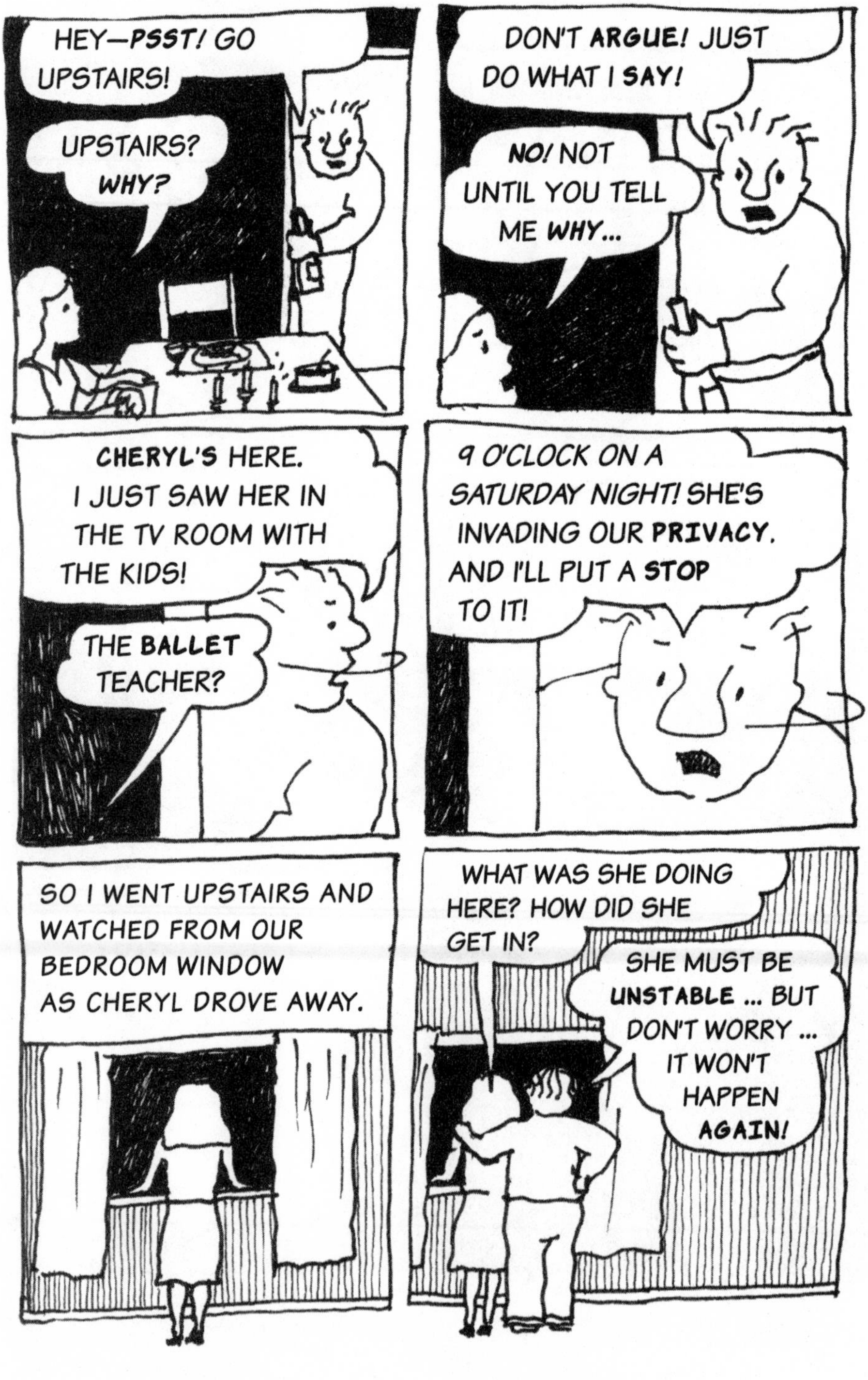
HEY—PSST! GO UPSTAIRS!
UPSTAIRS? WHY?
DON'T ARGUE! JUST DO WHAT I SAY!
NO! NOT UNTIL YOU TELL ME WHY...
CHERYL'S HERE. I JUST SAW HER IN THE TV ROOM WITH THE KIDS!
THE BALLET TEACHER?
9 O'CLOCK ON A SATURDAY NIGHT! SHE'S INVADING OUR PRIVACY. AND I'LL PUT A STOP TO IT!
SO I WENT UPSTAIRS AND WATCHED FROM OUR BEDROOM WINDOW AS CHERYL DROVE AWAY.
WHAT WAS SHE DOING HERE? HOW DID SHE GET IN?
SHE MUST BE UNSTABLE ... BUT DON'T WORRY ... IT WON'T HAPPEN AGAIN!

BUT THAT NIGHT HE TAUNTED ME...

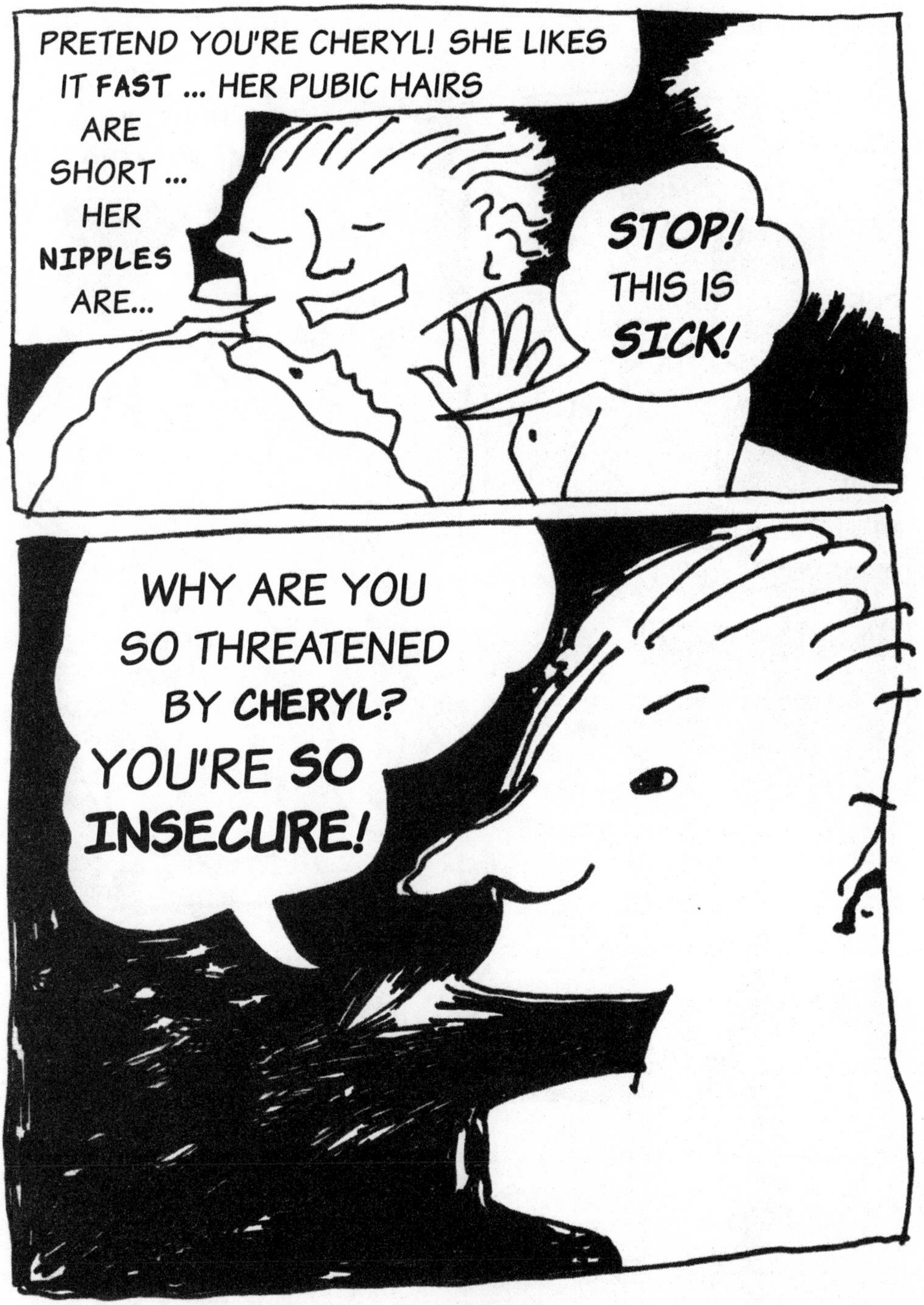
PRETEND YOU'RE CHERYL! SHE LIKES IT FAST ... HER PUBIC HAIRS ARE SHORT ... HER NIPPLES ARE...
STOP! THIS IS SICK!
WHY ARE YOU SO THREATENED BY CHERYL? YOU'RE SO INSECURE!

AND I DIDN'T KNOW WHAT TO THINK...

BRIAN BECAME MORE AND MORE DISTANT, BUT I PUT IT DOWN TO STRESS AT THE OFFICE. HE WAS EVASIVE ABOUT EVERYTHING.

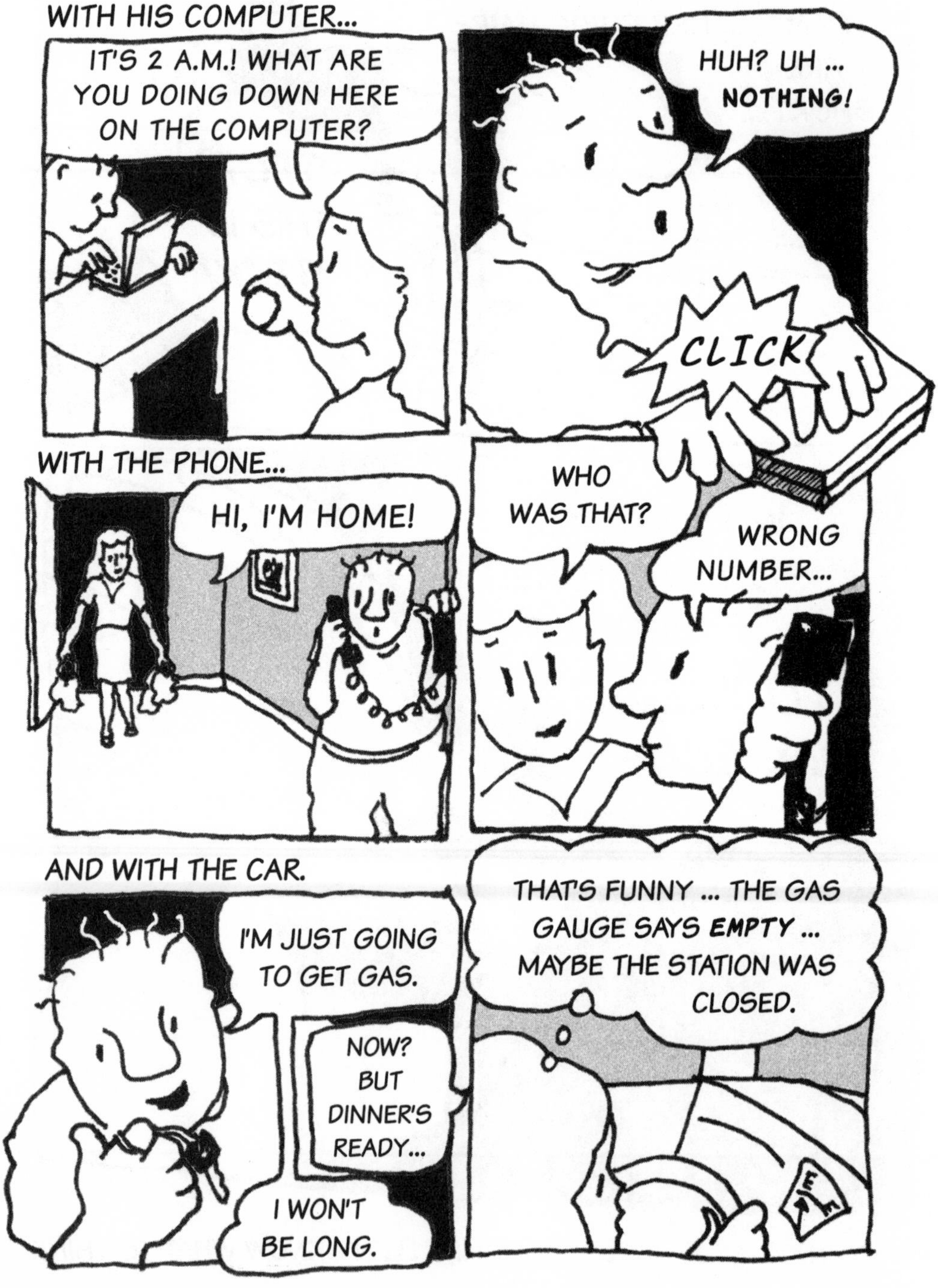

WITH HIS COMPUTER...
IT'S 2 A.M.! WHAT ARE YOU DOING DOWN HERE ON THE COMPUTER?
HUH? UH ... NOTHING!
CLICK
WITH THE PHONE...
HI, I'M HOME!
WHO WAS THAT?
WRONG NUMBER...
AND WITH THE CAR.
I'M JUST GOING TO GET GAS.
NOW? BUT DINNER'S READY...
I WON'T BE LONG.
THAT'S FUNNY ... THE GAS GAUGE SAYS EMPTY ... MAYBE THE STATION WAS CLOSED.

BUT THEN A CRISIS BROUGHT US CLOSER...

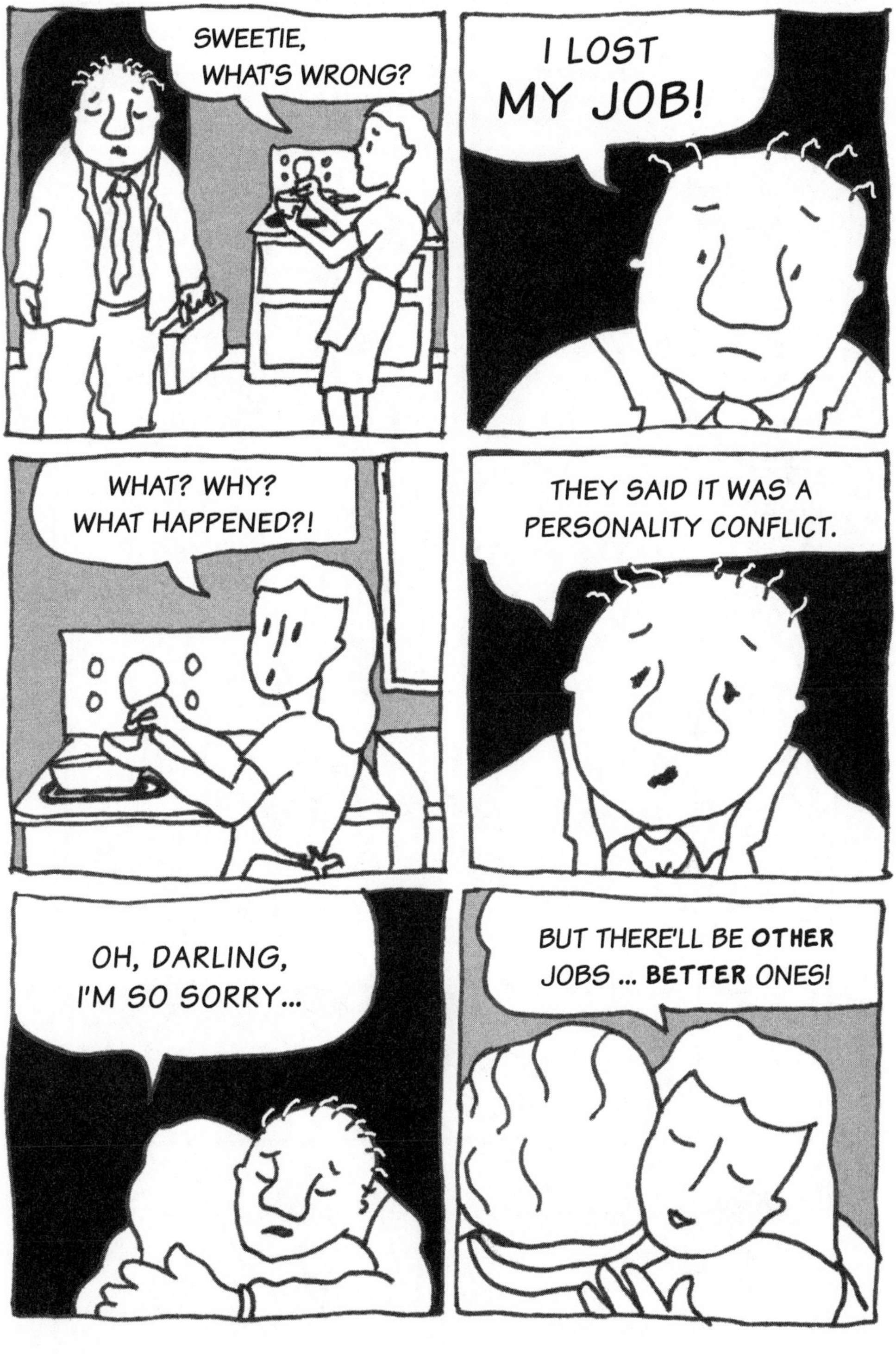
SWEETIE, WHAT'S WRONG?
I LOST MY JOB!
WHAT? WHY? WHAT HAPPENED?!
THEY SAID IT WAS A PERSONALITY CONFLICT.
OH, DARLING, I'M SO SORRY...
BUT THERE'LL BE **OTHER** JOBS ... **BETTER** ONES!

LATER THAT YEAR, BRIAN FLEW TO CALIFORNIA TO BE INTERVIEWED FOR A NEW JOB. HE CALLED FROM HIS HOTEL.

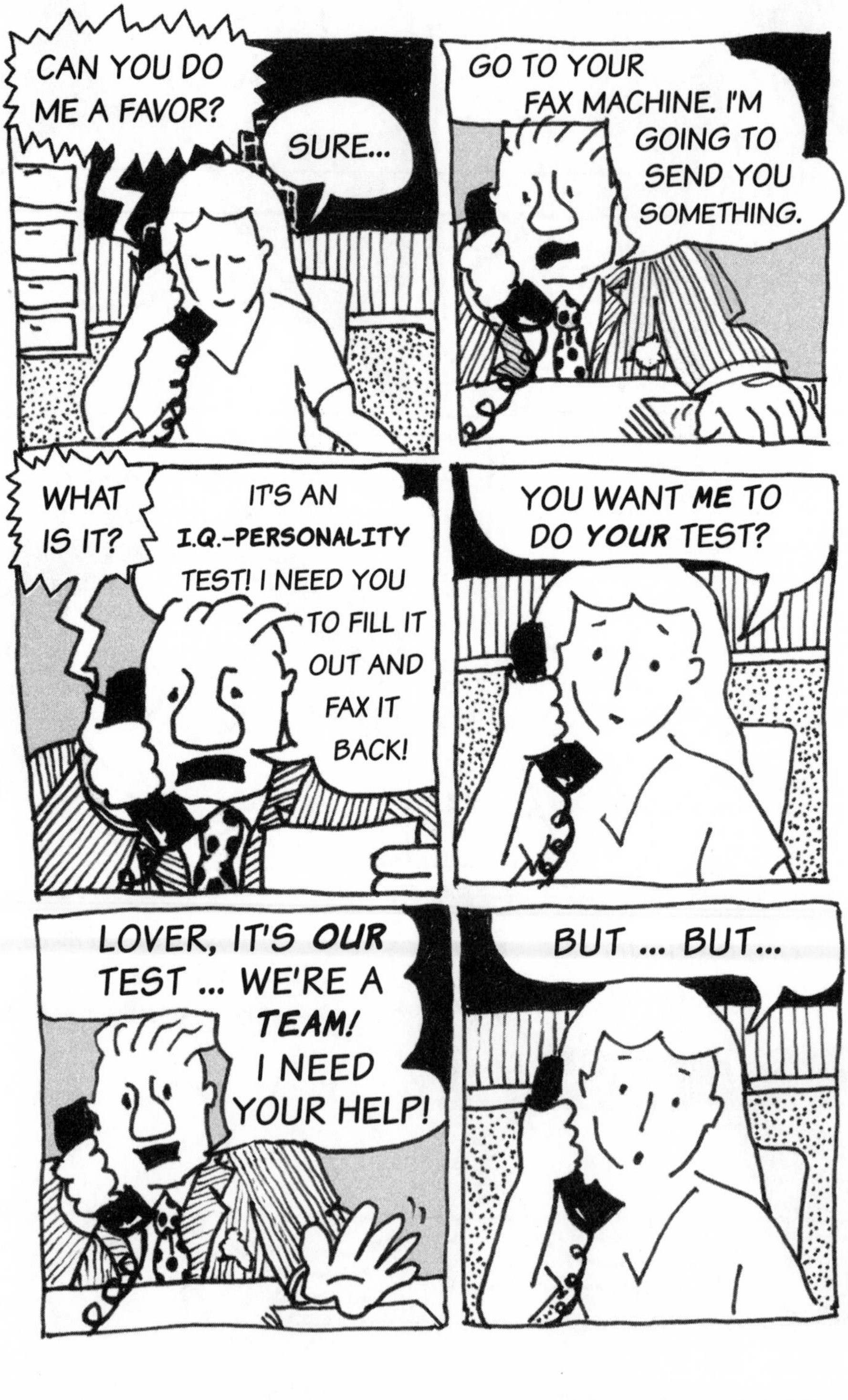
CAN YOU DO ME A FAVOR?
SURE...
GO TO YOUR FAX MACHINE. I'M GOING TO SEND YOU SOMETHING.
WHAT IS IT?
IT'S AN **I.Q.-PERSONALITY** TEST! I NEED YOU TO FILL IT OUT AND FAX IT BACK!
YOU WANT **ME** TO DO **YOUR** TEST?
LOVER, IT'S **OUR** TEST ... WE'RE A **TEAM!** I NEED YOUR HELP!
BUT ... BUT...

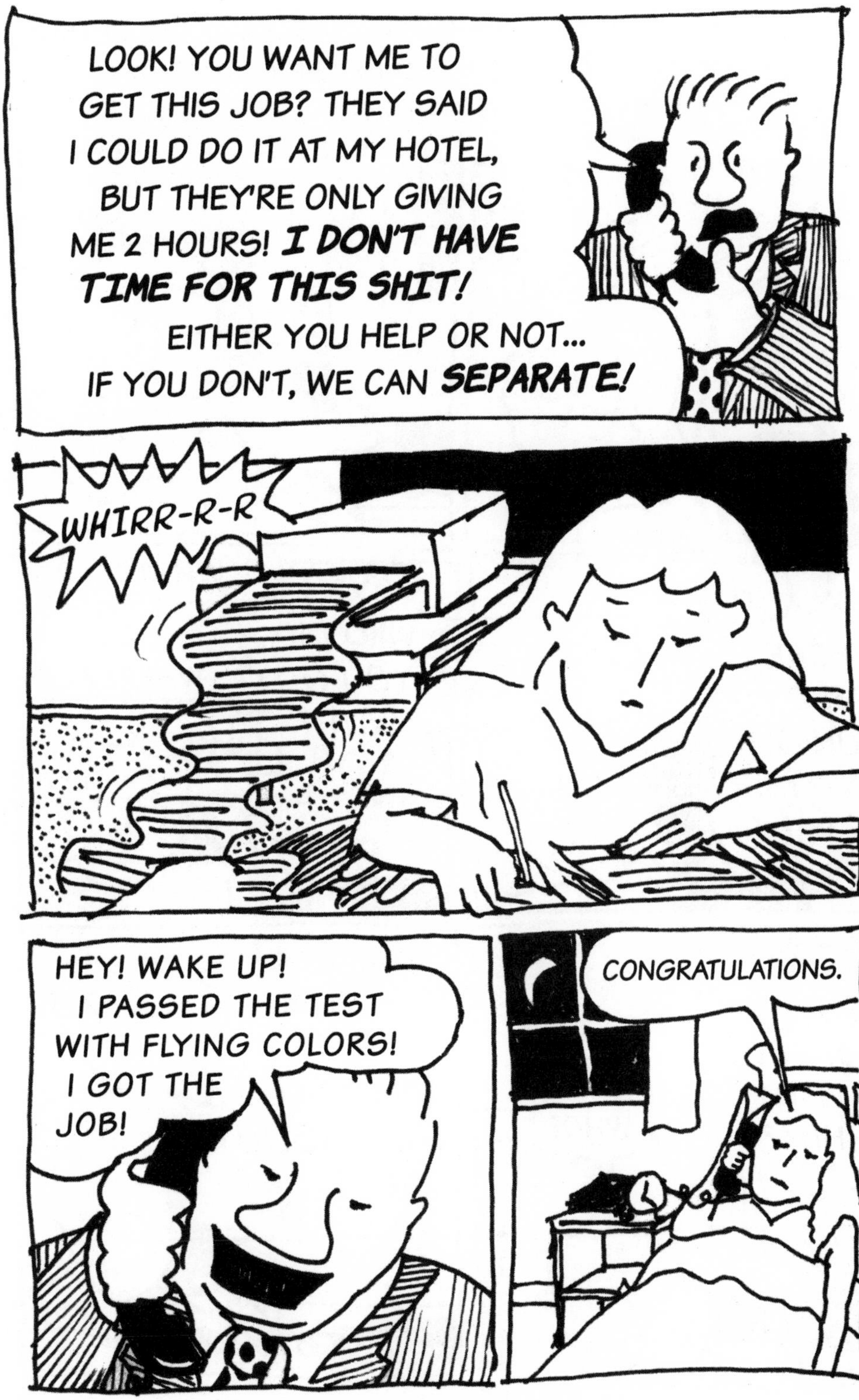
LOOK! YOU WANT ME TO GET THIS JOB? THEY SAID I COULD DO IT AT MY HOTEL, BUT THEY'RE ONLY GIVING ME 2 HOURS! I DON'T HAVE TIME FOR THIS SHIT!
EITHER YOU HELP OR NOT... IF YOU DON'T, WE CAN SEPARATE!
WHIRR-R-R
HEY! WAKE UP! I PASSED THE TEST WITH FLYING COLORS! I GOT THE JOB!
CONGRATULATIONS.

WHILE HE WAS AWAY, HE OFTEN CALLED IN THE MIDDLE OF THE NIGHT...

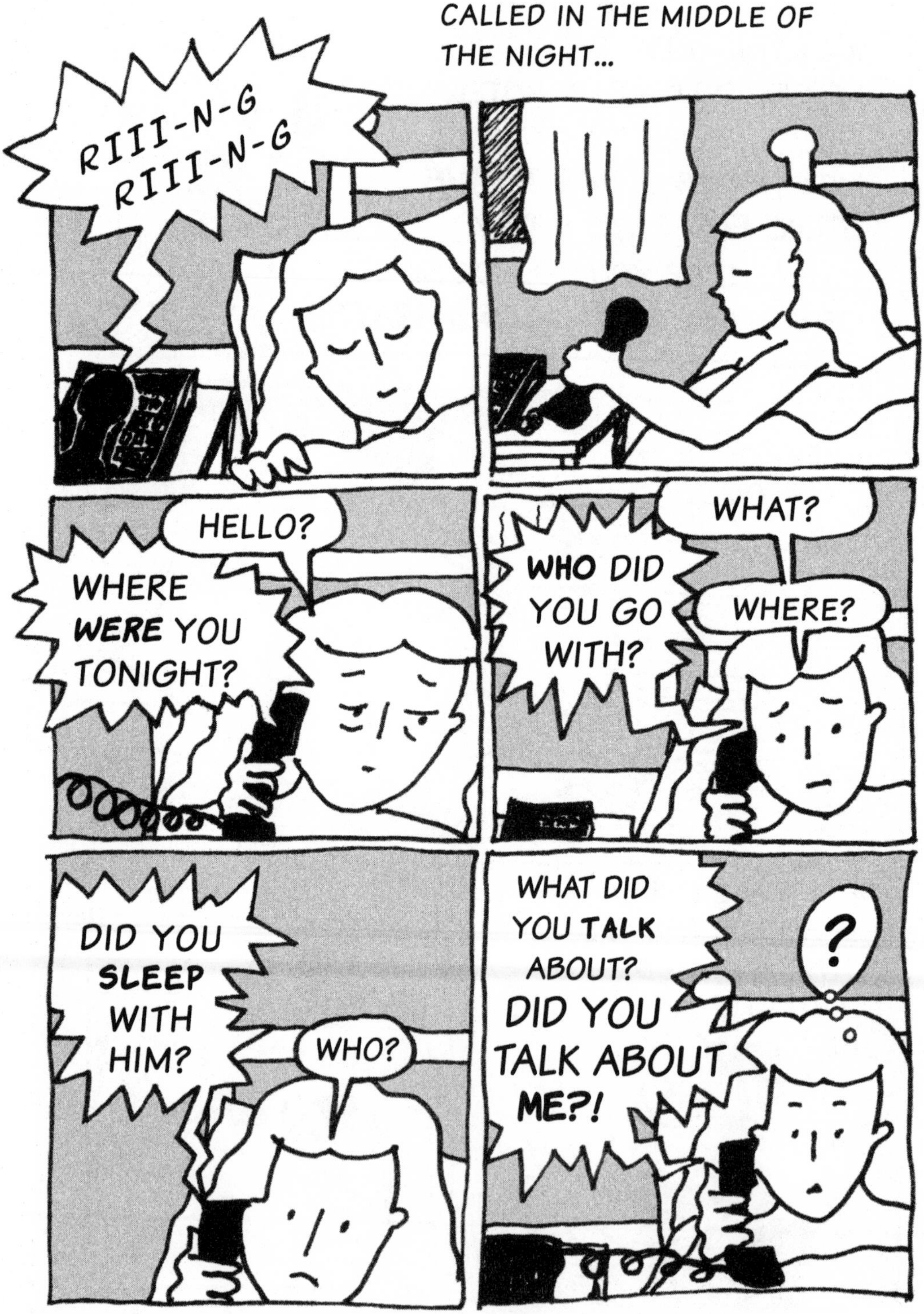

RIII-N-G
RIII-N-G
HELLO?
WHERE **WERE** YOU TONIGHT?
WHAT?
WHO DID YOU GO WITH?
WHERE?
DID YOU **SLEEP** WITH HIM?
WHO?
WHAT DID YOU **TALK** ABOUT?
DID YOU TALK ABOUT **ME?!**
?

BUT WHEN I NEEDED *HIM*...

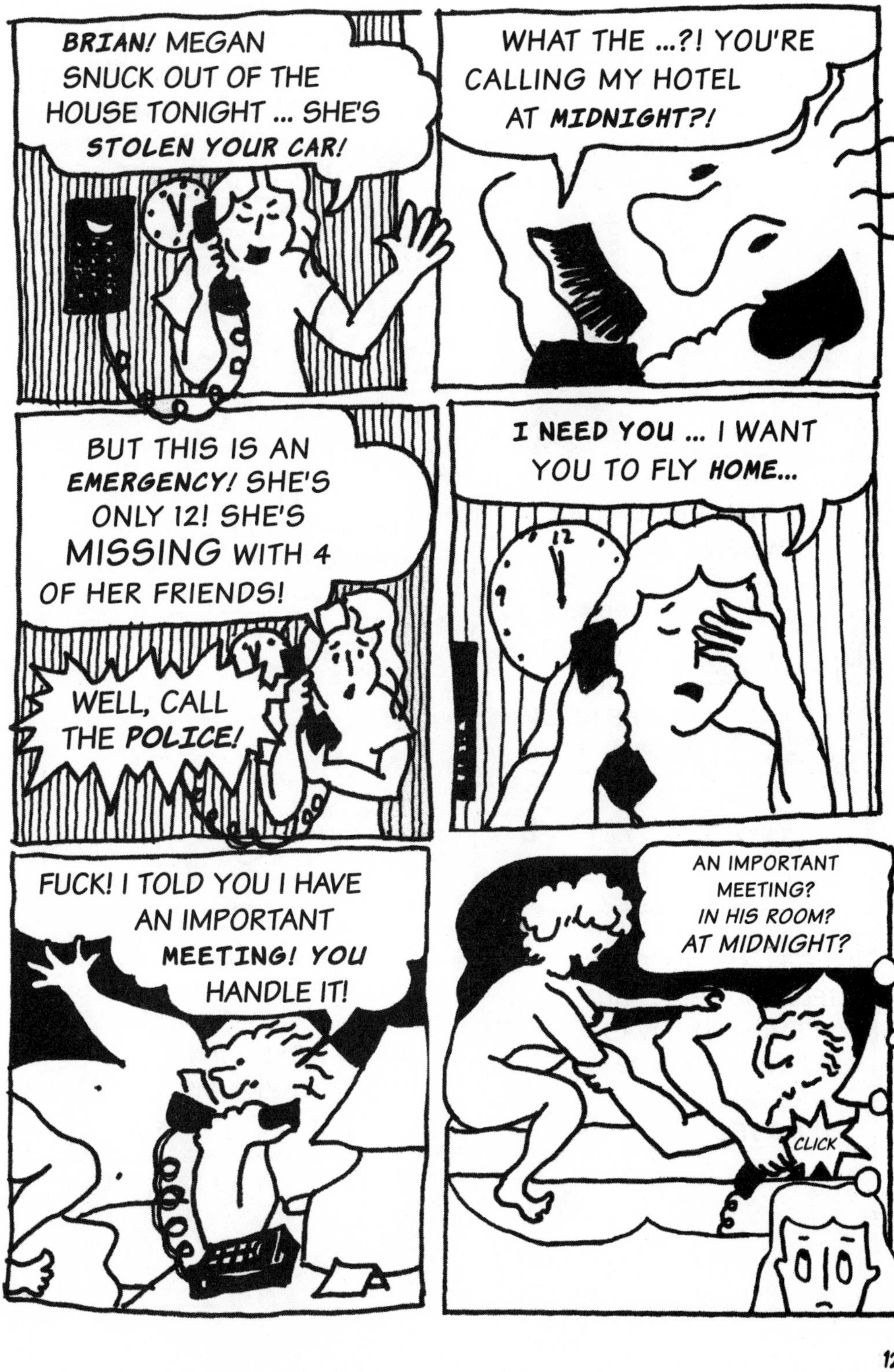
BRIAN! MEGAN SNUCK OUT OF THE HOUSE TONIGHT ... SHE'S **STOLEN YOUR CAR!**
WHAT THE ...?! YOU'RE CALLING MY HOTEL AT **MIDNIGHT?!**
BUT THIS IS AN **EMERGENCY!** SHE'S ONLY 12! SHE'S MISSING WITH 4 OF HER FRIENDS!
WELL, CALL THE **POLICE!**
I NEED YOU ... I WANT YOU TO FLY **HOME...**
FUCK! I TOLD YOU I HAVE AN IMPORTANT **MEETING! YOU** HANDLE IT!
AN IMPORTANT MEETING? *IN HIS ROOM?* AT MIDNIGHT?
CLICK

ONE NIGHT WE HAD A SURPRISE VISITOR...

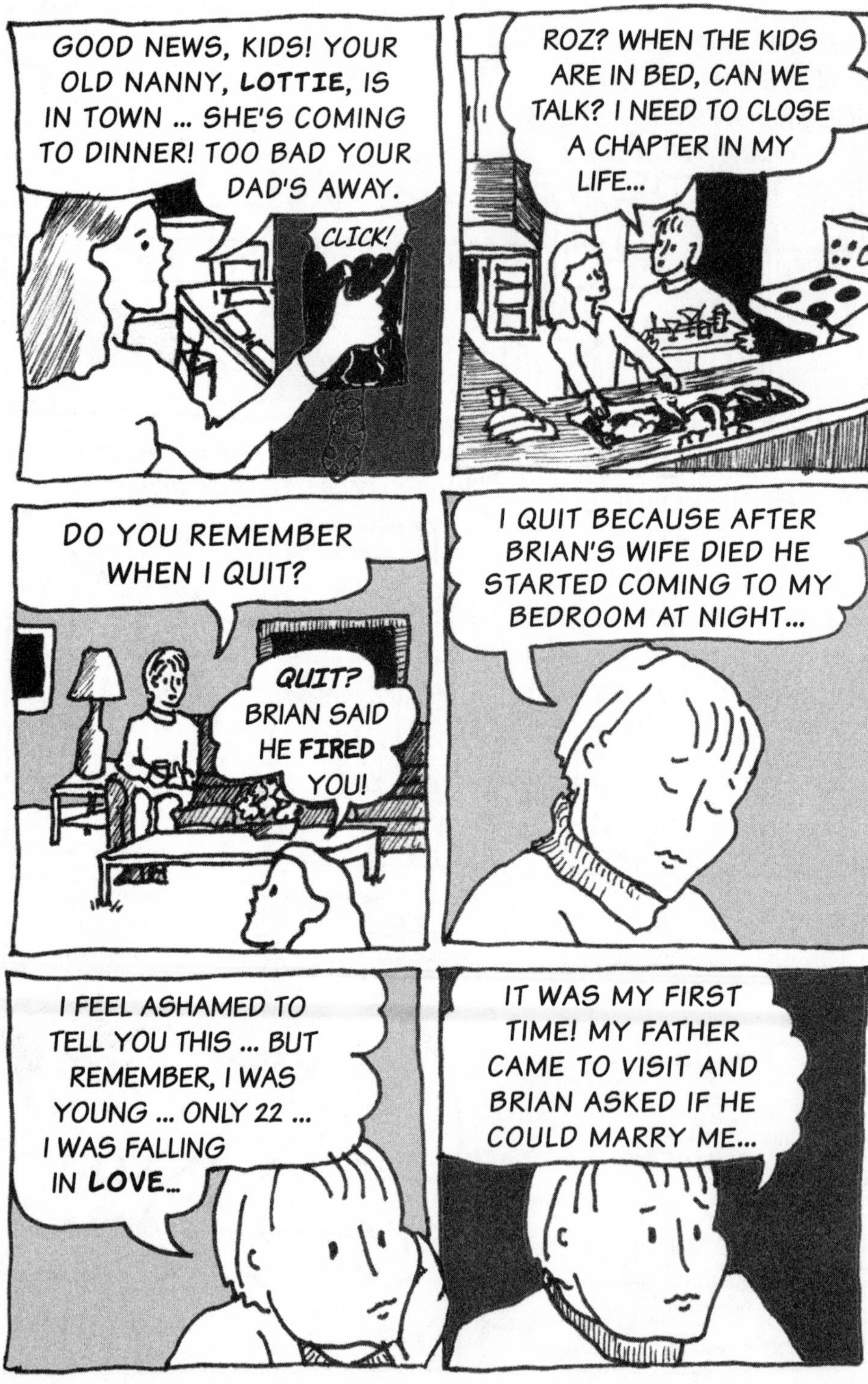
GOOD NEWS, KIDS! YOUR OLD NANNY, LOTTIE, IS IN TOWN ... SHE'S COMING TO DINNER! TOO BAD YOUR DAD'S AWAY.
CLICK!
ROZ? WHEN THE KIDS ARE IN BED, CAN WE TALK? I NEED TO CLOSE A CHAPTER IN MY LIFE...
DO YOU REMEMBER WHEN I QUIT?
QUIT? BRIAN SAID HE FIRED YOU!
I QUIT BECAUSE AFTER BRIAN'S WIFE DIED HE STARTED COMING TO MY BEDROOM AT NIGHT...
I FEEL ASHAMED TO TELL YOU THIS ... BUT REMEMBER, I WAS YOUNG ... ONLY 22 ... I WAS FALLING IN LOVE...
IT WAS MY FIRST TIME! MY FATHER CAME TO VISIT AND BRIAN ASKED IF HE COULD MARRY ME...

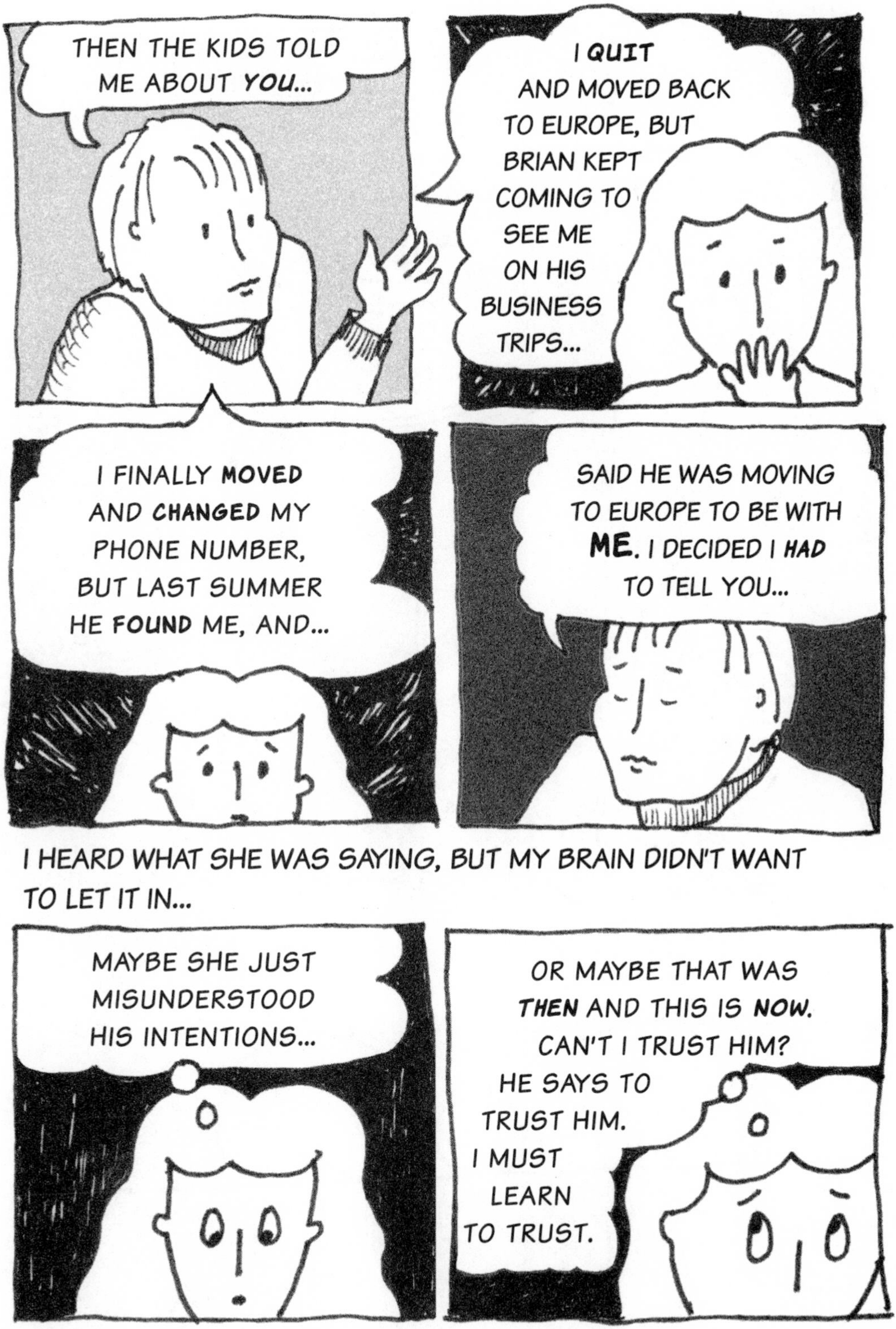
THEN THE KIDS TOLD ME ABOUT YOU...
I QUIT AND MOVED BACK TO EUROPE, BUT BRIAN KEPT COMING TO SEE ME ON HIS BUSINESS TRIPS...
I FINALLY MOVED AND CHANGED MY PHONE NUMBER, BUT LAST SUMMER HE FOUND ME, AND...
SAID HE WAS MOVING TO EUROPE TO BE WITH ME. I DECIDED I HAD TO TELL YOU...
I HEARD WHAT SHE WAS SAYING, BUT MY BRAIN DIDN'T WANT TO LET IT IN...
MAYBE SHE JUST MISUNDERSTOOD HIS INTENTIONS...
OR MAYBE THAT WAS THEN AND THIS IS NOW. CAN'T I TRUST HIM?
HE SAYS TO TRUST HIM. I MUST LEARN TO TRUST.

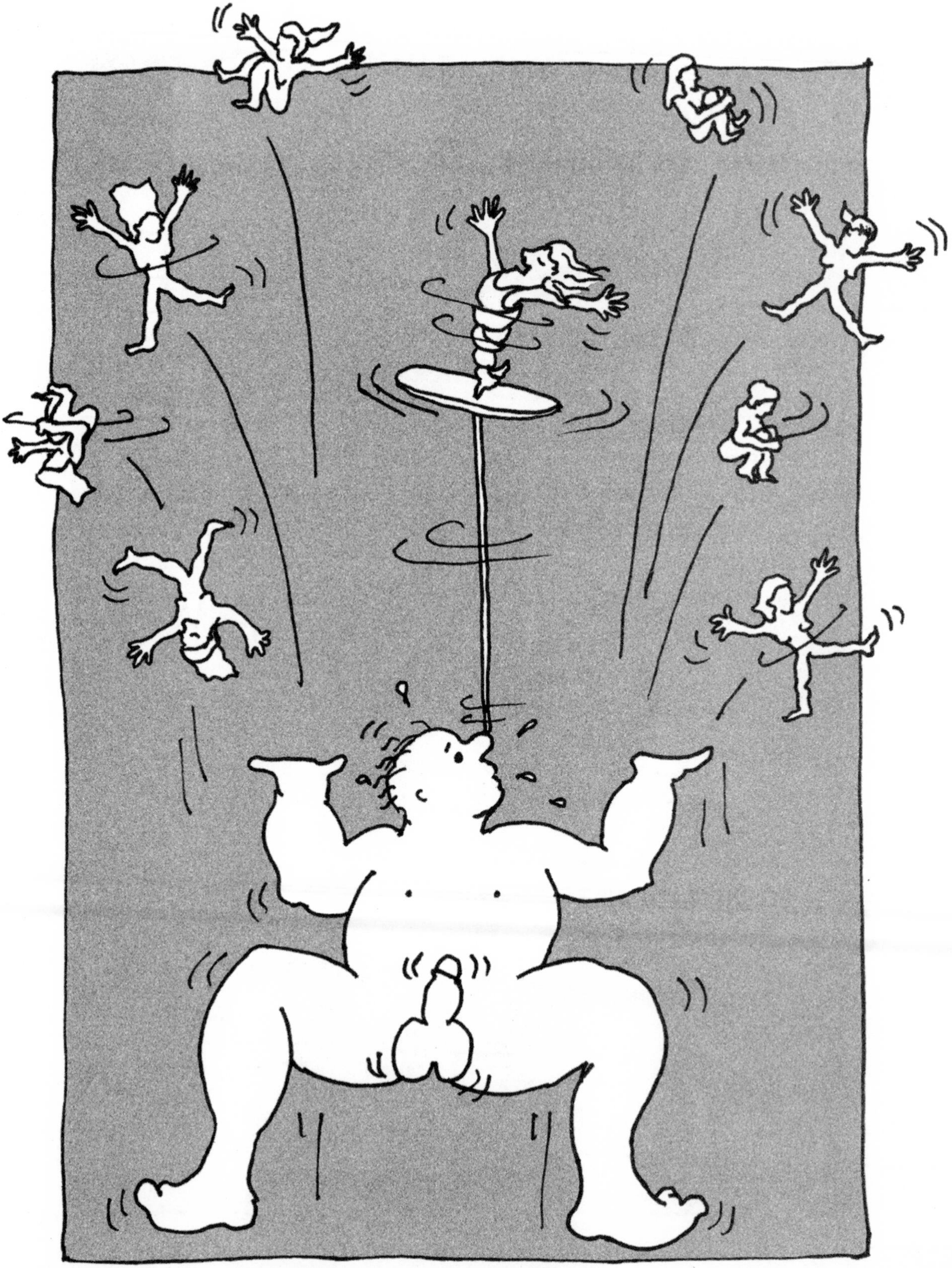

WHEN BRIAN CAME HOME...

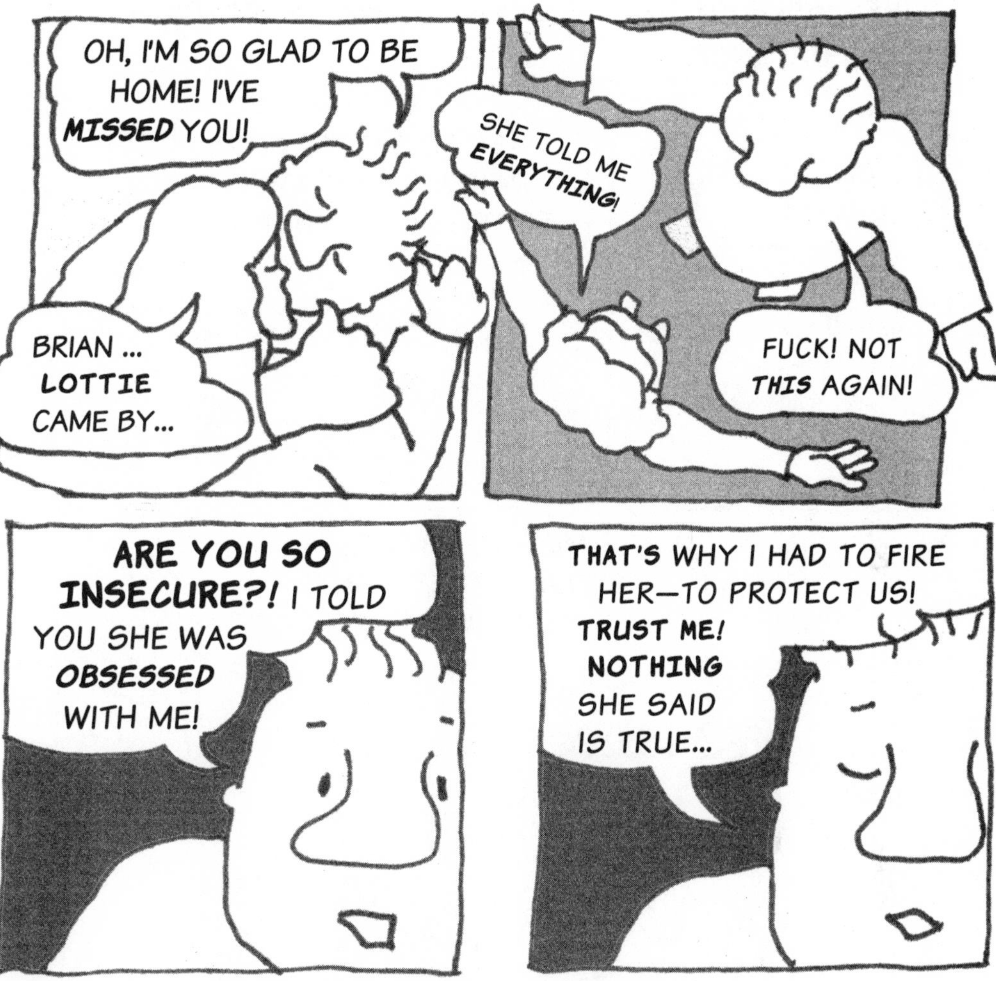
OH, I'M SO GLAD TO BE HOME! I'VE **MISSED** YOU!
BRIAN ... **LOTTIE** CAME BY...
SHE TOLD ME **EVERYTHING**!
FUCK! NOT **THIS** AGAIN!
ARE YOU SO INSECURE?! I TOLD YOU SHE WAS **OBSESSED** WITH ME!
THAT'S WHY I HAD TO FIRE HER—TO PROTECT US! **TRUST ME! NOTHING** SHE SAID IS TRUE...

LATER I GOT MAIL FROM LOTTIE.

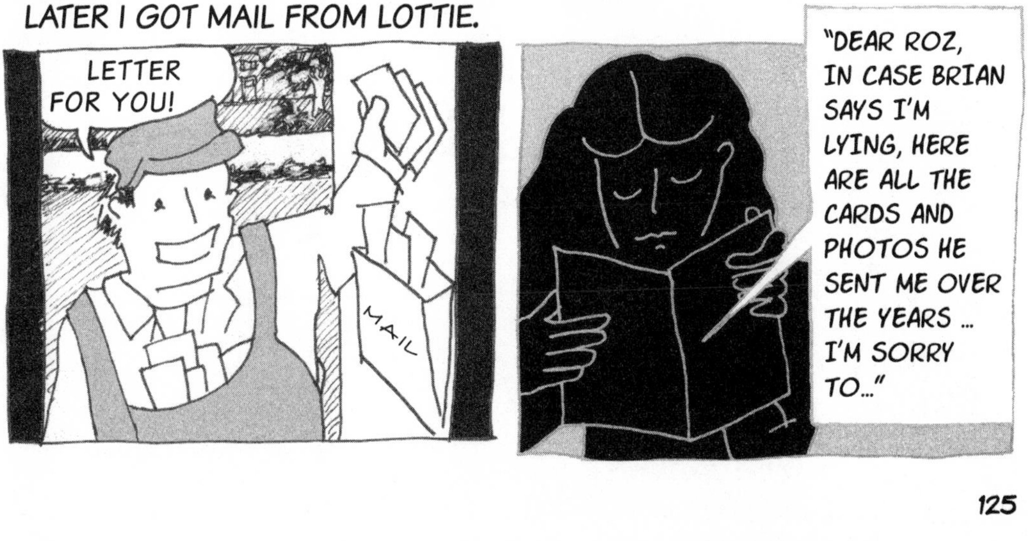
LETTER FOR YOU!
MAIL
"DEAR ROZ, IN CASE BRIAN SAYS I'M LYING, HERE ARE ALL THE CARDS AND PHOTOS HE SENT ME OVER THE YEARS ... I'M SORRY TO..."

I PREFERRED TO BELIEVE BRIAN. MEANWHILE, OTHER CRISES WERE HITTING ME LIKE TIDAL WAVES, KEEPING ME OFF BALANCE.

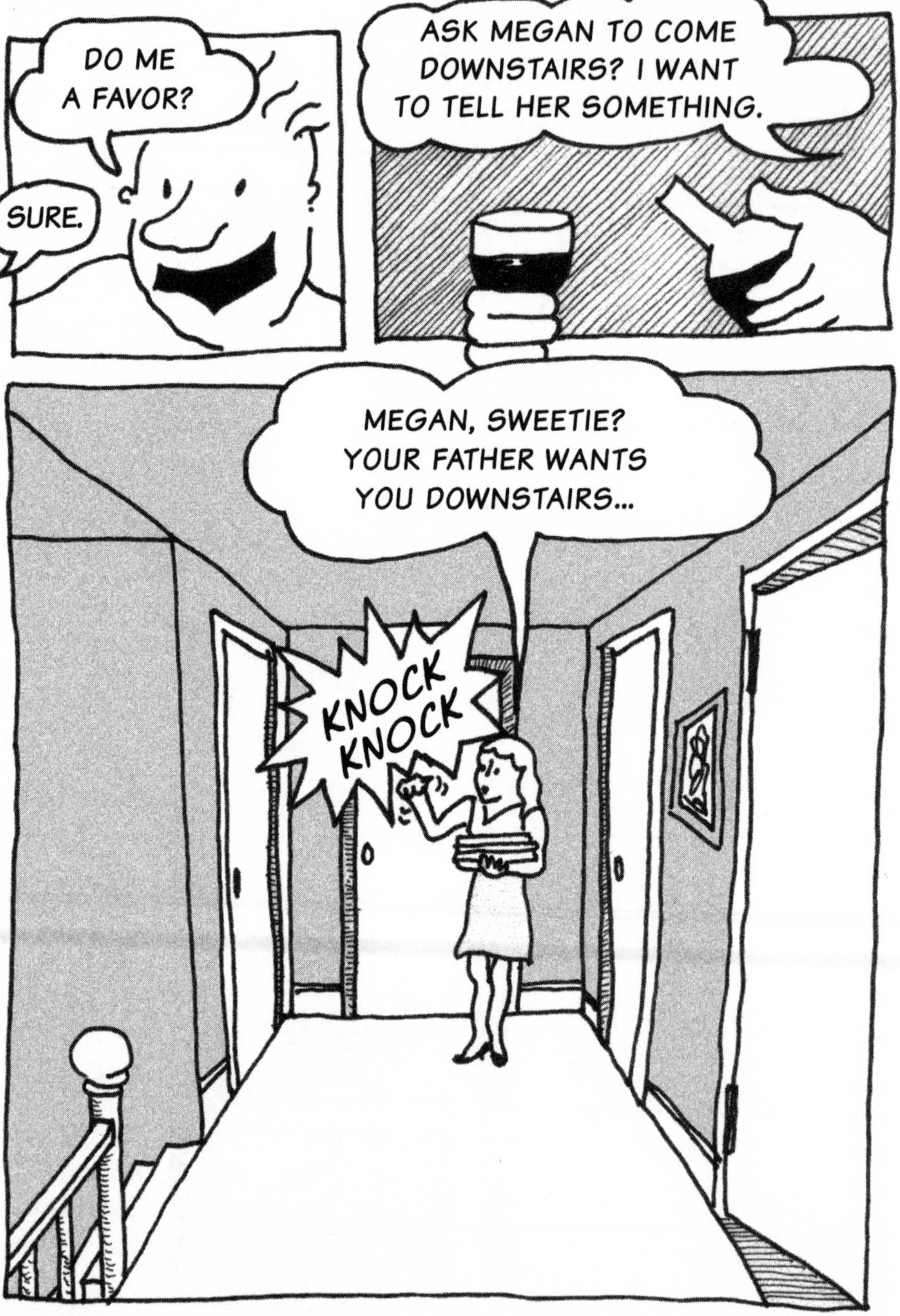
DO ME A FAVOR?
SURE.
ASK MEGAN TO COME DOWNSTAIRS? I WANT TO TELL HER SOMETHING.
MEGAN, SWEETIE? YOUR FATHER WANTS YOU DOWNSTAIRS...
KNOCK KNOCK

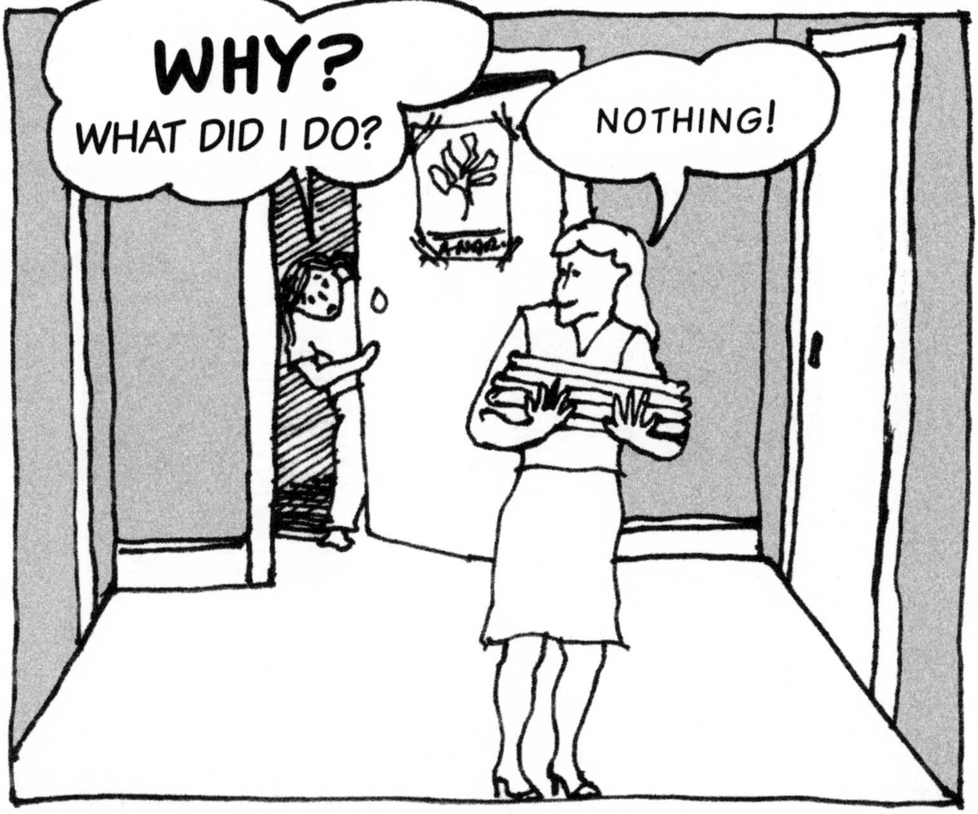
WHY?
WHAT DID I DO?
NOTHING!

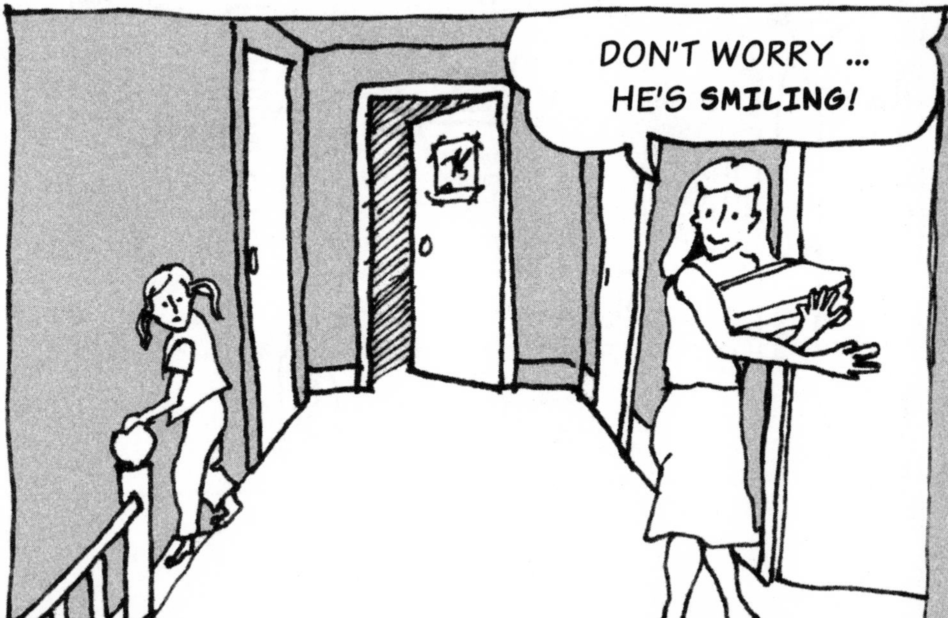
DON'T WORRY ...
HE'S SMILING!

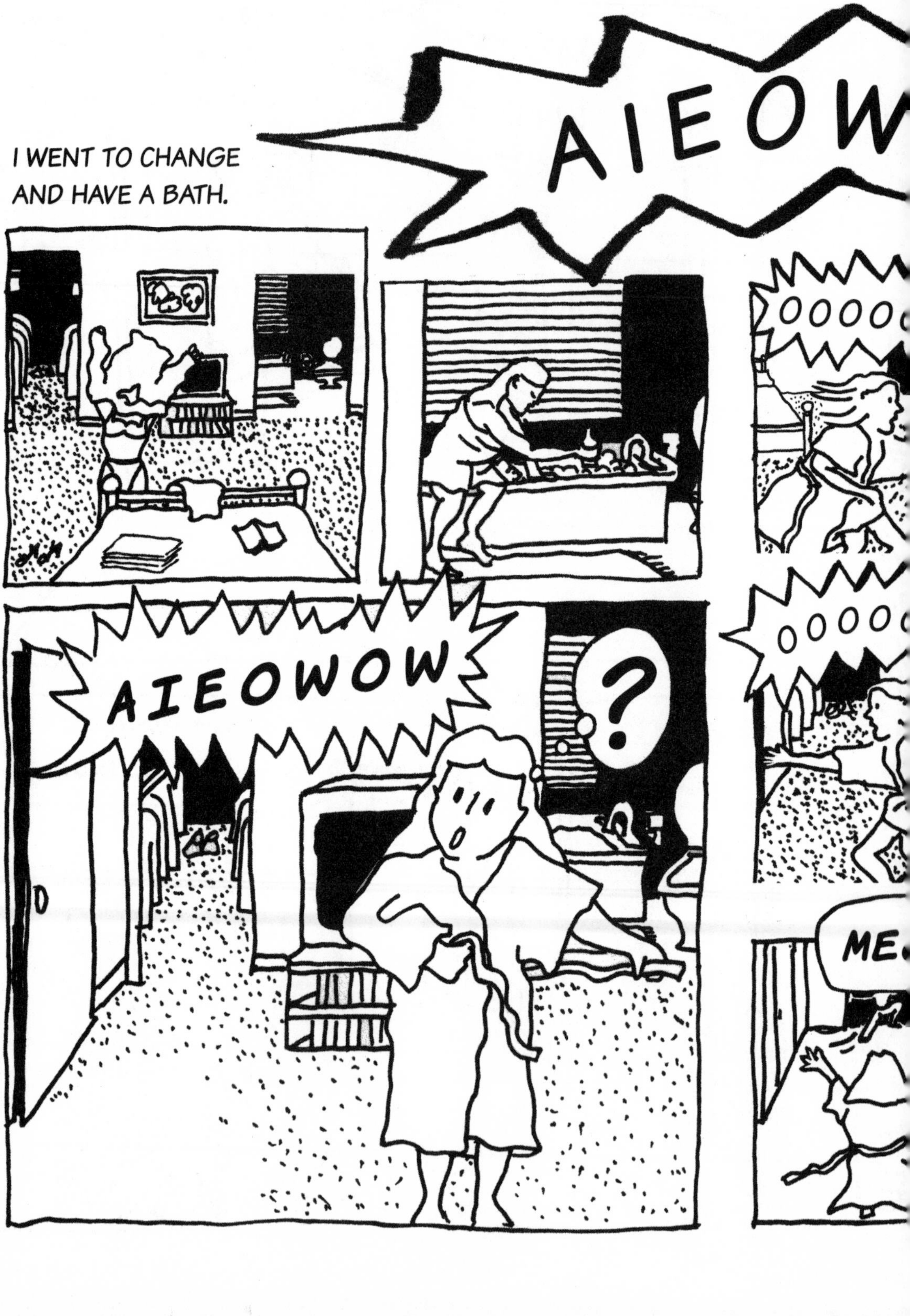
I WENT TO CHANGE AND HAVE A BATH.
AIEOW
OOOO
AIEOWOW
?
OOOO
ME.

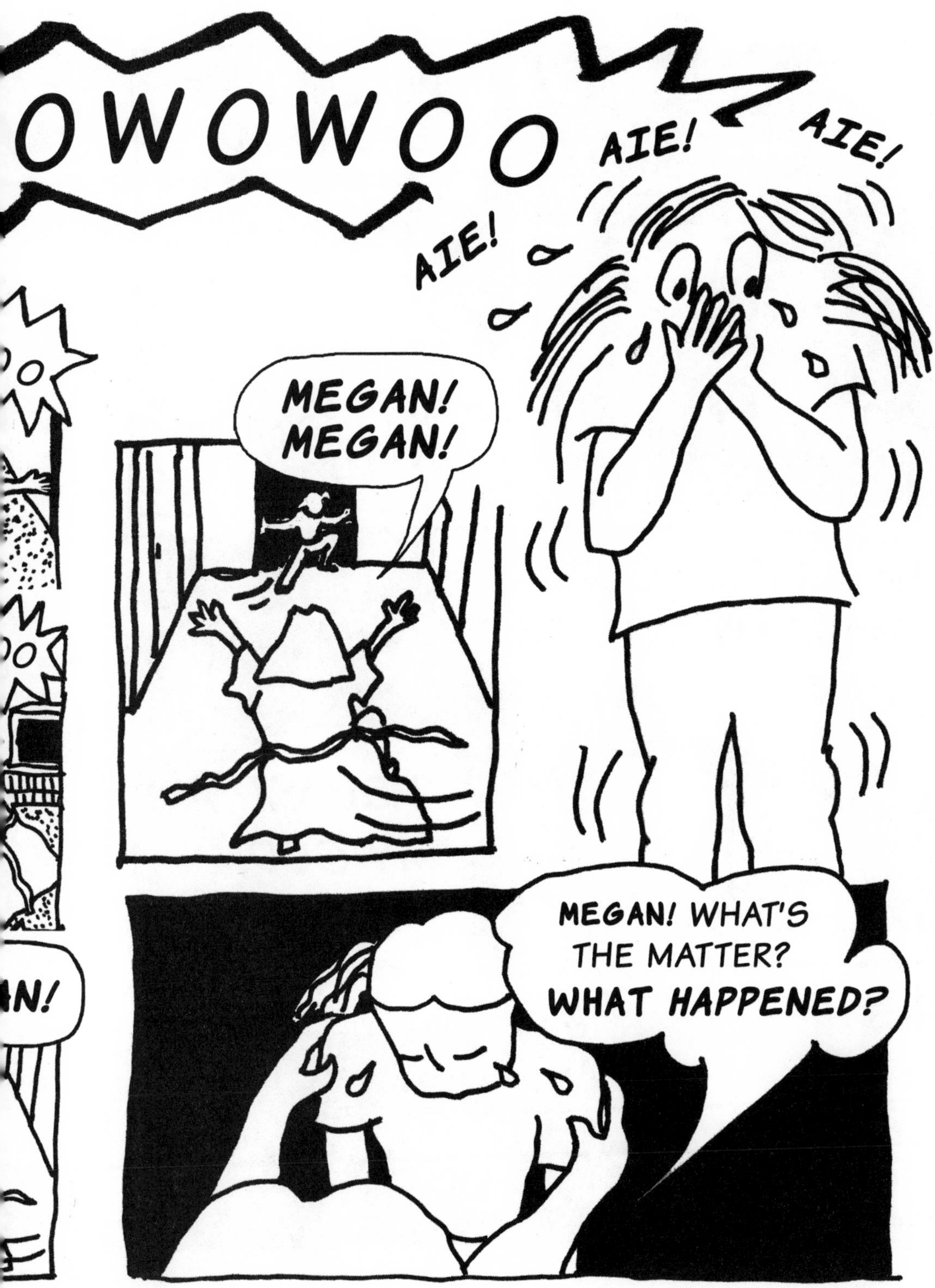
OWOWOO
AIE!
AIE!
AIE!
MEGAN! MEGAN!
AN!
MEGAN! WHAT'S THE MATTER? WHAT HAPPENED?

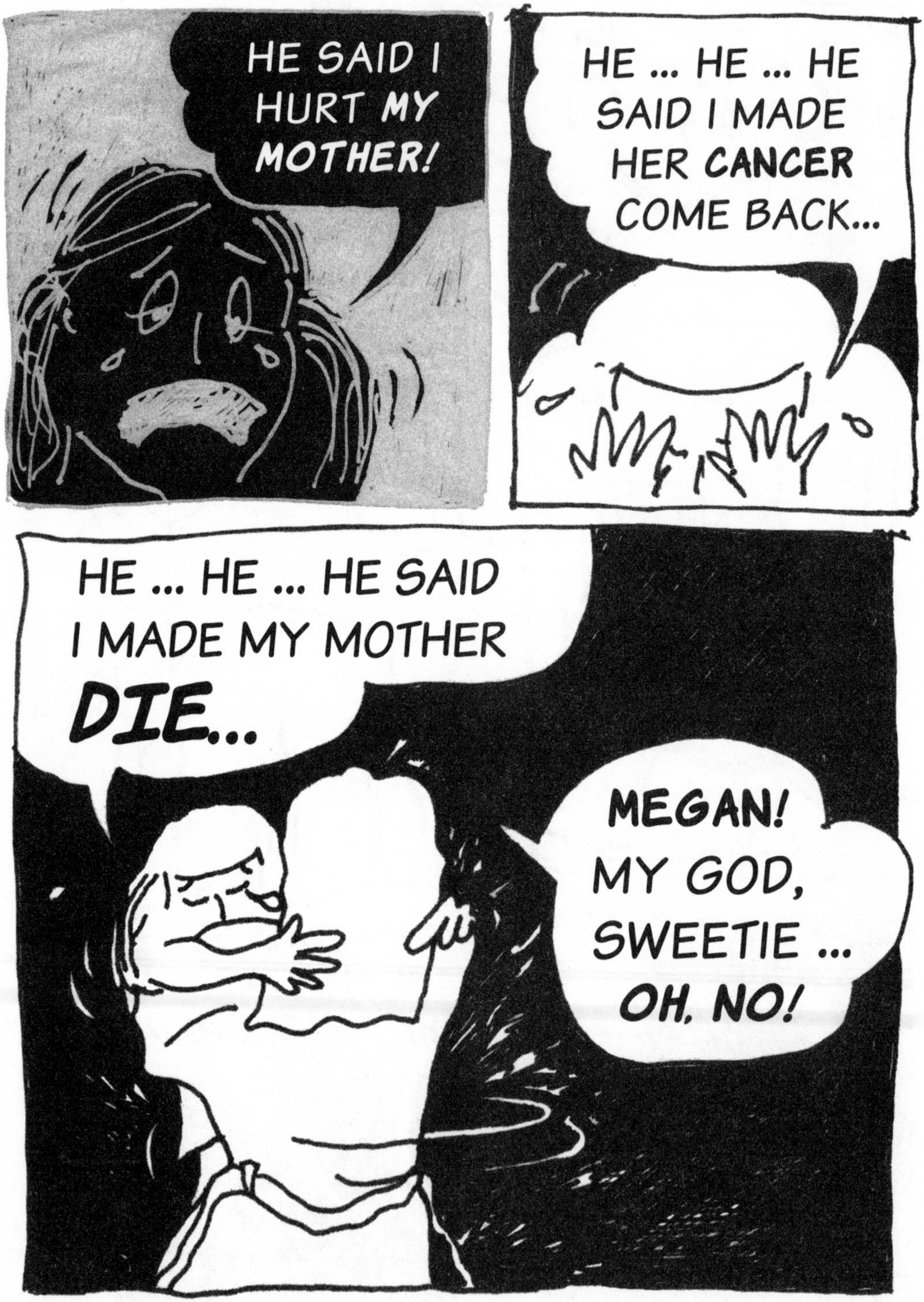
HE SAID I HURT MY MOTHER!
HE ... HE ... HE SAID I MADE HER CANCER COME BACK...
HE ... HE ... HE SAID I MADE MY MOTHER DIE...
MEGAN! MY GOD, SWEETIE ... OH, NO!

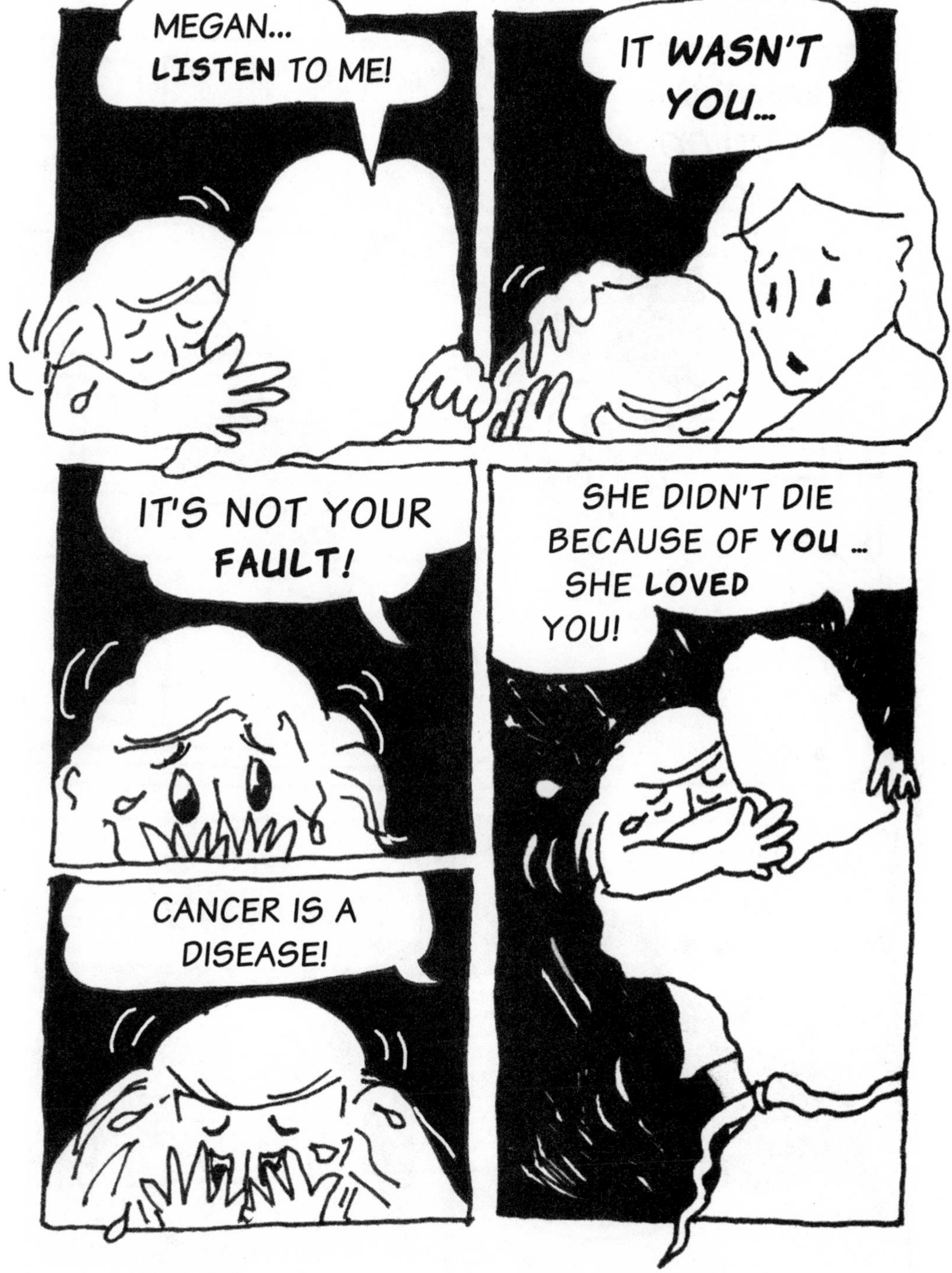
MEGAN... LISTEN TO ME!
IT WASN'T YOU...
IT'S NOT YOUR FAULT!
SHE DIDN'T DIE BECAUSE OF YOU ... SHE LOVED YOU!
CANCER IS A DISEASE!

I RAN DOWNSTAIRS, SHAKING WITH FURY. I FELT LIKE I HAD LED A LAMB TO SLAUGHTER.

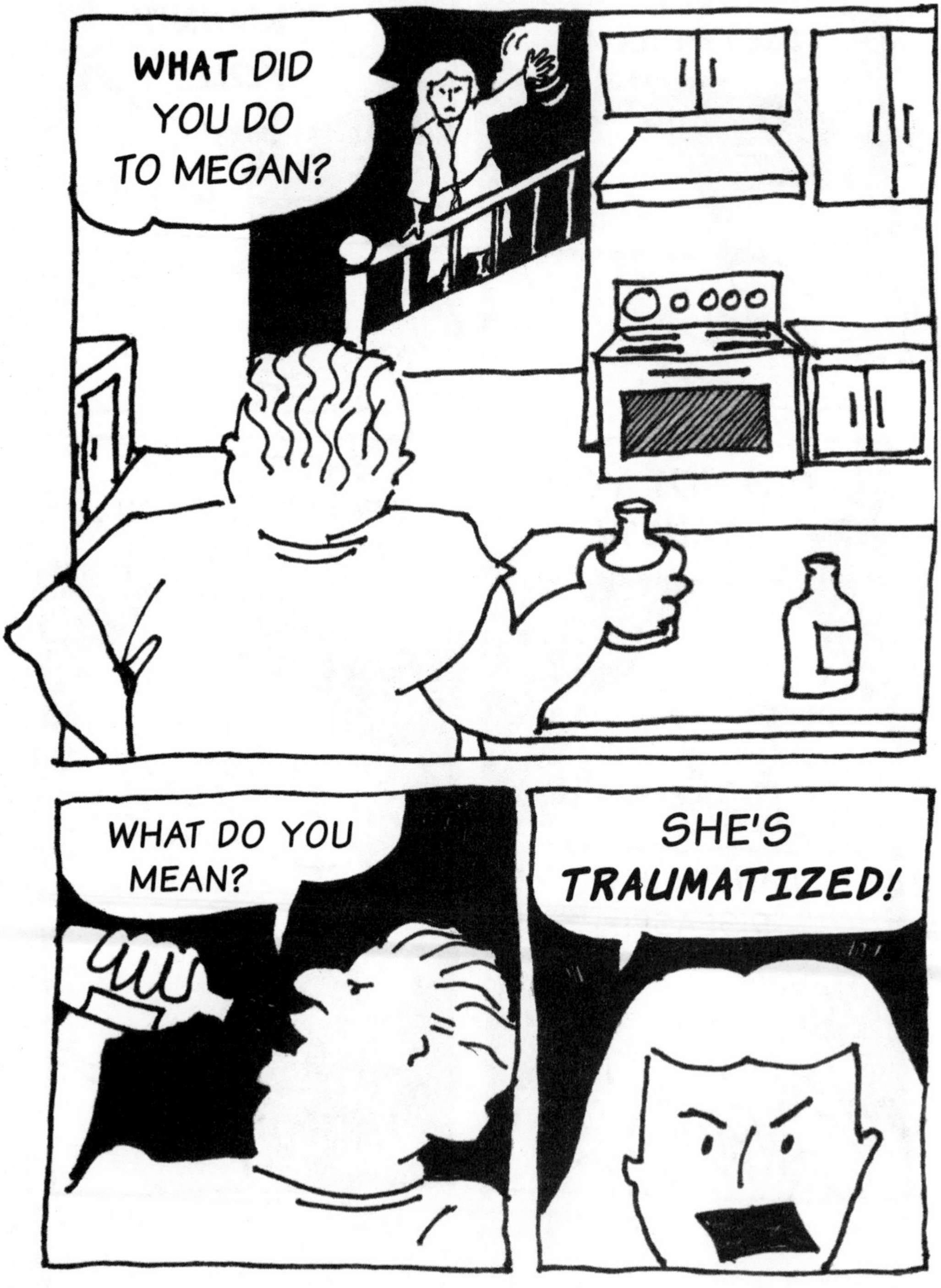
WHAT DID YOU DO TO MEGAN?
WHAT DO YOU MEAN?
SHE'S ***TRAUMATIZED!***

HE DANCED AROUND THE KITCHEN. I THOUGHT HE HAD GONE MAD.

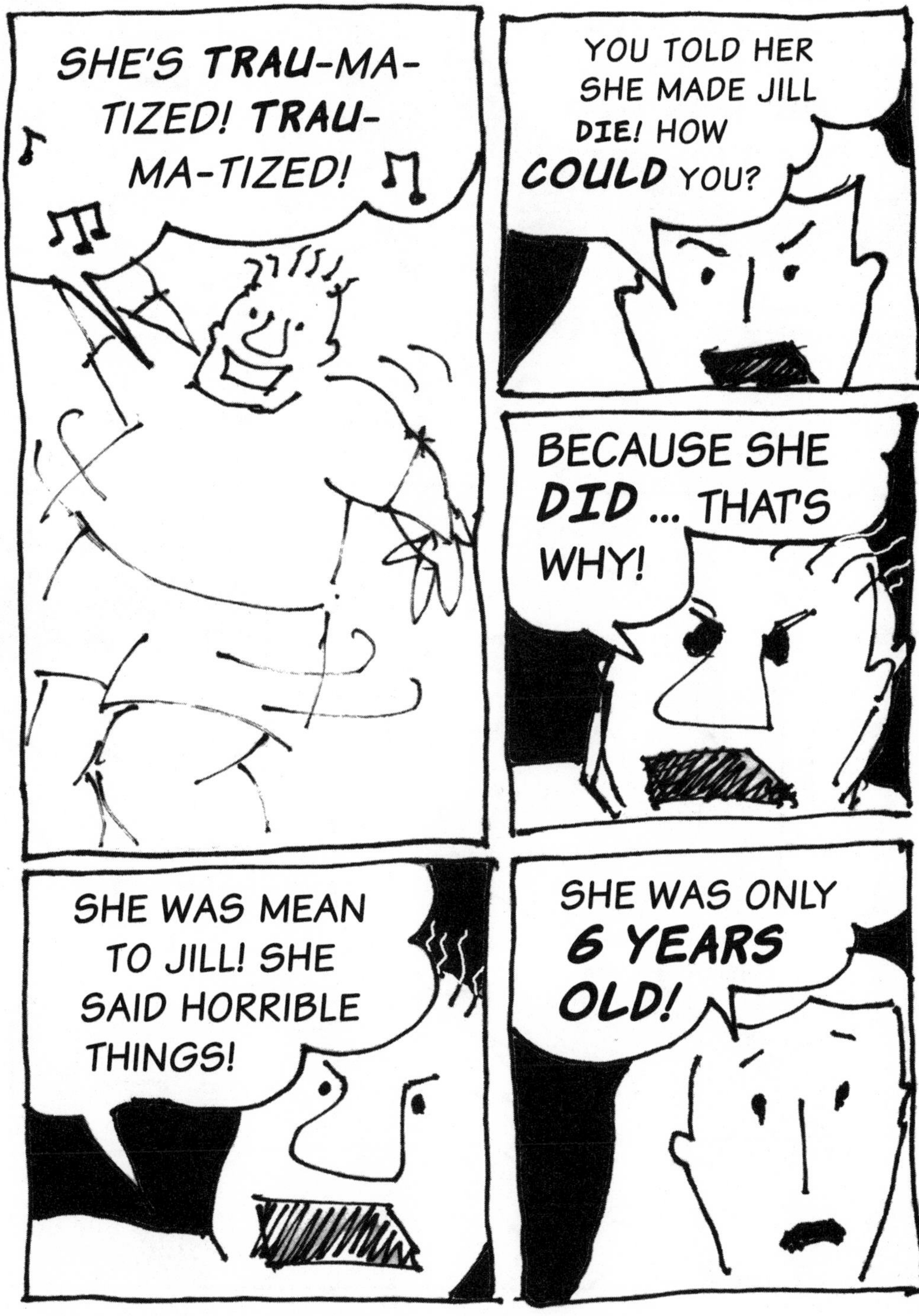
SHE'S **TRAU**-MA-TIZED! **TRAU**-MA-TIZED!
YOU TOLD HER SHE MADE JILL **DIE**! HOW **COULD** YOU?
BECAUSE SHE ***DID*** ... THAT'S WHY!
SHE WAS MEAN TO JILL! SHE SAID HORRIBLE THINGS!
SHE WAS ONLY ***6 YEARS OLD!***

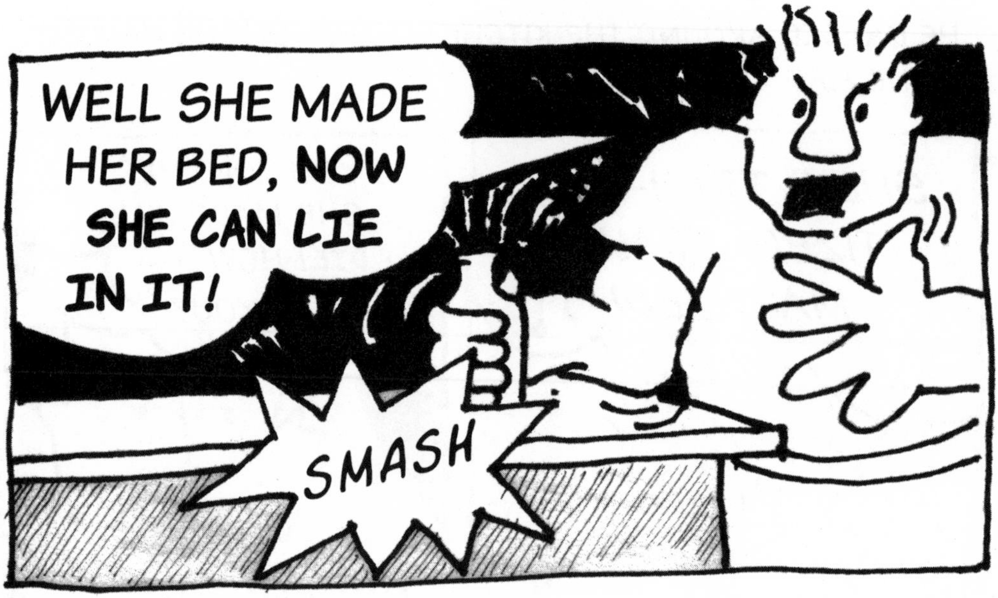
WELL SHE MADE HER BED, NOW SHE CAN LIE IN IT!
SMASH

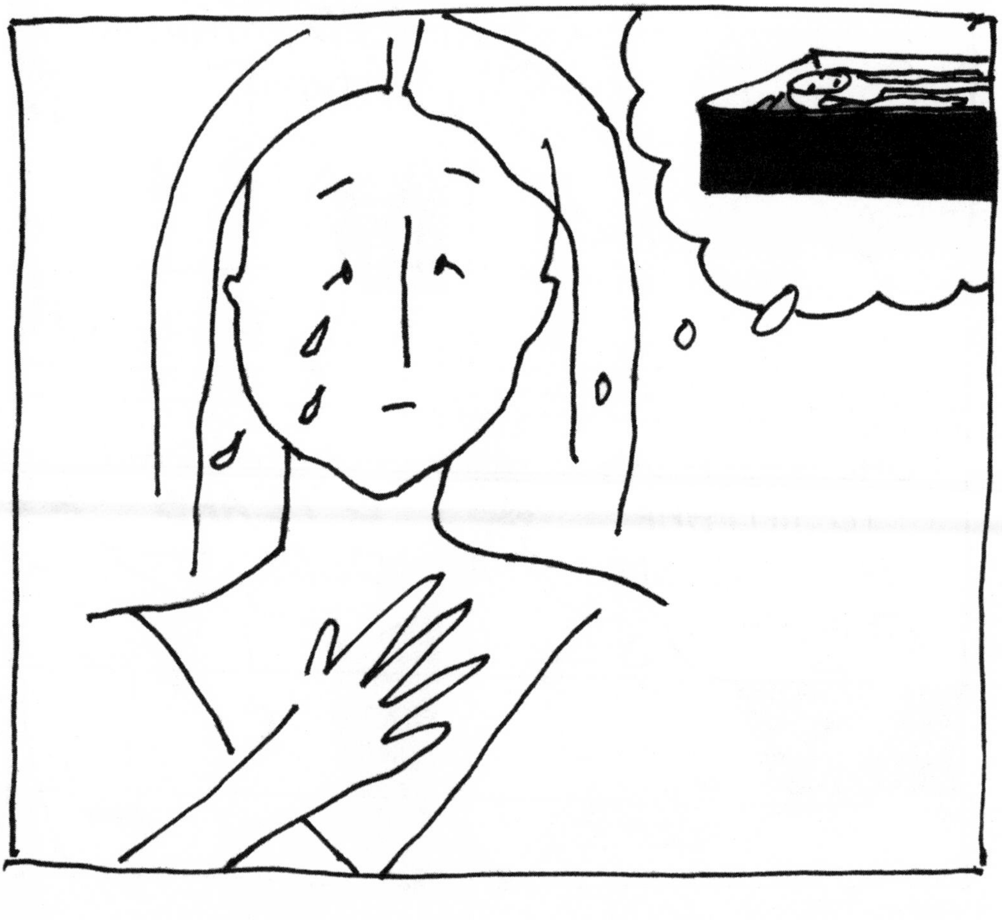

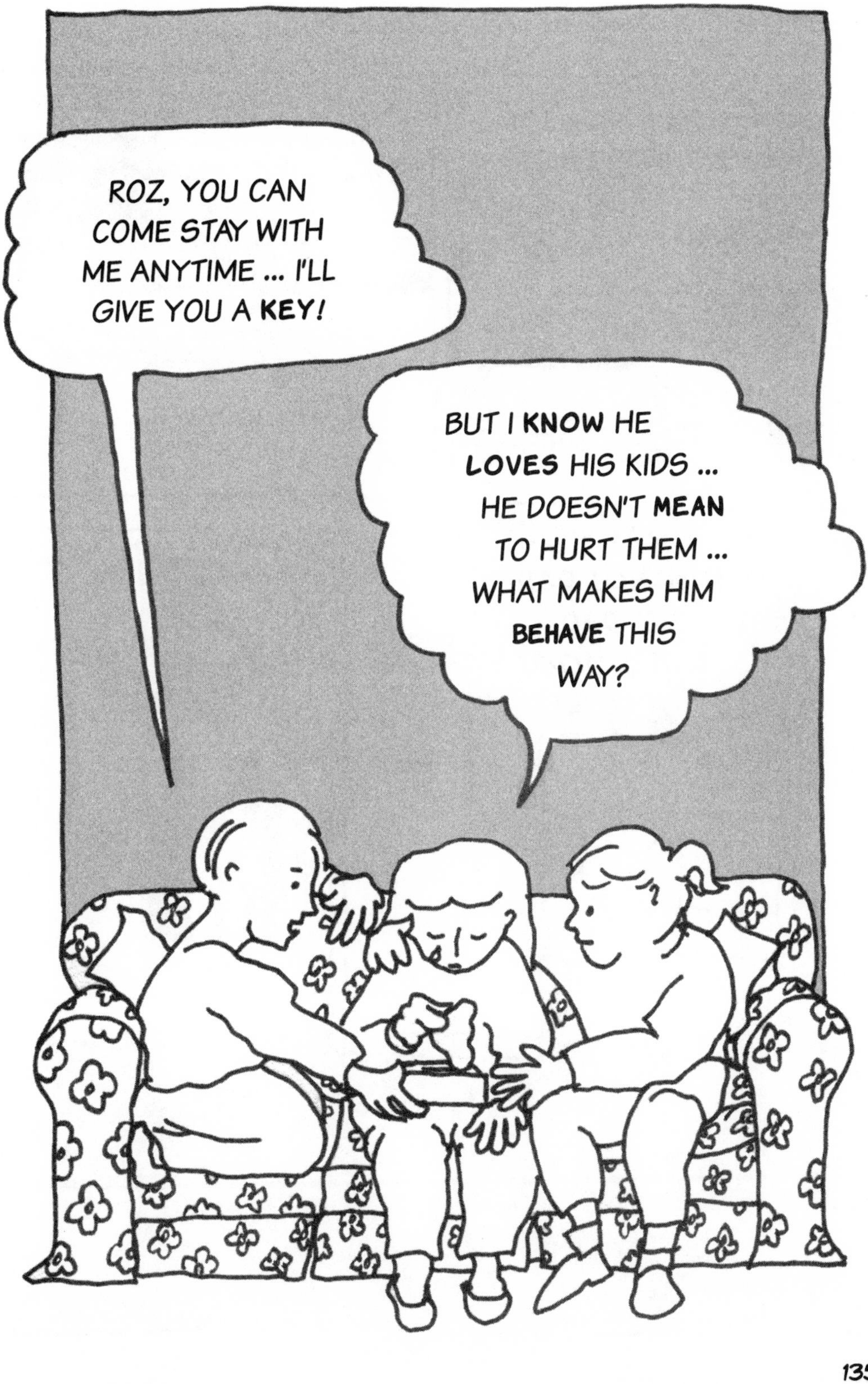
ROZ, YOU CAN COME STAY WITH ME ANYTIME ... I'LL GIVE YOU A KEY!
BUT I KNOW HE LOVES HIS KIDS ... HE DOESN'T MEAN TO HURT THEM ... WHAT MAKES HIM BEHAVE THIS WAY?

THEN ONE DAY I CAME HOME UNEXPECTEDLY...

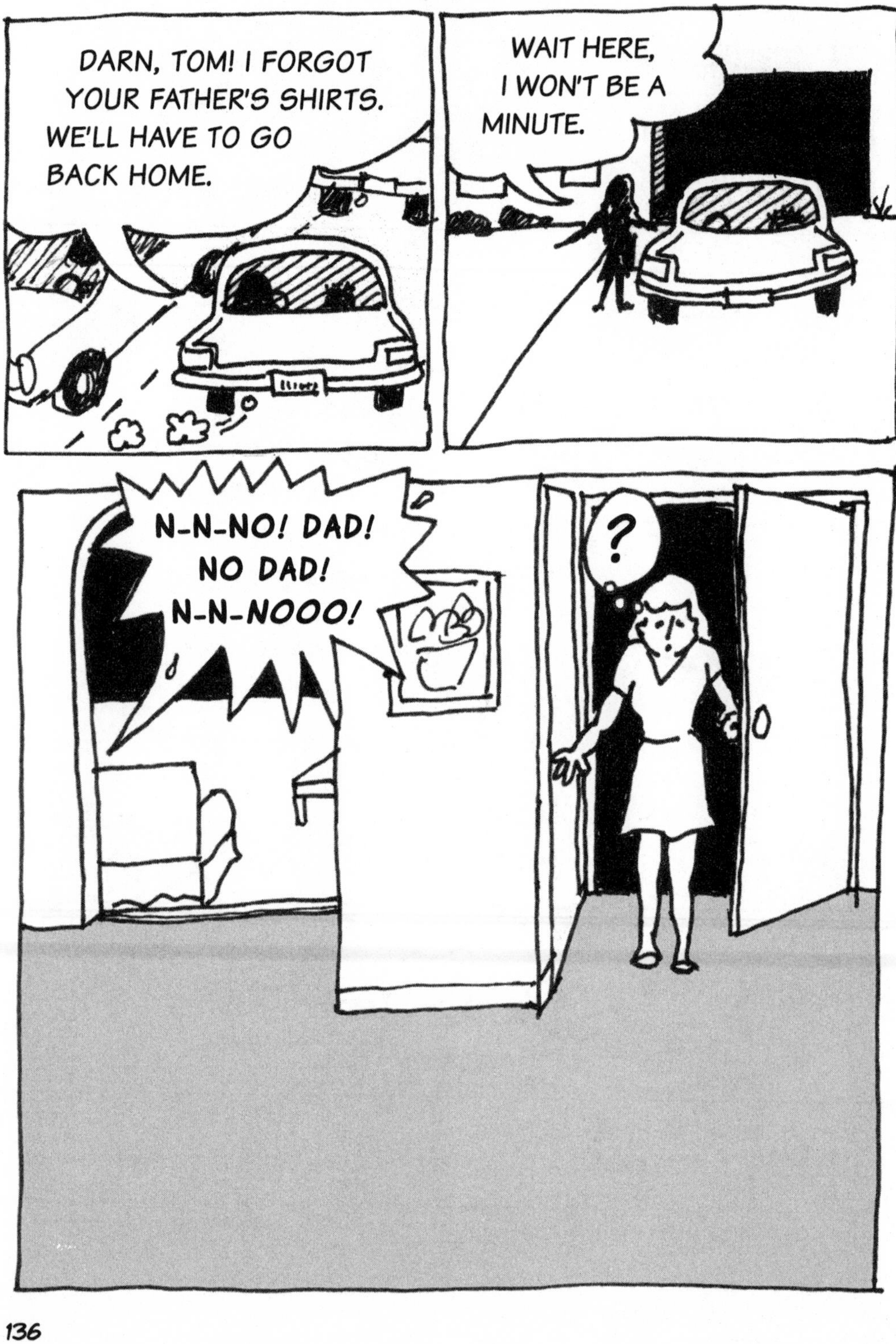
DARN, TOM! I FORGOT YOUR FATHER'S SHIRTS. WE'LL HAVE TO GO BACK HOME.
WAIT HERE, I WON'T BE A MINUTE.
N-N-NO! DAD! NO DAD! N-N-NOOO!
?

I CAN'T EXPLAIN WHAT I SENSED WHEN I ENTERED THE ROOM, BUT ALL THE HAIRS ON THE BACK OF MY NECK STOOD UP.

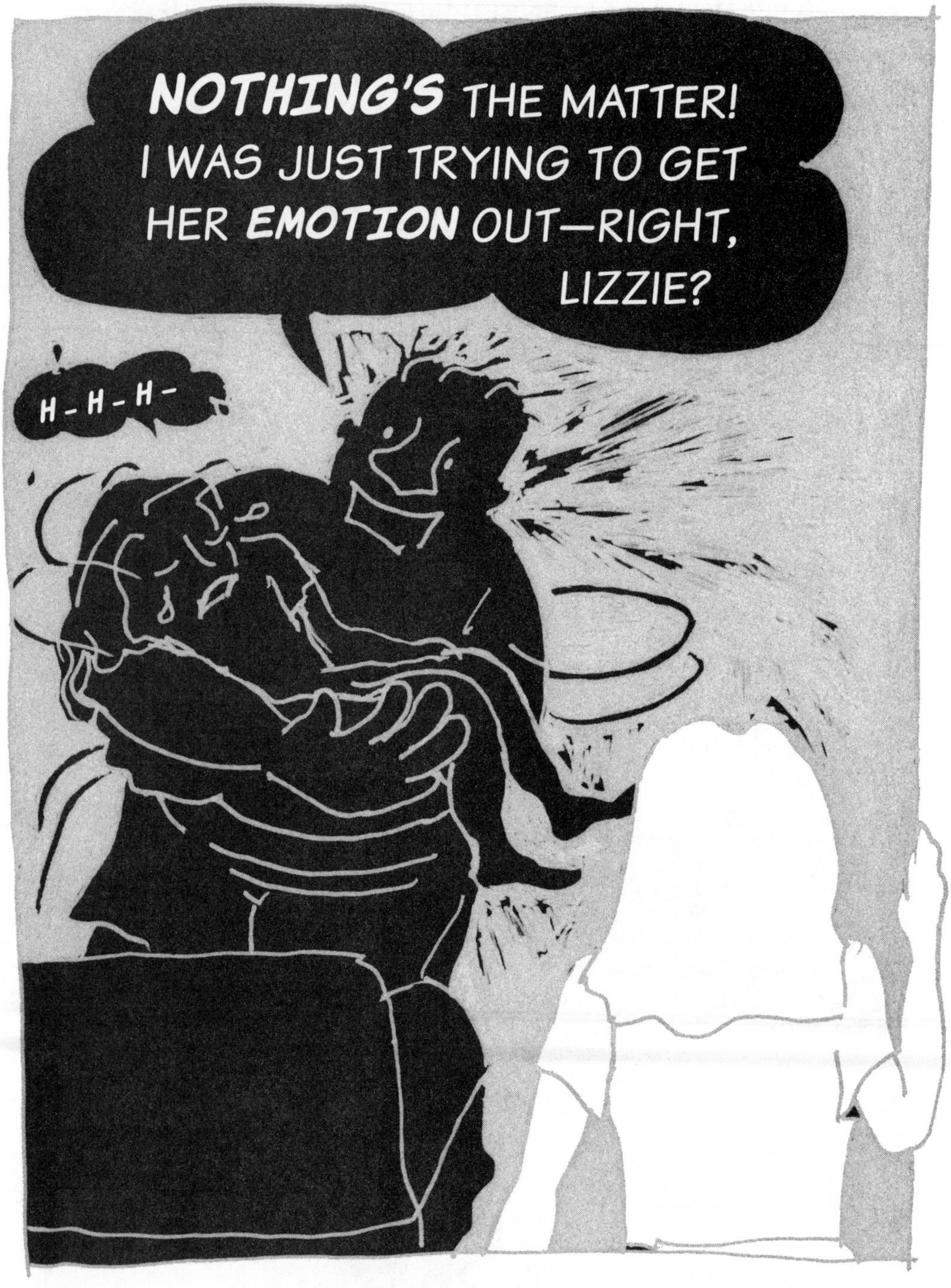
NOTHING'S THE MATTER! I WAS JUST TRYING TO GET HER EMOTION OUT—RIGHT, LIZZIE?
H-H-H-

I FELT LIKE SOMETHING DEEPLY DISTURBING HAD HAPPENED, EVEN THOUGH I HADN'T SEEN ANYTHING AT ALL.

I KNEW I SHOULD CONFIDE IN SOMEONE WITH AUTHORITY, SO I WENT, NERVOUSLY, TO THE CHILDREN'S PEDIATRICIAN...

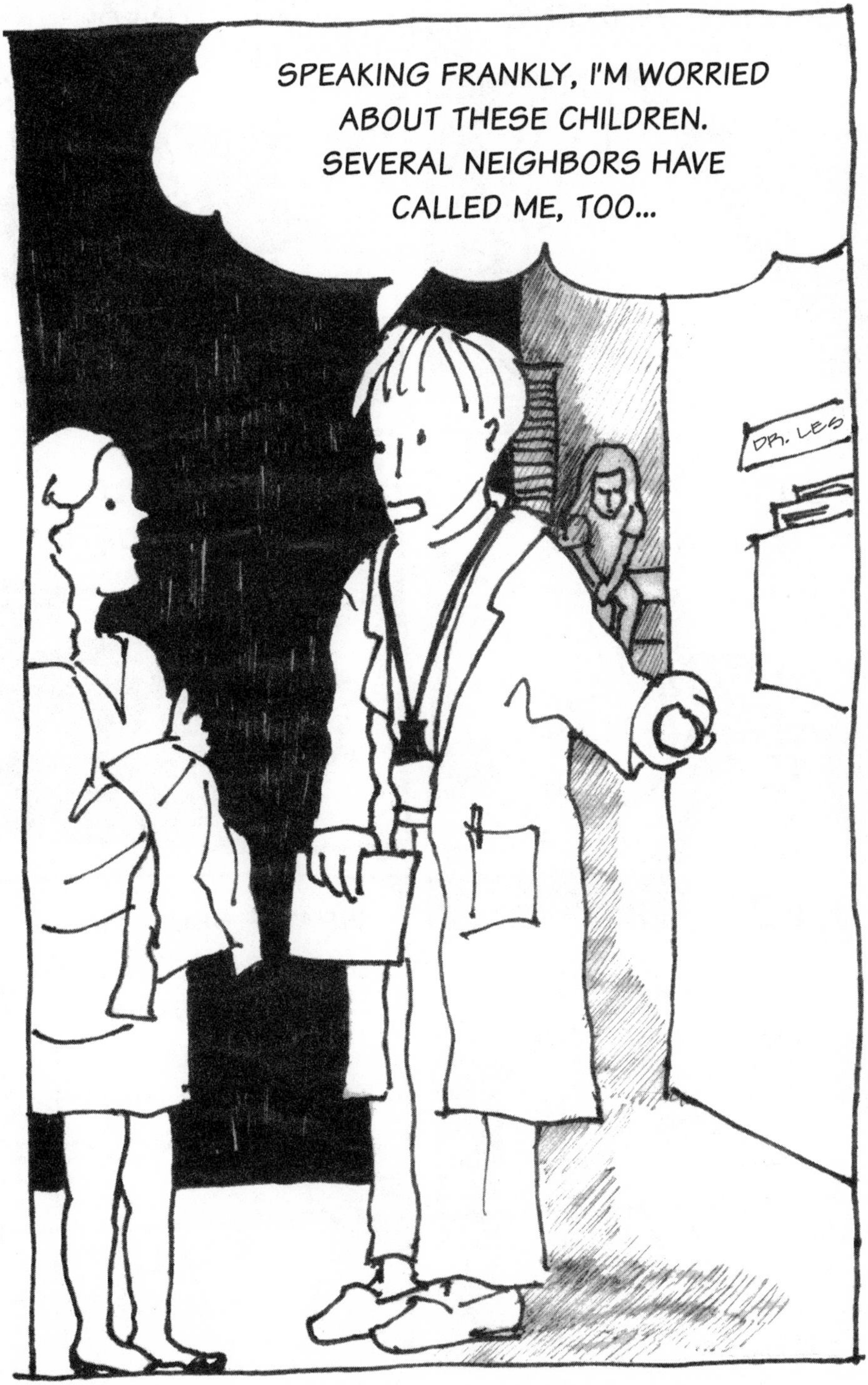
SPEAKING FRANKLY, I'M WORRIED ABOUT THESE CHILDREN. SEVERAL NEIGHBORS HAVE CALLED ME, TOO...
DR. LES

I'VE CONSIDERED CALLING CHILDREN'S AID...

BUT THERE IS NO PHYSICAL EVIDENCE...

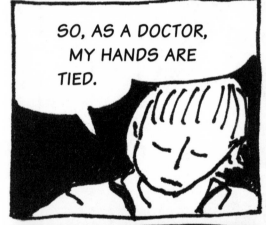

SO, AS A DOCTOR, MY HANDS ARE TIED.

YOU COULD CALL, THOUGH.

HOW CAN I DO THAT?

WHAT IF BRIAN FINDS OUT? WHAT IF IT JUST MAKES THINGS WORSE? MAYBE I'M IMAGINING THINGS.

FIVE YEARS IN, THINGS WENT FROM BAD TO WORSE. JIM WAS EXPERIMENTING WITH DRUGS, AND MEGAN KEPT RUNNING AWAY FROM HOME. WHEN LIZZIE TURNED 10...

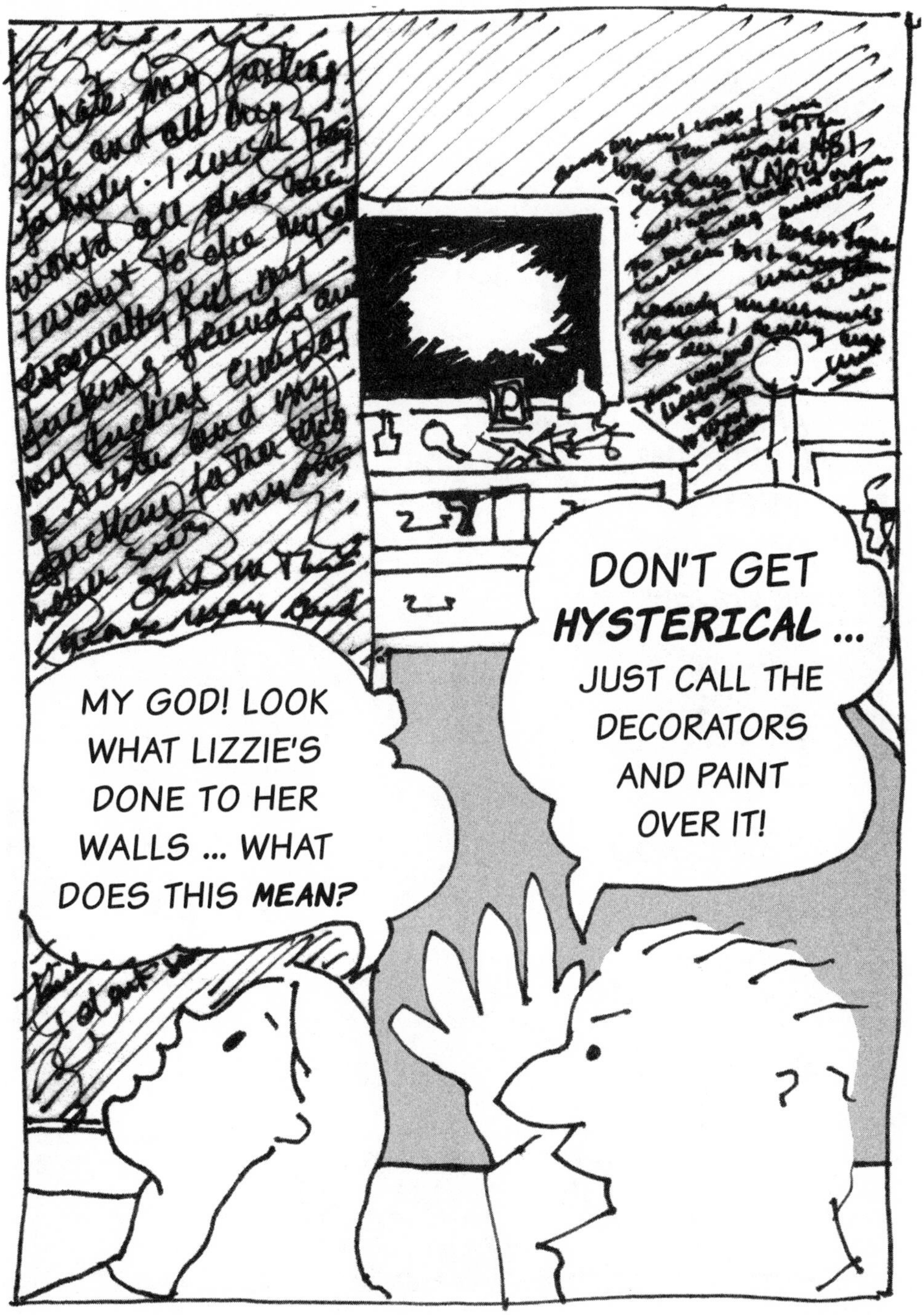
MY GOD! LOOK WHAT LIZZIE'S DONE TO HER WALLS ... WHAT DOES THIS MEAN?
DON'T GET HYSTERICAL ... JUST CALL THE DECORATORS AND PAINT OVER IT!

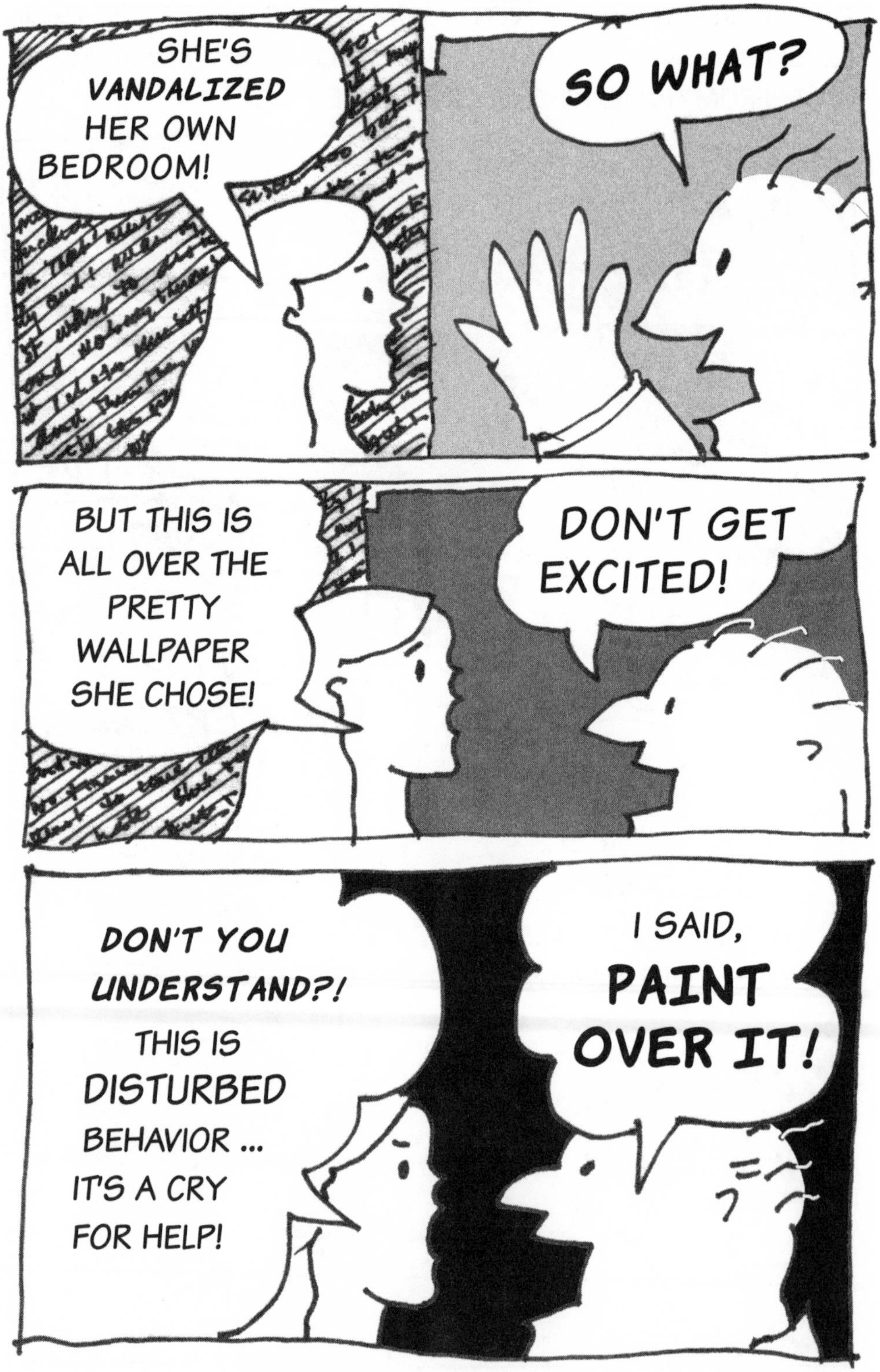
SHE'S VANDALIZED HER OWN BEDROOM!
SO WHAT?
BUT THIS IS ALL OVER THE PRETTY WALLPAPER SHE CHOSE!
DON'T GET EXCITED!
DON'T YOU UNDERSTAND?! THIS IS DISTURBED BEHAVIOR ... IT'S A CRY FOR HELP!
I SAID, PAINT OVER IT!

THEN AT DINNER ONE EVENING...

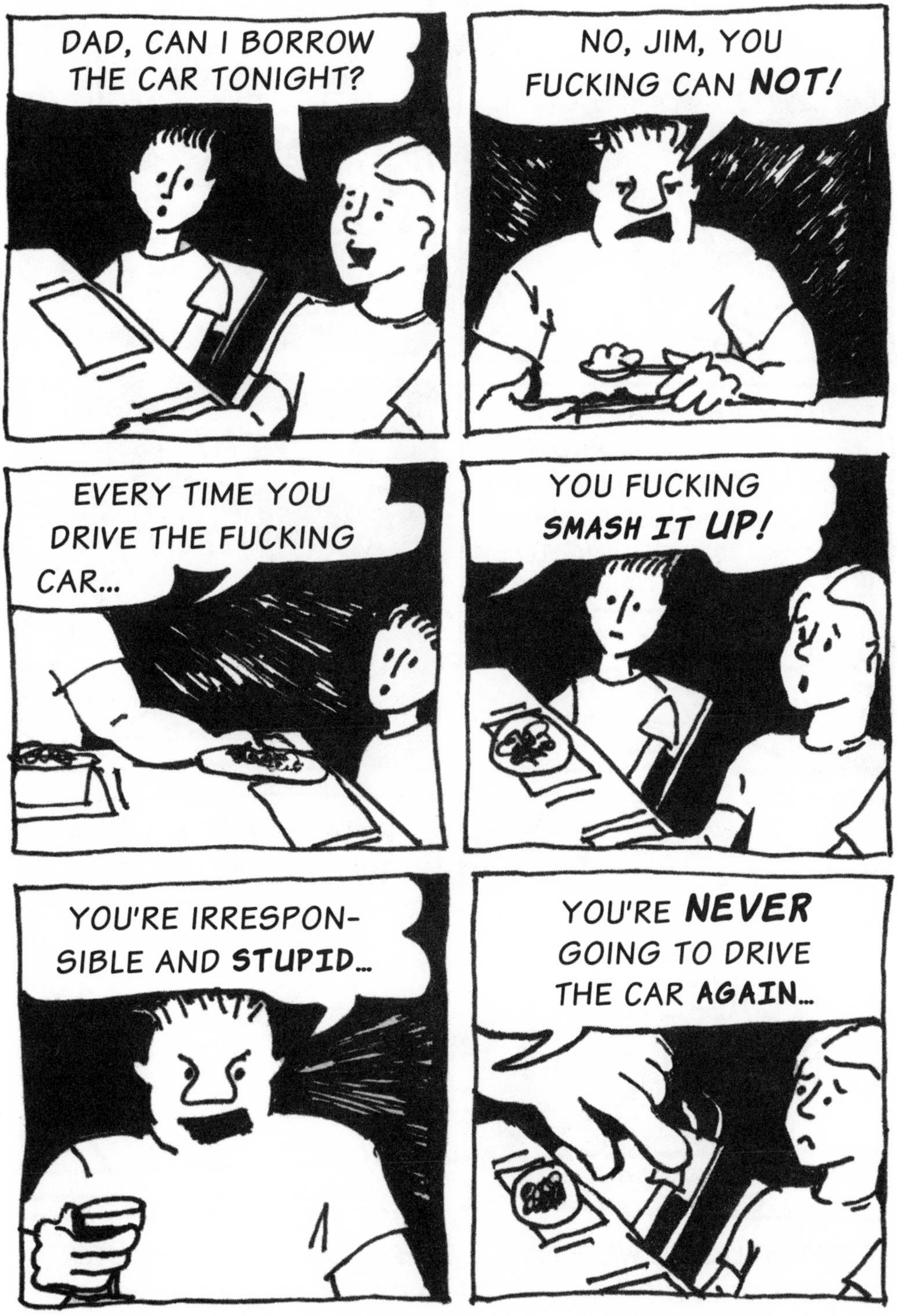
DAD, CAN I BORROW THE CAR TONIGHT?
NO, JIM, YOU FUCKING CAN NOT!
EVERY TIME YOU DRIVE THE FUCKING CAR...
YOU FUCKING SMASH IT UP!
YOU'RE IRRESPONSIBLE AND STUPID...
YOU'RE NEVER GOING TO DRIVE THE CAR AGAIN...

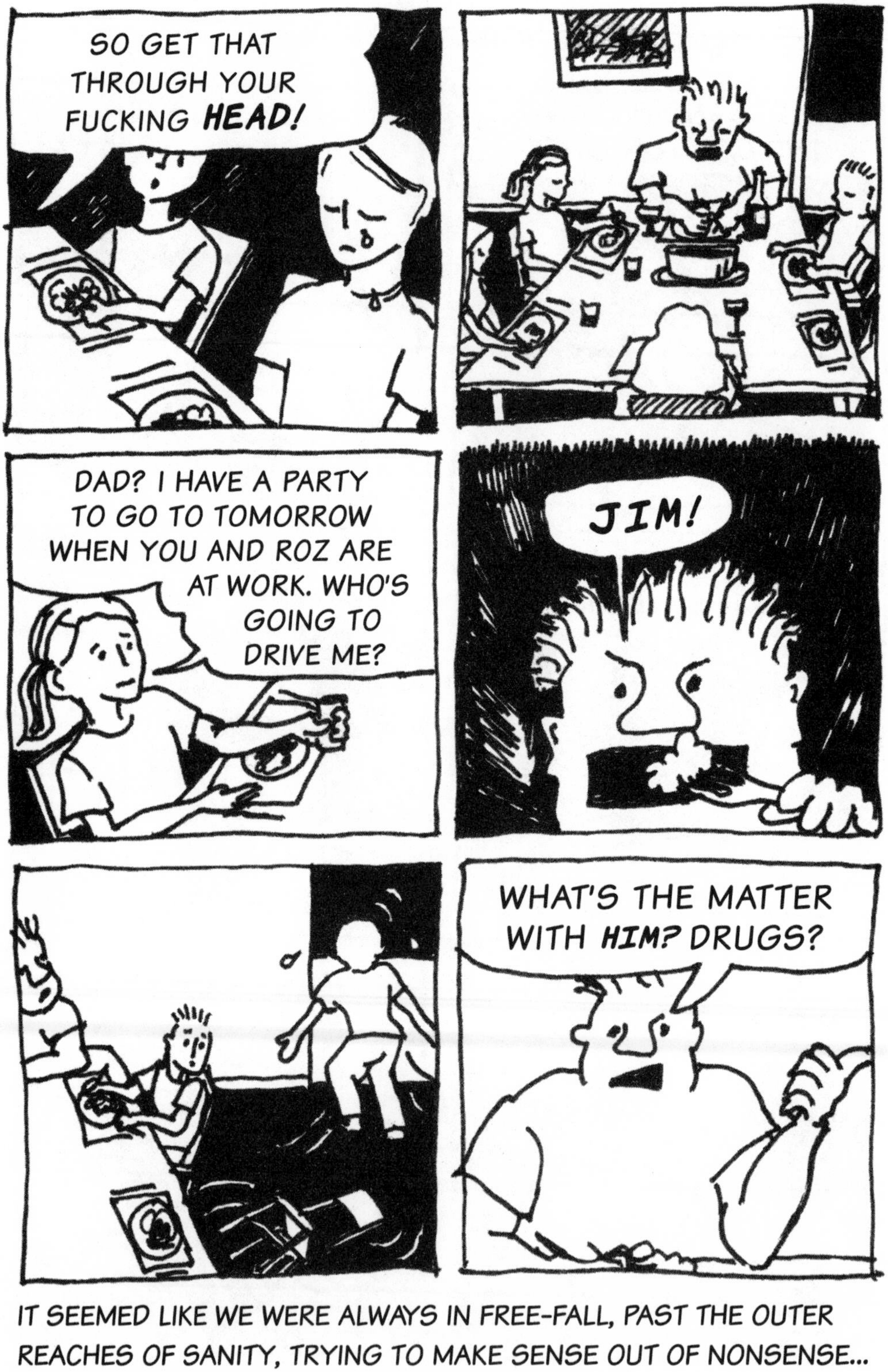
SO GET THAT THROUGH YOUR FUCKING **HEAD!**
DAD? I HAVE A PARTY TO GO TO TOMORROW WHEN YOU AND ROZ ARE AT WORK. WHO'S GOING TO DRIVE ME?
JIM!
WHAT'S THE MATTER WITH **HIM?** DRUGS?

IT SEEMED LIKE WE WERE ALWAYS IN FREE-FALL, PAST THE OUTER REACHES OF SANITY, TRYING TO MAKE SENSE OUT OF NONSENSE...

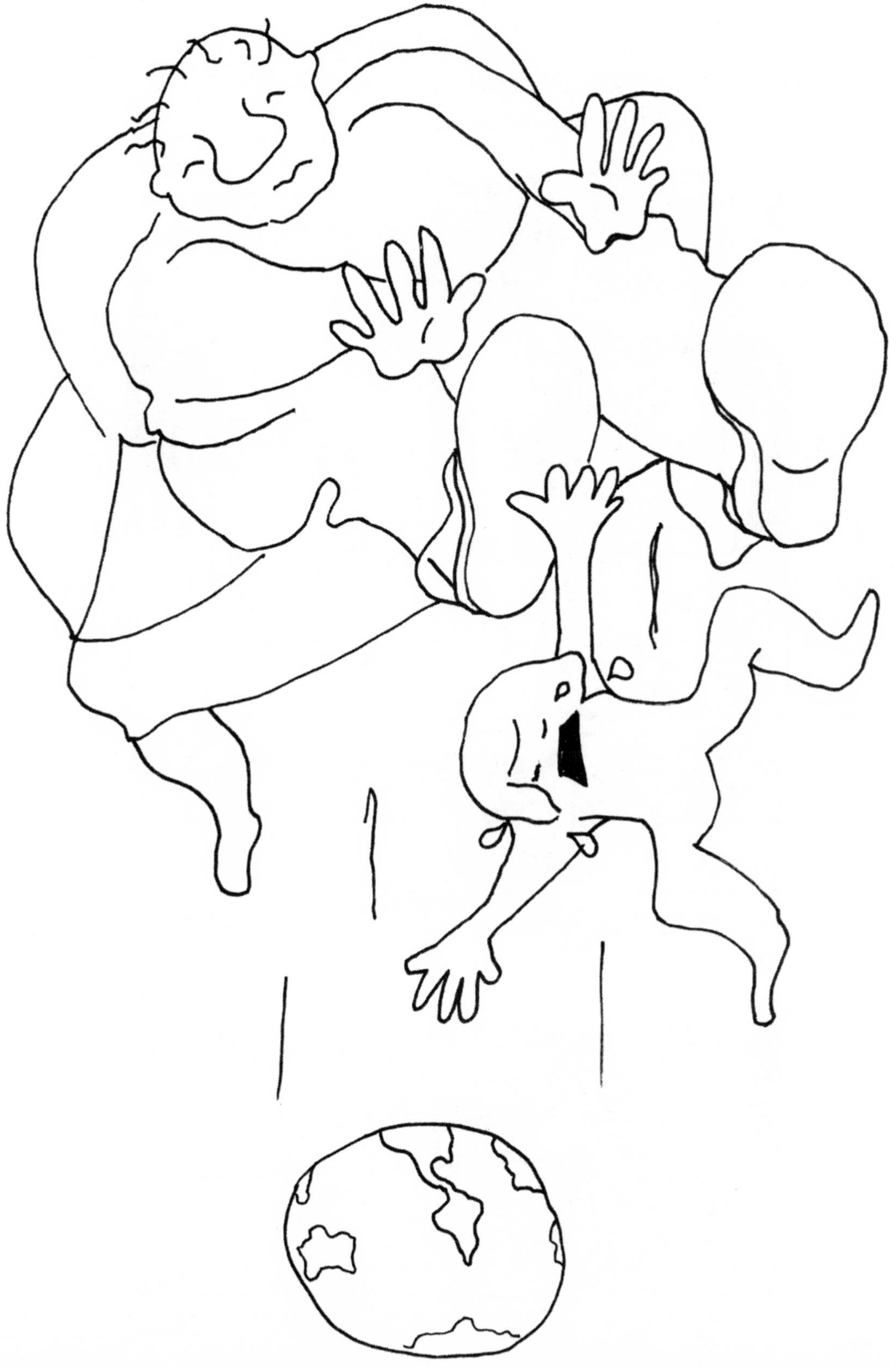

ONE EVENING, BRIAN WAS PREPARING AN EMPLOYEE'S REVIEW. HE BEGAN MUSING OUT LOUD, TALKING TO HIMSELF.

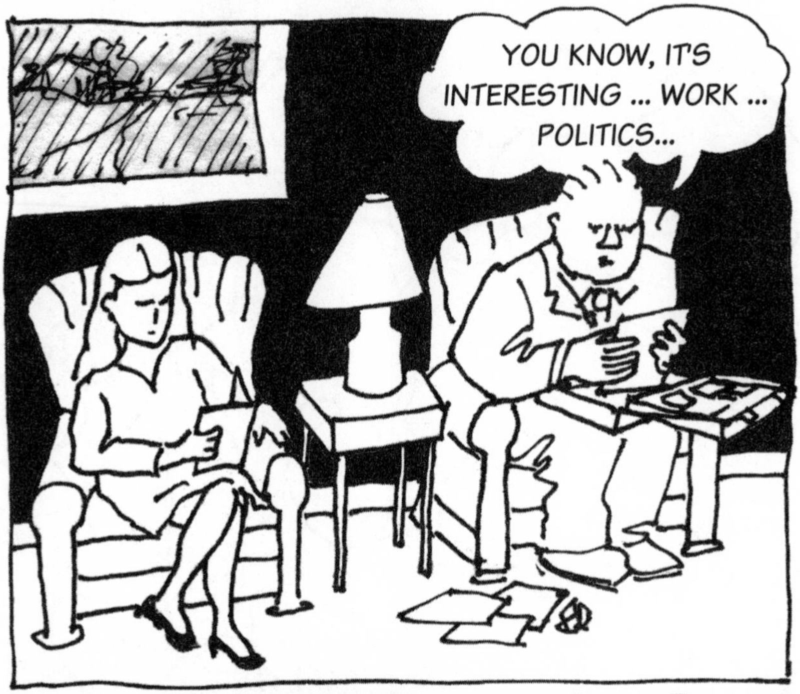
YOU KNOW, IT'S INTERESTING ... WORK ... POLITICS...

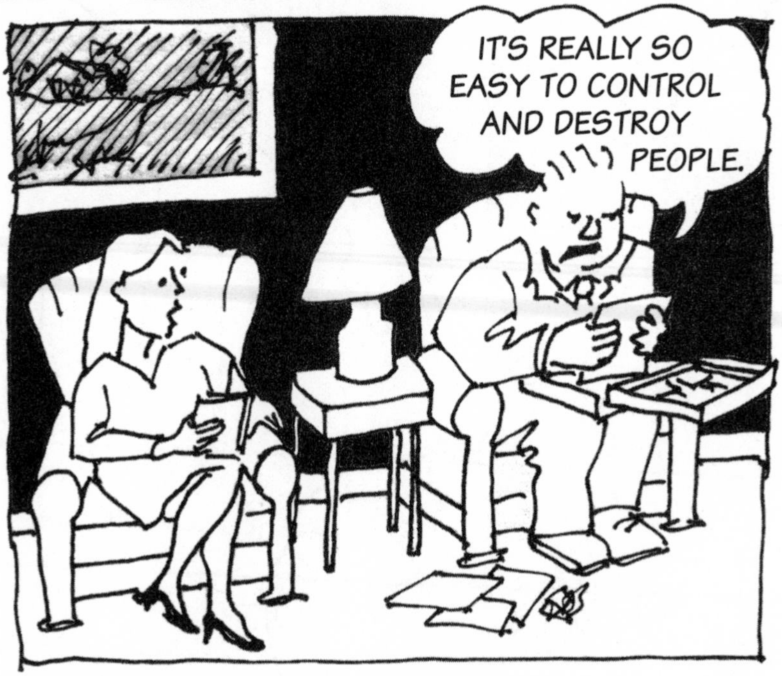
IT'S REALLY SO EASY TO CONTROL AND DESTROY PEOPLE.

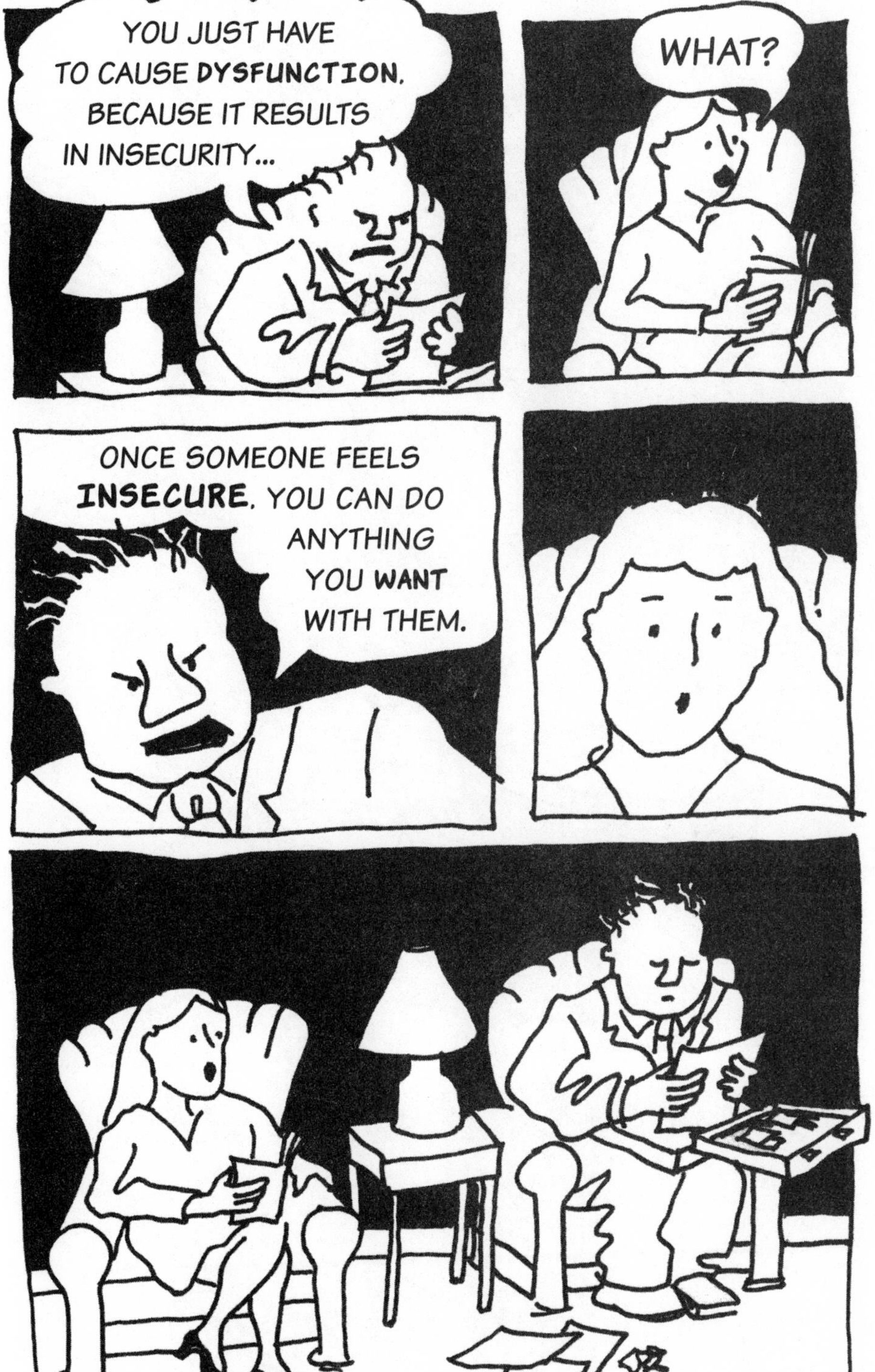
YOU JUST HAVE TO CAUSE DYSFUNCTION, BECAUSE IT RESULTS IN INSECURITY...
WHAT?
ONCE SOMEONE FEELS INSECURE, YOU CAN DO ANYTHING YOU WANT WITH THEM.

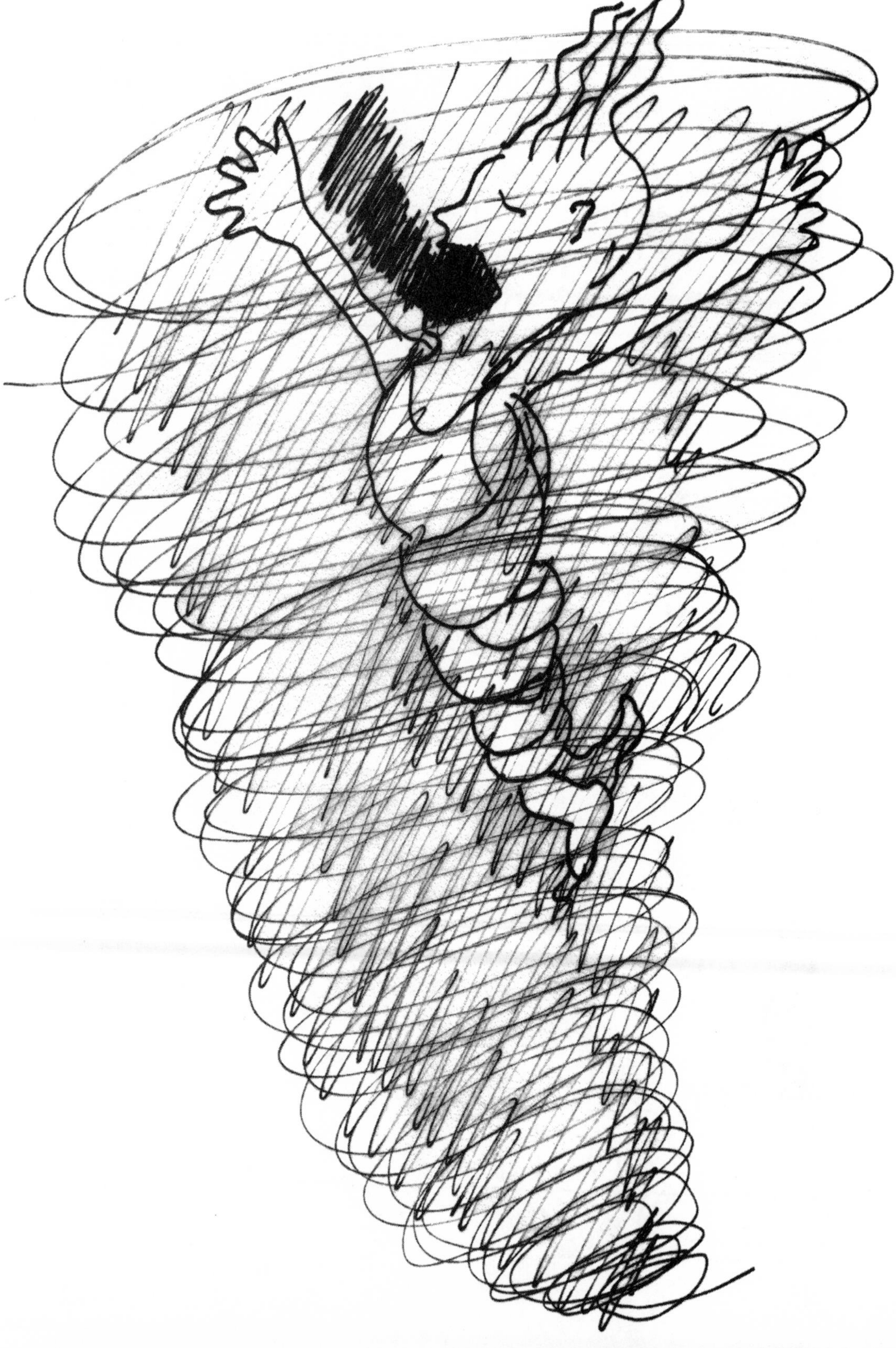

OUR SEX LIFE HAD BEEN GRADUALLY CHANGING, BUT I HADN'T WANTED TO ADMIT IT. HE HAD ASKED ME TO PRETEND TO BE OTHER WOMEN, WHICH MADE ME FEEL INTERCHANGEABLE. NOW HIS DEMANDS FELT INCREASINGLY DEMEANING.

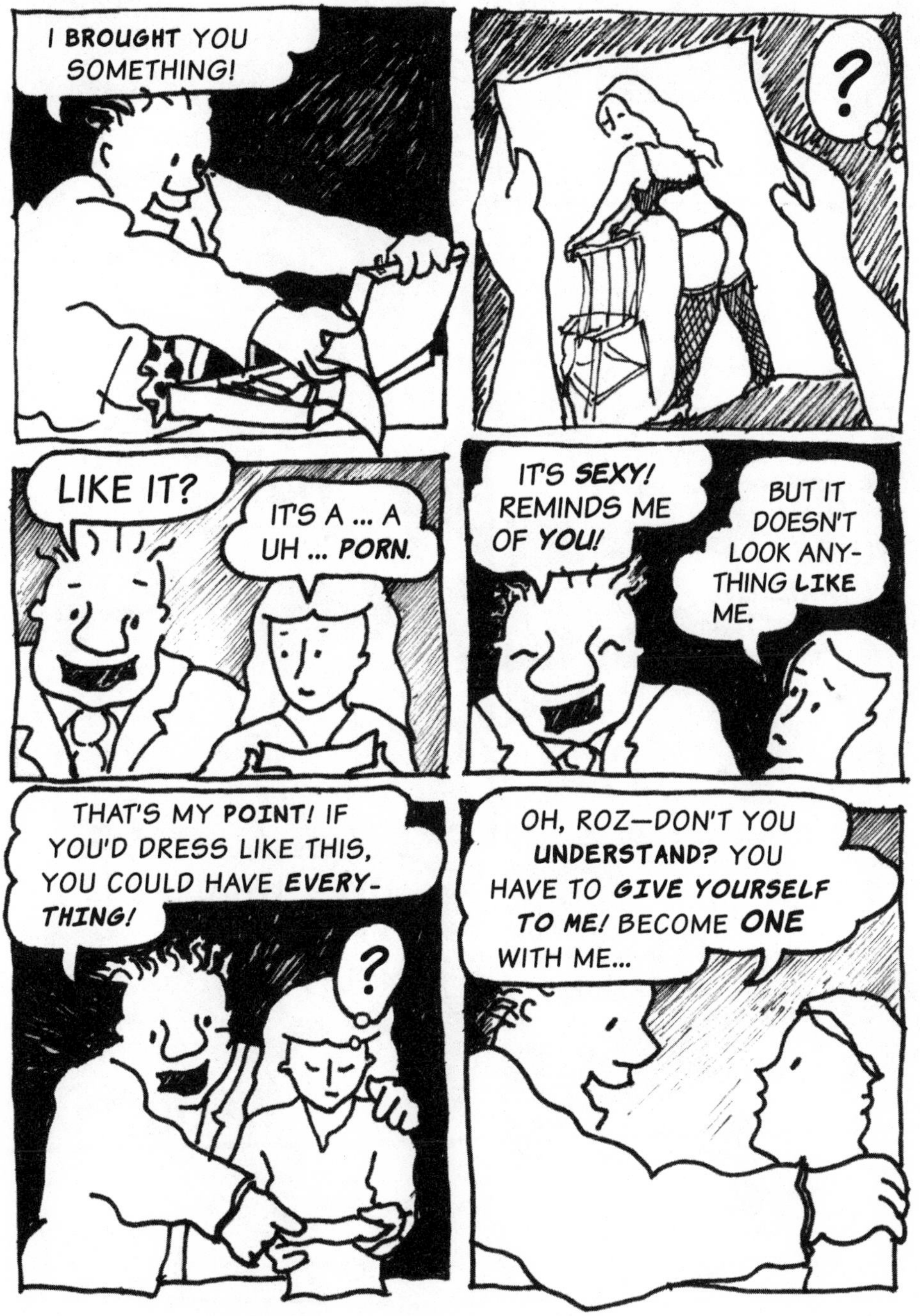
I BROUGHT YOU SOMETHING!
?
LIKE IT?
IT'S A ... A UH ... PORN.
IT'S SEXY! REMINDS ME OF YOU!
BUT IT DOESN'T LOOK ANY-THING LIKE ME.
THAT'S MY POINT! IF YOU'D DRESS LIKE THIS, YOU COULD HAVE EVERY-THING!
?
OH, ROZ—DON'T YOU UNDERSTAND? YOU HAVE TO GIVE YOURSELF TO ME! BECOME ONE WITH ME...

DESPITE WHAT HE PROMISED ME WHEN WE FIRST MET, THE POSSIBILITY OF BRIAN'S INFIDELITY STARTED TO SINK IN, SO I BEGAN TO WORRY ABOUT STD'S.

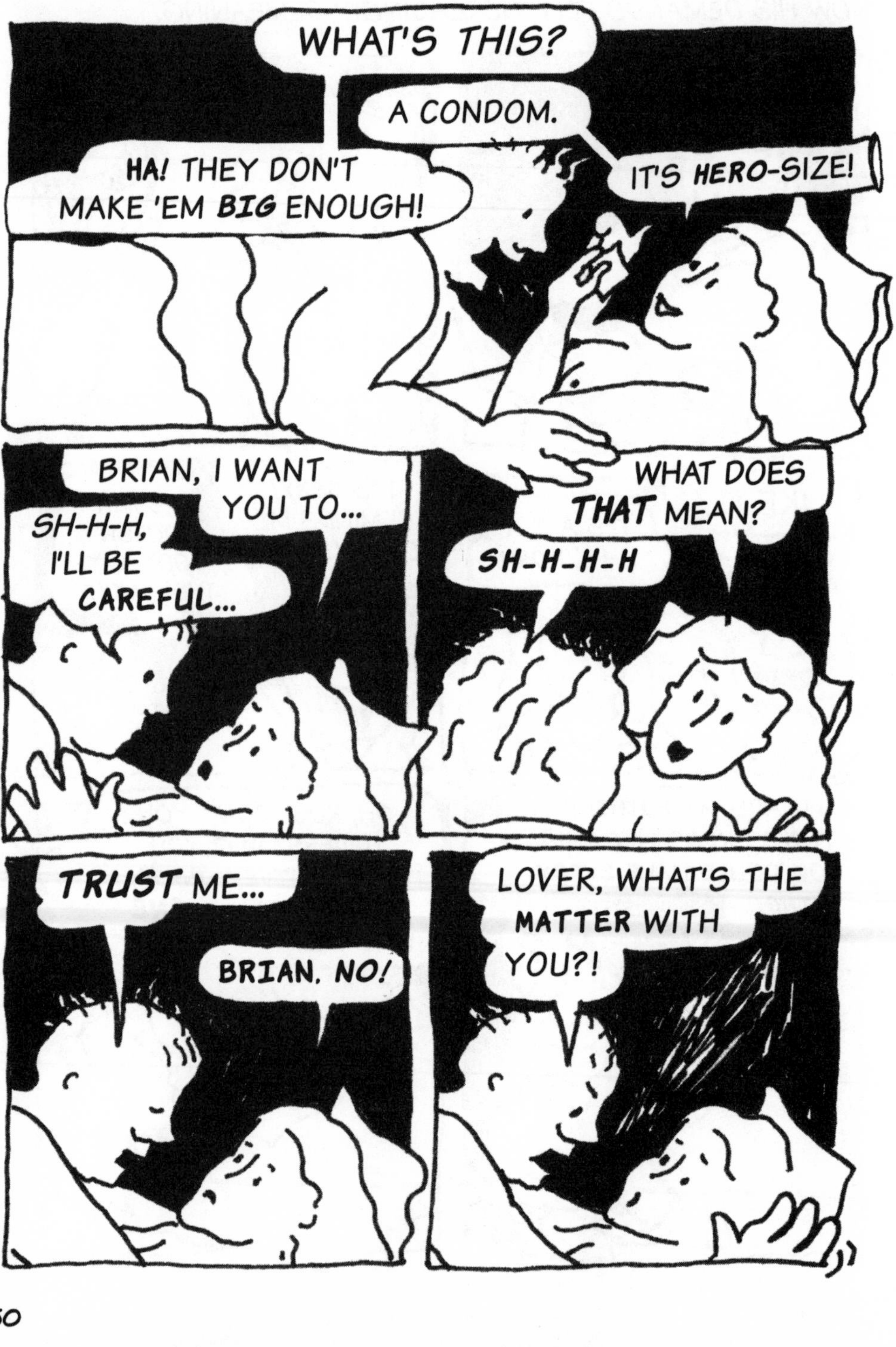
WHAT'S THIS?
A CONDOM.
HA! THEY DON'T MAKE 'EM BIG ENOUGH!
IT'S HERO-SIZE!
BRIAN, I WANT YOU TO...
SH-H-H, I'LL BE CAREFUL...
WHAT DOES THAT MEAN?
SH-H-H-H
TRUST ME...
BRIAN, NO!
LOVER, WHAT'S THE MATTER WITH YOU?!

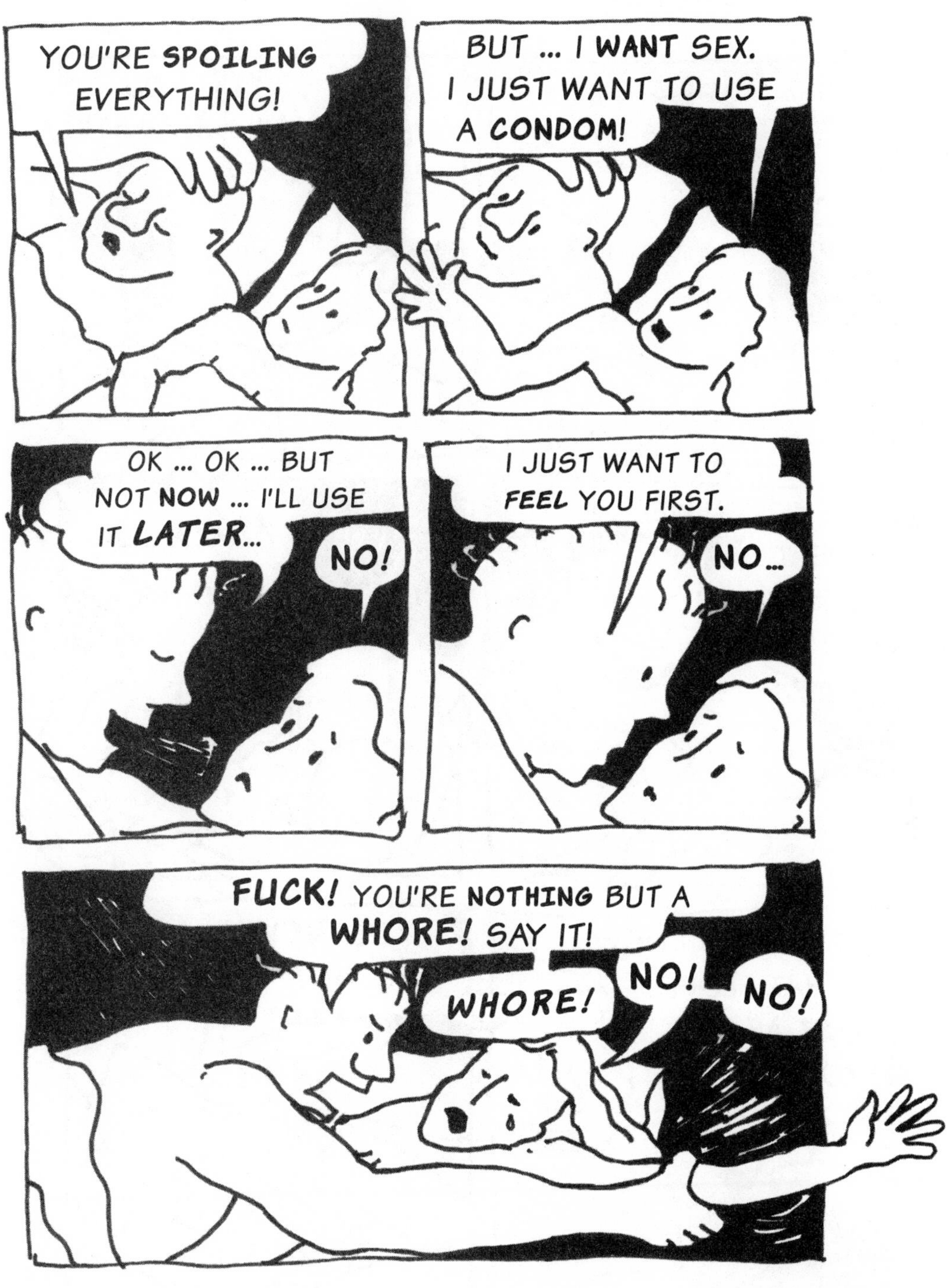
YOU'RE SPOILING EVERYTHING!
BUT ... I WANT SEX. I JUST WANT TO USE A CONDOM!
OK ... OK ... BUT NOT NOW ... I'LL USE IT LATER...
NO!
I JUST WANT TO FEEL YOU FIRST.
NO...
FUCK! YOU'RE NOTHING BUT A WHORE! SAY IT!
WHORE!
NO!
NO!

THE NEXT MORNING...

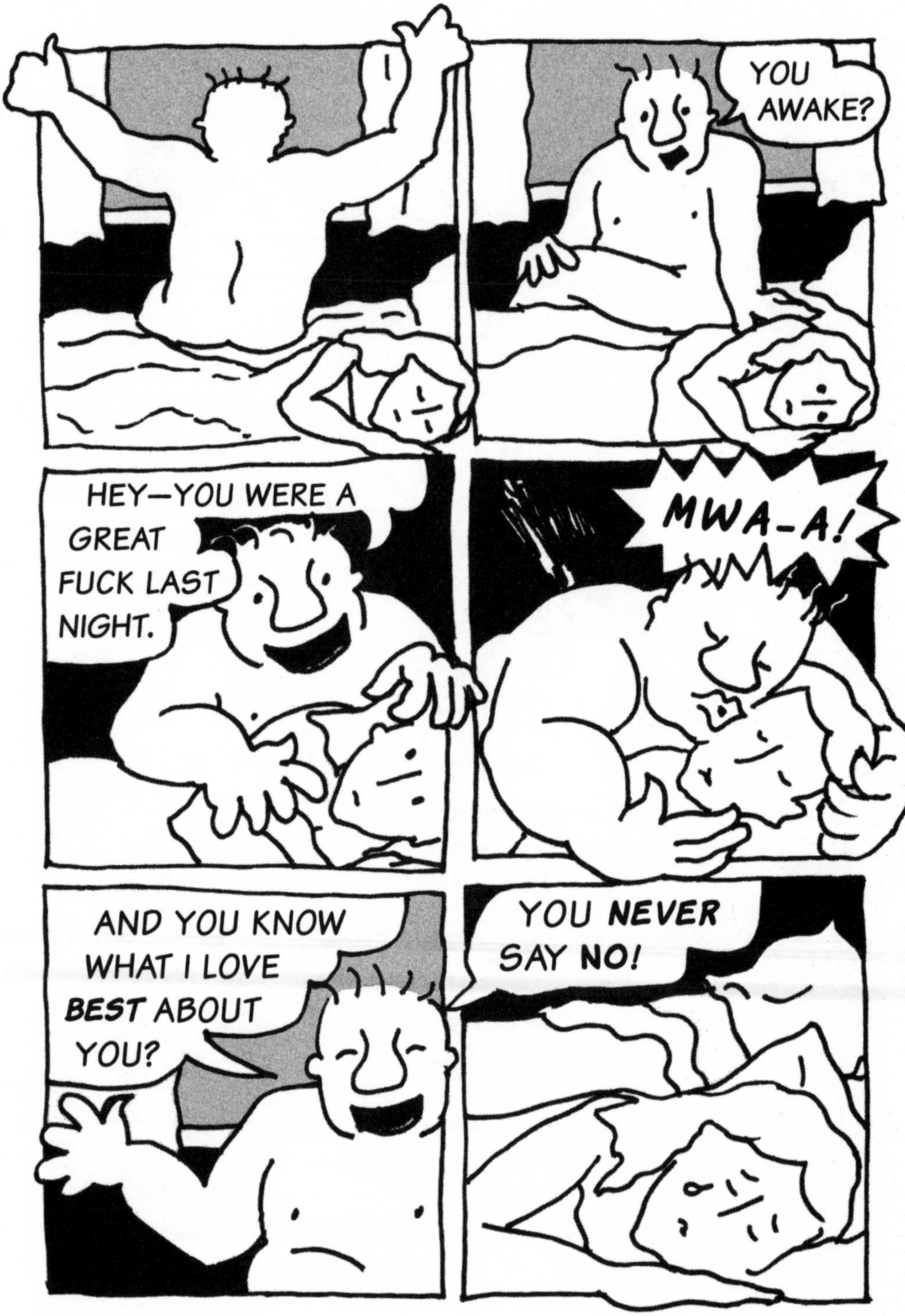
YOU AWAKE?
HEY—YOU WERE A GREAT FUCK LAST NIGHT.
MWA-A!
AND YOU KNOW WHAT I LOVE BEST ABOUT YOU?
YOU NEVER SAY NO!

AND THEN, JUST WHEN I THOUGHT THINGS COULDN'T GET WORSE, THEY *DID*...

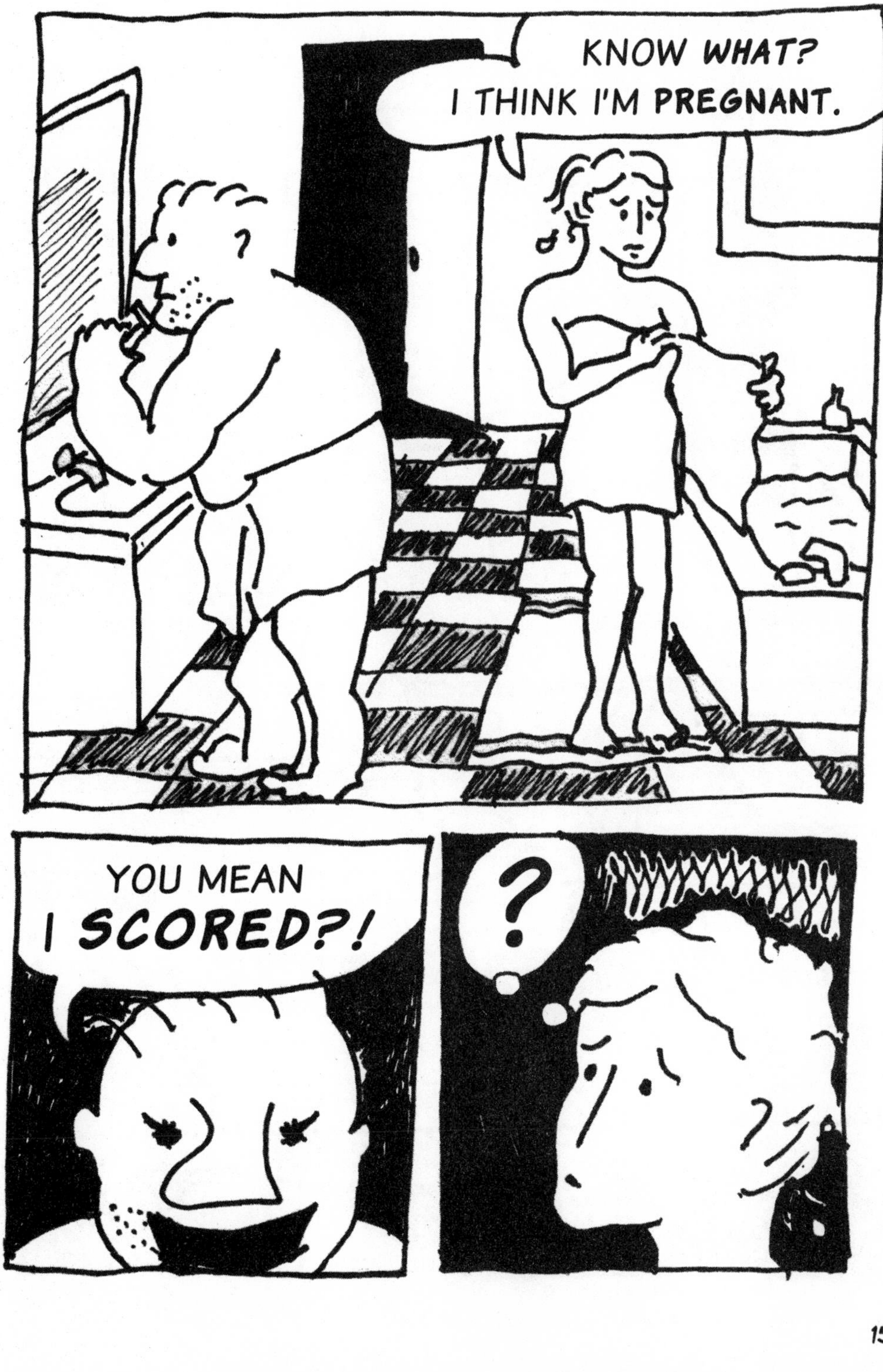
KNOW WHAT?
I THINK I'M PREGNANT.
YOU MEAN I SCORED?!
?

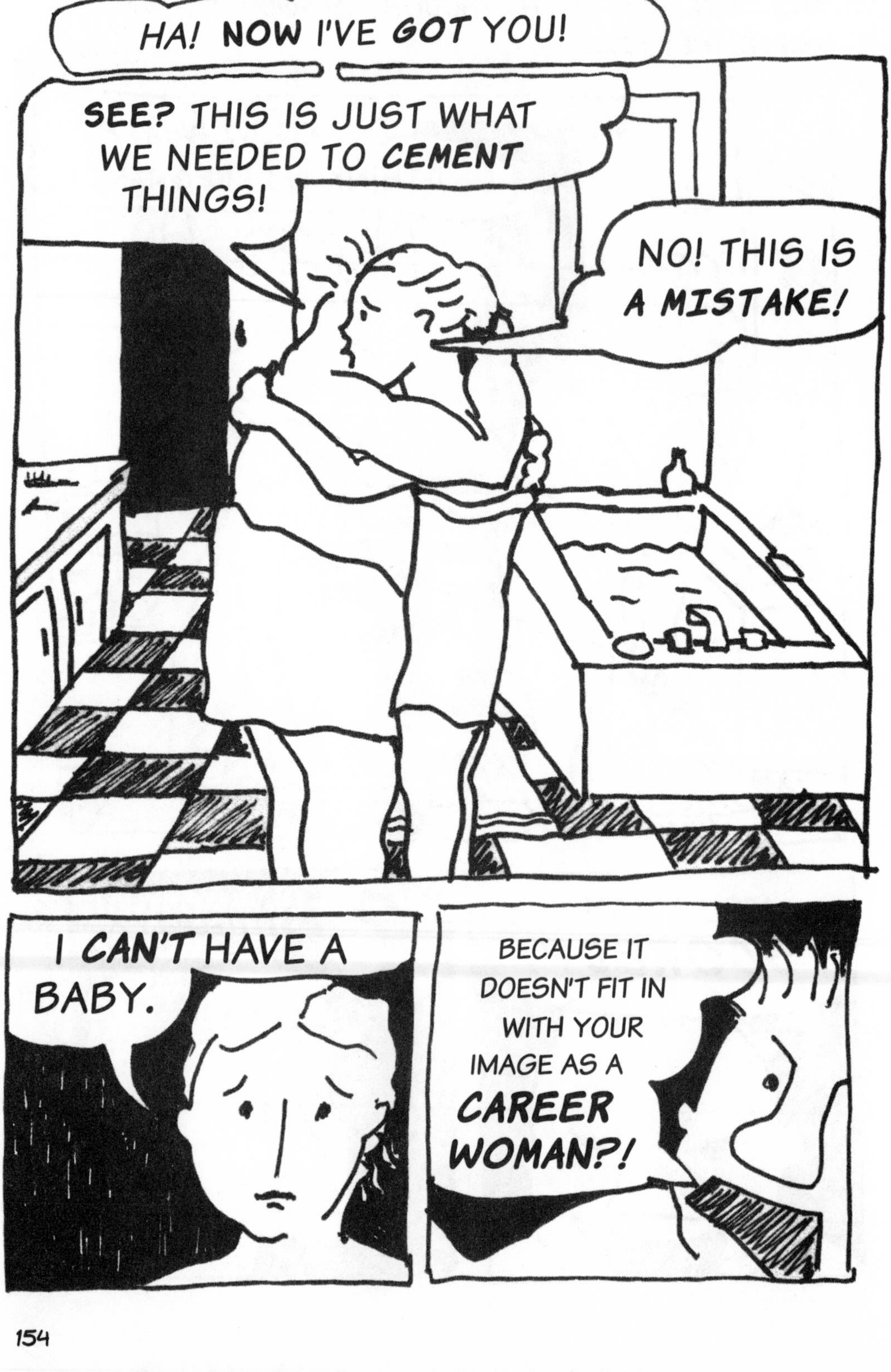
HA! NOW I'VE GOT YOU!
SEE? THIS IS JUST WHAT WE NEEDED TO CEMENT THINGS!
NO! THIS IS A MISTAKE!
I CAN'T HAVE A BABY.
BECAUSE IT DOESN'T FIT IN WITH YOUR IMAGE AS A CAREER WOMAN?!

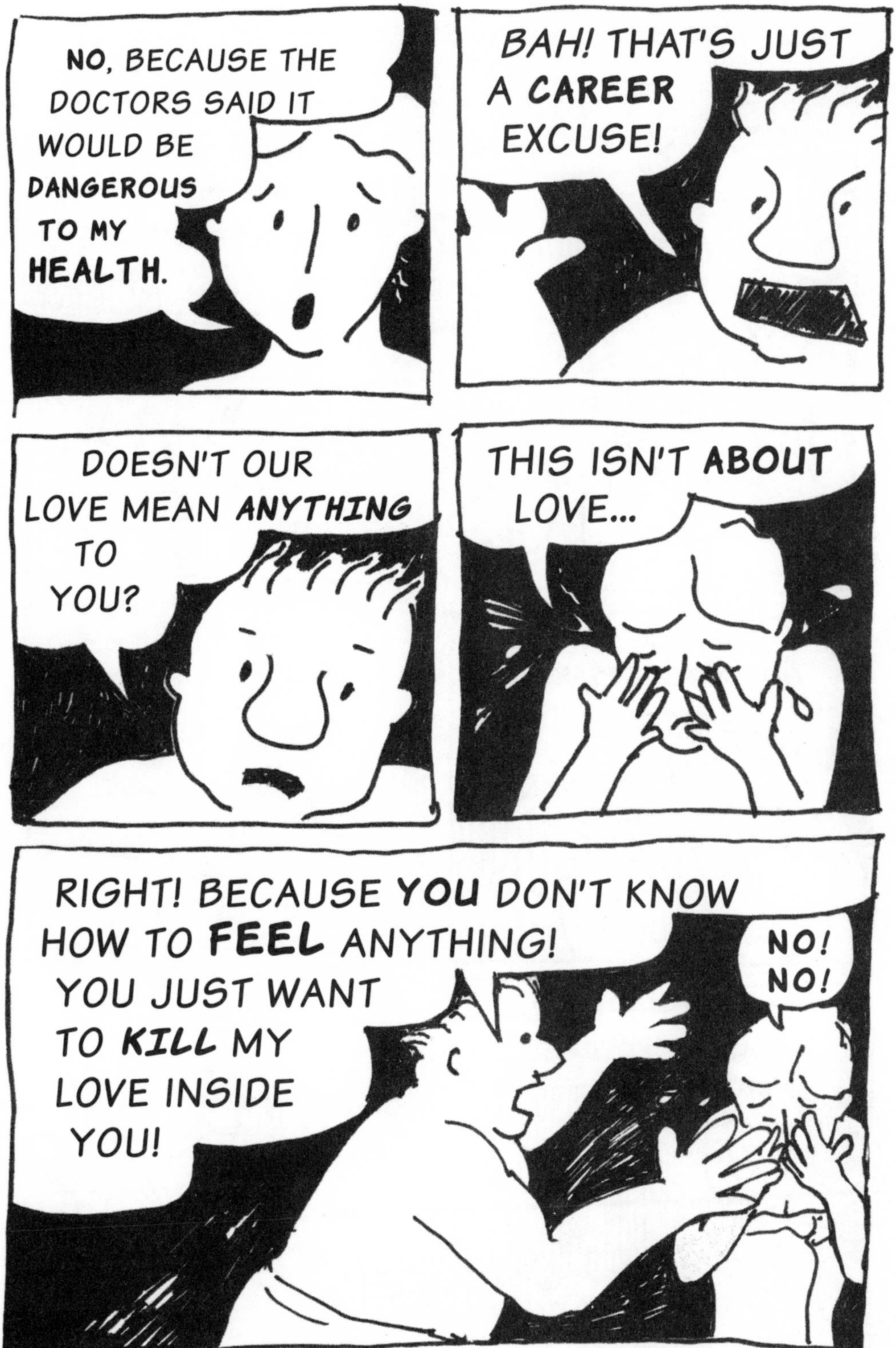

NO, BECAUSE THE DOCTORS SAID IT WOULD BE DANGEROUS TO MY HEALTH.
BAH! THAT'S JUST A CAREER EXCUSE!
DOESN'T OUR LOVE MEAN ANYTHING TO YOU?
THIS ISN'T ABOUT LOVE...
RIGHT! BECAUSE YOU DON'T KNOW HOW TO FEEL ANYTHING! YOU JUST WANT TO KILL MY LOVE INSIDE YOU!
NO! NO!

A WEEK WENT BY AND BRIAN IGNORED ME.

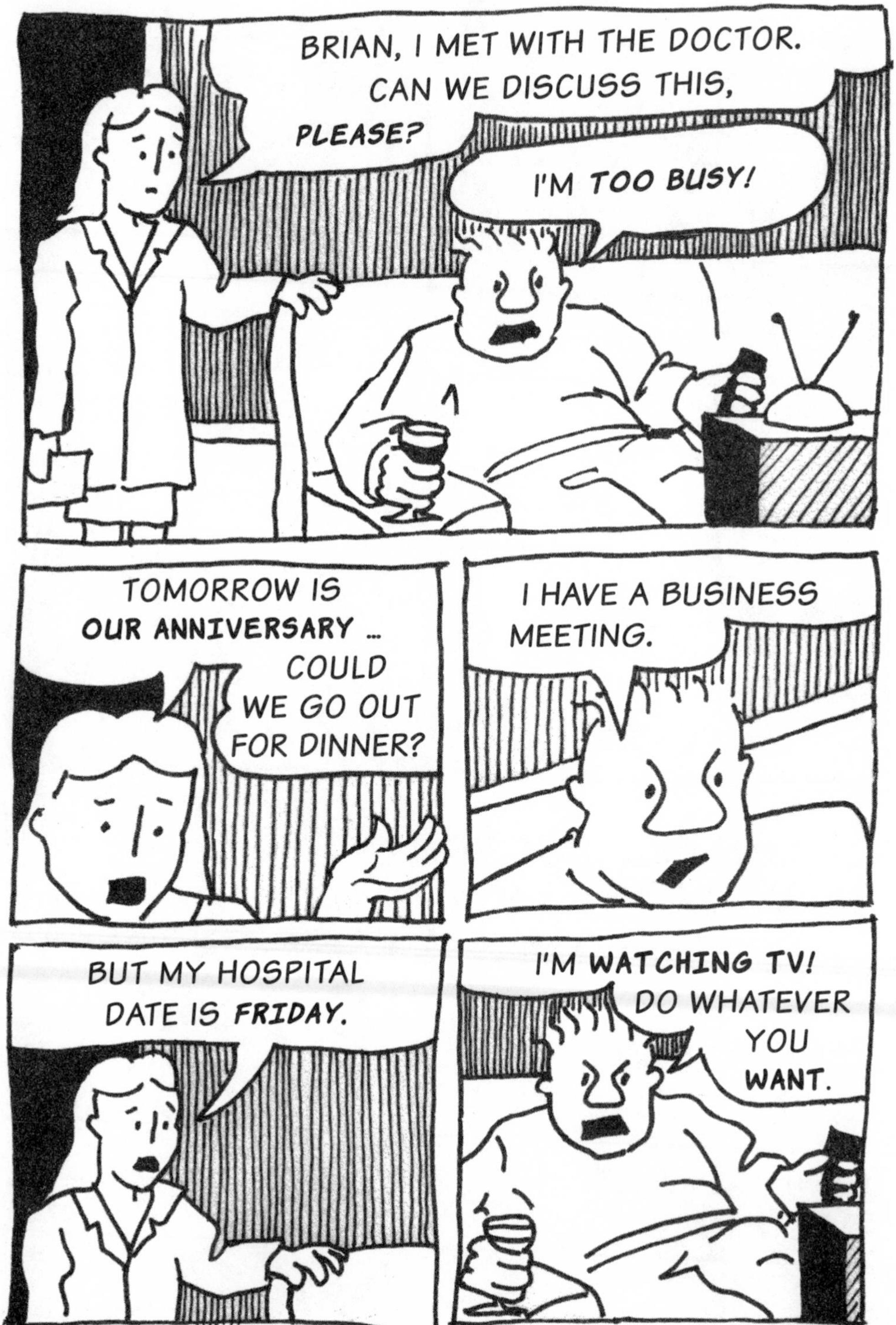
BRIAN, I MET WITH THE DOCTOR. CAN WE DISCUSS THIS, PLEASE?
I'M TOO BUSY!
TOMORROW IS OUR ANNIVERSARY ... COULD WE GO OUT FOR DINNER?
I HAVE A BUSINESS MEETING.
BUT MY HOSPITAL DATE IS FRIDAY.
I'M WATCHING TV! DO WHATEVER YOU WANT.

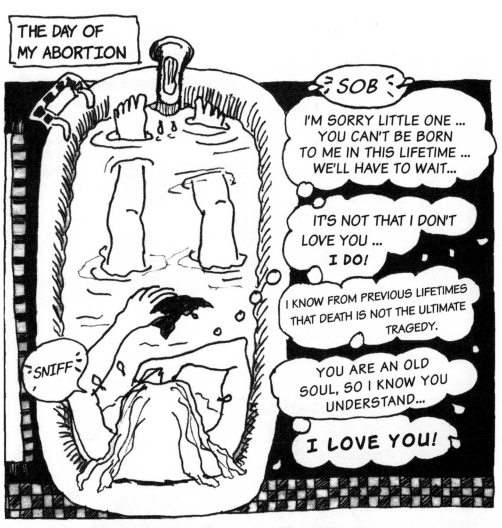

THE DAY OF MY ABORTION

SOB

I'M SORRY LITTLE ONE ... YOU CAN'T BE BORN TO ME IN THIS LIFETIME ... WE'LL HAVE TO WAIT...

IT'S NOT THAT I DON'T LOVE YOU ... I DO!

I KNOW FROM PREVIOUS LIFETIMES THAT DEATH IS NOT THE ULTIMATE TRAGEDY.

YOU ARE AN OLD SOUL, SO I KNOW YOU UNDERSTAND...

I LOVE YOU!

SNIFF

THEN I TOOK A TAXI TO THE HOSPITAL...

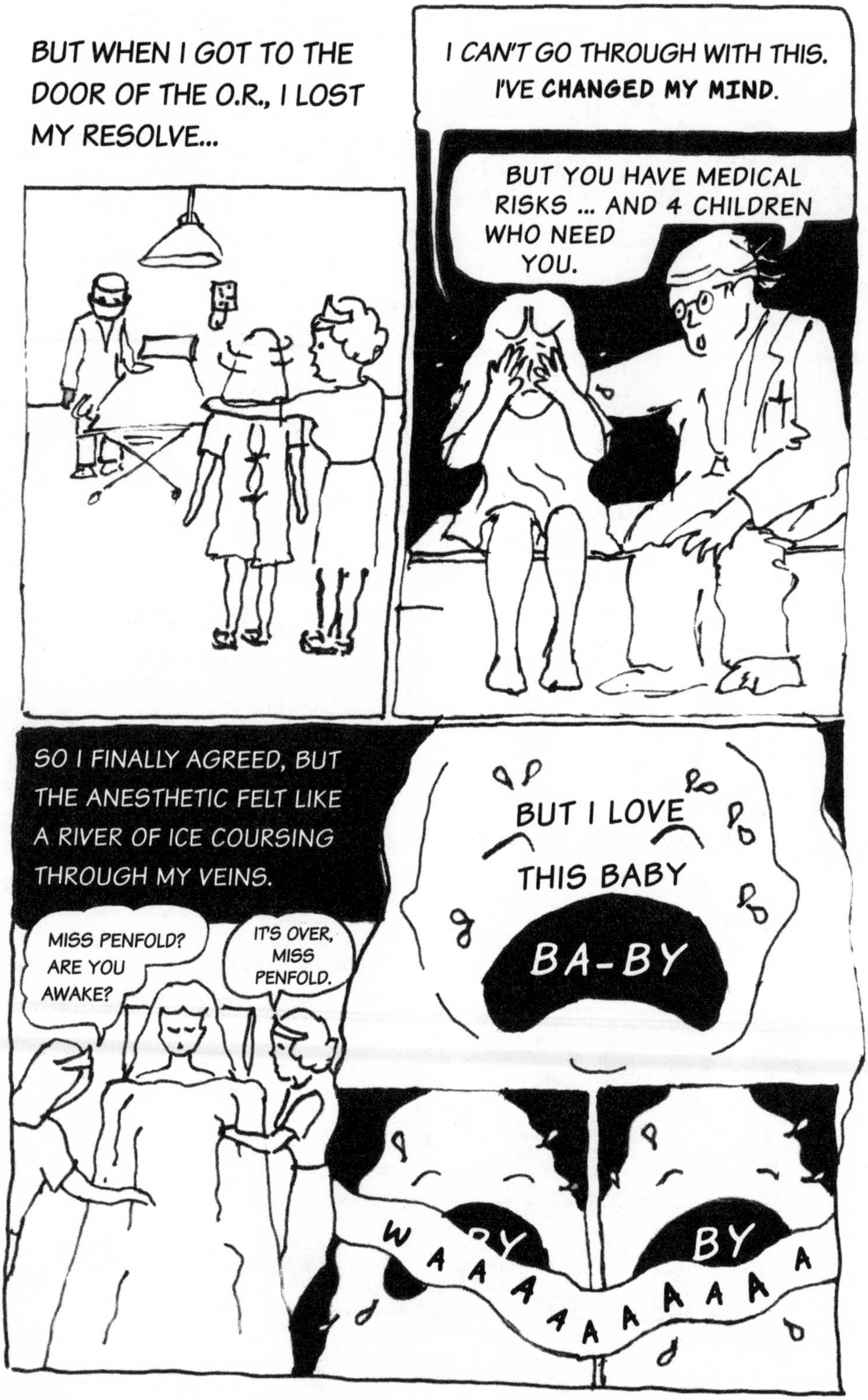
BUT WHEN I GOT TO THE DOOR OF THE O.R., I LOST MY RESOLVE...
I CAN'T GO THROUGH WITH THIS. I'VE CHANGED MY MIND.
BUT YOU HAVE MEDICAL RISKS ... AND 4 CHILDREN WHO NEED YOU.
SO I FINALLY AGREED, BUT THE ANESTHETIC FELT LIKE A RIVER OF ICE COURSING THROUGH MY VEINS.
BUT I LOVE THIS BABY
BA-BY
MISS PENFOLD? ARE YOU AWAKE?
IT'S OVER, MISS PENFOLD.
BY
WAAAAAAAAAAAAA

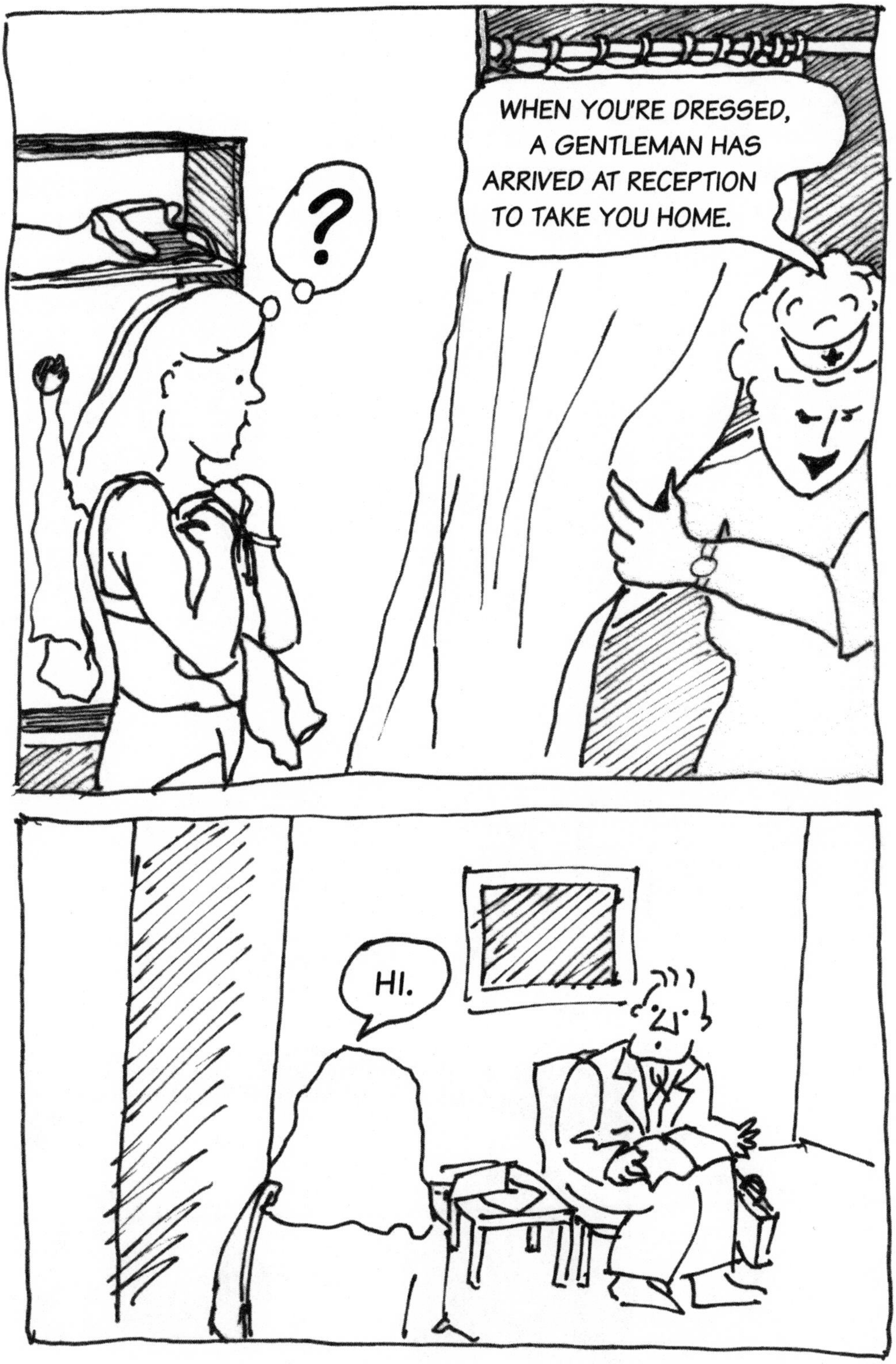
?
WHEN YOU'RE DRESSED, A GENTLEMAN HAS ARRIVED AT RECEPTION TO TAKE YOU HOME.
HI.

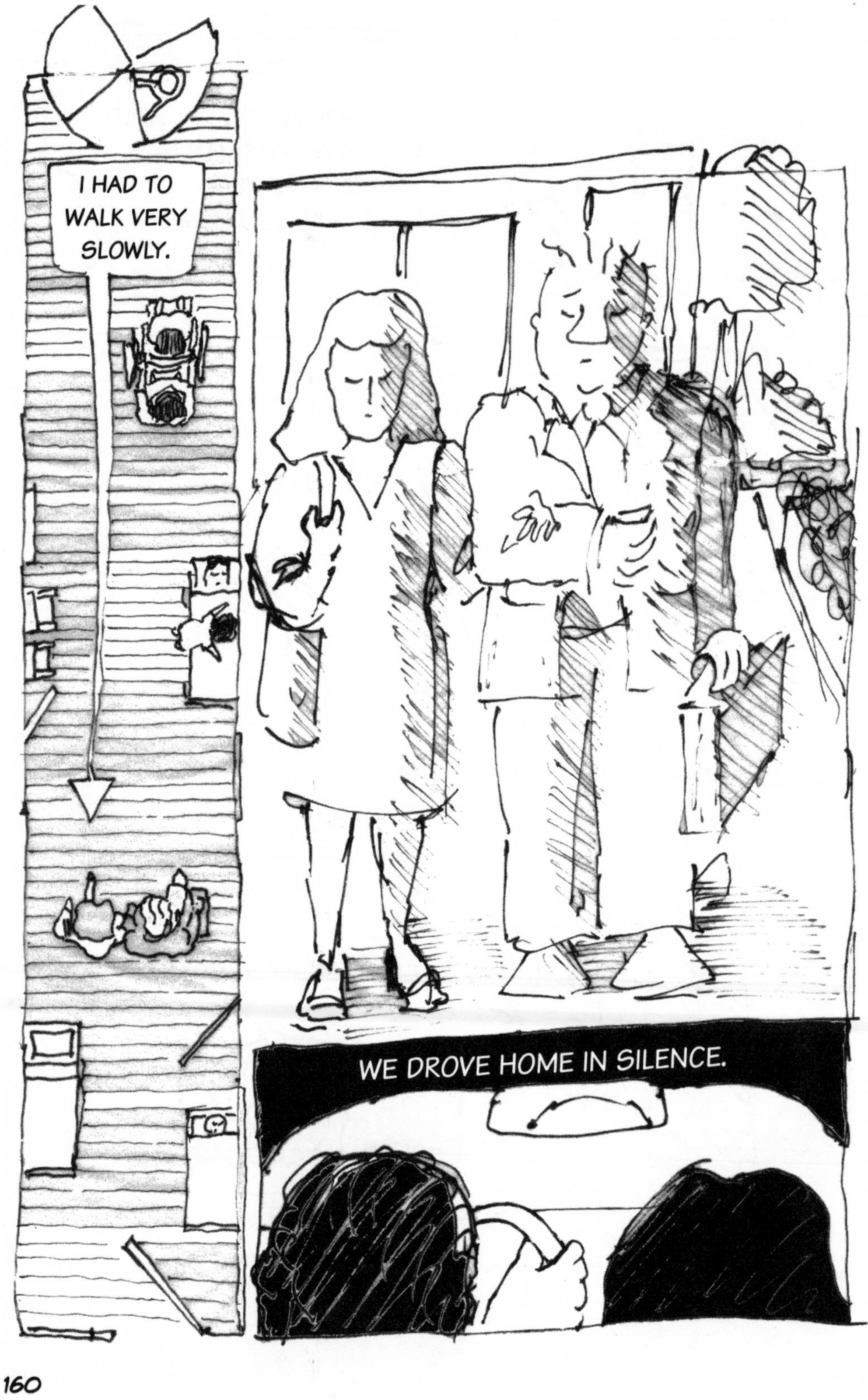
I HAD TO WALK VERY SLOWLY.
WE DROVE HOME IN SILENCE.

INSIDE THE HOUSE, WE SAT DOWN IN THE DINING ROOM. I STILL HAD MY HOSPITAL BRACELET ON. BRIAN WOULDN'T SPEAK TO ME.

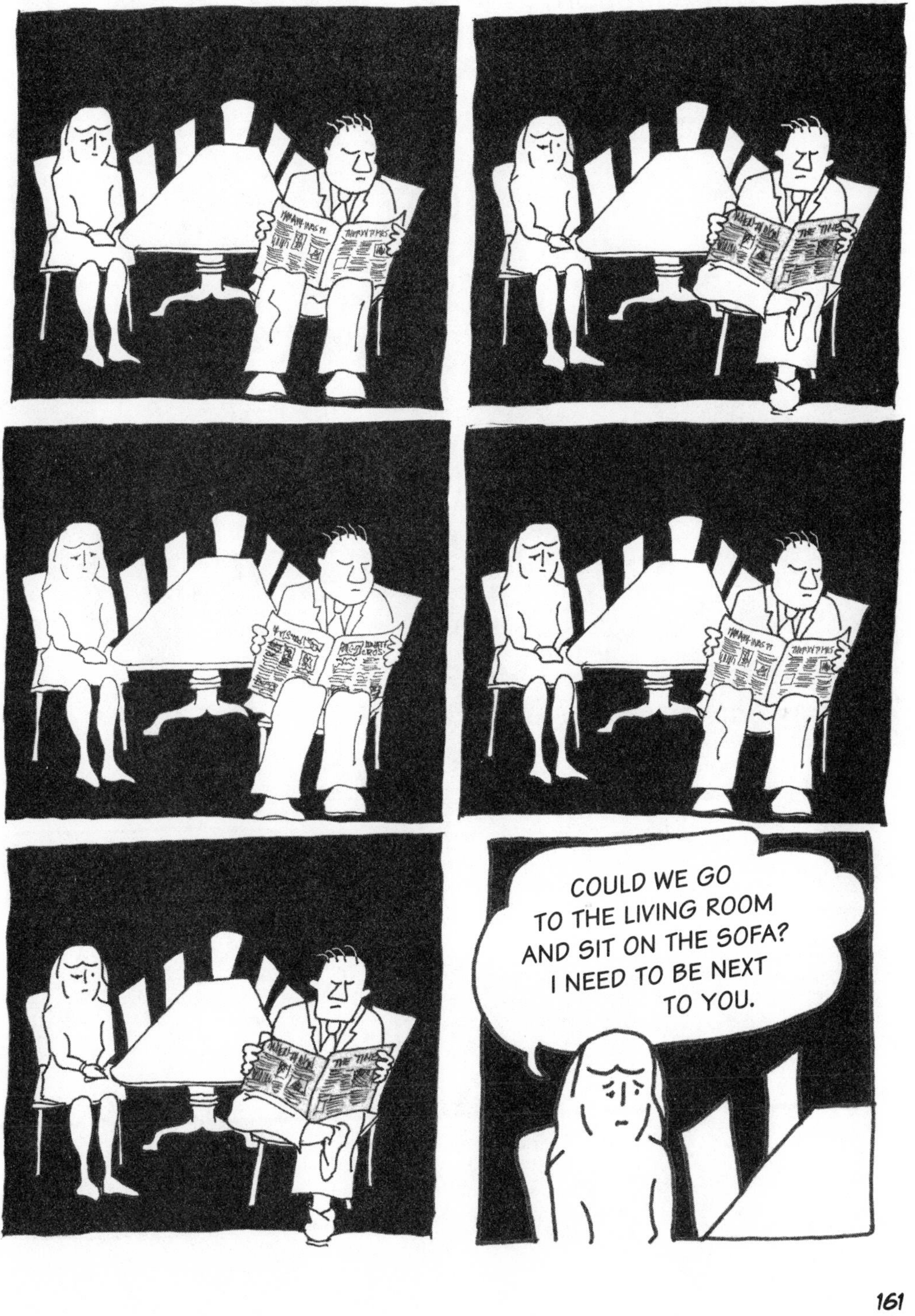
COULD WE GO TO THE LIVING ROOM AND SIT ON THE SOFA? I NEED TO BE NEXT TO YOU.

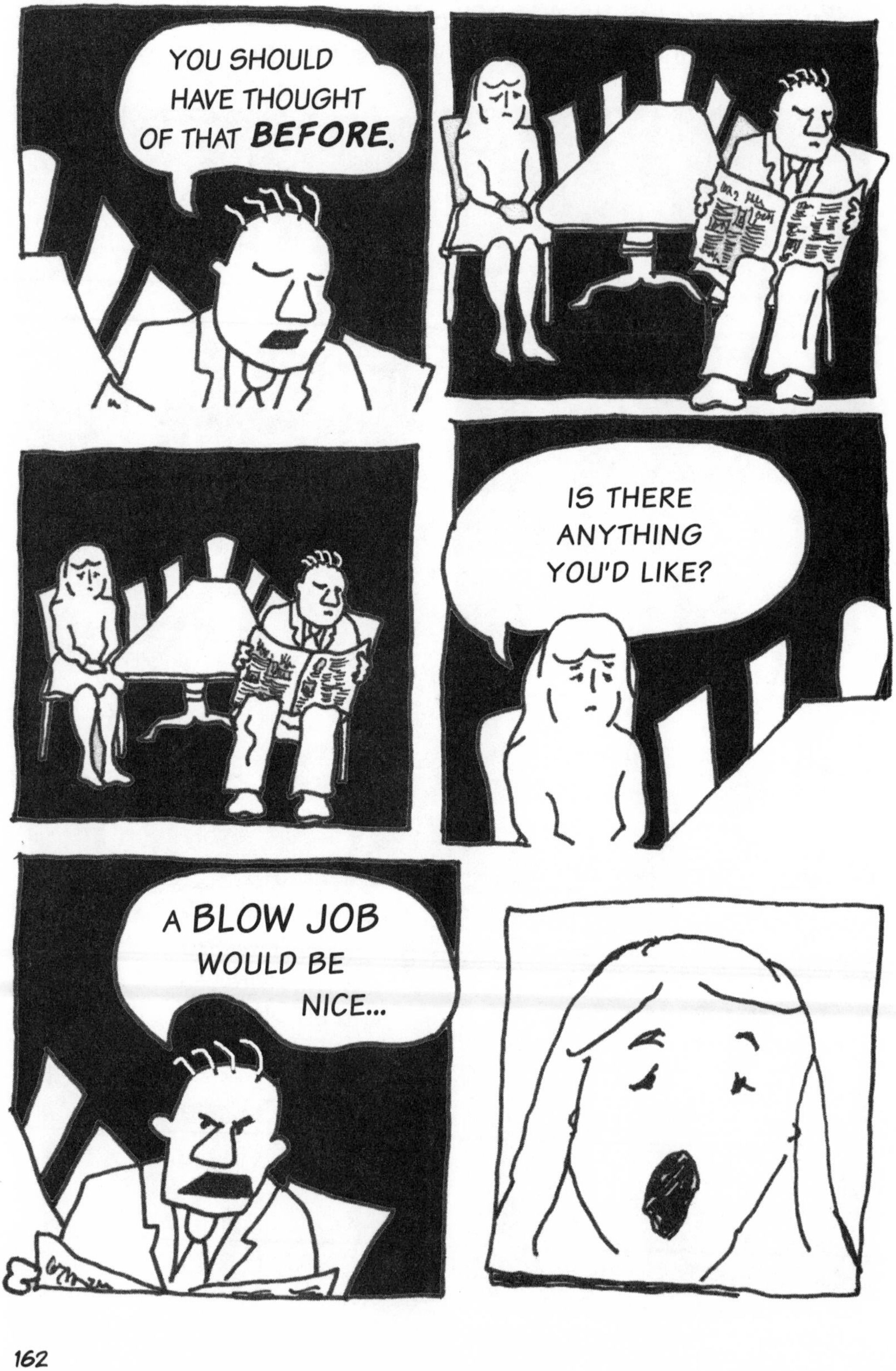
YOU SHOULD HAVE THOUGHT OF THAT BEFORE.
IS THERE ANYTHING YOU'D LIKE?
A BLOW JOB WOULD BE NICE...

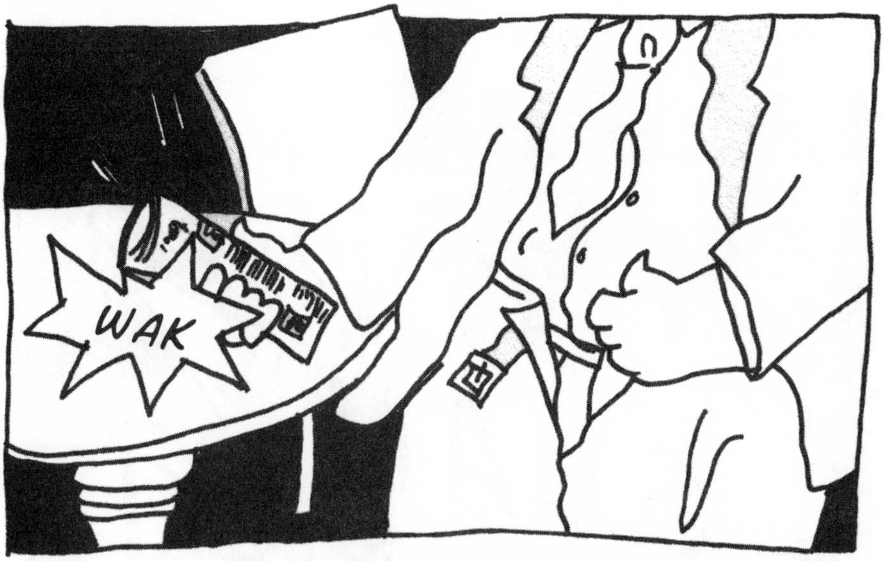
WAK

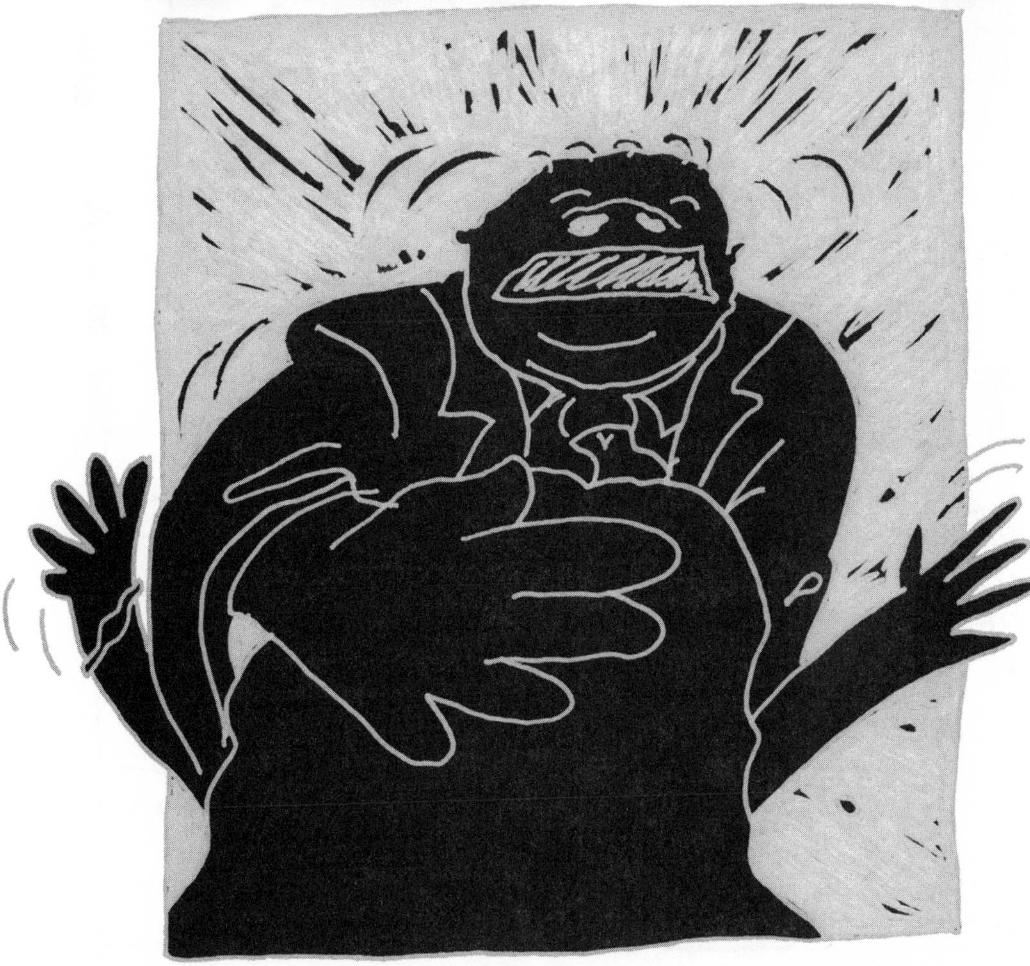

THEN HE WENT BACK TO THE OFFICE...

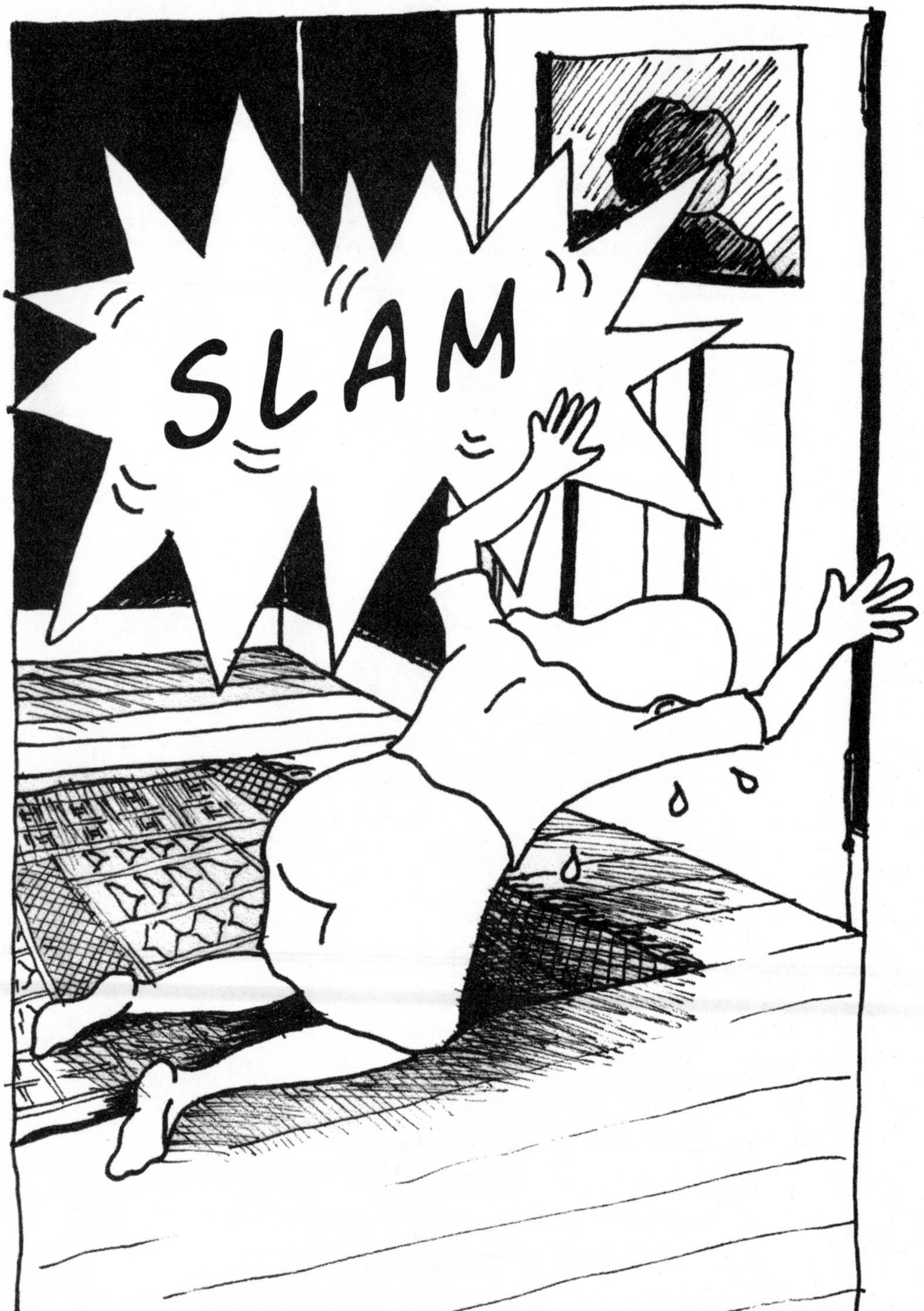
SLAM

MY PUNISHMENT WASN'T OVER, HOWEVER. BRIAN HAD BEEN GIVING ME THE SILENT TREATMENT FOR DAYS. THEN, ONE AFTERNOON, HE CALLED FROM THE OFFICE.

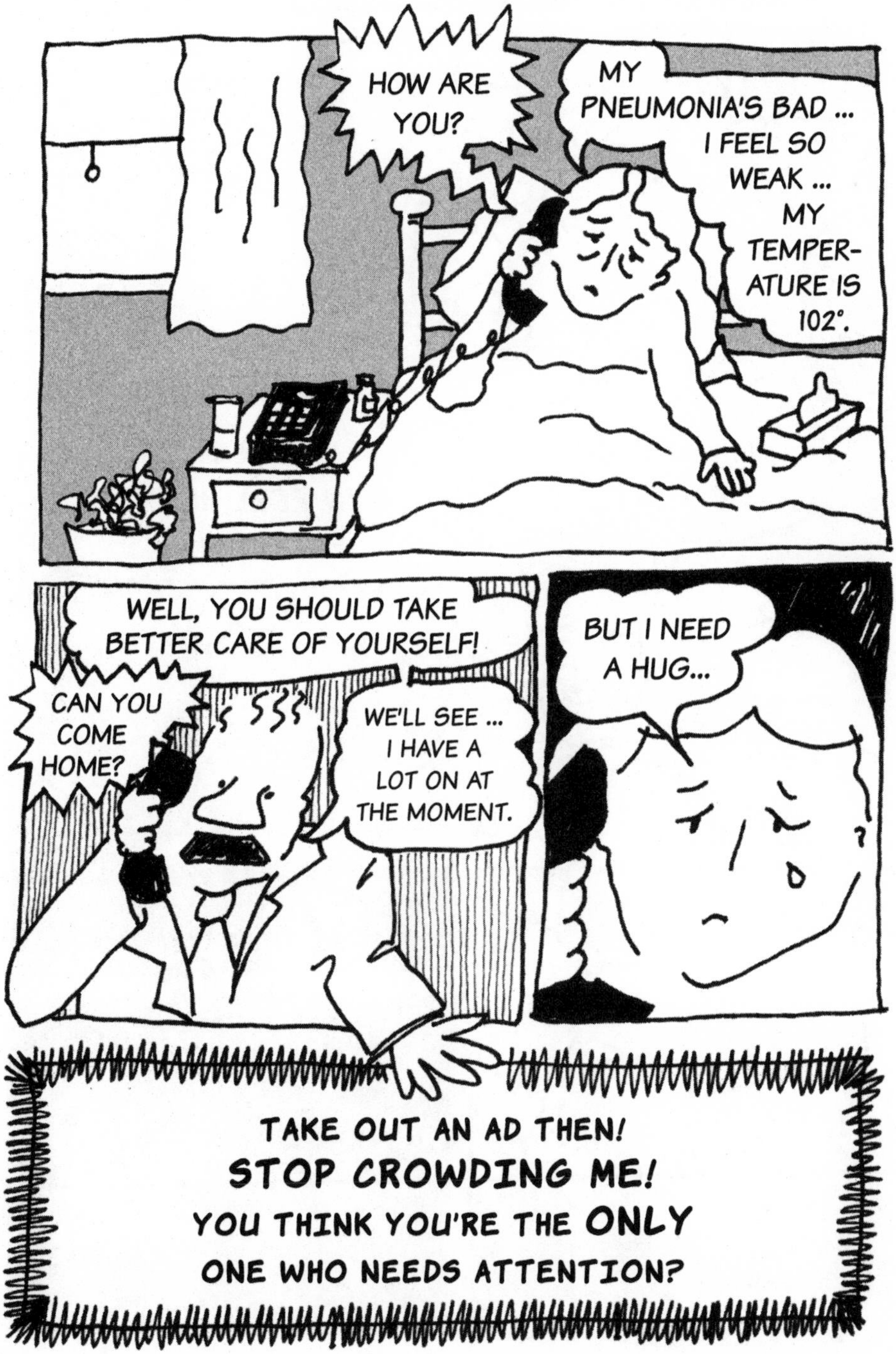
HOW ARE YOU?
MY PNEUMONIA'S BAD ... I FEEL SO WEAK ... MY TEMPERATURE IS 102°.
WELL, YOU SHOULD TAKE BETTER CARE OF YOURSELF!
CAN YOU COME HOME?
WE'LL SEE ... I HAVE A LOT ON AT THE MOMENT.
BUT I NEED A HUG...
TAKE OUT AN AD THEN!
STOP CROWDING ME!
YOU THINK YOU'RE THE ONLY ONE WHO NEEDS ATTENTION?

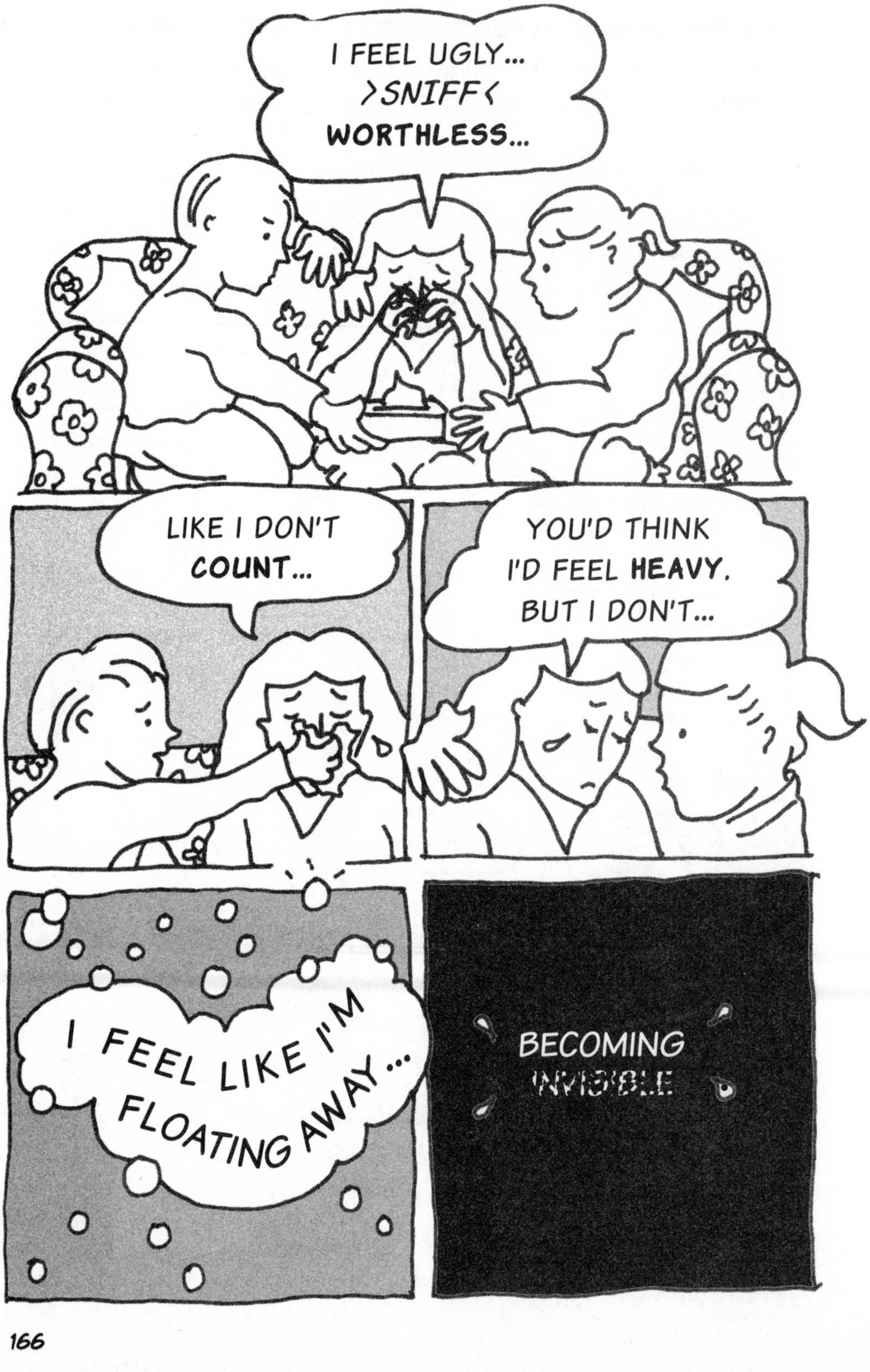
I FEEL UGLY... >SNIFF< WORTHLESS...
LIKE I DON'T COUNT...
YOU'D THINK I'D FEEL HEAVY, BUT I DON'T...
I FEEL LIKE I'M FLOATING AWAY...
BECOMING INVISIBLE

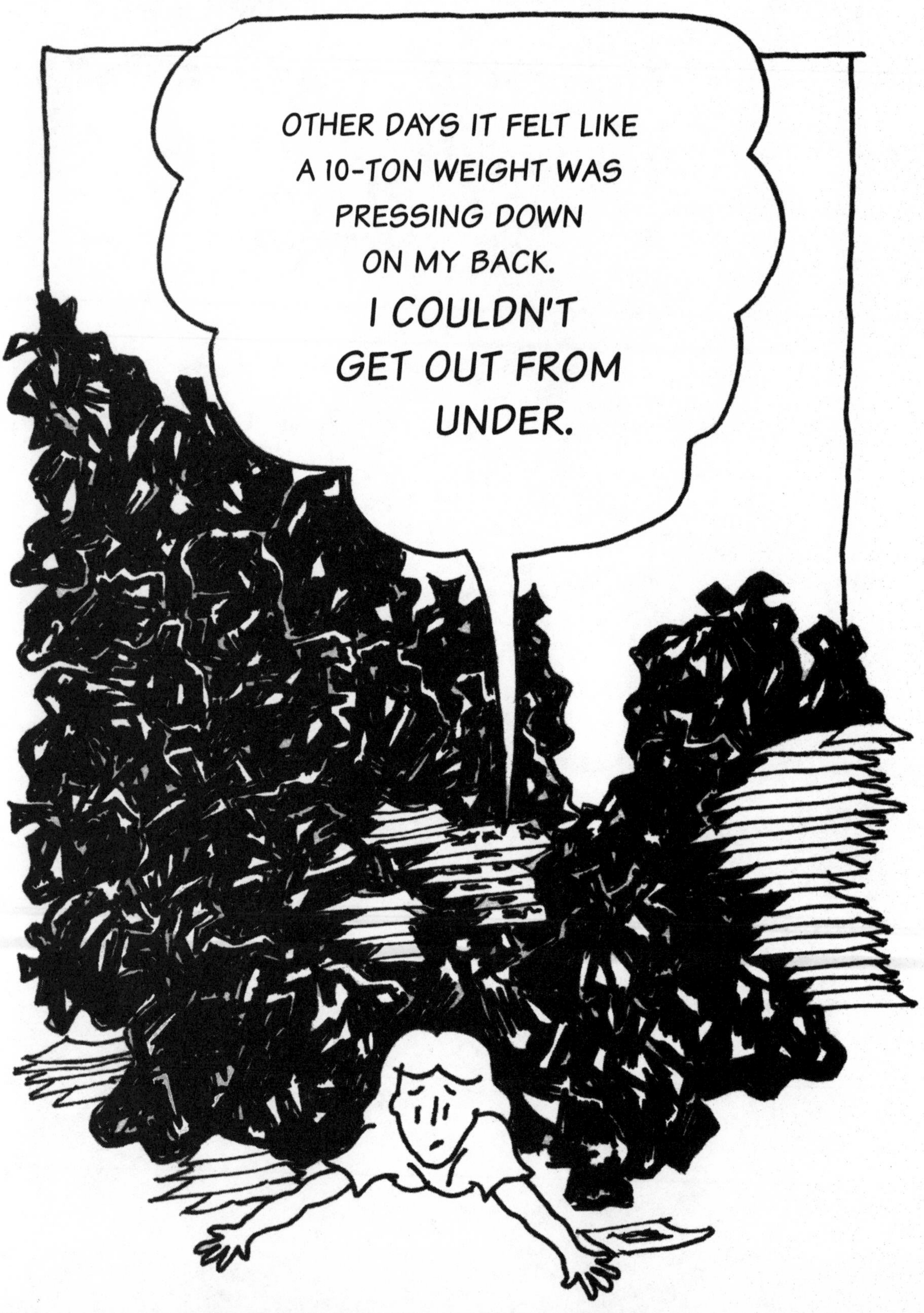
OTHER DAYS IT FELT LIKE A 10-TON WEIGHT WAS PRESSING DOWN ON MY BACK.
I COULDN'T GET OUT FROM UNDER.

Getting Out: Letting Go

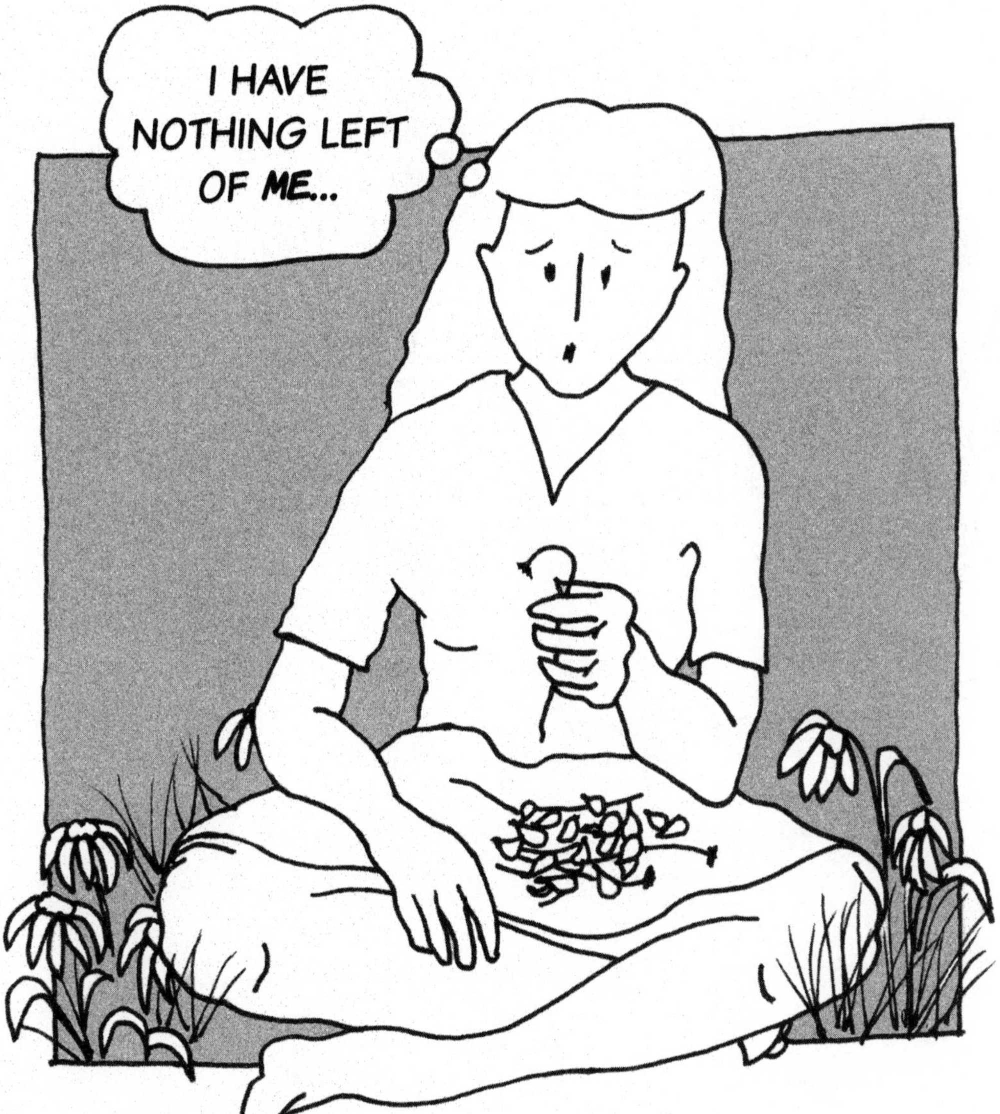
I HAVE NOTHING LEFT OF **ME**...

EVERYWHERE I LOOKED, PEOPLE WERE SMILING.
HOW DID THEY DO THAT?

BRIAN WAS LEAVING ON A BUSINESS TRIP TO EUROPE.
I CAN'T SAY I WAS SORRY TO SEE HIM GO.

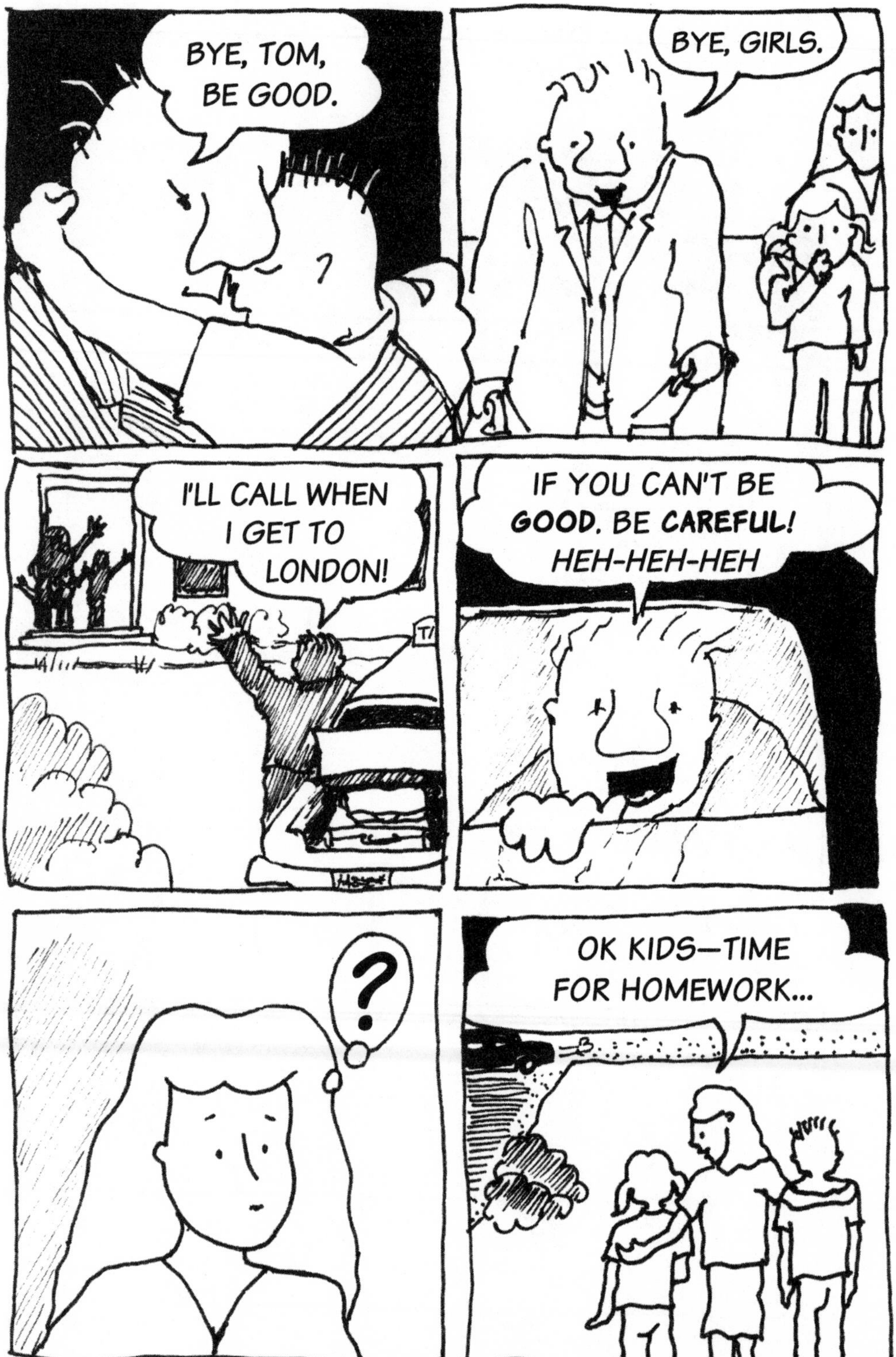
BYE, TOM, BE GOOD.
BYE, GIRLS.
I'LL CALL WHEN I GET TO LONDON!
IF YOU CAN'T BE **GOOD**. BE **CAREFUL**! HEH-HEH-HEH
?
OK KIDS—TIME FOR HOMEWORK...

WITH BRIAN GONE, THE CHILDREN AND I HAD FUN!

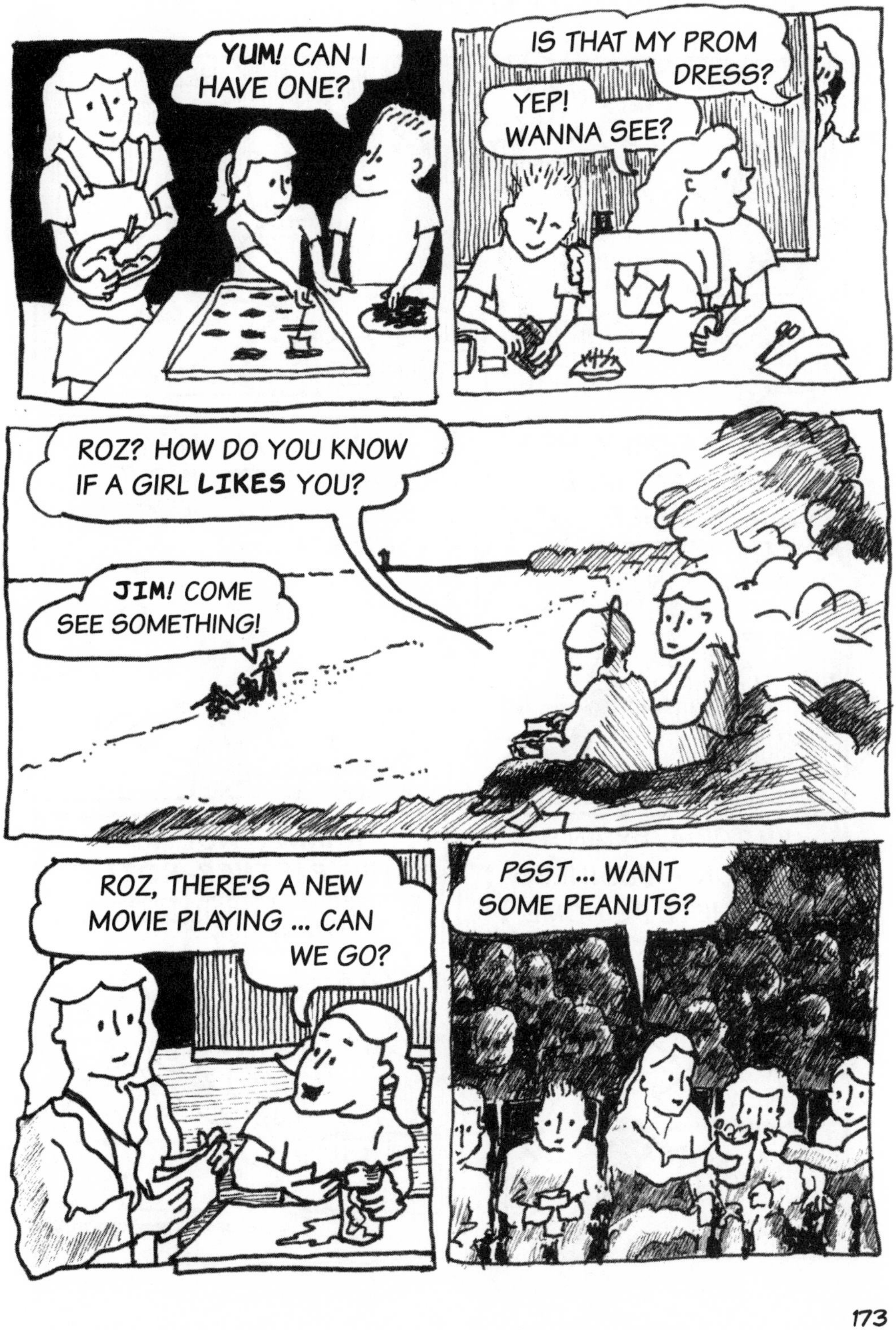

YUM! CAN I HAVE ONE?
IS THAT MY PROM DRESS?
YEP! WANNA SEE?
ROZ? HOW DO YOU KNOW IF A GIRL LIKES YOU?
JIM! COME SEE SOMETHING!
ROZ, THERE'S A NEW MOVIE PLAYING ... CAN WE GO?
PSST ... WANT SOME PEANUTS?

THEN ONE NIGHT AFTER THE CHILDREN HAD GONE TO BED, I WAS FINISHING IN THE KITCHEN ...

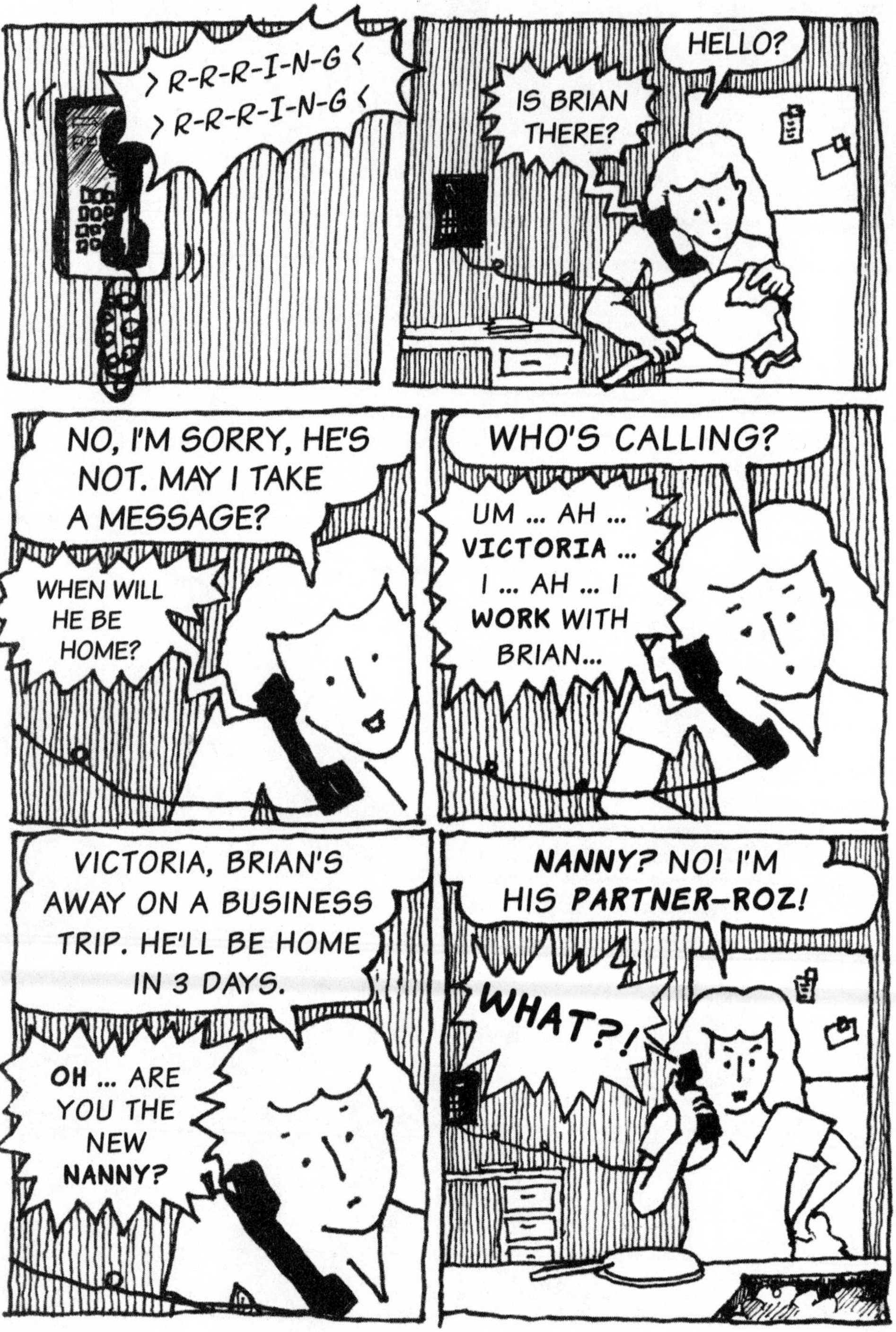
> R-R-R-I-N-G <
> R-R-R-I-N-G <
HELLO?
IS BRIAN THERE?
NO, I'M SORRY, HE'S NOT. MAY I TAKE A MESSAGE?
WHEN WILL HE BE HOME?
WHO'S CALLING?
UM ... AH ... VICTORIA ... I ... AH ... I WORK WITH BRIAN...
VICTORIA, BRIAN'S AWAY ON A BUSINESS TRIP. HE'LL BE HOME IN 3 DAYS.
OH ... ARE YOU THE NEW NANNY?
NANNY? NO! I'M HIS PARTNER–ROZ!
WHAT?!

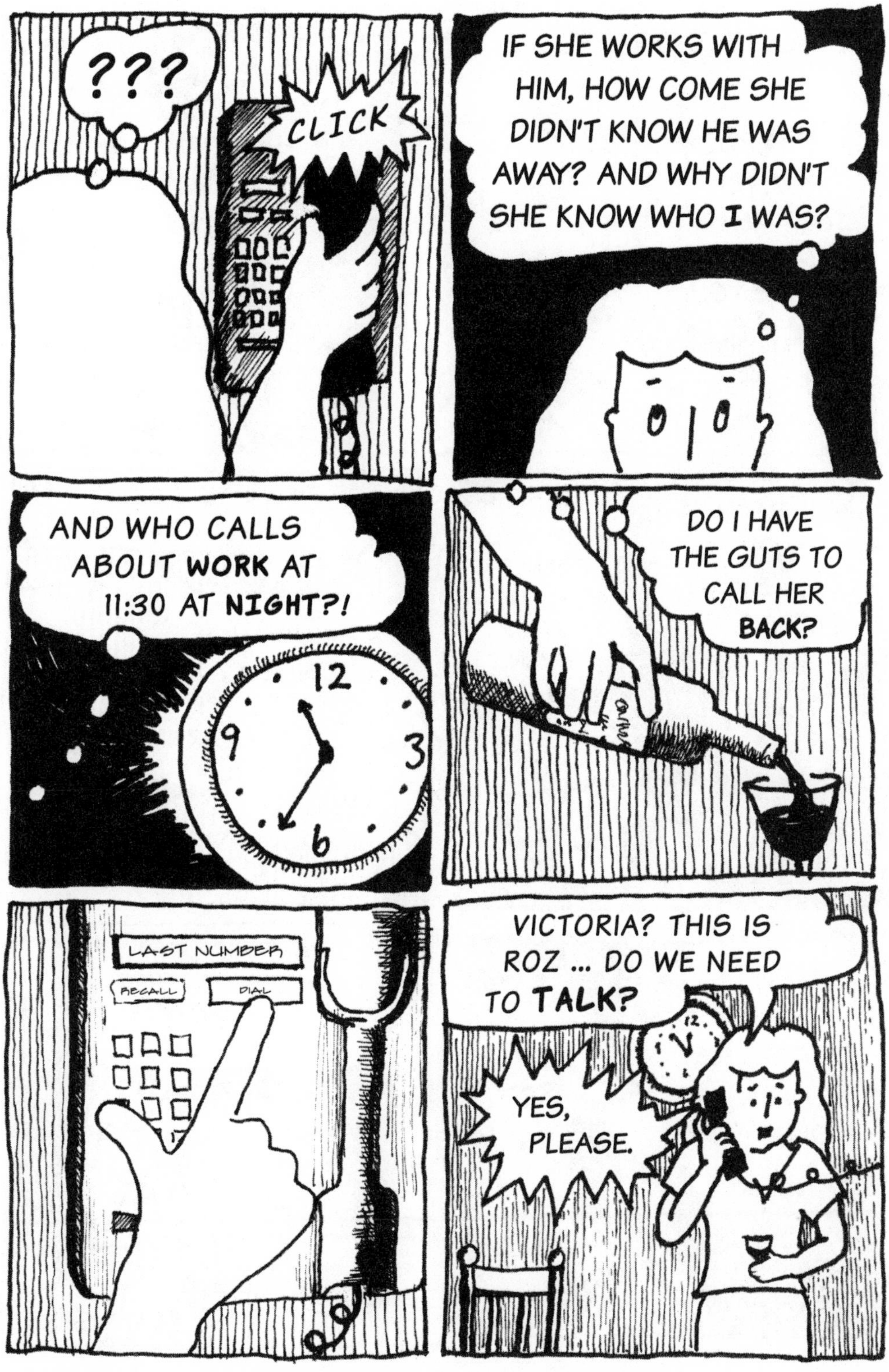
???
CLICK
IF SHE WORKS WITH HIM, HOW COME SHE DIDN'T KNOW HE WAS AWAY? AND WHY DIDN'T SHE KNOW WHO I WAS?
AND WHO CALLS ABOUT WORK AT 11:30 AT NIGHT?!
12
3
6
9
DO I HAVE THE GUTS TO CALL HER BACK?
LAST NUMBER
RECALL
DIAL
VICTORIA? THIS IS ROZ ... DO WE NEED TO TALK?
YES, PLEASE.

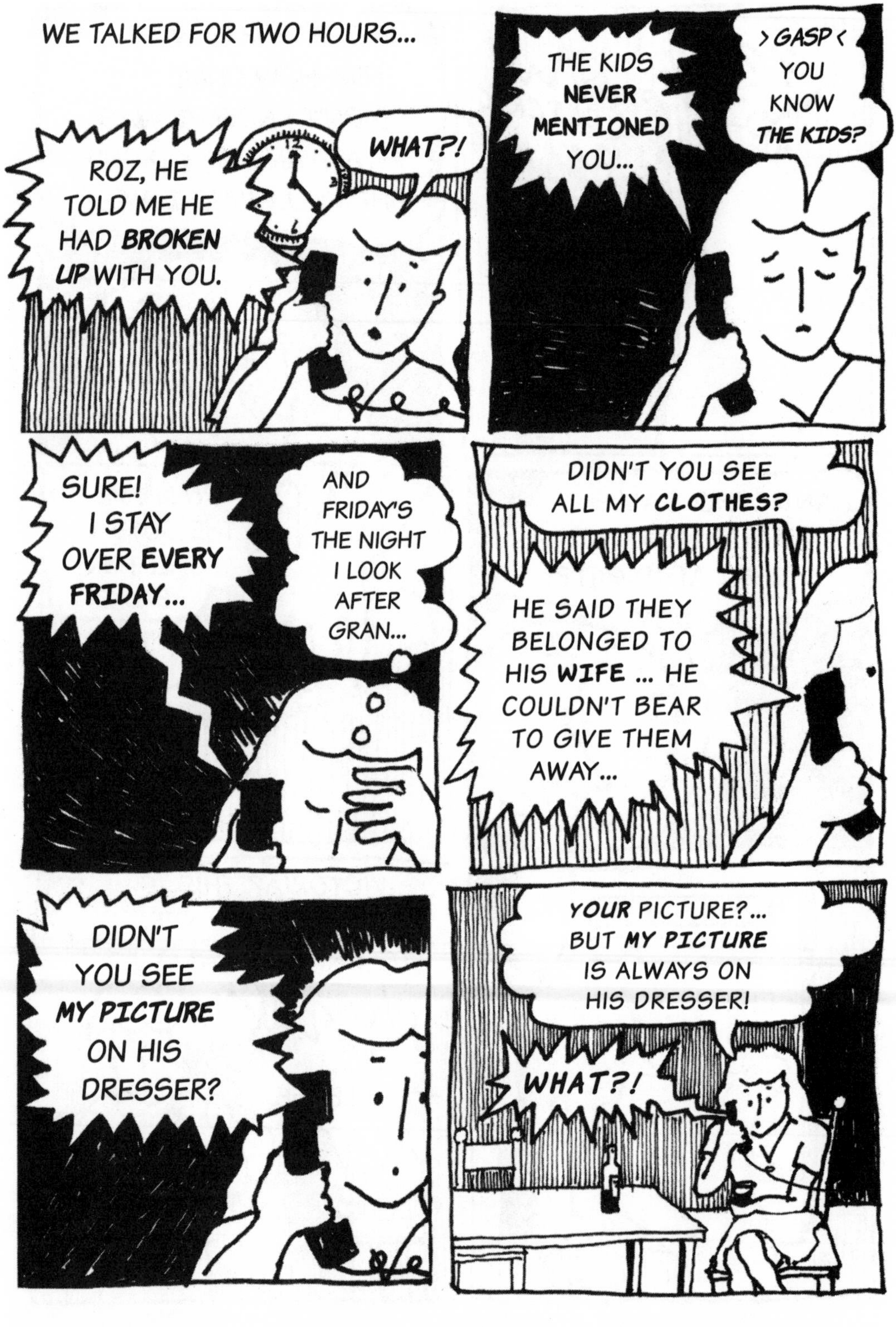
WE TALKED FOR TWO HOURS...
ROZ, HE TOLD ME HE HAD BROKEN UP WITH YOU.
WHAT?!
THE KIDS NEVER MENTIONED YOU...
>GASP< YOU KNOW THE KIDS?
SURE! I STAY OVER EVERY FRIDAY...
AND FRIDAY'S THE NIGHT I LOOK AFTER GRAN...
DIDN'T YOU SEE ALL MY CLOTHES?
HE SAID THEY BELONGED TO HIS WIFE ... HE COULDN'T BEAR TO GIVE THEM AWAY...
DIDN'T YOU SEE MY PICTURE ON HIS DRESSER?
YOUR PICTURE?... BUT MY PICTURE IS ALWAYS ON HIS DRESSER!
WHAT?!

WE AGREED TO MEET THE NEXT DAY FOR COFFEE. DEEP DOWN, I KNEW THIS WAS THE MOMENT OF TRUTH I HAD BEEN DREADING. THIS WAS THE OTHER SLIPPER DROPPING...

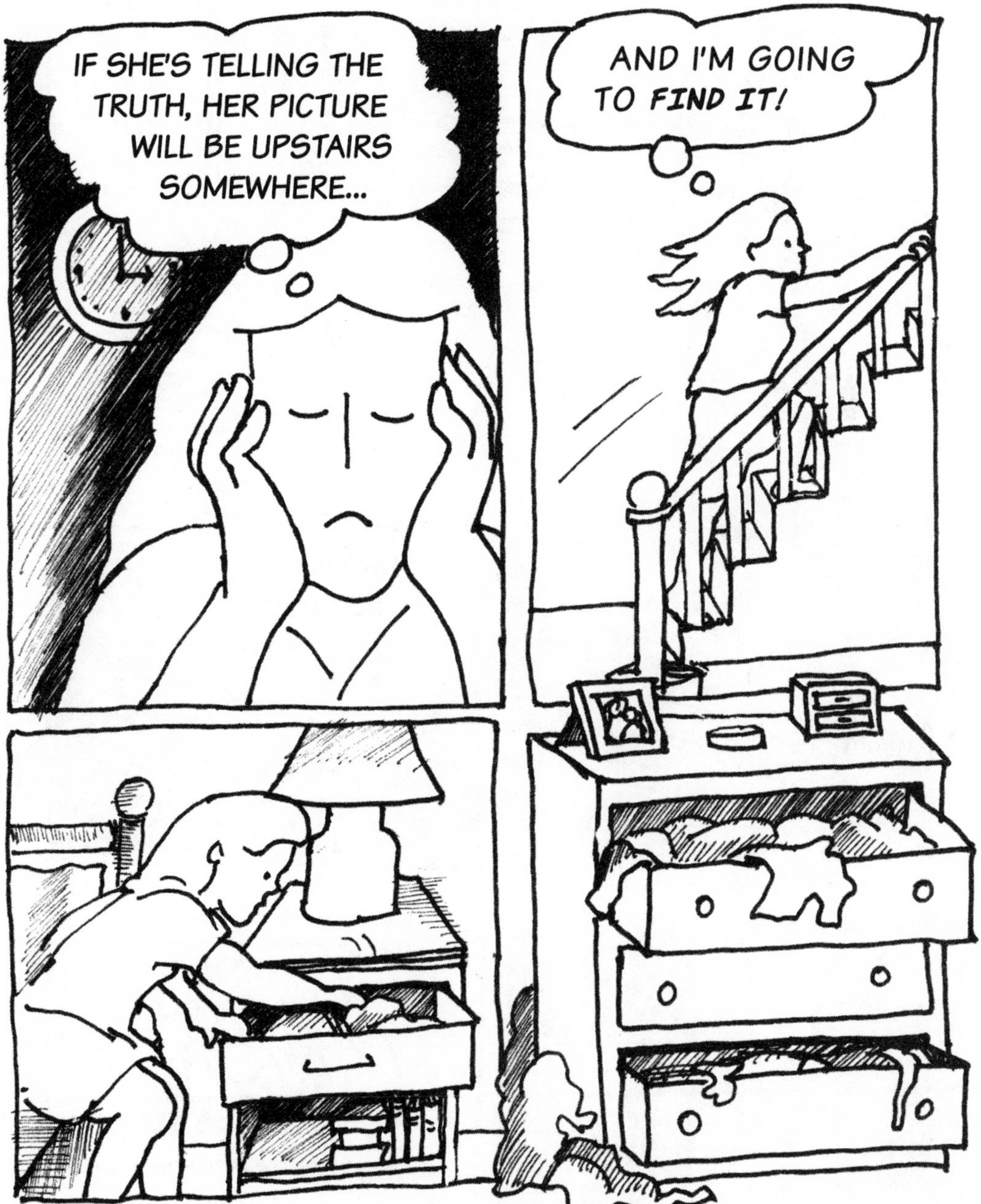
IF SHE'S TELLING THE TRUTH, HER PICTURE WILL BE UPSTAIRS SOMEWHERE...
AND I'M GOING TO FIND IT!

I TORE THE ROOM APART...

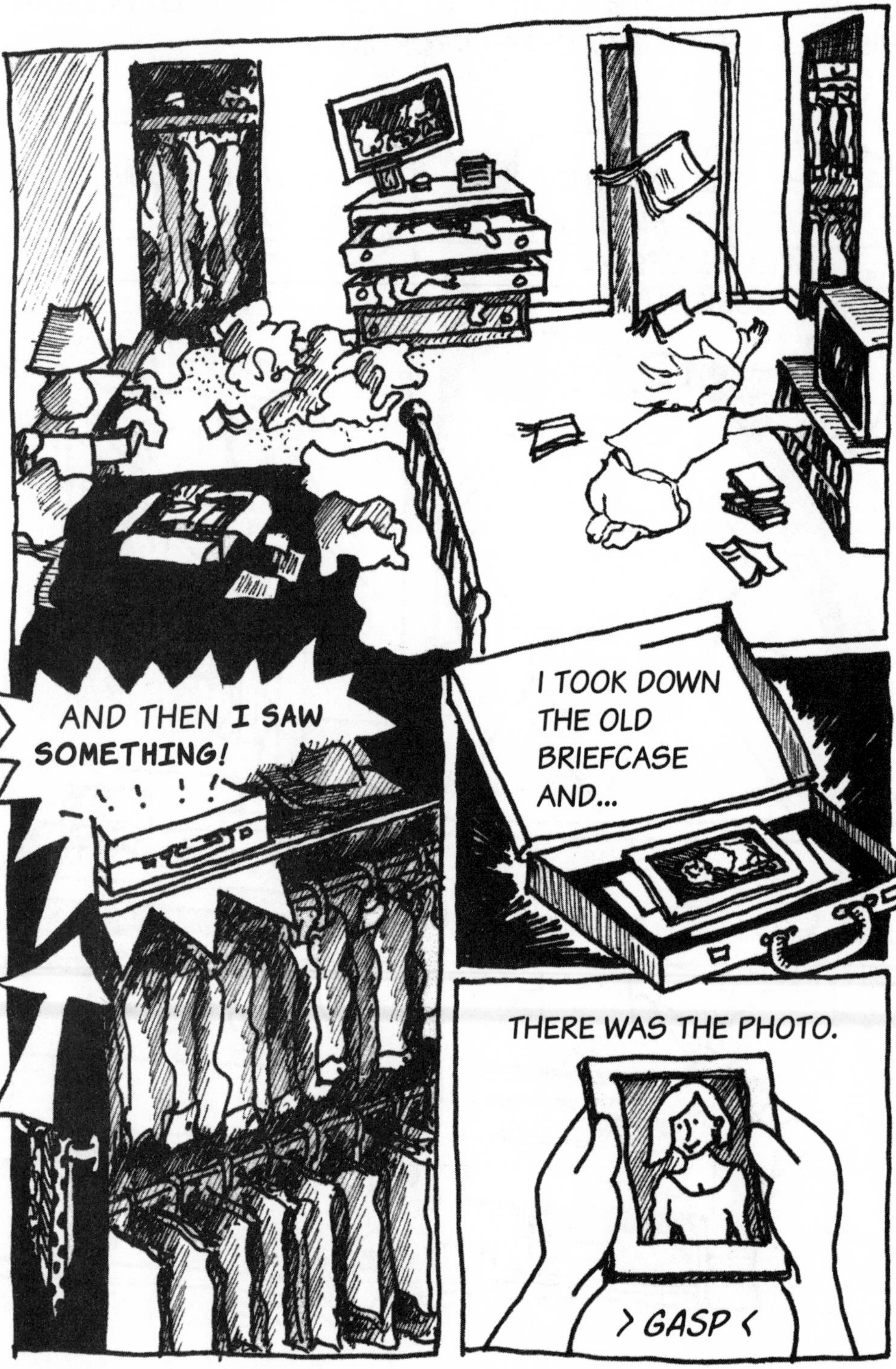
AND THEN I SAW SOMETHING!
I TOOK DOWN THE OLD BRIEFCASE AND...
THERE WAS THE PHOTO.
> GASP <

FINALLY I KNEW ALL OF THIS WASN'T ABOUT BRIAN'S DENIALS, BUT MY OWN. I COLLAPSED ONTO THE CARPET AND CRIED UNTIL I THOUGHT THE WHOLE HOUSE MIGHT FLOAT AWAY ON MY TEARS.

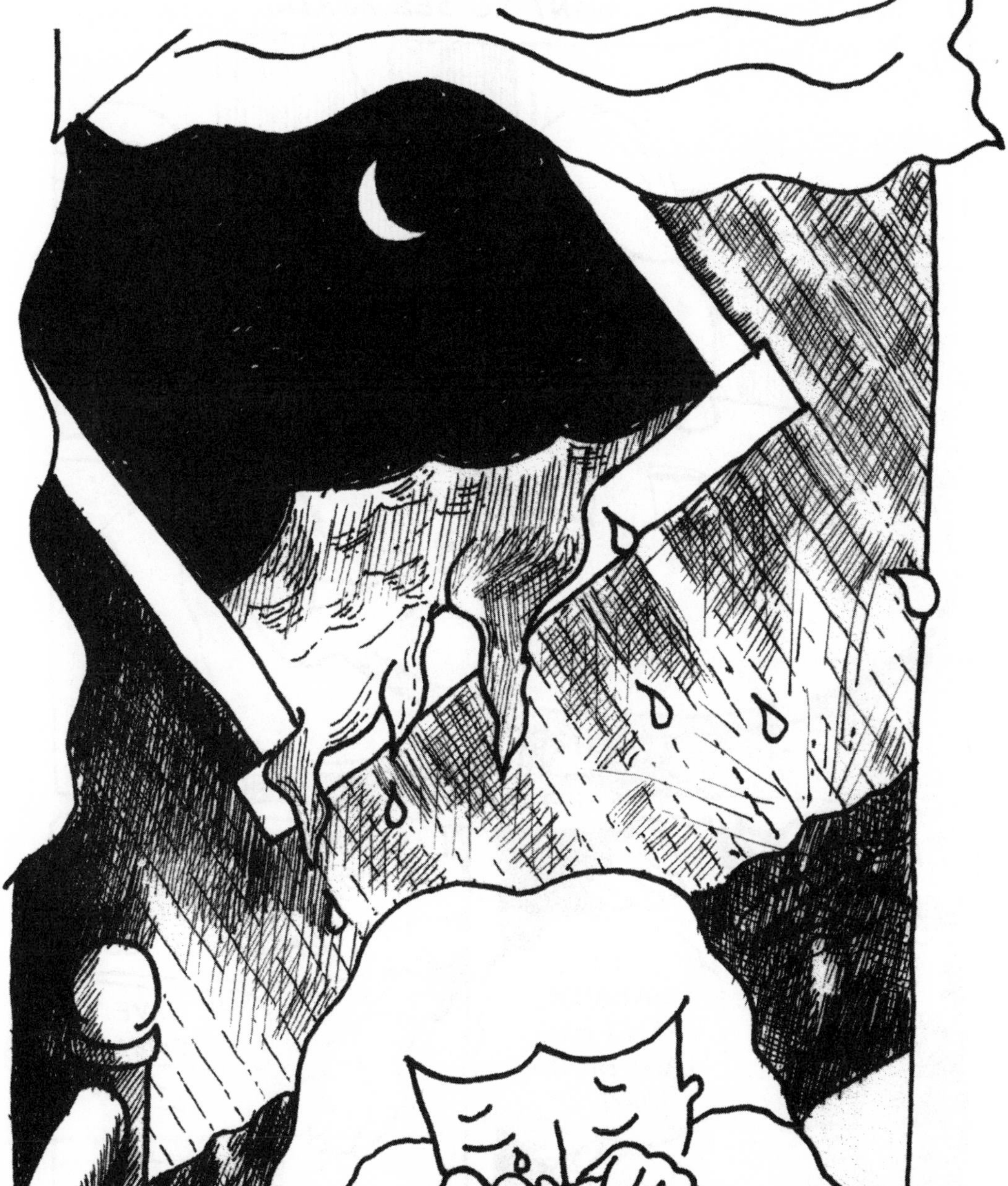

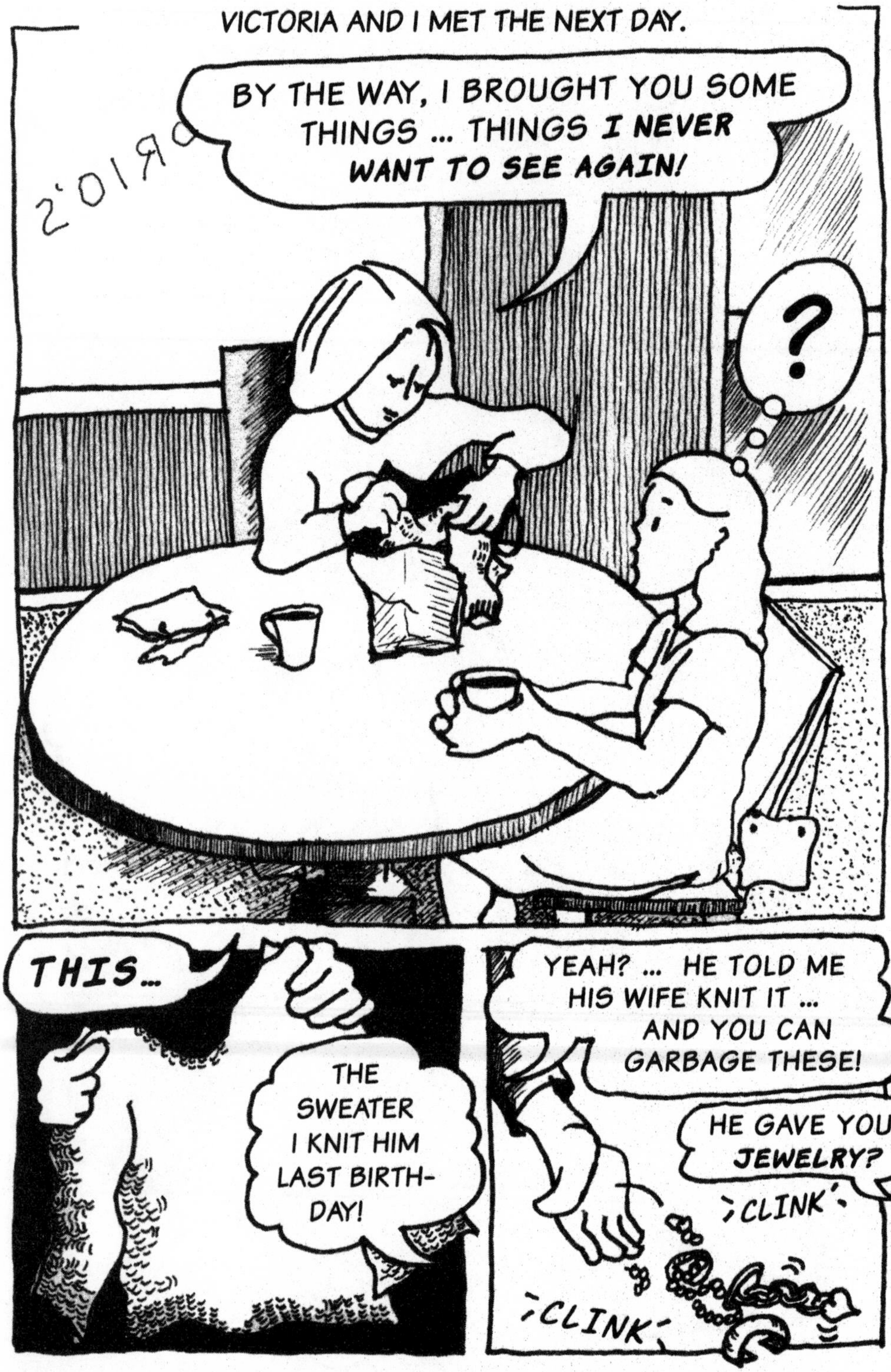
VICTORIA AND I MET THE NEXT DAY.
BY THE WAY, I BROUGHT YOU SOME THINGS ... THINGS I NEVER WANT TO SEE AGAIN!
?
THIS...
THE SWEATER I KNIT HIM LAST BIRTH-DAY!
YEAH? ... HE TOLD ME HIS WIFE KNIT IT ... AND YOU CAN GARBAGE THESE!
HE GAVE YOU JEWELRY?
CLINK
CLINK

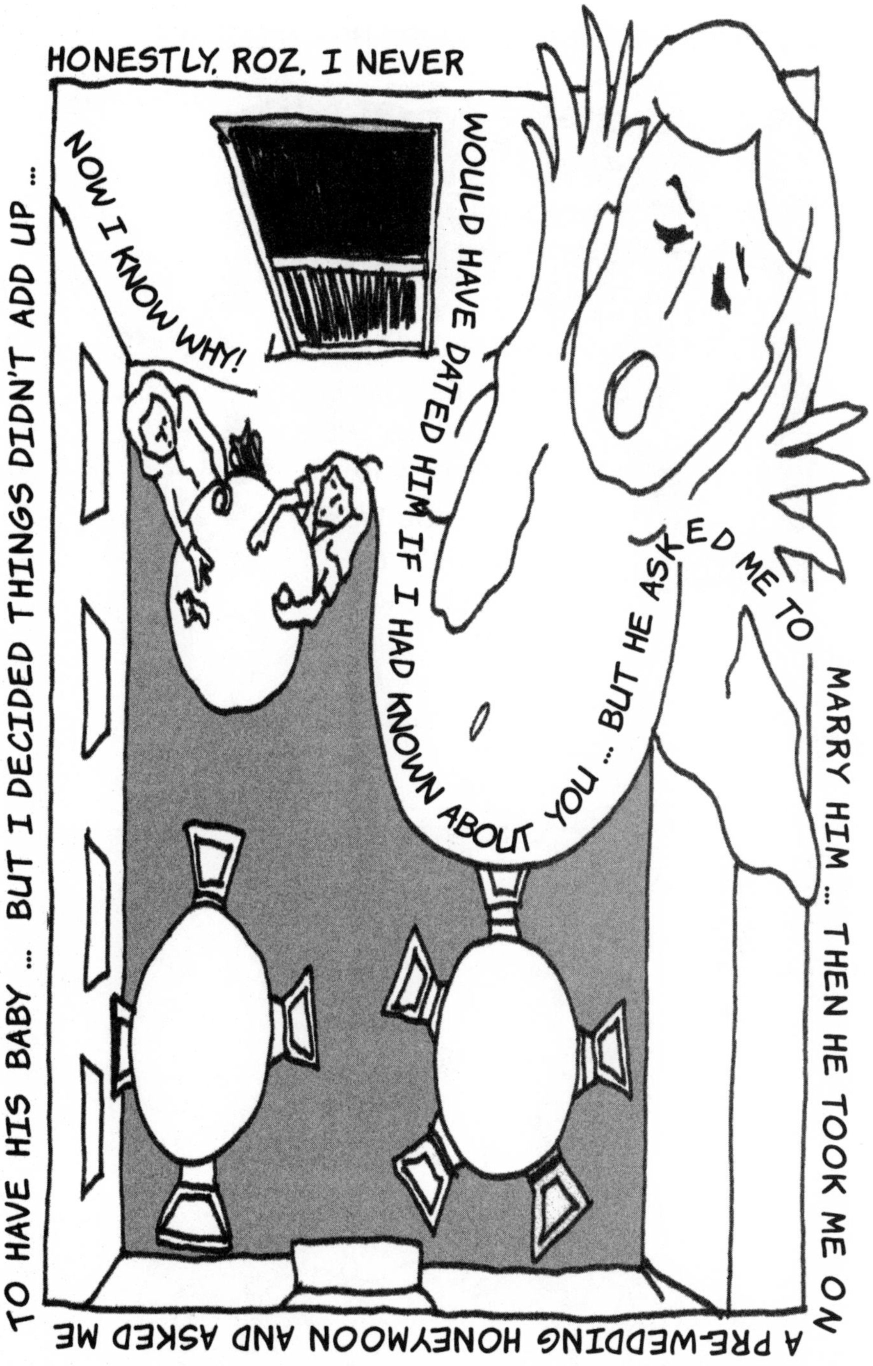
HONESTLY, ROZ, I NEVER
WOULD HAVE DATED HIM IF I HAD KNOWN ABOUT YOU ... BUT HE ASKED ME TO
MARRY HIM ... THEN HE TOOK ME ON
A PRE-WEDDING HONEYMOON AND ASKED ME
TO HAVE HIS BABY ... BUT I DECIDED THINGS DIDN'T ADD UP ...
NOW I KNOW WHY!

THE NEXT DAY WAS VALENTINE'S DAY. VICTORIA AND I EACH RECEIVED IDENTICAL FLOWERS FROM BRIAN. VICTORIA SUGGESTED WE MEET AT HER HOUSE FOR A VALENTINE DINNER OF OUR OWN...

I WAS AT VICTORIA'S HOUSE WHEN HE CALLED HER.

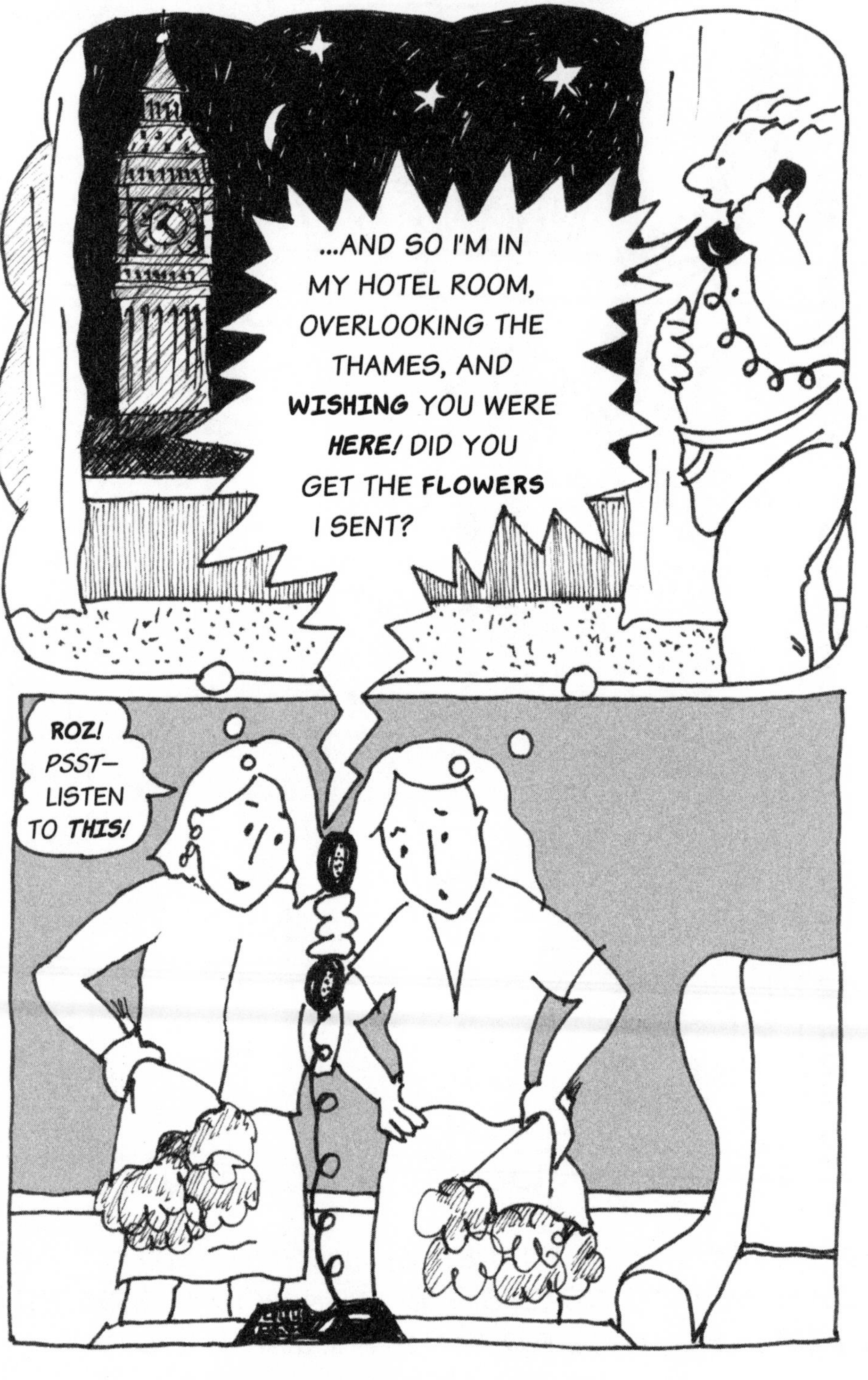
...AND SO I'M IN MY HOTEL ROOM, OVERLOOKING THE THAMES, AND WISHING YOU WERE HERE! DID YOU GET THE FLOWERS I SENT?
ROZ! PSST— LISTEN TO THIS!

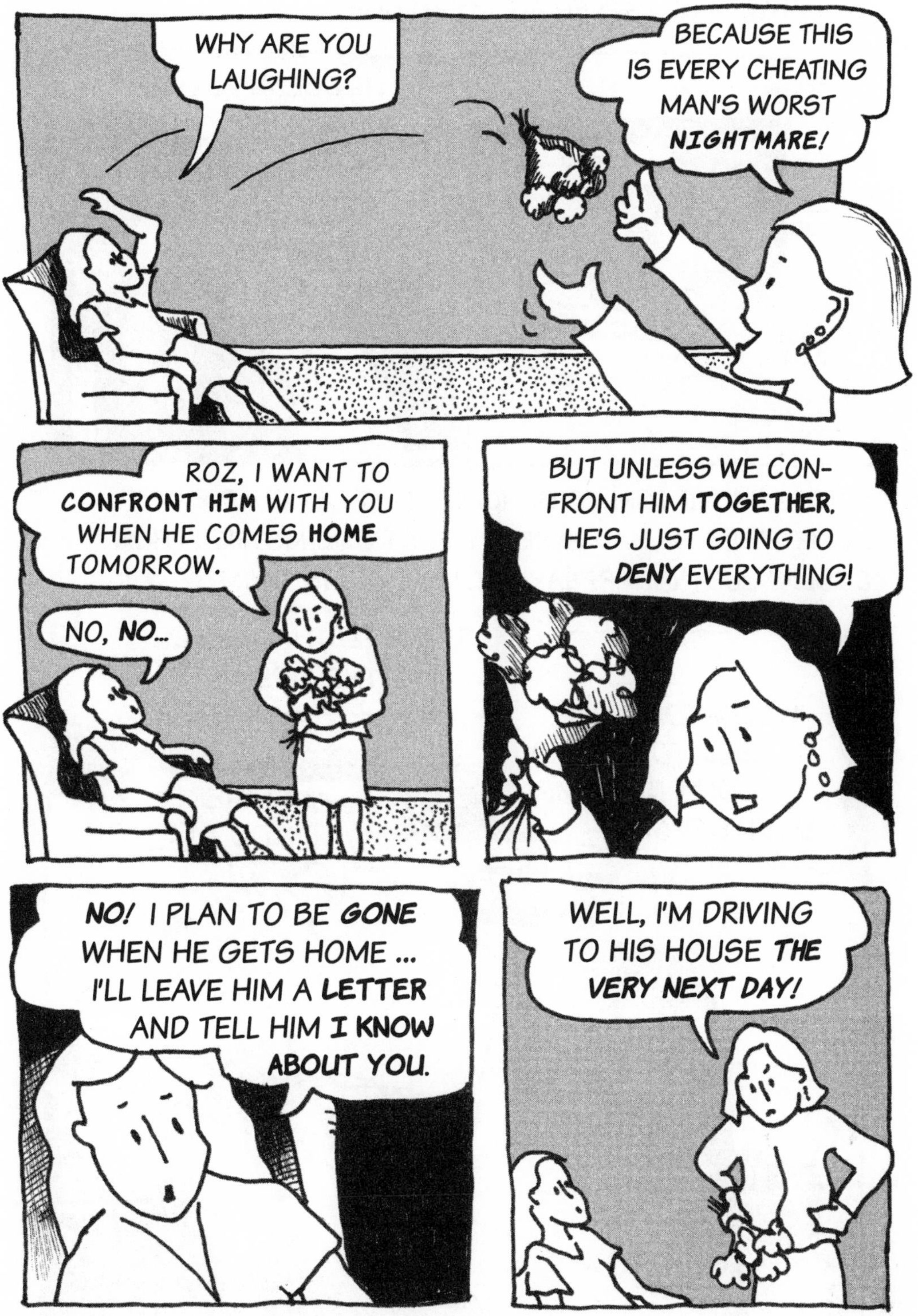
WHY ARE YOU LAUGHING?
BECAUSE THIS IS EVERY CHEATING MAN'S WORST NIGHTMARE!
ROZ, I WANT TO CONFRONT HIM WITH YOU WHEN HE COMES HOME TOMORROW.
NO, NO...
BUT UNLESS WE CON-FRONT HIM TOGETHER, HE'S JUST GOING TO DENY EVERYTHING!
NO! I PLAN TO BE GONE WHEN HE GETS HOME ... I'LL LEAVE HIM A LETTER AND TELL HIM I KNOW ABOUT YOU.
WELL, I'M DRIVING TO HIS HOUSE THE VERY NEXT DAY!

BY DAWN, I HAD PACKED ALL MY THINGS.

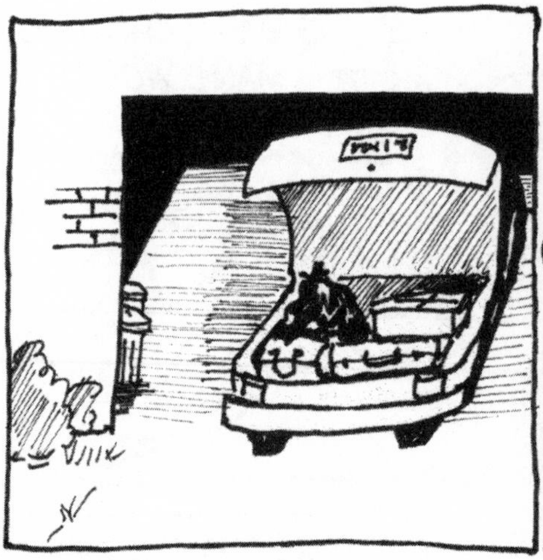

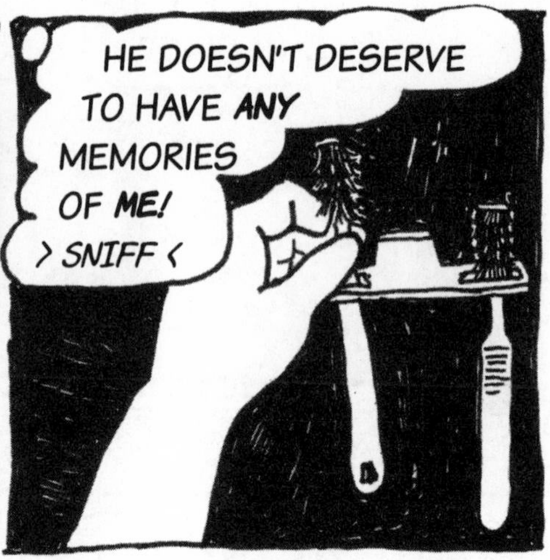
HE DOESN'T DESERVE TO HAVE **ANY** MEMORIES OF **ME!**
> SNIFF <

WHEN I DROVE TOM TO SCHOOL, I FELT I SHOULD SAY SOMETHING. HE HAD ALREADY LOST ONE MOTHER—HOW COULD I JUST DISAPPEAR WITHOUT TELLING HIM?

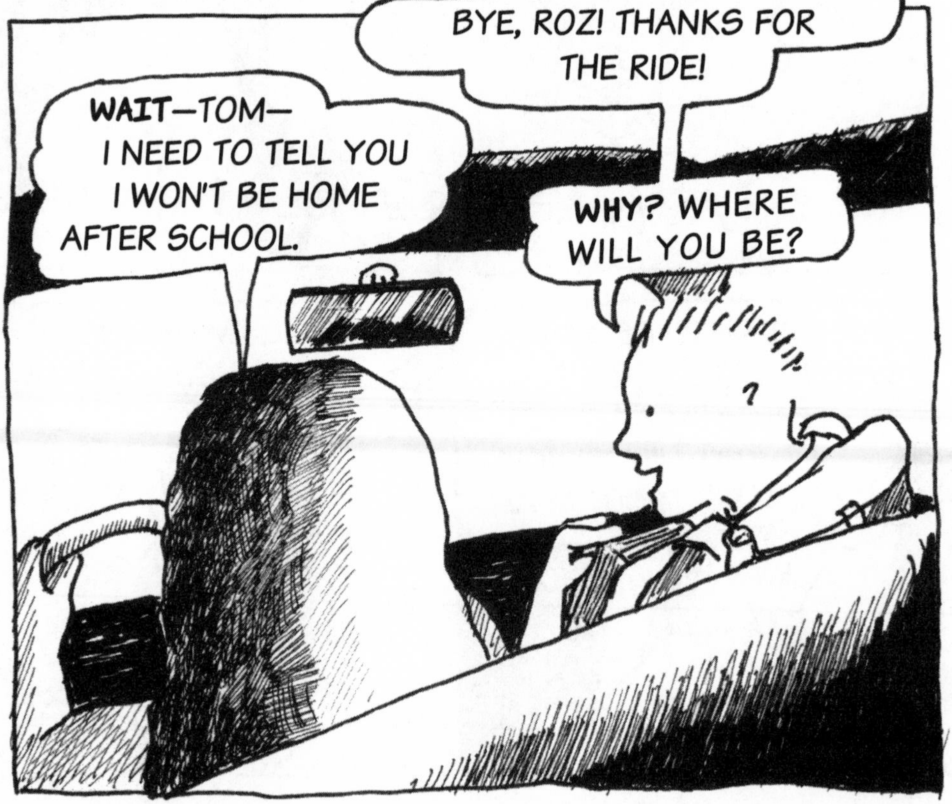
BYE, ROZ! THANKS FOR THE RIDE!
WAIT—TOM— I NEED TO TELL YOU I WON'T BE HOME AFTER SCHOOL.
WHY? WHERE WILL YOU BE?
?

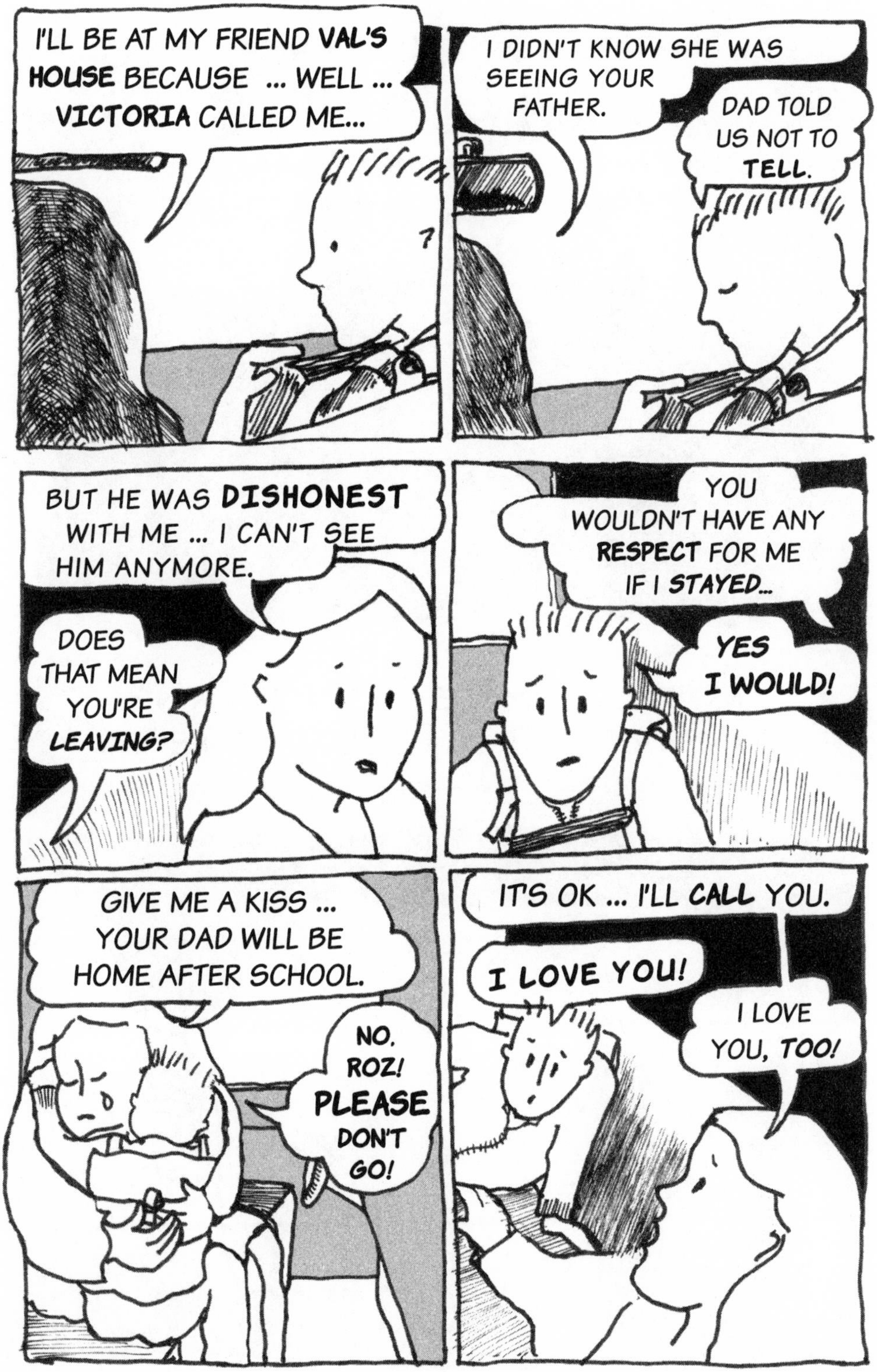
I'LL BE AT MY FRIEND VAL'S HOUSE BECAUSE ... WELL ... VICTORIA CALLED ME...
I DIDN'T KNOW SHE WAS SEEING YOUR FATHER.
DAD TOLD US NOT TO TELL.
BUT HE WAS DISHONEST WITH ME ... I CAN'T SEE HIM ANYMORE.
DOES THAT MEAN YOU'RE LEAVING?
YOU WOULDN'T HAVE ANY RESPECT FOR ME IF I STAYED...
YES I WOULD!
GIVE ME A KISS ... YOUR DAD WILL BE HOME AFTER SCHOOL.
NO, ROZ! PLEASE DON'T GO!
IT'S OK ... I'LL CALL YOU.
I LOVE YOU!
I LOVE YOU, TOO!

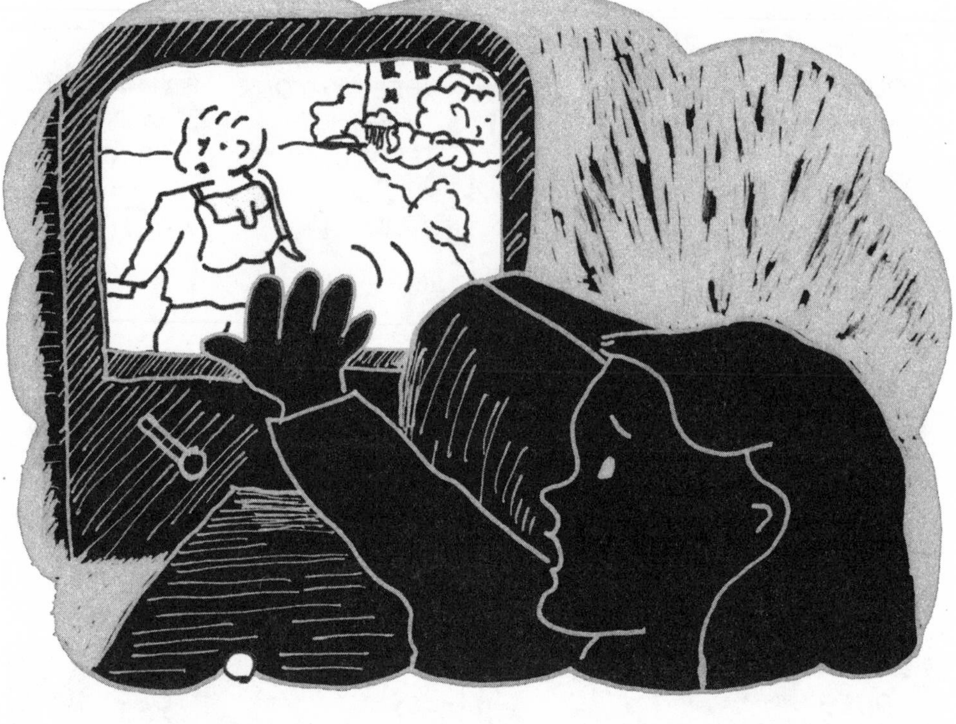

I KNEW THE IMAGE OF TOM WALKING AWAY WOULD BE IN MY HEART FOREVER.

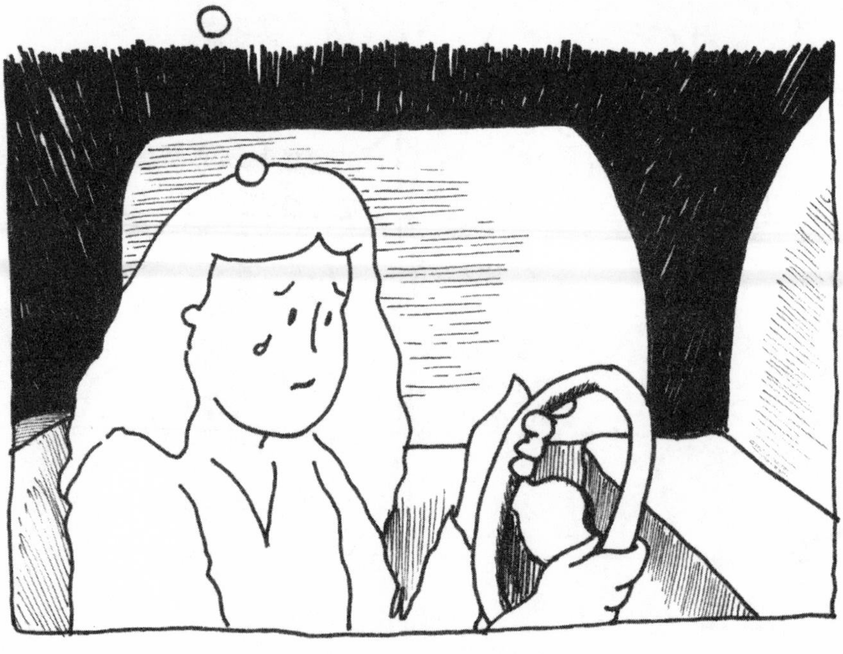

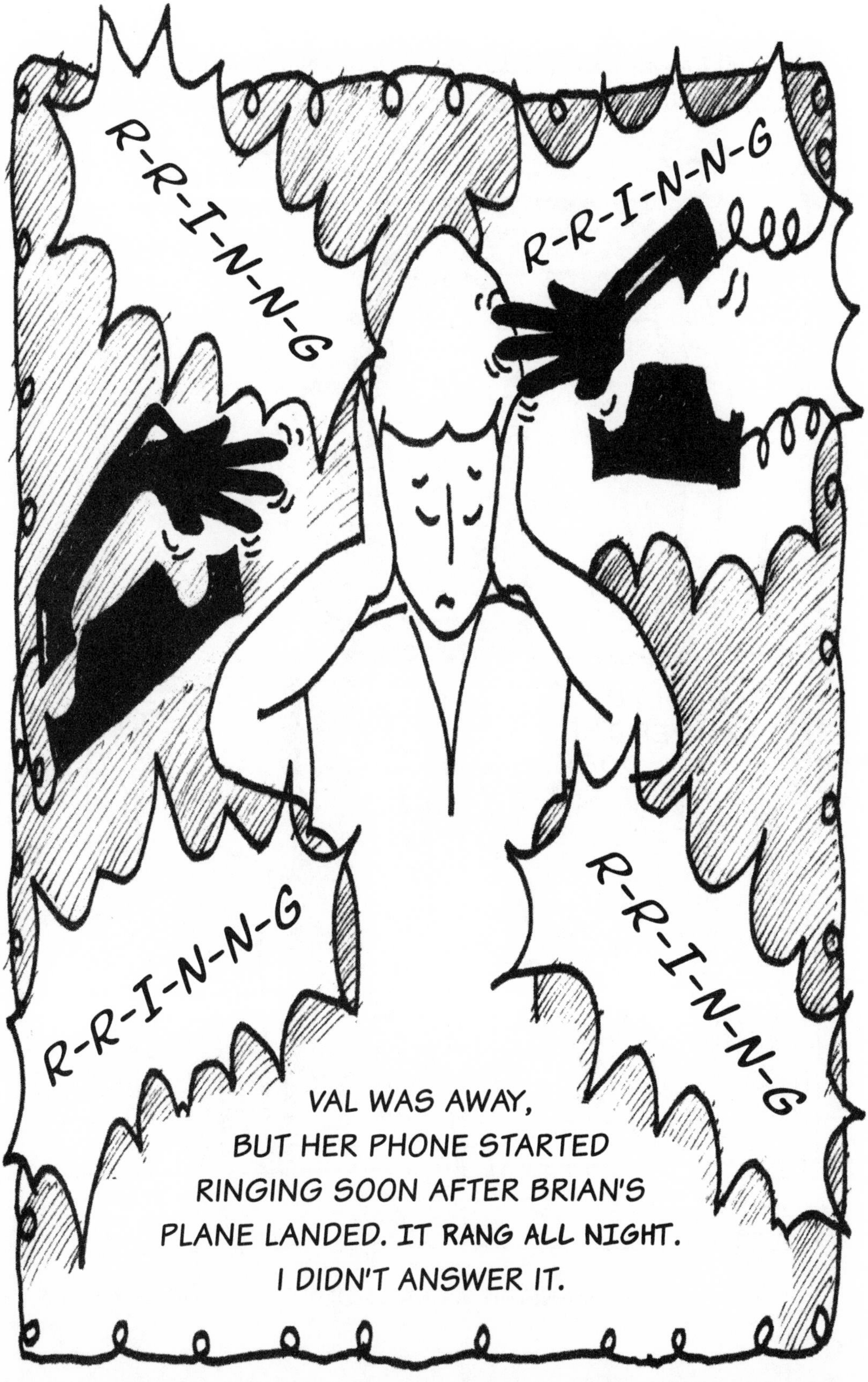
R-R-I-N-N-G
R-R-I-N-N-G
R-R-I-N-N-G
R-R-I-N-N-G
VAL WAS AWAY,
BUT HER PHONE STARTED
RINGING SOON AFTER BRIAN'S
PLANE LANDED. IT RANG ALL NIGHT.
I DIDN'T ANSWER IT.

THE NEXT MORNING I COULD HEAR BANGING AT VAL'S DOOR. I LOOKED OUT AT THE STREET AND SAW BRIAN'S CAR.

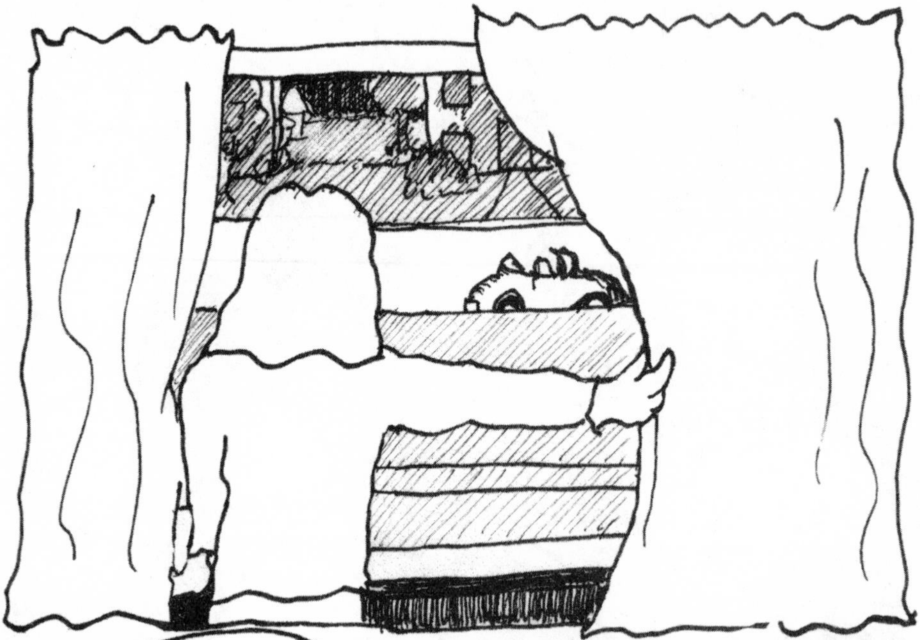

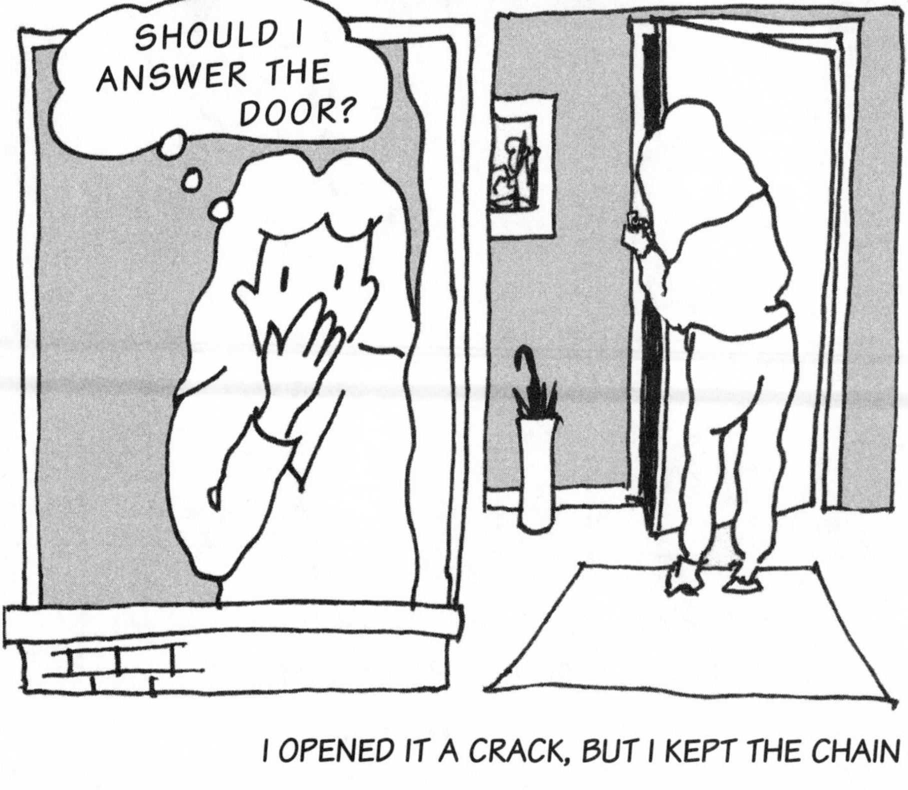
SHOULD I ANSWER THE DOOR?

I OPENED IT A CRACK, BUT I KEPT THE CHAIN ON.

BRIAN LOOKED LIKE HE HAD BEEN CRYING ALL NIGHT.
HE LOOKED LIKE HE WAS IN SHOCK. HE WAS HOLDING MY LETTER.

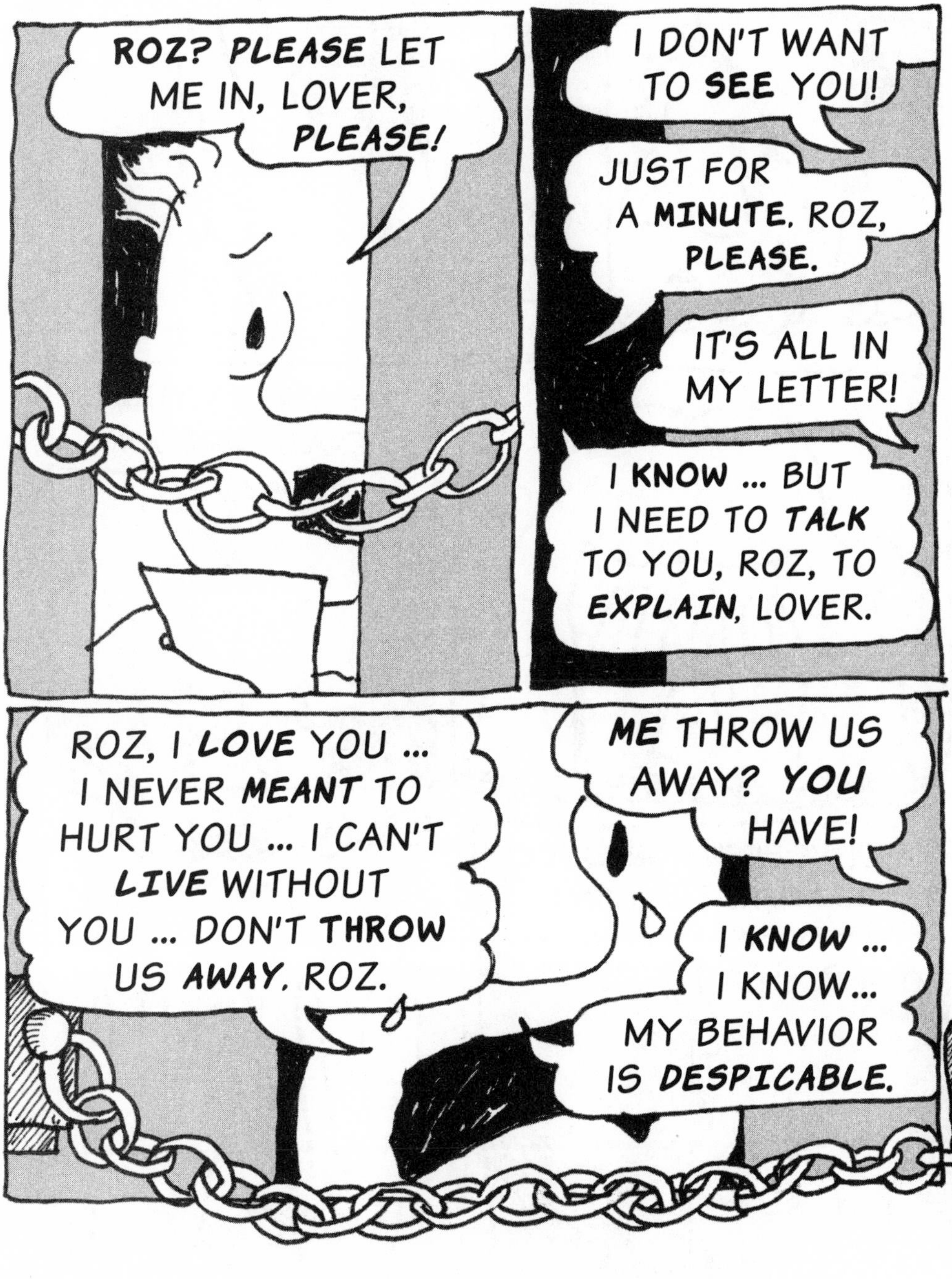
ROZ? PLEASE LET ME IN, LOVER, PLEASE!
I DON'T WANT TO SEE YOU!
JUST FOR A MINUTE. ROZ, PLEASE.
IT'S ALL IN MY LETTER!
I KNOW ... BUT I NEED TO TALK TO YOU, ROZ, TO EXPLAIN, LOVER.
ROZ, I LOVE YOU ... I NEVER MEANT TO HURT YOU ... I CAN'T LIVE WITHOUT YOU ... DON'T THROW US AWAY. ROZ.
ME THROW US AWAY? YOU HAVE!
I KNOW ... I KNOW... MY BEHAVIOR IS DESPICABLE.

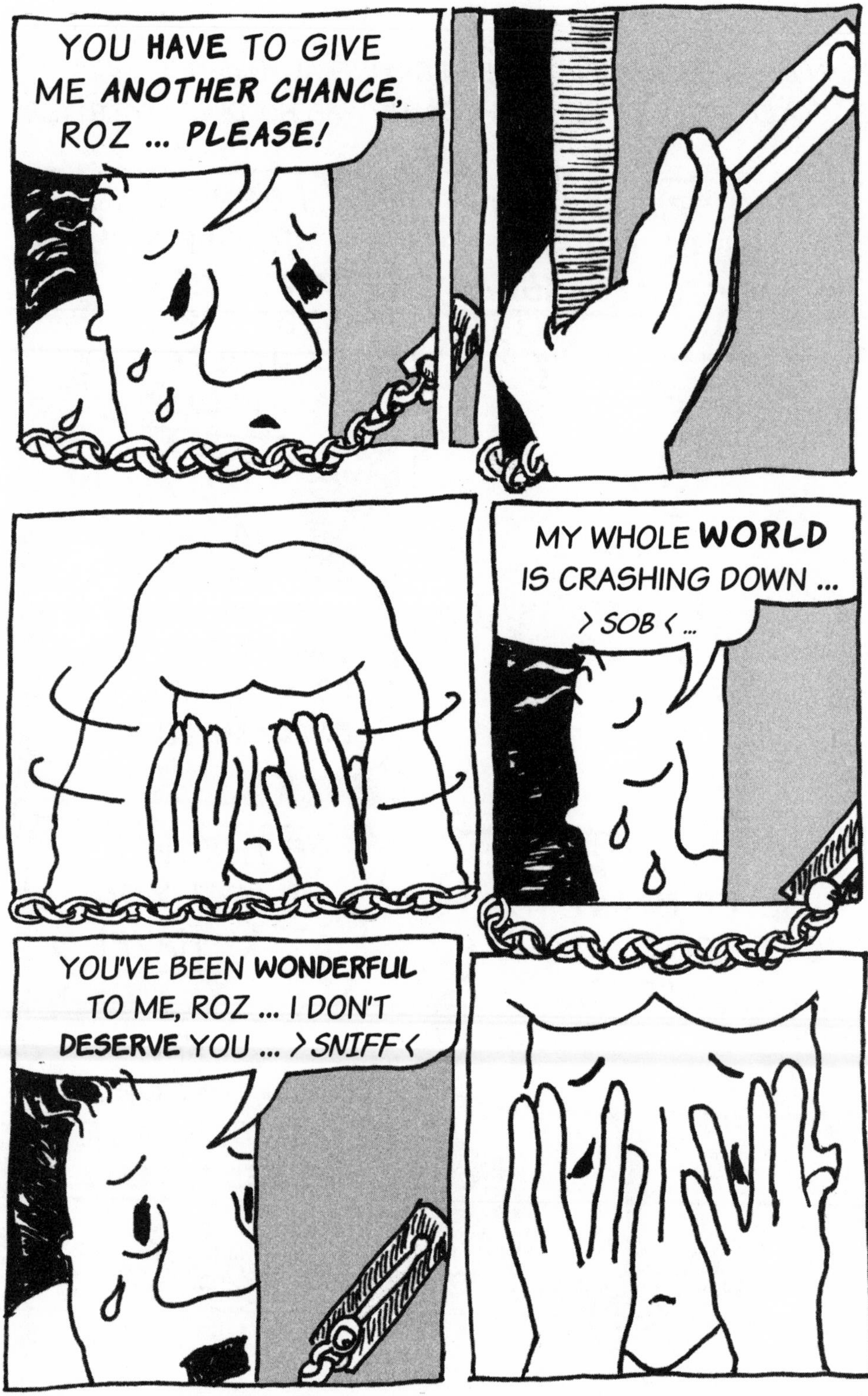
YOU HAVE TO GIVE ME ANOTHER CHANCE, ROZ ... PLEASE!
MY WHOLE WORLD IS CRASHING DOWN ... >SOB< ...
YOU'VE BEEN WONDERFUL TO ME, ROZ ... I DON'T DESERVE YOU ... >SNIFF<

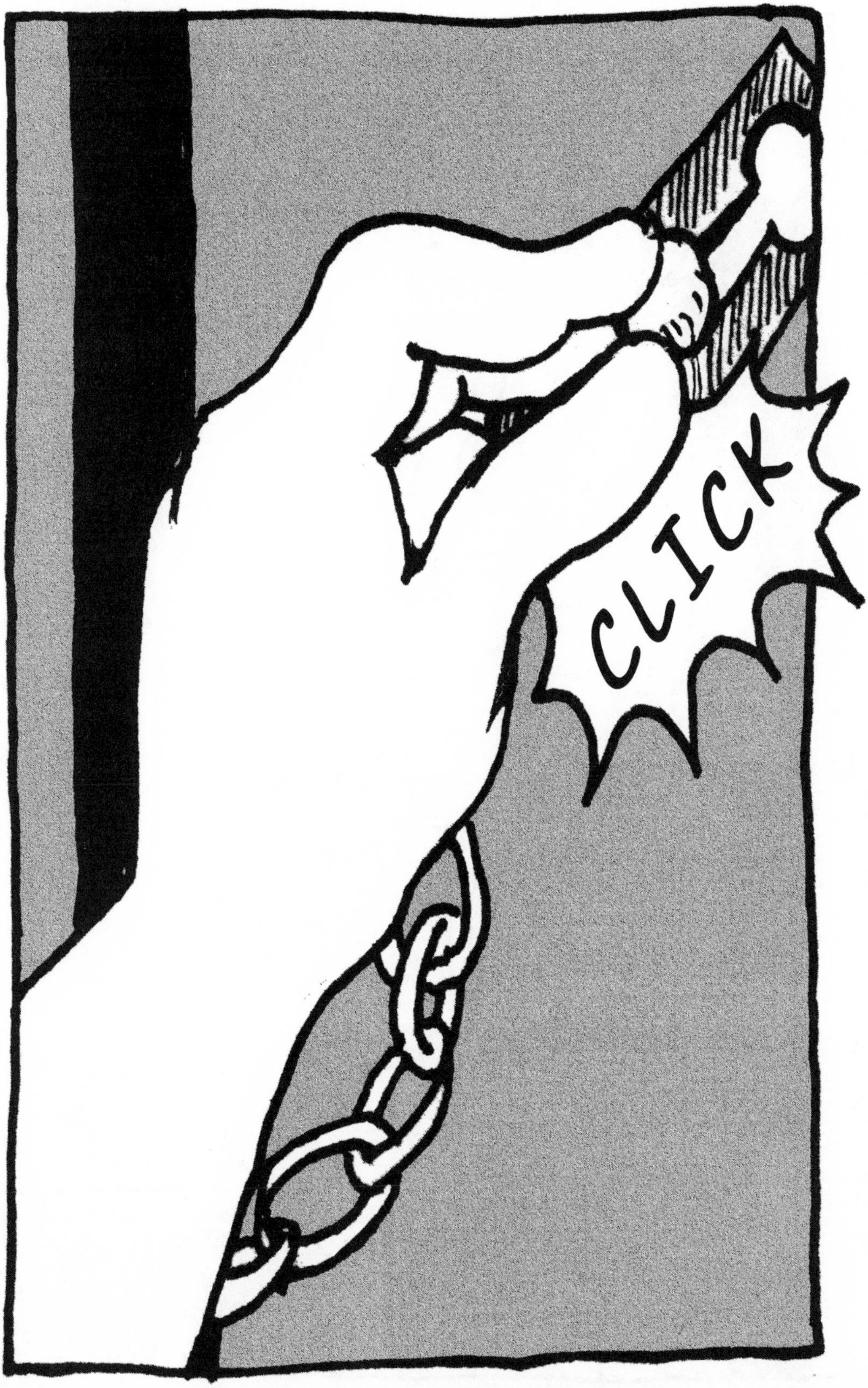
CLICK

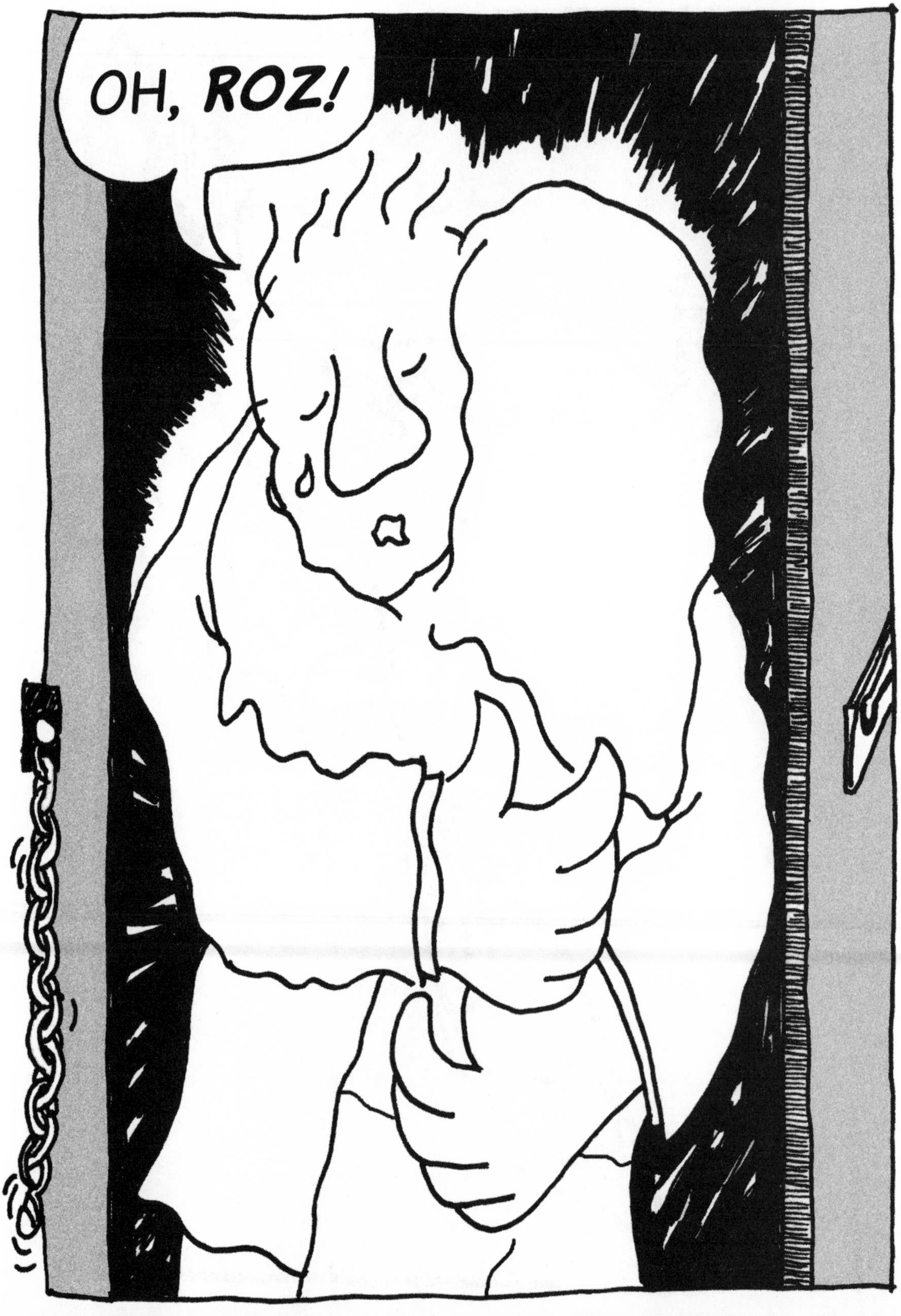
OH, ROZ!

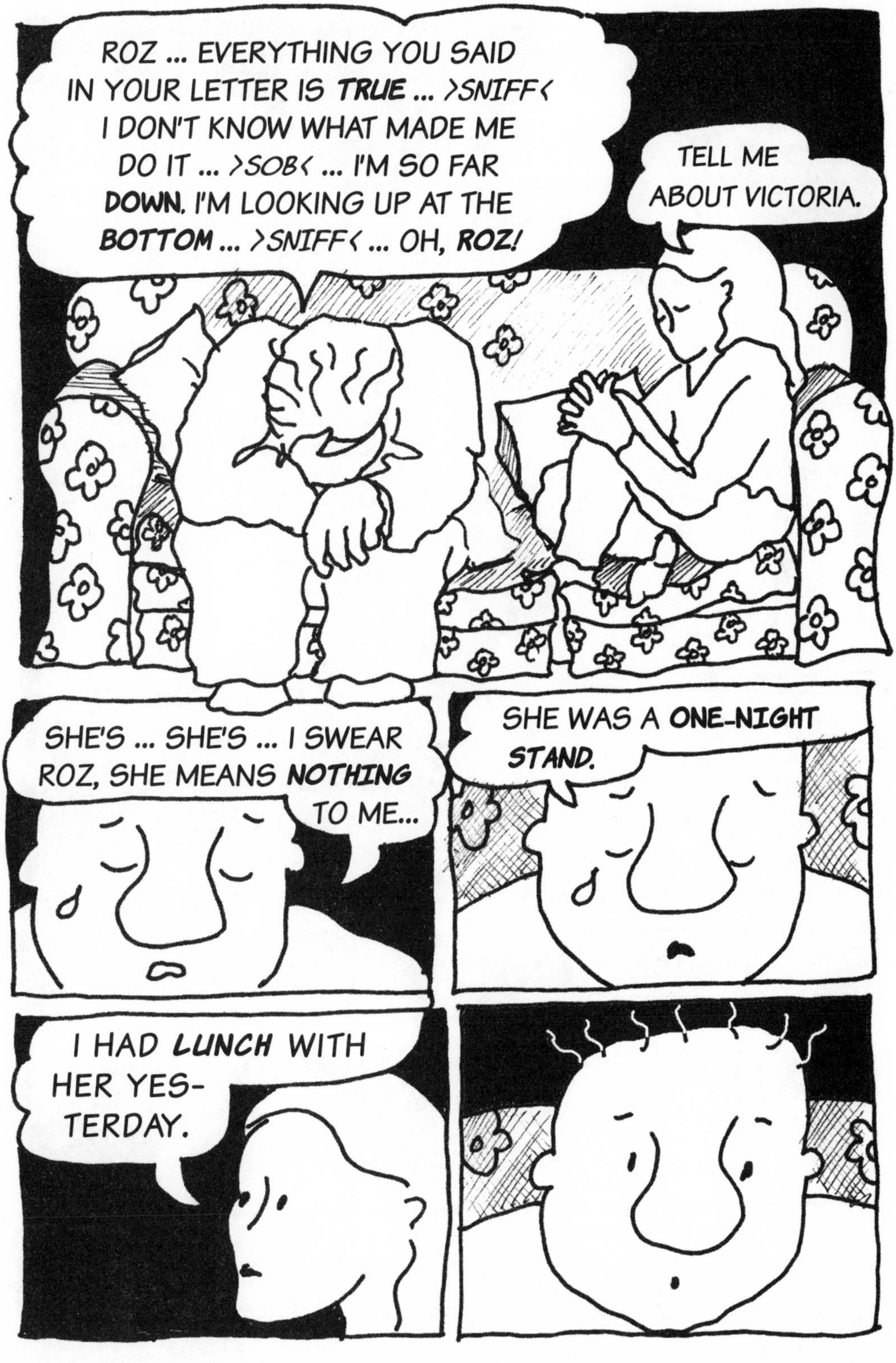
ROZ ... EVERYTHING YOU SAID IN YOUR LETTER IS **TRUE** ... >SNIFF< I DON'T KNOW WHAT MADE ME DO IT ... >SOB< ... I'M SO FAR **DOWN**. I'M LOOKING UP AT THE **BOTTOM** ... >SNIFF< ... OH, **ROZ!**
TELL ME ABOUT VICTORIA.
SHE'S ... SHE'S ... I SWEAR ROZ, SHE MEANS **NOTHING** TO ME...
SHE WAS A **ONE-NIGHT STAND.**
I HAD **LUNCH** WITH HER YES-TERDAY.

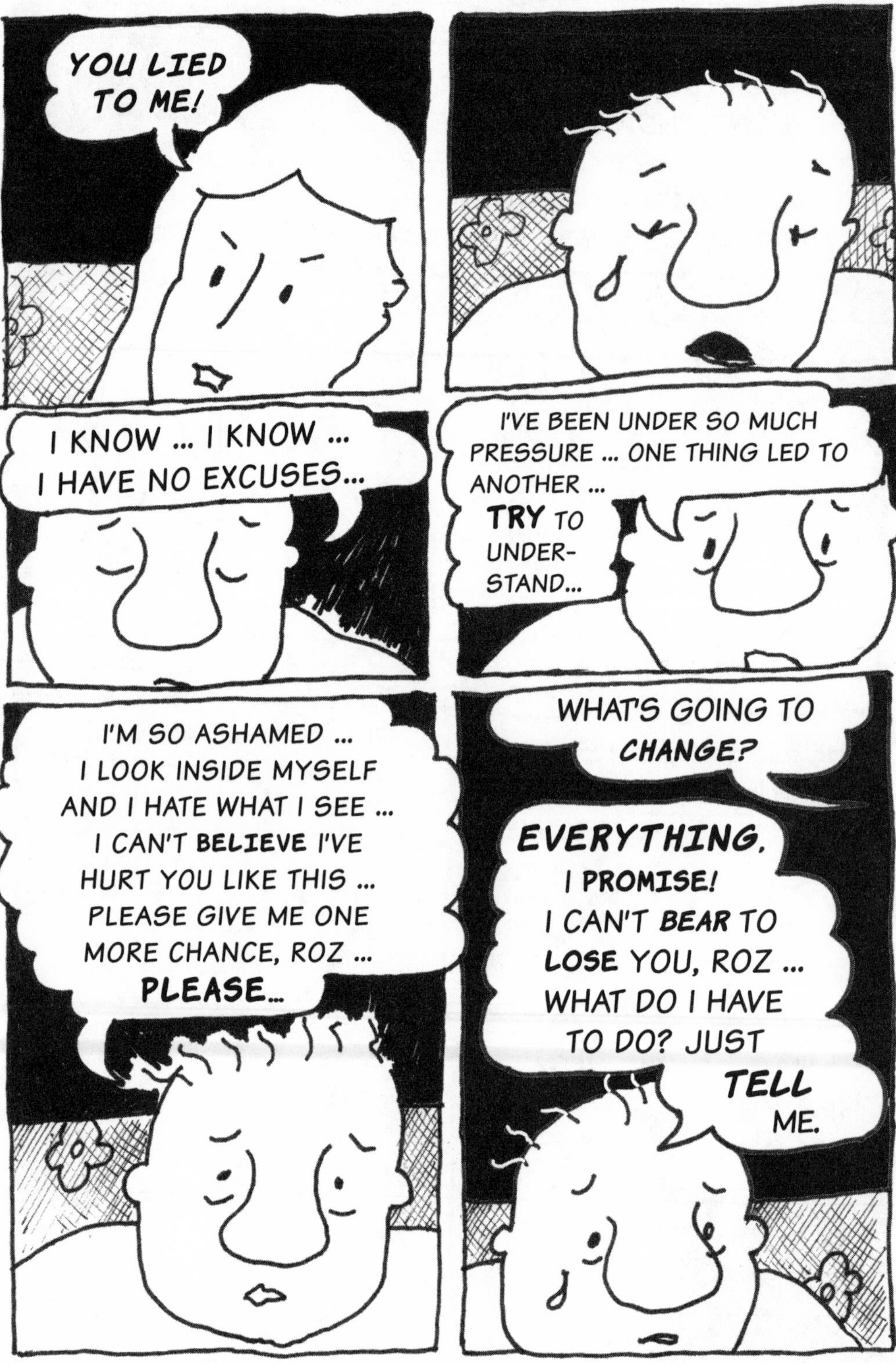
YOU LIED TO ME!
I KNOW ... I KNOW ... I HAVE NO EXCUSES...
I'VE BEEN UNDER SO MUCH PRESSURE ... ONE THING LED TO ANOTHER ... TRY TO UNDER-STAND...
I'M SO ASHAMED ... I LOOK INSIDE MYSELF AND I HATE WHAT I SEE ... I CAN'T BELIEVE I'VE HURT YOU LIKE THIS ... PLEASE GIVE ME ONE MORE CHANCE, ROZ ... PLEASE...
WHAT'S GOING TO CHANGE?
EVERYTHING. I PROMISE! I CAN'T BEAR TO LOSE YOU, ROZ ... WHAT DO I HAVE TO DO? JUST TELL ME.

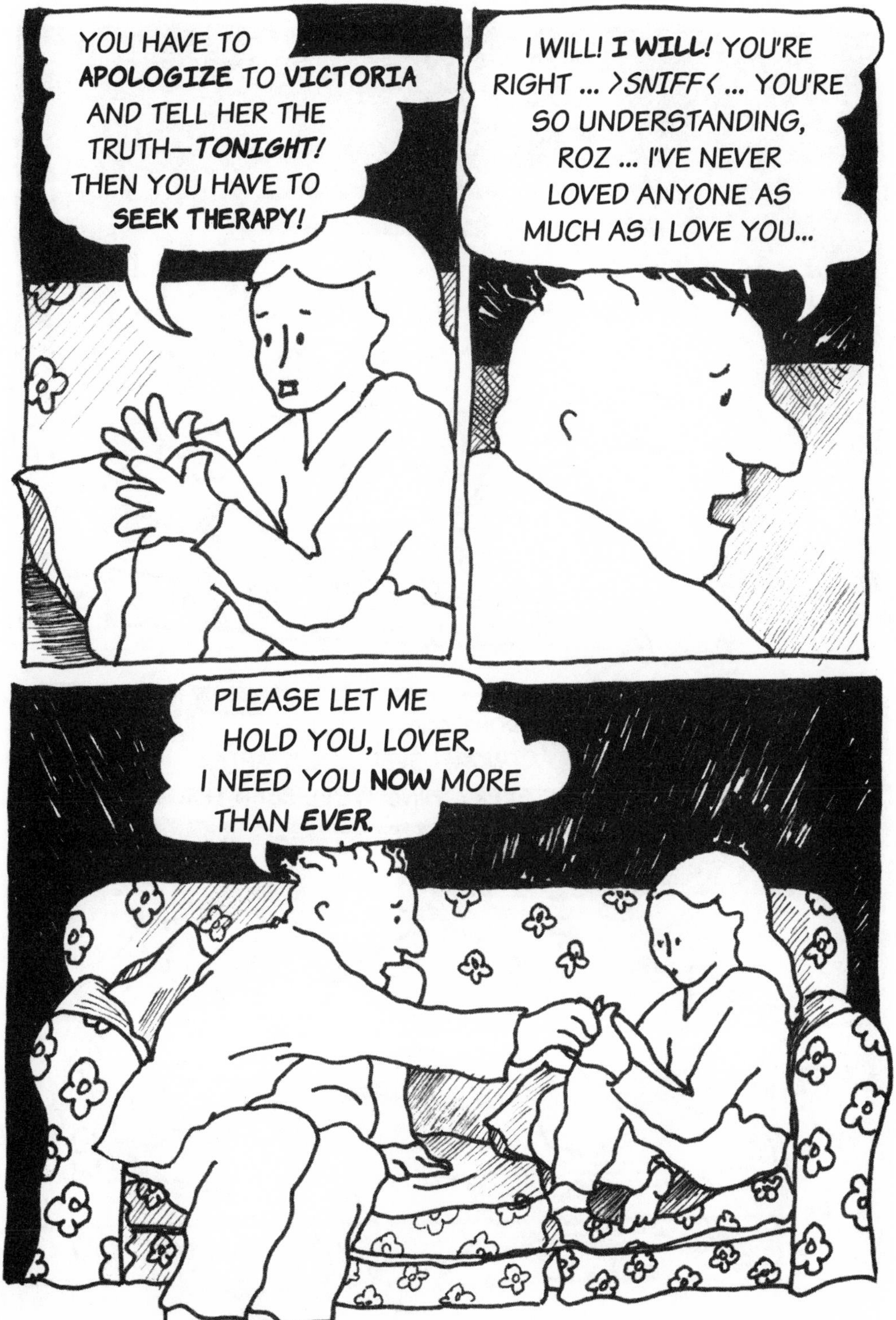
YOU HAVE TO APOLOGIZE TO VICTORIA AND TELL HER THE TRUTH—TONIGHT! THEN YOU HAVE TO SEEK THERAPY!
I WILL! I WILL! YOU'RE RIGHT ... >SNIFF< ... YOU'RE SO UNDERSTANDING, ROZ ... I'VE NEVER LOVED ANYONE AS MUCH AS I LOVE YOU...
PLEASE LET ME HOLD YOU, LOVER, I NEED YOU NOW MORE THAN EVER.

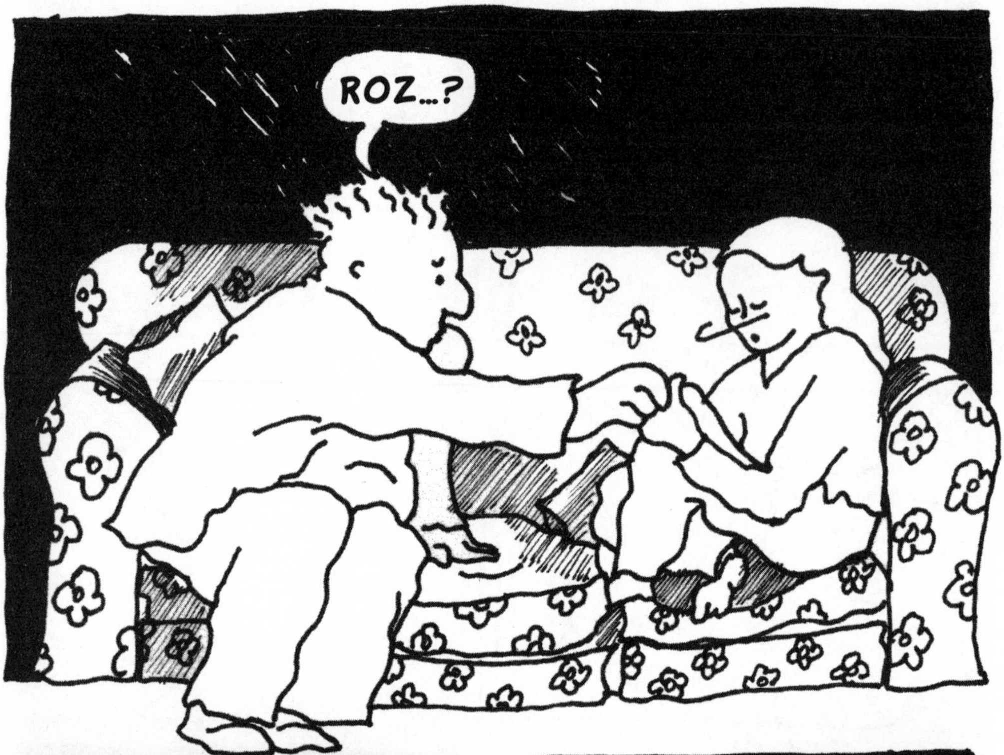
ROZ...?

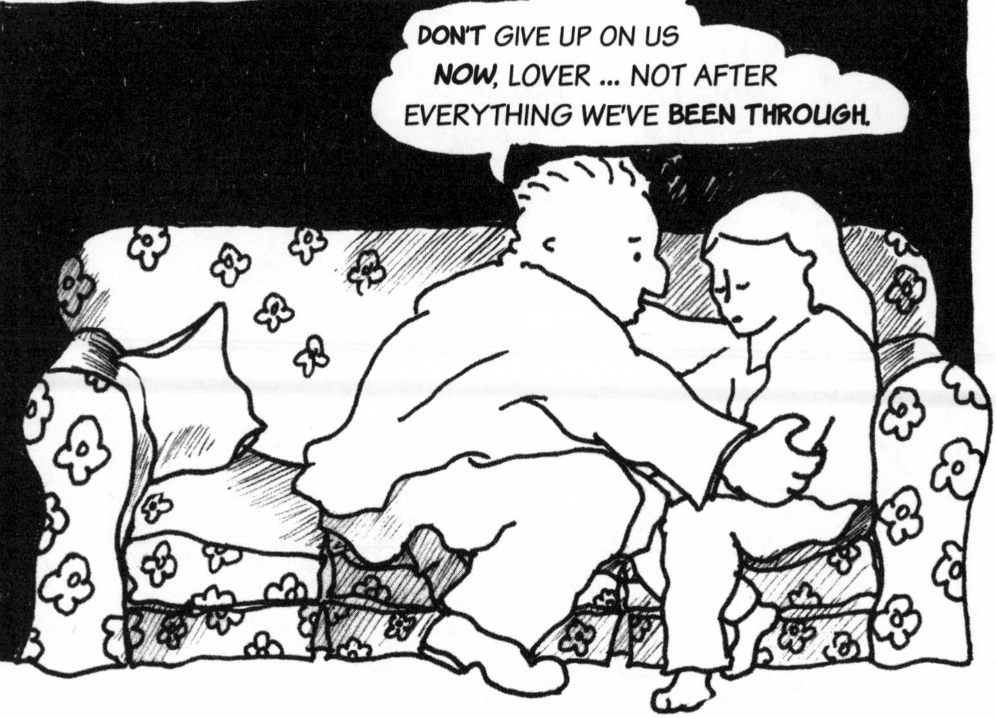
DON'T GIVE UP ON US NOW, LOVER ... NOT AFTER EVERYTHING WE'VE BEEN THROUGH.

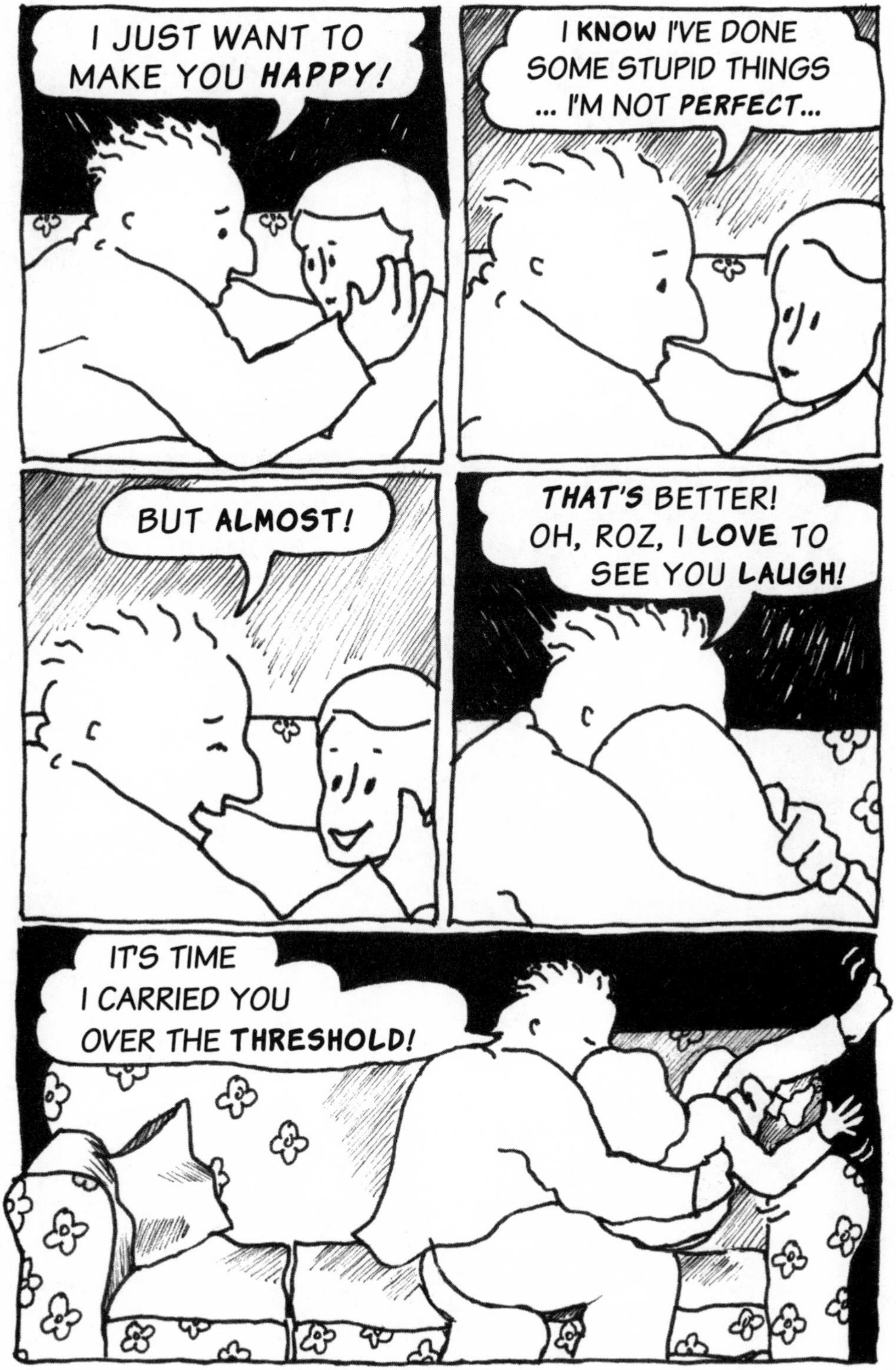
I JUST WANT TO MAKE YOU **HAPPY!**
I **KNOW** I'VE DONE SOME STUPID THINGS ... I'M NOT **PERFECT**...
BUT **ALMOST!**
THAT'S BETTER! OH, ROZ, I **LOVE** TO SEE YOU **LAUGH!**
IT'S TIME I CARRIED YOU OVER THE **THRESHOLD!**

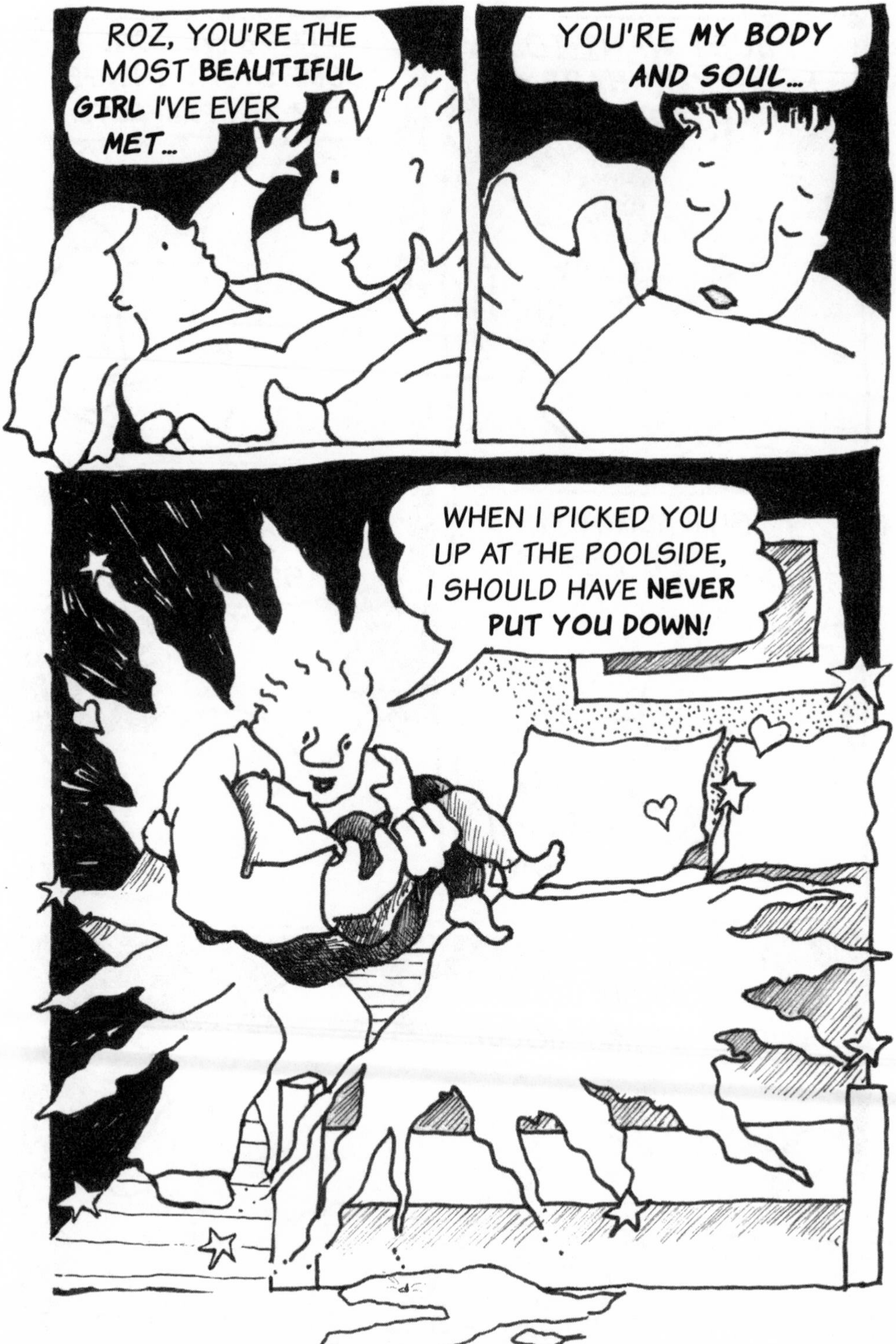
ROZ, YOU'RE THE MOST BEAUTIFUL GIRL I'VE EVER MET...
YOU'RE MY BODY AND SOUL...
WHEN I PICKED YOU UP AT THE POOLSIDE, I SHOULD HAVE NEVER PUT YOU DOWN!

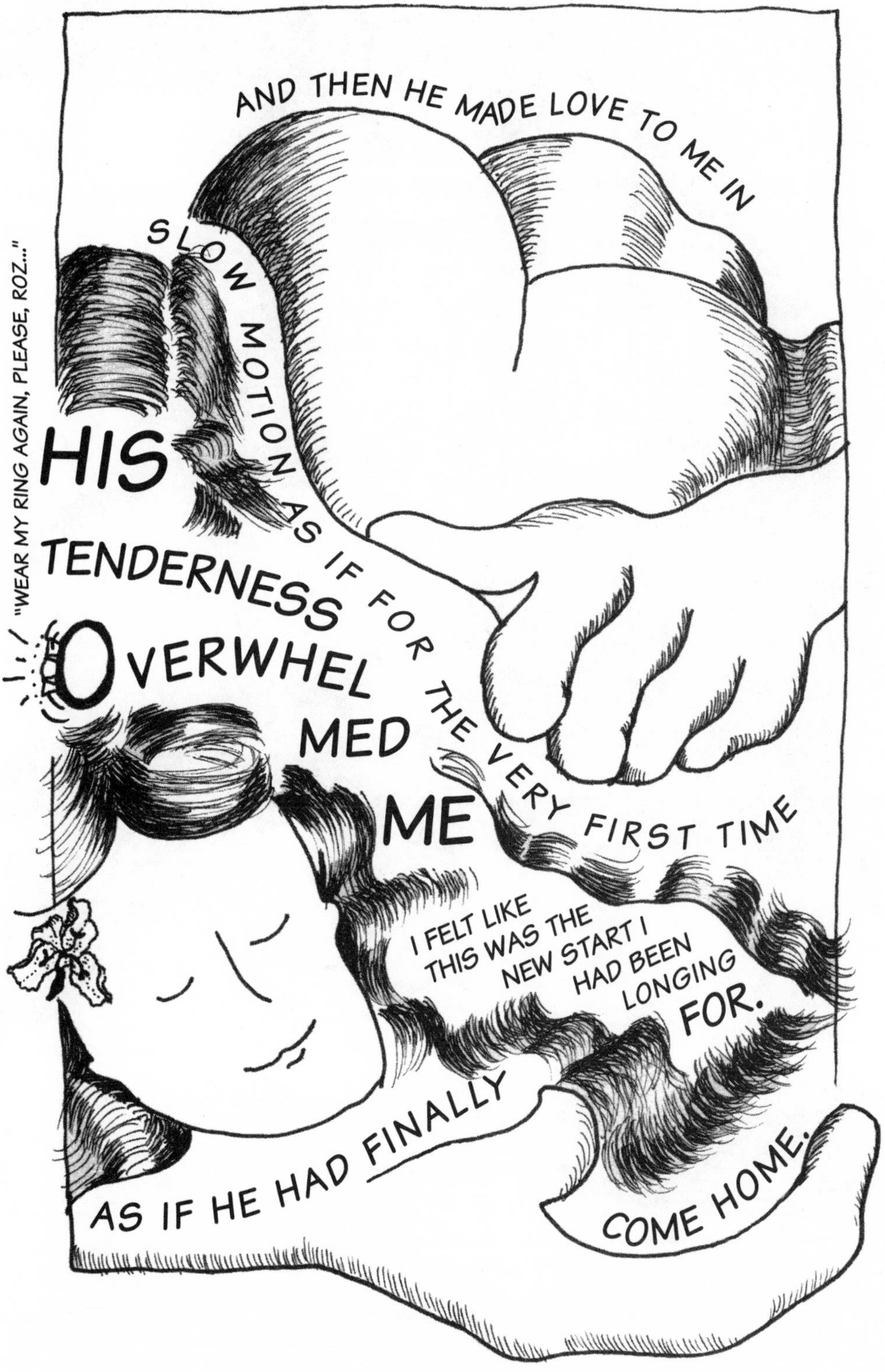

AND THEN HE MADE LOVE TO ME IN
SLOW MOTION AS IF FOR THE VERY FIRST TIME
"WEAR MY RING AGAIN, PLEASE, ROZ..."
HIS
TENDERNESS
OVERWHEL
MED
ME
I FELT LIKE THIS WAS THE NEW START I HAD BEEN LONGING FOR.
AS IF HE HAD FINALLY
COME HOME.

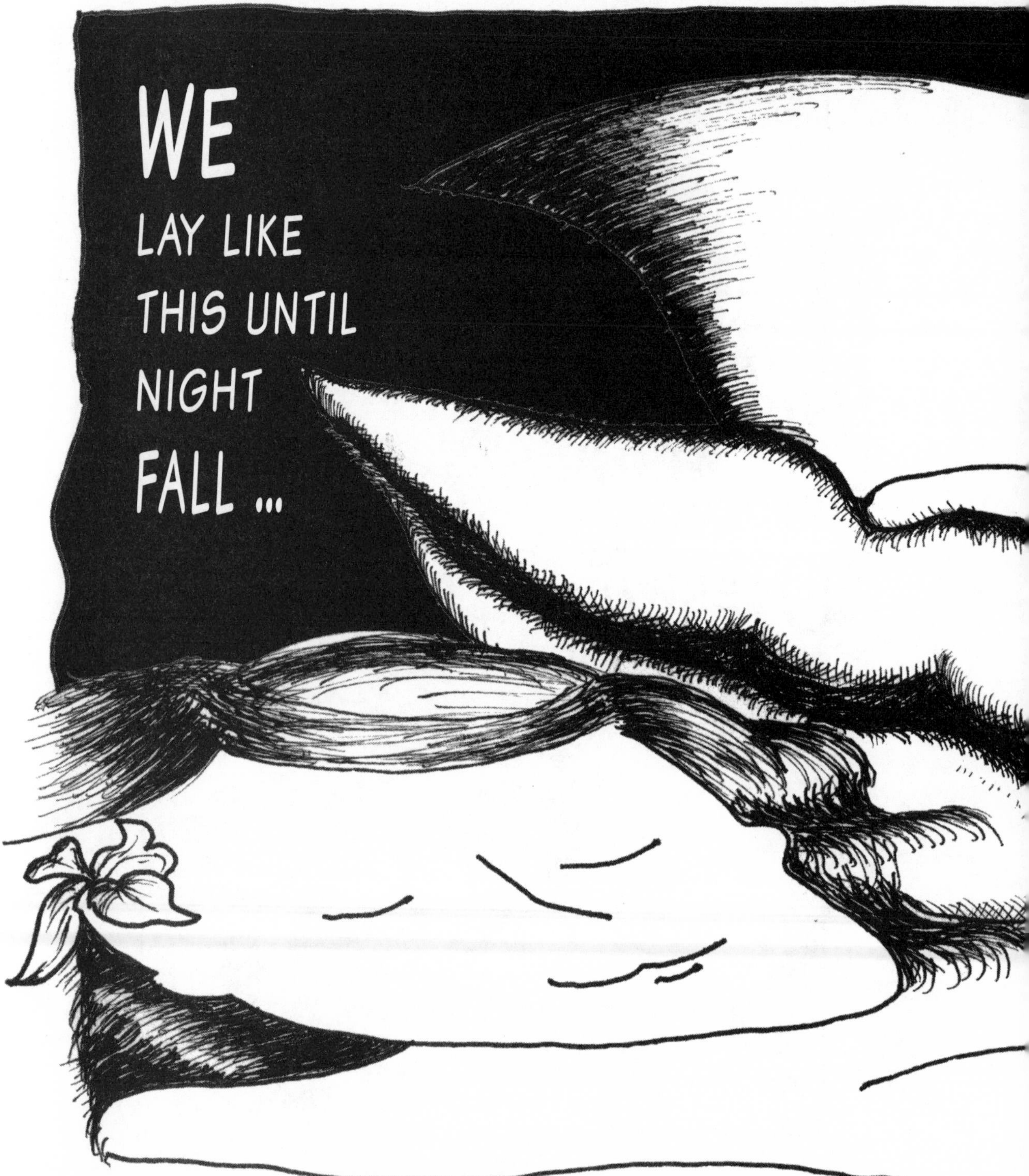
WE
LAY LIKE
THIS UNTIL
NIGHT
FALL ...

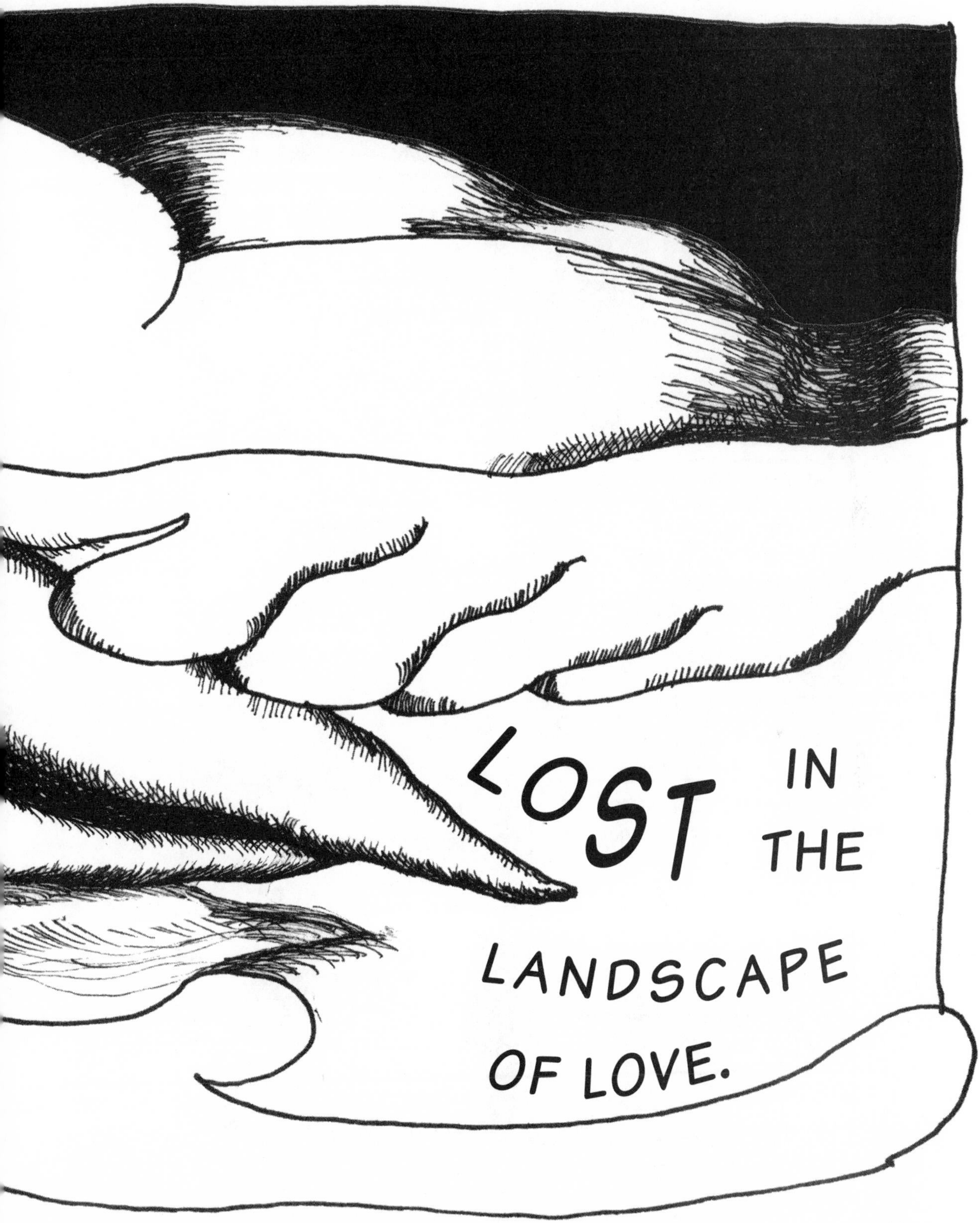
LOST IN THE LANDSCAPE OF LOVE.

BY THE TIME BRIAN LEFT, IT WAS DARK.

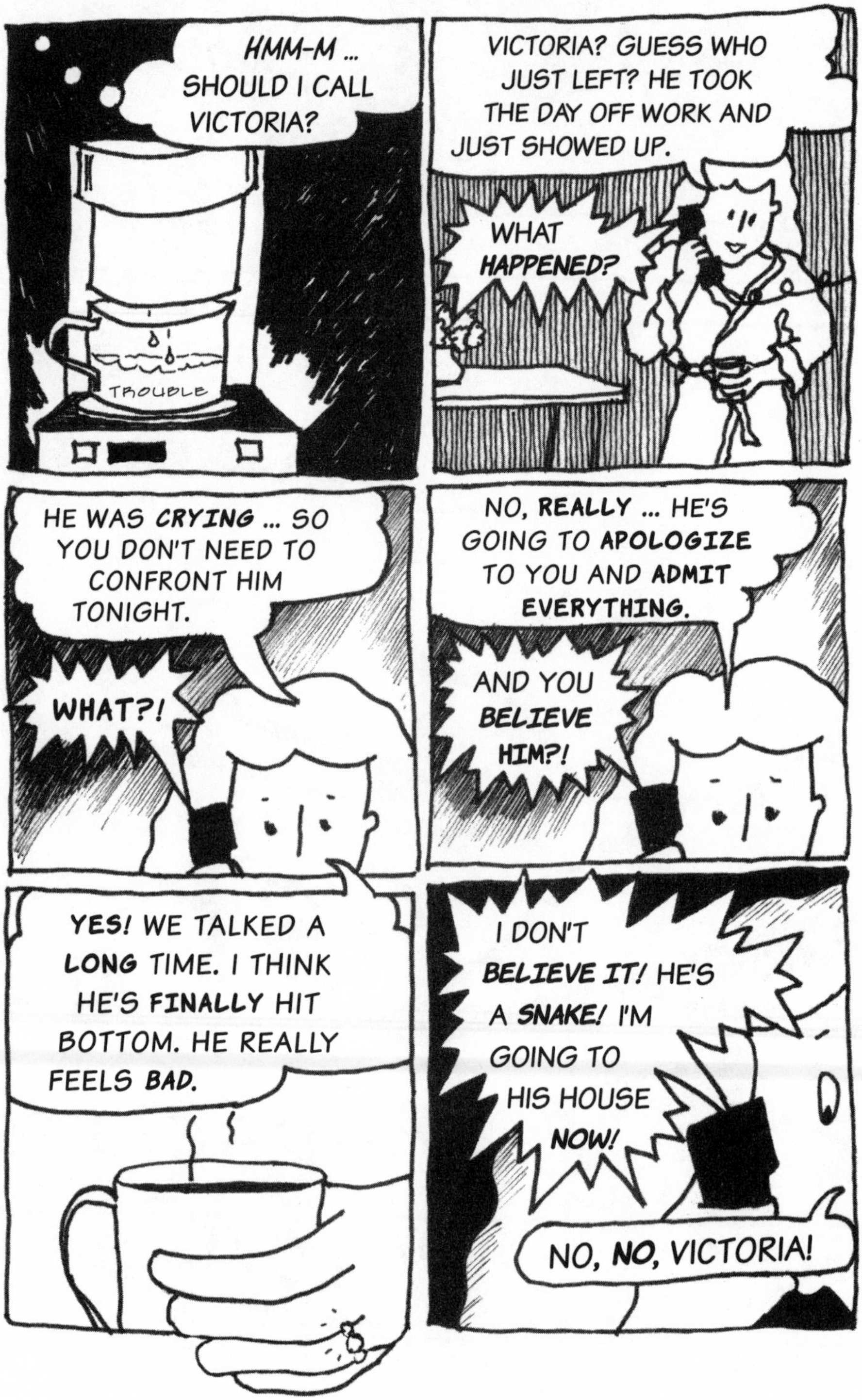
HMM-M ... SHOULD I CALL VICTORIA?
TROUBLE
VICTORIA? GUESS WHO JUST LEFT? HE TOOK THE DAY OFF WORK AND JUST SHOWED UP.
WHAT HAPPENED?
HE WAS CRYING ... SO YOU DON'T NEED TO CONFRONT HIM TONIGHT.
WHAT?!
NO, REALLY ... HE'S GOING TO APOLOGIZE TO YOU AND ADMIT EVERYTHING.
AND YOU BELIEVE HIM?!
YES! WE TALKED A LONG TIME. I THINK HE'S FINALLY HIT BOTTOM. HE REALLY FEELS BAD.
I DON'T BELIEVE IT! HE'S A SNAKE! I'M GOING TO HIS HOUSE NOW!
NO, NO, VICTORIA!

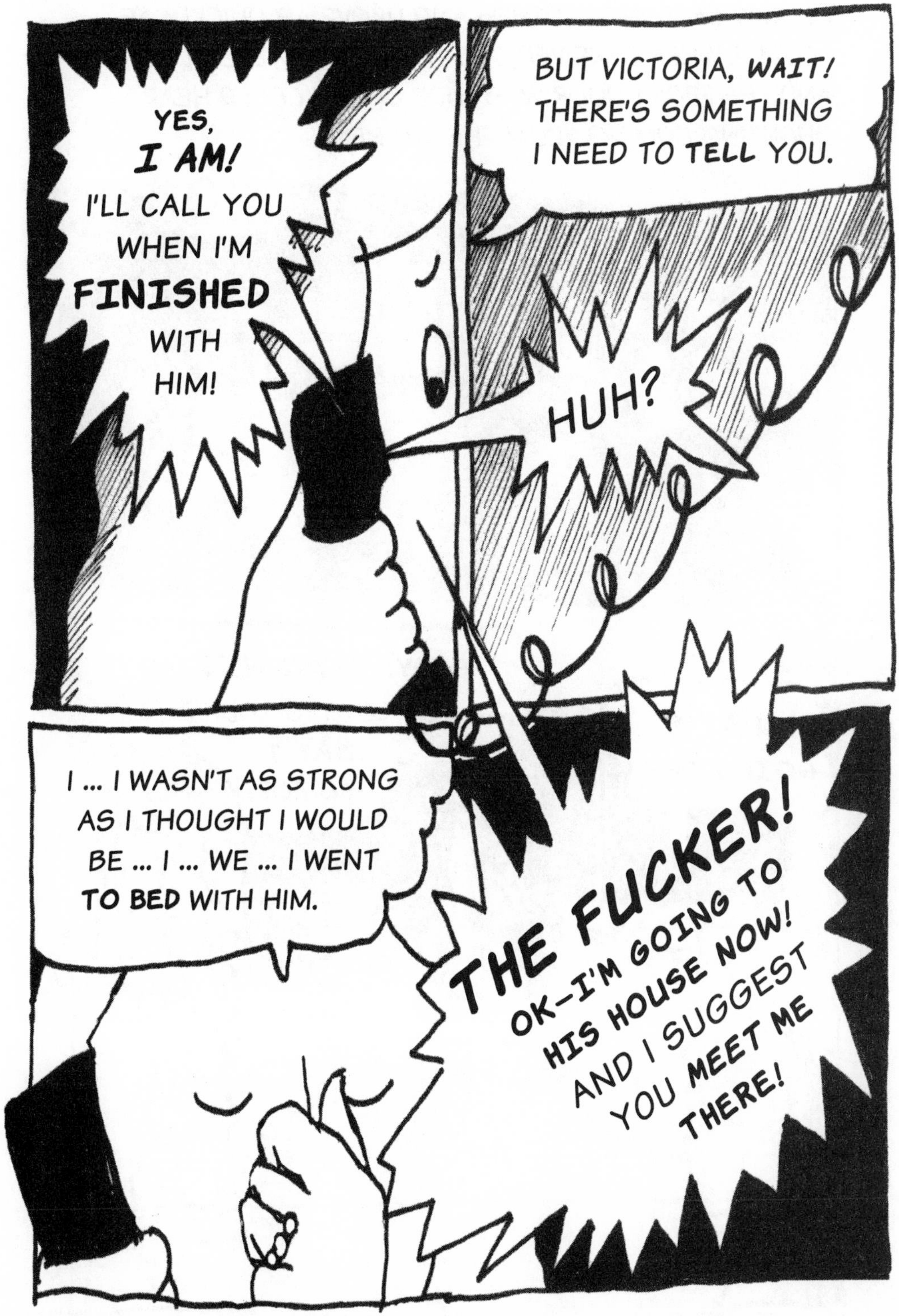
YES, I AM! I'LL CALL YOU WHEN I'M FINISHED WITH HIM!
BUT VICTORIA, WAIT! THERE'S SOMETHING I NEED TO TELL YOU.
HUH?
I ... I WASN'T AS STRONG AS I THOUGHT I WOULD BE ... I ... WE ... I WENT TO BED WITH HIM.
THE FUCKER! OK—I'M GOING TO HIS HOUSE NOW! AND I SUGGEST YOU MEET ME THERE!

I THREW ON SOME CLOTHES AND DROVE AS QUICKLY AS I COULD. WHEN I ARRIVED, ALL THE LIGHTS WERE BLAZING AND THE FRONT DOOR WAS WIDE OPEN. I COULD HEAR SHOUTING COMING FROM THE KITCHEN...

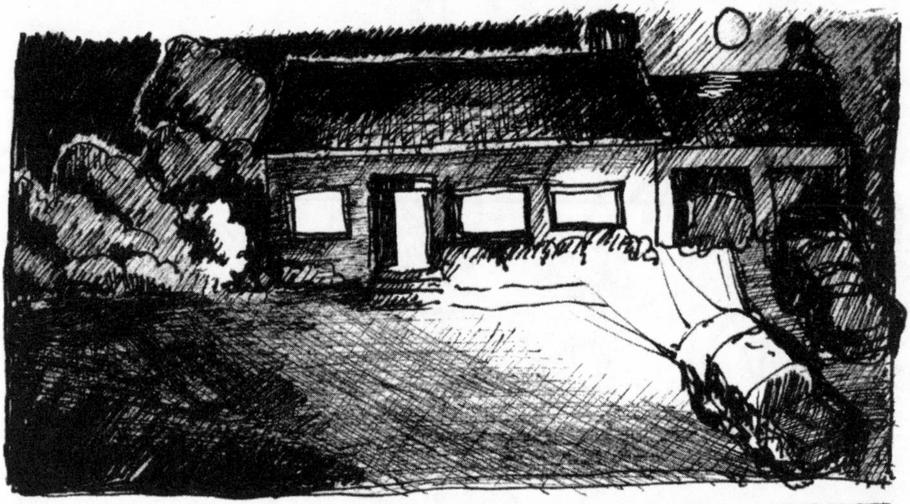

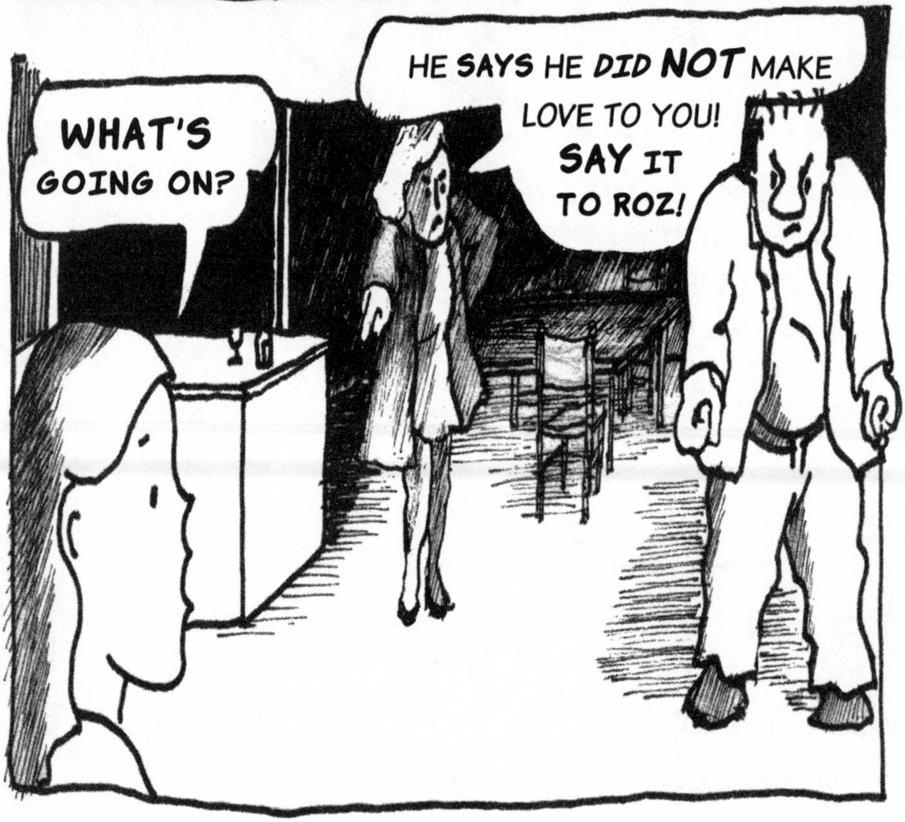
WHAT'S GOING ON?
HE SAYS HE DID NOT MAKE LOVE TO YOU! SAY IT TO ROZ!

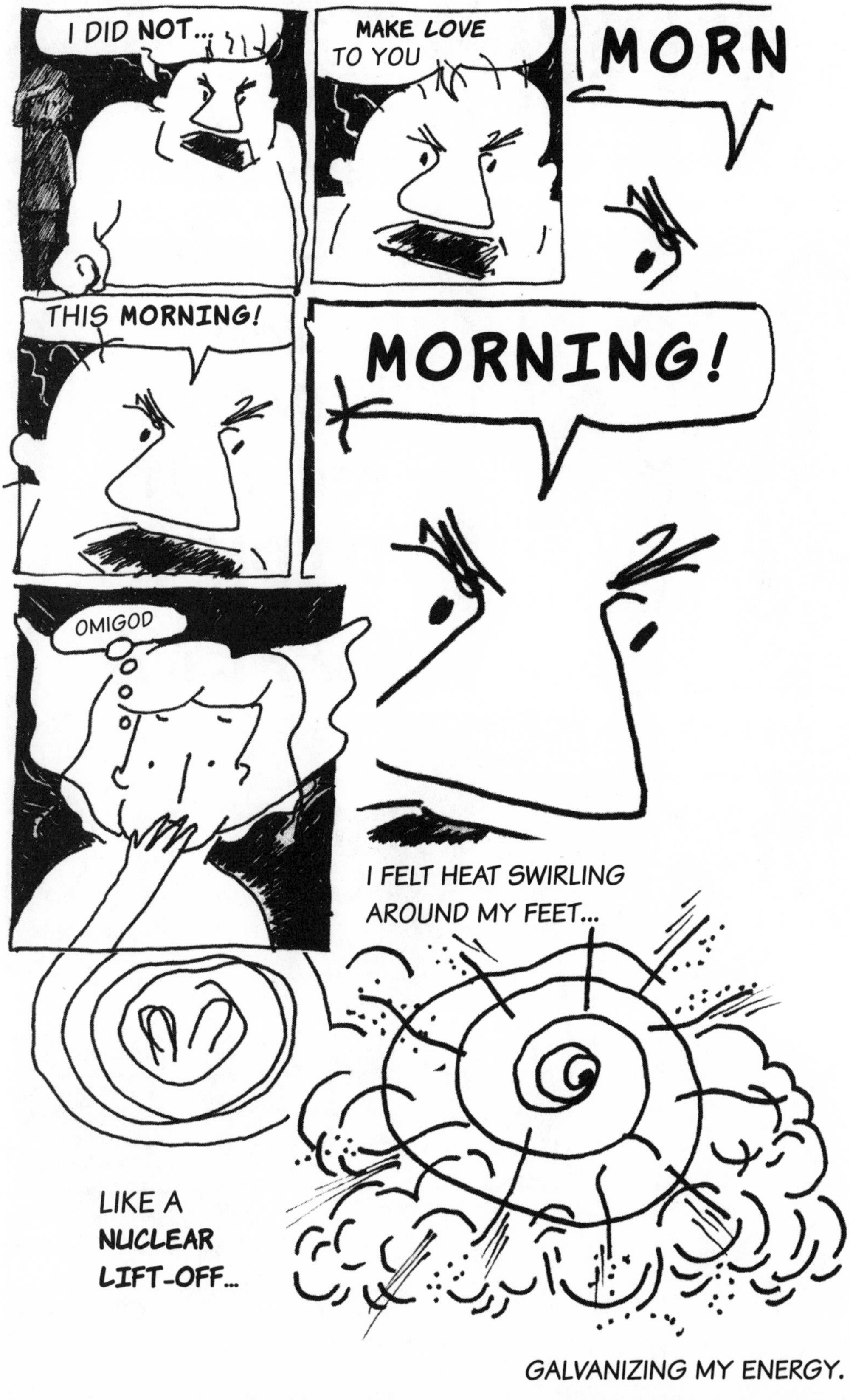
I DID NOT...
MAKE LOVE TO YOU
MORN
THIS MORNING!
MORNING!
OMIGOD
I FELT HEAT SWIRLING AROUND MY FEET...
LIKE A NUCLEAR LIFT-OFF...
GALVANIZING MY ENERGY.

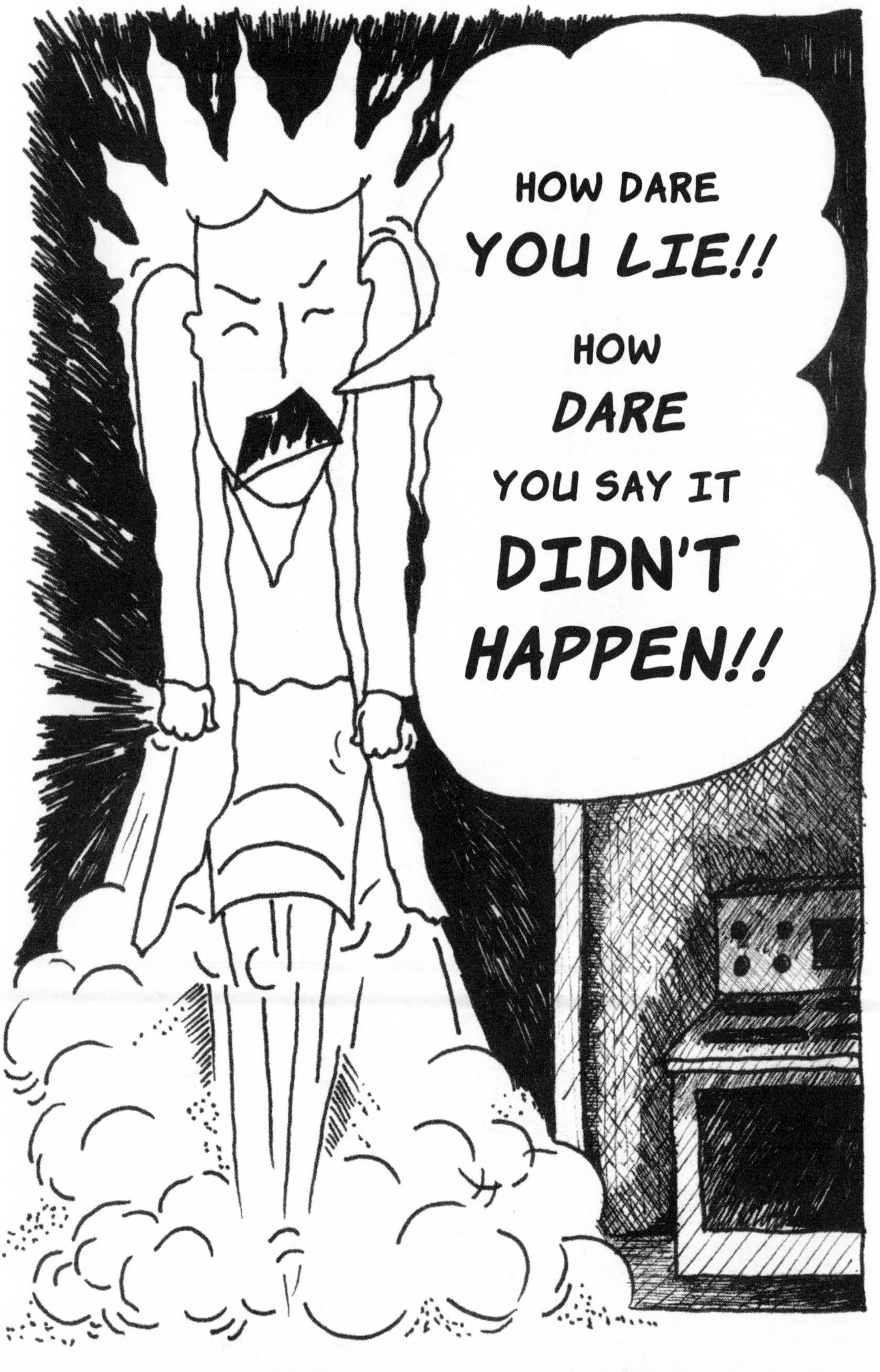
HOW DARE YOU LIE!! HOW DARE YOU SAY IT DIDN'T HAPPEN!!

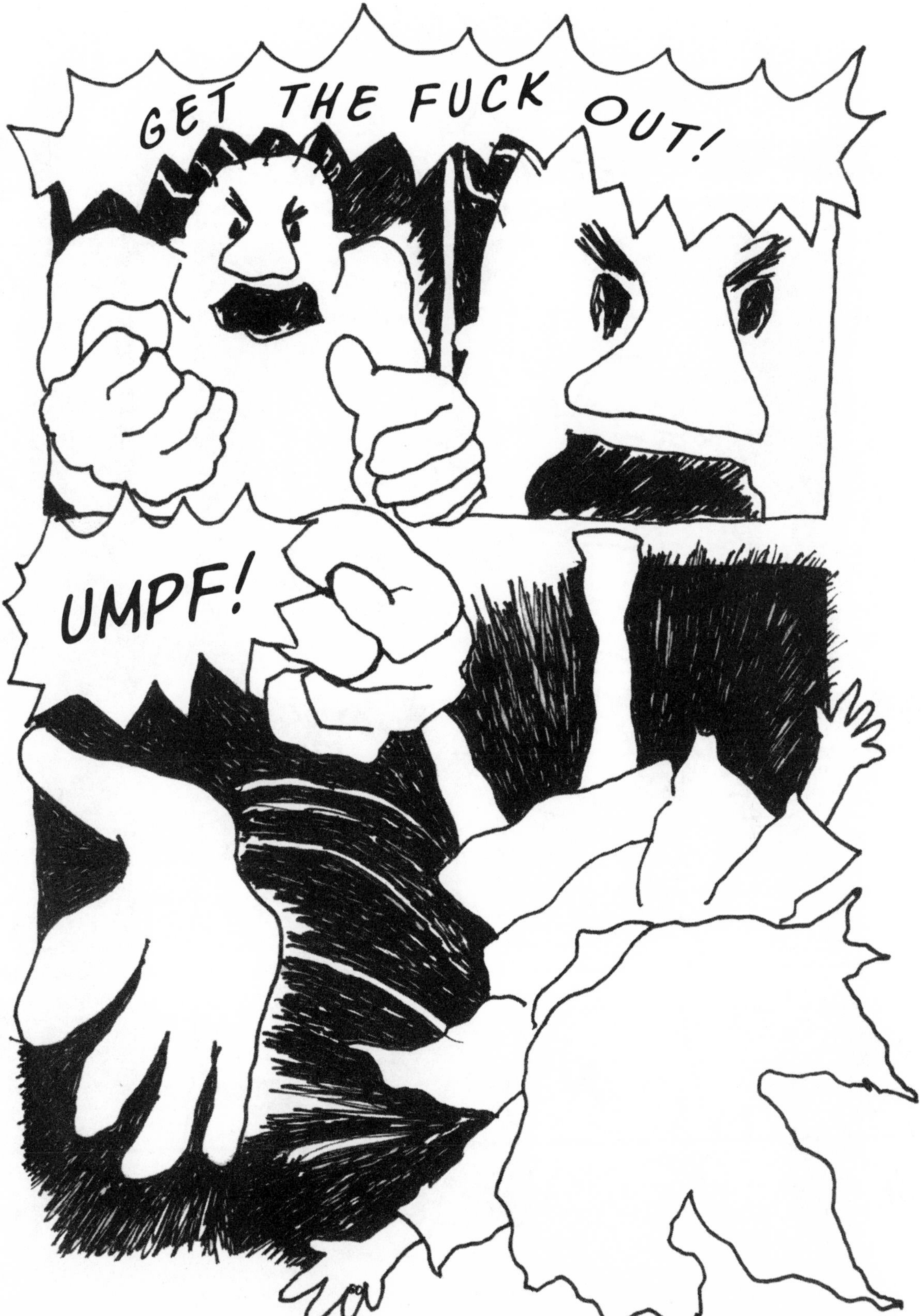
GET THE FUCK OUT!
UMPF!

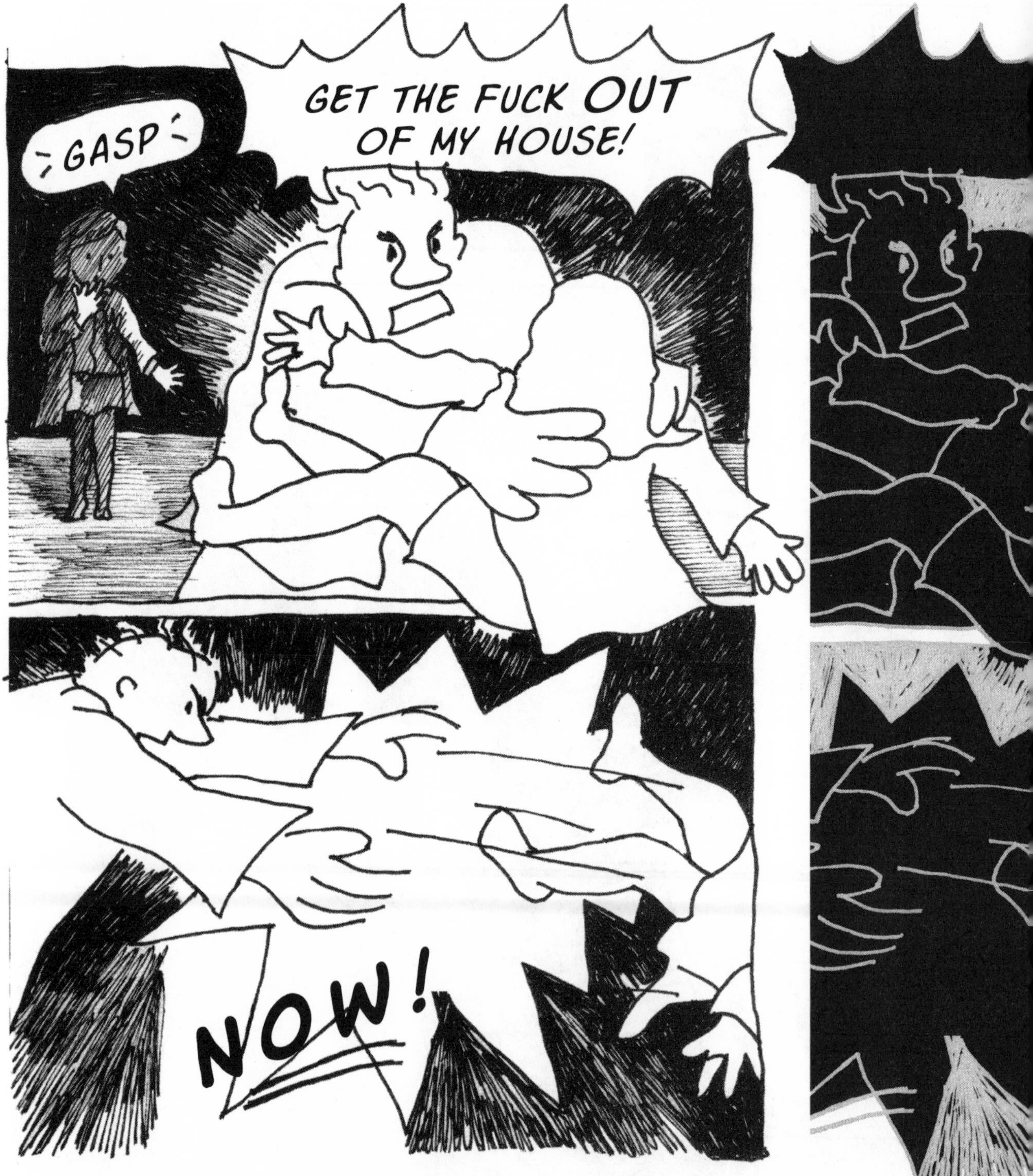
GASP
GET THE FUCK OUT OF MY HOUSE!
NOW!

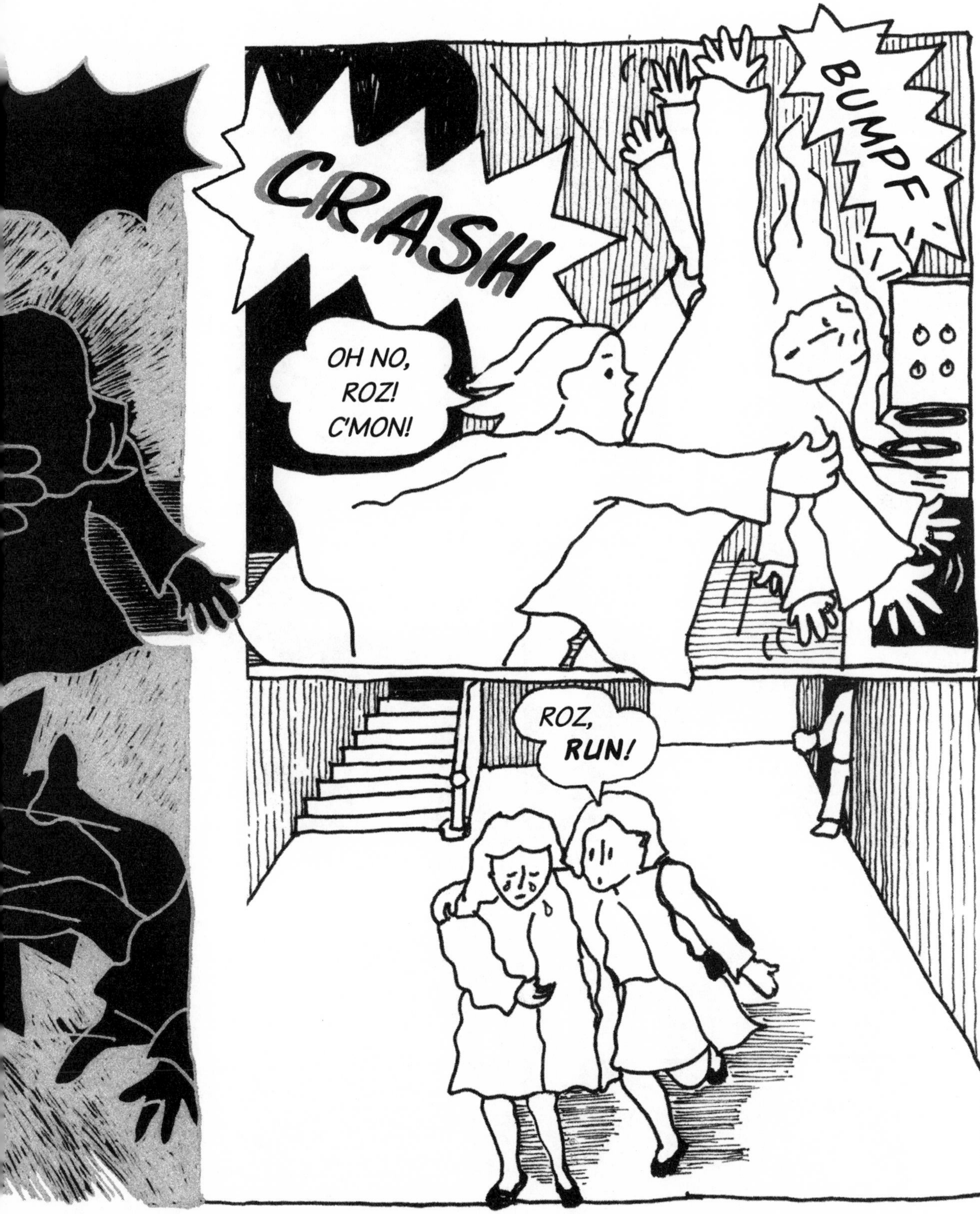
CRASH
BUMPF
OH NO, ROZ! C'MON!
ROZ, RUN!

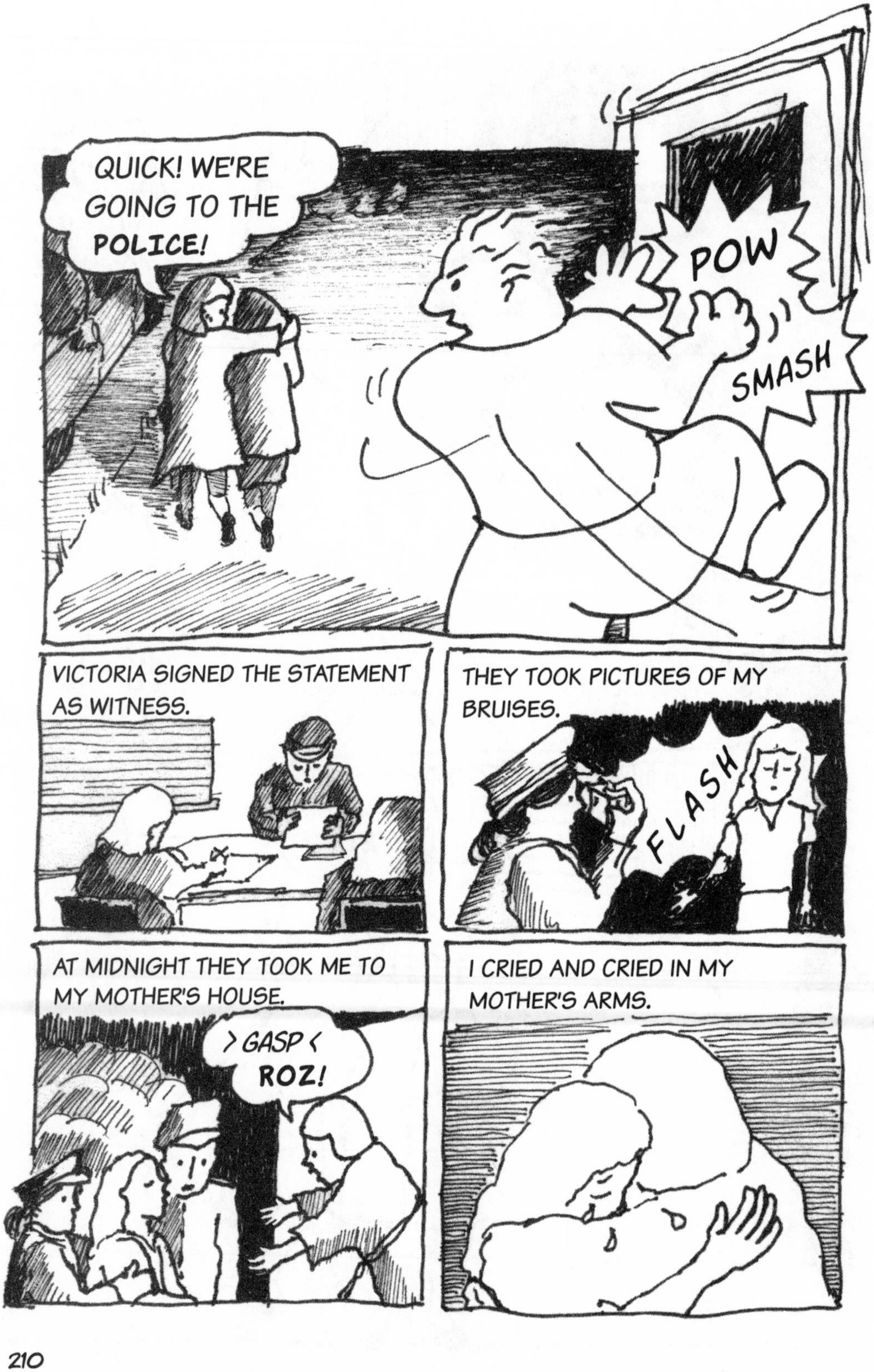
QUICK! WE'RE GOING TO THE POLICE!
POW
SMASH
VICTORIA SIGNED THE STATEMENT AS WITNESS.
THEY TOOK PICTURES OF MY BRUISES.
FLASH
AT MIDNIGHT THEY TOOK ME TO MY MOTHER'S HOUSE.
>GASP< ROZ!
I CRIED AND CRIED IN MY MOTHER'S ARMS.

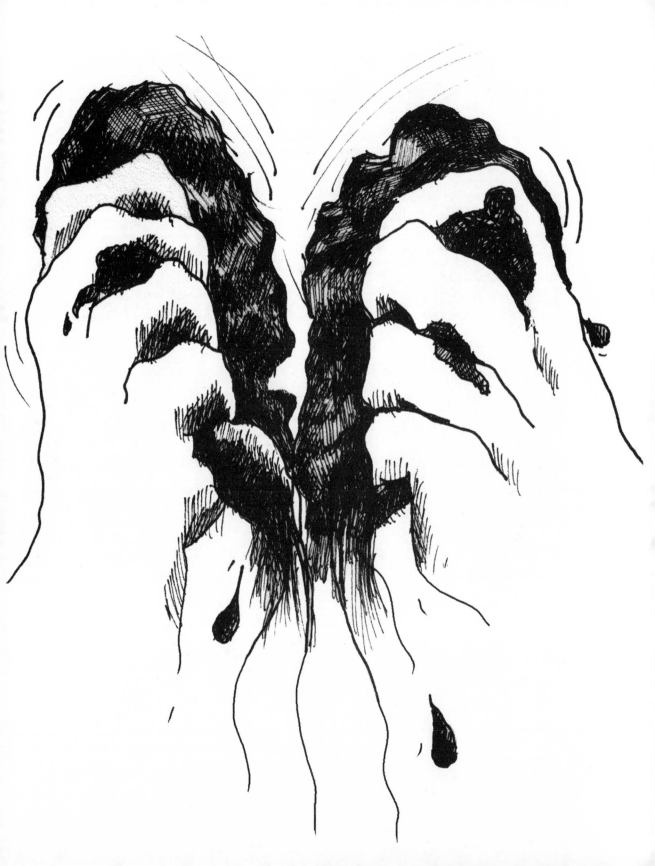

THREE MONTHS PASSED WITHOUT CONTACT...

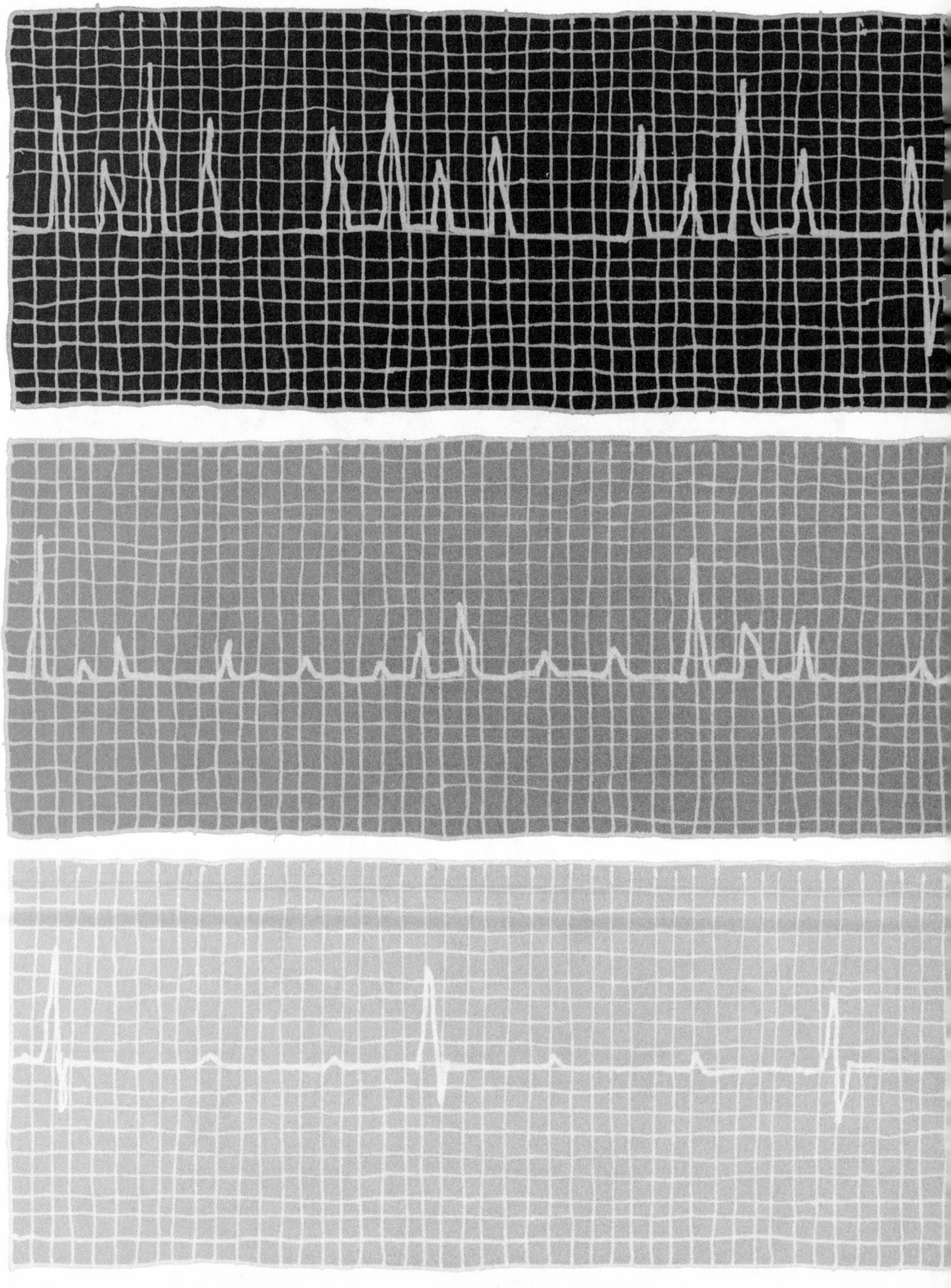

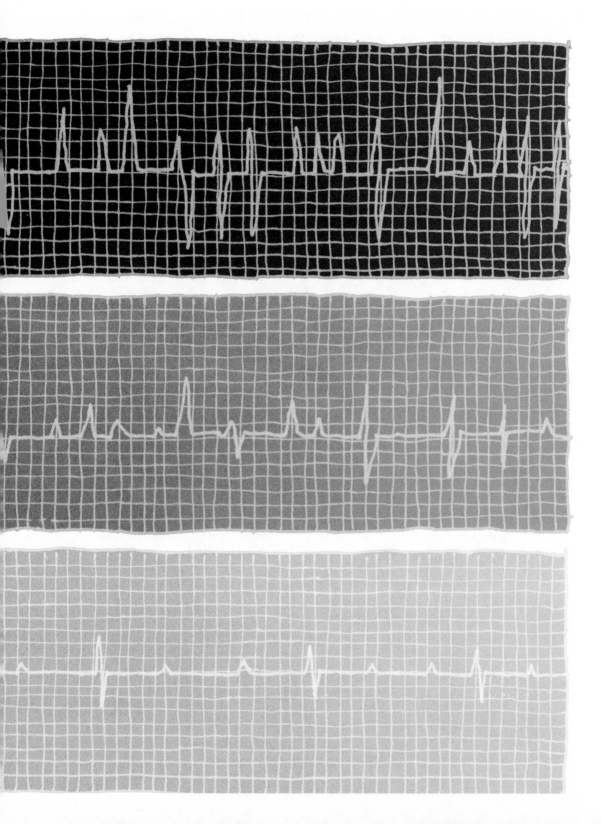

BRIAN HAD RETALIATED BY REMOVING ME AS A LEGAL GUARDIAN OF THE CHILDREN, AND I WASN'T ALLOWED TO SEE THEM. MY LAWYER WAS PREPARING FOR TRIAL.

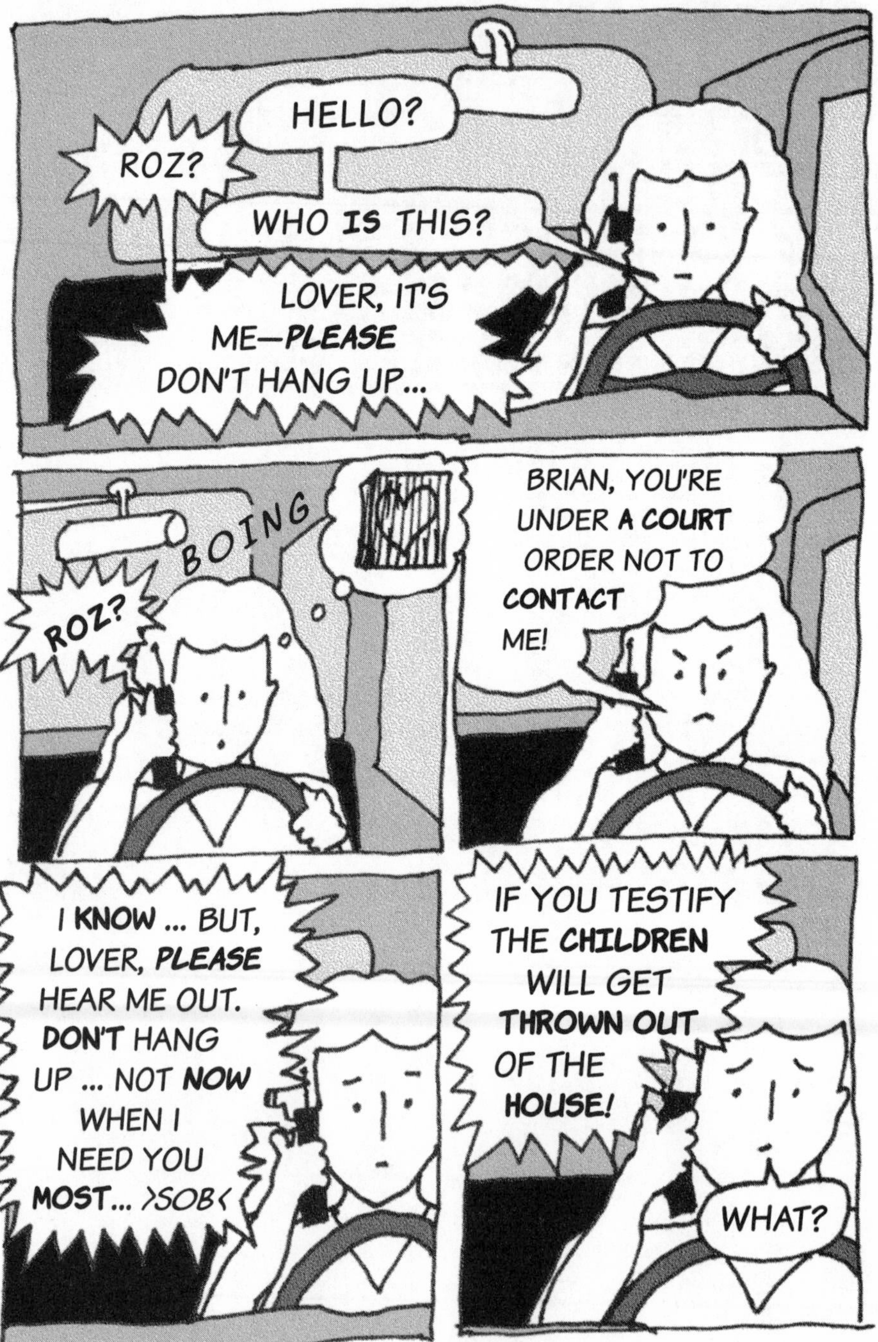

HELLO?
ROZ?
WHO **IS** THIS?
LOVER, IT'S ME—***PLEASE*** DON'T HANG UP...
BOING
ROZ?
BRIAN, YOU'RE UNDER **A COURT** ORDER NOT TO **CONTACT** ME!
I **KNOW** ... BUT, LOVER, **PLEASE** HEAR ME OUT. **DON'T** HANG UP ... NOT **NOW** WHEN I NEED YOU **MOST**... *>SOB<*
IF YOU TESTIFY THE **CHILDREN** WILL GET **THROWN OUT** OF THE **HOUSE!**
WHAT?

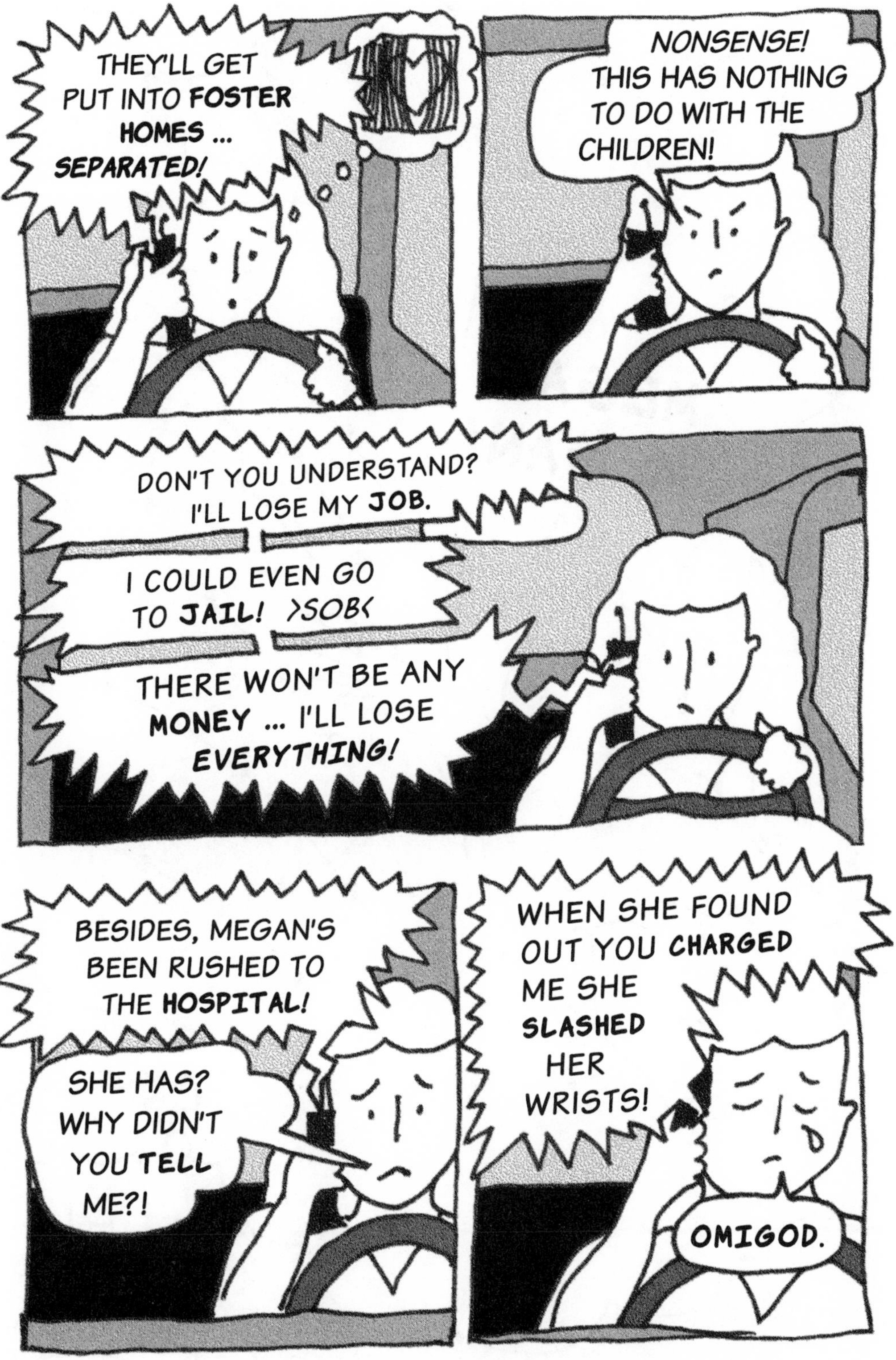
THEY'LL GET PUT INTO FOSTER HOMES ... SEPARATED!
NONSENSE! THIS HAS NOTHING TO DO WITH THE CHILDREN!
DON'T YOU UNDERSTAND? I'LL LOSE MY JOB.
I COULD EVEN GO TO JAIL! >SOB<
THERE WON'T BE ANY MONEY ... I'LL LOSE EVERYTHING!
BESIDES, MEGAN'S BEEN RUSHED TO THE HOSPITAL!
SHE HAS? WHY DIDN'T YOU TELL ME?!
WHEN SHE FOUND OUT YOU CHARGED ME SHE SLASHED HER WRISTS!
OMIGOD.

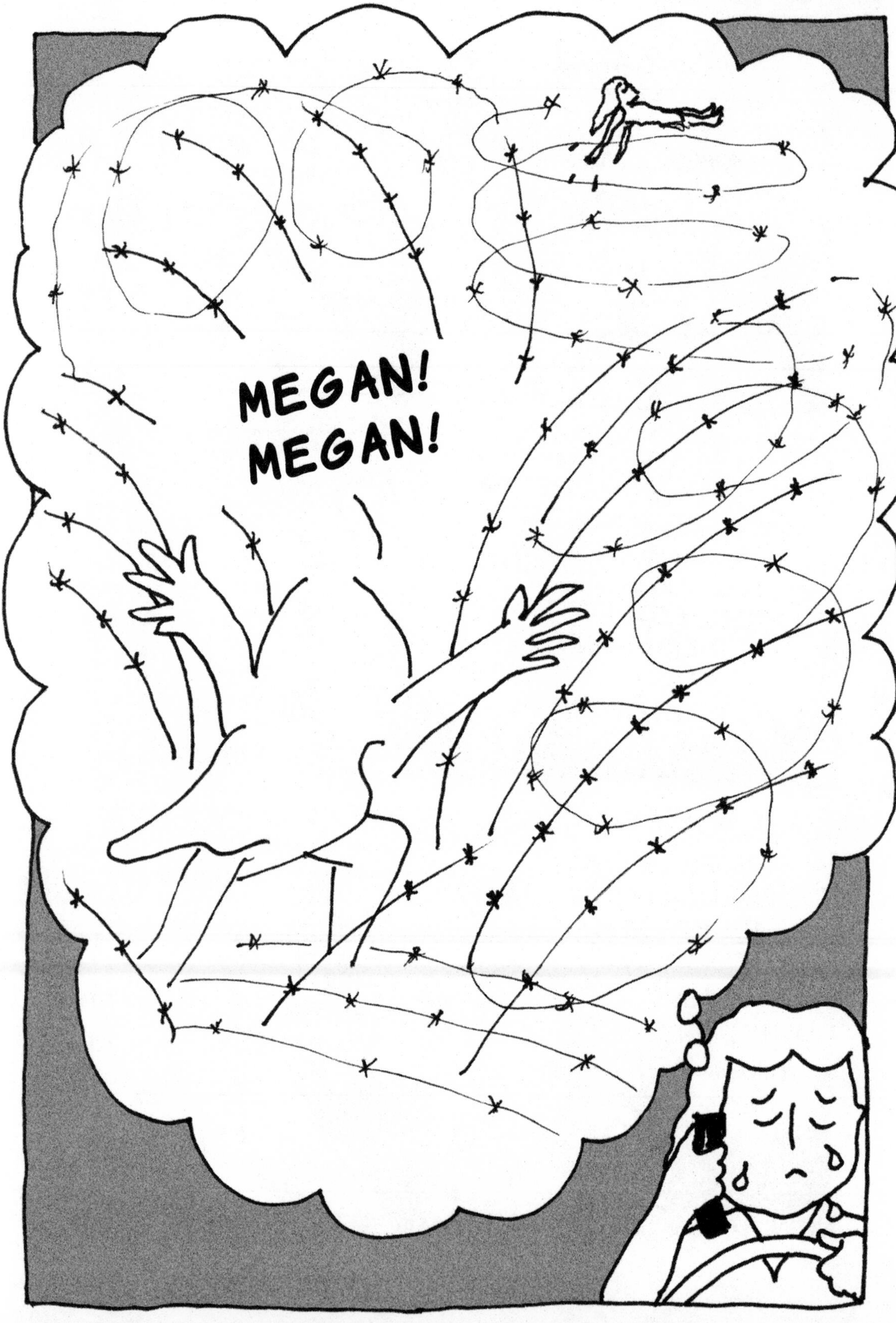
MEGAN!
MEGAN!

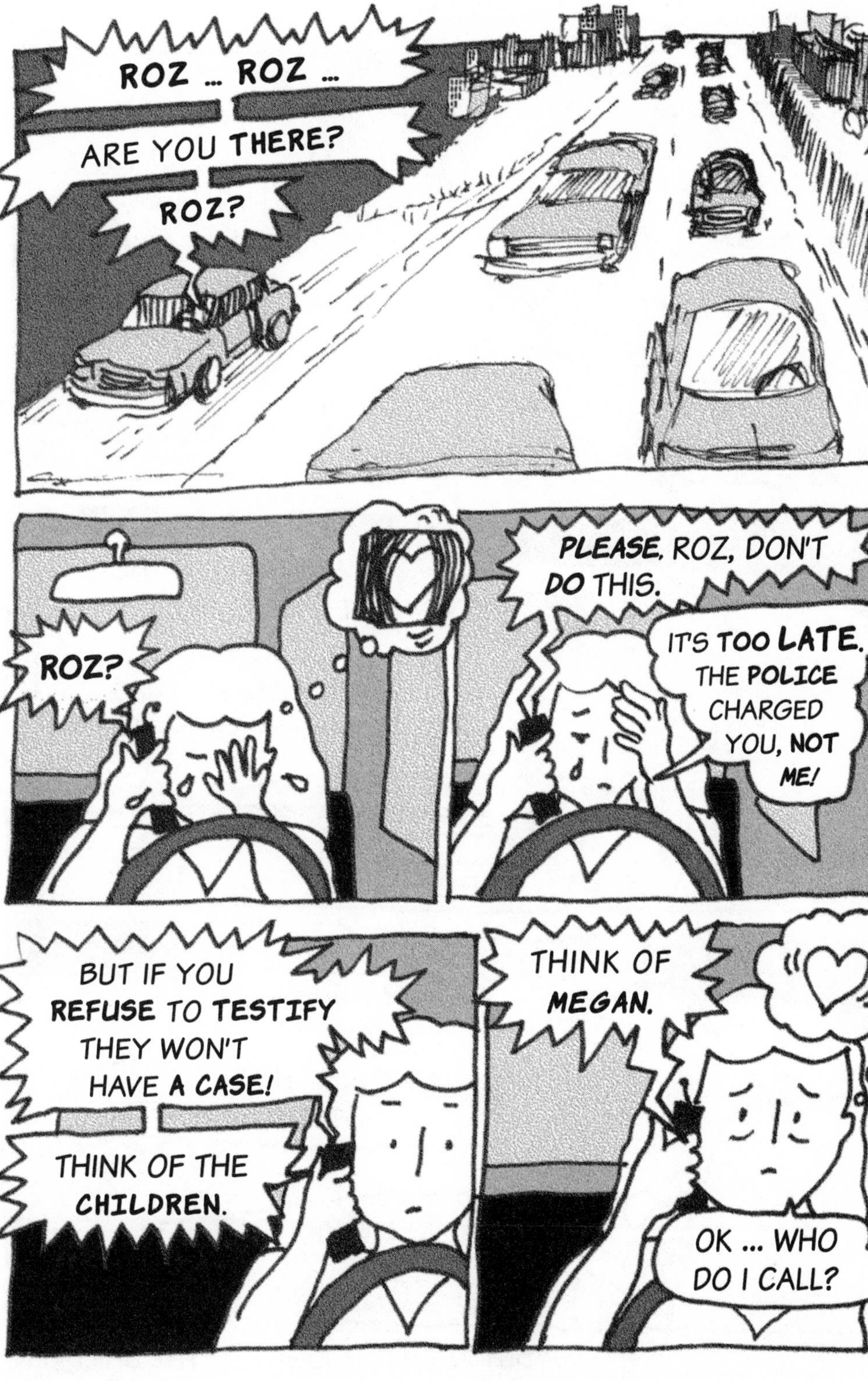
ROZ ... ROZ ...
ARE YOU THERE?
ROZ?
ROZ?
PLEASE, ROZ, DON'T DO THIS.
IT'S TOO LATE. THE POLICE CHARGED YOU, NOT ME!
BUT IF YOU REFUSE TO TESTIFY THEY WON'T HAVE A CASE!
THINK OF THE CHILDREN.
THINK OF MEGAN.
OK ... WHO DO I CALL?

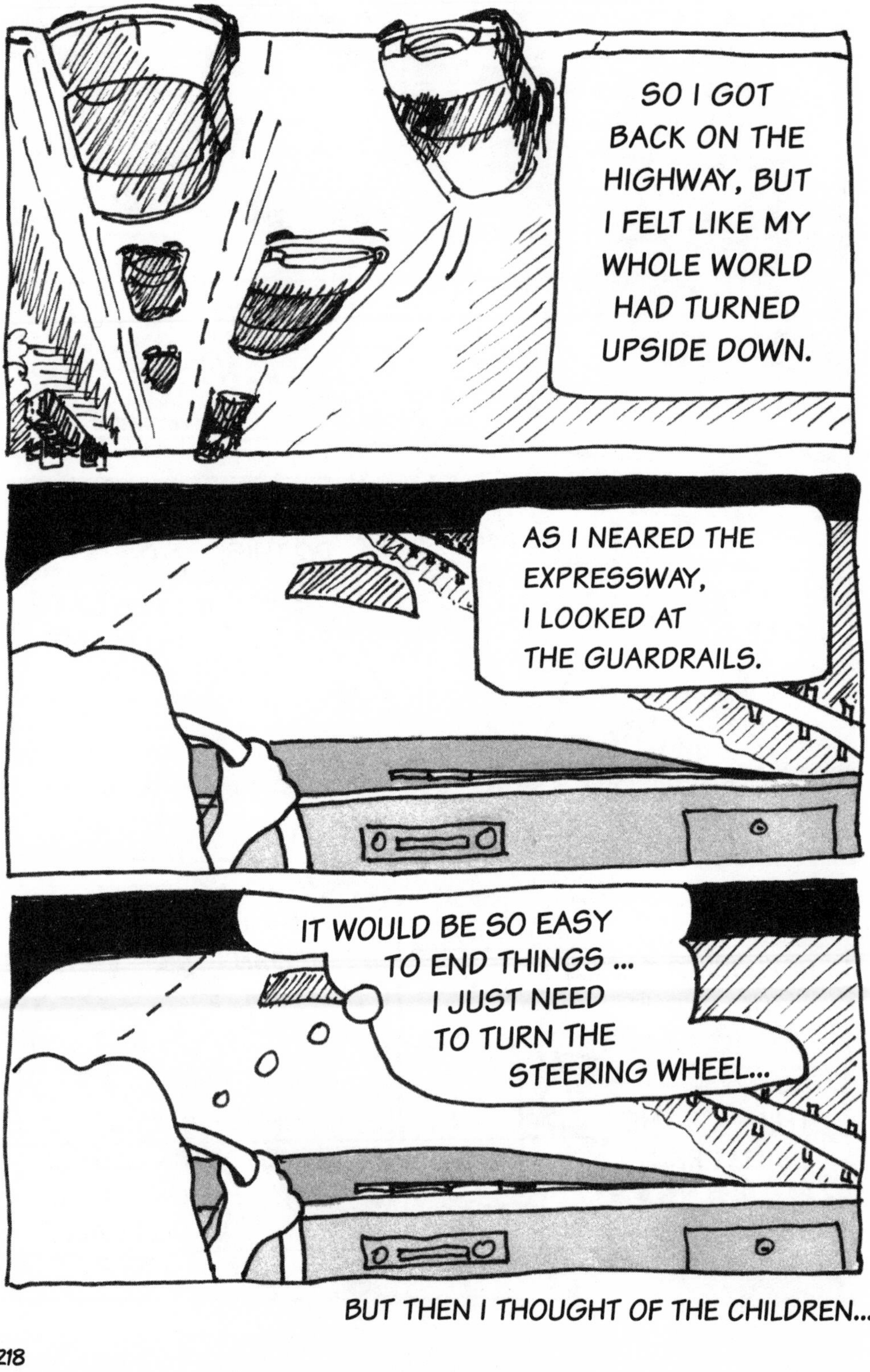
SO I GOT BACK ON THE HIGHWAY, BUT I FELT LIKE MY WHOLE WORLD HAD TURNED UPSIDE DOWN.
AS I NEARED THE EXPRESSWAY, I LOOKED AT THE GUARDRAILS.
IT WOULD BE SO EASY TO END THINGS ... I JUST NEED TO TURN THE STEERING WHEEL...

BUT THEN I THOUGHT OF THE CHILDREN...

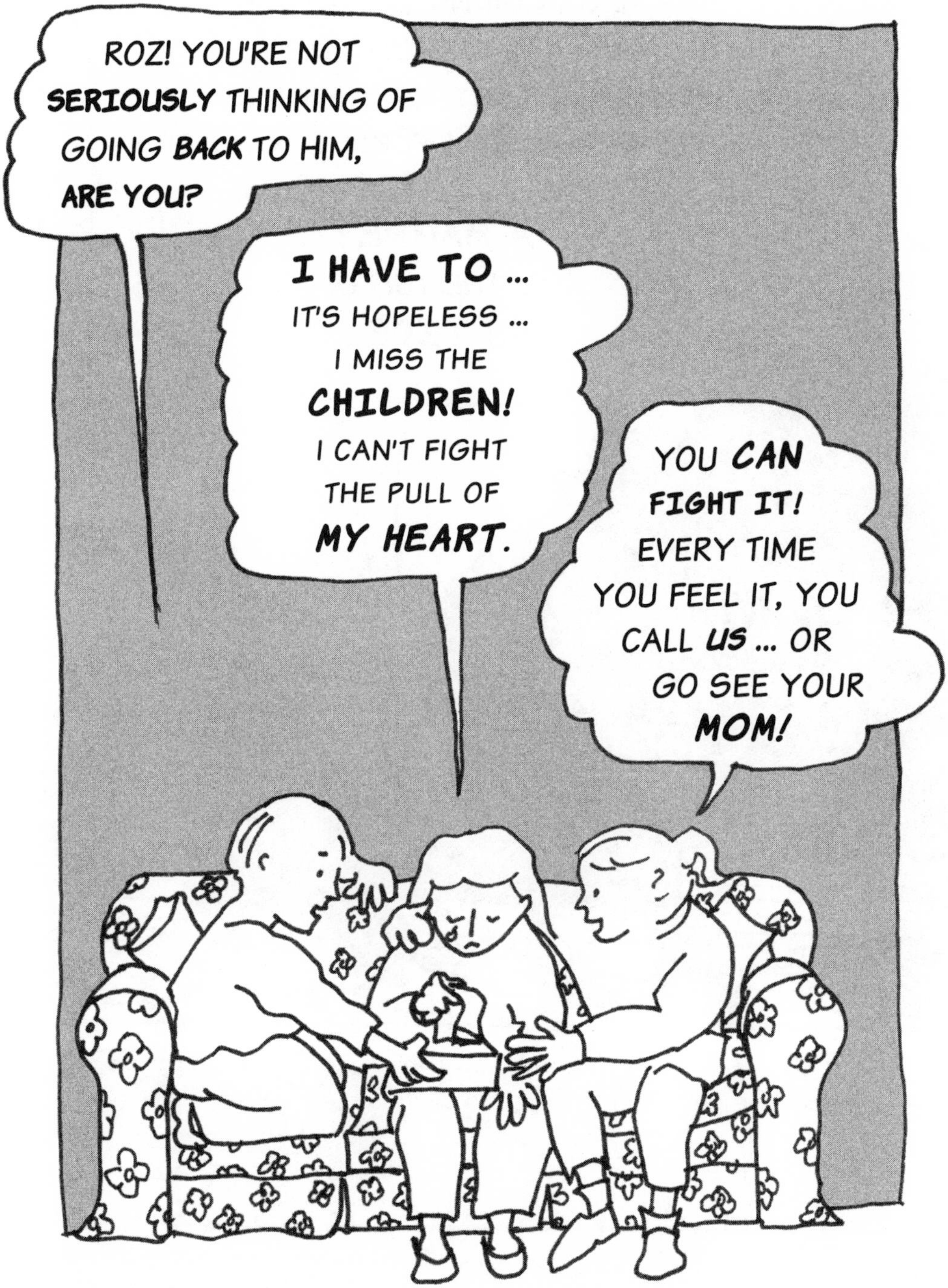
ROZ! YOU'RE NOT SERIOUSLY THINKING OF GOING BACK TO HIM, ARE YOU?
I HAVE TO ... IT'S HOPELESS ... I MISS THE CHILDREN! I CAN'T FIGHT THE PULL OF MY HEART.
YOU CAN FIGHT IT! EVERY TIME YOU FEEL IT, YOU CALL US ... OR GO SEE YOUR MOM!

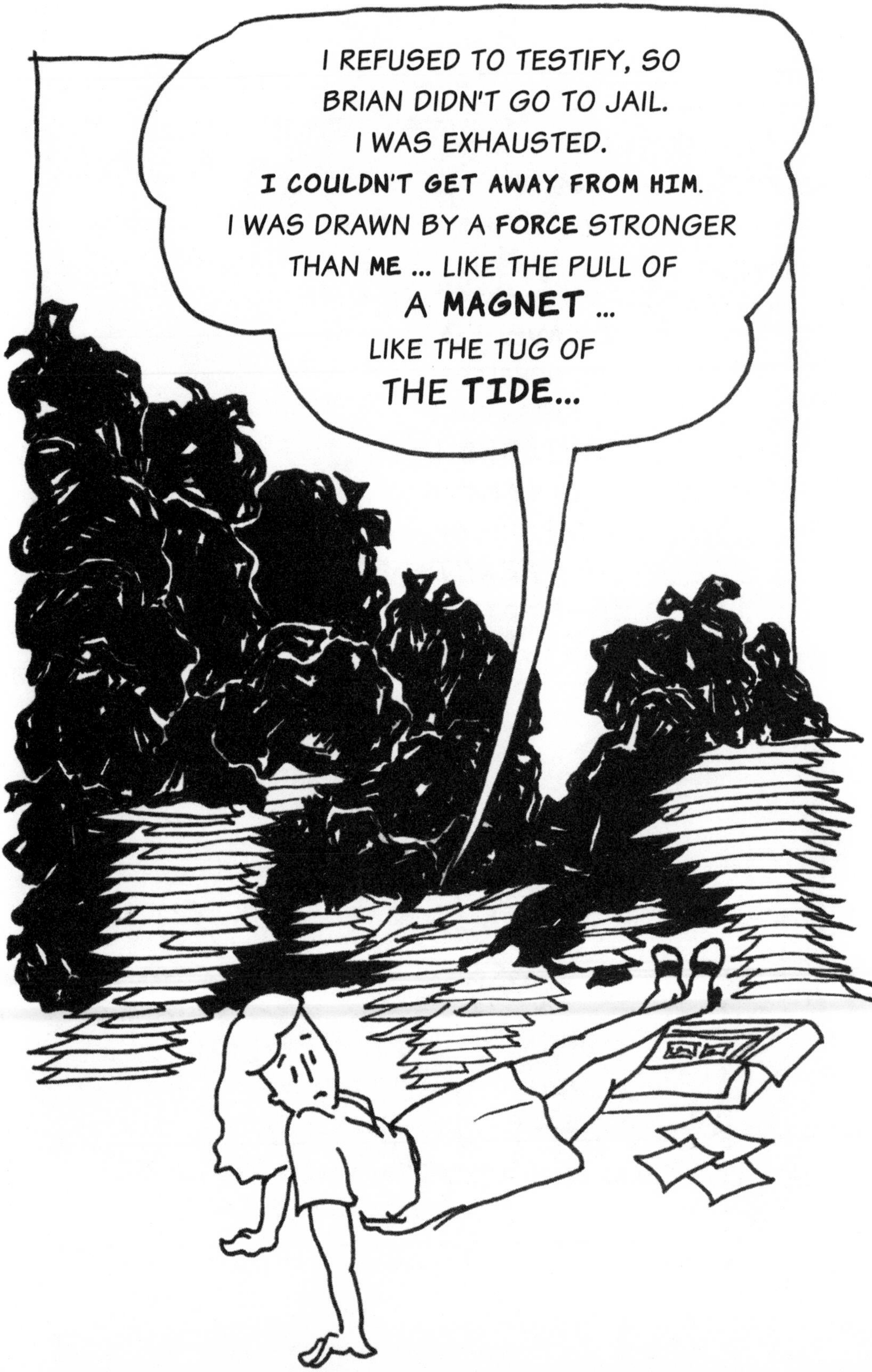
I REFUSED TO TESTIFY, SO BRIAN DIDN'T GO TO JAIL. I WAS EXHAUSTED. I COULDN'T GET AWAY FROM HIM. I WAS DRAWN BY A FORCE STRONGER THAN ME ... LIKE THE PULL OF A MAGNET ... LIKE THE TUG OF THE TIDE...

Coming Home: Finding Myself

MY MOTHER LISTENED TO ME ENDLESSLY...

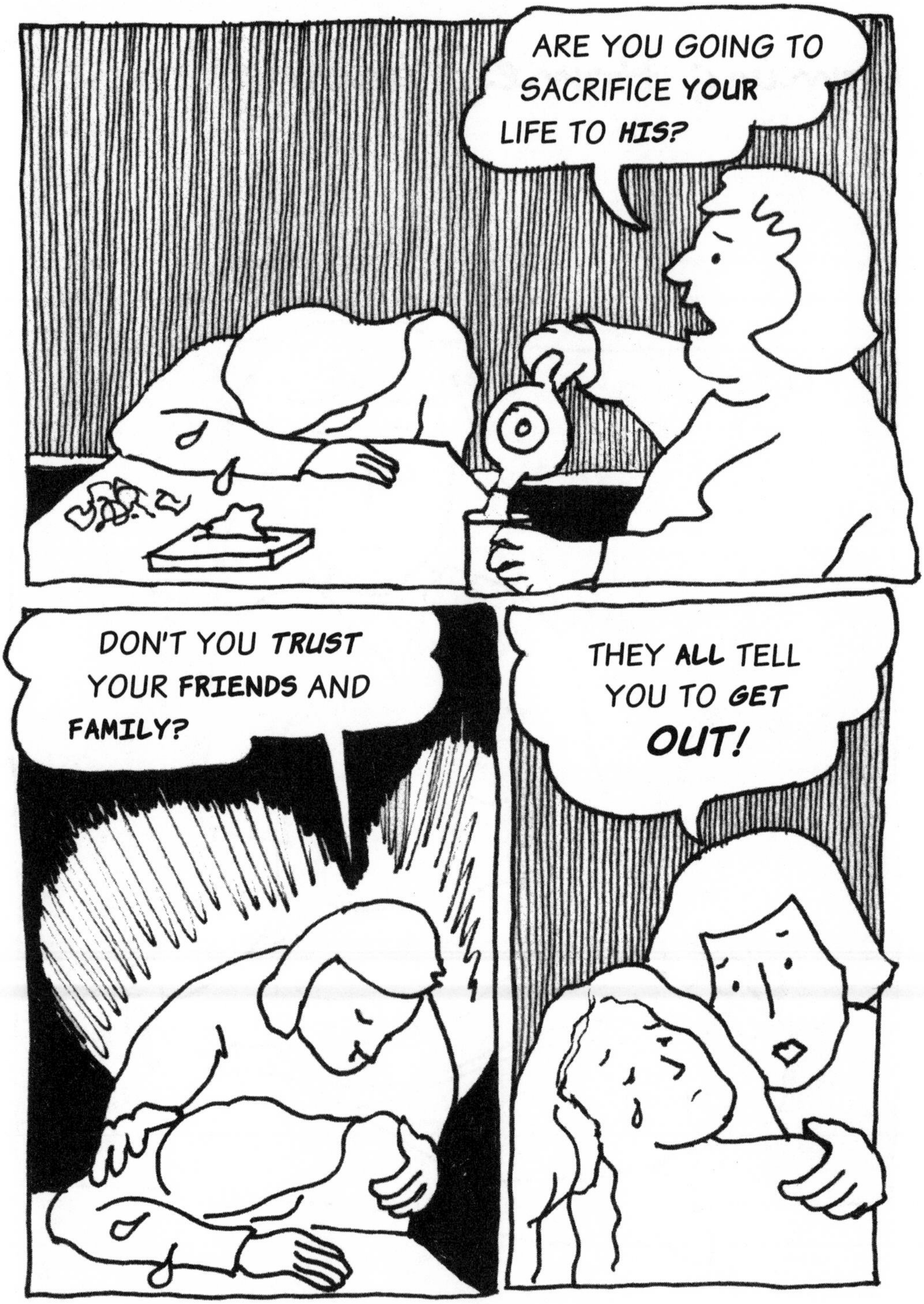
ARE YOU GOING TO SACRIFICE YOUR LIFE TO HIS?
DON'T YOU TRUST YOUR FRIENDS AND FAMILY?
THEY ALL TELL YOU TO GET OUT!

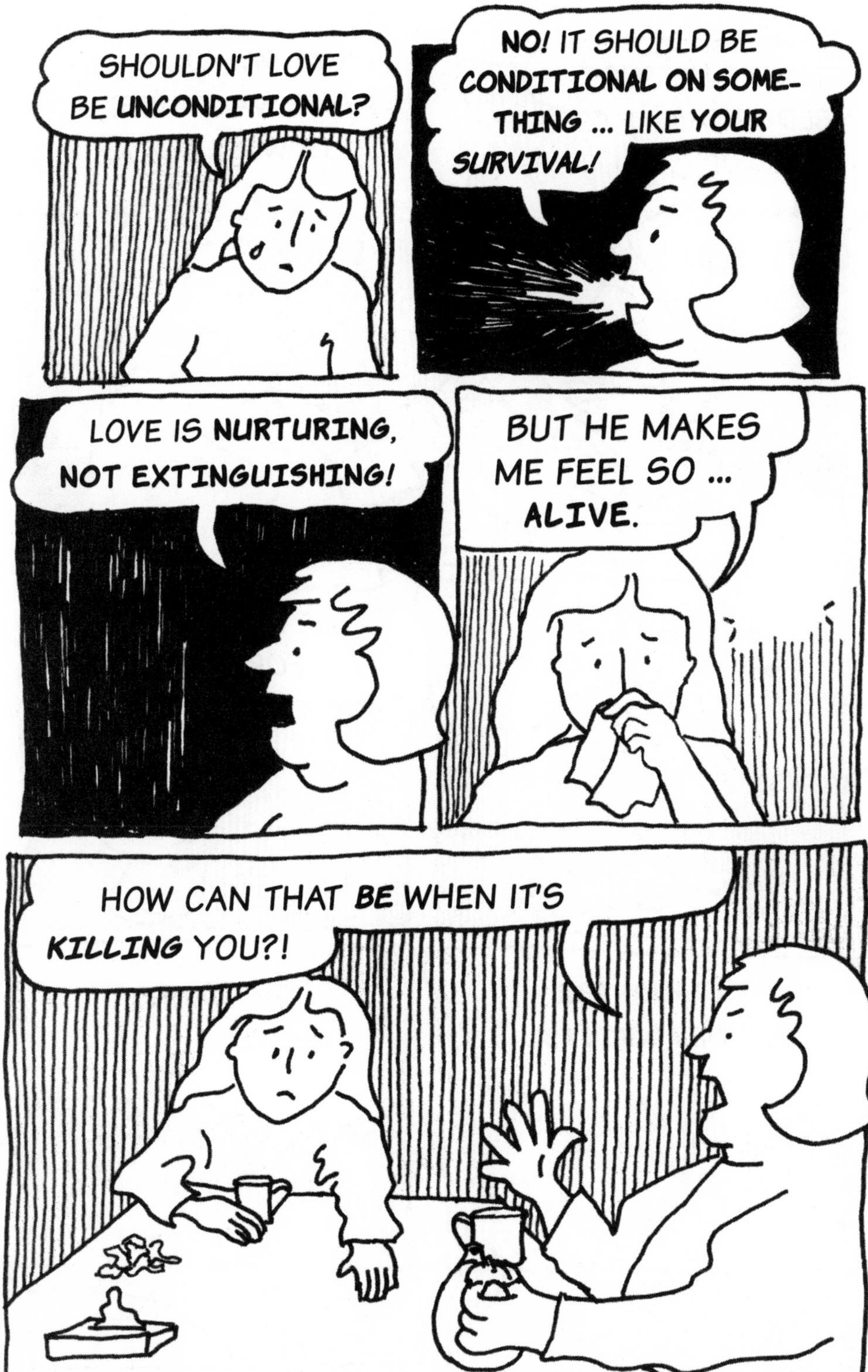
SHOULDN'T LOVE BE UNCONDITIONAL?
NO! IT SHOULD BE CONDITIONAL ON SOME-THING ... LIKE YOUR SURVIVAL!
LOVE IS NURTURING, NOT EXTINGUISHING!
BUT HE MAKES ME FEEL SO ... ALIVE.
HOW CAN THAT BE WHEN IT'S KILLING YOU?!

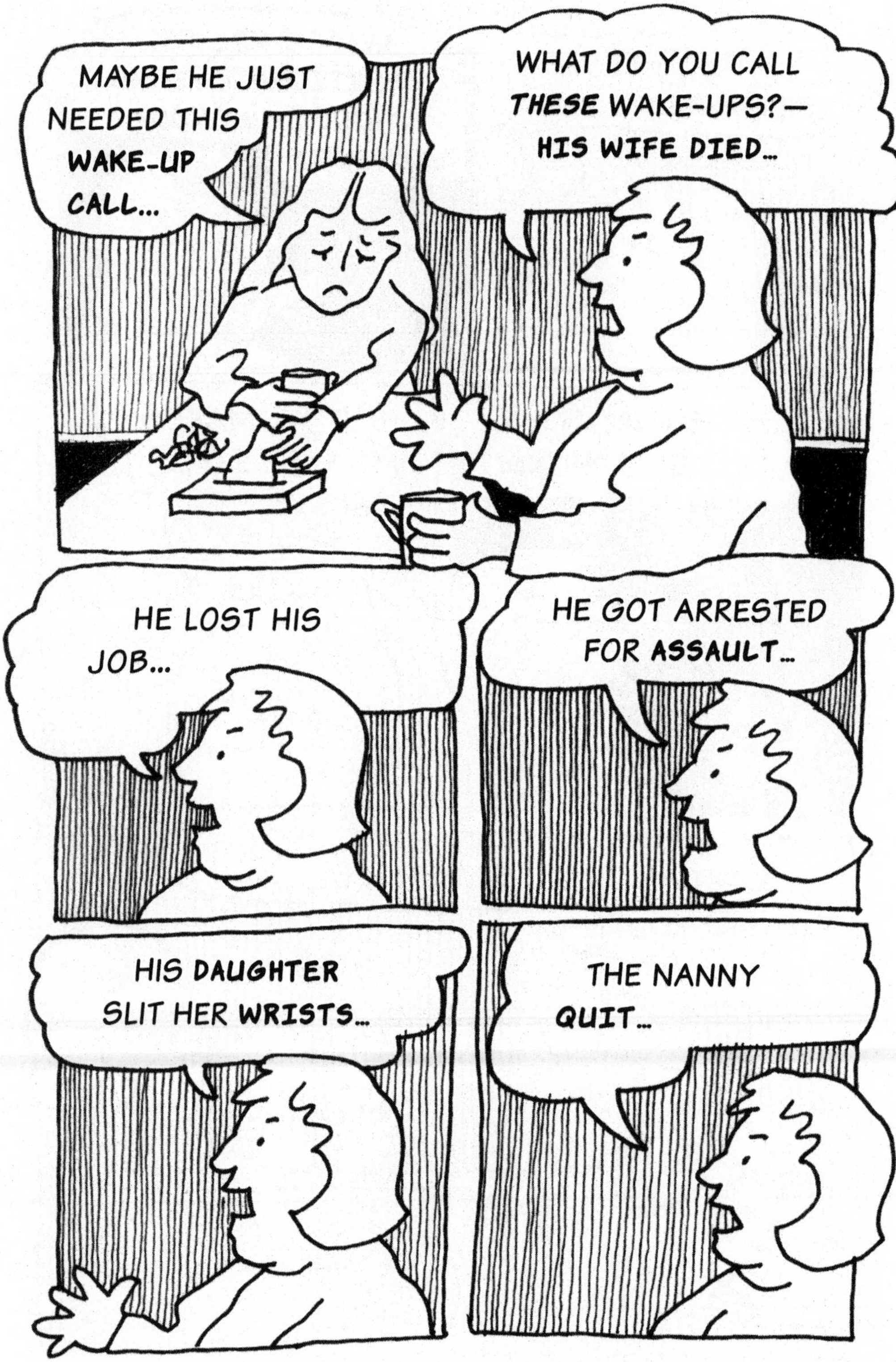
MAYBE HE JUST NEEDED THIS WAKE-UP CALL...
WHAT DO YOU CALL THESE WAKE-UPS?— HIS WIFE DIED...
HE LOST HIS JOB...
HE GOT ARRESTED FOR ASSAULT...
HIS DAUGHTER SLIT HER WRISTS...
THE NANNY QUIT...

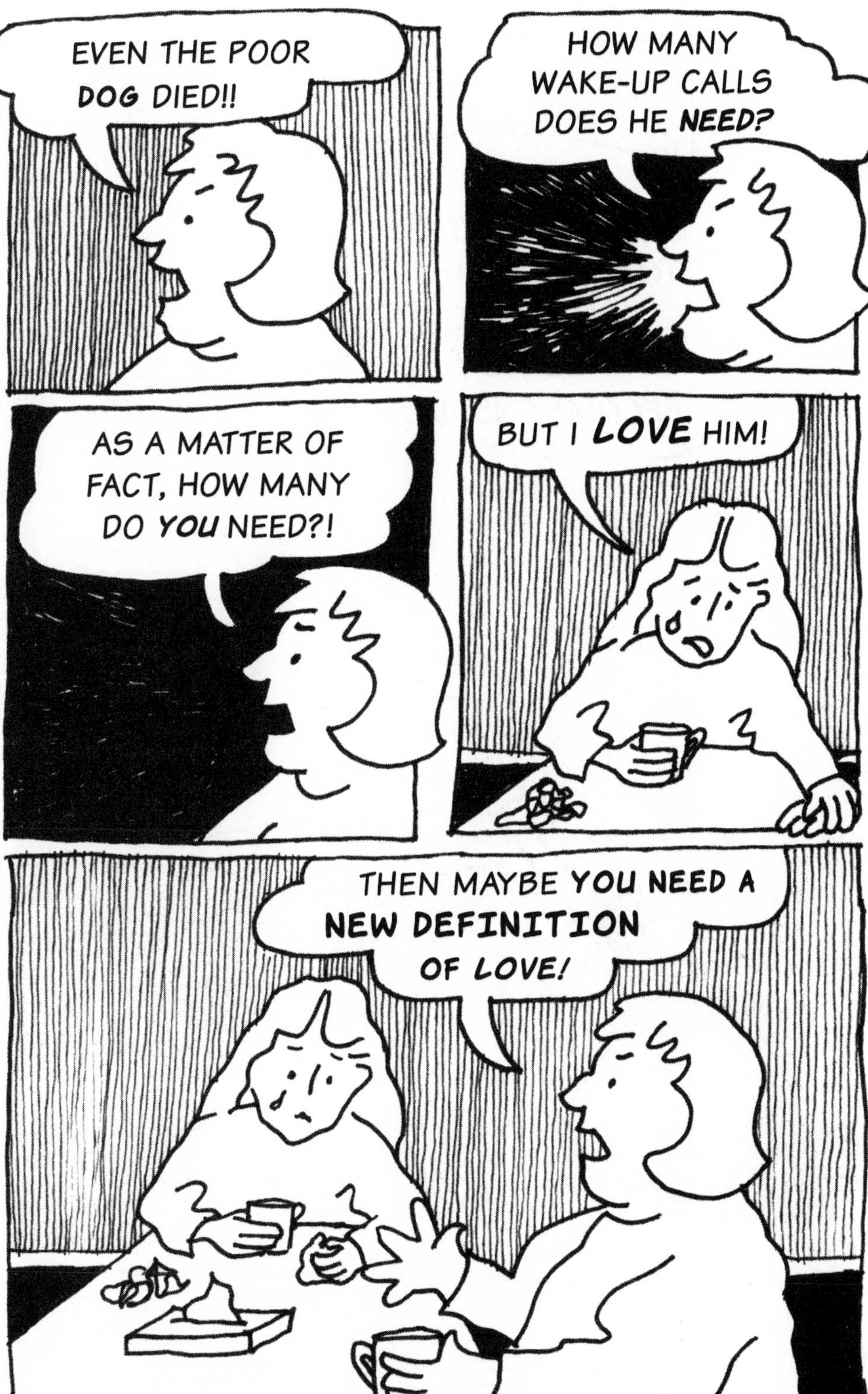
EVEN THE POOR DOG DIED!!
HOW MANY WAKE-UP CALLS DOES HE NEED?
AS A MATTER OF FACT, HOW MANY DO YOU NEED?!
BUT I LOVE HIM!
THEN MAYBE YOU NEED A NEW DEFINITION OF LOVE!

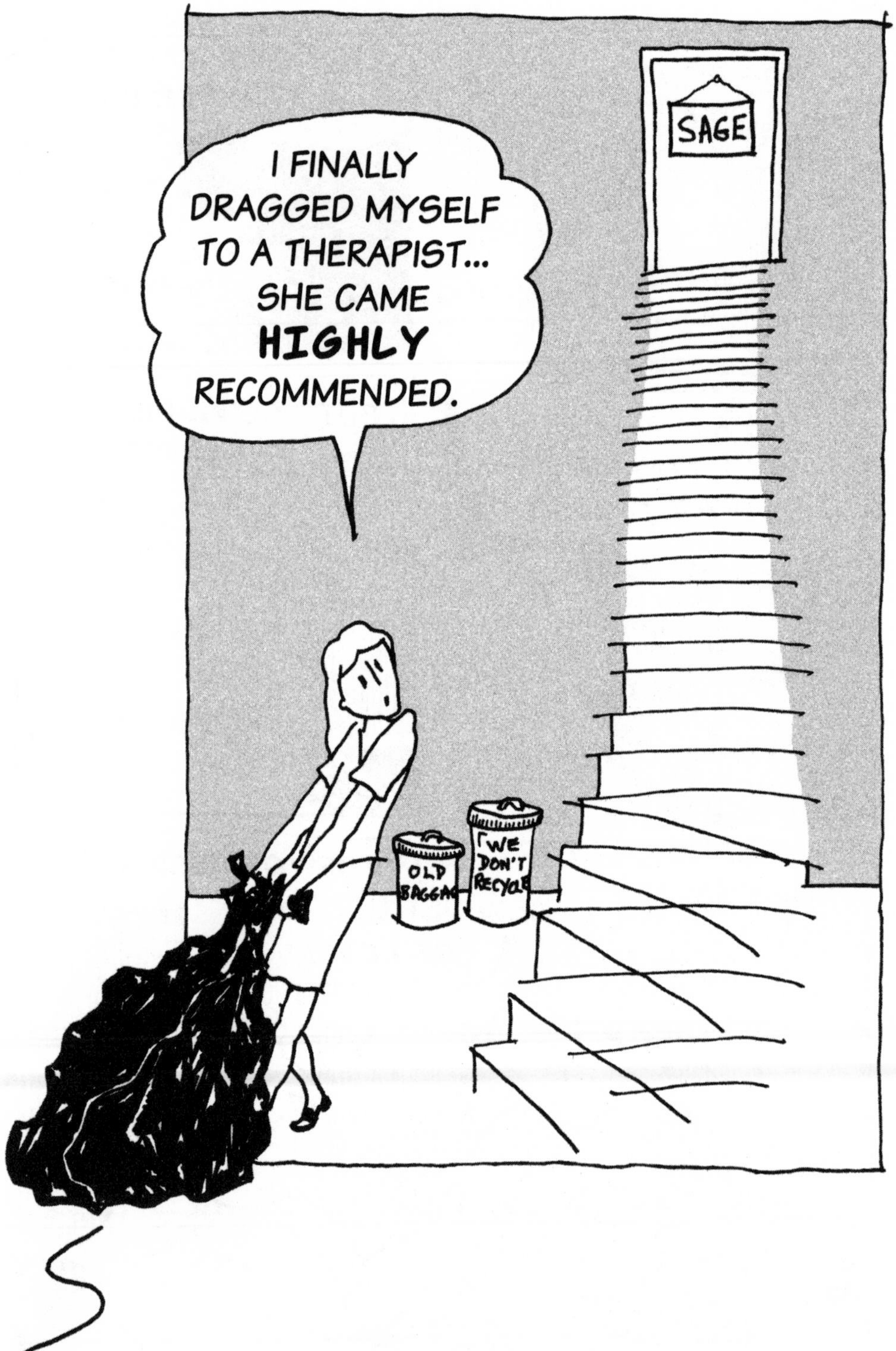
SAGE
I FINALLY DRAGGED MYSELF TO A THERAPIST... SHE CAME **HIGHLY** RECOMMENDED.
OLD BAGGAG
WE DON'T RECYCLE

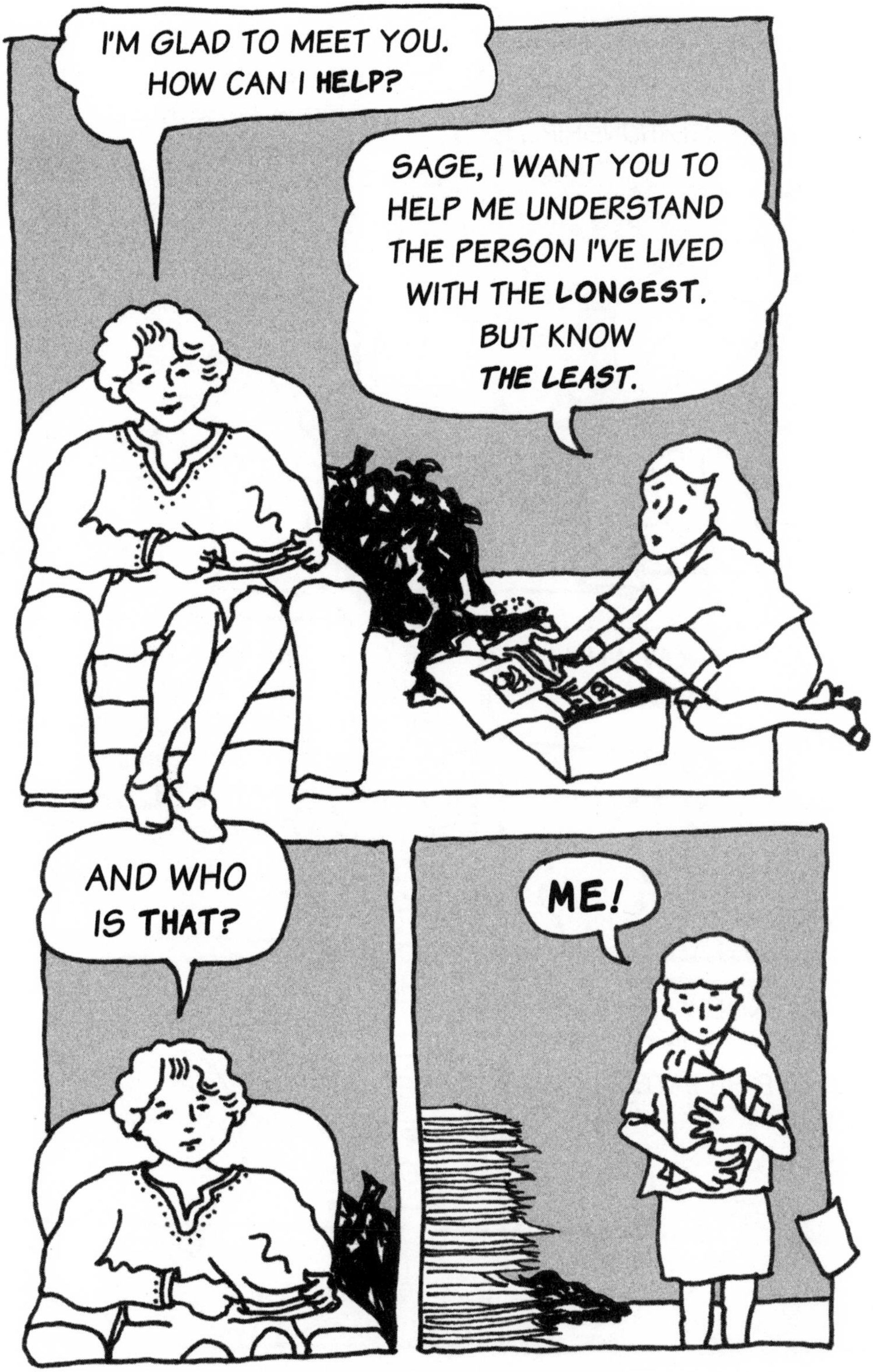
I'M GLAD TO MEET YOU. HOW CAN I HELP?
SAGE, I WANT YOU TO HELP ME UNDERSTAND THE PERSON I'VE LIVED WITH THE LONGEST. BUT KNOW THE LEAST.
AND WHO IS THAT?
ME!

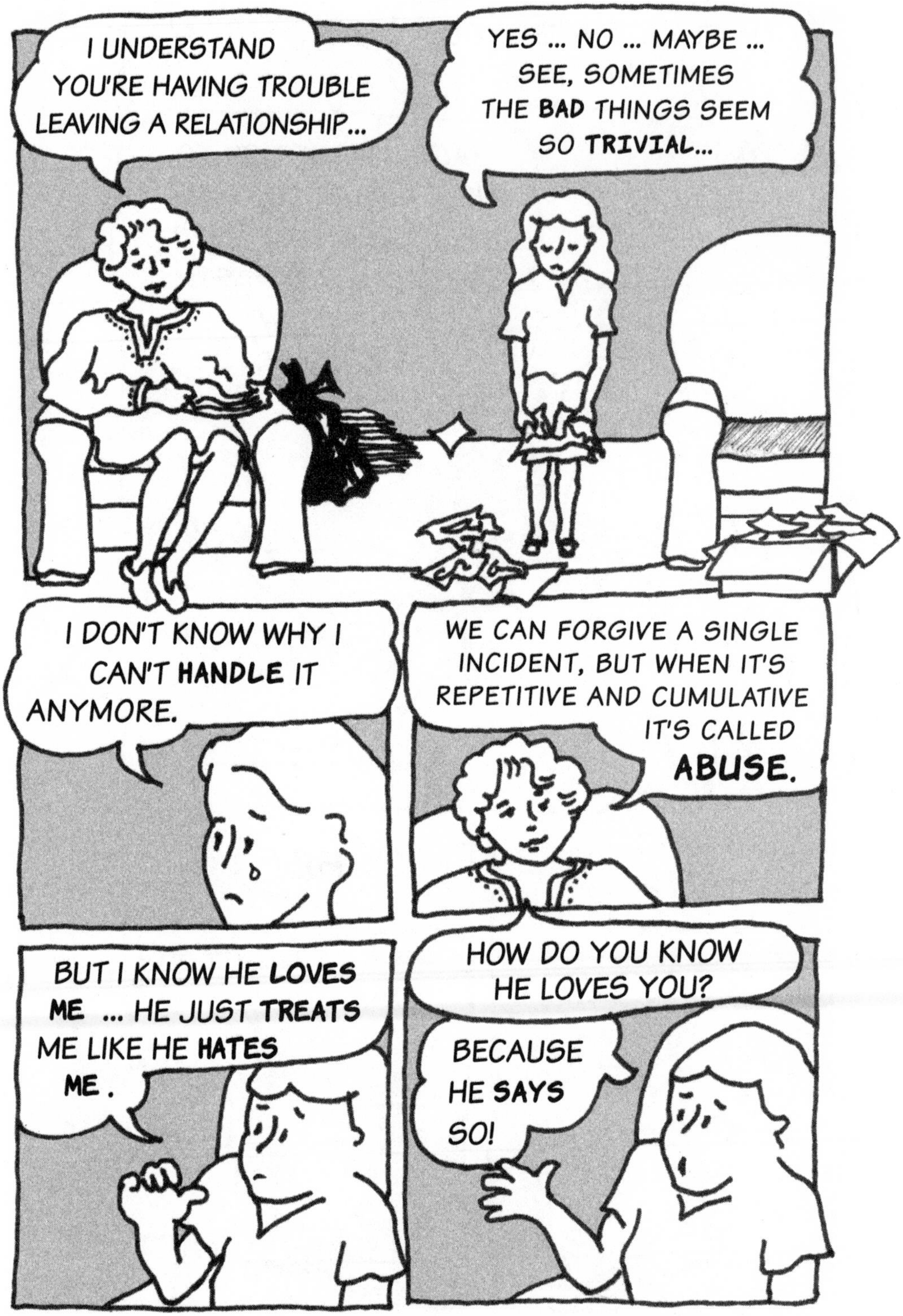
I UNDERSTAND YOU'RE HAVING TROUBLE LEAVING A RELATIONSHIP...
YES ... NO ... MAYBE ... SEE, SOMETIMES THE BAD THINGS SEEM SO TRIVIAL...
I DON'T KNOW WHY I CAN'T HANDLE IT ANYMORE.
WE CAN FORGIVE A SINGLE INCIDENT, BUT WHEN IT'S REPETITIVE AND CUMULATIVE IT'S CALLED ABUSE.
BUT I KNOW HE LOVES ME ... HE JUST TREATS ME LIKE HE HATES ME.
HOW DO YOU KNOW HE LOVES YOU?
BECAUSE HE SAYS SO!

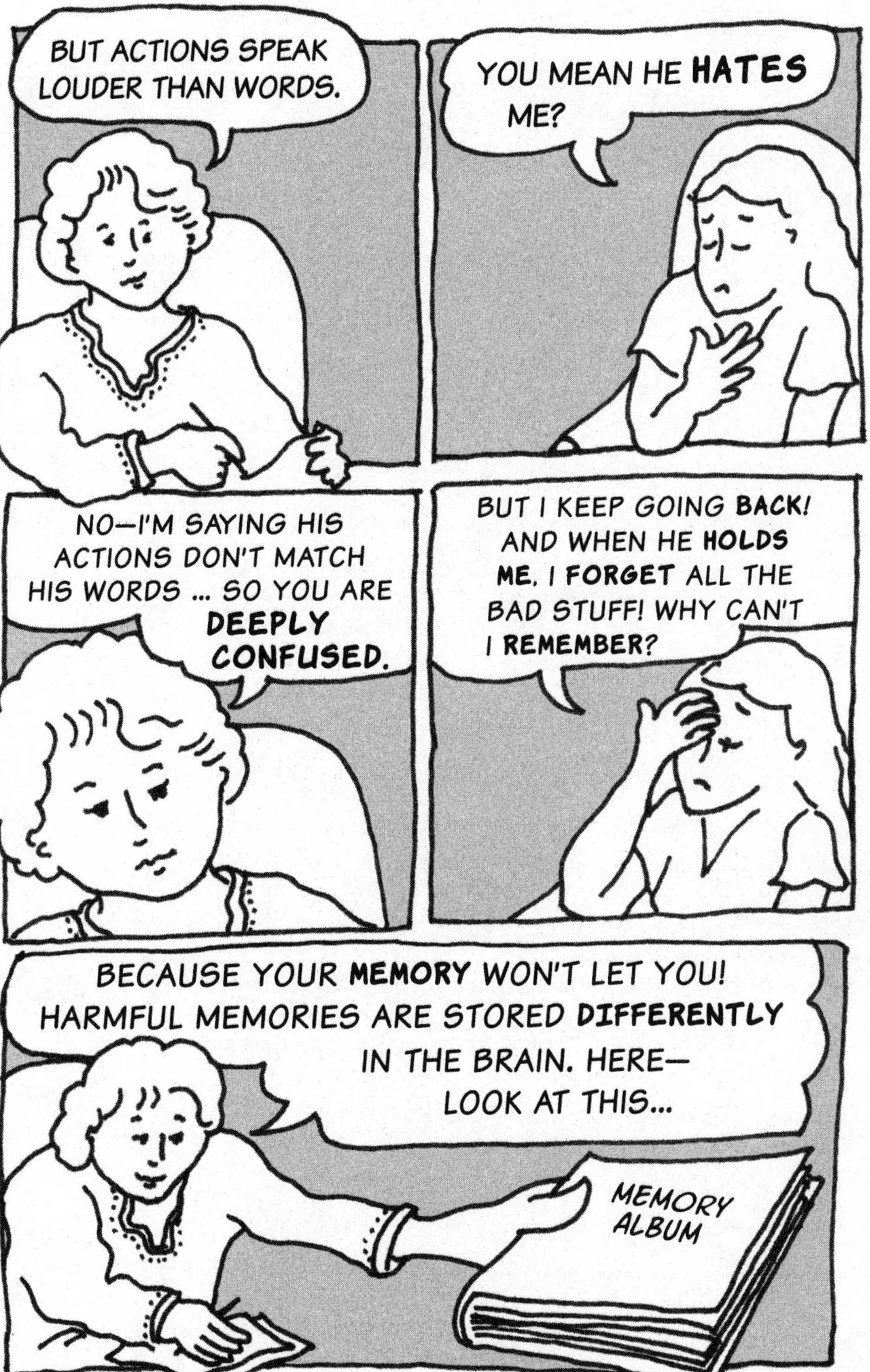
BUT ACTIONS SPEAK LOUDER THAN WORDS.
YOU MEAN HE HATES ME?
NO—I'M SAYING HIS ACTIONS DON'T MATCH HIS WORDS ... SO YOU ARE DEEPLY CONFUSED.
BUT I KEEP GOING BACK! AND WHEN HE HOLDS ME, I FORGET ALL THE BAD STUFF! WHY CAN'T I REMEMBER?
BECAUSE YOUR MEMORY WON'T LET YOU! HARMFUL MEMORIES ARE STORED DIFFERENTLY IN THE BRAIN. HERE— LOOK AT THIS...
MEMORY ALBUM

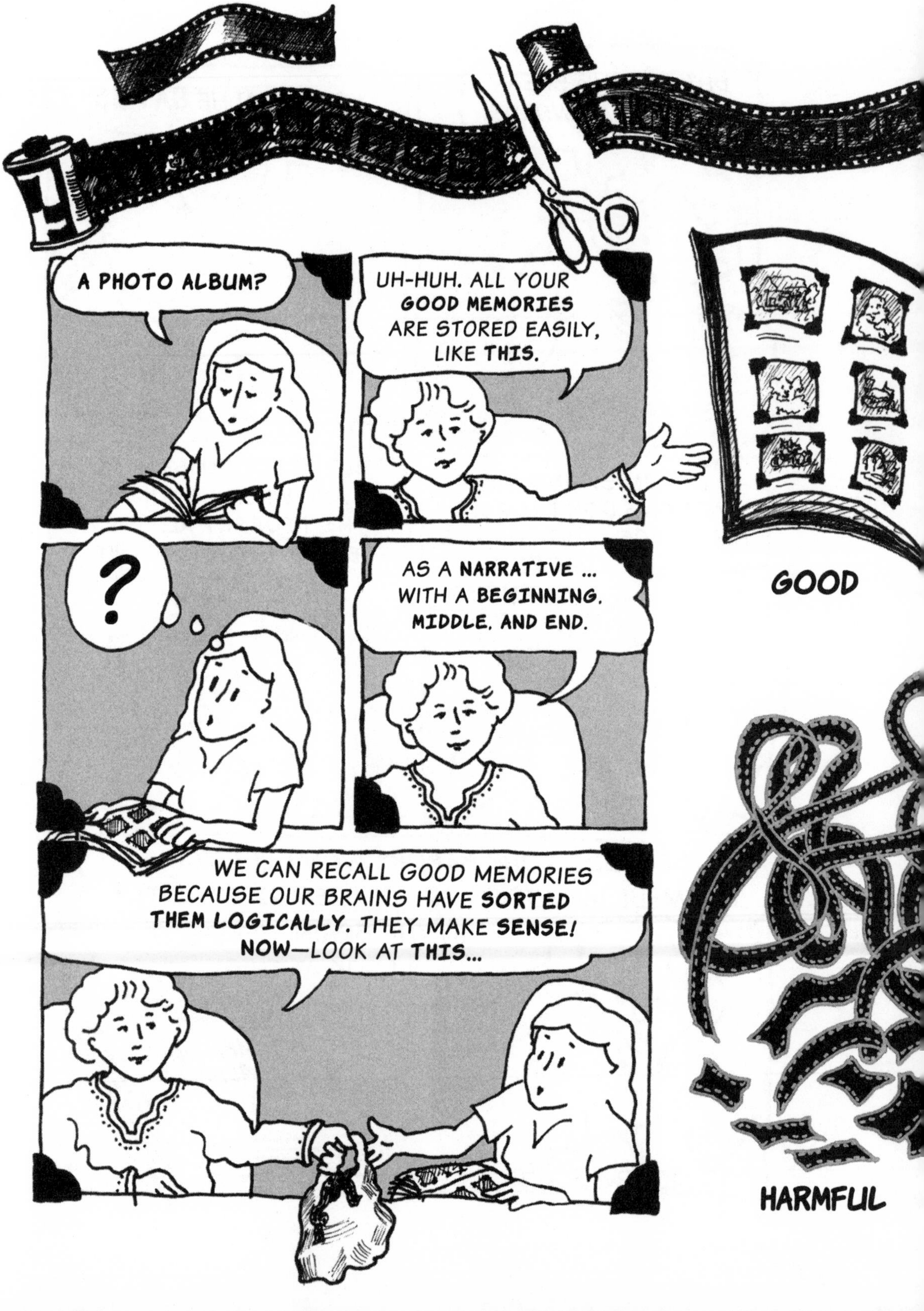
A PHOTO ALBUM?
UH-HUH. ALL YOUR GOOD MEMORIES ARE STORED EASILY, LIKE THIS.
?
AS A NARRATIVE ... WITH A BEGINNING, MIDDLE, AND END.
WE CAN RECALL GOOD MEMORIES BECAUSE OUR BRAINS HAVE SORTED THEM LOGICALLY. THEY MAKE SENSE! NOW—LOOK AT THIS...
GOOD
HARMFUL

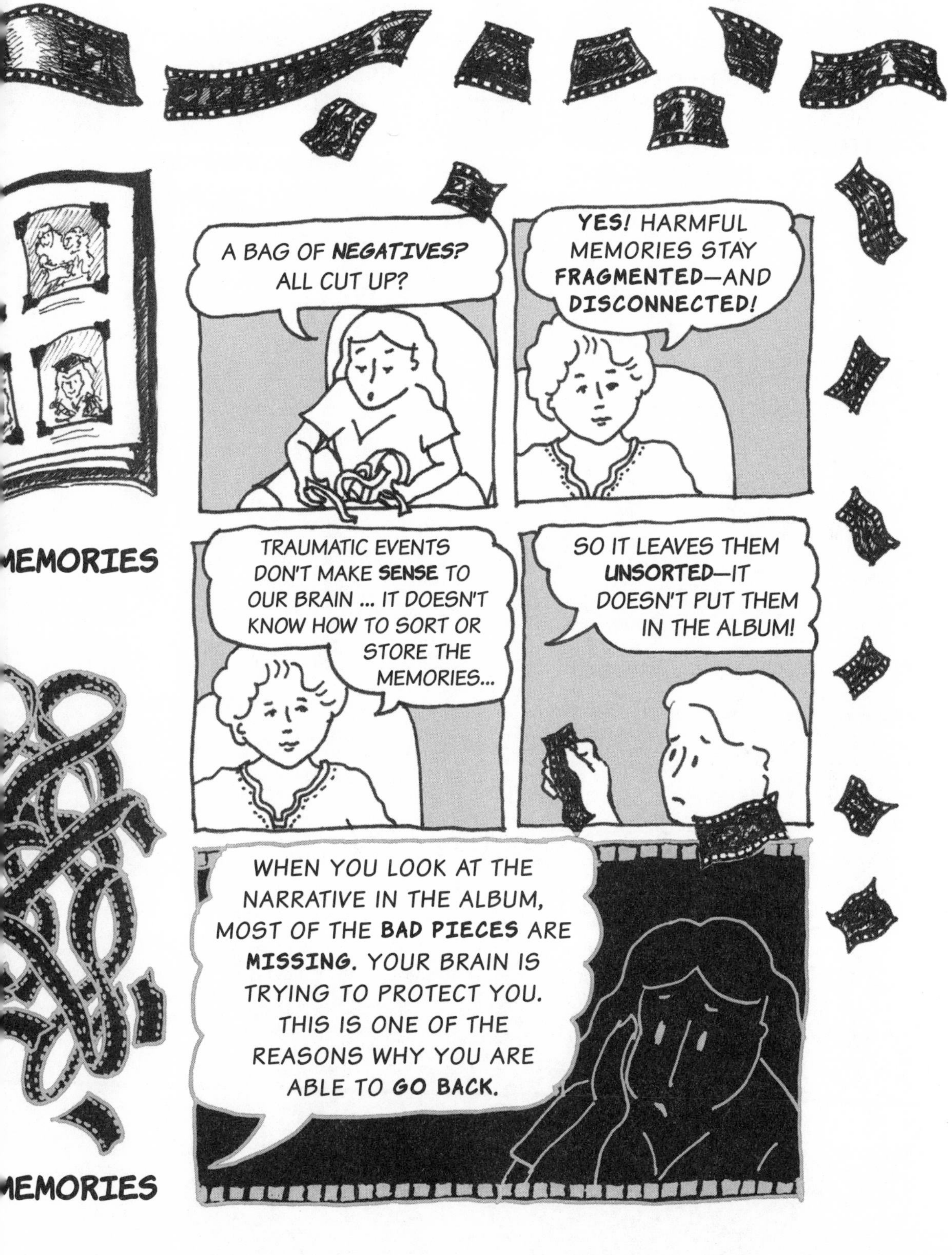
A BAG OF NEGATIVES? ALL CUT UP?
YES! HARMFUL MEMORIES STAY FRAGMENTED—AND DISCONNECTED!
TRAUMATIC EVENTS DON'T MAKE SENSE TO OUR BRAIN ... IT DOESN'T KNOW HOW TO SORT OR STORE THE MEMORIES...
SO IT LEAVES THEM UNSORTED—IT DOESN'T PUT THEM IN THE ALBUM!
WHEN YOU LOOK AT THE NARRATIVE IN THE ALBUM, MOST OF THE BAD PIECES ARE MISSING. YOUR BRAIN IS TRYING TO PROTECT YOU. THIS IS ONE OF THE REASONS WHY YOU ARE ABLE TO GO BACK.

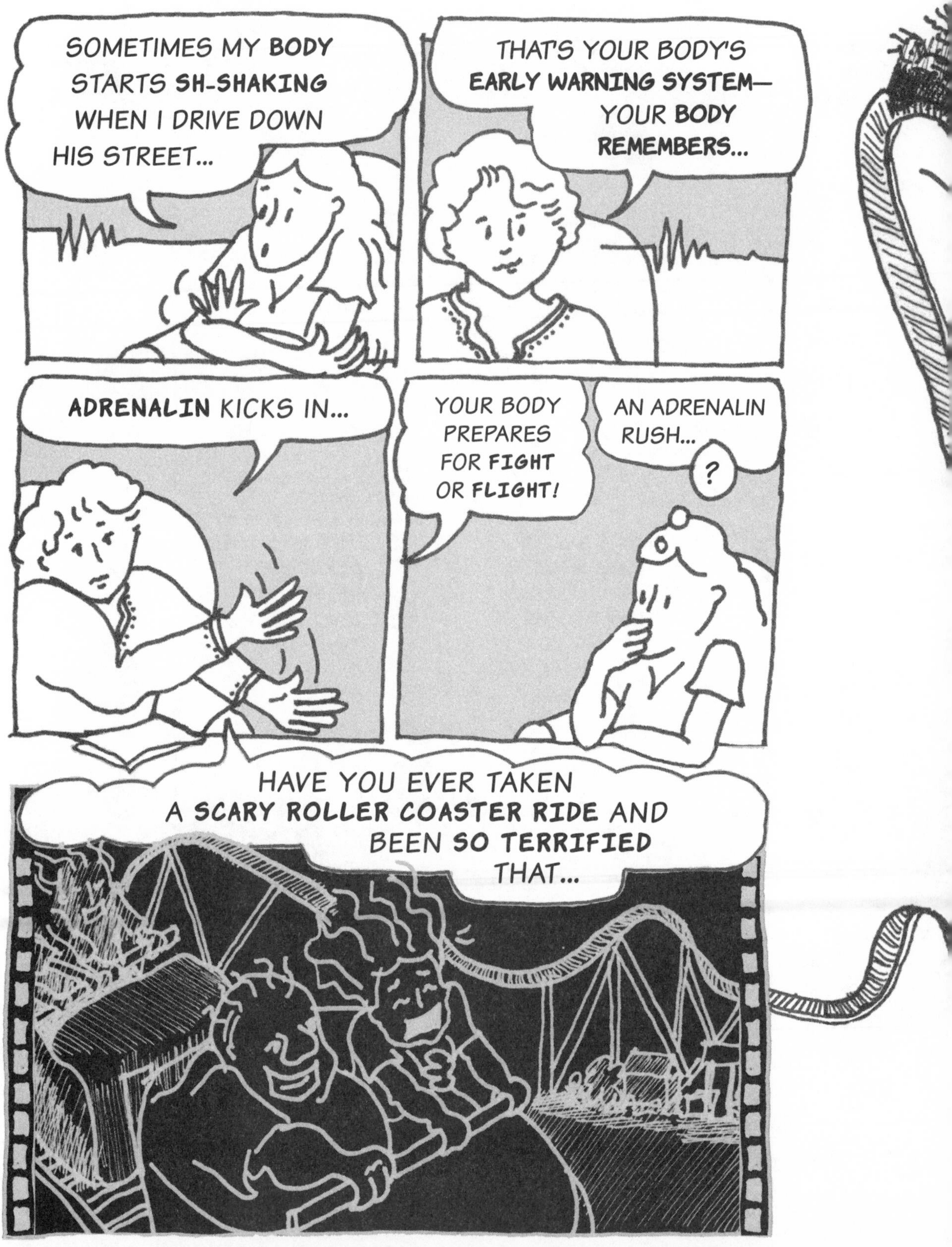
SOMETIMES MY BODY STARTS SH-SHAKING WHEN I DRIVE DOWN HIS STREET...
THAT'S YOUR BODY'S EARLY WARNING SYSTEM— YOUR BODY REMEMBERS...
ADRENALIN KICKS IN...
YOUR BODY PREPARES FOR FIGHT OR FLIGHT!
AN ADRENALIN RUSH...
?
HAVE YOU EVER TAKEN A SCARY ROLLER COASTER RIDE AND BEEN SO TERRIFIED THAT...

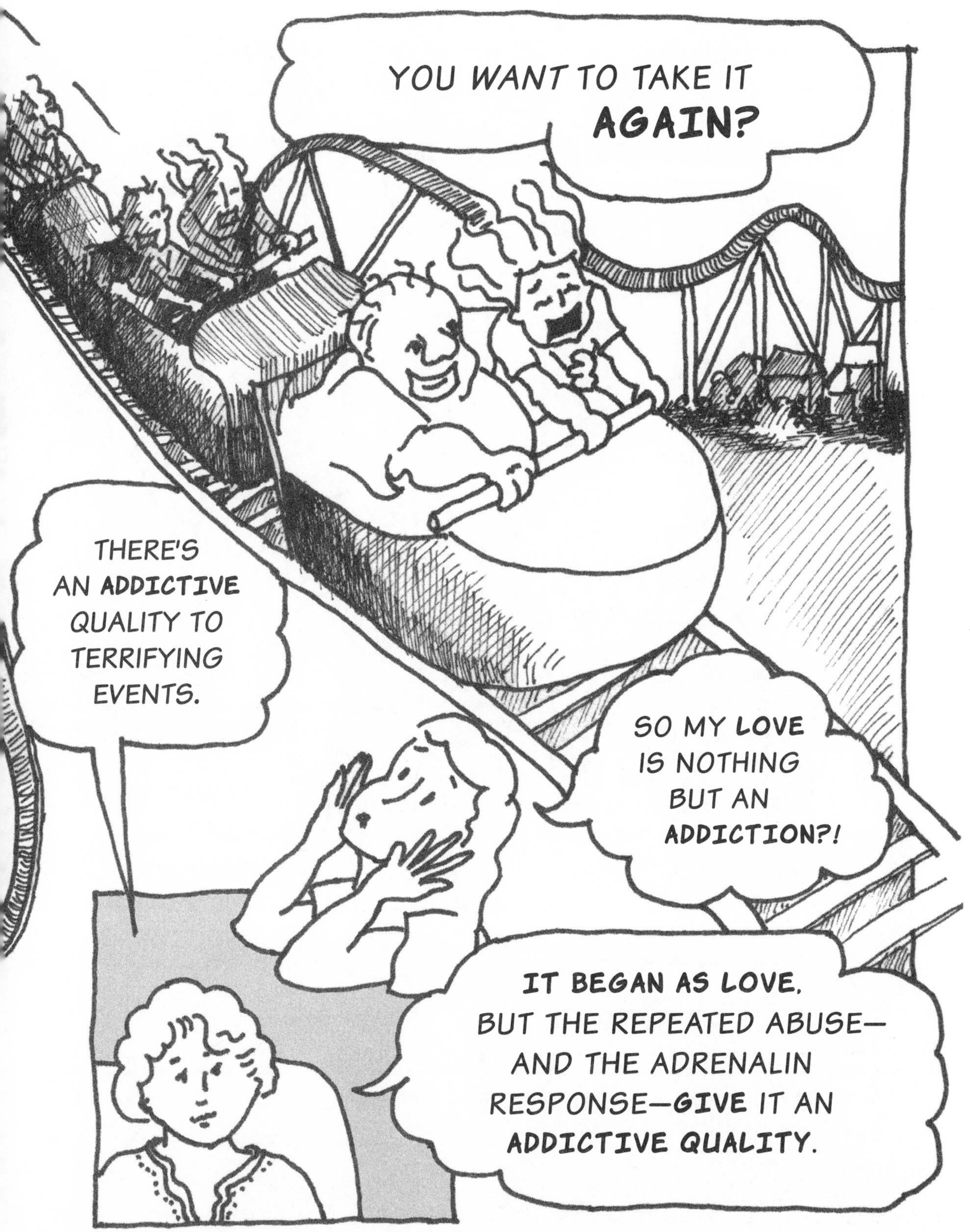
YOU WANT TO TAKE IT AGAIN?
THERE'S AN ADDICTIVE QUALITY TO TERRIFYING EVENTS.
SO MY LOVE IS NOTHING BUT AN ADDICTION?!
IT BEGAN AS LOVE. BUT THE REPEATED ABUSE—AND THE ADRENALIN RESPONSE—GIVE IT AN ADDICTIVE QUALITY.

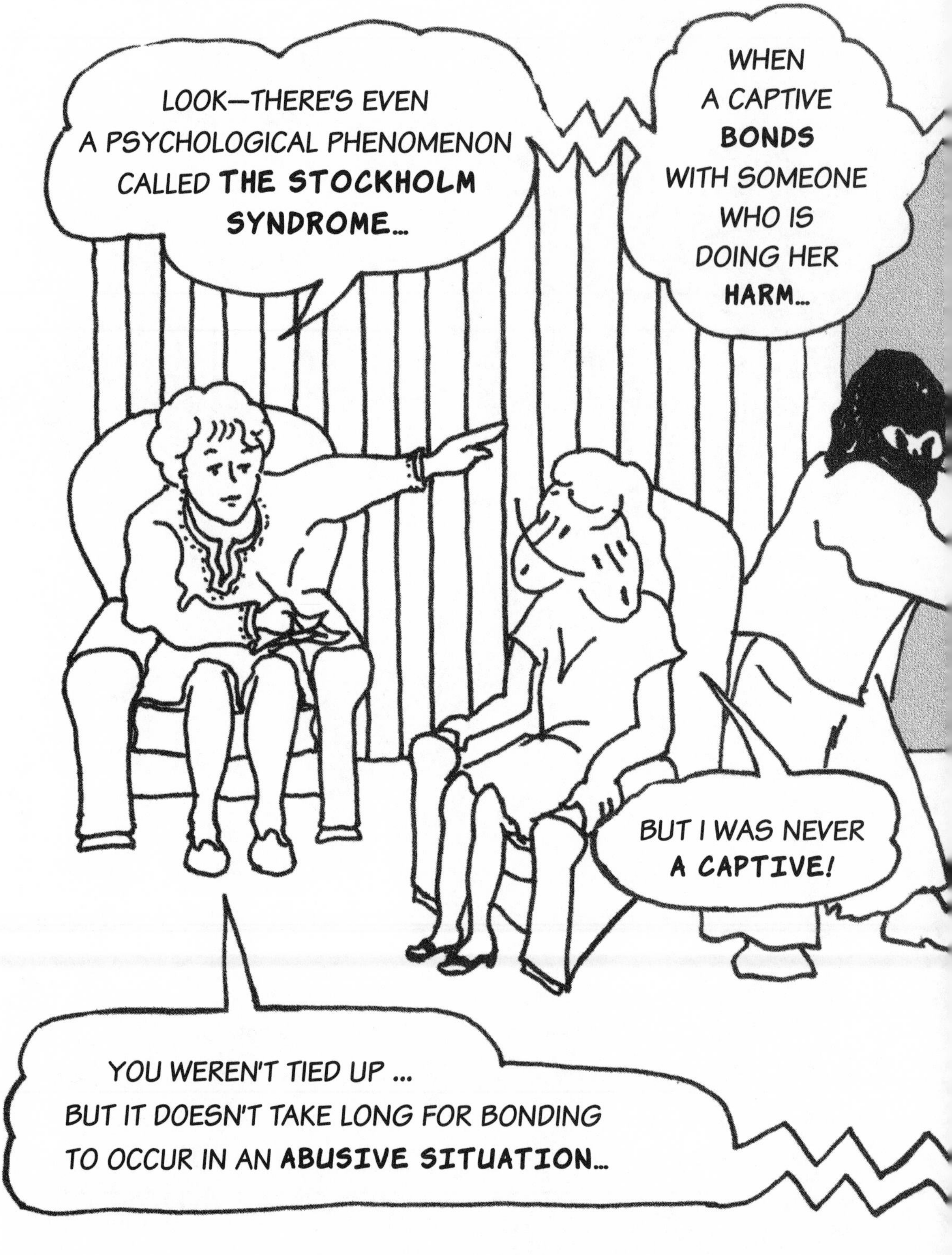
LOOK—THERE'S EVEN A PSYCHOLOGICAL PHENOMENON CALLED **THE STOCKHOLM SYNDROME**...
WHEN A CAPTIVE **BONDS** WITH SOMEONE WHO IS DOING HER **HARM**...
BUT I WAS NEVER **A CAPTIVE!**
YOU WEREN'T TIED UP ... BUT IT DOESN'T TAKE LONG FOR BONDING TO OCCUR IN AN **ABUSIVE SITUATION**...

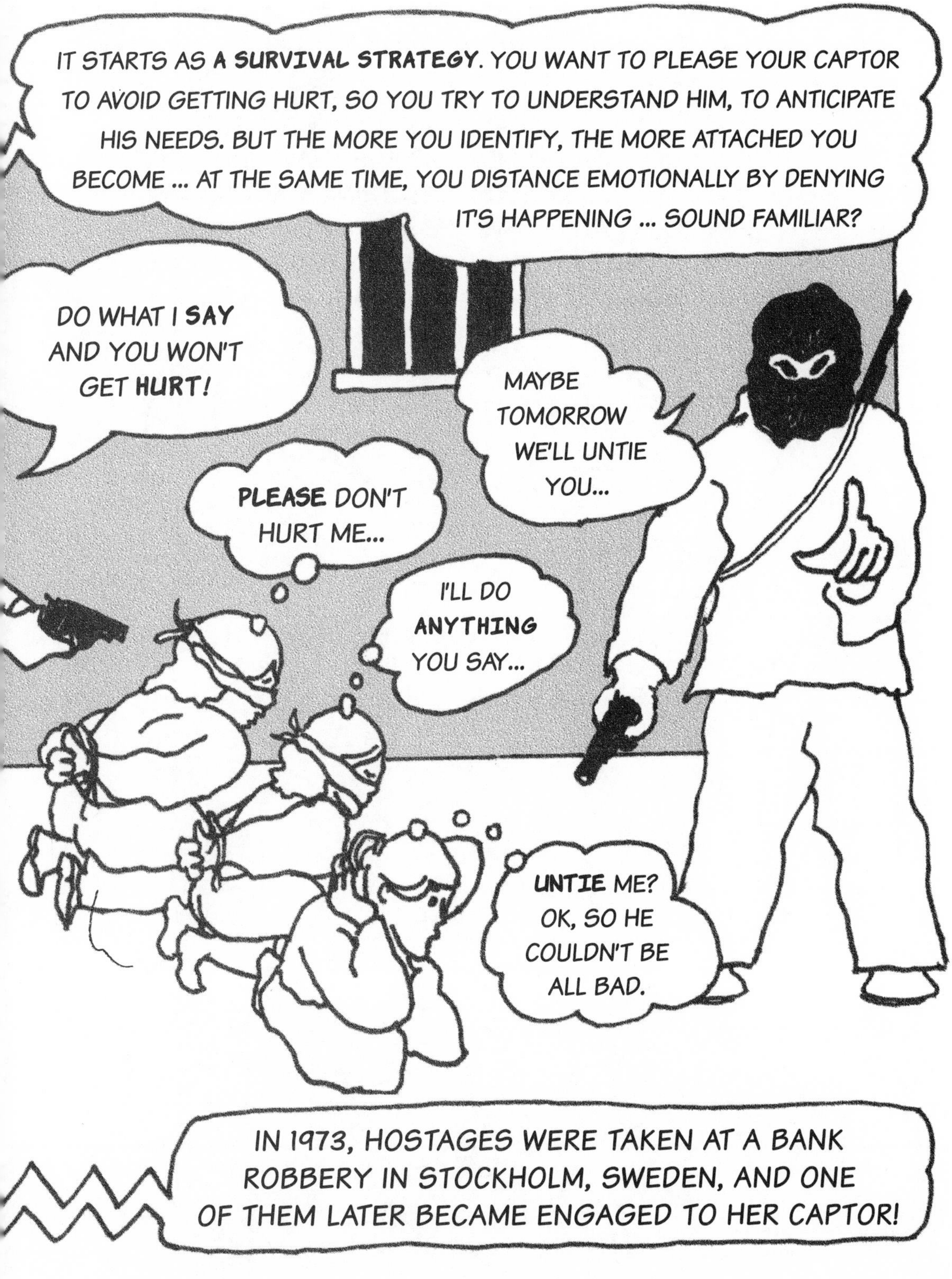

IT STARTS AS **A SURVIVAL STRATEGY**. YOU WANT TO PLEASE YOUR CAPTOR TO AVOID GETTING HURT, SO YOU TRY TO UNDERSTAND HIM, TO ANTICIPATE HIS NEEDS. BUT THE MORE YOU IDENTIFY, THE MORE ATTACHED YOU BECOME ... AT THE SAME TIME, YOU DISTANCE EMOTIONALLY BY DENYING IT'S HAPPENING ... SOUND FAMILIAR?
DO WHAT I **SAY** AND YOU WON'T GET **HURT**!
MAYBE TOMORROW WE'LL UNTIE YOU...
PLEASE DON'T HURT ME...
I'LL DO **ANYTHING** YOU SAY...
UNTIE ME? OK, SO HE COULDN'T BE ALL BAD.
IN 1973, HOSTAGES WERE TAKEN AT A BANK ROBBERY IN STOCKHOLM, SWEDEN, AND ONE OF THEM LATER BECAME ENGAGED TO HER CAPTOR!

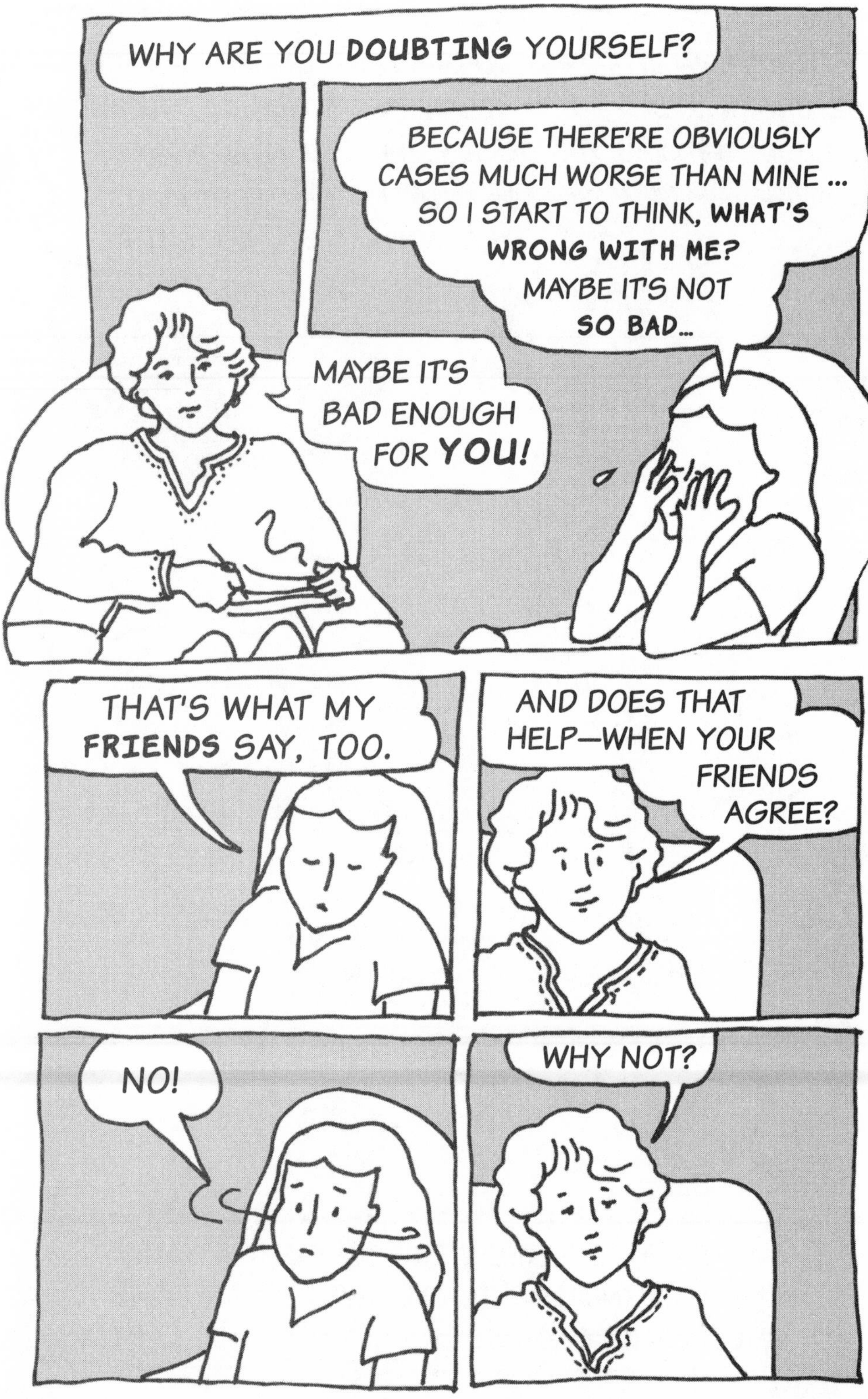
WHY ARE YOU DOUBTING YOURSELF?
BECAUSE THERE'RE OBVIOUSLY CASES MUCH WORSE THAN MINE ... SO I START TO THINK, WHAT'S WRONG WITH ME? MAYBE IT'S NOT SO BAD...
MAYBE IT'S BAD ENOUGH FOR YOU!
THAT'S WHAT MY FRIENDS SAY, TOO.
AND DOES THAT HELP—WHEN YOUR FRIENDS AGREE?
NO!
WHY NOT?

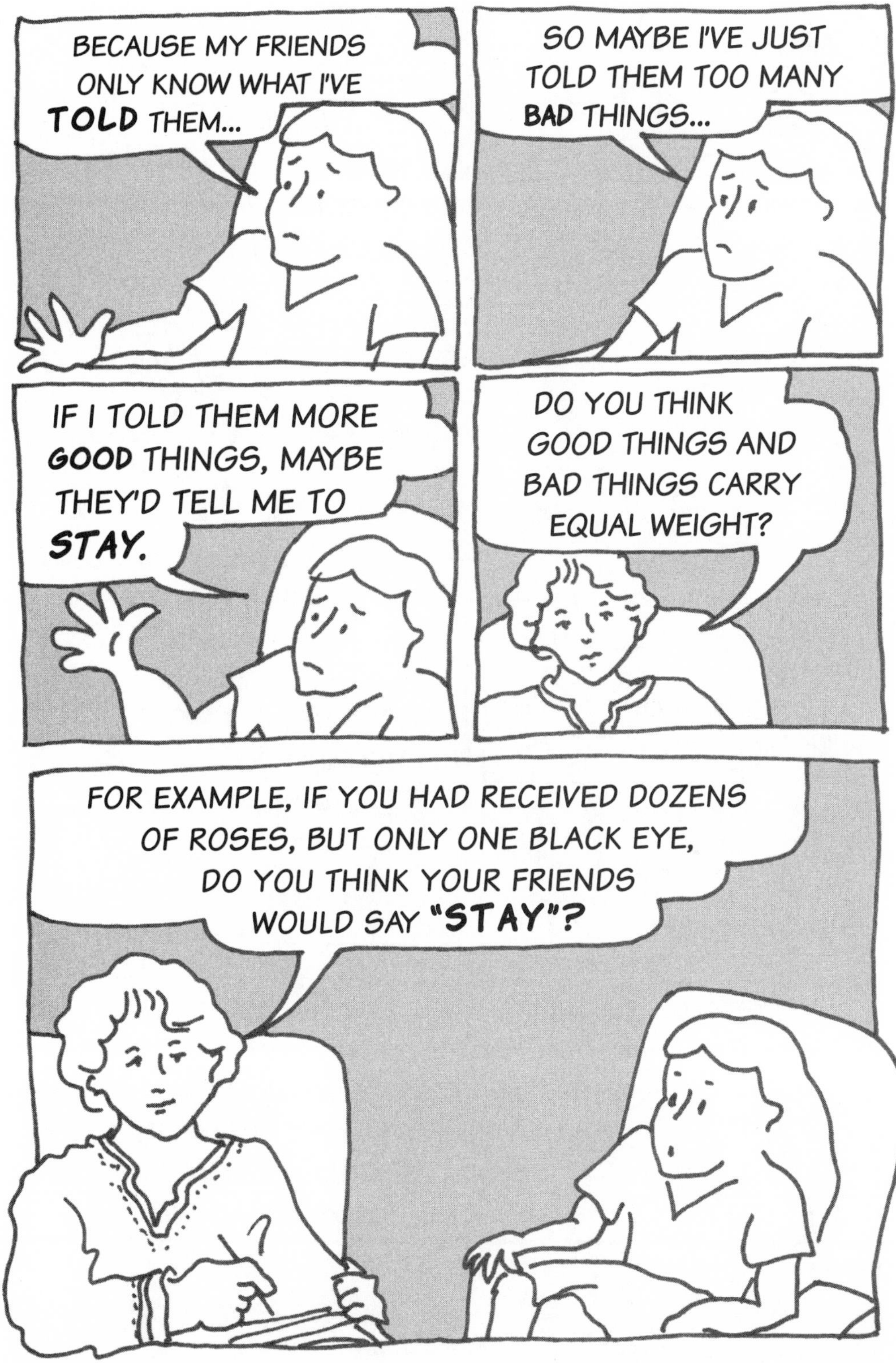
BECAUSE MY FRIENDS ONLY KNOW WHAT I'VE **TOLD** THEM...
SO MAYBE I'VE JUST TOLD THEM TOO MANY **BAD** THINGS...
IF I TOLD THEM MORE **GOOD** THINGS, MAYBE THEY'D TELL ME TO **STAY.**
DO YOU THINK GOOD THINGS AND BAD THINGS CARRY EQUAL WEIGHT?
FOR EXAMPLE, IF YOU HAD RECEIVED DOZENS OF ROSES, BUT ONLY ONE BLACK EYE, DO YOU THINK YOUR FRIENDS WOULD SAY **"STAY"**?

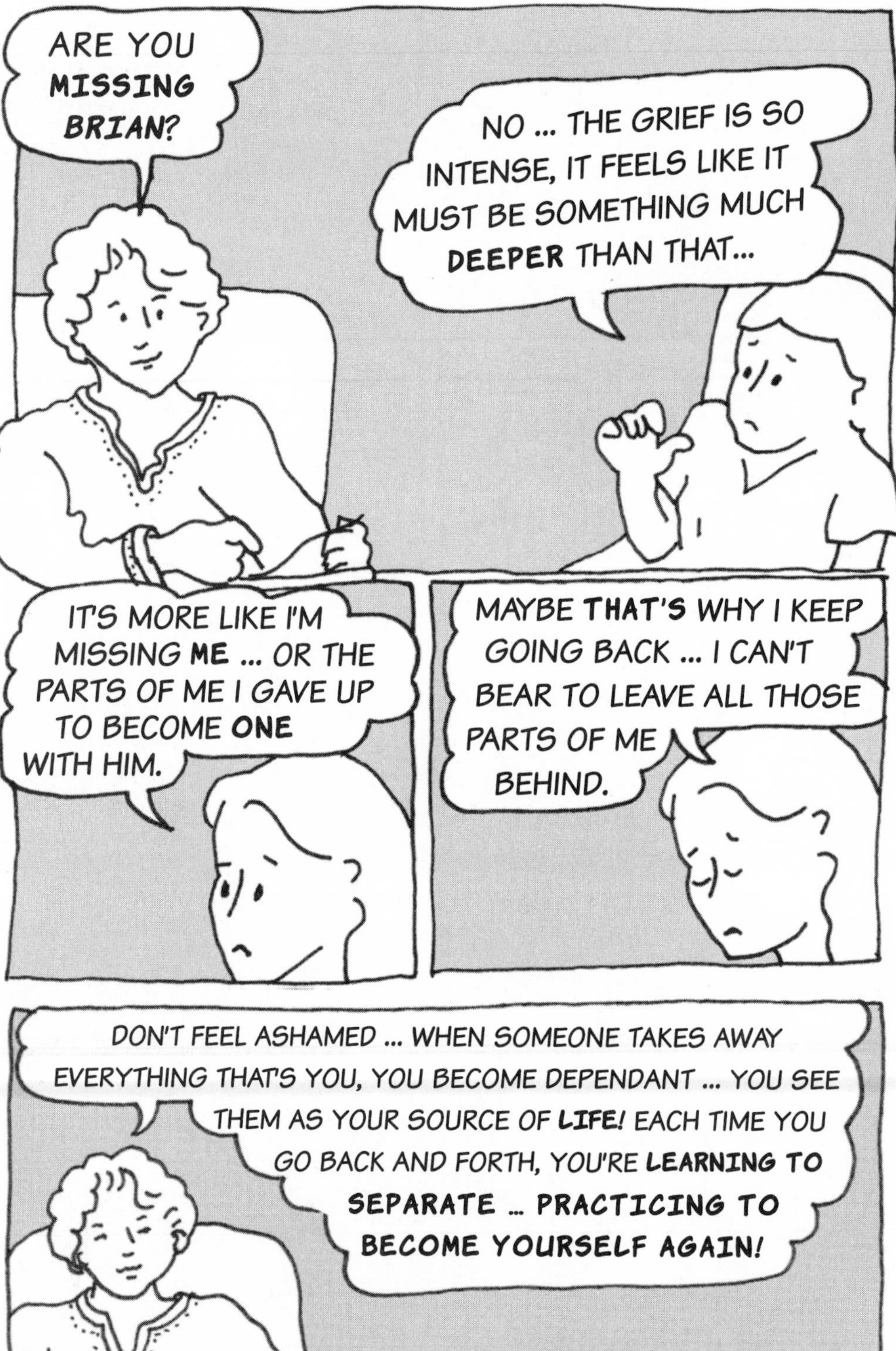
ARE YOU MISSING BRIAN?
NO ... THE GRIEF IS SO INTENSE, IT FEELS LIKE IT MUST BE SOMETHING MUCH DEEPER THAN THAT...
IT'S MORE LIKE I'M MISSING ME ... OR THE PARTS OF ME I GAVE UP TO BECOME ONE WITH HIM.
MAYBE THAT'S WHY I KEEP GOING BACK ... I CAN'T BEAR TO LEAVE ALL THOSE PARTS OF ME BEHIND.
DON'T FEEL ASHAMED ... WHEN SOMEONE TAKES AWAY EVERYTHING THAT'S YOU, YOU BECOME DEPENDANT ... YOU SEE THEM AS YOUR SOURCE OF LIFE! EACH TIME YOU GO BACK AND FORTH, YOU'RE LEARNING TO SEPARATE ... PRACTICING TO BECOME YOURSELF AGAIN!

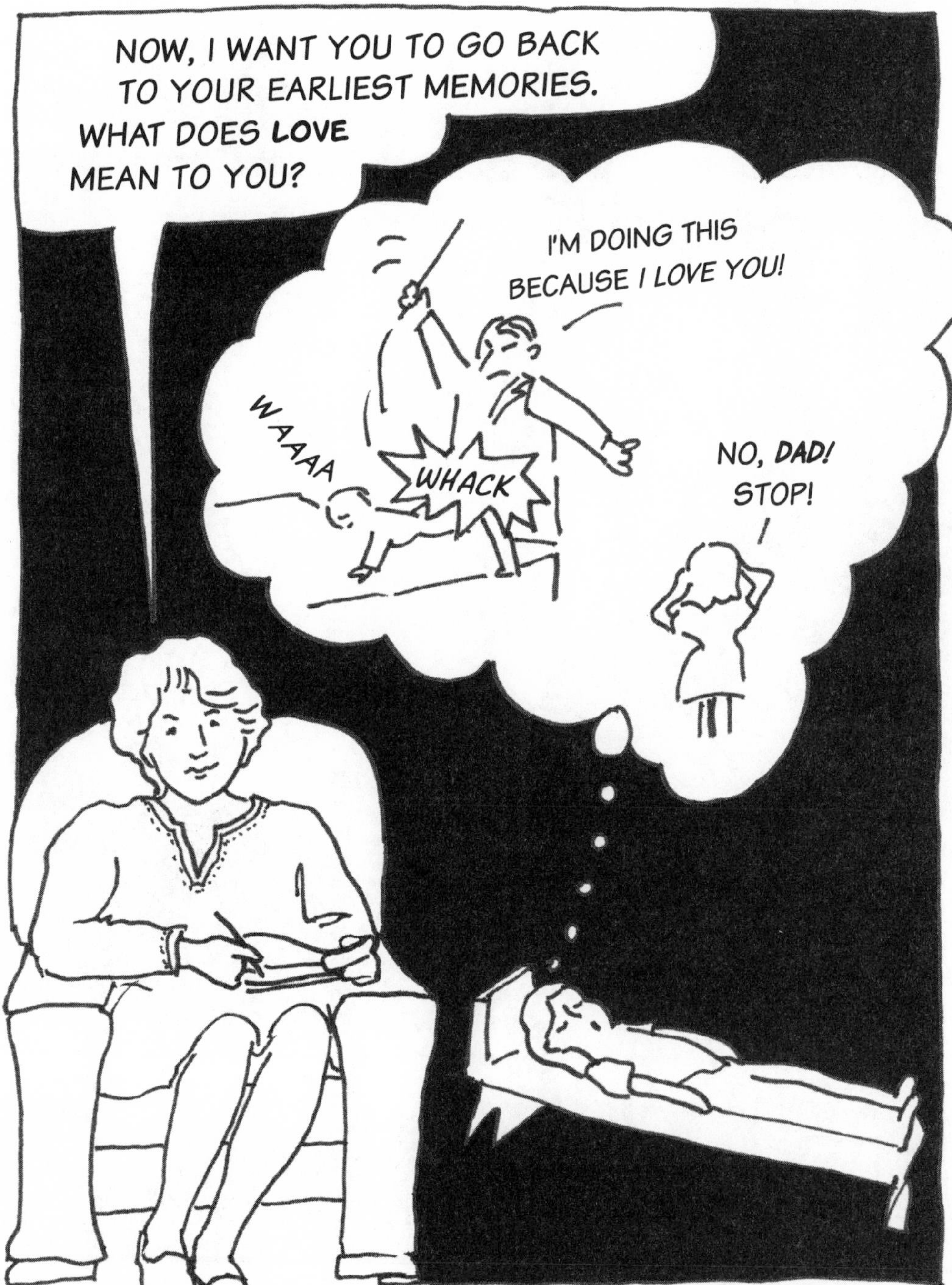
NOW, I WANT YOU TO GO BACK TO YOUR EARLIEST MEMORIES. WHAT DOES **LOVE** MEAN TO YOU?
I'M DOING THIS BECAUSE I LOVE YOU!
WAAAA
WHACK
NO, **DAD!** STOP!

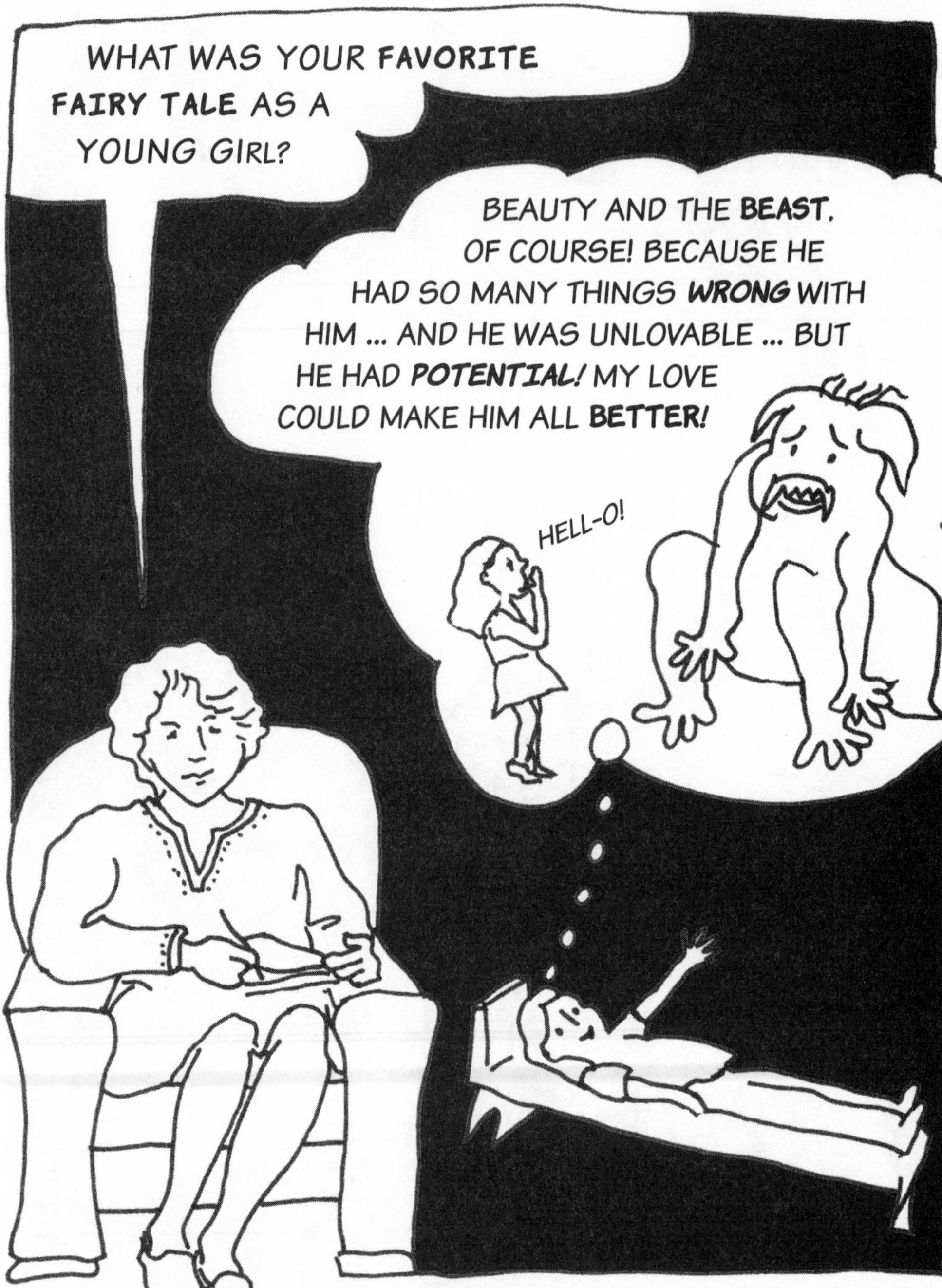
WHAT WAS YOUR FAVORITE FAIRY TALE AS A YOUNG GIRL?
BEAUTY AND THE BEAST, OF COURSE! BECAUSE HE HAD SO MANY THINGS WRONG WITH HIM ... AND HE WAS UNLOVABLE ... BUT HE HAD POTENTIAL! MY LOVE COULD MAKE HIM ALL BETTER!
HELL-O!

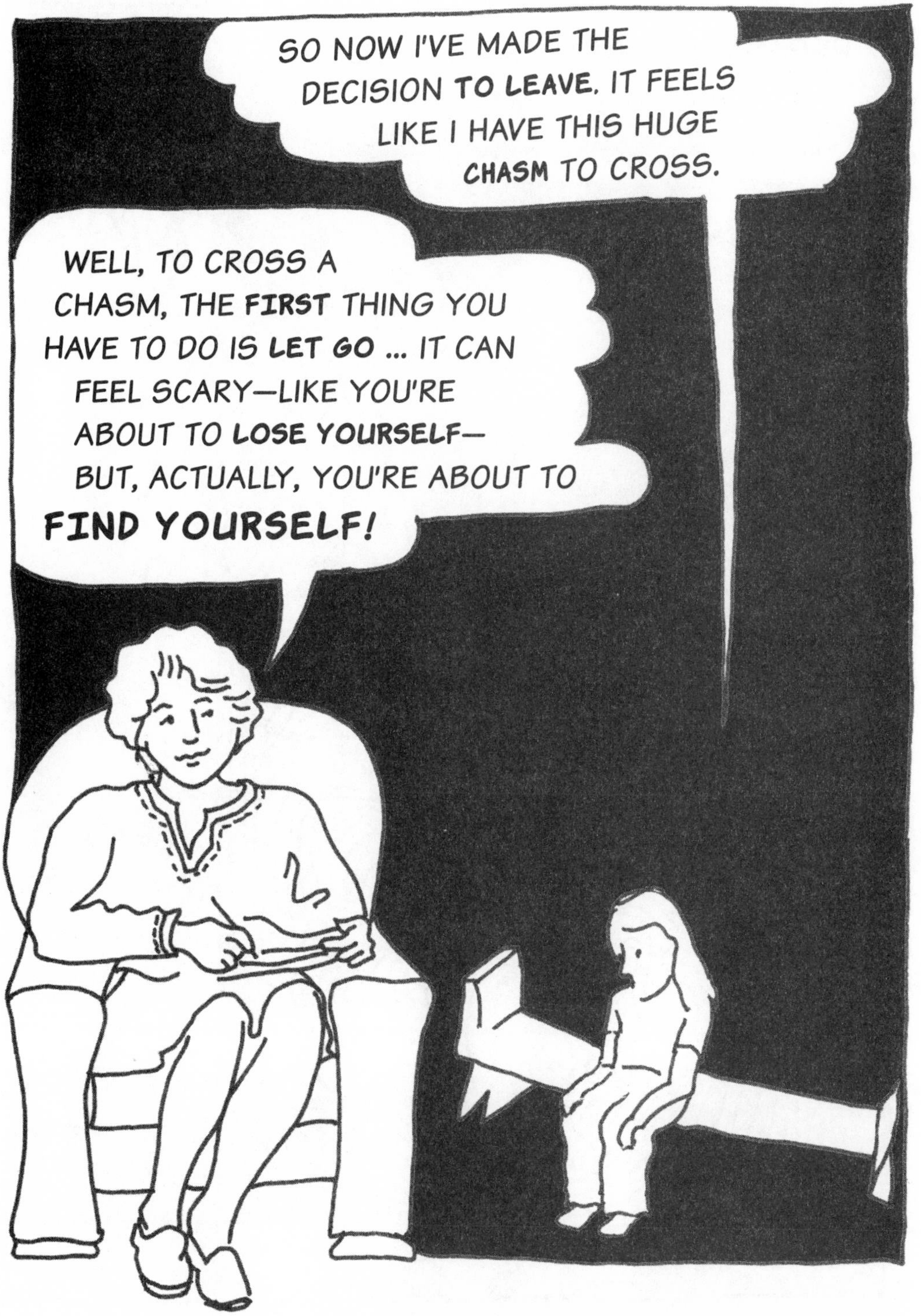
SO NOW I'VE MADE THE DECISION **TO LEAVE**. IT FEELS LIKE I HAVE THIS HUGE **CHASM** TO CROSS.
WELL, TO CROSS A CHASM, THE **FIRST** THING YOU HAVE TO DO IS **LET GO** ... IT CAN FEEL SCARY—LIKE YOU'RE ABOUT TO **LOSE YOURSELF**— BUT, ACTUALLY, YOU'RE ABOUT TO **FIND YOURSELF!**

THE ABUSED BRAIN

I'M ALWAYS CONFUSED ... NOTHING MAKES SENSE ... I CAN'T FIND MY WAY OUT.

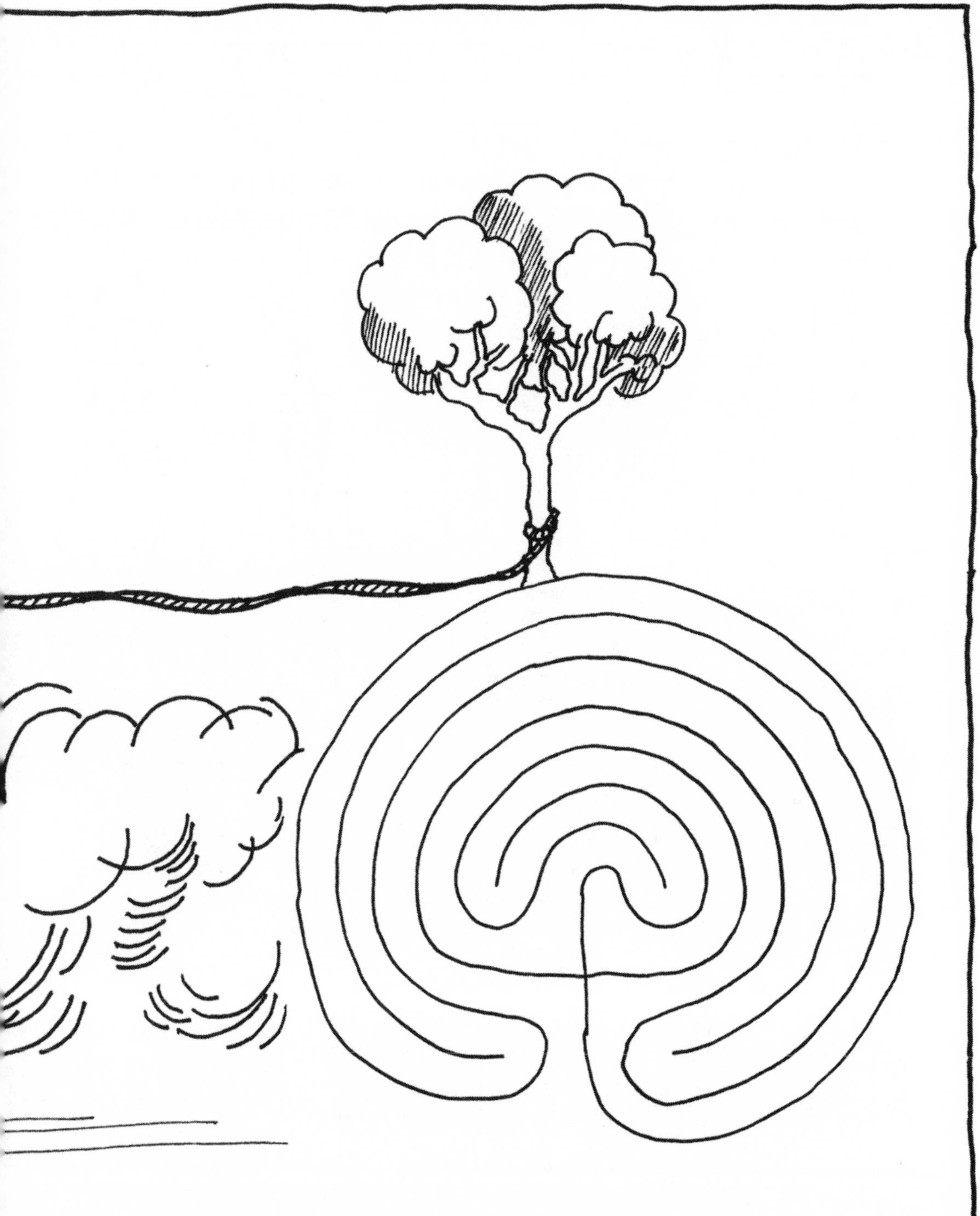

THE PEACEFUL BRAIN
THIS WILL GO SMOOTHLY ... I'LL HAVE ENERGY ... I'LL NEVER FEEL LOST.

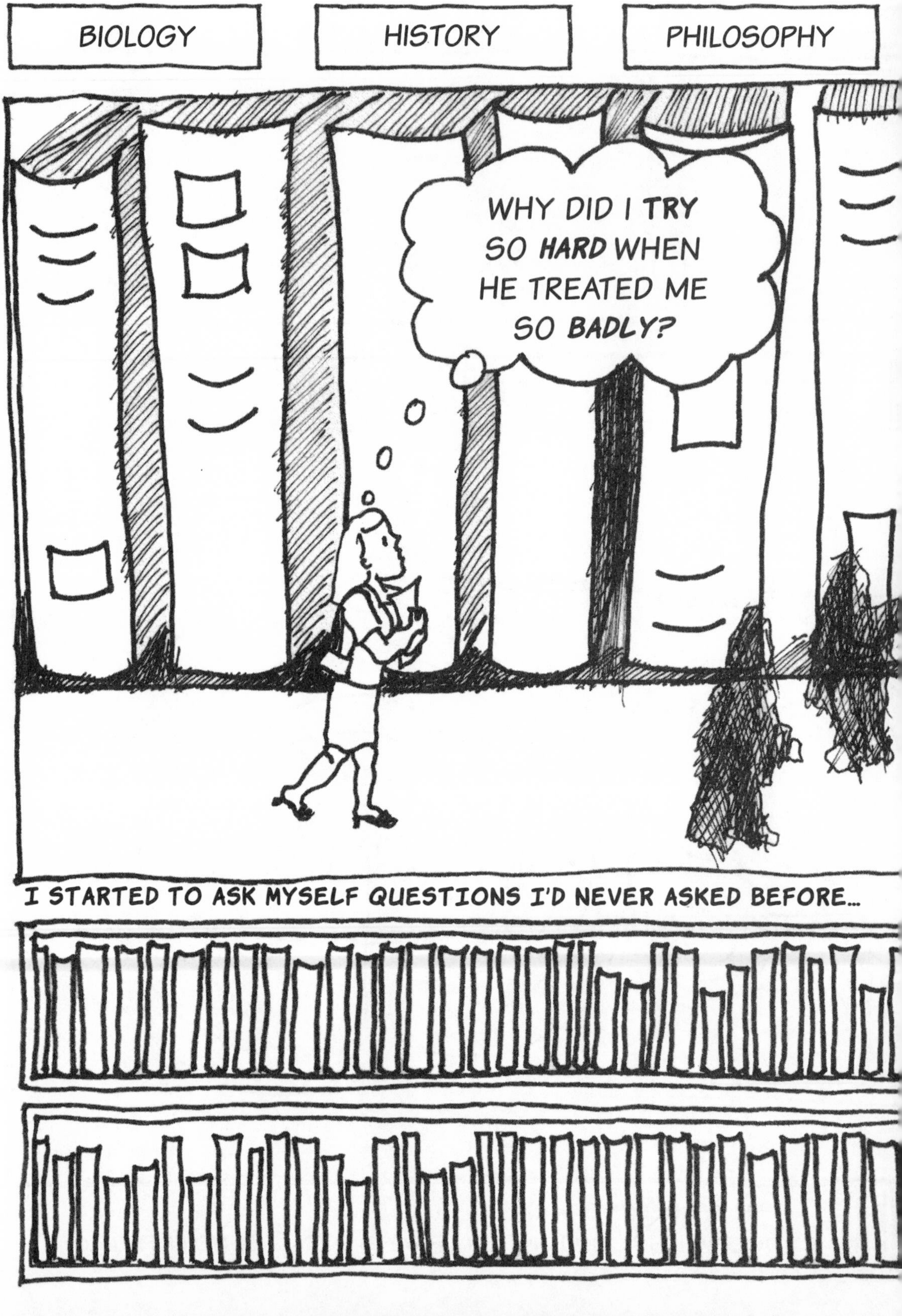
BIOLOGY
HISTORY
PHILOSOPHY
WHY DID I TRY SO HARD WHEN HE TREATED ME SO BADLY?
I STARTED TO ASK MYSELF QUESTIONS I'D NEVER ASKED BEFORE...

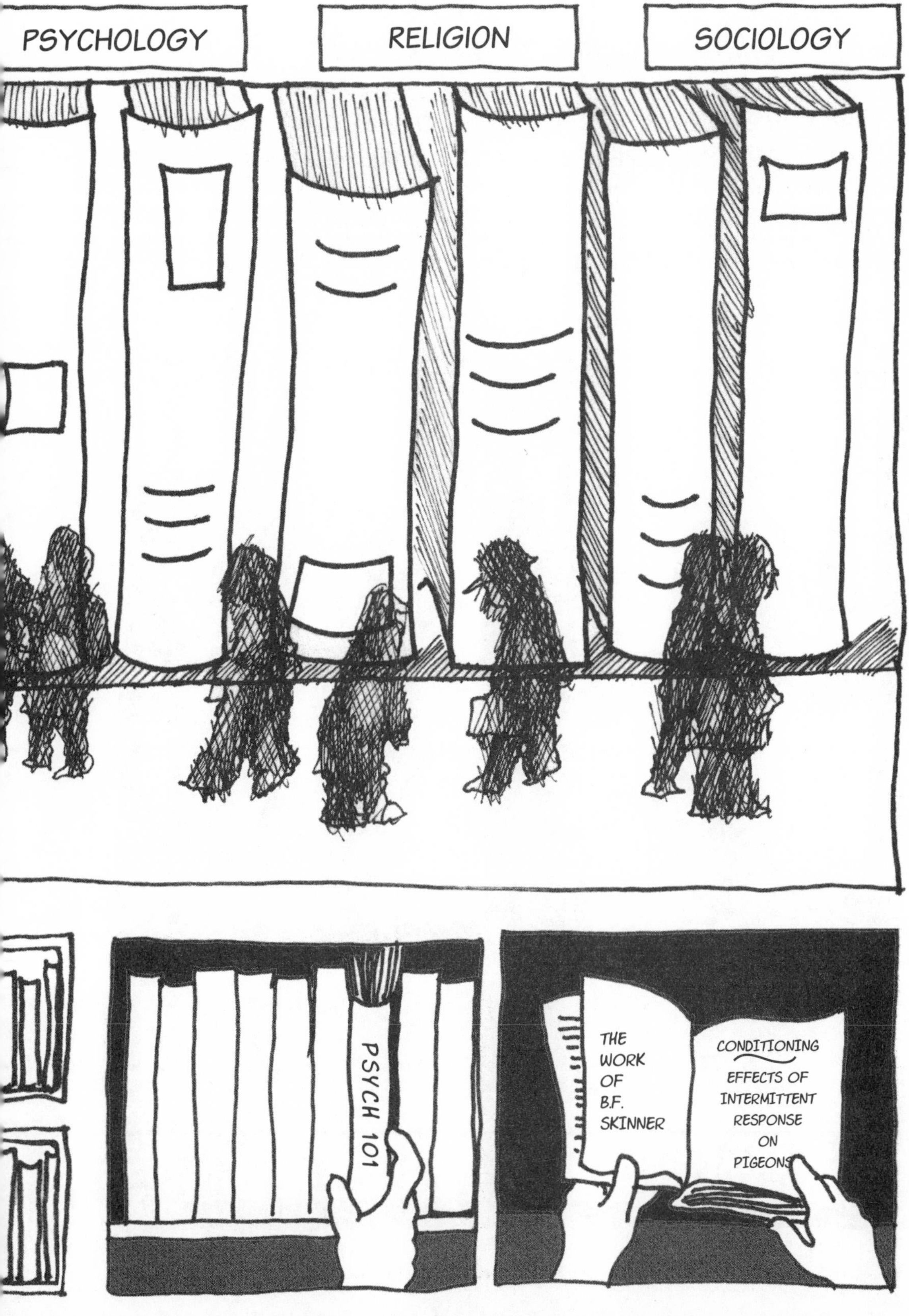
PSYCHOLOGY
RELIGION
SOCIOLOGY
PSYCH 101
THE WORK OF B.F. SKINNER
CONDITIONING
EFFECTS OF INTERMITTENT RESPONSE ON PIGEONS

I DISCOVERED WHAT I CALL "THE PIGEON PRINCIPLE"...

IN SKINNER'S EXPERIMENT, PIGEON ONE GOT A FOOD PELLET EVERY TIME IT PRESSED THE LEVER, *SO IT FELT SECURE.* PIGEON TWO, HOWEVER, NEVER KNEW WHEN OR IF IT WOULD GET FOOD. IT COULD NEVER FEEL SECURE, *SO IT KEPT TRYING HARDER.* I BEGAN TO WONDER ... HAD I BEEN CONDITIONED, JUST LIKE PIGEON TWO?

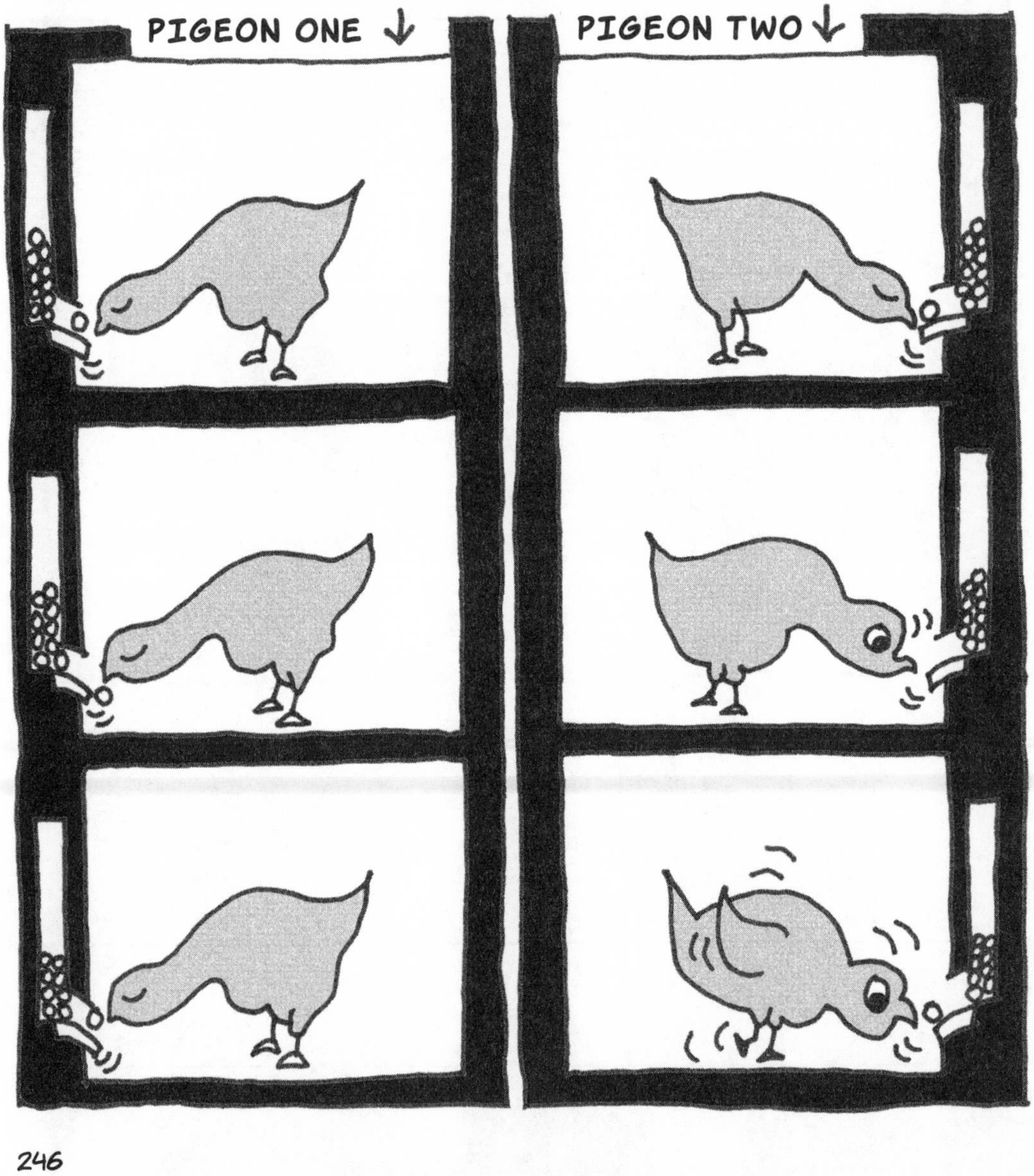
PIGEON ONE
PIGEON TWO

THEN SKINNER REMOVED THE FOOD FROM BOTH PIGEONS AND **LOOK WHAT HAPPENED!** PIGEON ONE GOT THE MESSAGE RIGHT AWAY. **BUT PIGEON TWO** KEPT TRYING HARDER AND HARDER UNTIL IT **ALMOST DIED FROM EXHAUSTION!** THAT SCARED ME.

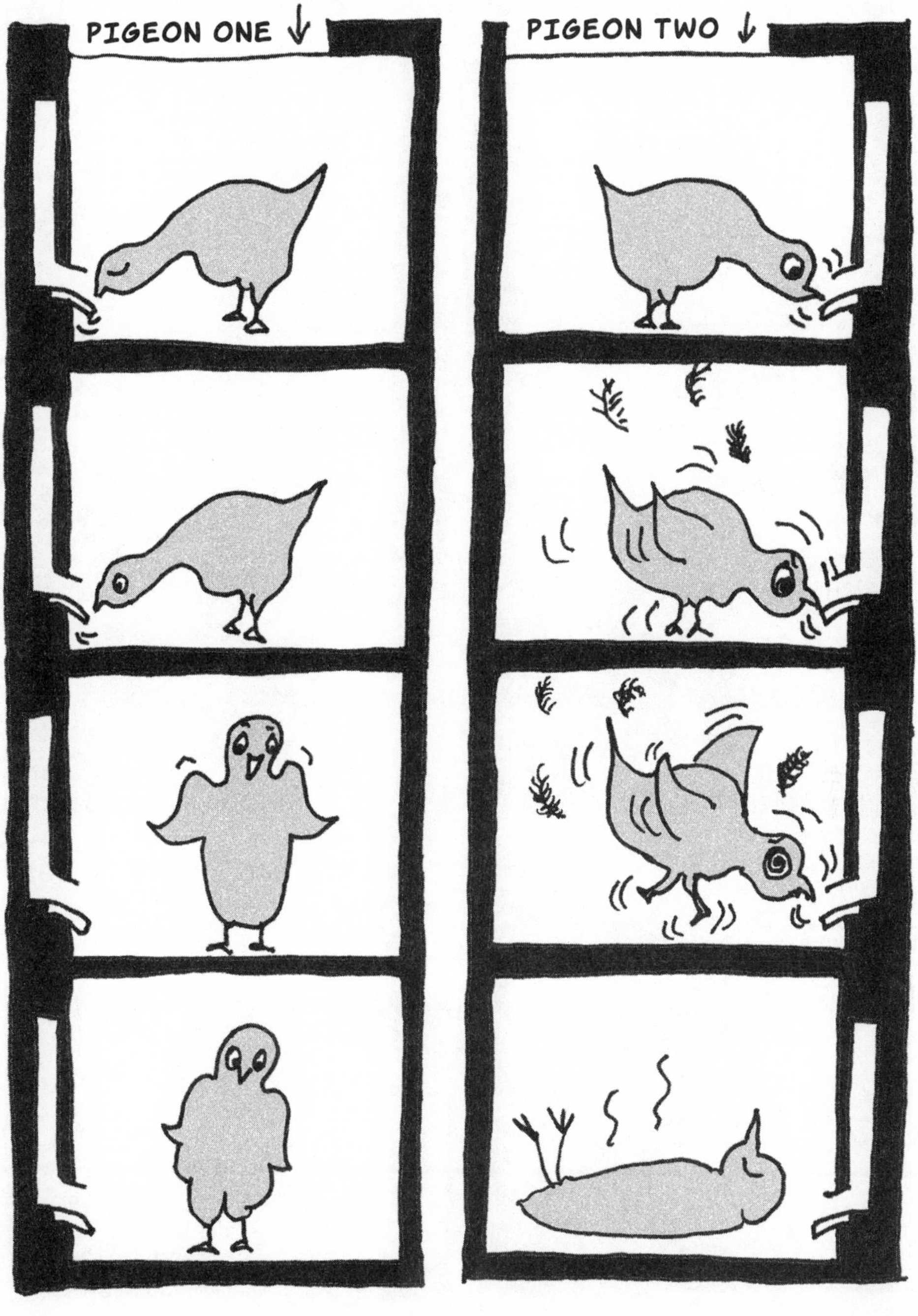
PIGEON ONE ↓
PIGEON TWO ↓

I WENT BACK TO SAGE...

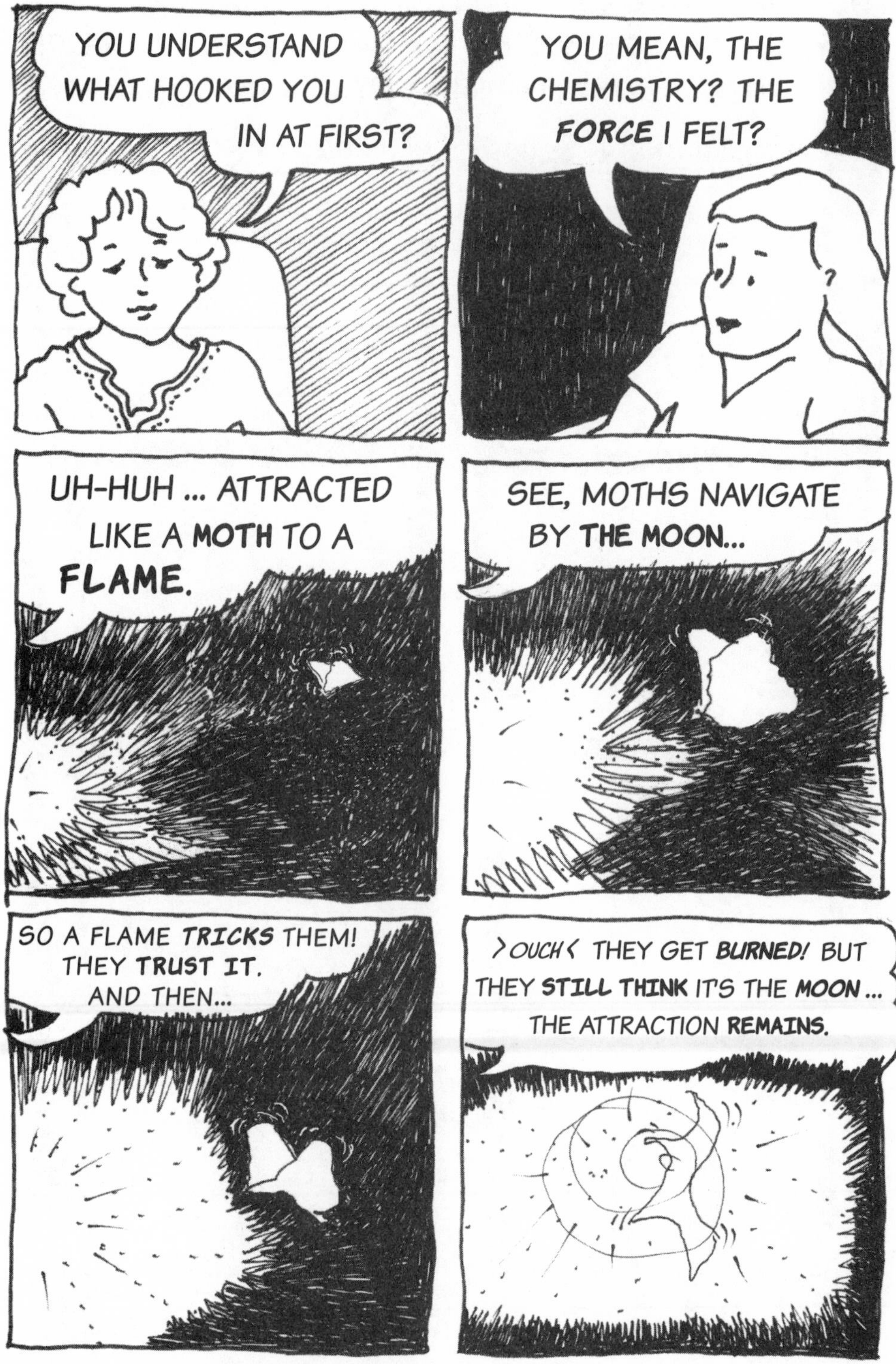
YOU UNDERSTAND WHAT HOOKED YOU IN AT FIRST?
YOU MEAN, THE CHEMISTRY? THE **FORCE** I FELT?
UH-HUH ... ATTRACTED LIKE A **MOTH** TO A **FLAME**.
SEE, MOTHS NAVIGATE BY **THE MOON**...
SO A FLAME **TRICKS** THEM! THEY **TRUST IT**. AND THEN...
>OUCH< THEY GET **BURNED!** BUT THEY **STILL THINK** IT'S THE **MOON** ... THE ATTRACTION **REMAINS**.

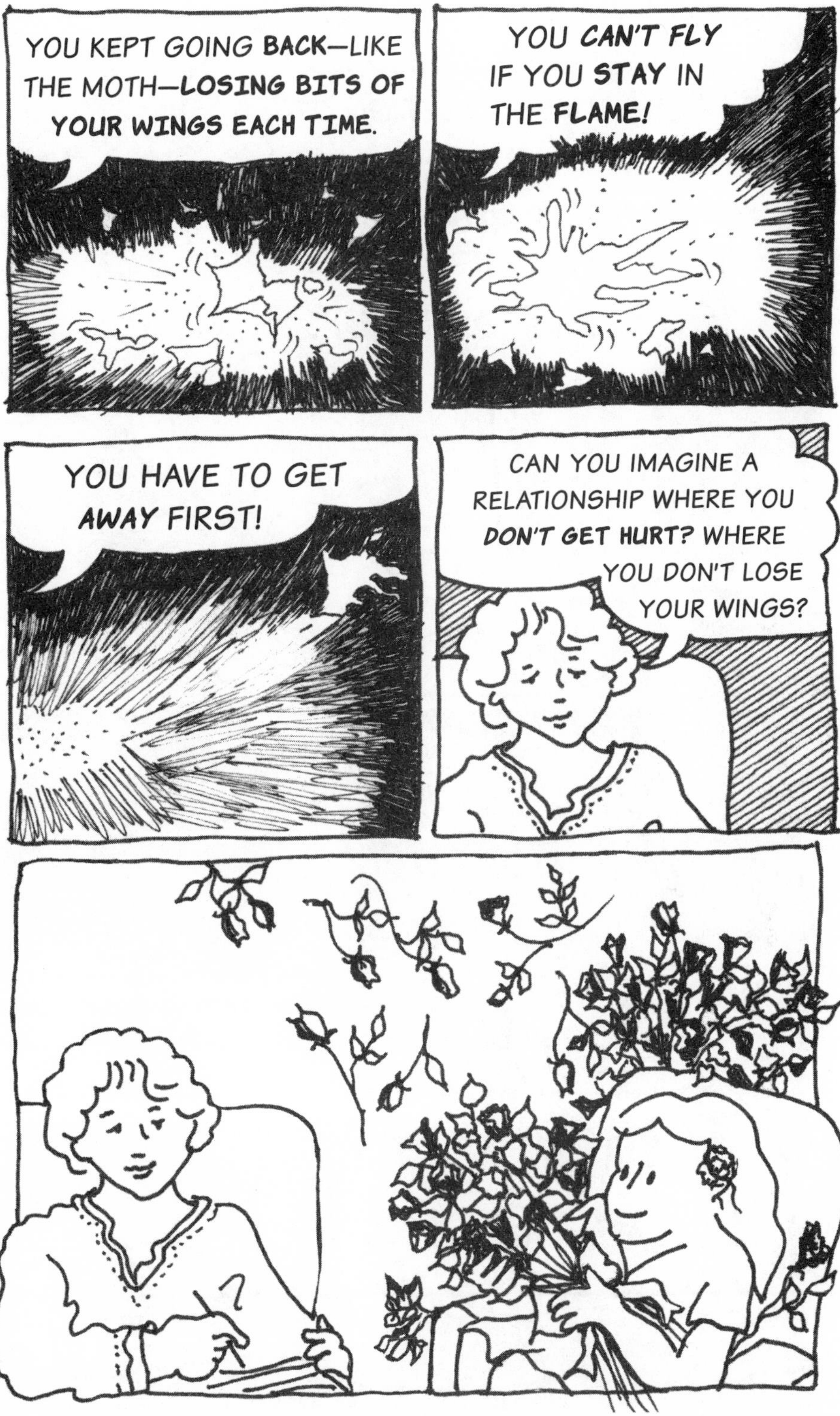
YOU KEPT GOING BACK—LIKE THE MOTH—LOSING BITS OF YOUR WINGS EACH TIME.
YOU CAN'T FLY IF YOU STAY IN THE FLAME!
YOU HAVE TO GET AWAY FIRST!
CAN YOU IMAGINE A RELATIONSHIP WHERE YOU DON'T GET HURT? WHERE YOU DON'T LOSE YOUR WINGS?

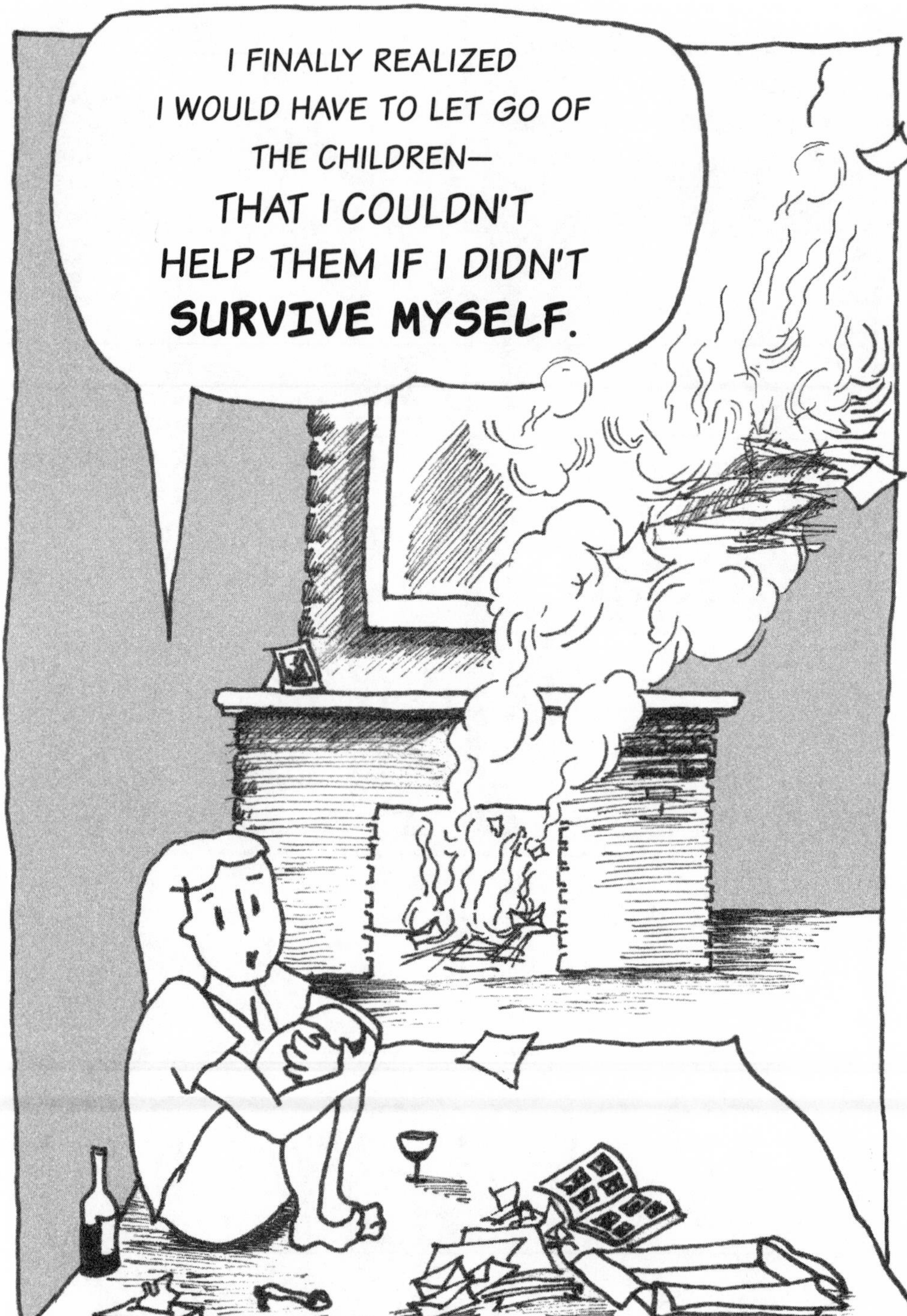
I FINALLY REALIZED I WOULD HAVE TO LET GO OF THE CHILDREN— THAT I COULDN'T HELP THEM IF I DIDN'T **SURVIVE MYSELF**.

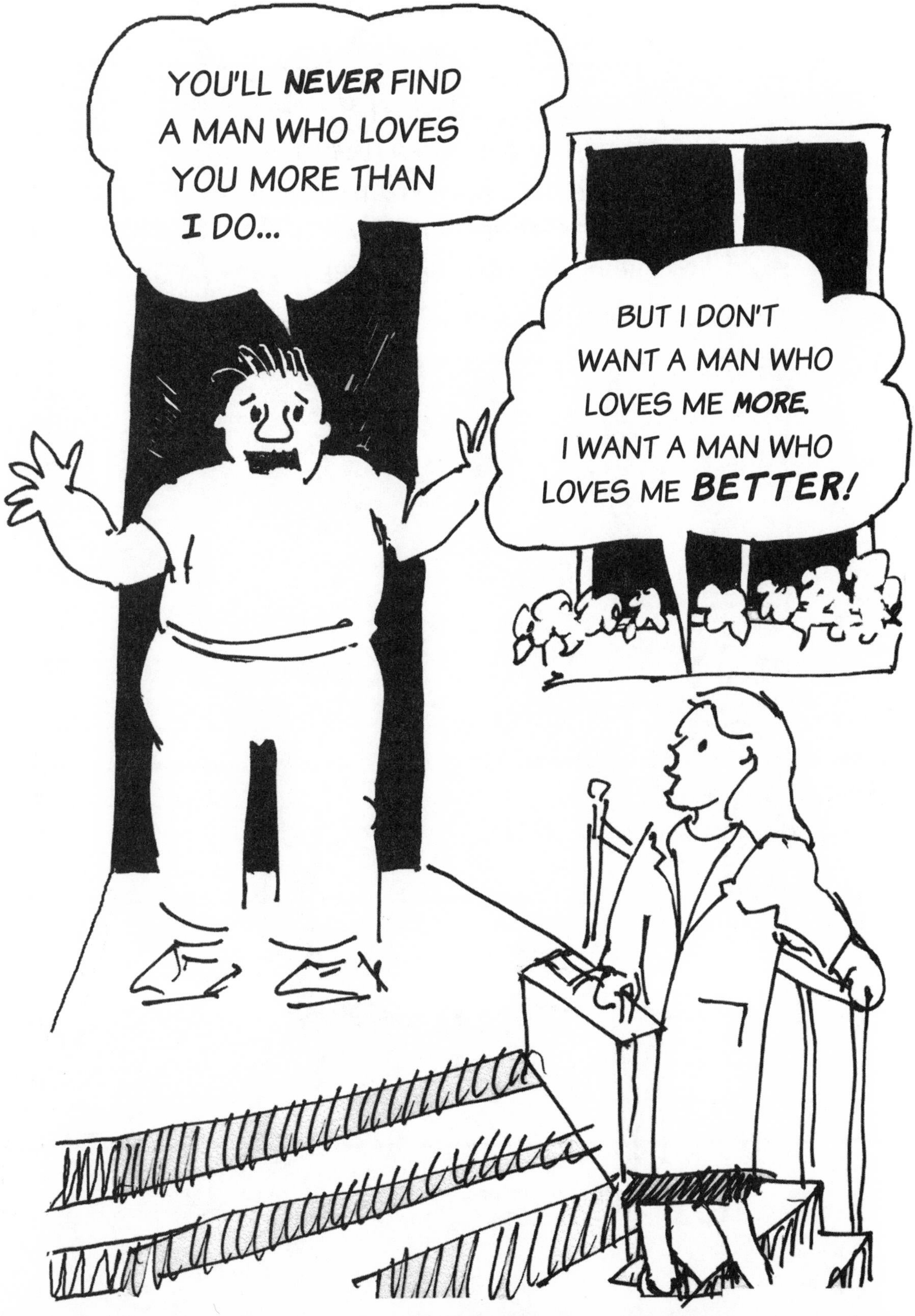
YOU'LL **NEVER** FIND A MAN WHO LOVES YOU MORE THAN **I** DO...
BUT I DON'T WANT A MAN WHO LOVES ME **MORE**. I WANT A MAN WHO LOVES ME **BETTER!**

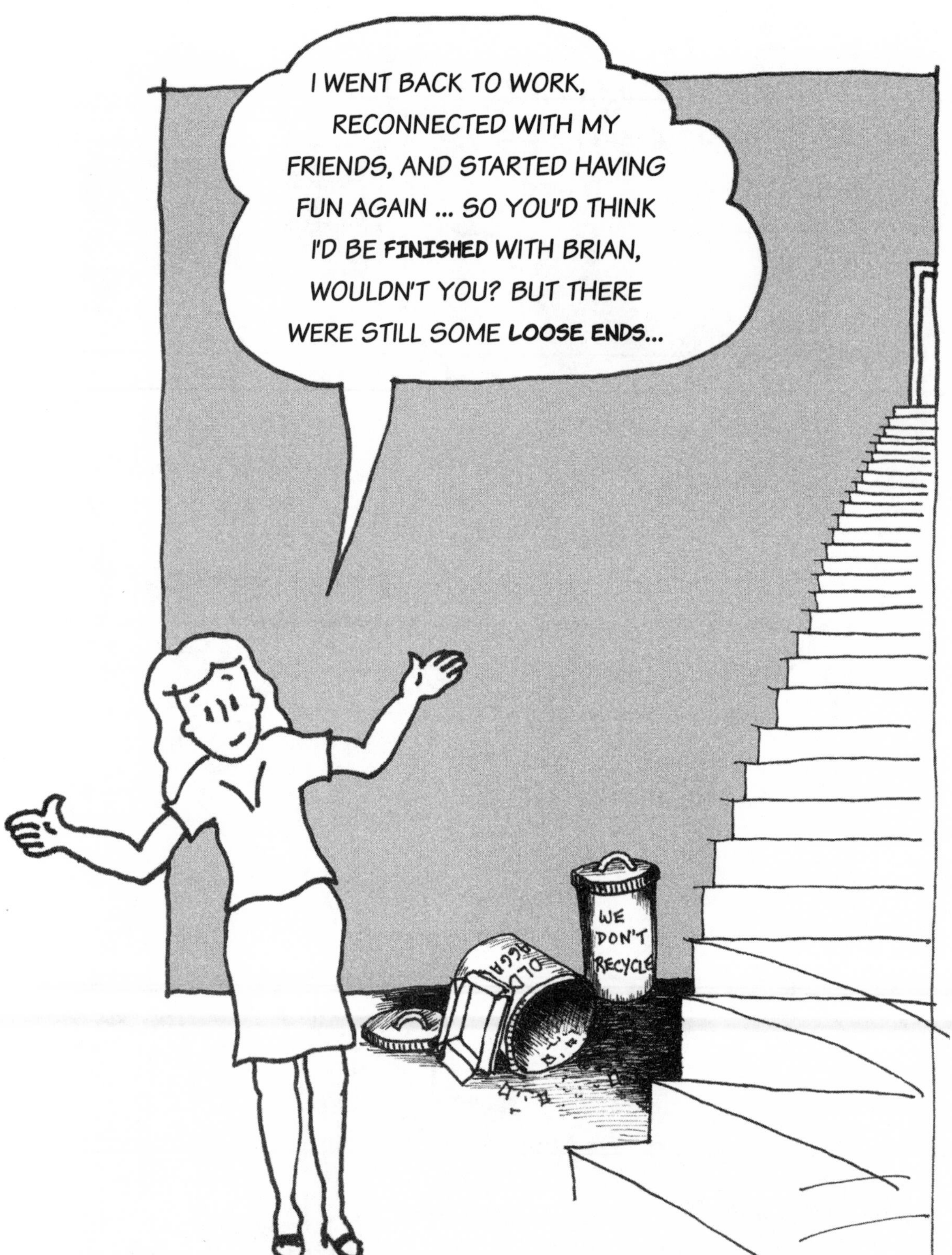
I WENT BACK TO WORK, RECONNECTED WITH MY FRIENDS, AND STARTED HAVING FUN AGAIN ... SO YOU'D THINK I'D BE **FINISHED** WITH BRIAN, WOULDN'T YOU? BUT THERE WERE STILL SOME **LOOSE ENDS...**
WE DON'T RECYCLE
OLD

EPILOGUE: 5 YEARS LATER...

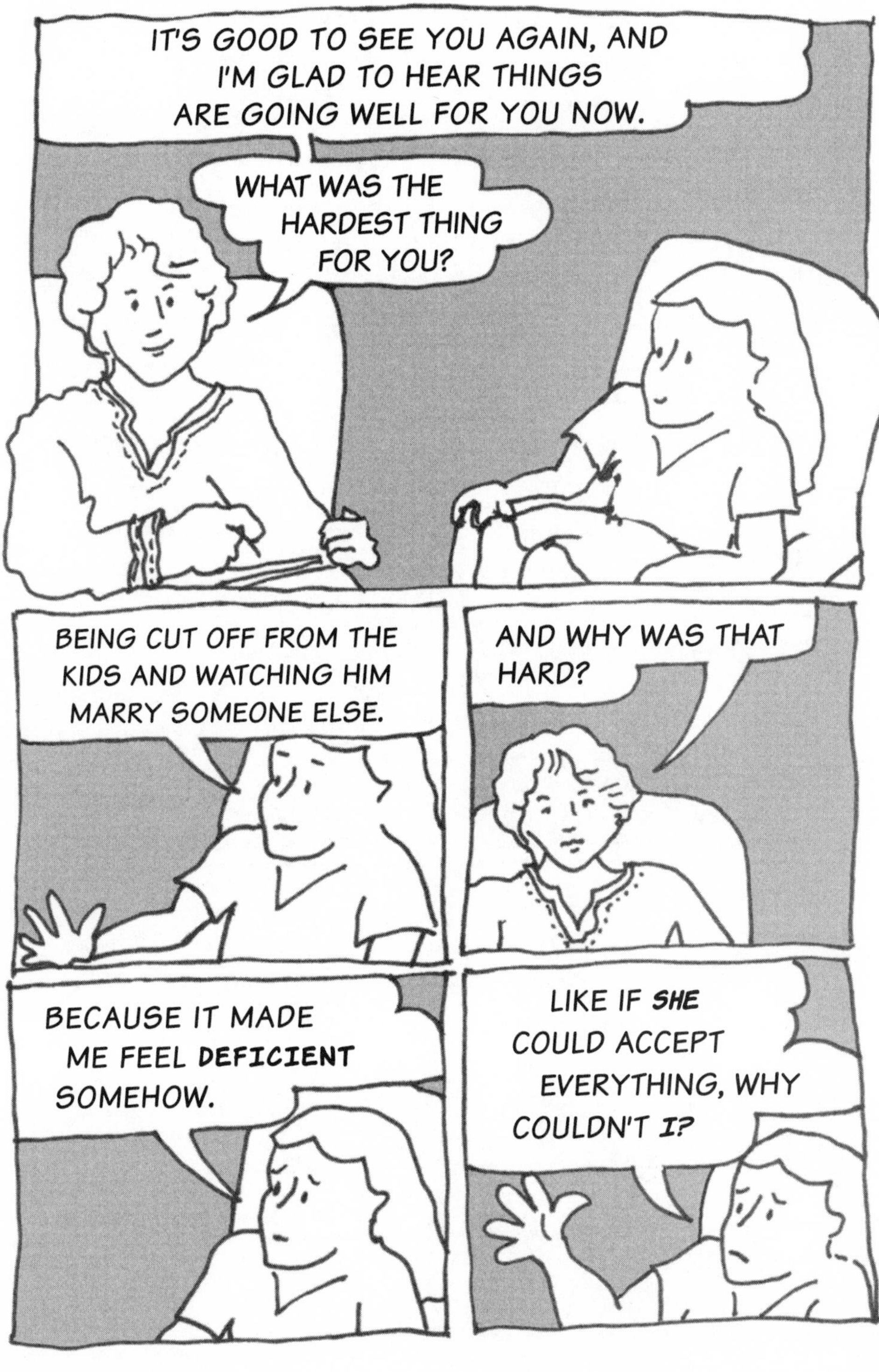
IT'S GOOD TO SEE YOU AGAIN, AND I'M GLAD TO HEAR THINGS ARE GOING WELL FOR YOU NOW.
WHAT WAS THE HARDEST THING FOR YOU?
BEING CUT OFF FROM THE KIDS AND WATCHING HIM MARRY SOMEONE ELSE.
AND WHY WAS THAT HARD?
BECAUSE IT MADE ME FEEL **DEFICIENT** SOMEHOW.
LIKE IF **SHE** COULD ACCEPT EVERYTHING, WHY COULDN'T ***I***?

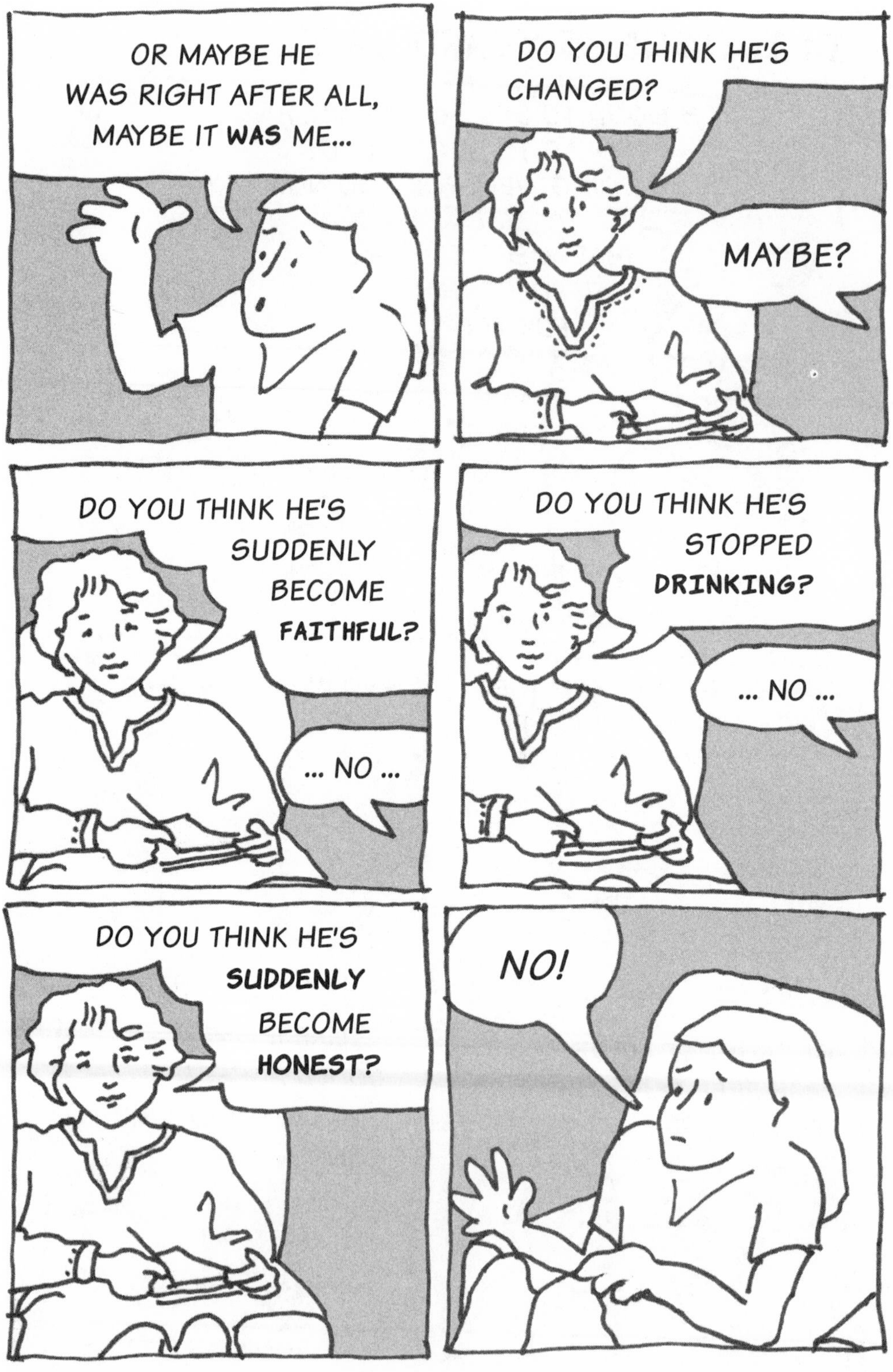
OR MAYBE HE WAS RIGHT AFTER ALL, MAYBE IT **WAS** ME...
DO YOU THINK HE'S CHANGED?
MAYBE?
DO YOU THINK HE'S SUDDENLY BECOME **FAITHFUL?**
... NO ...
DO YOU THINK HE'S STOPPED **DRINKING?**
... NO ...
DO YOU THINK HE'S **SUDDENLY** BECOME **HONEST?**
NO!

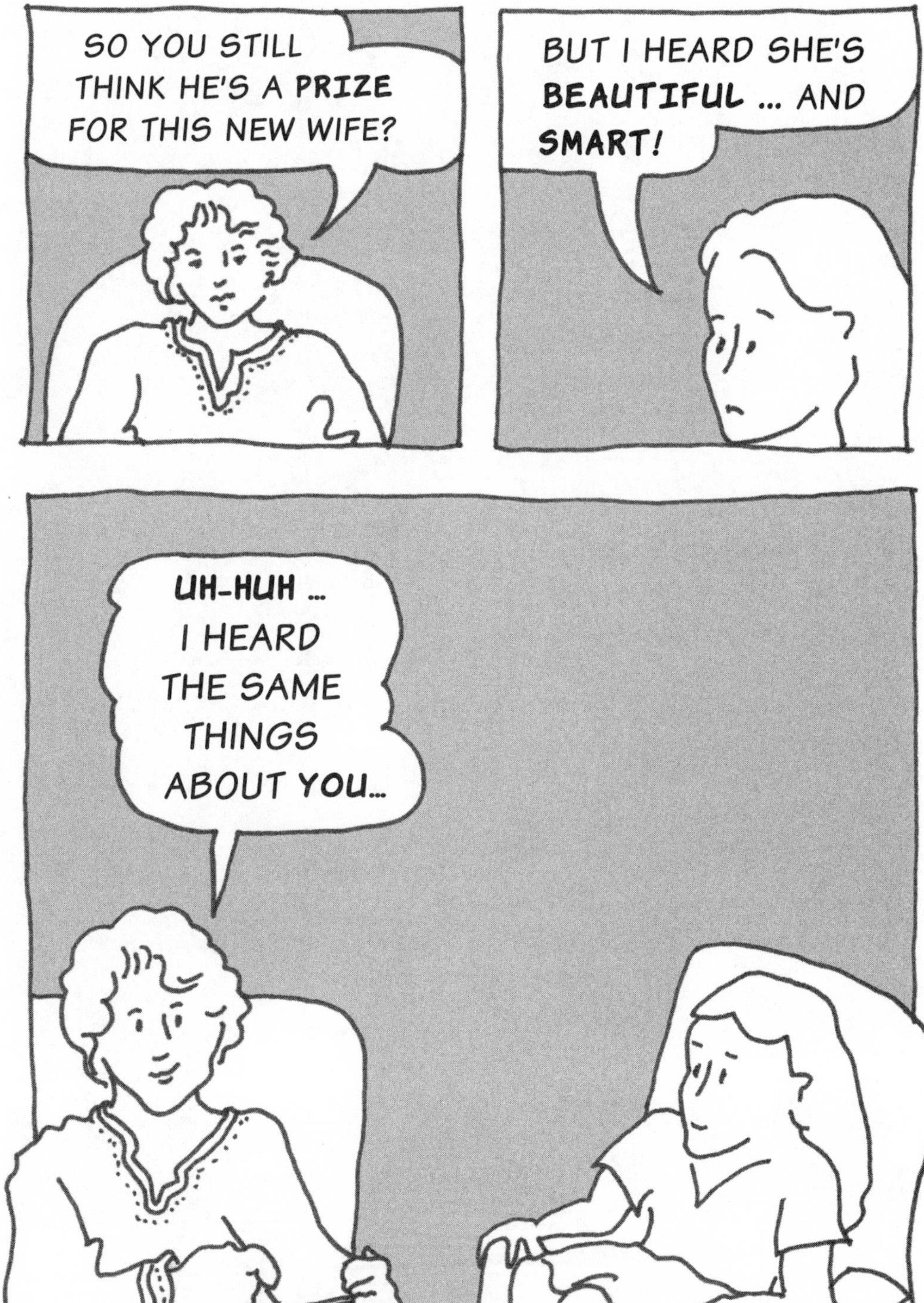
SO YOU STILL THINK HE'S A PRIZE FOR THIS NEW WIFE?
BUT I HEARD SHE'S BEAUTIFUL ... AND SMART!
UH-HUH ... I HEARD THE SAME THINGS ABOUT YOU...

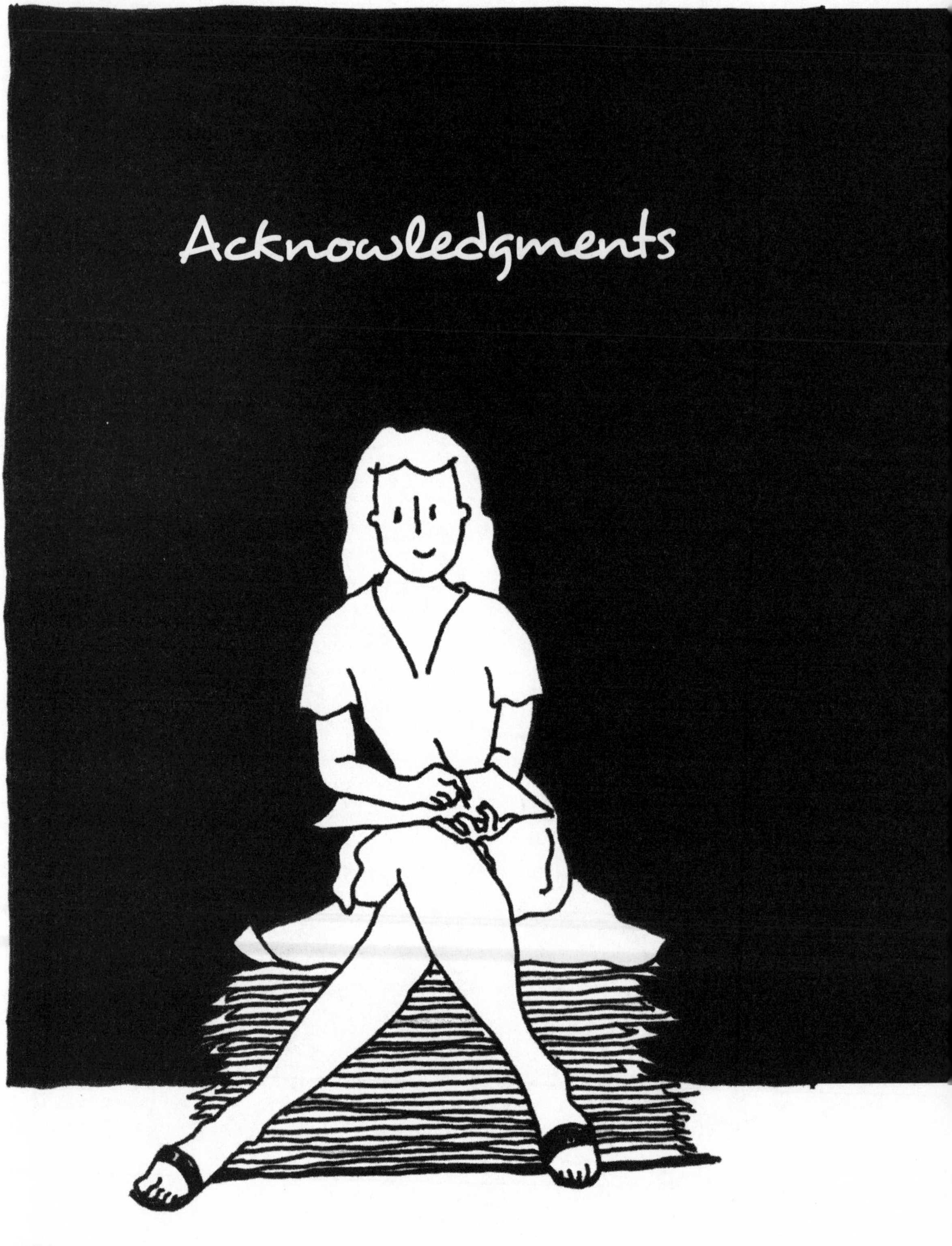
Acknowledgments

I WISH TO THANK MY ARMY OF FRIENDS who formed a phalanx
around me: who supported me, comforted me, and inspired me; and
a special thank you to our favorite "Robin Hood"—W.D.—and his men.

In particular, I thank those who would not let me stop drawing, those who
generously formed Friends-of-Rosalind, and those who became the group's
"Sages-in-residence." I also thank the first man to see my drawings,
because he said they were important. All of you gave me courage.

The final process was long and arduous. It was made easier by
the determined vision and commitment of my editors and publishers
worldwide, and by my wonderful agent, who makes all things possible.

I couldn't have survived without the love and safety net of my family
and those who make up the composite of "Sage" in this book—they
know who they are. Most of all, it is for the children that
I have made the promise to **BREAK THE CYCLE**.

FOR MORE OF ROZ, PLEASE VISIT WWW.FRIENDS-OF-ROSALIND.COM

Rosalind Penfold   Rosalind Penfold

Rosalind B. Penfold

Rosalind Penfold

Roz Penfold.

Rosalind Penfold

Rosalind Penfold

Roz Penfold.   Roz Penfold

Rosalind B Penfold

Roz Penfold.   Rosalind Penfold.

Rosalind B. Penfold

Rosalind Penfold

THERE ARE HUNDREDS OF THOUSANDS OF "ROSALIND B. PENFOLDS"
AROUND THE WORLD WHO WILL RECOGNIZE THEMSELVES IN THIS
STORY. SOME OF THESE WOMEN, THROUGH FRIENDS-OF-ROSALIND.COM,
HAVE VOLUNTEERED TO AUTOGRAPH THIS BOOK. I HOPE IT
HELPS TO KNOW THAT YOU ARE NOT ALONE. IT HELPED ME. I ALSO
HOPE THAT THIS BOOK WILL HELP YOU TO RECOGNIZE THAT
FINDING YOURSELF IN AN ABUSIVE RELATIONSHIP DOES NOT MEAN
YOU'RE STUPID OR UNAWARE OR UNWORTHY. IT MAY MEAN THAT
YOU'RE COMPASSIONATE AND SENSITIVE AND TRUSTING—AND
EASILY TAKEN ADVANTAGE OF...

THIS BOOK HAS BEEN AUTOGRAPHED BY:

Roz Penfold   *Rosalind Penfold*

Rosalind Penfold

Rosalind Penfold.   *Roz Penfold.*

Rosalind B. Penfold is a pseudonym.

Text and illustrations copyright © 2005 Rosalind B. Penfold

Originally published by Penguin Canada in 2005

Printed in the United States of America

FIRST AMERICAN EDITION

Library of Congress Cataloging-in-Publication Data
Penfold, Rosalind B.
Dragonslippers : this is what an abusive relationship looks like /
by Rosalind B. Penfold.
p. cm.
ISBN-10: 0-8021-7020-X
ISBN-13: 978-0-8021-7020-0
1. Abused wives—United States—Psychology. 2. Psychological abuse—United
States. 3. Man-woman relationships—United States. I. Title.
HV6626.2.P46 2005
616.85'822—dc22   2005057169

Black Cat
a paperback original imprint of Grove/Atlantic, Inc.
841 Broadway
New York, NY 10003

DISTRIBUTED BY PUBLISHERS GROUP WEST

www.groveatlantic.com

06 07 08 09 10 10 9 8 7 6 5 4 3 2 1

Roz on Drawing the Comics

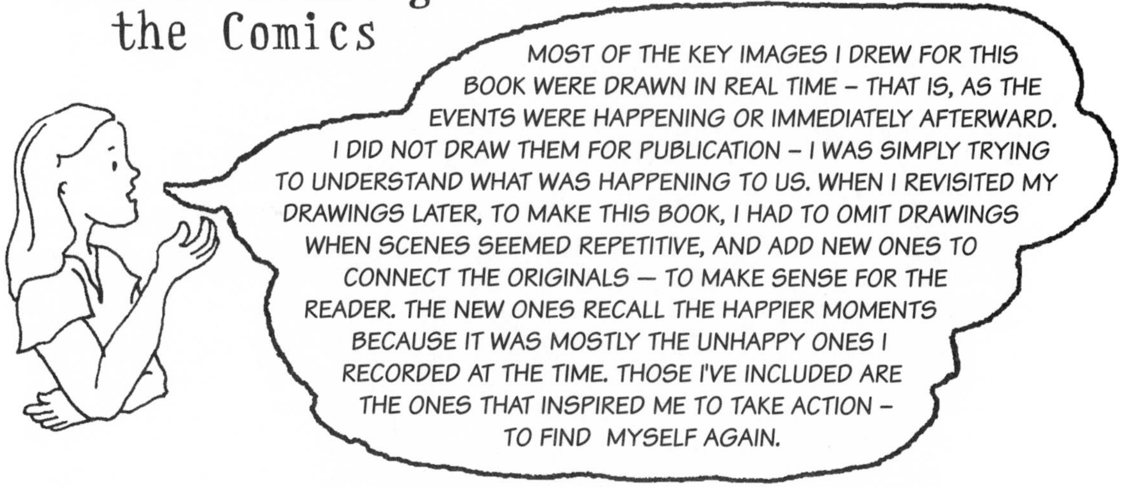
MOST OF THE KEY IMAGES I DREW FOR THIS BOOK WERE DRAWN IN REAL TIME – THAT IS, AS THE EVENTS WERE HAPPENING OR IMMEDIATELY AFTERWARD. I DID NOT DRAW THEM FOR PUBLICATION – I WAS SIMPLY TRYING TO UNDERSTAND WHAT WAS HAPPENING TO US. WHEN I REVISITED MY DRAWINGS LATER, TO MAKE THIS BOOK, I HAD TO OMIT DRAWINGS WHEN SCENES SEEMED REPETITIVE, AND ADD NEW ONES TO CONNECT THE ORIGINALS — TO MAKE SENSE FOR THE READER. THE NEW ONES RECALL THE HAPPIER MOMENTS BECAUSE IT WAS MOSTLY THE UNHAPPY ONES I RECORDED AT THE TIME. THOSE I'VE INCLUDED ARE THE ONES THAT INSPIRED ME TO TAKE ACTION – TO FIND MYSELF AGAIN.

More Praise for *Dragonslippers*:

"***DRAGONSLIPPERS*** is graphic in both senses of the word. The book takes less than an hour to read, yet conveys Roz's story with an immediacy and impact that a conventional 300-page account would struggle to match."

—*THE SUNDAY TELEGRAPH*

"A mesmerizing tale of how an independent, intelligent woman can get trapped in a relationship with an abusive male . . . ***DRAGONSLIPPERS*** pulled me into the vortex of Rosalind Penfold's experience and didn't let go. Why didn't someone think of telling this all-too-common story through a graphic novel before?"

—JUDY REBICK, THE SAM GINDIN CHAIR IN SOCIAL JUSTICE AND DEMOCRACY AT RYERSON UNIVERSITY AND AUTHOR OF *TEN THOUSAND ROSES*

"***DRAGONSLIPPERS*** brings new meaning to a picture being worth a thousand words. Rosalind Penfold has brought to the pages of this remarkable book graphic evidence that speaks louder than all the petitions and statistics surrounding abusive relationships. The warning signals she depicts are the litmus test for every relationship. Her story is painfully clear, horribly true, and thankfully triumphant."

—SALLY ARMSTRONG, AUTHOR OF *VEILED THREAT*

"Rosalind Penfold's words and images strike like an arrow deep into the poisoned heart of spousal abuse. Her visual shorthand—raw with flashes of brilliance—portray the relentless betrayals that destroy the victim without also annihilating the reader. Authentic and courageous."

—SYLVIA FRASER, AUTHOR OF *MY FATHER'S HOUSE*

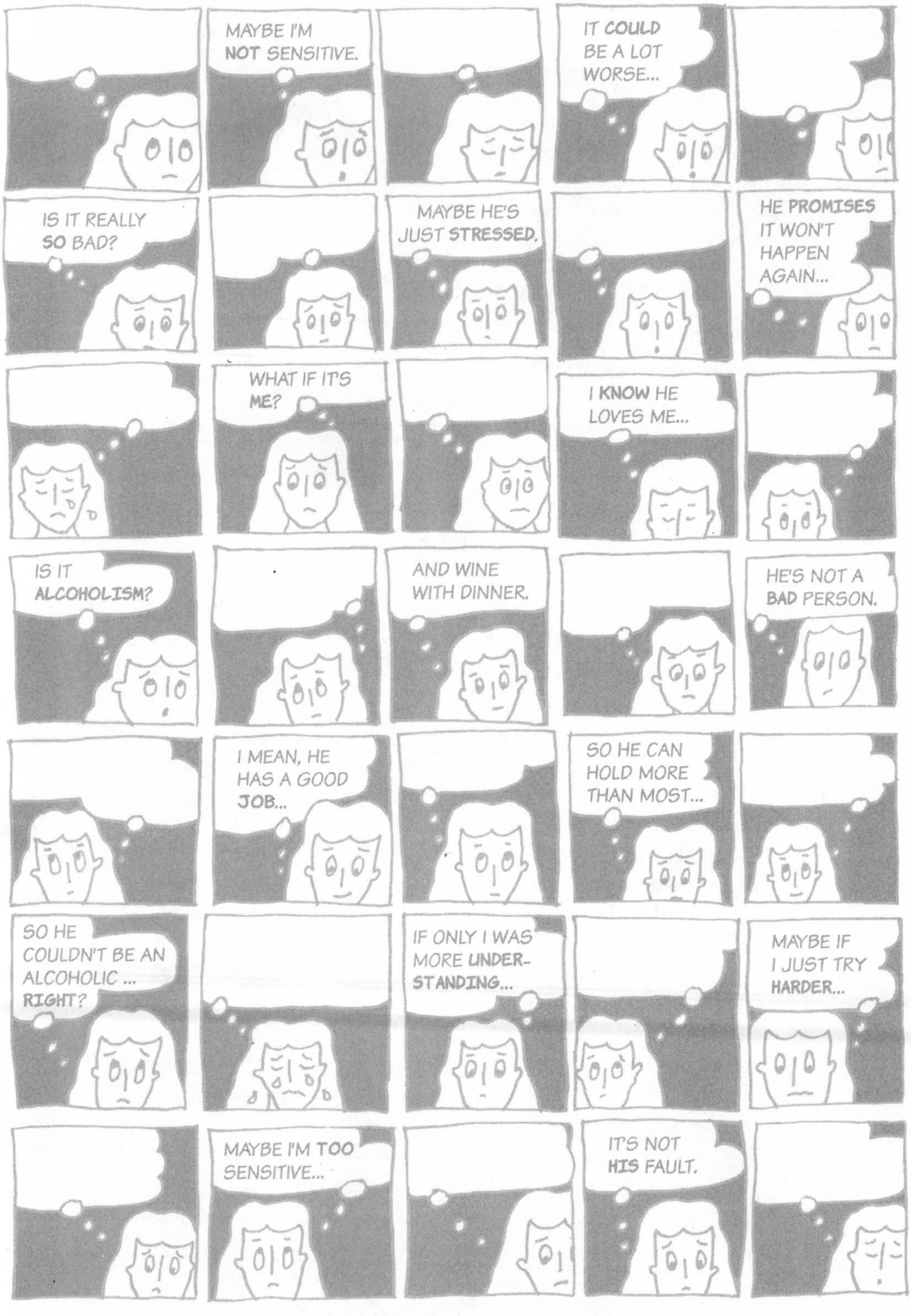
MAYBE I'M **NOT** SENSITIVE.
IT **COULD** BE A LOT WORSE...
IS IT REALLY **SO** BAD?
MAYBE HE'S JUST **STRESSED**.
HE **PROMISES** IT WON'T HAPPEN AGAIN...
WHAT IF IT'S **ME**?
I **KNOW** HE LOVES ME...
IS IT **ALCOHOLISM**?
AND WINE WITH DINNER.
HE'S NOT A **BAD** PERSON.
I MEAN, HE HAS A GOOD **JOB**...
SO HE CAN HOLD MORE THAN MOST...
SO HE COULDN'T BE AN ALCOHOLIC ... **RIGHT**?
IF ONLY I WAS MORE **UNDER-STANDING**...
MAYBE IF I JUST TRY **HARDER**...
MAYBE I'M **TOO** SENSITIVE...
IT'S NOT **HIS** FAULT.